Steps to Writing Well

with Additional Readings

Steps to Writing Well

with Additional Readings

FOURTH EDITION

JEAN WYRICK

Colorado State University

Harcourt Brace College Publishers

*Fort Worth   Philadelphia   San Diego   New York   Orlando   Austin   San Antonio
Toronto   Montreal   London   Sydney   Tokyo*

This book is dedicated to DAVID
and to SARAH, KATE, and AUSTIN

Publisher	**Earl McPeek**
Acquisitions Editor	**Julie McBurney**
Product Manager	**Laura Brennan**
Developmental Editor	**Camille Adkins**
Project Editor	**Louise Slominsky**
Production Manager	**Kathy Ferguson**
Art Director	**Garry Harman**

Cover image: *Rouen Cathedral: Facade and Tour d'Albane (Morning effect)*, 1892–1894. Oscar Claude Monet. Oil on canvas (41¾ × 29⅛ in.). Tompkins Collection, Courtesy Museum of Fine Arts, Boston.

ISBN: 0-15-505451-1
Library of Congress Catalog Card Number: 98-72582

Address for Orders
Harcourt Brace College Publishers, 6277 Sea Harbor Drive, Orlando, FL 32887-6777
1-800-782-4479

Address for Editorial Correspondence
Harcourt Brace College Publishers, 301 Commerce Street, Suite 3700, Fort Worth, TX 76102

Web Site Address
http://www.hbcollege.com

Harcourt Brace College Publishers will provide complimentary supplements or supplement packages to those adopters qualified under our adoption policy. Please contact your sales representative to learn how to qualify. If as an adopter or potential user you receive supplements you do not need, please return them to your sales representative or send them to: Attn: Returns Department, Troy Warehouse, 465 South Lincoln Drive, Troy, MO 63379.

Printed in the United States of America

9 0 1 2 3 4 5 6 7   039   9 8 7 6 5 4 3

Harcourt Brace College Publishers

To the Teacher

The fourth edition of *Steps to Writing Well with Additional Readings* has been written for teachers of composition who have had trouble finding a textbook that students can easily understand. Too many books on today's market, these teachers rightfully complain, are still unnecessarily complex, dry, or massive for the majority of students. Written simply in an informal style and addressed to the student, this textbook offers a step-by-step guide to writing a variety of 500-to-800-word essays. The combination of concise, practical advice, a number of student and professional samples, and a brief handbook should provide more than enough helpful information for students enrolled in a one-semester or one-quarter course without intimidating them with more material than they can possibly master.

Although many parts of the book have been revised or expanded for this edition, its organization remains essentially the same. Part One offers advice on "The Basics of the Short Essay"; Part Two discusses "Purposes, Modes, and Strategies"; Part Three focuses on "Special Assignments"; and Part Four presents "A Concise Handbook." Part Five contains additional professional essays. This textbook still begins with the essay "To the Student," which not only argues that students can learn to write better with practice and dedication but also gives them a number of practical reasons why they *should* learn to write better.

Part One, containing eight chapters, moves students through the process of writing the short essay. Chapter 1, on prewriting, stresses finding the proper attitude ("the desire to communicate") and presents helpful suggestions for selecting a subject. This chapter then offers students ten methods for finding a significant purpose and focus for their essays. In addition, a section on using the journal explains more than a dozen ways that students may improve their skills by writing a variety of nonthreatening—and even enjoyable—assignments. The section on audience should also help student writers identify their particular readers and communicate more effectively with them. After finding a topic and identifying their audience, students are ready for Chapter 2, devoted almost entirely to a discussion of the thesis statement. This chapter first explains the role of the "working thesis" in early drafts and then clearly outlines what a good thesis is and isn't by presenting a host of examples to illustrate the advice. Also included in this chapter is an explanation of the "essay map," an organizational tool that can help students outline their essays and plan their body paragraphs.

Chapter 3 discusses in detail the requirements of good body paragraphs: topic sentences, unity, order and coherence, adequate development, use of specific detail, and logical sequence. Over forty paragraphs illustrate both strengths and weaknesses of student writing. These paragraphs are not complex literary or professional excerpts but rather well-designed, precise examples of the principles under examination, written on subjects students can understand and appreciate. This chapter twice provides the opportunity for students to see how a topic may progress from a working thesis statement to an informal essay outline, which in turn helps produce well-developed paragraphs in the body of an essay. To complete the overview of the short essay, Chapter 4 explains, through a number of samples, how to write good introductions, conclusions, and titles.

Chapter 5, "Drafting and Revising: Creative Thinking, Critical Thinking," focuses on the revision process. Because too many students still think of revision as merely proofreading their essays rather than as an essential, recursive activity, this chapter emphasizes the importance of revision in all good writing. These pages offer a system for revising drafts in stages, while cautioning novice writers against trying to revise too many parts of their essays at once. A section on critical thinking shows students how to analyze and evaluate their ideas and those of others. This section stresses the role of critical thinking skills in the selection of evidence for all writing assignments. Chapter 5 also offers advice for participants in "peer workshops" (instructors may also find useful advice on organizing effective peer workshops in the Instructor's Manual for this edition). Also included in this chapter is a student essay, annotated to show how a writer (or a workshop partner) might use the questions suggested in the discussion of the revision process. This chapter ends with a list of suggestions for beating writer's block.

Chapter 6, on effective sentences, emphasizes the importance of clarity, conciseness, and vividness, with nearly one hundred and fifty sample sentences illustrating the chapter's advice. Chapter 7, on word choice, presents practical suggestions for selecting accurate, appropriate words that are specific, memorable, and persuasive. This chapter also contains sections on avoiding sexist language and "bureaucratese." Chapter 8, "The Reading–Writing Connection," maintains that by learning to read analytically, students can improve their own writing skills. The chapter contains step-by-step directions for reading and annotating essays and suggests many ways students may profit from studying the rhetorical choices of other writers. A professional essay annotated according to these steps is offered as a model. Teachers may wish to assign this chapter before asking students to read the professional essays that appear throughout this textbook.

Each chapter in Part One contains samples and exercises. As in the previous editions, the "Practicing What You've Learned" exercises follow each major section in each chapter so that both teacher and students may quickly discover if particular material needs additional attention. Moreover, by conquering small steps in the writing process, one at a time, students should feel more confident and should learn more rapidly. Assignments, which also follow each major section in these chapters, suggest class activities and frequently emphasize "peer teaching," a useful method that asks students to prepare appropriate exercises for classmates and then to evaluate the results. Such assignments, operating under the premise that "you don't truly learn a subject until you teach it," provide engaging classroom activity for all the students and also remove from the teacher some of the burden of creating exercises.

Throughout the chapters in Part One, activities called "Applying What You've Learned to *Your* Writing" follow the exercises and assignments. Each of these activities encourages students to "follow through" by incorporating into a current draft the skill they have just read about and practiced. By following a three-step procedure—reading the advice in the text, practicing the advice through the exercises, and then applying the advice directly to their own prose—students should improve their writing processes. In addition, each of the chapters in Part One concludes with a summary, designed to help students review the important points in the material under study.

Part Two presents discussion of the kinds of essays students are most often asked to write. Chapter 9, on exposition, is divided into separate discussions of the expository strategies: example, process, comparison/contrast, definition, division and classification, and causal analysis. Each discussion in Chapter 9 and each of the chapters on argument, description, and narration follow a similar format by offering the students (a) a clear definition of the mode (or strategy), explained with familiar examples; (b) practical advice on developing each essay; (c) warnings against common problems; (d) suggested essay topics on subjects that appeal to students' interests and capabilities; (e) a topic proposal sheet; (f) a sample student essay with marginal notes; (g) a professional essay followed by questions on content, structure, and style, a vocabulary list, and writing suggestions; (h) a revision worksheet to guide student writers through their rough drafts; and (i) a progress report. The advice on developing the essay and the section on common problems are both explained in easy-to-understand language accompanied by numerous examples.

The eleven student essays in this text should encourage student writers by showing them that others in their situation can indeed compose organized, thoughtful essays. The student essays that appear here are not perfect, however; consequently, teachers may use them in class to generate suggestions for still more revision. The twelve professional essays were also selected to spur class discussion and to illustrate the rhetorical principles presented in this part of the text. (The comparison/contrast section of Chapter 9 contains *two* professional essays so that students may see examples of the two common methods of organization.) The seven professional essays most popular with users of the third edition were retained in this edition; five new essays replace previous readings.

Chapter 10 presents advice on the argumentative essay; Chapters 11 and 12, on writing effective description and narration, follow. Some college writing courses (especially those limited to one semester) begin with expository essays; these instructors may assign Chapters 11 and 12 for advice on improving descriptive and narrative skills because they are incorporated in other kinds of essays outlined in Part Two. The placement of these chapters after the chapters on expository and argumentative essays reflects this kind of syllabus. However, those instructors who wish to begin their courses with descriptive and/or narrative essays may wish to assign these chapters first, before Chapter 9 on the expository strategies.

 New to this edition is Chapter 13, "Writing Essays Using Multiple Strategies." Although this text shows students how to master individual rhetorical strategies, one essay at a time, effective writers, in reality, must often choose a combination, or blending, of strategies to best accomplish their purpose. Chapter 13 is now included at the end of Part Two, offering advice to writers who are ready to address more complex topics and essay organization. The chapter also contains a new student essay and a new professional essay, each illustrating clear use of multiple strategies to achieve its purpose.

Users of previous editions may note that a central portion of this text has been reorganized and expanded into a new Part Three, called "Special Assignments." This section allows instructors to design their composition courses in a variety of ways, adding a research paper or literary analysis if they prefer. It also provides suggestions for writing various kinds of in-class essays or essay exams, "under pressure."

Chapter 14, "Writing a Paper Using Research," shows students how to focus a topic, search for and evaluate evidence, avoid plagiarism, and effectively incorporate source material into their essays. The chapter presents information on both MLA and APA documentation styles and includes updated samples illustrating the use of electronic sources.

NEW "Writing about Literature," Chapter 15, is new to this edition. It discusses ways literature may be used in the composition classroom, either as prompts for personal essays or for papers of literary analysis. Students are offered a detailed series of suggestions for both close reading and writing about poetry and short fiction. The chapter contains an annotated poem, short story, and two student essays; another poem, without marginal notes, is included for classroom discussion or assignment.

Chapter 16, "Writing In-Class Assignments," helps students respond quickly and accurately by understanding their task's purpose and by recognizing directional words. Advice for successfully completing timed writing is also designed to decrease students' anxiety.

Part Four contains a concise handbook with nontechnical explanations and easy-to-understand examples showing how to correct the most common errors in grammar, punctuation, and mechanics. A brief section on spelling hints may offer some limited relief to students who suffer from the malady of being poor spellers.

Part Five gives teachers the opportunity to choose among thirty-two additional professional essays. These essays—some serious, some humorous, some familiar, nine new to this edition—also illustrate the strategies discussed in Part Two and offer a variety of ideas, structures, and styles to consider. "Essays for Further Study" contains four selections that illustrate complex audience appeals and multiple strategies. This edition also includes two poems and a short story to complement the addition of Chapter 15. Studying the professional selections presented in Part Five should help novice writers as they make their own rhetorical choices.

Once again, readers of this edition may note an occasional attempt at humor. The lighthearted tone of some samples and exercises is the result of the author's firm belief that while learning to write is serious business, solemn composition classrooms are not always the most beneficial environments for anxious beginning writers. The author takes full responsibility (and all of the blame) for the bad jokes and even worse puns.

 Finally, a complimentary Instructor's Manual, updated for this edition by Anne Machin Norris, is available from Harcourt Brace. It contains suggestions for teaching, answers to exercises and essay questions, and questions and answers to accompany the essays in Part Five of this textbook. A new section on portfolio grading has been included in this updated edition. Interested instructors should contact their Harcourt Brace representative for more information.

Although a new edition of this textbook has allowed its author to make a number of changes and additions, the book's purpose remains as stated in the original preface: "While there are many methods of teaching composition, *Steps to Writing Well* tries to help inexperienced writers by offering a clearly defined sequential approach to writing the short essay. By presenting simple, practical advice directly to the students, this text is intended to make the demanding jobs of teaching and learning the basic principles of composition easier and more enjoyable for everyone."

ACKNOWLEDGMENTS

I would like to express my appreciation to Julie McBurney, English Acquisitions Editor, for her support during the completion of this edition, in a year of challenges and changes. Once more, to Senior Developmental Editor Camille Adkins, who generously provided assistance in countless ways, improving every part of this revision from beginning to end, I say thank you, thank you, thank you. I'm grateful, too, to Anne Machin Norris for her excellent revision of the Instructor's Manual and her textual suggestions.

A round of thanks goes to Garry Harman, Art Director; Kathy Ferguson, Production Manager; Louise Slominsky, Project Editor; and the other good people at Harcourt Brace, including the hard-working sales representatives (and their managers) for getting this book into the hands of the right folks. I am also indebted to Aimé Merizon for obtaining the literary permissions for this edition and to Kate Barnes for her thoughtful proofreading. Once more, Nancy Marcus Land and her staff at Publications Development Company did a fine job on production. I greatly appreciate those students at Colorado State University who allowed me to reprint their writing, and also Sharon Strauss, whose student essay "Treeclimbing" was a prize winner at the College of Charleston.

In addition, I would like to acknowledge a number of colleagues across the country who offered many useful suggestions for this edition: Rosemary Fithian Guruswamy, Radford University; Lauri Humberson, St. Philip's College; Linda Lightsey, Mississippi Gulf Coast Community College; Marian Wernicke, Pensacola Junior College; and Richard W. White, Edison Community College.

Finally, I am grateful to my husband, David Hall, and to our children, Sarah, Kate, and Austin, for their understanding and patience during this revision.

To the Student

FINDING THE RIGHT ATTITUDE

If you agree with one or more of the following statements, we have some serious myth-killing to do before you begin this book:

1. I'm no good in English—never have been, never will be.

2. Only people with natural talent for writing can succeed in composition class.

3. My composition teacher is a picky, comma-hunting old fogey/radical, who will insist I write just like him or her.

4. I write for myself, not for anyone else, so I don't need this class or this book.

5. Composition classes are designed to put my creativity in a straitjacket.

The notion that good writers are born, not made, is a widespread myth that may make you feel defeated before you start. But the simple truth is that good writers *are* made—simply because *effective writing is a skill that can be learned.* Despite any feelings of insecurity you may about composition, you should realize that you already know many of the basic rules of good writing; after all, you've been writing since you were six years old. What you need now is some practical advice on composition, some coaching to sharpen your skills, and a strong dose of determination to practice those skills until you can consistently produce the results you want. Talent, as the French writer Flaubert once said, is nothing more than long patience.

Think about learning to write well as you might consider your tennis game. No one is born a tennis star. You first learn the basic rules and movements and then go out on the court to practice. And practice. No one's tennis will improve if he or she stays off the court; similarly, you must write regularly and receive feedback to improve your composition skills. Try to see your teacher not as Dr. Frankenstein determined to reproduce his or her style of writing in you, but rather as your coach, your loyal trainer who wants you to do the very best you can. Like any good coach, your teacher will point out your strengths and weaknesses; she or he will often send you to this text for practical suggestions for improvement. And while there are no quick, magic solutions for learning to write well, the most important point to remember is this: with this text, your own common sense, and determination, *you can improve your writing.*

WHY WRITE?

"OK," you say, "so I can improve if I try—but why should I bother? Why should I write well? I'm not going to be a professional writer."

In the first place, writing helps us explore our own thoughts and feelings. Writing forces us to articulate our ideas, to discover what we really think about an issue. For example, let's suppose you're faced with a difficult decision and that the arguments pro and con are jumbled in your head. You begin to write down all the pertinent facts and feelings, and suddenly, you begin to see that you do, indeed, have stronger arguments for one side of the question than the other. Once you "see" what you are thinking, you may then scrutinize your opinions for any logical flaws or weaknesses and revise your argument accordingly. In other words, writing lays out our ideas for examination, analysis, and thoughtful reaction. Thus when we write, we (and the world at large) see who we are, and what we stand for, much more clearly. Moreover, writing can provide a record of our thoughts that we may study and evaluate in a way that conversation cannot. In short, writing well enables us to see and know ourselves—our feelings, ideas, and opinions—better.

On a more practical level, we need to write effectively to communicate with others. While some of our writing may be done solely for ourselves, the majority of it is created for others to share. In this world, it is almost impossible to claim that we write only for ourselves. We are constantly asked to put our feelings, ideas, and knowledge in writing for others to read. During your college years, no matter what your major, you will be repeatedly required to write essays, tests, reports, and exercises (and possibly letters home). Later, you may need to write formal letters of application for jobs or graduate training. And on a job you may have to write numerous kinds of reports, proposals, analyses, and requisitions. To be successful in any field, you must make your correspondence with business associates and co-workers clearly understood; remember that enormous amounts of time, energy, and profit have been lost because of a single unclear office memo.

There's still a third—more cynical—reason for studying writing techniques. Once you begin to improve your ability to use language, you will become more aware of the ways others write and speak. Through today's mass media and electronic highways, we are continually bombarded with words from politicians, advertisers, scientists, preachers, teachers, and self-appointed "authorities." We need to understand and evaluate what we are hearing, not only for our benefit but also for self-protection. Language is frequently manipulated to manipulate us. For example, years ago some government officials on trial preferred us to see Watergate as an "intelligence information gathering mission" rather than as simple breaking and entering. The CIA has long referred to the "neutralization" of enemies, and, more recently, Pentagon officials noted "collateral damage" rather than civilian deaths when our "physics packages" (bombs) fell on "soft" (human) targets during the Gulf War. (One year not so long ago, the National Council of Teachers of English gave their Doublespeak Award to the U.S. officers who, after accidentally shooting down a plane of civilians, reported that the plane didn't crash—rather, it had "uncontrolled contact with the ground.") Some members of Congress have seen no recessions, just "meaningful downturns in aggregate output," so they have treated themselves to a "pay equalization concept," rather than a raise. Advertisers frequently try to sell us "authentic art reproductions" that are, of course, cheap mass-produced copies; the television networks treat us to "encore presentations" that are the same old summer reruns. And "fenestration engineers" are still window cleaners; "environmental superintendents" are still janitors; "drain surgeons" are still plumbers.

By becoming better writers ourselves, we can learn to recognize and reject the irresponsible, cloudy, or dishonest language of others before we become victims of their exploitation.

Contents

PART
One

THE BASICS OF THE SHORT ESSAY

The first section of this text is designed to move you through the writing process as you compose a short essay, the kind you are most likely to encounter in composition class and in other college courses. Chapters 1 and 2, on prewriting and the thesis statement, will help you find a topic, purpose, and focus for your essay. Chapter 3, on paragraphs, will show you how to plan, organize, and develop your ideas; Chapter 4 will help you complete your essay. Chapter 5 offers suggestions for revising your writing, and Chapters 6 and 7 presents additional advice on selecting your words and composing your sentences. Chapter 8 explains the important reading-writing connection and shows how learning to read analytically can sharpen your writing skills.

CHAPTER

1

Prewriting

GETTING STARTED (OR SOUP-CAN LABELS CAN BE FASCINATING)

For many writers, getting started is the hardest part. You may have noticed that when it is time to begin a writing assignment, you suddenly develop an enormous desire to straighten your books, water your plants, or sharpen your pencils for the fifth time. If this situation sounds familiar, you may find it reassuring to know that many professionals undergo these same strange compulsions before they begin writing. Jean Kerr, author of *Please Don't Eat the Daisies,* admits that she often finds herself in the kitchen reading soup-can labels—or anything—in order to prolong the moments before taking pen in hand. John C. Calhoun, vice president under Andrew Jackson, insisted he had to plow his fields before he could write, and Joseph Conrad, author of *Lord Jim* and other novels, is said to have cried on occasion from the sheer dread of sitting down to compose his stories.

To spare you as much hand-wringing as possible, this chapter presents some practical suggestions on how to begin writing your short essay. Although all writers must find the methods that work best for them, you may find some of the following ideas helpful.

But no matter how you actually begin putting words on paper, it is absolutely essential to maintain two basic ideas concerning your writing task. Before you write a single sentence, you should always remind yourself that

1. You have some valuable ideas to tell your reader, and

2. More than anything, you want to communicate those ideas to your reader.

These reminders may seem obvious to you, but without a solid commitment to your own opinions as well as to your reader, your prose will be lifeless and boring. If *you* don't care about your subject, you can't very well expect anyone else to. Have confidence that your ideas are worthwhile and that your reader genuinely wants, or needs, to know what you think.

Equally important, you must also have a strong desire to tell others what you are thinking. One of the most common mistakes inexperienced writers make is failing to move past early stages in the writing process in which they are writing for—or writing to—themselves only. In the first stages of composing an essay, writers frequently "talk" on paper to themselves, exploring thoughts, discovering new insights, making connections, selecting examples, and so on. The ultimate goal of a finished essay, however, is to communicate your opinions to *others* clearly and persuasively. Whether you wish to inform your readers, change their minds, or stir them to action, you cannot accomplish your purpose by writing so that only you understand what you mean. The burden of communicating your thoughts falls on *you,* not the reader, who is under no obligation to struggle through confused, unclear prose, paragraphs that begin and end for no apparent reason or sentences that come one after another with no more logic than lemmings following one another to the sea.

Therefore, as you move through the drafting and revising stages of your writing process, commit yourself to becoming increasingly aware of your reader's reactions to your prose. Ask yourself as you revise your drafts, "Am I moving beyond writing just to myself? Am I making myself clear to others who may not know what I mean?" Much of your success as a writer depends on an unflagging determination to communicate clearly with your readers.

SELECTING A SUBJECT

Once you have decided that communicating clearly with others is your ultimate goal, you are ready to select the subject of your essay. Here are some suggestions on how to begin:

Start early. Writing teachers since the earth's crust cooled have been pushing this advice, and for good reason. It's not because teachers are egoists competing for the dubious honor of having the most time-consuming course; it is because few writers, even experienced ones, can do a good job when rushed. You need time to mull over ideas, organize your thoughts, revise and polish your prose. Rule of thumb: always give yourself twice as much time as you think you'll need to avoid the 2:00-A.M.-why-did-I-come-to-college panic.

Select something in which you currently have a strong interest. If the essay subject is left to you, think of something fun, fascinating, or frightening you've done or seen lately, perhaps something you've already told a friend about. The subject might be the pleasure of a new hobby, the challenge of a recent book or movie, or even the harassment of registration—anything in which you are personally involved. If you aren't enthusiastic enough about your subject to want to spread the word, pick something else. Bored writers write boring essays.

Don't feel you have nothing from which to choose your subject. Your days are full of activities, people, joys, and irritations. Essays do not have to be written on lofty intellectual or poetic subjects—in fact, some of the world's best essays have been written on such subjects as china teacups, roast pig, and chimney sweeps. Think: what have you been talking or thinking about lately? What have you been doing that you're excited about? Or what about your past? Reflect a few moments on some of your most vivid memories—special people, vacations, holidays, childhood hideaways, your first job or first date—all of which are possibilities.

If a search of your immediate or past personal experience doesn't turn up anything inspiring, you might try looking in the campus newspaper for stories that arouse your strong feelings; don't skip the "Letters to the Editor" column. What are the current topics of controversy on your campus? How do you feel about open admissions? A particular graduation requirement? Speakers or special-interest groups on campus? Financial aid applications? Registration procedures? Parking restrictions? Consider the material you are studying in your other classes: reading *The Jungle* in a literature class may spark an investigative essay on the hot dog industry today, or studying previous immigration laws in your history class may lead you to an argument for or against current immigration practices. Finally, your local newspaper or national magazines might suggest essay topics to you on local, national, or international affairs that affect your life.

In other words, when you're stuck for an essay topic, take a closer look at your environment: your own life—past, present, and future; your hometown; your college town; your state; your country; and your world. You'll probably discover more than enough subjects to satisfy the assignments in your writing class.

Narrow a large subject. Once you've selected a general subject to write on, you may find that it is too broad for effective treatment in a short essay;

therefore, you may need to narrow it somewhat. Suppose, for instance, you like to work with plants and have decided to make them the subject of your essay. The subject of "plants," however, is far too large and unwieldy for a short essay, perhaps even for a short book. Consequently, you must make your subject less general. "Houseplants" is more specific, but, again, there's too much to say. "Minimum-care houseplants" is better, but you still need to pare this large, complex subject further so that you may treat it in depth in your short essay. After all, there are many houseplants that require little attention. After several more tries, you might arrive at more specific, manageable topics such as "houseplants that thrive in dark areas" or "the easy-care Devil's Ivy."

Then again, let's assume you are interested in sports. A 500- to-800-word essay on "sports" would obviously be superficial since the subject covers so much ground. Instead, you might divide the subject into categories such as "sports heroes," "my years on the high school tennis team," "women in gymnastics," "my love of jogging," and so forth. Perhaps several of your categories would make good short essays, but after looking at your list, you might decide that your real interest at this time is jogging and that it will be the topic of your essay.

FINDING YOUR ESSAY'S PURPOSE AND FOCUS

Even after you've narrowed your large subject to a more manageable topic, you still must find a specific *purpose* for your essay. Why are you writing about this topic? Do your readers need to be informed, persuaded, entertained? What do you want your writing to accomplish?

In addition to knowing your purpose, you must also find a clear *focus* or direction for your essay. You cannot, for example, inform your readers about every aspect of jogging. Instead, you must decide on a particular part of the sport and then determine the main point you want to make. If it helps, think of a camera: you see a sweeping landscape you'd like to photograph but you know you can't get it all into one picture, so you pick out a particularly interesting part of the scene. Focus in an essay works in the same way; you zoom in, so to speak, on a particular part of your topic and make that the focus of your paper.

Sometimes part of your problem may be solved by your assignment; your teacher may choose the focus of your essay for you by asking for certain specific information or by prescribing the method of development you should use (compare jogging to aerobics, explain the process of jogging properly, analyze the effects of daily jogging, and so forth). But if the purpose and focus of your essay are decisions you must make, you should always allow your interest and knowledge to guide you. Often a direction or focus for your essay will surface as you narrow your subject, but don't become frustrated if you have to discard several ideas before you hit the one that's right. For instance, you might first consider writing on how to select running shoes and then realize that you know too little about the shoe market, or you might find that there's just too little of importance to say about jogging paths to make an interesting 500-word essay.

Let's suppose for a moment that you have thought of a subject that interests you—but now you're stuck. Deciding on something to write about this subject suddenly looks as easy as nailing Jell-O to your kitchen wall. What should you say? What would be the purpose of your essay? What would be interesting for you to write about and for readers to hear about?

At this point, you may profit from trying more than one prewriting exercise, designed to help you generate some ideas about your topic. The exercises described next are, in a sense, "pump primers" that will get your creative juices flowing again. Because all writers compose differently, not all of these exercises will work for you—in fact, some of them may lead you nowhere. Nevertheless, try all of them at least once or twice; you may be surprised to discover that some pump-primer techniques work better with some subjects than with others.

PUMP-PRIMER TECHNIQUES

1. Listing

Try jotting down all the ideas that pop into your head about your topic. Free-associate; don't hold back anything. Try to brainstorm for at least ten minutes.

A quick list on jogging might look like this:

fun	training for races
healthy	both sexes
relieves tension	any age group
no expensive equipment	running with friend or spouse
shoes	too much competition
poor shoes won't last	great expectations
shin splints	good for lungs
fresh air	improves circulation
good for heart	firming
jogging paths vs. streets	no weight loss
hard surfaces	warm-ups before run
muscle cramps	cool-downs after
going too far	getting discouraged
going too fast	hitting the wall
sense of accomplishment	marathons

As you read over the list, look for connections between ideas or one large idea that encompasses several small ones. In this list, you might first notice that many of the ideas focus on improving health (heart, lungs, circulation), but you discard that subject because a "jogging improves health" essay is too obvious; it's a topic that's been done too many times to say anything new. A closer look at your list, however, turns up a number of ideas that concern how *not* to jog or reasons why someone might get discouraged and quit a jogging program. You begin to think of friends who might have stuck with jogging as you have if only they'd warmed up properly beforehand, chosen the right places to run, paced themselves more realistically, and so on. You decide, therefore, to write an essay telling first-time joggers how to start a successful program, how to avoid a number of problems, from shoes to track surfaces, that might otherwise defeat their efforts before they've given the sport a chance.

2. Freewriting

Some people simply need to start writing to find a focus. Take out several sheets of blank paper, give yourself at least ten to fifteen minutes, and begin writing whatever comes to mind on your subject. Don't worry about spelling, punctuation, or even complete sentences. Don't change, correct, or delete anything. If you run out of things to say, write "I can't think of anything to say" until you can find a new thought. At the end of the time period you may discover that by continuously writing you will have written yourself into an interesting topic.

Here are examples of freewriting from students who were given ten minutes to write on the general topic of "nature."

STUDENT 1:

I'm really not the outdoorsy type. I'd rather be inside somewhere than out in Nature tromping through the bushes. I don't like bugs and snakes and stuff like that. Lots of my friends like to go hiking around or camping but I don't. Secretly, I think maybe one of the big reasons I really don't like being out in Nature is because I'm deathly afraid of bees. When I was a kid I was out in the woods and ran into a swarm of bees and got stung about a million times, well, it felt like a million times. I had to go to the hospital for a few days. Now every time I'm outside somewhere and something, anything, flies by me I'm terrified. Totally paranoid. Everyone kids me because I immediately cover my head. I

keep hearing about killer bees heading this way, my worst
nightmare come true. . . .

STUDENT 2:

We're not going to have any Nature left if people don't do
something about the environment. Despite all the media attention to recycling, we're still trashing the planet left and
right. People talk big about "saving the environment" but
then do such stupid things all the time. Like smokers who
flip their cigarette butts out their car windows. Do they
think those filters are just going to disappear overnight?
The parking lot by this building is full of butts this morning
where someone dumped their car ashtray. This campus is
full of pop cans, I can see at least three empties under desks
in this classroom right now. . . .

These two students reacted quite differently to the same general subject.
The first student responded personally, thinking about her own relationship
to "nature" (defined as being out in the woods), whereas the second student
obviously associated nature with environmental concerns. More freewriting
might lead student 1 to a humorous essay on her bee phobia or even to an in-
quiry about those dreaded killer bees; student 2 might write an interesting
paper suggesting ways college students could clean up their campus or easily
recycle their aluminum cans.

Often freewriting will not be as coherent as these two samples; sometimes
freewriting goes nowhere or in circles. But it's a technique worth trying. By
allowing our minds to roam freely over a subject, without worrying about
"correctness" or organization, we may remember or discover topics we want
to write about or investigate, topics we feel strongly about and wish to introduce to others.

3. Looping*

Looping is a variation on freewriting that works amazingly well for many
people, including those who are frustrated rather than helped by freewriting.

Let's assume you've been assigned that old standby "My Summer Vacation." Obviously you must find a focus, something specific and important to

* This technique is suggested by Peter Elbow in *Writing Without Teachers* (New York: Oxford
University Press, 1975).

say. Again, take out several sheets of blank paper and begin to freewrite, as described previously. Write for at least ten minutes. At the end of this period read over what you've written and try to identify a central idea that has emerged. This idea may be an important thought that occurred to you in the middle or at the end of your writing, or perhaps it was the idea you liked best for whatever reason. It may be the idea that was pulling you onward when time ran out. In other words, look for the thought that stands out, that seems to indicate the direction of your thinking. Put this thought or idea into one sentence called the "center-of-gravity sentence." You have now completed loop 1.

To begin loop 2, use your center-of-gravity sentence as a jumping-off point for another ten minutes of freewriting. Stop, read what you've written, and complete loop 2 by composing another center-of-gravity sentence. Use this second sentence to start loop 3. You should write at least three loops and three center-of-gravity sentences. At the end of three loops, you may find that you have focused on a specific topic that might lead to a good essay. If you're not satisfied with your topic at this point, by all means try two or three more loops until your subject is sufficiently narrowed and focused.

Here's an example of one student's looping exercise:

SUMMER VACATION

Loop 1

I think summer vacations are very important aspects of living. They symbolize getting away from daily routines, discovering places and people that are different. When I think of vacations I think mostly of traveling somewhere too far to go, say, for a weekend. It is a chance to get away and relax and not think about most responsibilities. Just have a good time and enjoy yourself. Vacations can also be a time of gathering with family and friends.

Center-of-gravity sentence
Loop 2

Vacations are meant to be used for traveling.

Vacations are meant for traveling. Last summer my family and I drove to Yellowstone National Park. I didn't want to go at first. I thought looking at geysers would be dumb and boring. I was really obnoxious all the way up there and made lots of smart remarks about getting eaten by bears. Luckily, my parents ignored me and I'm glad they did, because Yellowstone turned out to be wonderful. It's not just Old Faithful—there's lots more to see and learn about, like these colorful boiling pools and boiling patches of mud. I got interested in the thermodynamics of the pools and how new ones are surfacing all the time, and how algae make the pools different colors.

Center-of-gravity
sentence

Once I got interested in Yellowstone's amazing pools, my vacation turned out great.

Loop 3

Once I got interested in the pools, I had a good time, mainly because I felt I was seeing something really unusual. I knew I'd never see anything like this again unless I went to Iceland or New Zealand (highly unlikely!). I felt like I was learning a lot, too. I liked the idea of learning a lot about the inside of the earth without having to go to class and study books. I really hated to leave—Mom and Dad kidded me on the way back about how much I'd griped about going on the trip in the first place. I felt pretty dumb. But I was really glad I'd given the Park a closer look instead of holding on to my view of it as a boring bunch of water fountains. I would have had a terrible time, but now I hope to go back some-day. I think the experience made me more open-minded about trying new places.

Center-of-gravity
sentence

My vacation this summer was special because I was willing to put aside my expectations of boredom and learn some new ideas about the strange environment at Yellowstone.

At the end of three loops, this student has moved from the general subject of "summer vacation" to the more focused idea that her willingness to learn about a new place played an important part in the enjoyment of her vacation. Although her last center-of-gravity sentence still contains some vague words ("special," "new ideas," "strange environment"), the thought stated here may eventually lead to an essay that will not only say something about this student's vacation but may also persuade the readers to reconsider their attitude toward taking trips to new places.

4. The Boomerang

Still another variation on freewriting is the technique called the boome-rang, named appropriately because, like the Australian stick, it invites your mind to travel over a subject from opposite directions to produce new ideas.

Suppose, for example, members of your class have been asked to write about their major field of study, which in your case is Liberal Arts. Begin by writing a statement that comes into your mind about majoring in the Liberal

Arts and then freewrite on that statement for five minutes. Then write a second statement that approaches the subject from an opposing point of view, and freewrite again for five minutes. Continue this pattern several times. Boomeranging, like looping, can help writers see their subject in a new way and consequently help them find an idea to write about.

Here's an abbreviated sample of boomeranging:

1. Majoring in the Liberal Arts is impractical in today's world.

    [Freewrite for five minutes.]

2. Majoring in the Liberal Arts is practical in today's world.

    [Freewrite for five minutes.]

3. Liberal Arts is a particularly enjoyable major for me.

    [Freewrite for five minutes.]

4. Liberal Arts is not always an enjoyable major for me.

    [Freewrite for five minutes.]

And so on.

By continuing to "throw the boomerang" across your subject, you may not only find your focus but also gain insight into other people's views of your topic, which can be especially valuable if your paper will address a controversial issue or one that you feel is often misunderstood.

5. Clustering

Another excellent technique is clustering (sometimes called "mapping"). Place your general subject in a circle in the middle of a blank sheet of paper and begin to draw other lines and circles that radiate from the original subject. Cluster those ideas that seem to fall together. At the end of ten minutes see if a topic emerges from any of your groups of ideas.

Ten minutes of clustering on the subject of "A Memorable Holiday" might look like the drawing on page 13.

This student may wish to brainstorm further on the Christmas he spent in the hospital with a case of appendicitis or perhaps the Halloween he first experienced a house of horrors. By using clustering, he has recollected some important details about a number of holidays that may help him focus on an occasion he wants to describe in his paper.

6. Cubing

Still another way to generate ideas is cubing. Imagine a six-sided cube that looks something like the figure on page 14.

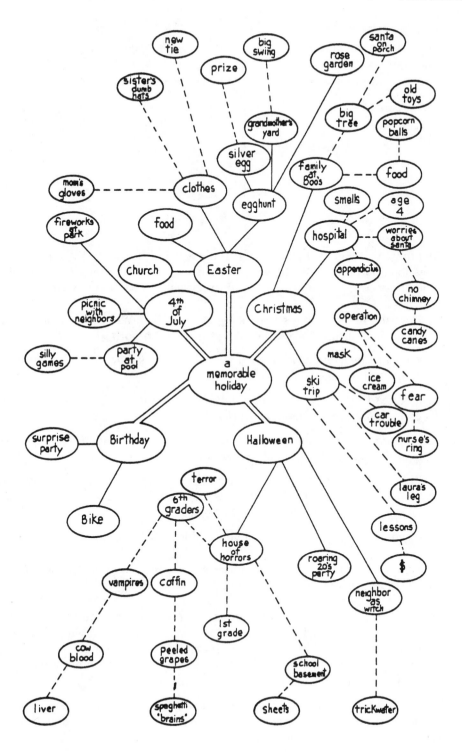

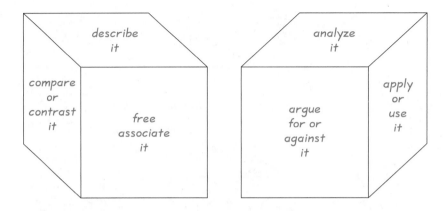

Mentally, roll your subject around the cube and freewrite the answers to the questions that follow. Write whatever comes to mind for ten or fifteen minutes; don't concern yourself with the "correctness" of what you write.

a. *Describe it:* What does your subject look like? What size, colors, textures does it have? Any special features worth noting?

b. *Compare or contrast it:* What is your subject similar to? What is your subject different from? In what ways?

c. *Free-associate it:* What does this subject remind you of? What does it call to mind? What memories does it conjure up?

d. *Analyze it:* How does it work? How are the parts connected? What is its significance?

e. *Argue for or against it:* What arguments can you make for or against your subject? What advantages or disadvantages does it have? What changes or improvements should be made?

f. *Apply it:* What are the uses of your subject? What can you do with it?

A student who had recently volunteered at a homeless shelter wrote the following responses about her experience:

a. *Describe it:* I and five other members of my campus organization volunteered three Saturdays to work at the shelter here in town. We mainly helped in the kitchen, preparing, serving, and cleaning up after meals. At the dinners we served about 70 homeless people, mostly men but also some families with small children and babies.

b. *Compare or contrast it:* I had never done anything like this before so it's hard to compare or contrast it to anything. It was different though from what I expected. I hadn't really thought much about the people who would be there—or to be honest I think I thought they would be pretty weird or sad and I was kind of dreading going there after I volunteered. But the people were just regular normal people. And they were very, very polite to us.

c. *Free-associate it:* Some of the people there reminded me of some of my relatives! John, the kitchen manager, said most of the people were just temporarily "down on their luck" and that reminded me of my aunt and uncle who came to stay with us for a while when I was in high school after my uncle lost his job.

d. *Analyze it:* I feel like I got a lot out of my experience. I think I had some wrong ideas about "the homeless" and working there made me think more about them as real people not just a faceless group.

e. *Argue for or against it:* I would encourage others to volunteer there. The work isn't hard and it isn't scary. It makes you appreciate what you've got and also makes you think about what you or your family might do if things went wrong for a while. It also makes you feel good to do something for people you don't even know.

f. *Apply it:* I feel like I am more knowledgeable when I hear people talk about the poor or the homeless in this town, especially those people who criticize those who use the shelter.

After you've written your responses, see if any one or more of them give you an idea for a paper. The student who wrote the preceding responses decided she wanted to write an article for her campus newspaper encouraging people to volunteer at the shelter not only to provide much-needed help but also to challenge their own preconceived notions about the homeless in her college town. Cubing helped her realize she had something valuable to say about her experience and gave her a purpose for writing.

7. Interviewing

Another way to find a direction for your paper is through interviewing. Ask a classmate or friend to discuss your subject with you. Let your thoughts range over your subject as your friend asks you questions that arise naturally in the conversation. Or your friend might try asking what are called "reporter's questions" as she or he "interviews" you on your subject:

Who?   When?
What?   Why?
Where?   How?

Listen to what you have to say about your subject. What were you most interested in talking about? What did your friend want to know? Why? By talking about your subject, you may find that you have talked your way into an interesting focus for your paper. If, after the interview, you are still stumped, question your friend: if he or she had to publish an essay based on the information from your interview, what would that essay focus on? Why?

8. The Cross-Examination

If a classmate isn't available for an interview, try interviewing, or cross-examining, yourself. Ask yourself questions about your general subject, just as a lawyer might if you were on the witness stand. Consider using the five categories described below, which are adapted from those suggested by Aristotle, centuries ago, to the orators of his day. Ask yourself as many questions in each category as you can think of, and then go on to the next category. Jot down brief notes to yourself as you answer.

Here are the five categories, plus six sample questions for each to illustrate the possibilities:

1. Definition

    a. How does the dictionary or encyclopedia define or explain this subject?
    b. How do most people define or explain it?
    c. How do I define or explain it?
    d. What do its parts look like?
    e. What is its history or origin?
    f. What are some examples of it?

2. Comparison and Contrast

    a. What is it similar to?
    b. What does it differ from?
    c. What does it parallel?
    d. What is it opposite to?
    e. What is it better than?
    f. What is it worse than?

3. Relationship

    a. What causes it?
    b. What are the effects of it?
    c. What larger group or category is it a part of?
    d. What larger group or category is it in opposition to?
    e. What are its values or goals?
    f. What contradictions does it contain?

4. Circumstance

    a. Is it possible?

    b. Is it impossible?

    c. When has it happened before?

    d. What might prevent it from happening?

    e. Why might it happen again?

    f. Who has been or might be associated with it?

5. Testimony

    a. What do people say about it?

    b. What has been written about it?

    c. What authorities exist on the subject?

    d. Are there any relevant statistics?

    e. What research has been done?

    f. Have I had any direct experience with it?

Some of the questions suggested here, or ones you think of, may not be relevant or useful to your subject. But some may lead you to ideas you wish to explore in more depth, either in a discovery draft or by using another prewriting technique described in this chapter, such as looping or mapping.

9. Sketching

Sometimes when you have found or been assigned a general subject, the words to explain or describe it just won't come. Although listing or freewriting or one of the other methods suggested here work well for some people, other writers find these techniques intimidating or unproductive. Some of these writers are visual learners—that is, they respond better to pictorial representations of material than they do to written descriptions or explanations. If, on occasion, you are stuck for words, try drawing or sketching or even cartooning the pictures in your mind.

You may be surprised at the details that you remember once you start sketching. For example, you might have been asked to write about a favorite place or a special person in your life or to compare or contrast two places you have lived or visited. See how many details you can conjure up by drawing the scenes or the people; then look at your details to see if some dominant impression or common theme has emerged. Your Aunt Sophie's insistence on wearing two pounds of costume jewelry might become the focus of a paragraph on her sparkling personality, or the many details you recalled about your grandfather's barn might lead you to a paper on the hardships of farm life. For some writers, a picture can be worth a thousand words—especially if that picture helps them begin putting those words on paper.

10. Dramatizing the Subject

Some writers find it helpful to visualize their subject as if it were a drama or play unfolding in their minds. Kenneth Burke, a thoughtful writer himself, suggests that writers might think about human action in dramatists' terms and then see what sorts of new insights arise as the "drama" unfolds. Burke's dramatists' terms might be adapted for our use and pictured this way:

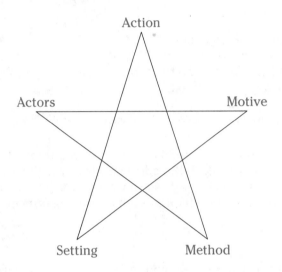

Action

Actors   Motive

Setting   Method

Just as you did in the cubing exercise, try mentally rolling your subject around the star above and explore the possibilities that emerge. For example, suppose you want to write about your recent decision to return to college after a long period of working, but you don't know what you want to say about your decision. Start thinking about this decision as a drama and jot down brief answers to such questions as these:

Action: What happened?
           What were the results?
           What is going to happen?

Actors: Who was involved in the action?
           Who was affected by the action?
           Who caused the action?
           Who was for it and who was opposed?

Motive: What were the reasons behind the action?
           What forces motivated the actors to perform as they did?

Method: How did the action occur?
           By what means did the actors accomplish the action?

Setting: What was the time and place of the action?

What did the place look like?

What positive or negative feelings are associated with this time or place?

These are only a few of the dozens of questions you might ask yourself about your "drama." (If it helps, think of your "drama" as a murder mystery and answer the questions the police detective might ask: what happened here? to whom? who did it? why? with what? when? where? and so on.)

You may find that you have a great deal to write about the combination of actor and motive but very little to say in response to the questions on setting or method. That's fine—simply use the "dramatists' approach" to help you find a specific topic or idea you want to write about.

> If at any point in this stage of the writing process, you are experiencing *Writer's Block,* you might turn to the suggestions for overcoming this common affliction, which appear on pages 123–125 in Chapter 5. You might also find it helpful to read the section on *Keeping a Journal,* pages 27–30 in this chapter, as writing in a relaxed mood on a regular basis may be the best long-term cure for your writing anxiety.

AFTER YOU'VE FOUND YOUR FOCUS

Once you think you've found the focus of your essay, you may be ready to compose a *working thesis statement,* an important part of your essay discussed in great detail in the next chapter. If you've used one of the prewriting exercises outlined in this chapter, by all means hang onto it. The details and observations you generated as you focused your topic may be useful to you as you begin to organize and develop your body paragraphs.

 PRACTICING WHAT YOU'VE LEARNED

A. Some of the subjects listed below are too broad for a 500- to 800-word essay. Identify those topics that might be treated in short papers and those that still need to be narrowed.

    1. The role of the modern university

    2. My first (and last) experience with roller blading

3. The characters of William Shakespeare

4. Solar energy

5. Collecting baseball cards

6. Gun-control laws

7. Down with throw-away bottles

8. Computers

9. The best teacher I've ever had

10. Selecting the right bicycle

B. Select two of the large subjects that follow, and, through looping or listing details or another prewriting technique, find focused topics that would be appropriate for essays of 500 to 800 words.

1. music

2. cars

3. education

4. jobs

5. television commercials

6. politics

7. animals

8. childhood

9. pollution

10. athletics

DISCOVERING YOUR AUDIENCE

Once you have a focused topic and perhaps some ideas about developing your essay, you need to stop a moment to consider your *audience*. Before you can decide what information needs to go in your essay and what should be omitted, you must know who will be reading your paper and why. Knowing your audience will also help you determine what *voice* you should use to achieve the proper tone in your essay.

Suppose, for example, you are attending a college organized on the quarter system, and you decide to write an essay arguing for a switch to the semester system. If your audience is composed of classmates, your essay will probably focus on the advantages to the student body, such as better opportunities for in-depth study in one's major, the ease of making better grades, and the benefits of longer mid-winter and summer vacations. However, if you are addressing the Board of Regents, you might emphasize the power of the semester system to attract more students, cut registration costs, and use professors more efficiently. If your audience is composed of townspeople who know little about either system, you will have to devote more time to explaining the logistics of each one and then discuss the semester plan's advantages to the local merchants, realtors, restauranteurs, and so on. *In other words, such factors as the age, education, profession, and interests of your audience can make a difference in determining which points of your argument to stress or omit, which ideas need additional explanation, and what kind of language to adopt.*

HOW TO IDENTIFY YOUR READERS

To help you analyze your audience before you begin writing your working thesis statement and rough drafts, here are some steps you may wish to follow:

1. First, see if your writing assignment specifies a particular audience (editors of a journal in your field or the Better Business Bureau of your town, for example) or a general audience of your peers (your classmates or readers of the local newspaper, for instance). Even if your assignment does not mention an intended audience, try to imagine one anyway. Imagining specific readers will help you stick to your goal of communicating with others. Forgetting that they have an audience of real people often causes writers to address themselves to their typing paper, a mistake that usually results in dull or unclear prose.

2. If a specific audience is designated, ask yourself some questions about their motivation or *reasons for reading* your essay.

- What do these readers want to learn?
- What do they hope to gain?
- Do they need your information to make a decision? Formulate a new plan? Design a new project?
- What action do you want them to take?

The answers to such questions will help you find both your essay's purpose and its content. If, for example, you're trying to persuade an employer to hire you for a particular job, you certainly would write your application in a way that stresses the skills and training the company is searching for. You may have a fine hobby or wonderful family, but if your prospective employer-reader doesn't need to hear about that particular part of your life, toss it out of this piece of writing.

3. Next, try to discover what *knowledge* your audience has of your subject.

- What, if anything, can you assume that your readers already know about your topic?

- What background information might they need to know to understand a current situation clearly?

- What facts, explanations, or examples will best present your ideas? How detailed should you be?

- What terms need to be defined? Equipment explained?

Questions like these should guide you as you collect and discard information for your paper. An essay written to your colleagues in electrical engineering, for instance, need not explain commonly used technical instruments; to do so might even insult your readers. But the same report read by your composition classmates would probably need more detailed explanation in order for you to make yourself understood. Always put yourself in your readers' place and then ask: what else do they need to know to understand this point completely?

4. Once you have decided what information is necessary for your audience, dig a little deeper into your readers' identities. Pose some questions about their *attitudes* and emotional states.

- Are your readers already biased for or against your ideas in some way?

- Do they have positive or negative associations with your subject?

- Are they fearful or anxious, reluctant or bored?

- Do they have radically different expectations or interests?

It helps enormously to know the emotional attitudes of your readers toward your subject. Let's suppose you were arguing for the admission of a child with AIDS into a local school system, and your audience was the parent-teacher organization. Some of your readers might be frightened or even hostile; knowing this, you would wisely begin your argument with a disarming array of information showing that no cases of AIDS have developed from the casual contact of schoolchildren. In other words, the more you know about your audience's attitudes before you begin writing, the more convincing your prose, because you will make the best choices about both content and organization.

5. Last, think of any *special qualities* that might set your audience apart from any other.

- Are they older or younger than your peers?

- Do they share similar educational experiences or training?

- Are they from a particular part of the world or country that might affect their perspective? Urban or rural?

- Are they in positions of authority?

Knowing special facts about your audience makes a difference, often in your choice of words and tone. You wouldn't, after all, use the same level of vocabulary addressing a group of fifth-graders as you would writing to the children's teacher or principal. Similarly, your tone and word choice probably wouldn't be as formal in a letter to a friend as in a letter to the telephone company protesting your most recent bill.

Without question, analyzing your specific audience is an important step to take before you begin to shape your rough drafts. And before you move on to writing a working thesis, here are a few tips to keep in mind about *all* audiences, no matter who your readers are or what their reasons for reading your writing.

1. Readers don't like to be bored. Grab your readers' attention and fight to keep it. Remember the last dull movie you squirmed—or slept—through? How much you resented wasting not only your money but your valuable time as well? How you turned it off mentally and drifted away to someplace more exciting? As you write and revise your drafts, keep imagining readers who are as intelligent—and busy—as you are. Put yourself in their place: would you find this piece of writing stimulating enough to keep reading?

2. Readers hate confusion and disorder. Can you recall a time when you tried to find your way to a party, only to discover that a friend's directions were so muddled you wound up hours later, out of gas, cursing in a cornfield? Or the afternoon you spent trying to follow a friend's notes for setting up a chemistry experiment, with explanations that twisted and turned as often as a wandering stray cat? Try to relive such moments of intense frustration as you struggle to make *your* writing clear and direct.

3. Readers want to think and learn (whether they realize it or not). Every time you write, you strike a bargain of sorts with your readers: in return for their time and attention, you promise to inform and interest them, to tell them something new or show them something familiar in a different light. You may enlighten them or amuse them or even try to frighten them—

but they must feel, in the end, that they've gotten a fair trade. As you plan, write, and revise, ask yourself, "What are my readers learning?" If the honest answer is "nothing important," you may be writing only for yourself. (If you yourself are bored rereading your drafts, you're probably not writing for anybody at all.)

4. Readers want to see what you see, feel what you feel. Writing that is vague keeps your readers from fully sharing the information or experience you are trying to communicate. Clear, precise language—full of concrete details and specific examples—lets your readers know that you understand your subject and that you want them to understand it, too. Even a potentially dull topic such as tuning a car can become engaging to a reader if the right details are provided in the right places: your terror as blue sparks leap under your nose when the wrong wire is touched, the depressing sight of the screwdriver squirming from your greasy fingers and disappearing into the oil pan, the sudden shooting pain when the wrench slips and turns your knuckles to raw hamburger. Get your readers involved and interested—and they'll listen to what you have to say. (Details also persuade your reader that you're an authority on your subject; after all, no reader likes to waste time listening to someone whose tentative, vague prose style announces "I only sort-of know what I'm talking about here.")

5. Readers are turned off by writers with pretentious, phony voices. Too often inexperienced writers feel they must sound especially scholarly, scientific, or sophisticated for their essays to be convincing. In fact, the contrary is true. When you assume a voice that is not yours, when you pretend to be someone you're not, you don't sound believable at all—you sound phony. Your readers want to hear what *you* have to say, and the best way to communicate with them is in a natural voice. You may also believe that to write a good essay it is necessary to use a host of unfamiliar, unpronounceable, polysyllabic words gleaned from the pages of your thesaurus. Again, the opposite is true. Our best writers agree with Mark Twain, who once said, "Never use a twenty-five-cent word when a ten-cent word will do." In other words, avoid pretension in your writing just as you do in everyday conversation. Select simple, direct words you know and use frequently; keep your voice natural, sincere, and reasonable. (For additional help choosing the appropriate words and the level of your diction, see Chapter 7.)

DON'T EVER FORGET YOUR READERS!

Thinking about them as you write will help you choose your ideas, organize your information effectively, and select the best words.

PRACTICING WHAT YOU'VE LEARNED

The article that follows appeared in newspapers across the country some time ago. Read about the new diet called "Breatharianism" and then write the assignments that follow the article.

The Ultimate in Diet Cults: Don't Eat Anything at All

1   CORTE MADERA, CALIF.—Among those seeking enlightenment through diet cults, Wiley Brooks seemed to have the ultimate answer—not eating at all. He called himself a "Breatharian" and claimed to live on air, supplemented only by occasional fluids taken to counteract the toxins of urban environments.

2   "Food is more addictive than heroin," the tall, gaunt man told hundreds of people who paid $500 each to attend five-day "intensives," at which he would stand before them in a camel velour sweatsuit and talk for hours without moving, his fingers meditatively touching at their tips.

3   Brooks, 46, became a celebrity on the New Age touring circuit. ABC-TV featured him in October, 1980, as a weight lifter; he allegedly hoisted 1,100 pounds, about 10 times his own weight. He has also been interviewed on radio and in newspapers.

4   Those who went to his sessions during the past six months on the West Coast and in Hawaii were not just food faddists, but also physicians and other professionals who—though not necessarily ready to believe—thought this man could be onto something important. Some were convinced enough by what they saw to begin limiting their own diets, taking the first steps toward Breatharianism.

5   In his intensives, Brooks did not recommend that people stop eating altogether. Rather, he suggested they "clean their blood" by starting with the "yellow diet"—24 food items including grapefruit, papaya, corn products, eggs, chicken, fish, goat's milk, millet, salsa piquante (Mexican hot sauce) and certain flavors of the Häagen Dazs brand ice cream, including "rum raisin." These foods, he said, have a less toxic effect because, among other things, "their vibrational quality is yellow."

6   Last week, however, aspirants toward Breatharianism were shocked by reports that Brooks had been eating—and what's more, eating things that to health food purists are the worst kind of junk.

7   Word spread that during an intensive in Vancouver, Brooks was seen emerging from a 7-Eleven store with a bag of groceries. The next morning there were allegedly room service trays outside his hotel room, while inside, the trash basket held empty containers of chicken pot pie, chili and biscuits.

8   Kendra Wagner, regional Breatharian coordinator, said she herself had seen Brooks drinking a Coke. "When I asked him about it he said, 'That's how dirty the air is here,'" she explained. "We (the coordinators) sat down with Wiley after the training and said, 'We want you to tell us the truth.' He denied everything. We felt tricked and deceived."

9   As the rumors grew, some Breatharians confronted their leader at a lecture in San Francisco. Brooks denied the story and said that the true message of Breatharianism did not depend on whether he ate or not, anyway.

10   The message in his promotional material reads that "modern man is the degenerate descendant of the Breatharian," and that "living on air alone leads to perfect health and perfect happiness." Though followers had the impression Brooks has not eaten for 18 years, his leaflets merely declare that "he does not eat, and seldom drinks any fluid. He sleeps less than seven hours a week and is healthier, more energetic and happier than he ever dreamed possible."

11   In a telephone interview, Brooks acknowledged that this assertion is not quite correct. "I'm sure I've taken some fruit, like an apple or an orange, but it's better in public to keep it simple." He again staunchly denied the 7-Eleven story.

12   Among those who have been on the yellow diet for months is Jime Collison, 24, who earlier tried "fruitarianism," fasting and other special regimens, and moved from Texas to the San Francisco Bay area just to be around the Breatharian movement. "Now I'm a basket case," he said. "My world revolved around Wiley's philosophy." He had thought Wiley "made the jump to where all of us health food fanatics were going," Collison said.

13   Other Brooks disciples, though disappointed, feel they nevertheless benefitted from their experience. Said a physician who has been on the yellow diet for four months: "I feel very good. I still don't know what the truth is, but I do know that Wiley is a good salesman. So I'll be patient, keep an open mind and continue to observe."

14   "Breatharianism is the understanding of what the body really needs, not whether Wiley eats or doesn't," said James Wahler, 35, who teaches a self-development technique called "rebirthing," in Marin County. "I'm realizing that the less I eat the better I feel." He also suggested that Brooks may have lied for people's own good, to get them to listen.

15   "Everyone has benefitted from what I'm saying," Brooks said. "There will be a food shortage and a lot of unhappy people when they realize that I was trying to save their lives."

Each of the assignments that follow is directed to a different audience, none of whom know much about Breatharianism. What information does each audience need to know? What kinds of details will be the most persuasive? What sort of organization will work best for each purpose and audience?

1. Write a brief radio advertisement for the five-day intensives. What appeals will persuade people to pay $500 each to attend a seminar to learn to eat air?

2. Assume you are a regional Breatharian coordinator. Write a letter to your City Council petitioning for a parade permit that will allow members of your organization to parade down your main street in support of this diet and its lifestyle. What do Council members need to know and understand before they vote for such a permit?

3. You are a former Breatharian who is now unhappy with the diet and its unfulfilled promises. Write a report for the Vice Squad calling for an investigation into the organization. Convince the investigators that the organization is defrauding local citizens and should be stopped.

After writing these assignments, you might exchange them with those written by some of your classmates. Which ads, petitions, and reports are the most persuasive and why?

KEEPING A JOURNAL
(TALKING TO YOURSELF *DOES* HELP)

Many professional writers carry small notebooks with them so they can jot down ideas and impressions for future use. Other people have kept daily logs or diaries for years to record their thoughts for their own enjoyment. In your composition class, you may find it useful to keep a journal that will help you with your writing process, especially in the early stages of prewriting. Journals can also help you to prepare for class discussions and to remember important course material.

You may have kept a journal in another class. There, it may have been called a daybook or learning log or some other name. Although the journal has a variety of uses, it frequently is assigned to encourage you to record your responses to the material read or discussed in class as well as your own thoughts and questions. Most often the journal is kept in a notebook of some kind (spiral is fine, although you may find a prong or ring notebook more convenient because it will allow you to add or remove pages where and when you wish). Even if a journal is not an assigned part of your composition class, it is still a useful notebook for you to keep.

Writers who have found journal writing effective advise trying to write a minimum of three entries a week, with each entry at least a half page. To keep your entries organized, you might start each entry on a new page and date each entry you write. You might also leave the backs of your pages blank so that you can return and respond to an entry at a later date if you wish.

Uses of the Journal

Here are some suggested uses for your journal as you begin and move through the writing process. You may want to experiment with a number of these suggestions to see which are the most productive for you.

1. Use the journal, especially in the first weeks of class, to confront your fears of writing, to conquer the blank page. Write anything you want to—thoughts, observations, notes to yourself, letters home, anything at all. Best your enemy by writing down that witty retort you thought of later and wished you had said. Write about your ideal job, vacation, car, or home. Write a self-portrait or make a list of all the subjects that you are (or would like to become) an "authority" on. The more you write, the easier writing becomes—or at least, the easier it is to begin writing because, like a sword swallower, you know you have accomplished the act before and lived to tell about it.

2. Improve your powers of observation. Record interesting snippets of conversations you overhear or catalog noises you hear in a ten-minute period in a crowded place, such as your student center, a bookstore, or a mall. Eat something with multiple layers (a piece of fruit such as an orange) and list all the tastes, textures, and smells you discover. Look around your room and write down a list of everything that is yellow. By becoming sensitive to the sights, sounds, smells, and textures around you, you may find that your powers of description and explanation will expand, enabling you to help your reader "see" what you're talking about in your next essay.

3. Save your own brilliant ideas. Jot down those bright ideas that might turn into great essays. Or save those thoughts you have now for the essay you know is coming later in the semester so you won't forget them. Expand or elaborate on any ideas you have; you might be able to convert your early thoughts into a paragraph when it's time to start drafting.

4. Save other people's brilliant ideas. Record interesting quotations, facts, and figures from other writers and thinkers. You may find some of this information useful in one of your later essays. It's also helpful to look at the ways other writers make their words emphatic, moving, and arresting so you can try some of their techniques in your own prose. (Important: Don't forget to note the source of any material you record, so if you do quote any of it in a paper later, you will be able to document it properly.)

5. Be creative. Write a poem or song or story or joke. Parody the style of someone you've heard or read. Become an inanimate object and complain to the humans around you (for example, what would a soft-drink machine like to say to those folks constantly beating on its stomach?). Become a little green creature from Mars and convince a human to accompany you back to your planet as a specimen of Earthlings (or be the invited guest and explain to the creature why you are definitely not the person to go). The possibilities are endless, so go wild.

6. Prepare for class. If you've been given a reading assignment (an essay or article or pages from a text, for instance), try a split-page entry. Draw a line down the middle of a page in your journal and on the left side of the page write a summary of what you've read or perhaps list the main points. Then on the right side of the same page, write your responses to the material. Your responses might be your personal reaction to the content (what struck you hardest? why?), or it might be your agreement or disagreement with a particular point or two. Or the material might call up some long-forgotten idea or memory. By thinking about your class material both analytically and personally, you almost certainly will remember it for class discussion. You might also find that a good idea for an essay will arise as you think about the reading assignments in different ways.

7. Record responses to class discussions. A journal is a good place to jot down your reactions to what your teacher and your peers are saying in class. You can ask yourself questions ("What did Megan mean when she said . . .") or note any confusion ("I got mixed up when . . .") or record your own reactions ("I disagree with Jason when he argued that . . ."). Again, some of your reactions might become the basis of a good essay.

8. Focus on a problem. You can restate the problem or explore the problem or solve the problem. Writing about a problem often encourages the mind to flow over the information in ways that allow discoveries to happen. Sometimes, too, we don't know exactly what the problem is or how we feel about it until we write about it. (You can see the truth of this statement almost every week if you're a reader of advice columns such as "Dear Abby"—invariably someone will write a letter asking for help and end by saying, "Thanks for letting me write; I know now what I should do.")

9. Practice audience awareness. Write letters to different companies, praising or panning their product; then write advertising copy for each product. Become the third critic on a popular movie-review program and show the other two commentators why your review of your favorite movie is superior to theirs. Thinking about a specific audience when you write will help you plan the content, organization, and tone of each writing assignment.

10. Describe your own writing process. It's helpful sometimes to record how you go about writing your essays. How do you get started? How much time do you spend getting started? Do you write an "idea" draft or work from an outline? How do you revise? Do you write multiple drafts? These and many other questions may give you a clue to any problems you may have as you write your next essay. If, for example, you see that you're having trouble again and again with conclusions, you can turn to Chapter 4 for some extra help. Sometimes it's hard to see that there's a pattern in our writing process until we've described it several times.

11. Write a progress report. List all the skills you've mastered as the course progresses. You'll be surprised at how much you have learned. Read the list over if you're ever feeling frustrated or discouraged, and take pride in your growth.

12. Become sensitive to language. Keep a record of jokes and puns that play on words. Record people's weird-but-funny uses of language (overheard at the dorm cafeteria: "She was so skinny she was emancipated" and "I'm tired of being the escape goat"). Rewrite some of today's bureaucratic jargon or retread a cliché. Come up with new images of your own. Playing with language in fun or even silly ways may make writing tasks seem less threatening.

13. Write your own textbook. Make notes on material that is important for you to remember. For instance, make your own grammar or punctuation handbook with only those rules you find yourself referring to often. Or keep a list of spelling rules that govern the words you misspell frequently. Writing out the rules in your own words and having a convenient place to refer to them may help you teach yourself quicker than studying any textbook (including this one).

These suggestions are some of the many uses you may find for your journal once you start writing in one on a regular basis. Obviously, not all of the suggestions here will be appropriate for you, but some might be, so you might consider using a set of divider tabs to separate the different functions of your journal (one section for class responses, one section for your own thoughts, one for your own handbook, and so on).

You may find, as some students have, that the journal is especially useful during the first weeks of your writing course when putting pen to paper is often hardest. Many students, however, continue to use the journal throughout the entire course, and others adapt their journals to record their thoughts and responses to their other college courses and experiences. Whether you continue using a journal beyond this course is up to you, but consider trying the journal for at least six weeks. You may find that it will improve your writing skills more than anything else you have tried before.

CHAPTER 1 SUMMARY

Here is a brief summary of what you should know about the prewriting stage of your writing process:

1. Before you begin writing anything, remember that you have valuable ideas to tell your readers.

2. Moreover, it's not enough that these valuable ideas are clear to you, the writer. Your single most important goal is to communicate those ideas clearly to your readers, who cannot know what's in your mind until you tell them.

3. Whenever possible, select a subject to write on that is of great interest to you, and always give yourself more time than you think you'll need to work on your essay.

4. Try a variety of prewriting techniques to help you find your essay's purpose and a narrowed, specific focus.

5. Review your audience's knowledge of and attitudes toward your topic before you begin your first draft; ask yourself questions such as "Who needs to know about this topic, and why?"

6. Consider keeping a journal to help you explore good ideas and possible topics for writing in your composition class.

CHAPTER

2

The Thesis Statement

The famous American author Thomas Wolfe had a simple formula for beginning his writing: "Just put a sheet of paper in the typewriter and start bleeding." For some writers, the "bleeding" method works well. You may find that, indeed, you are one of those writers who must begin by freewriting or by writing an entire "discovery draft"* to find your purpose and focus—you must write yourself into your topic, so to speak. Other writers are more structured; they may prefer prewriting in lists, maps, or cubes. Sometimes writers begin certain projects by composing one way, whereas other kinds of writing tasks profit from another method. There is no right or wrong way to find a topic or to begin writing; simply try to find the methods that work best for you.

Let's assume at this point that you have identified a topic you wish to write about—perhaps you found it by working through one of the prewriting activities mentioned in Chapter 1 or by writing in your journal. Perhaps you had an important idea you have been wanting to write about for some time, or perhaps the assignment in your class suggested the topic to you. Suppose

---

*If you do begin with a discovery draft, you may wish to turn at this point to the manuscript suggestions on pages 104–105 in Chapter 5.

that through one of these avenues you have focused on a topic and you have given some thought to a possible audience for your paper. You may now find it helpful to formulate a *working thesis*.

WHAT IS A THESIS? WHAT DOES A "WORKING THESIS" DO?

The thesis statement declares the main point or controlling idea of your entire essay. Frequently located near the beginning of a short essay, the thesis answers the questions "What is the subject of this essay?"; "What is the writer's opinion on this subject?"; "What is the writer's purpose in this essay?" (to explain something? to argue a position? to move people to action? to entertain?).

Consider a "working thesis" a statement of your main point in its trial or rough-draft form. Allow it to "work" for you as you move from prewriting through drafts and revision. Your working thesis may begin as a very simple sentence. For example, one of the freewriting exercises on nature in Chapter 1 (p. 9) might lead to a working thesis such as "Our college needs an on-campus recycling center." Such a working thesis states an opinion about the subject (the need for a center) and suggests what the essay will do (give arguments for building such a center). Similarly, the prewriting list on jogging (p. 7) might lead to a working thesis such as "Before beginning a successful jogging program, novice runners must learn a series of warm-up and cool-down exercises." This statement not only tells the writer's opinion and purpose (the value of the exercises) but also indicates an audience (novice runners).

A working thesis statement can be your most valuable organizational tool. Once you have thought about your essay's main point and purpose, you can begin to draft your paper to accomplish your goals. *Everything in your essay should support your thesis.* Consequently, if you write your working thesis statement at the top of your first draft and refer to it often, your chances of drifting away from your purpose should be reduced.

CAN A "WORKING THESIS" CHANGE?

It's important for you to know at this point that there may be a difference between the working thesis that appears in your rough drafts and your final thesis. As you begin drafting, you may have one main idea in mind that surfaced from your prewriting activities. But as you write, you discover that what you really want to write about is different. Perhaps you discover that one particular part of your essay is really what you want to concentrate on (instead of covering three or four problems you have with your current job, for instance, you decide you want to explore in depth only the difficulties with your boss), or perhaps in the course of writing you find another approach to your subject more satisfying or persuasive (explaining how employees may avoid problems with a particular kind of difficult boss as opposed to describing various kinds of difficult bosses in your field).

Changing directions is not uncommon: *writing is an act of discovery.* Frequently we don't know exactly what we think or what we want to say until we write it. A working thesis appears in your early drafts to help you focus and organize your essay; don't feel it's carved in stone.

A warning comes with this advice, however. If you do write yourself into another essay—that is, if you discover that as you write you are finding a better topic or main point to make, consider this piece of writing a "discovery draft," extended prewriting that has helped you find your real focus. Occasionally, your direction changes so slightly that you can rework or expand your thesis to accommodate your new ideas. But more frequently you may find that it's necessary to begin another draft with your newly discovered working thesis as the controlling idea. When this is the case, don't be discouraged—this kind of "reseeing" or revision of your topic is a common practice among experienced writers (for more advice on revising as rethinking, see Chapter 5). Don't be tempted at this point to leave your original thesis in an essay that has clearly changed its point, purpose, or approach—in other words, don't try to pass off an old head on the body of a new statue! Remember that ultimately you want your thesis to guide your readers rather than confuse them by promising an essay they can't find as they read on.

GUIDELINES FOR WRITING A GOOD THESIS

To help you draft your thesis statement, here is some advice:

A good thesis states the writer's clearly defined opinion on some subject. You must tell your reader what you think. Don't dodge the issue; present your opinion specifically and precisely. For example, if you were asked to write a thesis statement expressing your position on the national law that designates twenty-one the legal minimum age to purchase or consume alcohol, the first three theses listed below would be confusing:

Poor Many people have different opinions on whether people under twenty-one should be permitted to drink alcohol, and I agree with some of them. [The writer's opinion on the issue is not clear to the reader.]

Poor The question of whether we need a national law governing the minimum age to drink alcohol is a controversial issue in many states.

[This statement might introduce the thesis, but the writer has still avoided stating a clear opinion on the issue.]

Poor   I want to give my opinion on the national law that sets twenty-one as the legal age to drink alcohol and the reasons I feel this way. [What is the writer's opinion? The reader still doesn't know.]

Better   To reduce the number of highway fatalities, our country needs to enforce the national law that designates twenty-one as the legal minimum age to purchase and consume alcohol. [The writer clearly states an opinion that will be supported in the essay.]

Better   The legal minimum age for purchasing alcohol should be eighteen rather than twenty-one. [Again, the writer has asserted a clear position on the issue that will be argued in the essay.]

   A good thesis asserts one main idea. Many essays drift into confusion because the writer is trying to explain or argue two different, large issues in one essay. You can't effectively ride two horses at once; pick one main idea and explain or argue it in convincing detail.

Poor   The proposed no-smoking ordinance in our town will violate a number of our citizens' civil rights, and no one has proved secondary smoke is dangerous anyway. [This thesis contains two main assertions—the ordinance's violation of rights and secondary smoke's lack of danger—that require two different kinds of supporting evidence.]

Better   The proposed no-smoking ordinance in our town will violate our civil rights. [This essay will show the various ways the ordinance will infringe on personal liberties.]

Better   The most recent U.S. Health Department studies claiming that secondary smoke is dangerous to nonsmokers are based on faulty research. [This essay will also focus on one issue: the validity of the studies on secondary smoke danger.]

Poor   High school athletes shouldn't have to maintain a certain grade-point average to participate in school sports, and the value of sports is often worth the lower academic average. [Again, this essay moves in two different directions.]

Better   High school athletes shouldn't have to maintain a certain grade-point average to participate in school sports. [This essay will focus on one issue: reasons why a particular average shouldn't be required.]

Better   For some students, participation in sports may be more valuable than achieving a high grade-point average. [This essay will focus on why the benefits of sports may sometimes outweigh those of academics.]

Incidentally, at this point you may recall from your high school days a rule about always expressing your thesis in one sentence. Writing teachers often insist on this rule to help you avoid the double-assertion problem just illustrated. Although not all essays have one-sentence theses, many do, and it's a good habit to strive for in this early stage of your writing.

A good thesis has something worthwhile to say. Although it's true that almost any subject can be made interesting with the right treatment, some subjects are more predictable and therefore more boring than others. Before you write your thesis, think hard about your subject: does your position lend itself to stale or overly obvious ideas? For example, most readers would find the following theses tiresome unless the writers had some original method of developing their essays:

Poor   Dogs have always been man's best friends. [This essay might be full of ho-hum clichés about dogs' faithfulness to their masters.]

Poor   Friendship is a wonderful thing. [Again, watch out for tired truisms that restate the obvious.]

Poor   Food in my dorm is horrible. [Although this essay might be enlivened by some vividly repulsive imagery, the subject itself is ancient.]

Frequently in composition classes you will be asked to write about yourself; after all, you are the world's authority on that subject, and you have many significant interests to talk about whose subject matter will naturally intrigue your readers. However, some topics you may consider writing about may not necessarily appeal to other readers because the material is simply too personal or restricted to be of general interest. In these cases, it often helps to *universalize* the essay's thesis so your readers can also identify with or learn something about the general subject, while learning something about you at the same time:

Poor   The four children in my family have completely different personalities. [This statement may be true, but would anyone other than the children's parents really be fascinated with this topic?]

Better   Birth order can influence children's personalities in startling ways. [The writer is wiser to offer this controversial statement, which is of more interest to readers than the preceding one because many readers have brothers and sisters of their own. The writer can then illustrate her claims with examples from her own family, and from other families, if she wishes.]

Poor   I don't like to take courses that are held in big lecture classes at this school. [Why should your reader care one way or another about your class preference?]

Better   Large lecture classes provide a poor environment for the student who learns best through interaction with both teachers and peers. [This thesis will allow the writer to present personal examples that the reader may identify with or challenge, without writing an essay that is exclusively personal.]

In other words, try to select a subject that will interest, amuse, challenge, persuade, or enlighten your readers. If your subject itself is commonplace, find a unique approach or an unusual, perhaps even controversial, point of view. If your subject is personal, ask yourself if the topic alone will be sufficiently interesting to readers; if not, think about universalizing the thesis to include your audience. Remember that a good thesis should encourage readers to read on with enthusiasm rather than invite groans of "not this again" or shrugs of "so what."

A good thesis is limited to fit the assignment. Your thesis should show that you've narrowed your subject matter to an appropriate size for your essay. Don't allow your thesis to promise more of a discussion than you can adequately deliver in a short essay. You want an in-depth treatment of your subject, not a superficial one. Certainly you may take on important issues in your essays; don't feel you must limit your topics to local or personal subjects. But one simply cannot refight Vietnam or effectively defend U.S. foreign policy in Central America in five to eight paragraphs. Focus your essay on an important part of a broader subject that interests you. (For a review of ways to narrow and focus your subject, see pp. 4–19.)

Poor   Nuclear power should be banned as an energy source in this country. [Can the writer give the broad subject of nuclear power a fair treatment in three to five pages?]

Better   Because of its poor safety record during the past two years, the Collin County nuclear power plant should be closed. [This writer could probably argue this focused thesis in a short essay.]

Poor   The parking permit system at this college should be completely revised. [An essay calling for the revision of the parking permit system would involve discussion of permits for various kinds of students, faculty, administrators, staff, visitors, delivery personnel, disabled persons, and so forth. Therefore, the thesis is probably too broad for a short essay.]

Better   Because of the complicated application process, the parking permit system at this university penalizes disabled students. [This thesis is focused on a particular problem and could be argued in a short paper.]

Poor   African-American artists have always contributed a lot to many kinds of American culture. ["African-American artists," "many kinds," "a lot," and "culture" cover more ground than can be dealt with in one short essay.]

Better   Scott Joplin was a major influence in the development of the uniquely American music called ragtime. [This thesis is more specifically defined.]

A good thesis is clearly stated in specific terms. More than anything, a vague thesis reflects lack of clarity in the writer's mind and almost inevitably leads to an essay that talks around the subject but never makes a coherent point. Try to avoid words whose meanings are imprecise or those that depend largely on personal interpretation, such as "interesting," "good," and "bad."

Poor   The women's movement is good for our country. [What group does the writer refer to? How is it good? For whom?]

Better   The Colorado Women's Party is working to ensure the benefits of equal pay for equal work for both males and females in our state. [This tells who will benefit and how—clearly defining the thesis.]

Poor   Registration is a big hassle. [No clear idea is communicated here. How much trouble is a "hassle"?]

Better   Registration's alphabetical fee-paying system is inefficient. [The issue is specified.]

Poor   Living in an apartment for the first time can teach you many things about taking care of yourself. ["Things" and "taking care of yourself" are both too vague—what specific ideas does the writer want to discuss? And who is the "you" the writer has in mind?]

Better   By living in an apartment, freshmen can learn valuable lessons in financial planning and time management. [The thesis is now clearly defined and directed.]

A good thesis is easily recognized as the main idea, and is often located in the first or second paragraph. Many students are hesitant to spell out a thesis at the beginning of an essay. To quote one student, "I feel as if I'm giving everything away." Although you may feel uncomfortable "giving away" the main point so soon, the alternative of waiting until the last page to present your thesis can seriously weaken your essay.

Without an assertion of what you are trying to prove, your reader does not know how to assess the supporting details your essay presents. For example, if your roommate comes home one afternoon and points out that the roof on your apartment leaks, the rent is too high, and the closet space is too small, you may agree but you may also be confused. Does your roommate want you to call the owner or is this merely a gripe session? How should you respond? On the other hand, if your roommate first announces that he wants the two of you to look for a new place, you can put the discussion of the roof, rent, and closets into its proper context and react accordingly. Similarly, you write an essay to have a specific effect on your readers. You will have a better chance of producing this effect if the readers understand what you are trying to do.

Granted, some essays whose position is unmistakably obvious from the outset can get by with a strongly *implied thesis,* and it's true that some essays, often those written by professional writers, are organized to build dramatically to a climax. But if you are an inexperienced writer, the best choice at this point still may be to give a clear statement of your main idea. It is, after all, your responsibility to make your purpose clear, with as little expense of time and energy on the readers' part as possible. Readers should not be forced to puzzle out your essay's main point—it's your job to tell them.

Remember: an essay is not a detective story, so don't keep your readers in suspense until the last minute. Until you feel comfortable with more sophisticated patterns of organization, plan to put your clearly worded thesis statement near the beginning of your essay.

AVOIDING COMMON ERRORS IN THESIS STATEMENTS

Here are five mistakes to avoid when forming your thesis statements:

1. Don't make your thesis merely an announcement of your subject matter or a description of your intentions. State an attitude toward the subject.

Poor   The subject of this theme is my experience with a pet boa constrictor. [This is an announcement of the subject, not a thesis.]

Poor   I'm going to discuss boa constrictors as pets. [This represents a statement of intention but not a thesis.]

Better   Boa constrictors do not make healthy indoor pets. [The writer states an opinion that will be explained and defended in the essay.]

Better   My pet boa constrictor, Sir Pent, was a much better bodyguard than my dog, Fang. [The writer states an opinion that will be explained and illustrated in the essay.]

2. Don't clutter your thesis with expressions such as "in my opinion," "I believe," and "in this essay I'll argue that. . . ." These unnecessary phrases weaken your thesis statement because they often make you sound timid or uncertain. This is your essay; therefore, the opinions expressed are obviously yours. Be forceful: speak directly, with conviction.

Poor   My opinion is that the federal government should devote more money to solar energy research.

Poor   My thesis states that the federal government should devote more money to solar energy research.

Better The federal government should devote more money to solar energy research.

Poor   In this essay I will present lots of reasons why horse racing should not be legalized in Texas.

Better Horse racing should not be legalized in Texas.

3. Don't be unreasonable. Making irrational or oversimplified claims will not persuade your reader that you have a thorough understanding of the issue. Don't insult any reader; avoid irresponsible charges, name calling, and profanity.

Poor   Radical religious fanatics across the nation are trying to impose their right-wing views by censoring high school library books. [Words such as "radical," "fanatics," "right-wing," and "censoring" will antagonize many readers immediately.]

Better Only local school board members—not religious leaders or parents— should decide which books high school libraries should order.

Poor   Too many corrupt books in our high school libraries selected by liberal, atheistic educators are undermining the morals of our youth. [Again, some readers will be offended.]

Better To ensure that high school libraries contain books that reflect community standards, parents should have a voice in selecting new titles.

4. Don't merely state a fact. A thesis is an assertion of opinion that leads to discussion. Don't select an idea that is self-evident or dead-ended.

Poor   Child abuse is a terrible problem. [Yes, of course; who wouldn't agree that child abuse is terrible?]

Better Child-abuse laws in this state are too lenient for repeat offenders. [This thesis will lead to a discussion in which supporting arguments and evidence will be presented.]

Poor   Advertisers often use attractive models in their ads to sell products. [True, but rather obvious. How could this essay be turned into something more than a list describing one ad after another?]

Better   A number of liquor advertisers, well known for using pictures of attractive models to sell their products, are now using special graphics to send subliminal messages to their readers. [This claim is controversial and will require persuasive supporting evidence.]

Better   Although long criticized for their negative portrayal of women in television commercials, the auto industry is just as often guilty of stereotyping men as brainless idiots unable to make a decision. [This thesis makes a point that may lead to an interesting discussion.]

   5. Don't express your thesis in the form of a question unless the answer is already obvious to the reader.

Poor   Why should every college student be required to take two years of foreign language?

Better   Chemistry majors should be exempt from the foreign language requirement.

REMEMBER

Many times writers "discover" a better thesis near the end of their first draft. That's fine—consider that draft a prewriting or focusing exercise and begin another draft, using the newly discovered thesis as a starting point.

 PRACTICING WHAT YOU'VE LEARNED

A. Identify each of the following thesis statements as adequate or inadequate. If the thesis is weak or insufficient in some way, explain the problem.

   1. I think *Titanic* is a really interesting movie that everyone should see.

   2. Which cars are designed better, Japanese imports or those made in America?

   3. Some people think that the state lottery is a bad way to raise money for parks.

4. My essay will tell you how to apply for a college loan with the least amount of trouble.

5. During the fall term, final examinations should be given before the Winter break, not after the holidays as they are now.

6. Raising the cost of tuition will be a terrible burden on the students and won't do anything to help the quality of education at this school.

7. I can't stand to even look at people who are into body piercing, especially in their face.

8. The passage of the newly proposed health-care bill for the elderly will lead to socialized medicine in this country.

9. Persons over seventy-five should be required to renew their driver's licenses every year.

10. Having a close friend you can talk to is very important.

B. Rewrite the sentences below so that each one is a clear thesis statement. Be prepared to explain why you changed the sentences as you did.

1. Applying for a job can be a negative experience.

2. Skiing is a lot of fun, but it can be expensive and dangerous.

3. There are many advantages and disadvantages to the county's new voting machines.

4. The deregulation of the telephone system has been one big headache.

5. In this paper I will debate the pros and cons of the controversial motorcycle helmet law.

6. We need to do something about the billboard clutter on the main highway into town.

7. The insurance laws in this country need to be rewritten.

8. Bicycle riding is my favorite exercise because it's so good for me.

9. In my opinion, Santa Barbara is a fantastic place.

10. The Civil Rights Movement of the 1960s had a tremendous effect on this country.

ASSIGNMENT

Narrow the subject and write one good thesis sentence for five of the following topics:

1. A political or social issue

2. College or high school

3. Family

4. A hobby or pastime

5. A recent book or movie

6. Vacations

7. An environmental issue

8. A current fad or fashion

9. A job or profession

10. A rule, law, or regulation

USING THE ESSAY MAP*

Many thesis sentences will benefit from the addition of an *essay map,* a brief statement in the introductory paragraph introducing the major points to be discussed in the essay. Consider the analogy of beginning a trip by checking your map to see where you are headed. Similarly, an essay map allows the readers to know in advance where you, the writer, will be taking them in the essay.

Let's suppose you have been assigned the task of praising or criticizing some aspect of your campus. You decide that your thesis will be "The Study Skills Center is an excellent place for freshmen to receive help with basic courses." Although your thesis does take a stand ("excellent place"), your reader will not know why the Center is helpful or what points you will cover in your argument. With an essay map added, the reader will have a brief but specific idea where the essay is going and how it will be developed:

Thesis	The Study Skills Center is an excellent place for freshmen to receive help with basic courses. The Center's numerous free ser-
Essay map (underlined)	vices, well-trained tutors, and variety of supplementary learning

---

*I am indebted to Susan Wittig for this useful concept, introduced in *Steps to Structure: An Introduction to Composition and Rhetoric* (Cambridge, MA: Winthrop Publishers, 1975), pages 125–126.

materials can often mean the difference between academic success and failure for many students.

Thanks to the essay map, the reader knows that the essay will discuss the Center's free services, tutors, and learning materials.

Here's another example—this time let's assume you have been frustrated trying to read materials that have been placed "on reserve" in your campus library, so you decided to criticize your library's reserve facility:

Thesis Essay map (underlined)	The library's reserve facility is badly managed. Its unpredictable hours, poor staffing, and inadequate space discourage even the most dedicated students.

After reading the introductory paragraph, the reader knows the essay will discuss the reserve facility's problematic hours, staff, and space. In other words, the thesis statement defines the main purpose of your essay, and the essay map indicates the route you will take to accomplish that purpose.

The essay map often follows the thesis, but it can also appear before it. It is, in fact, frequently part of the thesis statement itself, as illustrated in the following examples:

Thesis with underlined essay map	Because of its free services, well-trained tutors, and useful learning aids, the Study Skills Center is an excellent place for freshmen seeking academic help.
Thesis with underlined essay map	For those freshmen who need extra help with their basic courses, the Study Skills Center is one of the best resources because of its numerous free services, well-trained tutors, and variety of useful learning aids.
Thesis with underlined essay map	Unreasonable hours, poor staffing, and inadequate space make the library reserve facility difficult to use.

In addition to suggesting the main points of the essay, the map provides two other benefits. It will provide a set of guidelines for organizing your essay, and it will help keep you from wandering off into areas only vaguely related to your thesis. A clearly written thesis statement and essay map provide a skeletal outline for the sequence of paragraphs in your essay, frequently with one body paragraph devoted to each main point mentioned in your map. (Chapter

3, on paragraphs, will explain in more detail the relationships among the thesis, the map, and the body of your essay.) Note that the number of points in the essay map may vary, although three or four may be the number found most often in 500- to 800-word essays. (More than four main points in a short essay may result in underdeveloped paragraphs; see pp. 64–69 for additional information.)

Some important advice: although essay maps can be helpful to both writers and readers, they can also sound too mechanical, repetitive, or obvious. If you choose to use a map, always strive to blend it with your thesis as smoothly as possible.

Poor The Study Skills Center is a helpful place for three reasons. The reasons are its free services, good tutors, and lots of learning materials.

Better Numerous free services, well-trained tutors, and a variety of useful learning aids make the Study Skills Center a valuable campus resource.

If you feel your essay map is too obvious or mechanical, try using it only in your rough drafts to help you organize your essay. Once you're sure it isn't necessary to clarify your thesis or to guide your reader, consider dropping it from your final draft.

 PRACTICING WHAT YOU'VE LEARNED

A. Identify the thesis and the essay map in the following sentences by underlining the map.

1. *Citizen Kane* deserves to appear on a list of "Top Movies of All Times" because of its excellent ensemble acting, its fast-paced script, and its innovative editing.

2. Our state should double the existing fines for first-offense drunk drivers. Such a move would lower the number of accidents, cut the costs of insurance, and increase the state revenues for highway maintenance.

3. To guarantee sound construction, lower costs, and personalized design, more people should consider building their own log cabin home.

4. Apartment living is preferable to dorm living because it's cheaper, quieter, and more luxurious.

5. Not everyone can become an astronaut. To qualify, a person must have intelligence, determination, and training.

6. Through unscrupulous uses of propaganda and secret assassination squads, Hitler was able to take control of an economically depressed Germany.

7. Because it builds muscles, increases circulation, and burns harmful fatty tissue, weight lifting is a sport that benefits the entire body.

8. The new tax bill will not radically reform the loophole-riddled revenue system: deductions on secondary residences will remain, real estate tax shelters are untouched, and nonprofit health organizations will be taxed.

9. Avocados make excellent plants for children. They're inexpensive to buy, easy to root, quick to sprout, and fun to grow.

10. His spirit of protest and clever phrasing blended into unusual musical arrangements have made Bob Dylan a recording giant for over twenty-five years.

B. Review the thesis statements you wrote for the Assignment on page 44. Write an essay map for each thesis statement. You may place the map before or after the thesis, or you may make it part of the thesis itself. Identify which part is the thesis and which is the essay map by underlining the map.

 ASSIGNMENT

Use one of the following quotations to help you think of a subject for an essay of your own. Don't merely repeat the quotation itself as your thesis statement but, rather, allow the quotation to lead you to your subject and a main point of your own creation that is appropriately narrowed and focused. Don't forget to designate an audience for your essay, a group of readers who need or want to hear what you have to say.

1. "Few things are harder to put up with than the annoyance of a good example"—Mark Twain, writer and humorist

2. "It is amazing how complete is the delusion that beauty is goodness"—Leo Tolstoy, writer

3. "The world is a book and those who don't travel read only a page"—St. Augustine, cleric

4. "Sports do not build character. They reveal it"—Heywood Hale Broun, sportscaster

5. "It is never too late to give up your prejudices"—Henry Thoreau, writer and naturalist

6. "When a thing is funny, search it carefully for a hidden truth"—George Bernard Shaw, writer

7. "I am a great believer in luck, and I find the harder I work the more I have of it"—Stephen Leacock, economist and humorist

8. "Noncooperation with evil is as much a moral obligation as is cooperation with good"—Martin Luther King, Jr., statesman and civil-rights activist

9. "Though familiarity may not breed contempt, it takes the edge off admiration"—William Hazlitt, writer

10. "In this world there are only two tragedies. One is not getting what one wants, and the other is getting it"—Oscar Wilde, writer

11. "It is never too late to be what one might have been"—George Eliot, writer

12. "Happiness is not something you experience; it's something you remember"—Oscar Levant, writer

13. "People change and forget to tell each other"—Lillian Hellman, writer

14. "Nobody can make you feel inferior without your consent"—Eleanor Roosevelt, stateswoman

15. "When a person declares that he's going to college, he's announcing that he needs four more years of coddling before he can face the real world"—Al Capp, creator of the *Li'l Abner* cartoon

16. "Family jokes are the bond that keeps most families alive"—Stella Benson, writer

17. "Nobody ever went broke underestimating the intelligence of the American public"—H.L. Mencken, writer and critic

18. "Even if you are on the right track, you will get run over if you just sit there"—Will Rogers, humorist and writer

19. "No matter what accomplishments you make, somebody helps you"—Althea Gibson, tennis champion

20. "Human beings are like tea bags. You don't know your own strength until you get into hot water"—Bruce Laingen, U.S. diplomat

CHAPTER 2 SUMMARY

Here's a brief review of what you need to know about the thesis statement:

1. A thesis statement declares the main point of your essay; it tells the reader what clearly defined opinion you hold.

2. Everything in your essay should support your thesis statement.

3. A good thesis statement asserts one main idea, narrowed to fit the assignment, and is stated in clear, specific terms.

4. A good thesis statement makes a reasonable claim about a topic that is of interest to its readers as well as to its writer.

5. The thesis statement is often presented near the beginning of the essay, frequently in the first or second paragraph, or is so strongly implied that readers cannot miss the writer's main point.

6. A "working" or trial thesis is an excellent organizing tool to use as you begin drafting because it can help you decide which ideas to include.

7. Because writing is an act of discovery, you may write yourself into a better thesis statement by the end of your first draft. Don't hesitate to begin a new draft with the new thesis statement.

8. Some writers may profit from using an essay map, a brief statement accompanying the thesis that introduces the supporting points discussed in the body of the essay.

CHAPTER 3

The Body Paragraphs

The middle or *body* of your essay is composed of paragraphs that support the thesis statement. By citing examples, explaining causes, offering reasons, or using other strategies in these paragraphs, you supply enough specific evidence to persuade your reader that the opinion expressed in your thesis is a sensible one. Each paragraph in the body usually presents and develops one main point in the discussion of your thesis. Generally, but not always, a new body paragraph signals another major point in the discussion.

PLANNING THE BODY OF YOUR ESSAY

Many writers like to have a plan before they begin drafting the body of their essay. To help you create a plan, first look at your thesis. If you used an essay map, as suggested in Chapter 2, you may find that the points mentioned there will provide the basis for the body paragraphs of your essay. For example, recall from Chapter 2 the thesis and essay map praising the Study Skills Center (p. 45): "Because of its free services, well-trained tutors, and useful learning aids, the Study Skills Center is an excellent place for freshmen seeking academic help." Your plan for developing the body of your essay might look like this:

Body paragraph one: discussion of free services
Body paragraph two: discussion of tutors
Body paragraph three: discussion of learning aids

At this point in your writing process you may wish to sketch in some of the supporting evidence you will include in each paragraph. You might find it helpful to go back to your prewriting activities (listing, looping, freewriting, mapping, cubing, and so on) to see what ideas surfaced then. Adding some examples and supporting details might make an informal outline of the Study Skills paper appear like this:

I.   Free services

    A Mini-course on improving study skills

    B. Tutoring < composition / math

    C. Weekly seminars < stress management / test anxiety / building vocabulary

    D. Testing for learning disabilities

II.   Tutors

    A. Top graduate students in their fields
    B. Experienced teachers
    C. Some bilingual
    D. Have taken training course at Center

III. Learning aids

    A. Supplementary texts
    B. Workbooks
    C. Audiovisual aids

Notice that this plan is an *informal* or *working outline* rather than a *formal outline*—that is, it doesn't have strictly parallel parts nor is it expressed in complete sentences. Unless your teacher requests a formal sentence or topic outline, don't feel you must make one at this early stage. Just consider using the informal outline to plot out a tentative plan that will help you start your first draft.

Here's an example of an informal outline at work: let's suppose you have been asked to write about your most prized possession—and you've chosen your 1966 Mustang, a car you have restored. You already have some ideas but as yet they're scattered and too few to make an interesting, well-developed essay. You try an informal outline, jotting down your ideas thus far:

I. Car is special because it was a gift from Dad

II. Fun to drive

III. Looks great—new paint job

IV. Engine in top condition

V. Custom features

VI. Car shows—fun to be part of

After looking at your outline, you see that some of your categories overlap and could be part of the same discussion. For example, your thoughts about the engine are actually part of the discussion of "fun to drive" and "custom features" are what make the car look great. Moreover, the outline may help you discover new ideas—custom features could be divided into those on the interior as well as those on the exterior of the car. The revised outline might look like this:

I. Gift from Dad

II. Fun to drive

    A. Engine
    B. Steering

III. Looks great

    A. New paint job
    B. Custom features
        1. exterior
        2. interior

IV. Car shows

You could continue playing with this outline, even moving big chunks of it around; for example, you might decide that what really makes the car so special is that it was a graduation gift from your dad and that is the note you want to end on. So you move "I. Gift from Dad" down to the last position in your outline.

The important point to remember about an informal or working outline is that it is there to help you—not control you. The value of an outline is its ability to help you plan, to help you see logical connections between your ideas, and to help you see obvious places to add new ideas and details. (The informal outline is also handy to keep around in case you're interrupted for a long period while you're drafting; you can always check the outline to see where you were and where you were going when you stopped.) In other words, *don't be intimidated by the outline!*

Here's one more example of an informal outline, this time for the thesis and essay map on the library reserve facility, from Chapter 2:

Thesis-map: Unpredictable hours, poor staffing, and inadequate space make the library's reserve facility difficult for students to use.

I.   Unpredictable hours

   A. Hours of operation vary from week to week
   B. Unannounced closures
   C. Closed on some holidays, open on others

II. Poor staffing

   A. Uninformed personnel at reserve desk
   B. Too few on duty at peak times

III. Inadequate space

   A. Room too small for number of users
   B. Too few chairs, tables
   C. Weak lighting

You may have more than three points to make in your essay. And, on occasion, you may need more than one paragraph to discuss a single point. For instance, you might discover that you need two paragraphs to explain fully the services at the Study Skills Center (for advice on splitting the discussion of a single point into two or more paragraphs, see p. 70). At this stage, you needn't bother trying to guess whether you'll need more than one paragraph per point; just use the outline to get going. Most writers don't know how much they have to say before they begin writing—and that's fine because writing itself is an act of discovery and learning.

When you are ready to begin drafting, read Chapter 5 for advice on composing and revising. Remember, too, that Chapter 5 contains suggestions for beating Writer's Block, should this condition arise while you are planning or drafting any part of your essay.

COMPOSING THE BODY PARAGRAPHS

There are many ways to organize and develop body paragraphs. Paragraphs developed by common patterns such as example, comparison, and definition will be discussed in specific chapters in Part Two; at this point, however, here are some comments about the general nature of all good body paragraphs that should help as you draft your essay.

> Most of the body paragraphs in your essay will profit from a focused *topic sentence*. In addition, body paragraphs should have adequate *development, unity, and coherence.*

THE TOPIC SENTENCE

Most body paragraphs present one main point in your discussion, expressed in a *topic sentence.* The topic sentence of a body paragraph has three important functions:

1. It supports the thesis by clearly stating a main point in the discussion.

2. It announces what the paragraph will be about.

3. It controls the subject matter of the paragraph. The entire discussion—the examples, details, and explanations—in a particular paragraph must directly relate to and support the topic sentence.

Think of a body paragraph (or a single paragraph) as a kind of mini-essay in itself. The topic sentence is, in a sense, a smaller thesis. It too asserts one main idea on a limited subject that the writer can explain or argue in the rest of the paragraph. Like the thesis, the topic sentence should be stated in as specific language as possible.

To see how a topic sentence works in a body paragraph, study this sample:

Essay thesis: The Study Skills Center is an excellent place for freshmen who need academic help.

Topic Sentence
1. The topic sentence supports the thesis by stating a main point (one reason why the Center provides excellent academic help).

2. The topic sentence announces the subject matter of the paragraph (a variety of free services that improve basic skills).

3. The topic sentence controls the subject matter (all the

The Center offers students a variety of free services designed to improve basic skills. Freshmen who discover their study habits are poor, for instance, may enroll in a six-week mini-course in study skills that offers advice on such topics as how to read a text, take notes, and organize material for review. Students whose math or writing skills are below par can sign up for free tutoring sessions held five days a week throughout each semester. In addition, the Center presents weekly seminars on special topics such as stress management and overcoming test anxiety for those students who are finding college more of a nerve-wracking experience than they expected; other students can attend evening seminars in such worthwhile endeavors as vocabulary building examples—the mini-course, the tutoring, the seminars, and the testing—support the claim of the topic sentence).

or spelling tips. Finally, the Center offers a series of tests to identify the presence of any learning disabilities, such as dyslexia, that might prevent a student from succeeding academically. With such a variety of free services, the Center can help almost any student.

Here's another example from the essay on the library reserve:

Essay thesis: The library's reserve facility is difficult for students to use.

Topic Sentence
1. The topic sentence supports the thesis by stating a main point (one reason why the facility is difficult to use).

2. The topic sentence announces the subject matter of the paragraph (the unpredictable hours).

3. The topic sentence controls the subject matter (all the examples—the changing hours, the sudden closures, the erratic holiday schedule).

The library reserve facility's unpredictable hours frustrate even the most dedicated students. Instructors who place articles on reserve usually ask students to read them by a certain date. Too often, however, students arrive at the reserve desk only to find it closed. The facility's open hours change from week to week: students who used the room last week on Tuesday morning may discover that this week on Tuesday the desk is closed, which means another trip. Perhaps even more frustrating are the facility's sudden, unannounced closures. Some of these closures allow staff members to have lunch or go on breaks, but, again, they occur without notice on no regular schedule. A student arrives, as I did two weeks ago, at the desk to find a "Be Back Soon" sign. In my case, I waited for nearly an hour. Another headache is the holiday schedule, which is difficult to figure out. For example, this year the reserve room was closed without advance notice on Presidents' Day but open on Easter; open during Winter Break but closed some days during Spring Break, a time many students use to catch up on their reserve assignments. Overall, the reserve facility would be much easier for students to use if it adopted a set schedule of operating hours, announced these times each semester, and maintained them.

Always be sure your topic sentences actually support the particular thesis of your essay. For example, the second topic sentence presented here doesn't belong in the essay promised by the thesis:

Thesis: Elk hunting should be permitted because it financially aids people in our state.

Topic Sentences

1. Fees for hunting licenses help pay for certain free, state-supported social services.

2. Hunting helps keep the elk population under control.

3. Elk hunting offers a means of obtaining free food for those people with low incomes.

Although topic sentence 2 is about elk and may be true, it doesn't support the thesis's emphasis on financial aid and therefore should be tossed out of this essay.

Here's another example:

> **Thesis:** During the past fifty years, movie stars have often tried to change the direction of America's politics.

Topic Sentences

1. During World War II, stars sold liberty bonds to support the country's war effort.

2. Many stars refused to cooperate with the blacklisting of their colleagues in the 1950s.

3. Some stars were actively involved in protests against the Vietnam War.

4. More recently, stars have appeared in Congress criticizing the lack of legislative help for struggling farmers.

Topic sentences 2, 3, and 4 all show how stars have tried to effect a change. But topic sentence 1 says only that stars sold bonds to support, not *change*, the political direction of the nation. Although it does show stars involved in politics, it doesn't illustrate the claim of this particular thesis.

Sometimes a topic sentence needs only to be rewritten or slightly recast to fit:

> **Thesis:** The recent tuition hike will discourage students from attending our college.

Topic Sentences

1. Students already pay more here than at other in-state schools.

2. Out-of-state students would have to pay an additional "penalty" to attend.

3. Tuition funds should be used to give teachers raises.

As written, topic sentence 3 doesn't show why students won't want to attend the school. However, a rewritten topic sentence does support the thesis:

3. Because the tuition money will not be used for teachers' salaries, many top professors may take job offers elsewhere, and their best students may follow them there.

In other words, always check carefully to make sure that *all* your topic sentences clearly support your thesis's assertion.

Focusing Your Topic Sentence

A vague, fuzzy, or unfocused topic sentence most often leads to a paragraph that touches only on the surface of its subject or that wanders away from the writer's main idea. On the other hand, a topic sentence that is tightly focused and stated precisely will not only help the reader to understand the point of the paragraph but will also help you select, organize, and develop your supporting details.

Look, for example, at these unfocused topic sentences and their revisions:

Unfocused	Too many people treat animals badly in experiments. (What people? Badly how? What kinds of experiments?)
Focused	The cosmetic industry often harms animals in unnecessary experiments designed to test their products.
Unfocused	Grades are an unfair pain in the neck. (Again, the focus is too broad: all grades? Unfair how?)
Focused	A course grade based on one multiple-choice exam doesn't accurately measure a student's knowledge of the subject.
Unfocused	Getting the right job is important and can lead to rewarding experiences. (Note both vague language and a double focus—"important" and "can lead to rewarding experiences.")
Focused	Getting the right job can lead to an improved sense of self-esteem.

Before you practice writing focused topic sentences, you may wish to review pages 35–42, the advice on composing good thesis statements, as the same rules generally apply.

Placing Your Topic Sentence

Although the topic sentence most frequently occurs as the first sentence in the body paragraph, it also often appears as the second or last sentence. A topic sentence that directly follows the first sentence of a paragraph usually does so because the first sentence provides an introductory statement or some kind of a "hook" to the preceding paragraph. A topic sentence frequently appears at the end of a paragraph that first presents particular details and then concludes with its central point. Here are two paragraphs in which the topic sentences do not appear first:

Introductory sentence

Topic sentence

Millions of Americans have watched the elaborate Rose Bowl Parade televised nationally each January from Pasadena, California. *Less well-known, but growing in popularity, is Pasadena's Doo Dah Parade, an annual parody of the Rose Bowl spectacle, that specializes in wild-and-crazy participants.* Take this year's Doo Dah Precision Drill Team, for instance. Instead of marching in unison, the members cavorted down the avenue displaying—what else—a variety of precision electric drills. In heated competition with this group was the Synchronized Briefcase Drill Team, whose male and female members wore gray pinstripe suits and performed a series of tunes by tapping on their briefcases. Another crowd-pleasing entry was the Citizens for the Right to Bare Arms, whose members sang while carrying aloft unclothed mannequin arms. The zany procession, led this year as always by the All-Time Doo Dah Parade Band, attracted more than 150,000 fans and is already preparing for its next celebration.

In the previous paragraph, the first sentence serves as an introduction leading into the topic sentence; in the following paragraph, the writer places the topic sentence last to make a general comment about the importance of VCRs.

Because of VCRs, we no longer have to miss a single joke on our favorite sitcom. Sporting events can be recorded in their entirety even though we may have to go to work or class after the fifth inning or second quarter. Even our dose of television violence does not have to be postponed forever just because a popular special is on another channel at the same time. Moreover, events of historical significance can be captured and replayed for future generations even if Aunt Tillie keeps us eating tacos until after the show begins. *In but a few years, VCRs have radically changed America's television viewing habits.*

Topic sentence

As you can see, the position of topic sentences largely depends on what you are trying to do in your paragraph. And it's true that the purposes of some paragraphs are so obvious that no topic sentence is needed. However, if you are a beginning writer, you may want to practice putting your topic sentences first for a while to help you organize and unify your paragraphs.

Some paragraphs with a topic sentence near the beginning also contain a concluding sentence that makes a final general comment based on the supporting details. The last sentence below, for example, sums up and restates the main point of the paragraph.

Topic sentence   *Of all nature's catastrophes, tornadoes cause the most bizarre destruction.* Whirling out of the sky at speeds up to 300 miles per hour, tornadoes have been known to drive broom handles through brick walls and straws into tree trunks. In one extreme case, a Kansas farmer reported that his prize rooster had been sucked into a two-gallon distilled-water bottle. More commonly, tornadoes lift autos and deposit them in fields miles away or uproot trees and drop them on lawns in neighboring towns. One tornado knocked down every wall in a house but one—luckily, the very wall shielding the terrified family. *Whenever a tornado touches*

Concluding sentence *the earth, spectacular headlines are sure to follow.*

Warning: Although topic sentences may appear in different places in a paragraph, there is one common error you should be careful to avoid. Do *not* put a topic sentence at the end of one body paragraph that belongs to the paragraph that follows it. For example, let's suppose you were writing an essay discussing a job you had held recently, one that you enjoyed because of the responsibilities you were given, the training program you participated in, and the interaction you experienced with your coworkers. The body paragraph describing your responsibilities may end with its own topic sentence or with a concluding sentence about those responsibilities. However, that paragraph should not end with a sentence such as "Another excellent feature of this job was the training program for the next level of management." This "training program" sentence belongs in the *following body* paragraph as its topic sentence. Similarly, you would not end the paragraph on the training program with a topic sentence praising your experience with your coworkers.

If you feel your paragraphs are ending too abruptly, consider using a concluding sentence, as described previously. Later in this chapter you will also learn some ways to smooth the way from one paragraph to the next by using transition devices and idea "hooks" (pp. 86–88). For now, remember: do *not* place a topic sentence that introduces and controls paragraph "B" at the end of paragraph "A." In other words, always place your topic sentence in the paragraph to which it belongs, to which it is topic-related, not at the end of the preceding paragraph.

PRACTICING WHAT YOU'VE LEARNED

A. Point out the topic sentences in the following paragraphs; identify those paragraphs that also contain concluding sentences. Cross out any stray topic sentences that belong elsewhere.

Denim is one of America's most widely used fabrics. It was first introduced during Columbus's voyage, when the sails of the Santa Maria were made of the strong cloth. During our pioneer days, denim was used for tents, covered wagons, and the now-famous blue jeans. Cowboys found denim an ideal fabric for protection against sagebrush, cactus, and saddle sores. World War II also gave denim a boost in popularity when sailors were issued jeans as part of their dress code. Today, denim continues to be in demand as more and more casual clothes are cut from the economical fabric. Because of its low cost and durability, manufacturers feel that denim will continue as one of America's most useful fabrics.

Adlai Stevenson, American statesman and twice an unsuccessful presidential candidate against Eisenhower, was well-known for his intelligence and wit. Once on the campaign trail, after he had spoken eloquently and at length about several complex ideas, a woman in the audience was moved to stand and cheer, "That's great! Every thinking person in America will vote for you!" Stevenson immediately retorted, "That's not enough. I need a majority!" Frequently a reluctant candidate but never at a loss for words, Stevenson once reflected on the country's highest office: "Yes, in America any boy may become President. . . . I suppose it's just one of the risks he takes." Stevenson was also admired for his opposition to McCarthyism in the 1950s.

Almost every wedding tradition has a symbolic meaning that originated centuries ago. For example, couples have been exchanging rings to symbolize unending love for over a thousand years. Most often, the rings are worn on the third finger of the left hand, which was thought to contain a vein that ran directly to the heart. The rings in ancient times were sometimes made of braided grass, rope, or leather, giving rise to the expression "tying the knot." Another tradition, the bridal veil, began when marriages were arranged by the families and the groom was not allowed to see their choice until the wedding. The tossing of rice at newlyweds has long signified fertility blessings, and the sweet smell of the bride's bouquet was present to drive away evil spirits, who were also diverted by the surrounding bridal attendants. Weddings may vary enormously today, but many couples still include ancient traditions to signify their new life together.

You always think of the right answer five minutes after you hand in the test. You always hit the red light when you're already late for class. The one time you skip class is the day of the pop quiz. Back-to-back classes are always held in buildings at opposite ends of campus. The one course you need to graduate will not be offered your last semester. If any of these sound familiar, you've obviously been a victim of the "Murphy's Laws" that govern student life.

Want to win a sure bet? Then wager that your friends can't guess the most widely sold musical instrument in America today. Chances are they won't get the answer right—not even on the third try. In actuality, the most popular instrument in the country is neither the guitar nor the trumpet but the lowly kazoo. Last year alone, some three and one-half million kazoos were sold to music lovers of all ages. Part of the instrument's popularity arises from its availability, since kazoos are sold in variety stores and music centers nearly everywhere; another reason is its inexpensiveness—it ranges from the standard thirty-nine-cent model to the five-dollar gold-plated special. But perhaps the main reason for the kazoo's popularity is the ease with which it can be played by almost anyone—as can testify the members of the entire Swarthmore College marching band, who have now added a marching kazoo number to their repertoire. Louie Armstrong, move over!

It's a familiar scenario: Dad won't stop the car to ask directions, despite the fact that he's been hopelessly lost for over forty-five minutes. Mom keeps nagging Dad to slow down and finally blows up because your little sister suddenly remembers she's left her favorite doll, the one she can't sleep without, at the rest stop you left over an hour ago. Your legs are sweat-glued to the vinyl seats, you need desperately to go to the bathroom, and your big brother has just kindly acknowledged that he will relieve you of your front teeth if you allow any part of your body to extend over the imaginary line he has drawn down the back seat. The wonderful institution known as the "family vacation" has begun.

B. Rewrite these topic sentences so that they are clear and focused rather than fuzzy or too broad.

1. My personality has changed a lot in the last year.

2. His blind date turned out to be really great.

3. The movie's special effects were incredible.

4. The Memorial Day celebration was more fun than ever before.

5. The evening with her parents was an unforgettable experience.

C. Add topic sentences to the following paragraphs:

Famous inventor Thomas Edison, for instance, did so poorly in his first years of school that his teachers warned his parents that he'd never be a success at anything. Similarly, Henry Ford, the father of the auto industry, had trouble in school with both reading and writing. But perhaps the best example is Albert Einstein, whose parents and teachers suspected that he was retarded because he responded to questions so slowly and in a stuttering voice. Einstein's high school record was poor in everything but math, and he failed his college entrance exams the first time. Even out of school the man had trouble holding a job—until he announced the theory of relativity.

A 1950s felt skirt with Elvis's picture on it, for example, now sells for $150, and Elvis scarves go for as much as $200. Elvis handkerchiefs, originally 50 cents or less, fetch $150 in today's market as do wallets imprinted with the singer's face. Posters from the Rock King's movies can sell for $500, and cards from the chewing gum series can run $30 apiece. Perhaps one of the most expensive collectors' items is the Emene Elvis guitar that can cost a fan from $500 to $700, regardless of musical condition.

When successful playwright Jean Kerr once checked into a hospital, the receptionist asked her occupation and was told, "Writer." The receptionist said, "I'll just put down 'housewife.'" Similarly, when a British official asked W. H. Auden, the late award-winning poet and essayist, what he did for a living, Auden replied, "I'm a writer." The official jotted down "no occupation."

Cumberland College, for example, set the record back in 1916 for the biggest loss in college ball, having allowed Georgia Tech to run up 63 points in the first quarter and ultimately succumbing to them with a final score of 222 to nothing. In pro ball, the Washington Redskins are the biggest losers, going down in defeat 73 to 0 to the Chicago Bears in 1940. The award for the longest losing streak, however, goes to Northwestern University's team, who by 1981 had managed to lose 29 consecutive games. During that year, morale was so low that one disgruntled fan passing a local highway sign that read "Interstate 94" couldn't resist adding "Northwestern 0."

D. Write a focused topic sentence for five of the following subjects:

  1. Job interviews

  2. Friends

3. Food

4. Money

5. Selecting a major or occupation

6. Clothes

7. Music

8. Dreams

9. Housing

10. Childhood

 ASSIGNMENT

Review the thesis statements with essay maps you wrote for the practice exercise on page 47. Choose two, and from each thesis create at least three topic sentences for possible body paragraphs.

 APPLYING WHAT YOU'VE LEARNED TO YOUR WRITING

If you currently have a working thesis statement you have written in response to an assignment in your composition class, try sketching out an outline or plan for the major ideas you wish to include. After you write a draft, underline the topic sentences in your body paragraphs. Do your topic sentences directly support your thesis? If you find that they do not clearly support your thesis, you must decide if you need to revise your draft's organization or whether you have, in fact, discovered a new, and possibly better, subject to write about. If the latter is true, you'll need to redraft your essay so that your readers will not be confused by a paper that announces one subject but discusses another. (See Chapter 5 for more information on revising your drafts.)

PARAGRAPH DEVELOPMENT

Possibly the most serious—and most common—weakness of all essays by novice writers is *the lack of effectively developed body paragraphs*. The information in each paragraph must adequately explain, exemplify, define, or in some other way *support* your topic sentence. Therefore, you must include *enough supporting information* or *evidence* in each paragraph to make your readers understand your topic sentence. Moreover, you must make the information in the paragraph clear and specific enough for the readers to accept your ideas.

The next paragraph is *underdeveloped*. Although the topic sentence promises a discussion of Jesse James as a Robin Hood figure, the paragraph does not provide enough specific supporting evidence (in this case, examples) to explain this unusual view of the gunfighter.

> Although he was an outlaw, Jesse James was considered a Robin Hood figure in my hometown in Missouri. He used to be generous to the poor, and he did many good deeds, not just robberies. In my hometown people still talk about how lots of the things James did weren't all bad.

Rewritten, the paragraph might read as follows:

> Although he was an outlaw, Jesse James was considered a Robin Hood figure in my hometown in Missouri. Jesse and his gang chose my hometown as a hiding place, and they set out immediately to make friends with the local people. Every Christmas for four years, the legend goes, he dumped bags of toys on the doorsteps of poor children. The parents knew the toys had been bought with money stolen from richer people, but they were grateful anyway. On three occasions, Jesse gave groceries to the dozen neediest families—he seemed to know when times were toughest—and once he supposedly held up a stage to pay for an old man's operation. In my hometown, some people still sing the praises of Jesse James, the outlaw who wasn't all bad.

The topic sentence promises a discussion of James's generosity and delivers just that by citing specific examples of his gifts to children, the poor, and the sick. The paragraph is, therefore, better developed.

The following paragraph offers supporting reasons but no specific examples or details to support those reasons:

> Living with my ex-roommate was unbearable. First, she thought everything she owned was the best. Second, she possessed numerous filthy habits. Finally, she constantly exhibited immature behavior.

The writer might provide more evidence this way:

> Living with my ex-roommate was unbearable. First, she thought everything she owned, from clothes to cosmetics,

was the best. If someone complimented my pants, she'd point out that her designer jeans looked better and would last longer because they were made of better material. If she borrowed my shampoo, she'd let me know that it didn't get her hair as clean and shiny as hers did. My hand cream wasn't as smooth; my suntan lotion wasn't as protective; not even my wire clothes hangers were as good as her padded ones! But despite her pickiness about products, she had numerous filthy habits. Her dirty dishes remained in the sink for ages before she got the incentive to wash them. Piles of the "best" brand of tissues were regularly discarded from her upper bunk and strewn about the floor. Her desk and closets overflowed with heaps of dirty clothes, books, cosmetics, and whatever else she owned, and she rarely brushed her teeth (when she did brush, she left oozes of toothpaste on the sink). Finally, she constantly acted immaturely by throwing tantrums when things didn't go her way. A poor grade on an exam or paper, for example, meant books, shoes, or any other small object within her reach would hit the wall flying. Living with such a person taught me some valuable lessons about how not to win friends or keep roommates.

By adding more supporting evidence—specific examples and details—to this paragraph, the writer has a better chance of convincing the reader of the roommate's real character.

Where does evidence come from? Where do writers find their supporting information? Evidence comes from many sources. Personal experiences, memories, observations, hypothetical examples, reasoned arguments, facts, statistics, testimony from authorities, many kinds of studies and research—all these and more can help you make your points clear and persuasive. In the paragraph on Jesse James, for example, the writer relied on stories and memories from his hometown. The paragraph on the obnoxious roommate was supported by examples gained through the writer's personal observation. The kind of supporting evidence you choose for your paragraphs depends on your purpose and your audience; as the writer, you must decide what will work best to make your readers understand and accept each important point in your discussion. (For advice on ways to think critically about evidence, see Chapter 5; for more information on incorporating research material into your essays, see Chapter 14.)

Having a well-developed paragraph is more than a matter of additional material or expanding length, however. The information in each paragraph must effectively explain or support your topic sentence. *Vague generalities or repetitious ideas are not convincing.* Look, for example, at the following paragraph, in which the writer offers only generalities:

> We ought to get rid of cellular telephones in cars. Some people who have them think they're a really good idea but a lot of us don't agree. A car phone can cause too many dangerous accidents to happen, and even if there's no terrible accident, people using them have been known to do some really stupid things in traffic. Drivers using car phones are constantly causing problems for other drivers; pedestrians are in big trouble from these people too. I think car phones are getting to be a really dangerous nuisance and we ought to do something about them soon.

This paragraph is weak because it is composed of repetitious general statements stated in vague, unclear language. None of its general statements are supported with specific evidence. Why are car phones not a "good" idea? How do they cause accidents? What "stupid things" happened because of them? What are the "problems" and "trouble" the writer refers to? What exactly does "do something about them" mean? The writer obviously had some ideas in mind, but these ideas are not clear to the reader because they are not adequately developed with specific evidence and language. By adding supporting examples and details, the writer might revise the paragraph this way:

> Although cellular telephones may be a time-saving convenience for busy executives or commuters, they are too distracting for use by drivers of moving vehicles, whose lack of full attention poses a serious threat to other drivers and to pedestrians. The simple act of dialing or answering a telephone, for example, may take a driver's eyes away from traffic signals or other cars. Moreover, involvement in a complex or emotional conversation could slow down a driver's response time just when fast action is needed to avoid an accident. Last week I drove behind a man using his car phone. As he drove and talked, I could see him gesturing wildly, obviously agitated with the other caller. His speed repeatedly slowed and then picked up, slowed and increased, and his car drifted more than once, on a street frequently crossed by schoolchildren. Because the man was clearly not in full, conscious control of his driving, he was dangerous. My experience is not isolated; a recent study by the Foundation for Traffic Safety has discovered that using a cellular phone is

far more distracting to drivers than listening to the radio or talking to a rider. With additional studies in progress, voters should soon be able to demand legislation to restrict use of car telephones to passengers or to drivers when the vehicles are not in motion.

The reader now has a better idea why the writer feels cellular phones are distracting and, consequently, dangerous to drivers. By using two hypothetical examples (looking away, slowed response time), one personal experience (observing the agitated man), and one reference to research (the safety study), the writer offers the reader three kinds of supporting evidence for the paragraph's claim.

After examining the following two paragraphs, decide which explains its point more effectively.

1

Competing in an Ironman triathlon is one of the most demanding feats known to amateur athletes. First, they have to swim many miles and that takes a lot of endurance. Then they ride a bicycle a long way, which is also hard on their bodies. Last, they run a marathon, which can be difficult in itself but is especially hard after the first two events. Competing in the triathlon is really tough on the participants.

2

Competing in an Ironman triathlon is one of the most demanding feats known to amateur athletes. During the first stage of the triathlon, the competitors must swim 2.4 miles in the open ocean. They have to battle the constantly choppy ocean, the strong currents, and the frequent swells. The wind is often an adversary, and stinging jellyfish are a constant threat. Once they have completed the ocean swim, the triathletes must ride 112 miles on a bicycle. In addition to the strength needed to pedal that far, the bicyclists must use a variety of hand grips to assure the continued circulation in their fingers and hands as well as to ease the strain on the neck and shoulder muscles. Moreover, the concentration necessary to steady the bicycle as well as the attention to the inclines on the course and the consequent shifting of gears causes mental fatigue for the athletes. After completing these two grueling segments, the triathletes must then run 26.2 miles, the length of a regular marathon. Dehydration is a constant concern as is the prospect of cramping. Even the pain and swelling of a friction blister can be enough to eliminate a contestant at this late stage of the event. Finally, disorientation and fatigue can set in and distort the athlete's judgment. Competing in an Ironman triathlon takes incredible physical and mental endurance.

The first paragraph contains, for the most part, repetitious generalities; it repeats the same idea (the triathlon is hard work) and gives few specific details to illustrate the point presented in the topic sentence. The second paragraph, however, does offer many specific examples and details—the exact mileage figures, the currents, jellyfish, inclines, grips, blisters, and so forth—that help the reader understand why the event is so demanding.

Joseph Conrad, the famous British novelist, once remarked that a writer's purpose was to use "the power of the written word to make you hear, to make you feel . . . before all, to make you *see*. That—and no more, and it is everything." By using specific details instead of vague, general statements, you can write an interesting, convincing essay. Ask yourself as you revise your paragraphs, "Have I provided enough information, presented enough clear, precise details to make my readers *see* what I want them to?" In other words, a well-developed paragraph effectively makes its point with *an appropriate amount of specific supporting evidence.* (Remember that a handwritten paragraph in your rough draft will look much shorter when it is typed. Therefore, if you can't think of much to say about a particular idea, you should gather more information or consider dropping it as a major point in your essay.)

PARAGRAPH LENGTH

"How long is a good paragraph?" is a question novice writers often ask. Like a teacher's lecture or a preacher's sermon, paragraphs should be long enough to accomplish their purpose and short enough to be interesting. In truth, there is no set length, no prescribed number of lines or sentences, for any of your paragraphs. In a body paragraph, your topic sentence presents the main point, and the rest of the paragraph must give enough supporting evidence to convince the reader. While too much unnecessary or repetitious detail is boring, too little discussion will leave the reader uninformed, unconvinced, or confused.

Although paragraph length varies, beginning writers should avoid the one- or two-sentence paragraphs frequently seen in newspapers or magazine articles. (Journalists have their own rules to follow; paragraphs are shorter in newspapers, for one reason, because large masses of print in narrow columns are hard to read quickly.) Essay writers do occasionally use the one-sentence paragraph, most often to produce some special effect, when the statement is especially dramatic or significant and needs to call attention to itself or when an emphatic transition is needed. For now, however, you should concentrate on writing well-developed body paragraphs.

One more note on paragraph length: sometimes you may discover that a particular point in your essay is so complex that your paragraph is growing far too long—well over a typed page, for instance. If this problem occurs, look for a logical place to divide your information and start a new paragraph. For example, you might see a convenient dividing point between a series of actions you're describing or a break in the chronology of a narrative or between explanations of arguments or examples. Just make sure you begin your next paragraph with some sort of transition phrase or key words to let the reader know you are still discussing the same point as before ("Still another problem caused by the computer's faulty memory circuit is . . .").

 ## PRACTICING WHAT YOU'VE LEARNED

Analyze the following paragraphs. Explain how you might improve the development of each one.

1. Professor Wilson is the best teacher I've ever had. His lectures are interesting, and he's very concerned about his students. He makes the class challenging but not too hard. On tests he doesn't expect more than one can give. I think he's a great teacher.

2. Newspaper advice columns are pretty silly. The problems are generally stupid or unrealistic, and the advice is out of touch with today's world. Too often the columnist just uses the letter to make a smart remark about some pet peeve. The columns could be put to some good uses, but no one tries very hard.

3. Driving tests do not adequately examine a person's driving ability. Usually the person being tested does not have to drive very far. The test does not require the skills that are used in everyday driving situations. Supervisors of driving tests tend to be very lenient.

4. Nursing homes are often sad places. They are frequently located in ugly old buildings unfit for anyone. The people there are lonely and bored. What's more, they're sometimes treated badly by the people who run the homes. It's a shame something better can't be done for the elderly.

5. There is a big difference between acquaintances and friends. Acquaintances are just people you know slightly, but friends give you some

important qualities. For example, they can help you gain self-esteem and confidence just by being close to you. By sharing intimate things, they also help you feel happy about being alive.

 ASSIGNMENT

A. Select two of the paragraphs from above and rewrite them, adding enough specific details to make well-developed paragraphs.

B. Write a paragraph composed of generalities and vague statements. Exchange this paragraph with a classmate's, and turn each other's faulty paragraph into a clearly developed one.

C. Find at least two well-developed paragraphs in an essay or book; explain why you think the two paragraphs are successfully developed.

 APPLYING WHAT YOU'VE LEARNED TO YOUR WRITING

If you are currently drafting an essay, look closely at your body paragraphs. Find the topic sentence in each paragraph and circle the key words that most clearly communicate the main idea of the paragraph. Then ask yourself if the information in each paragraph effectively supports, explains, or illustrates the main idea of the paragraph's topic sentence. Is there enough information? If you're not sure, try numbering your supporting details. Are there too few to be persuasive? Does the paragraph present clear, specific supporting material or does it contain too many vague generalities to be convincing? Where could you add more details to help the reader understand your ideas better and to make each paragraph more interesting? (For more help revising your paragraphs, see Chapter 5.)

PARAGRAPH UNITY

Every sentence in a body paragraph should directly relate to the main idea presented by the topic sentence. A paragraph must stick to its announced subject; it must not drift away into another discussion. In other words, a good paragraph has *unity*.

Examine the unified paragraph on page 72; note that the topic sentence clearly states the paragraph's main point and that each sentence thereafter supports the topic sentence.

(1)Frank Lloyd Wright, America's leading architect of the first half of the twentieth century, believed that his houses should blend naturally with their building sites. (2)Consequently, he designed several "prairie houses," whose long, low lines echoed the flat earth plan. (3)Built of brick, stone, and natural wood, the houses shared a similar texture with their backgrounds. (4)Large windows were often used to blend the interior and exterior of the houses. (5)Wright also punctuated the lines and spaces of the houses with greenery in planters to further make the buildings look like part of nature.

The first sentence states the main idea, that Wright thought houses should blend with their location, and the other sentences support this assertion:

Topic sentence: Wright's houses blend with their natural locations

(2) long, low lines echo flat prairie

(3) brick, stone, wood provide same texture as location

(4) windows blend inside with outside

(5) greenery in planters imitates the natural surroundings.

Now look at the next paragraph, in which the writer strays from his original purpose:

(1)Cigarette smoke is unhealthy even for people who don't have the nicotine habit themselves. (2)Secondhand smoke can cause asthmatics and sufferers of sinusitis serious problems. (3)Doctors regularly advise heart patients to avoid confined smoky areas because coronary attacks might be triggered by the lack of clean air. (4)Moreover, having the smell of smoke in one's hair and clothes is a real nuisance. (5)Even if a person is without any health problems, exhaled smoke doubles the amount of carbon monoxide in the air, a condition that may cause lung problems in the future.

Sentence 4 refers to smoke as a nuisance and therefore does not belong in a paragraph that discusses smoking as a health hazard to nonsmokers.

Sometimes a large portion of a paragraph will drift into another topic. In the paragraph below, did the writer wish to focus on her messiness or on the beneficial effects of her engagement?

> I have always been a very messy person. As a child, I was a pack rat, saving every little piece of insignificant paper that I thought might be important when I grew up. As a teenager, my pockets bulged with remnants of basketball tickets, hall passes, gum wrappers, and other important articles from my high school education. As a college student, I became a boxer—not a fighter, but someone who cannot throw anything away and therefore it winds up in a box in my closet. But my engagement has changed everything. I'm really pleased with the new stage of my life, and I owe it all to my fiancé. My overall outlook on life has changed because of his influence on me. I'm neater, much more cheerful, and I'm even getting places on time like I never did before. It's truly amazing what love can do.

Note shift from the topic of messiness

This writer may wish to discuss the changes her fiancé has inspired and then use her former messiness, tardiness, and other bad habits as examples illustrating those changes; however, as presented here, the paragraph is not unified around a central idea. On the contrary, it first seems to promise a discussion of her messiness but then wanders into comments on "what love can do."

Also beware a tendency to end your paragraph with a new idea. A new point calls for an entirely new paragraph. For example, the paragraph below focuses on the *origins* of Muzak; the last sentence, on Muzak's *effects* on workers, should be omitted or moved to a paragraph on Muzak's uses in the workplace.

> Muzak, the ever-present sound of music that pervades elevators, office buildings, and reception rooms, was created over fifty years ago by George Owen Squier, an army general. A graduate of West Point, Squier was also an inventor and scientist. During World War I he headed the Signal Corps where he began experimenting with the notion of transmitting simultaneous messages over power lines. When he retired from the army in 1922, he founded Wired Radio, Inc., and later, in 1934, the first Muzak medley was heard in Cleveland, Ohio, for homeowners willing to pay the great sum of $1.50 a month. That year he struck upon the now-famous name, which combined the idea of music with

the brand name of the country's most popular camera, Kodak. *Today, experiments show that workers get more done when they listen to Muzak.*

In general, think of paragraph unity in terms of the diagram below:

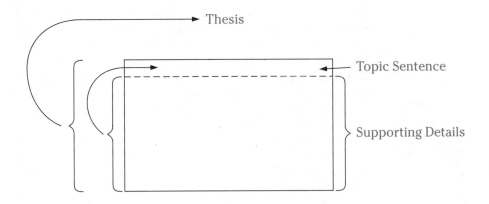

The sentences in the paragraph support the paragraph's topic sentence; the paragraph, in turn, supports the thesis statement.

 PRACTICING WHAT YOU'VE LEARNED

In each of the following examples, delete or rewrite any information that interferes with the unity of the paragraph:

> In the Great Depression of the 1930s, American painters suffered severely because few people had the money to spend on the luxury of owning art. To keep our artists from starving, the government ultimately set up the Federal Art Project, which paid then little-known painters such as Jackson Pollock, Arshile Gorky, and Willem de Kooning to paint murals in post offices, train stations, schools, housing projects, and other public places. During this period, songwriters were also affected by the depression, and they produced such memorable songs as "Buddy, Can You Spare a Dime?" The government-sponsored murals, usually depicting familiar American scenes and historical events, gave our young artists an opportunity to develop their skills and new techniques; in return, our country obtained thousands of elaborate works of art in over one thousand American cities. Sadly, many of these art works were destroyed in later years, as public buildings were torn down or remodeled.

After complaining in vain about the quality of food in the campus restaurant, University of Colorado students are having their revenge after all. The student body recently voted to rename the grill after Alferd Packer, the only American ever convicted of cannibalism. Packer was a Utah prospector trapped with an expedition of explorers in the southwest Colorado mountains during the winter of 1874; the sole survivor of the trip, he was later tried by a jury and sentenced to hang for dining on at least five of his companions. Colorado students are now holding an annual "Alferd Packer Day" and have installed a mural relating the prospector's story on the main wall of the restaurant. Some local wits have also suggested a new motto for the bar and grill: "Serving our fellow man since 1874." Another well-known incident of cannibalism in the West occurred in the winter of 1846, when the Donner party, a wagon train of eighty-seven California-bound immigrants, became trapped by ice and snow in the Sierra Nevada mountain range.

Inventors of food products often name their new creations after real people. In 1896 Leo Hirschfield hand-rolled a chewy candy and named it after his daughter Tootsie. In 1920 Otto Schnering gave the world the Baby Ruth candy bar, named after the daughter of former President Grover Cleveland. To publicize his new product, Schnering once dropped the candy tied to tiny parachutes from an airplane flying over Pittsburgh. And one of our most popular soft drinks was named by a young suitor who sought to please his sweetheart's physician father, none other than old Dr. Pepper. Despite the honor, the girl's father never approved of the match and the young man, Wade Morrison, married someone else.

States out West have often led the way in recognizing women's roles in politics. Wyoming, for example, was the first state to give women the right to vote and hold office, back in 1869 while the state was still a territory. Colorado was the second state to grant women's suffrage; Idaho, the third. Wyoming was also the first state to elect a woman as governor, Nellie Tayloe Ross, in 1924. Montana elected Jeanette Rankin as the nation's first congresswoman. Former U.S. Representative from Colorado, Patricia Schroeder, claims to be the first person to take the congressional oath of office while clutching a handbag full of diapers. Ms. Schroeder later received the National Motherhood Award.

Living in a college dorm is a good way to meet people. There are activities every weekend such as dances and parties where one can get acquainted with all kinds of students. Even just sitting by someone in the cafeteria during a meal can start a friendship. Making new friends from foreign countries can teach students more about international relations. A girl on my dorm floor, for example, is from Peru, and I've learned a lot about the customs and culture in her country. She's also helping me with my study of Spanish. I hope to visit her in Peru some day.

 APPLYING WHAT YOU'VE LEARNED TO YOUR WRITING

If you have written a draft of an essay, underline the topic sentence in each body paragraph and circle the key words. For example, if in an essay on America's growing health consciousness, one of your topic sentences reads "In an effort to improve their health, Americans have increased the number of vitamins they consume," you might circle "Americans," "increased," and "vitamins." Then look closely at your paragraph. All the information in that paragraph should support the idea expressed in your topic sentence; nothing should detract from the idea of showing that Americans have increased their vitamins. Now study the paragraphs in your draft, one by one. Cross out any sentences or material that interferes with the ideas in your topic sentences. If one of your paragraphs begins to drift away from its topic-sentence idea, you will need to rethink the purpose of that paragraph and rewrite so that the reader will understand what the paragraph is about. (For additional help revising your drafts, turn to Chapter 5.)

PARAGRAPH COHERENCE

In addition to unity, *coherence* is essential to a good paragraph. Coherence means that all the sentences and ideas in your paragraph flow together to make a clear, logical point about your topic. Your paragraph should not be a confusing collection of ideas set down in random order. The readers should be able to follow what you have written and see easily and quickly how each sentence grows out of, or is related to, the preceding sentence. To achieve coherence, you should have a smooth connection or transition between the sentences in your paragraphs.

There are five important means of achieving coherence in your paragraphs:

1. A natural or easily recognized order

2. Transition words and phrases

3. Repetition of key words

4. Substitution of pronouns for key nouns

5. Parallelism

These transition devices are similar to the couplings between railroad cars; they enable the controlling engine to pull the train of thought along as a unit.

A Recognizable Ordering of Information

Without consciously thinking about the process, you may often organize paragraphs in easily recognized patterns that give the reader a sense of logical movement and order. Four common patterns of ordering sentences in a paragraph are discussed next:

The Order of Time

Some paragraphs are composed of details arranged in chronological order. You might, for example, explain the process of changing an oil filter on your car by beginning with the first step, draining the old oil, and concluding with the last step, installing the new filter. Here is a paragraph on black holes in which the writer chronologically orders her details:

> A black hole in space, from all indications, is the result of the death of a star. Scientists speculate that stars were first formed from the gases floating in the universe at the beginning of time. In the first stage in the life of a star, the hot gas is drawn by the force of gravity into a burning sphere. In the middle stage—our own sun being a middle-aged star—the burning continues at a regular rate, giving off enormous amounts of heat and light. As it grows old, however, the star eventually explodes to become what is called a nova, a superstar. But gravity soon takes over again, and the exploded star falls back in on itself with such force that all the matter in the star is compacted into a mass no larger than a few miles in diameter. At this point, no heavenly body can be seen in that area of the sky, as the tremendous pull of gravity lets nothing escape, not even light. A black hole has thus been formed.

The Order of Space

When your subject is a physical object, you should select some orderly means of describing it: from left to right, top to bottom, inside to outside, and so forth. For example, you might describe a sculpture as you walk around it from front to back. Below is a paragraph describing a cowboy in which the writer has ordered the details of his description in a head-to-feet pattern.

> Big Dave was pure cowboy. He wore a black felt hat so big that it kept his face in perpetual shade. Around his neck was knotted a red bandana stained with sweat from long hot days in the saddle. His over-sized blue denim shirt hung from his shoulders to give him plenty of arm freedom; one pocket bulged with a pouch of chewing tobacco. His faded

jeans were held up by a broad brown leather belt with a huge silver buckle featuring a snorting bronc in full buck. His boots were old and dirt-colored and kicked up little dust storms as he sauntered across the corral.

Deductive Order

A paragraph ordered deductively moves from a generalization to particular details that explain or support the general statement. Perhaps the most common pattern of all paragraphs, the deductive paragraph begins with its topic sentence and proceeds to its supporting details, as illustrated in the following example:

> If 111 ninth-graders in Honolulu are typical of today's teenagers, spelling and social science teachers may be in for trouble. In a recent experiment, not one of the students tested could write the Pledge of Allegiance correctly. In addition, the results showed that the students apparently had little understanding of the pledge's meaning. For example, several students described the United States as a "nation under guard" instead of "under God," and the phrase "to the Republic for which it stands" appeared in several responses as "of the richest stand" or "for Richard stand." Many students changed the word "indivisible" to the phrase "in the visible," and over nine percent of the students, all of whom are Americans from varying racial and ethnic backgrounds, misspelled the word "America."

Inductive Order

An inductive paragraph begins with an examination of particular details and then concludes with a larger point or generalization about those details. Such a paragraph often ends with its topic sentence, as does the following paragraph on Little League baseball:

> At almost every Little League baseball game, one or another adult creates a minor scene by yelling obscenely at an umpire or a coach. Similarly, it is fairly common to see such adults arguing loudly with one another in the stands over whose child should have caught a missed ball. Perhaps the most astounding spectacle of all, however, is an irate father or mother yanking a child off the field after a bad play for a humiliating lecture in front of the whole team. Sadly, Little League baseball today often seems intended more for childish parents than for the children who actually play it.

Transition Words and Phrases

Some paragraphs may need internal transition words to help the reader move smoothly from one thought to the next so that the ideas do not appear disconnected or choppy.

Here is a list of common transition words and phrases and their uses:

giving examples	for example, for instance, specifically, in particular, namely, another
comparison	similarly, not only . . . but also, in comparison
contrast	although, but, while, in contrast, however, though, on the other hand
sequence	first . . . second . . . third, and finally, moreover, also, in addition, next, then, after, furthermore
results	therefore, thus, consequently, as a result

Notice the difference the use of transition words makes in the paragraphs below:

> Working in the neighborhood grocery store as a checker was one of the worst jobs I've ever had. In the first place, I had to wear an ugly, scratchy uniform cut at least three inches too short. My schedule of working hours was another inconvenience; because my hours were changed each week, it was impossible to make plans in advance, and getting a day off was out of the question. In addition, the lack of working space bothered me. Except for a half-hour lunch break, I was restricted to three square feet of room behind the counter and consequently felt as if I were no more than a cog in the cash register.

The same paragraph rewritten without transition words sounds choppy and childish:

> Working in the neighborhood grocery store as a checker was one of the worst jobs I've ever had. I had to wear an ugly, scratchy uniform. It was cut at least three inches too short. My schedule of working hours was inconvenient. My hours changed each week. It was impossible to make plans in advance. Getting a day off was out of the question. The lack of working space bothered me. Except for a half-hour break, I was restricted to three square feet of room behind the counter. I felt like a cog in the cash register.

Although transition words and phrases are useful in bridging the gaps between your ideas, don't overuse them. Not every sentence needs a transition phrase, so use one only when the relationship between your thoughts needs clarification. It's also a mistake to place the transition word in the same position in your sentence each time. Look at the paragraph that follows:

> It's a shame that every high school student isn't required to take a course in first aid. *For example,* you might need to treat a friend or relative for drowning during a family picnic. Or, *for instance,* someone might break a bone or receive a snakebite on a camping trip. *Also,* you should always know what to do for a common cut or burn. *Moreover,* it's important to realize when someone is in shock. *However,* very few people take the time to learn the simple rules of first aid. *Thus,* many injured or sick people suffer more than they should. *Therefore,* everyone should take a first aid course in school or at the Red Cross center.

As you can see, a series of sentences each beginning with a transition word quickly becomes repetitious and boring. To hold your reader's attention, use transition words only when necessary to avoid choppiness, and vary their placement in your sentences.

Repetition of Key Words

Important words or phrases (and their synonyms) may be repeated throughout a paragraph to connect the thoughts into a coherent statement:

> One of the most common, and yet most puzzling, phobias is the *fear* of *snakes.* It's only natural, of course, to be afraid of a poisonous *snake,* but many people are just as frightened of the harmless varieties. For such people, a tiny green grass *snake* is as terrifying as a cobra. Some researchers say this unreasonable *fear* of any and all *snakes* is a legacy left to us by our cave-dwelling ancestors, for whom these *reptiles* were a real and constant danger. Others maintain that the *fear* is a result of our associating the *snake* with the notion of evil, as in the Garden of Eden. Whatever the reason, the fact remains that for many otherwise normal people, the mere sight of a *snake* slithering through the countryside is enough to keep them city dwellers forever.

The repeated words "fear" and "snake" and the synonym "reptile" help tie one sentence to another so that the reader may follow the ideas easily.

Pronouns Substituted for Key Nouns

A pronoun is a word that stands for a noun. In your paragraph you may use a key noun in one sentence and then use a pronoun in its place in the following sentences. The pronoun "it" often replaces "shark" in the description below:

> [1]The great white shark is perhaps the best equipped of all the ocean's predators. [2]*It* can grow up to twenty-one feet and weigh three tons, with two-inch teeth that can replace themselves within twenty-four hours when damaged. [3]The shark's sense of smell is so acute *it* can detect one ounce of fish blood in a million ounces of water. [4]In addition, *it* can sense vibrations from six hundred feet away.

Sentences 2, 3, and 4 are tied to the topic sentence by the use of the pronoun "it."

Parallelism

Parallelism in a paragraph means using the same grammatical structure in several sentences to establish coherence. The repeated use of similar phrasing helps tie the ideas and sentences together. Next, for example, is a paragraph predominantly unified by its use of grammatically parallel sentences:

> The weather of Texas offers something for everyone. If you are the kind who likes to see snow drifting onto mountain peaks, a visit to the Big Bend area will satisfy your eye. If, on the other hand, you demand a bright sun to bake your skin a golden brown, stop in the southern part of the state. And for hardier souls, who ask from nature a show of force, the skies of the Panhandle regularly release ferocious springtime tornadoes. Finally, if you are the fickle type, by all means come to central Texas, where the sun at any time may shine unashamed throughout the most torrential rainstorm.

The parallel structures of sentences 2, 3, and 5 ("if you" + verb) keep the paragraph flowing smoothly from one idea to the next.

Using a Variety of Transition Devices

Most writers use a combination of transition devices in their paragraphs. In the following example, three kinds of transition devices are circled. See if you can identify each one.

Transitions are the glue that holds a paragraph together. These devices lead the reader from sentence to sentence, smoothing over the gaps between by indicating the relationship between the sentences. If this glue is missing, the paragraph will almost inevitably sound choppy or childish, even if every sentence in it responds to a single topic commitment. However, transitions are not substitutes for topic unity: like most glue, they are most effective when joining similar objects, or, in this case, similar ideas. For example, in a paragraph describing a chicken egg, no transition could bridge the gap created by the inclusion of a sentence concerned with naval losses in the Civil War. In other words, transitions can call attention to the topic relationships between sentences, but they cannot create those relationships.

transition words	repetition of pronouns	repetition of key words

PRACTICING WHAT YOU'VE LEARNED

A. Identify each of the following paragraphs as ordered by time, space, or parallelism:

My apartment is so small that it will no longer hold all my posses-sions. Every day when I come in the door, I am shocked by the clutter. The wall to my immediate left is completely obscured by art and movie posters that have become so numerous they often overlap, hiding even each other. Along the adjoining wall is my sound system: CDs and tapes are stacked several feet high on two long, low tables. The big couch that runs across the back of the room is always piled so high with schoolbooks and magazines that a guest usually ends up sitting on the floor. To my right is a large sliding glass door that opens onto a balcony—or at least it used to, before it was permanently blocked by my tennis gear, golf clubs, and ten-speed bike. Even the tiny closet next to the front door is bursting with clothes, both clean and dirty. I think the time has come for me to move.

Once-common acts of greeting may be finding renewed popularity after three centuries. According to one historian, kissing was at the height of its popularity as a greeting in seventeenth-century England, when ladies and gentlemen of the court often saluted each other in this affectionate manner. Then the country was visited by a strange plague, whose cause was unknown. Because no one knew how the plague was spread, people tried to avoid physical contact with others as much as possible. Both kissing and the handshake went out of fashion and were replaced by the bow and curtsy, so people could greet others without having to touch them. The bow and curtsy remained in vogue for over a hundred years, until the handshake—for men only—returned to popularity in the nineteenth century. Today, both men and women may shake hands upon meeting others, and kissing as a greeting is making a comeback—especially among the jet-setters and Hollywood stars.

Students have diverse ways of preparing for final exams. Some stay up the night before, trying to cram into their brains what they avoided all term. Others pace themselves, spending a little time each night going over the notes they took in class that day. Still others cross their fingers and hope they absorbed enough from lectures. In the end, though, everyone hopes the tests are easy.

B. Circle and identify the transition devices in the following paragraphs:

Each year I follow a system when preparing firewood to use in my stove. First, I hike about a mile from my house with my bow saw in hand. I then select three good size oak trees and mark them with orange ties. Next, I saw through the base of each tree about two feet from the ground. After I fell the trees, not only do I trim away the branches, but I also sort the scrap from the usable limbs. I find cutting the trees into manageable length logs is too much for one day; however, I roll them off the ground so they will not begin to rot. The next day I cut the trees into eight-foot lengths, which allows me to handle them more easily. Once they are cut, I roll them along the fire lane to the edge of the road where I stack them neatly but not too high. The next day I borrow my uncle's van, drive to the pile of logs, and load as many logs as I can, thus reducing the number of trips. When I finally have all the logs in my backyard, I begin sawing them into eighteen-inch lengths. I create large piles that consequently have to be split and finally stacked. The logs will age and dry until winter when I will make daily trips to the woodpile.

Fans of professional baseball and football argue continually over which is America's favorite spectator sport. Though the figures on attendance for each vary with every new season, certain arguments remain the same, spelling out both the enduring appeals of each game and something about the people who love to watch. Football, for instance, is a quicker, more physical sport, and football fans enjoy the emotional involvement they feel while watching. Baseball, on the other hand, seems more mental, like chess, and attracts those fans who prefer a quieter, more complicated game. In addition, professional football teams usually play no more than fourteen games a year, providing fans with a whole week between games to work themselves up to a pitch of excitement and expectation. Baseball teams, however, play almost every day for six months, so that the typical baseball fan is not so crushed by missing a game, knowing there will be many other chances to attend. Finally, football fans seem to love the half-time pageantry, the marching bands, and the pretty cheerleaders, whereas baseball fans are more content to concentrate on the game's finer details and spend the breaks between innings filling out their own private scorecards.

C. This paragraph lacks common transition devices. Fill in each blank with the appropriate transition word or key word.

Scientists continue to debate the cause of the dinosaurs' disappearance. One group claims the _____ vanished after a comet smashed into the Earth; dust and smoke _____ blocked the sun for a long time. _____ of no direct sunlight, the Earth underwent a lengthy "winter," far too cold for the huge _____ to survive. A University of California paleontologist, _____, disputes this claim. He argues that _____ we generally think of _____ living in swampy land, fossils found in Alaska show that _____ could live in cold climates _____ warm ones. _____ group claims that the _____ became extinct following an intense period of global volcanic activity. _____ to killing the _____ themselves, these scientists _____ believe the volcanic activity killed much of the plant life that the _____ ate and, _____, many of the great _____ who survived the volcanic eruptions starved to death. Still _____ groups of _____ claim the _____ were destroyed by acid rain, _____ by a passing "death star," _____ even by visitors from outer space.

D. The sentences in each of the following exercises are out of order. By noting the various transition devices, you should be able to arrange each group of sentences into a coherent paragraph.

Paragraph 1: How to Purchase a New Car

- If you're happy with the car's performance, find out about available financing arrangements.
- Later, at home, study your notes carefully to help you decide which car fits your needs.
- After you have discussed various loans and interest rates, you can negotiate the final price with the salesperson.
- A visit to the showroom also allows you to test-drive the car.
- Once you have agreed on the car's price, feel confident you have made a well-chosen purchase.
- Next, a visit to a nearby showroom should help you select the color, options, and style of the car of your choice.
- First, take a trip to the library to read the current auto magazines.
- As you read, take notes on models and prices.

Paragraph 2: Henry VIII and the Problems of Succession

- After Jane, Henry took three more wives, but all these marriages were childless.
- Jane did produce a son, Edward VI, but he died at age fifteen.
- The problem of succession was therefore an important issue during the reign of Henry VIII.
- Still hoping for a son, Henry beheaded Anne and married Jane Seymour.

- Thus, despite his six marriages, Henry failed in his attempts to secure the succession.

- In sixteenth-century England it was considered essential for a son to assume the throne.

- Henry's first wife, Catherine of Aragon, had only one child, the Princess Mary.

- But Anne also produced a daughter, the future Queen Elizabeth I.

- Consequently, he divorced Catherine and married Anne Boleyn.

PARAGRAPH SEQUENCE

The order in which you present your paragraphs is another decision you must make. In some essays, the subject matter itself will suggest its own order.* For instance, in an essay designed to instruct a beginning jogger, you might want to discuss the necessary equipment—good jogging shoes, loose-fitting clothing, and sweatband—before moving to a discussion of where to jog and how to jog. Other essays, however, may not suggest a natural order, in which case you yourself must decide which order will most effectively reach and hold the attention of your audience. Frequently, writers withhold their strongest point until last. (Lawyers often use this technique; they first present the jury with the weakest arguments, then pull out the most incriminating evidence—the "smoking pistol." Thus the jury members retire with the strongest argument freshest in their minds.) Sometimes, however, you'll find it necessary to present one particular point first so that the other points make good sense. Study your own major points and decide which order will be the most logical, successful way of persuading your reader to accept your thesis.

TRANSITIONS BETWEEN PARAGRAPHS

As you already know, each paragraph usually signals a new major point in your discussion. These paragraphs should not appear as isolated blocks of thought but rather as parts of a unified, step-by-step progression. To avoid a choppy essay, link each paragraph to the one before it with *transition devices*. Just as the sentences in your paragraphs are connected, so are the paragraphs themselves; therefore, you can use the same transition devices suggested on pages 79–82.

* For more information on easily recognized patterns of order, see pages 77–78.

The first sentence of most body paragraphs frequently contains the transition device. To illustrate this point, here are some topic sentences lifted from the body paragraphs of a student essay criticizing a popular sports car, renamed the 'Gator to protect the guilty and to prevent lawsuits. The transition devices are italicized.

Thesis: The 'Gator is one of the worst cars on the market.

- When you buy a 'Gator, you buy physical inconvenience. [repetition of key word from thesis]

- *Another* reason the 'Gator is a bad buy is the cost of insurance. [transition word, key word]

- You might overlook the *inconvenient* size and exorbitant *insurance* rates if the 'Gator were a strong, reliable car, *but* this automobile constantly needs repair. [key words from preceding paragraphs, transition word]

- When you decide to sell this *car*, you face *still another* unpleasant surprise: the extremely low resale value. [key word, transition phrase]

- The most serious drawback, *however,* is the 'Gator's safety record. [transition word, key word]

Sometimes, instead of using transition words or repetition of key words or their synonyms, you can use an *idea* hook. The last idea of one paragraph may lead you smoothly into your next paragraph. Instead of repeating a key word from the previous discussion, find a phrase that refers to the entire idea just expressed. If, for example, the previous paragraph discussed the highly complimentary advertising campaign for the 'Gator, the next paragraph might begin, "This view of the 'Gator as an economy car is ridiculous to anyone who's pumped a week's salary into this gas guzzler." The phrase "this view" connects the idea of the first paragraph with the one that follows. Idea hooks also work well with transition words: "This view, however, is ridiculous. . . ."

If you do use transition words, don't allow them to make your essay sound mechanical. For example, a long series of paragraphs beginning "first . . . second . . . third . . ." quickly becomes boring. Vary the type and position of your transition devices so that your essay has a subtle but logical movement from point to point.

 ## APPLYING WHAT YOU'VE LEARNED TO **YOUR** WRITING

If you are currently working on a draft of an essay, check each body paragraph for coherence, the smooth connection of ideas and sentences in a logical, easy-to-follow order. You might try placing brackets around key words, pronouns, and transition words that carry the reader's attention from thought to thought and from sentence to sentence. Decide whether you have enough ordering devices, placed in appropriate places, or whether you need to add (or delete) others. (For additional help revising your drafts, turn to Chapter 5.)

CHAPTER 3 SUMMARY

Here is a brief restatement of what you should know about the paragraphs in the body of your essay:

1. Each body paragraph usually contains one major point in the discussion promised by the thesis statement.

2. Each major point is presented in the topic sentence of a paragraph.

3. Each paragraph should be adequately developed with clear supporting detail.

4. Every sentence in the paragraph should support the topic sentence.

5. There should be an orderly, logical flow from sentence to sentence and from thought to thought.

6. The sequence of your essay's paragraphs should be logical and effective.

7. There should be a smooth flow from paragraph to paragraph.

8. The body paragraphs should successfully persuade your reader that the opinion expressed in your thesis is valid.

CHAPTER

4

Beginnings and Endings

As you work on your rough drafts, you might think of your essay as a coherent, unified whole composed of three main parts: the introduction (lead-in, thesis, and essay map), the body (paragraphs with supporting evidence), and the conclusion (final address to the reader). These three parts should flow smoothly into one another, presenting the reader with an organized, logical discussion. The following pages will suggest ways to begin, end, and also name your essay effectively.

HOW TO WRITE A GOOD LEAD-IN

The first few sentences of your essay are particularly important; first impressions, as you know, are often lasting ones. The beginning of your essay, then, must catch the readers' attention and make them want to keep reading. Recall the way you read a magazine: if you are like most people, you probably skim the magazine, reading a paragraph or two of each article that looks promising. If the first few paragraphs hold your interest, you read on. When you write your own introductory paragraph, assume that you have only a few sentences to attract your reader. Consequently, you must pay particular attention to making those first lines especially interesting and well written.

In some essays, your thesis statement alone may be controversial or striking enough to capture the readers. At other times, however, you will want to use the introductory device called a *lead-in*.* The lead-in (1) catches the readers' attention; (2) announces the subject matter and tone of your essay (humorous, satiric, serious, etc.); and (3) sets up, or leads into, the presentation of your thesis and essay map.

Here are some suggestions and examples of lead-ins:

1. A paradoxical or intriguing statement

> "Eat two chocolate bars and call me in the morning," says the psychiatrist to his patient. Such advice sounds like a sugar fanatic's dream, but recent studies have indeed confirmed that chocolate positively affects depression and anxiety.

2. An arresting statistic or shocking statement

> One of every seven women living in Smith County will be raped this year, according to a recent report prepared by the County Rape Information and Counseling Services.

3. A question

> It is three times the number of people who belong to the Southern Baptist Convention, nine times the number who serve in the U.S. armed forces, and more than twice the number who voted for Barry Goldwater for President in 1964. What is it? It's the number of people in the United States who admit to having smoked marijuana: a massive 62 million.

4. A quotation or literary allusion

> "I think onstage nudity is disgusting, shameful, and damaging to all things American," says actress Shelley

---

* Do note that for some writing assignments, such as certain kinds of technical reports, attention-grabbing lead-ins are not appropriate. Frequently, these reports are directed toward particular professional audiences and have their own designated format; they often begin, for example, with a statement of the problem under study or with a review of pertinent information or research.

Winters. "But if I were twenty-two with a great body, it would be artistic, tasteful, patriotic, and a progressive religious experience."

5. A relevant story, joke, or anecdote

Writer and witty critic Dorothy Parker was once assigned a remote, out-of-the-way office. According to the story, she became lonely, so desperate for company, that she ultimately painted "Gentlemen" on the door. Although this university is large, no one on this campus needs to feel as isolated as Parker obviously did: our excellent Student Activity Office has numerous clubs, programs, and volunteer groups to involve students of all interests.

6. A description, often used for emotional appeal

With one eye blackened, one arm in a cast, and third-degree burns on both her legs, the pretty, blond two-year-old seeks corners of rooms, refuses to speak, and shakes violently at the sound of loud noises. Tammy is not the victim of a war or a natural disaster; rather, she is the helpless victim of her parents, one of the thousands of children who suffer daily from America's hidden crime, child abuse.

7. A factual statement or a summary who-what-where-when-and-why lead-in

Texas's first execution of a woman in twenty-two years occurred September 17 at the Huntsville Unit of the state's Department of Corrections, despite the protests of various human rights groups around the country.

8. An analogy or comparison

The Romans kept geese on their Capitol Hill to cackle alarm in the event of attack by night. Modern Americans, despite their technology, have hardly improved on that old system of protection. According to the latest Safety Council report, almost any door with standard locks can be opened easily with a common plastic credit card.

9. A contrast

> I used to search for toast in the supermarket. I used to think "blackened"—as in blackened Cajun shrimp—referred to the way I cooked anything in a skillet. "Poached" could only have legal ramifications. But all that has changed! Attending a class in basic cooking this summer has transformed the way I purchase, prepare, and even talk about food.

10. A personal experience

> I realized times were changing for women when I overheard my six-year-old nephew speaking to my sister, a prominent New York lawyer. As we left her elaborate, luxurious office one evening, Tommy looked up at his mother and queried, "Mommy, can little boys grow up to be lawyers, too?"

11. A catalog of relevant examples

> A two-hundred-pound teenager quit school because no desk would hold her. A three-hundred-pound chef who could no longer stand on his feet was fired. A three-hundred-fifty-pound truck driver broke furniture in his friends' houses. All these people are now living healthier, happier, and thinner lives, thanks to the remarkable intestinal bypass surgery first developed in 1967.

12. Statement of a problem or a popular misconception

> Some people believe that poetry is written only by aging beatniks or solemn, mournful men and women with suicidal tendencies. The Poetry in the Schools Program is working hard to correct that erroneous point of view.

Thinking of a good lead-in is often difficult when you sit down to begin your essay. Many writers, in fact, skip the lead-in until the first draft is written. They compose their working thesis first and then write the body of the essay, saving the lead-in and conclusion for last. As you write the middle of your essay, you may discover an especially interesting piece of information you might want to save to use as your lead-in.

AVOIDING ERRORS IN LEAD-INS

In addition to the previous suggestions, here is some advice to help you avoid common lead-in errors:

Make sure your lead-in introduces your thesis. A frequent weakness in introductory paragraphs is an interesting lead-in but no smooth or clear transition to the thesis statement. To avoid a gap or awkward jump in thought in your introductory paragraph, you may need to add a connecting sentence or phrase between your lead-in and thesis. Study the paragraph below, which uses a comparison as its lead-in. The italicized transition sentence takes the reader from a general comment about Americans who use wheelchairs to information about those in Smallville, smoothly preparing the reader for the thesis that follows.

Lead-in

Transition sentence

Thesis

In the 1950s African-Americans demanded and won the right to sit anywhere they pleased on public buses. Today, Americans who use wheelchairs are fighting for the simple right to board those same buses. *Here in Smallville, as well as in other cities, the lack of proper boarding facilities often denies disabled citizens basic transportation to jobs, grocery stores, and medical centers.* To give persons in wheelchairs the same opportunities as other residents, the Smallville City Council should vote the funds necessary to convert the public transportation system.

Keep your lead-in brief. Long lead-ins in short essays often give the appearance of a tail wagging the dog. Use a brief, attention-catching hook to set up your thesis; don't make your introduction the biggest part of your essay.

Don't begin with an apology or complaint. Statements such as "It's difficult to find much information on this topic . . ." and "This controversy is hard to understand, but . . ." do nothing to entice your reader.

Don't assume your audience already knows your subject matter. Identify the pertinent facts even though you know your teacher knows the assignment. ("The biggest problem with the new requirement. . . ." What requirement?) If you are writing about a particular piece of literature, identify the title of the work and its author, using the writer's full name in the first reference.

Stay clear of overused lead-ins. If composition teachers had a nickel for every essay that began with a dry dictionary definition, they could all retire to

Bermuda. Leave *Webster's* alone and find a livelier way to begin. Asking a question as your lead-in is becoming overused, too, so use it only when it is obviously the best choice for your opener.

 PRACTICING WHAT YOU'VE LEARNED

Find three good lead-ins from essays, magazine articles, or newspaper feature stories. Identify the kinds of lead-ins you found, and tell why you think each effectively catches the reader's attention and sets up the thesis.

HOW TO WRITE A GOOD CONCLUDING PARAGRAPH

Like a good story, a good essay should not stop in the middle. It should have a satisfying conclusion, one that gives the reader a sense of completion on the subject. Don't allow your essay to drop off or fade out at the end—instead, use the concluding paragraph to emphasize the validity and importance of your thinking. Remember that the concluding paragraph is your last chance to convince the reader. (As one cynical but realistic student pointed out, the conclusion is the last part of your essay the teacher reads before putting a grade on your paper.) Therefore, make your conclusion count.

Some people feel that writing an essay shares a characteristic with a romantic fling—both activities are frequently easier to begin than they are to end. If you find, as many writers do, that you often struggle long while searching for an exit with the proper emphasis and grace, here are some suggestions, by no means exhaustive, that might spark some good ideas for your conclusions:

1. A restatement of both the thesis and the essay's major points (for long essays only)

    > As much as we may dislike the notion, it's time to reinstate the military draft. With the armed services' failure to meet its recruitment goals, the rising costs of defense, and the racism and sexism inherent in our volunteer system, we have no other choice if we wish a protected future.

2. An evaluation of the importance of the essay's subject

    > These amazing, controversial photographs of the comet will continue to be the subject of debate because, according

to some scientists, they yield the most important clues yet revealed about the origins of our universe.

3. A statement of the essay's broader implications

Because these studies of feline leukemia may someday play a crucial role in the discovery of a cure for AIDS in human beings, the experiments, as expensive as they are, must continue.

4. A call to action

The fate of the World War II hero Raoul Wallenberg is still unknown. Although Congress has awarded him honorary citizenship, such a tribute is not enough. We must write our congressional representatives today to voice our demand that they investigate his disappearance or produce proof of his death. No hero deserves less.

5. A warning based on the essay's thesis

Understanding the politics that led up to Hiroshima is essential for all Americans—indeed, for all the world's peoples. Without such knowledge, the frightful possibility exists that somewhere, sometime, someone may drop the bomb again.

6. A witticism that emphasizes or sums up the point of the essay

No one said dieting was easy. But for some of us who have surrendered, the cliché "half a loaf is better than none" has taken on new meaning!

7. A quotation, story, or joke that emphasizes or sums up the point of the essay

Bette Davis's role on and off the screen as the catty, wisecracking woman of steel helped make her an enduring star. After all, no audience, past or present, could ever resist a dame who drags on a cigarette and then mutters about a passing starlet, "There goes a good time that was had by all."

8. An image or description that lends finality to the essay

> As the last of the Big Screen's giant ants are incinerated by the army scientist, one can almost hear the movie audiences of the 1950s breathing a collective sigh of relief, secure in the knowledge that once again the threat of nuclear radiation had been vanquished by the efforts of the U.S. military.

(For another brief image that captures the essence of an essay, see also the "open house" scene that concludes "To Bid the World Farewell," p. 223.)

9. A rhetorical question that makes the readers think about the essay's main point

> No one wants to see hostages put in danger. But what nation can afford to let terrorists know they can get away with murder?

10. A forecast based on the essay's thesis

> Soap operas will continue to be popular not only because they distract us from our daily chores but also because they present life as we want it to be: fast-paced, glamorous, and full of exciting characters.

AVOIDING ERRORS IN CONCLUSIONS

Try to omit the following common errors in your concluding paragraphs:

Avoid a mechanical ending. One of the most frequent weaknesses in student essays is the conclusion that merely restates the thesis, word for word. A short essay of 500–750 words rarely requires a flat, point-by-point conclusion—in fact, such an ending often insults the readers' intelligence by implying that their attention spans are extremely short. Only after reading long essays do most readers need a precise recap of all the writer's main ideas. Instead of recopying your thesis and essay map, try finding an original, emphatic way to conclude your essay—or as a well-known newspaper columnist described it, a good ending should snap with grace and authority, like the close of an expensive sports car door.

Don't introduce new points. Treat the major points of your essay in separate body paragraphs rather than in your exit.

Don't tack on a conclusion. There should be a smooth flow from your last body paragraph into your concluding statements.

Don't change your stance. Sometimes writers who have been critical of something throughout their essays will soften their stance or offer apologies in their last paragraph. For instance, someone complaining about the poor quality of a particular college course might abruptly conclude with statements that declare the class wasn't so bad after all, maybe she should have worked harder, or maybe she really did learn something after all. Such reneging may seem polite, but in actuality it undercuts the thesis and confuses the reader who has taken the writer's criticisms seriously. Instead of contradicting themselves, writers should stand their ground, forget about puffy clichés or "niceties," and find an emphatic way to conclude that is consistent with their thesis.

Avoid trite expressions. Don't begin your conclusions by declaring, "in conclusion," "in summary," or "as you can see, this essay proves my thesis that. . . ." End your essay so that the reader clearly senses completion; don't merely announce that you're finished.

 PRACTICING WHAT YOU'VE LEARNED

Find three good concluding paragraphs. Identify each kind of conclusion and tell why you think it is an effective ending for the essay or article.

HOW TO WRITE A GOOD TITLE

As in the case of lead-ins, your title may be written at any time, but many writers prefer to finish their essays before naming them. A good title is similar to a good newspaper headline in that it attracts the readers' interest and makes them want to investigate the essay. Like the lead-in, the title also helps announce the tone of the essay. An informal or humorous essay, for instance, might have a catchy, funny title. Some titles show the writer's wit and love of wordplay; a survey of recent magazines revealed these titles: "Bittersweet News about Saccharin," "Coffee: New Grounds for Concern," and "The Scoop on the Best Ice Cream."

On the other hand, a serious, informative essay should have a more formal title that suggests its content as clearly and specifically as possible. Let's suppose, for example, that you are doing research on the meaning of color in dreams, and you run across an essay listed in the library's *Readers' Guide* titled merely "Dreams." You don't know whether you should read it. To avoid such confusion in your own essay and to encourage readers' interest, always use a specific title: "Animal Imagery in Dreams," "Dream Research in Dogs," and so forth. Moreover, if your subject matter is controversial, let the reader know which side you're on (e.g., "The Advantages of Solar Power"). Never substitute a mere label, such as "Football Games" or "Euthanasia," for a meaningful title. And never, never label your essays "Theme One" or "Comparison and Contrast Essay." In all your writing, including the title, use your creativity to attract the readers' attention and to invite their interest in your ideas.

If you're unsure about how to present your title, here are two basic rules:

1. Your own title should *not* be underlined or put in quotation marks. It should be written at the top of page one of your essay or on an appropriate cover sheet with no special marks of punctuation.

2. Only the first word and the important words of your title should be capitalized. Generally, do not capitalize words such as "an," "and," "a," or "the," or prepositions, unless they appear as the first word of the title.

 ## ASSIGNMENT

Select any three of the student or professional essays in this text; give the first one a new title; the second, an interesting lead-in; the third, a different conclusion. Why are your choices as effective or even better than those of the original writers?

 ## APPLYING WHAT YOU'VE LEARNED TO **YOUR** WRITING

Look at the draft of the essay you are currently working on and ask yourself these questions:

- Does the opening of my essay make my reader want to continue reading? Does the lead-in smoothly set up my thesis or do I need to add some sort of transition to help move the reader to my main idea? Is the lead-in appropriate in terms of the tone and length of my essay?

- Does the conclusion of my essay offer an emphatic ending, one that is consistent with my essay's purpose? Have I avoided a mechanical, trite, or tacked-on closing paragraph? Have I refrained from adding a new point in my conclusion that belongs in the body of my essay or in another essay?

- Does my title interest my reader? Is its content and tone appropriate for this particular essay?

If you have answered "no" to any of the above questions, you should continue revising your essay. (For more help revising your prose, turn to Chapter 5.)

CHAPTER 4 SUMMARY

Here is a brief restatement of what you should remember about writing introductions, conclusions, and titles:

1. Many essays will profit from a lead-in, the first sentences of the introductory paragraph that attract the reader's attention and smoothly set up the thesis statement.
2. Essays should end convincingly, without being repetitious or trite, with thoughts that emphasize the writer's main purpose.
3. Titles should invite the reader's interest by indicating the general nature of the essay's content and its tone.

CHAPTER

5

Drafting and Revising: Creative Thinking, Critical Thinking

There is no good writing, only rewriting.

—James Thurber

When I say writing, O, believe me, it is rewriting that I have chiefly in mind.

—Robert Louis Stevenson

The absolute necessity of revision cannot be overemphasized. All good writers rethink, rearrange, and rewrite large portions of their prose. The French novelist Colette, for instance, wrote everything over and over. In fact, she often spent an entire morning working on a single page. Hemingway, to cite another example, rewrote the ending to *A Farewell to Arms* thirty-nine times "to get the words right." While no one expects you to make thirty-nine drafts of each essay, the point is clear: writing well means revising. All good writers revise their prose.

WHAT IS REVISION?

Revision is a *thinking process* that occurs any time you are working on a writing project. It means looking at your writing with a "fresh eye"—that is, reseeing your writing in ways that will enable you to make more effective choices throughout your essay. Revision often entails rethinking what you have written and asking yourself questions about its effectiveness; it involves discovery as well as change. As you write, new ideas surface, prompting you to revise what you have planned or have just written. Or perhaps these new ideas will cause changes in earlier parts of your essay. In some cases, your new ideas will encourage you to begin an entirely new draft with a different focus or approach. Revision means making important decisions about the best ways to focus, organize, develop, clarify, and emphasize your ideas.

WHEN DOES REVISION OCCUR?

Revision, as noted above, occurs throughout your writing process. Early on, you are revising as you sort through ideas to write about, and you almost certainly revise as you define your purpose and audience and sharpen your thesis. Some revising may be done in your head, and some may be on paper as you plan, sketch, or "discovery-write" your ideas. Later, during drafting, revision becomes more individualized and complex. Many writers find themselves sweeping back and forth over their papers, writing for a bit and then rereading what they wrote, making changes, and then moving ahead. Some writers like to revise "lumps," or pieces of writing, perhaps reviewing one major idea or paragraph at a time. Frequently, writers discover that a better idea is occurring almost at the very moment they are putting another thought on paper. And virtually all writers revise after "reseeing" a draft in its entirety.

Revision, then, occurs before drafting, during drafting, between parts of drafts, and at the ends of drafts. You can revise a word, a sentence, a paragraph, or an entire essay. If you are like most writers, you sometimes revise almost automatically as you write (crossing out one word or line and quickly replacing it with another as you move on, for example), and at other times you revise very deliberately (concentrating on a conclusion you know is weak, for example). Revision is "rethinking," and that activity can happen anytime, in many ways, in any part of your writing.

MYTHS ABOUT REVISION

If revision is rethinking, what is it not? Three misconceptions about revision are addressed here.

1. *Revision is not autopsy.*

Revision is not an isolated stage of writing that occurs *only* after your last draft is written or right before your paper is to be handed in. Revising is not merely a postmortem procedure, to be performed only after your creative juices have ceased to flow. Good writing, as Thurber noted, *is* revision, and revision occurs throughout the writing process.

2. *Revision is not limited to editing or proofreading.*

Too many writers mistakenly equate revision with editing and proofreading. *Editing* means revising for "surface errors"—mistakes in spelling, grammar, punctuation, sentence sense, and word choice. Certainly, good writers comb their papers for such errors, and they edit their prose extensively for clarity, conciseness, and emphasis, too. *Proofreading* to search out and destroy errors and typos that distort meaning or distract the reader is also important. Without question, both editing and proofreading are essential to a polished paper. But revision is not *limited* to such activities. It includes them but also encompasses those larger, global changes writers may make in purpose, focus, organization, and development. Writers who revise effectively not only change words and catch mechanical errors but also typically add, delete, rearrange, and rewrite large chunks of prose. In other words, revision is not cosmetic surgery on a body that may need major resuscitation.

3. *Revision is not punishment or busywork.*

At one time or another, most of us have found ourselves guilty of racing too quickly through a particular job and then moving on. And perhaps just as often we have found ourselves redoing such jobs because the results were so disappointing. Some people may regard revising in a similar light—as the repeat performance of a job done poorly the first time. But that attitude isn't productive. Revising isn't punishment for failing to produce a perfect first draft. Rarely, if ever, does anyone—even our most admired professional writers—produce the results they want without revising.* Remember that revising is not a tacked-on stage nor is it merely a quick touch-up; it's an integral part of the entire writing process itself. It's an ongoing opportunity to discover, remember, reshape, and refine your ideas.

If you've ever created something you now treasure—a piece of jewelry, furniture, painting, or music—recall the time you put into it. You probably thought about it from several angles, experimented with it, crafted it, worked

---

*All of us have heard stories about famous essays or poems composed at one quick sitting. Bursts of creativity do happen. But it's also highly likely that authors of such pieces revise extensively in their heads before they write. They rattle ideas around in their brains for such a prolonged period that the actual writing does in fact flow easily or may even seem "dictated" by an inner voice. This sort of lengthy internal "cooking" may work well at various times for you, too.

it through expected and unexpected problems, and smoothed out its minor glitches, all to achieve the results you wanted. Similarly, with each revision you make, your paper becomes clearer, truer, more satisfying to you and to your readers. With practice, you will produce writing you are proud of—and you will discover that revising has become not only an essential but also a natural part of your writing process.

CAN I LEARN TO IMPROVE MY REVISION SKILLS?

Because revision is such a multifaceted and individual activity, no textbook can guide you through all the rethinking you may do as you move through each sentence of every writing project. But certainly you can learn to improve your ability to think creatively and critically about your prose. To sharpen your thinking and revision skills, this chapter will suggest a step-by-step method of self-questioning designed to help you achieve your writing goals.

PREPARING TO DRAFT AND REVISE

Before you begin drafting (either a "discovery" draft or a draft from your working thesis), remember this important piece of advice: no part of your draft is sacred or permanent. No matter what you write at this point, you can always change it. Drafting is discovering and recollecting as well as recording ideas from your earlier plans. Take the pressure off yourself: no one expects blue-ribbon prose in early drafts. (If you can't seem to get going or if you do become stuck along the way, try turning to pp. 123–125 of this chapter for suggestions to help you confront your writer's block.)

At this point, too, you might consider the actual format of your drafts. Because you will be making many changes in your writing, you may find revising less cumbersome and time-consuming if you prepare your manuscripts as described below.

If you are handwriting your drafts:

1. Always write on one side of your paper only, in case you want to cut and tape together portions of drafts or you want to experiment with interchanging parts of a particular draft. (If you have written on both sides, you may have to recopy the parts of your essay you want to save; your time is better spent creating and revising.)

2. Leave big margins on *both* sides of each page of your drafts so you can add information later or jot down new ideas as they occur. (Some writers also skip lines for this reason. If you choose to write every other line, however, do

remember that you may not be getting a true picture of your paragraph development or essay length. A handwritten double-spaced body paragraph, for example, may appear skimpy in your typed final copy.)

3. Devise a system of symbols (circles, stars, checks, asterisks, etc.) that will remind you of changes you want to make later. For example, if you're in hot pursuit of a great idea but can't think of the exact word you want, put down a word that's close, circle it, and go on so that your thinking is not derailed. Similarly, a check in the margin might mean "return to this tangled sentence." A question mark might mean a fuzzy idea, and a star, a great idea that needs expanding. A system of signals can save you from agonizing over every inch of your essay while you are still trying to discover and clarify your ideas.

4. If your ideas are flowing well but you realize you need more supporting evidence for some of your points, consider leaving some blank spots to fill in later. For example, let's say you are writing about the role of television in our presidential elections; your ideas are good but in a particular body paragraph you decide some statistics on commercial frequency would be most convincing. Or perhaps you need to cite an example of a particular kind of advertisement but you just can't think of a good one at that moment. Leave a spot for the piece of evidence with a key word or two to remind you of what's needed, and keep writing. Later, when you come back to that spot, you can add the appropriate support; if you can't find or think of the right supporting evidence to insert, you may decide to delete that point.

5. If you do decide to delete something—a sentence or an entire passage—mark a single "X" or line through it lightly. Don't scratch it out or destroy it completely; you may realize later you want to reinsert the material there or move it to another, better place.

6. At some point do try to work from a typed copy. Frankly, the more compact spacing of typed prose allows you to see better the relationship of the parts in your essay, making it easier for you to organize and develop your ideas. It is also far more likely that you will catch spelling and other mechanical errors if they are printed.

7. Always keep your drafts. Never burn your bridges—or your manuscripts! Sometimes essays change directions, and writers find they can return to prewriting or earlier drafts to recover ideas, once rejected, that now work well. Drafts also may contain ideas that didn't work in one paper but that look like great starts for another assignment. Tracking revisions from draft to draft can give writers a sense of accomplishment and insight into their composing processes. And drafts can be good insurance in case final copies of papers are lost or accidentally destroyed.

A Special Note for Writers with Word Processors

If you have access to a computer and any of the many word-processing programs available today, you have probably already discovered how helpful this technology can be to writers in all stages of the writing process. You can, for example, store your prewriting activities, journal entries, notes, or good ideas in various files until you need to recall certain information, and you can easily produce extra copies of your drafts or finished essays without having to search out a copy machine and correct change. Spell-checkers or dictionaries may identify many of your obvious errors and typos.

But the most important use of the computer to a writer may be what it can do as you draft and revise your prose. At your command, a word-processing program enables you to add, delete, or change words easily; it allows you to move words, sentences, and even paragraphs or larger pieces of your essay. On any computer, for example, you can play "what if" by dropping the cursor below what you have written and try to phrase your idea in another way. Then you can delete the less effective passage. With some programs, you can even compare drafts side by side or with special "windows" that help you to see your choices more clearly. In other words, computers can help us as writers do the kind of deep-structure revision that is necessary to produce our best, most effective prose—the kind of major changes that, in the past, we may have been hesitant to make because of the time involved in recopying or retyping major portions of our drafts.

Whether the program you are using at home or at school is a series of simple commands or an elaborate instructional system that can ask questions or provide a sophisticated analysis of your writing, make a point of getting to know how to use the computer in the most effective ways. Study the manual that accompanies your word-processing program (or one of the many self-help manuals now on the market), and don't be afraid to ask your instructor or computer-lab monitor for assistance. The more you practice using your program to help you organize, develop, and revise your prose, the better your writing will be. (Remember, to avoid the "agony of delete," always "save" what you have written every ten minutes or so, and do print out a copy of each major draft or set of revisions in case your system crashes or you accidentally hit the wrong keys.)

A REVISION PROCESS FOR YOUR DRAFTS

Let's assume at this point that you have completed a draft, using the first four chapters of this book as a guide. You feel you've chosen an interesting topic and presented some good ideas. Perhaps the ideas came quickly or perhaps you had to coax them. However your thoughts came, they're now on paper— you have a draft with meaning and general order, although it's probably much rougher in some spots than in others. Now it's time to "resee" this draft in a comprehensive way.

But wait. If possible, put a night's sleep or at least a few hours between this draft and the advice that appears on the next few pages. All writers become tired when they work on any project for too long at one sitting, and then they lose a sense of perspective. When you've looked at a piece of prose again and again, you may begin to read what's written in your head instead of what's on the page—that is, you may begin to "fill in" for yourself, reading into your prose what you meant to say rather than what your reader will actually see. Always try to start your writing process early enough to give yourself a few breaks from the action. You'll find that you will be better able to evaluate the strengths and weaknesses of your prose when you are fresh.

When you do return to your draft, *don't try to look at all the parts of your paper, from ideas to organization to mechanics, at the same time.* Trying to resee everything at once is rarely possible and will only overload and frustrate you. It may cause you to overlook some important part of your paper that needs your full attention. Overload can also block your creative ideas. Therefore, instead of trying to revise an entire draft in one swoop, break your revising process into a series of smaller, more manageable steps. Here is a suggested process:

I.	rethink	purpose, thesis, and audience
II.	rethink	ideas and evidence
III.	rethink	organization
IV.	rethink	clarity and style
V.	edit	grammar, punctuation, and spelling
VI.	proofread	entire essay

IMPORTANT: Please note that these steps are not necessarily distinct, nor must you always follow this suggested order. You certainly might, for instance, add details to a paragraph when you decide to move or reorder it. Or you might replace a vague word with a specific one after thinking about your audience and their needs. After strengthening a particular point, you might decide to offer it last, and therefore you rearrange the order of your paragraphs. In other words, the steps offered above are not part of a forced march—they are here simply to remind you to rethink and improve any part of your essay that needs work.

Now let's look at each of the steps in the revision process suggested above in more detail.

I. Revising for Purpose, Thesis, and Audience

To be effective, writers need a clear sense of purpose and audience. Their essays must present (or clearly imply) a main idea or thesis designed to fulfill

that purpose and to inform their audience. As you reread your draft, ask yourself the following questions:

> Have I fulfilled the objectives of my assignment? (For example, if you were
> asked to analyze the causes of a problem, did you merely describe or sum-
> marize it instead?)
>
> Did I follow directions carefully? (If you were given a three-part assign-
> ment, did you treat all parts as requested?)
>
> Do I understand the purpose of my essay? Am I trying to inform, persuade,
> or amuse my readers? Spur them to action? Convince them to change their
> minds? Give them a new idea? Am I myself clear about my exact intent—
> what I want to do or say—in this essay?
>
> Does my essay reflect my clearly understood purpose by offering an ap-
> propriately narrowed and focused thesis? (After reading through your
> essay once, could a reader easily state its purpose and main point?)
>
> Do I have a clear picture of my audience—their character, knowledge, and
> expectations?
>
> Have I addressed both my purpose and my readers' needs by selecting an
> appropriate strategy of development for my essay? (For example, would it
> be better to write an essay developed with examples illustrating the com-
> munity's need for a new hospital or should you present a more formal ar-
> gument that also rebuffs objections to the project? Should you narrate the
> story of your accident or analyze its effects on your family?)

If you feel that your draft needs work in any of these areas, make changes.
You might find it helpful to review Chapters 1 and 2 of this text to guide you as
you revise.

II. Revising for Ideas and Evidence

If you're satisfied that your purpose and thesis are clear to your readers,
begin to look closely at the development of your essay's ideas.

You want your readers to accept your thesis. To achieve this goal, you
must offer body paragraphs whose major points clearly support that main
idea. As you examine the body of your essay, you might ask yourself questions
such as these:

> Is there a clear relationship between my thesis and each of the major points
> presented in the body of my essay? That is, does each major point in my
> essay further my readers' understanding, and thus their acceptance, of my
> thesis's general claim?

Did I write myself into a new or slightly different position as I drafted my essay? If so, do I need to begin another draft with a new working thesis?

Have I included all the major points necessary to the readers' understanding of my subject or have I omitted pertinent ones? (On the other hand, have I included major ideas that aren't relevant or that actually belong in a different essay?)

Are my major points located and stated clearly in specific language so readers can easily see what position I am taking in each part of my discussion?

If you are happy with your choice and presentation of the major ideas in the body of your essay, it's time to look closely at the evidence you are offering to support your major ideas (which, in turn, support the claim of your thesis). To choose the best supporting evidence for their major points, effective writers use *critical thinking skills*.

WHAT IS CRITICAL THINKING?

Critical thinking means the ability to analyze and evaluate our own ideas and those of others. Because we are constantly bombarded today with all kinds of information and differing points of view, we need skills to examine ideas carefully before we accept or reject them.

Here's a common situation in which critical thinking comes into play: two of your friends are arguing over the use of fetal tissue in medical research. Each friend has many points to offer; each is presenting statistics, examples of actual case studies, the words of experts, and hypothetical situations that might arise. Many of the statistics and experts on one side of the argument seem to contradict directly the figures and authorities on the other side. Which side do you take? Why? Are there other points of view to consider? How can you know what to think?

Every day we are faced with just such decisions. We must be able to judge intelligently the merits of what we hear and read before we can feel confident about what we think of a particular issue. We must practice studying our beliefs and those held by others to analyze the reasons for maintaining those views. To think critically about ideas doesn't mean being constantly hostile or negative; it simply means that we need to examine opinions closely and carefully before we accept them.

THINKING CRITICALLY AS A WRITER

As a writer, you will be thinking critically in two important ways. First, you will need to think critically about any information you may be collecting to use as evidence in your essay. You will, for example, need to be a critical reader as you consider information from books, journals, or electronic sources. You almost certainly will need to be a critical listener as you hear other people talk about their experiences and beliefs.

As you draft and revise your essay, you must become a critical thinker in a second way: you must become your own toughest reader-critic. To convince your readers that your essay has merit, you must stand back and try to assess objectively what you have written. Are your ideas clear not only to you but to your readers as well? Will readers find your opinions well developed, logical, and supported? In other words, to revise more effectively, try role-playing one of your own most thoughtful critical readers, someone who will be closely examining the ideas and evidence in your essay before agreeing with its position.

Here are six suggestions to help you think critically as you draft and revise:

1. Learn to distinguish fact from opinion.

A *fact* is an accepted truth whose verification is not affected by its source. No matter who presents it, a fact remains true. We accept some statements as facts because we can test them personally (fire is hot) or because they have been verified frequently by others (penguins live in Antarctica). We accept as fact, for example, that President John Kennedy was killed in Dallas, Texas, on November 22, 1963. However, the identity of the assassin remains, for some people, a matter of *opinion*. That is, depending on the speaker, Kennedy's killer(s) could be Lee Harvey Oswald, a CIA assassin, a foreign agent, a disgruntled politician, a member of organized crime, or someone else. As you think about your evidence, be careful that you don't present your opinions as facts accepted by everyone. Opinions are debatable, and therefore you must always support them before your readers will be convinced.

2. Support your opinions with evidence.

To support your opinions, you must offer evidence of one or more kinds. You have a variety of options to choose from. You might support one idea by using personal experiences. Or you might describe the experiences of friends or family. In another place you might decide to offer detailed examples or to cite statistics or to quote an expert on your subject. You can also use hypothetical examples, researched material, vivid descriptions, reasoned arguments, revealing comparisons, case studies, or testimony of relevant participants, just to name a few other strategies. Consider your purpose and your audience, review the possibilities, and choose the most effective kind of support. The more convincing the support, the more likely your readers are to accept your opinions as true. (If you need to review some sample paragraphs developed by various types of evidence, turn to pp. 64–69 of Chapter 3.)

3. Evaluate the strength of your evidence.

As you choose your evidence, you should consider its value for the particular point it will support. Scrutinize the nature and source of your evidence carefully. If you are using examples, do they clearly illustrate your claim? Does this example or another one (or both?) provide the best illustration of your particular point? Is description alone enough support here? Are your statistics or researched material from a reliable, current source? Was information from your research collected in a careful, professional way? Are your experts unbiased authorities from the field under discussion? Where did your experts obtain their information? (For example, are you claiming that crystals possess healing powers because a woman on a talk show said so and she sounded reasonable to you? Just how much do you know about the source of a particular web site?) Asking yourself the kinds of questions posed here (and others suggested throughout Part Two of this text) will help you develop a critical eye for choosing the best evidence to support your opinions.

4. Use enough specific supporting evidence.

Readers need to see strong, relevant supporting evidence throughout your essay. You must be sure, therefore, that you have enough clearly stated evidence for each of your major points. If you present, for instance, too few examples or only a vague reference to an event that supports one of your ideas, a reader may remain unconvinced or may even be confused. As you revise, ask yourself questions such as these: "Do I need to provide additional information here?" "Do I need more details to develop the supporting evidence already present?" "Is any of my evidence concealed by vague or fuzzy language?" If you feel additional supporting evidence or details are needed, take another look at any prewriting you did—or use one of the "pump-primer" techniques described in Chapter 1 now to discover some new creative thoughts. For some topics, you may need to do more research or interviewing to find the information you need. (Writers occasionally need to prune ideas too, especially if they're repetitious or off the topic. But, in general, most early drafts are thin and will profit from more, rather than less, specific supporting evidence.)

5. Watch for biases and strong emotions that may undermine evidence.

As you think critically about evidence you are using, monitor any biases and emotional attitudes that may distort information you wish to incorporate into your essay. If you are using personal experiences, for example, have you calmed down enough from your anger over your landlord's actions to write about the clash in a rational, persuasive way? In an essay criticizing a particular product, are you so familiar with the frustrating item that you are making ambiguous claims? (If you write, "The new instructions for use are more confusing than ever," have you shown that they were confusing in the first place? Or why they are more so now?) Be sensitive to any racial, ethnic, cultural, religious, or gender-based assumptions you or your sources may have. Opinions based on generalizations and stereotypes ("Japanese cars are better because Orientals are more efficient workers than Americans"; "Women should stay home because they are better with children than men") are not convincing to thinking readers.

6. Check your evidence for logical fallacies.

Thinking critically about your drafts should help you support your ideas with reasonable, logical explanations and arguments. Logical fallacies are common errors in reasoning that good writers try to avoid. Those fallacies found most often today are explained on pages 294–297 of this text; reviewing them will enable you to identify problems in logic that might appear in the writing of others or in your own drafts.

Critical thinking is not, of course, limited to the six suggestions offered here. But by practicing this advice, you will begin to develop and sharpen analytical skills that should improve any writing project.

III. Revising for Organization

In reality, you have probably already made several changes in the order and organization of ideas in your draft. As noted before, it's likely that when you thought about your essay's meaning—its major points and their supporting evidence—you also thought about the arrangement of those ideas. As you take another look at your draft's organization, use these questions as a guide:

Am I satisfied with the organizational strategy I selected for my purpose? (For example, as you wrote did you decide that an essay primarily developed by comparison and contrast would achieve your purpose better than a narrative approach?)

Are my major points ordered in a logical, easy-to-follow pattern? Would readers understand my thinking better if certain paragraphs or major ideas were rearranged? Added? Divided? Omitted?

Are my major points presented in topic sentences that state each important idea clearly and specifically? (If any of your topic sentences are implied rather than stated, are you absolutely, 100 percent sure that your ideas cannot be overlooked or even slightly misunderstood by your readers?)

Is there a smooth flow between my major ideas? Between paragraphs? Within paragraphs? Have I used enough transition devices to guide the reader along?

Are any parts of my essay out of proportion? Too long or too short to do their job effectively?

Do my title and lead-in draw readers into the essay and toward my thesis?

Does my conclusion end my discussion thoughtfully? Emphatically or memorably?

Don't be afraid to restructure your drafts. Most good writers rearrange and recast large portions of their prose. Reviewing Chapters 3 and 4 may help you address questions on organization, beginnings, or endings.

IV. Revising for Clarity and Style

As you've revised for purpose, ideas, and organization, you have also taken steps to clarify your prose. Making a special point now of focusing on sentences and word choice will ensure your readers' complete understanding of your thinking. Read through your draft, asking these kinds of questions:

Is each of my sentences as clear and precise as it could be for readers who do not know what I know? Are there sentences that contain misplaced words or convoluted phrases that might cause confusion?

Are there any sentences that are unnecessarily wordy? Is there deadwood that could be eliminated? (Remember that concise prose is more effective than wordy, "fat" prose because readers can find and follow key ideas and terms easier. Nearly every writer has a wordiness problem that chokes communication, so now is the season to prune.)

Do any sentences run on for too long to be fully understood? Can any repetitive or choppy sentences be combined to achieve clarity and a pleasing variation of sentence style? (To help you decide if you need to combine sentences, you might try this experiment. Select a body paragraph and count the number of words it contains. Then count the number of sentences; divide the number of words by the number of sentences to discover the average number of words per sentence. If your score is less than 15–18, you may need to combine *some* sentences. Good prose offers a variety of sentence lengths and patterns.)

Are all my words and their connotations accurate and appropriate?

Can I clarify and energize my prose by adding "showing" details and by replacing bland, vague words with vivid, specific ones? By using active verbs rather than passive ones?

Can I eliminate any pretentious or unnecessary jargon or language that's inappropriate for my audience? Replace clichés and trite expressions with fresh, original phrases?

Is my voice authentic, or am I trying to sound like someone else? Is my tone reasonable, honest, and consistent?

The issues raised by these questions—and many others—are discussed in detail in Chapters 6 and 7, on effective sentences and words, which offer more advice on clarifying language and improving style.

V. Editing for Errors

Writers who are proud of the choices they've made in content, organization, and style are, to use a baseball metaphor, rounding third base and heading for home. But there's more to be done. Shift from a baseball metaphor to car maintenance for a moment. All good essays are not only fine-tuned but also waxed and polished—they are edited and proofread repeatedly for errors until they shine. To help you polish your prose by correcting errors in punctuation, grammar, spelling, and diction, here are some hints for effective editing:

Read aloud. In addition to repeatedly reading your draft silently, reading your draft aloud is a good technique because it allows your ears to hear ungrammatical "clunks" or unintended gaps in sense or sound you may otherwise miss.

Know your enemies. Learn to identify your particularly troublesome areas in punctuation and grammar and then read through your draft for one of these problems at a time: once for fragments, once for comma splices, once for run-ons, and so on. (If you try to look for too many errors at each reading, you'll probably miss quite a few.)

Read backwards. Try reading your draft one sentence at a time starting at the *end* of your essay and working toward the beginning. Don't read each sentence word-for-word backwards—just read the essay one sentence at a time from back to front. When writers try to edit (or proofread) starting at the beginning of their essays, they tend to begin thinking about the ideas they're reading rather than concentrating on the task of editing for errors. By reading one sentence at a time from the back, you will find that the sentences will still make sense but that you are less likely to wander away from the job at hand.

Learn some tricks. There are special techniques for treating some punctuation and grammar problems. If you have trouble, for example, with comma splices, turn to the FANBOYS hint on page 465. If fragments plague your writing, try the "it is true that" test explained on page 457. Consider designating a special part of your journal or class notebook to record in your own words these tricks and other useful pieces of advice so that you can refer to them easily and often.

Eliminate common irritants. Review your draft for those diction and mechanical errors many readers find especially annoying because they often reflect sheer carelessness. For example, look at these frequently confused words: *it's/its, your/you're, there/their/they're, who's/whose* (other often confused words are listed on page 158). Some readers are ready for a national march to protest the public's abandonment of the apostrophe, the Amelia

Earhart of punctuation. (Apostrophes *can* change the meaning of sentences: "The teacher called the students names." Was the instructor being rude or just taking roll?) It's a grammatical jungle out there, so be sensitive to your weary readers.

Use your tools. Keep your dictionary handy to check the spelling, usage, and meanings of words in doubt. A thesaurus can also be useful if you can restrain any tendencies you have for growing overly exotic prose. If you are using a word processor with a spell-checker, by all means run it after your last revisions are completed. Do remember, however, that computers only flag words whose spelling they don't recognize; they will not alert you to omitted or confused words (*affect/effect*), nor will they signal when you've typed in a wrong, but correctly spelled, word (*here* for *her*).

Use Part Four of this text to help resolve any questions you may have about grammar, mechanics, and spelling. Advice on untangling sentences and clarifying word choice in Chapters 6 and 7 may be useful, too.

VI. Proofreading

Proofread your final draft several times, putting as much time between the last two readings as possible. Fresh eyes catch more typographical or careless errors. Remember that typing errors—even the simple transposing of letters—can change the meaning of an entire thought and occasionally bring unintended humor to your prose (imagine, for example, the surprise of restaurant owners whose new lease instructed them to "Please sing the terms of the agreement as stated above." Was the contract presented a cappella or with music? Or consider the ramifications of the newspaper ad that offered "Great dames for sale").

Make sure, too, that your paper looks professional before you turn it in. You wouldn't, after all, expect to be taken seriously if you went to an executive job interview dressed in cutoffs. Turning in a paper with a coffee stain or ink blot on it has about the same effect as spinach in your teeth—it distracts folks from hearing what you have to say. If your final draft has typos or small blemishes, use correction fluid to conceal them; if you've patched so frequently that your paper resembles the medicine-dotted face of a kindergartner with chicken pox, photocopy your pages for a fresh look.

Check to be sure you've formatted your paper exactly as your assignment requested. Some instructors ask for a title page; others want folders containing all your drafts and prewriting. Most teachers appreciate papers with pages that are numbered, ordered correctly, clipped or stapled, with clean edges (not sheets violently ripped from a spiral notebook still dribbling the remains of angry confetti down one side nor computer paper with printer edges still attached). Putting your name on each page will identify your work if papers from a particular class are accidentally mixed up.

As it's often been said, essays are never really done—only due. Take a last reading using the checklist that follows, make some notes on your progress as a writer and thinker, and congratulate yourself on your fine efforts and accomplishment.

A FINAL CHECKLIST FOR YOUR ESSAY

If you have written an effective essay, you should be able to answer "yes" to the following questions:

1. Do I feel I have something important to say to my reader?

2. Am I sincerely committed to communicating with my reader and not just with myself?

3. Have I considered my audience's needs? (See Chapter 1.)

4. Do my title and lead-in attract the reader's attention and help set up my thesis? (See Chapter 4.)

5. Does my thesis statement assert one clearly focused idea? (See Chapter 2.)

6. Does my thesis and/or essay map give the reader an indication of what points the essay will cover? (See Chapter 2.)

7. Do my body paragraphs contain the necessary main points in the essay's discussion, and are those points expressed in clearly stated or implied topic sentences? (See Chapter 3.)

8. Is each major point in my essay well developed with enough detailed supporting evidence? (See Chapter 3.)

9. Does each body paragraph have unity and coherence? (See Chapter 3.)

10. Are all the paragraphs in my essay smoothly linked in a logical order? (See Chapter 3.)

11. Does my concluding paragraph provide a suitable ending for the essay? (See Chapter 4.)

12. Are all my sentences clear, concise, and coherent? (See Chapter 6.)

13. Are my words accurate, necessary, and meaningful? (See Chapter 7.)

14. Have I edited and proofread for errors in grammar, punctuation, spelling, or typing? (See Part Four.)

And most important:

15. Has my essay been effectively revised so that I am proud of this piece of writing?

BENEFITING FROM REVISION WORKSHOPS

Many writing courses today include revision workshops in which students comment helpfully on one another's drafts. This sort of revision activity may also be called peer editing, classroom critique, or reader review. Peer workshops may be arranged in a variety of ways, though frequently students will work in pairs or in small groups of three to five. Sometimes writers will simply talk about their papers or read them aloud; at other times students will be asked to write suggestions on one another's drafts. Sometimes instructors will give student-reviewers a list of questions to answer; at other times, the writers themselves will voice their concerns directly to their reviewers. Structured in many effective ways, peer workshops can be extremely valuable to writers, who will invariably profit from seeing their drafts from a reader's point of view.

Students taking part in revision workshops for the first time often have questions about the reviewing process. Some student-reviewers may feel uneasy about their role, wondering, "What if I can't think of any suggestions for the writer? How can I tell someone that their paper's really terrible? What if I sense something's wrong but I'm not sure what it is—or how to fix it?" Writers, too, may feel apprehensive or even occasionally defensive about receiving criticism of their papers. Because these concerns are genuine and widespread, here is some advice to help you get the most out of your participation in revision workshops, in the role of writer or reviewer.

When you are the writer:

1. Develop a constructive attitude. Admittedly, receiving criticism—especially on a creation that has required hard work—can sometimes be difficult, particularly if your self-image has become mixed up with your drafts. Try to realize that your reviewer is not criticizing *you* personally but rather is trying to help you by offering fresh insights. All drafts can be improved, and no writer need feel embarrassed about seeking or receiving advice. (Take comfort in the words of writer Somerset Maugham: "Only the mediocre person is always at his best.") See the workshop as a nonthreatening opportunity to reconsider your prose and improve your audience awareness.

2. Come prepared. If your workshop structure permits, tell your reviewer what sort of help you need at this point in your drafting or revising process.

Ask for suggestions to fix a particularly troublesome area or ask for feedback on a choice you've made but are feeling unsure of. Don't hesitate to ask your reviewer for assistance with any part of your essay.

3. Evaluate suggestions carefully. Writing isn't math: most of the time there are no absolutely right or wrong answers—just better or worse rhetorical choices. That is, there are many ways to communicate an idea to a set of readers. You, as the writer, must decide on an effective way, the way that best serves your purpose and your readers' needs. Sometimes your reviewer will suggest a change that is brilliant or one so obviously right you will wonder why in the world you didn't think of it yourself. At other times you may weigh your reviewer's suggestion and decide that your original choice is just as good or perhaps even better. Be open to suggestions, but learn to trust thyself as well.

4. Find the good in bad advice. Occasionally you may have a reviewer who seems to miss a crucial point or misunderstands your purpose entirely, whose suggestions for revising your paper seem uniformly unproductive for one reason or another. You certainly shouldn't take bad advice—but do think about the issues it raises. Although it's helpful to receive a dynamite suggestion you can incorporate immediately, the real value of a revision workshop is its ability to encourage you to rethink your prose. Readers' responses (yes, even the bizarre ones) challenge writers to take still another look at their rhetorical choices and ask themselves, "Is this clear after all? Does this example really work here? Did something in my essay throw this reader off the track?" Revision workshops offer you benefits, even if you ultimately decide to reject many of your reviewer's suggestions.

When you are the reviewer:

1. Develop a constructive attitude. Sometimes it's hard to give honest criticism—most of us are uncomfortable when we think we might hurt someone's feelings—but remember that the writer has resolved to develop a professional attitude, too. The writer expects (and is sometimes desperately begging for) sincere feedback, so be honest as you offer your best advice.

2. Be clear and specific. Vague or flippant responses ("This is confusing"; "Huh?") don't help writers know what or how to revise. Try putting some of your comments into this format: your response to X, the reason for your response, a request for change, and, if possible, a specific suggestion for the change ("I'm confused when you say you enjoy some parts of breakfast because this seems to contradict your thesis claim of 'wretched dorm food.' Would it be clearer to modify your thesis to exclude breakfast or to revise this paragraph to include only discussion of the rubbery eggs?").

3. Address important issues. Unless you have workshop directions that request certain tasks, read through the draft entirely at least once and then comment on the larger issues first. Writers want to know if they are achieving their overall purpose, if their thesis is clear and convincing, if their major points and evidence make sense, and if their paper seems logical and ordered. Editing tips are fine, too, but because workshops encourage authors to rewrite large portions of their prose, attention to minor details may be less valuable early on than feedback on ideas, organization, and development. (Of course, an editing workshop later in the revision process may be exclusively focused on sentence and word problems. Workshops may be designed to address specific problems that writers face.)

4. Encourage the writer. Writers with confidence write and revise better than insecure or angry writers. Praise honestly wherever you can, as specifically as you can. When weaknesses do appear, show the writer that you know she or he is capable of doing better work by linking the weakness to a strength elsewhere in the draft. ("Could you add more 'showing' details here so that your picture of the dentist is as vivid as your description of the nurse?") Substitute specific responses and suggestions for one-word labels such as "awk" (awkward) or "unclear." Even positive labels don't always help writers repeat effective techniques. ("Good!" enthusiastically inscribed in the margin by a well-developed paragraph feels nice but might cause the writer to wonder, "'Good' what? Good point? Good supporting evidence? Good detail? How can I do 'good' again if I don't know exactly what it is?")

5. Understand your role as critical reader. Sometimes it's easy for a reviewer to take ownership of someone else's paper. Keep the writer's purpose in mind as you respond; don't insist on revisions that produce an essay that's in *your* head. Be sensitive to your own voice and language as a reviewer. Instead of making authoritative pronouncements that might offend, ask reader-based questions. ("Will all your readers know the meaning of this technical term?" "Would some readers profit from a brief history of this controversy?") If you're unsure about a possible error, request verification. ("Could you recheck this quotation? Its wording here is confusing me because. . . .") Practice offering criticism in language that acknowledges the writer's hard work and accentuates the positive nature of revision. ("Would citing last year's budget figures make your good argument against the fish market even stronger?")

Last, always look over your own draft in light of the insightful suggestions you are offering your classmates. You may feel at first that it is far simpler to analyze someone else's writing than your own. As you participate in revision workshops, however, you will find it increasingly easy to transfer those same critical reading skills to your own work. Becoming a good reader-reviewer for your composition colleagues can be an important part of your training as a first-rate writer.

PRACTICING WHAT YOU'VE LEARNED

A. The draft of the student essay below has been annotated by its writer according to some—*but not all*—of the questions presented in this chapter's discussion of revision. As you read the draft and the writer's marginal comments, think of specific suggestions you might offer to help this writer improve her essay. What other changes, in addition to the ones mentioned here, would you encourage this writer to make? What strengths do you see in this draft?

My title and lead-in are too bland to attract reader's attention.

Would my thesis be clearer if I said what I did find?

My supporting examples could use more "showing" details so the readers can really see the unfriendliness.

This paragraph has some specific details but it rambles and repeats ideas. Needs tighter organization.

DORM LIFE

Dorm life is not at all what I had expected it to be. I had anticipated meeting friendly people, quiet hours for studying, eating decent food, and having wild parties on weekends. My dreams, I soon found out, were simply illusions, erroneous perceptions of reality.

My roommate, Kathy, and I live in Holland Hall on the third floor. The people on our dorm floor are about as unfriendly as they can possibly be. I wonder whether or not they're just shy and afraid or if they are simply snobs. Some girls, for example, ignore my roommate and me when we say "hello." Occasionally, they stare straight ahead and act like we aren't even there. Other girls respond, but it's as if they do it out of a sense of duty rather than being just friendly. The guys seem nice, but some are just as afraid or snobby as the girls.

I remember signing up for "quiet hours" when I put in my application for a dorm room last December. Unfortunately, I was assigned to a floor that doesn't have any quiet hours at all. I am a person who requires peace and quiet when studying or reading. The girls in all the rooms around us love to stay up until early in the morning and yell and turn up their music full blast. They turn music on at about eight o'clock at night and turn it off early in the morning. There is always at least one girl who has a CD playing at maximum volume. Now, I am very appreciative of music, but listening to "hard rock" until three in the morning isn't really my idea of what music is. The girls right across from

Breaks unity.

us usually play Bonnie Raitt or Celine Dion and I enjoy them. On the other hand, though, the girls on either side of our room love to listen to Metallica or Marilyn Manson into the wee hours of the morning. It is these girls who run up and down the hall, yell at each other, laugh obnoxiously, and try to attract attention. All this continuous racket makes it nearly impossible to study, read, or get any sleep. Kathy and I usually end up going to the library or student cafeteria to study. As far as sleep goes, it doesn't matter what time we go to bed, but rather it depends on how noisy it is, and how late the music is on. Sometimes the noise gets so loud and rambles on for so long that even when it stops, my ears are ringing and my stomach keeps churning. It is on nights like this that I never go to sleep. I wish the people here were a little more considerate of the people around them.

This paragraph doesn't support my thesis claim—do I mean the dorm has no good parties or no floor parties? Rethink so my point is clear.

Parties, on weekends, are supposedly the most important part of dorm life. Parties provide the opportunity to meet others and have a good time. Holland Hall has had two parties that are even worth mentioning. One of them was a Fifties dance held in the courtyard approximately three weeks ago. Unfortunately, all the other dormitories, the fraternities, and the sororities heard about it, and by eight o'clock at night there were masses of people. It was so packed that it was hard to move around. The other party, much to my dismay, turned out to be a luau party. I do not really care for roast pig, and my stomach turned from the scent of it when I entered the room. Our floor never has parties. Everyone leaves their doors open, turns up the music, yells back and forth. I suppose that there will be more dorm parties once everyone becomes adjusted to this life and begins to socialize.

As stated, this topic sentence contradicts my thesis.

Dorm food is what I anticipated it would be, terrible, and I was right, it is awful. Breakfast is probably the hardest meal to digest. The bacon and sausage are cold, slightly uncooked, and very greasy. Sometimes, it's as though I am eating pure grease.

Some good examples—could I use even more descriptive language?

Unity?

The eggs look and taste like nothing I ever had before. They look like plastic and they are never hot. I had eggs once and I vowed I would never have another one as long as I lived in Holland Hall. The most enjoyable part of breakfast is the orange juice. It's always cold and it seems to be fresh. No one can say dorm food is totally boring because the cooks break up the monotony of the same food by serving "mystery meat" at least once every two weeks. This puts a little excitement in the student's day because everyone cracks jokes and wonders just what's in this "mystery meat." I think a lot of students are afraid to ask, fearful of the answer, and simply make snide remarks and shovel it in.

Can I conclude emphatically without switching positions?

All in all, I believe dorm life isn't too great, even though there are some good times. Even though I complain about dorm food, the people, the parties, and everything else, I am glad I am here. I am happy because I have learned a lot about other people, responsibilities, consideration, and I've even learned a lot about myself.

B. Assume that the essay below is a draft written by one of your classmates who has asked you for help during a class workshop. Using your best critical thinking skills, offer some marginal comments and questions that will guide this writer through an effective revision process.

MAYBE YOU SHOULDN'T GO AWAY TO COLLEGE

Going away to college is not for everyone. There are good reasons why a student might choose to live at home and attend a local school. Money, finding stability while changes are occurring, and accepting responsibility are three to consider.

Money is likely to be most important. Not only is tuition more expensive, but extra money is needed for room and board. Whether room and board is a dorm or an apartment, the expense is great.

Most students never stop to consider that the money that could be saved from room and board may be better spent in future years on graduate school, which is likely to be more important in their careers.

Going to school is a time of many changes anyway, without adding the pressure of a new city or even a new state. Finding stability will be hard enough, without going from home to a dorm. Starting college could be an emotional time for some, and the security of their home and family might make everything easier.

When students decide to go away to school, sometimes because their friends are going away, or maybe because the school is their parents' alma mater, something that all need to decide is whether or not they can accept the responsibility of a completely new way of life.

Everyone feels as if they are ready for total independence when they decide to go away to college, but is breaking away when they are just beginning to set their futures a good idea?

Going away to school may be the right road for some, but those who feel that they are not ready might start looking to a future that is just around the corner.

 ASSIGNMENT

Select a body paragraph from one of the preceding student essays and revise it, making any change in focus, organization, development, sentence construction, or word choice, you feel is necessary. Feel free to elaborate on, eliminate, or change the content to improve the paragraph's organization and development.

SOME LAST ADVICE: HOW TO PLAY WITH YOUR MENTAL BLOCKS

Every writer, sooner or later, suffers from some form of writer's block, the inability to think of or organize ideas. Symptoms may include sweaty palms, pencil chewing, and a pronounced tendency to sit in corners and weep. Although not every "cure" works for everyone, here are a few suggestions to help minimize your misery:

Try to give yourself as much time as possible to write your essay. Don't try to write the entire paper in one sitting. By doing so, you may place yourself under too much pressure. Writer's Block often accompanies the "up against the wall" feeling that strikes at 2:00 A.M. the morning your essay is due at 9:00. Rome wasn't constructed in a day, and neither are most good essays.

Since most of you have had more experience talking than writing, try verbalizing your ideas. Sometimes it's helpful to discuss your ideas with a friend or classmate. Their questions and comments (not to mention their sympathy for your temporary block) will often trigger the thoughts you need to begin writing again. Or you might want to talk into a tape recorder so you can hear what you want to say.

When an irresistible force meets an immovable object, something's going to give. Conquer the task: break the paper into manageable bits. Instead of drooping with despair over the thought of a ten-page research paper, think of it as a series of small parts (explanation of the problem, review of current research, possible solutions, or whatever). Then tackle one part at a time and reward yourself when that section's done.

Get the juices flowing and the pen moving. Try writing the easiest or shortest part of your essay first. A feeling of accomplishment may give you the boost of confidence you need to undertake the other, more difficult sections. If no part looks easy or inviting, try more prewriting exercises, like the ones described in Chapter 1, until you feel prepared to begin the essay itself.

Play "Let's Make a Deal" with yourself. Sometimes we just can't face the failure that we are predicting for ourselves. Strike a bargain with yourself: promise yourself that you are only going to work on your paper for fifteen minutes—absolutely, positively fifteen minutes, not a second more, no sir, no way. If in fifteen minutes, you're on to something good, ignore your promise to yourself and keep going. If you're not, then leave and come back for another fifteen-minute session later (if you started early enough, you can do this without increasing your anxiety).

Give yourself permission to write garbage. Take the pressure off yourself by agreeing in advance to tear up the first page or two of whatever you write. You can always change your mind if the trash turns out to be treasure; if it isn't, so what? You said you were going to tear it up anyway.

Imagine that your brain is a water faucet. If you're like most people, you've probably lived in a house or apartment that contained a faucet that needed to run a few minutes before the hot water started to come out. Think of your brain in the same way, and do some other, easier writing task to warm up. Write a letter, make a grocery list, copy notes, whatever, to get your brain running. When you turn to your paper, your thoughts may be hotter than you thought.

Remove the threat by addressing a friendly face. Sometimes we can't write because we are too worried about what someone else will think about us or maybe we can't write because we can't figure out who would want to read this stuff anyway. Instead of writing into a void or to an audience that seems threatening, try writing to a friend. Imagine what that friend's responses might be and try to elaborate or clarify wherever necessary. If it helps, write the first draft as a letter ("Dear Clyde, I want to tell you what happened to me last week . . ."), and then redraft your ideas as an essay when you've found your purpose and focus, making whatever changes in tone or development are necessary to fit your real audience.

If Writer's Block does hit, remember that it is a temporary bogdown, not a permanent one. Other writers have had it—and survived to write again. Try leaving your papers and taking a walk outdoors or at least into another room. Think about your readers—what should they know or feel at this point in your essay? As you walk, try to complete the sentence "What I am trying to say is. . . ." Keep repeating this phrase and your responses aloud until you find the answer you want.

Sometimes while you're blocked at one point, a bright idea for another part of your essay will pop into your head. If possible, skip the section that's got you stuck and start working on the new part. (At least jot down the new idea somewhere so it won't be lost when you need it later.)

Change partners and dance. If you're thoroughly overcome by the vast white wasteland on the desk before you, get up and do something else for a while. Exercise, balance your checkbook, or put on music and dance. (Mystery writer Agatha Christie claimed she did her best planning while washing the dishes.) Give your mind a break and refresh your spirit. When you come back to the paper, you may be surprised to discover that your subconscious writer has been working while the rest of you played.

Here's the single most important piece of advice to remember: relax. No one—not even the very best professional writer—produces perfect prose every time pen hits paper. If you're blocked, you may be trying too hard; if your expectations of your first draft are too high, you may not be able to write at all for fear of failure. You just might be holding yourself back by being a perfectionist at this point. You can always revise and polish your prose in another draft—the first important step is jotting down your ideas. Remember that once the first word or phrase appears on your blank page, a major battle has been won.

CHAPTER 5 SUMMARY

Here is a brief summary of what you should remember about revising your writing:

1. Revision is an activity that occurs in all stages of the writing process.

2. All good writers revise their prose extensively.

3. Revision is not merely editing or last-minute proofreading; it involves important decisions about the essay's ideas, organization, and development.

4. To revise effectively, novice writers might review their drafts in steps, to avoid the frustration that comes with trying to fix everything at once.

5. Critical thinking skills are vitally important today to all good readers and writers.

6. Most writers experience Writer's Block at some time but live through it to write again.

CHAPTER

6

Effective Sentences

An insurance agent was shocked to open his mail one morning and read the following note from one of his clients: "In accordance with your instructions, I have given birth to twins in the enclosed envelope." However, he may not have been more surprised than the congregation who read this announcement in their church bulletin: "There will be a discussion tomorrow on the problem of adultery in the minister's office." Or the patrons of a health club who learned that "guest passes will not be given to members until the manager has punched each of them first."

Certainly, there were no babies born in an envelope, nor was there adultery in the minister's office, and one doubts that the club manager was planning to assault the membership. But the implications (and the unintended humor) are nevertheless present—solely because of the faulty ways in which the sentences were constructed.

To improve your own writing, you must express your thoughts in clear, coherent sentences that produce precisely the reader response you want. Effective sentences are similar to the threads in a piece of knitting or weaving: each thread helps form the larger design; if any one thread becomes tangled or lost, the pattern becomes muddled. In an essay, the same is true: if any sentence is fuzzy or obscure, the reader may lose the point of your discussion and in some cases never bother to regain it. Therefore, to retain your reader, you must concentrate on writing informative, effective sentences that continuously clarify the purpose of your essay.

Many problems in sentence clarity involve errors in grammar, usage, and word choice; the most common of these errors are discussed in Chapter 7 and Part Four of this text. In this chapter you'll find some general suggestions for writing clear, concise, engaging sentences. However, *don't try to apply all the rules to the first draft of your essay.* Revising sentences before your ideas are firmly in place may be a waste of effort if your essay's stance or structure changes. Concentrate first on your essay's content and general organization; then, in a later draft, rework your sentences so that each one is informative and clear. Your reader reads only the words on the page, not those in your mind—so it's up to you to make sure the sentences in your essay approximate the thoughts in your head as closely and vividly as possible.

REMEMBER

All good writers revise and polish their sentences.

DEVELOPING A CLEAR STYLE

When you are ready to revise the sentences in your rough draft for clarity, try to follow the next five rules.

Give Your Sentences Content

Fuzzy sentences are often the result of fuzzy thinking. When you examine your sentences, ask yourself, "Do I know what I'm talking about here? Or are my sentences vague or confusing because I'm really not sure what my point is or where it's going?" Look at this list of content-poor sentences taken from student essays; how could you reword and put more information into each one?

If you were to view a karate class, you would become familiar with all the aspects that make it up.

The meaning of the poem isn't very clear the first time you read it, but after several readings, the poet's meaning comes through.

One important factor that is the basis for determining a true friend is the ability that person has for being a real human being.

Listening is important because we all need to be able to sit and hear all that is said to us.

Don't pad your paragraphs with sentences that run in circles, leading nowhere; rethink your ideas and revise your writing so that every sentence—like each brick in a wall—contributes to the construction of a solid discussion. In other words, commit yourself to a position and make each sentence contain information pertinent to your point; leave the job of padding to mattress manufacturers.

Sometimes, however, you may have a definite idea in mind but still continue to write "empty sentences"—statements that alone do not contain enough information to make a specific point in your discussion. Frequently, an empty sentence may be revised by combining it with the sentence that follows, as shown in the examples below. The empty, or overly general, sentences are underlined.

Poor   There are many kinds of beautiful tropical fish. The kind most popular with aquarium owners is the angelfish.

Better   Of the many kinds of beautiful tropical fish, none is more popular with aquarium owners than the angelfish.

Poor   D. W. Griffith introduced many new cinematic techniques. Some of these techniques were contrast editing, close-ups, fade-outs, and freeze-frame shots.

Better   D. W. Griffith made movie history by introducing such new cinematic techniques as contrast editing, close-ups, fade-outs, and the freeze-frame shot.

Poor   There is a national organization called The Couch Potatoes. The group's 8,000 members are devoted television watchers.

Better   The Couch Potatoes is a national organization whose 8,000 members are devoted television watchers.

For more help on combining sentences, see pages 149–152.

Make Your Sentences Specific

In addition to containing an informative, complete thought, each of your sentences should give readers enough clear details for them to "see" the picture you are creating. Sentences full of vague words produce blurry, boring prose and drowsy readers. Remember your reaction the last time you asked a friend about a recent vacation? If the only response you received was something like, "Oh, it was great—a lot of fun," you probably yawned and proceeded quickly to a new topic. But if your friend had begun an exciting account of a wilderness rafting trip, with detailed stories about narrow escapes from freezing white water, treacherous rocks, and uncharted whirlpools, you'd probably have stopped and listened. The same principle works in your writing—clear, specific details are the only sure way to attract and hold the reader's interest. Therefore, make each sentence contribute something new and interesting to the overall discussion.

The examples below first show sentences far too vague to sustain anyone's attention. Rewritten, these sentences contain specific details that add clarity and interest:

Vague   She went home in a bad mood. [What kind of a bad mood? How did she act or look?]

Specific   She stomped home, hands jammed in her pockets, angrily kicking rocks, dogs, small children, and anything else that crossed her path.

Vague   His neighbor bought a really nice old desk. [Why nice? How old? What kind of desk?]

Specific   His neighbor bought a solid oak rolltop desk made in 1885 that contains a secret drawer triggered by a hidden spring.

Vague   My roommate is truly gross. ["Gross" in what ways? To what extent? Do you "see" this person?]

Specific   My roommate leaves dirty dishes under the bed, sweaty clothes in the closet, and toenail clippings in the sink.

Keep Your Sentences Simple

Because our society is becoming increasingly specialized and highly technical, we tend to equate complexity with excellence and simplicity with simplemindedness. This assumption is unfortunate because it often leads to a preference for unnecessarily complicated and even contorted writing. In a recent survey, for example, a student chose a sample of bureaucratic hogwash over several well-written paragraphs, explaining his choice by saying that it must have been better since he didn't understand it.

Our best writers have always worked hard to present their ideas simply and specifically so that their readers could easily understand them. Mark Twain, for instance, once praised a young author this way: "I notice that you use plain simple language, short words, and brief sentences. This is the way to write English. It is the modern way and the best way. Stick to it." And when a critic asked Hemingway to define his theory of writing, he replied, "[I] put down what I see and what I feel in the best and simplest way I can tell it."

In your own writing, therefore, work for a simple, direct style. Avoid sentences that are overpacked (too many ideas or too much information at once) as in the following example on racquetball:

John told Phil that to achieve more control over the ball, he should practice flicking or snapping his wrist, because this action is faster in the close shots and placing a shot requires only a slight change of the wrist's angle instead of an acute movement of the whole arm, which gives a player less reaction time.

To make the overpacked sentence easier to understand, try dividing the ideas into two or more sentences:

John told Phil that to achieve more control over the ball, he should practice flicking or snapping his wrist, because this action is faster in the close shots. Placing a shot requires only a slight change of the wrist's angle instead of an acute movement of the whole arm, which gives a player less reaction time.

Don't ever run the risk of losing your reader in a sentence that says too much to comprehend in one bite. This confusing notice, for example, came from a well-known credit card company:

The Minimum Payment Due each month shall be reduced by the amounts paid in excess of the Minimum Payment Due during the previous three months which have not already been so applied in determining the Minimum Payment Due in such earlier months, unless you have exceeded your line of credit or have paid the entire New Balance shown on your billing statement.

Or consider the confusion of soccer players whose coach warned them in this manner:

It is also a dangerous feeling to consider that where we are in the league is of acceptable standard because standard is relevant to the standards we have set, which thereby may well indicate that we have not aspired to the standard which we set ourselves.

Try too for a straightforward construction; former-president Ronald Reagan's sentence below, for example, takes far too many twists and turns for anyone to understand it easily on the first reading:

My goal is an America where something or anything that is done to or for anyone is done neither because of nor in spite of any difference between them, racially, religiously or ethnic-origin-wise.

If the sentences in your rough draft are contorted, try rephrasing your meaning in short sentences and then combining thoughts where most appropriate.

Pay Attention to Word Order

The correct word order is crucial for clarity. Always place a modifier near the word it modifies. The position of a modifier can completely change the meaning of your sentence; for example, each sentence presented here offers a different idea because of the placement of the modifier "only."

A. Eliza said she loves only me. [Eliza loves me and no one else.]

B. Only Eliza said she loves me. [No other person said she loves me.]

C. Eliza only said she loves me. [Eliza said she loves me, but said nothing other than that.]

D. Eliza said only she loves me. [Eliza says no one else loves me.]

To avoid confusion, therefore, place your modifiers close to the words or phrases they modify.

A modifier that seems to modify the wrong part of a sentence is called "misplaced." Not only can misplaced modifiers change or distort the meaning of your sentence, they can also provide unintentional humor as well, as illustrated by the following excerpt from the 1929 Marx Brothers' movie *Coconuts:*

Woman   There's a man waiting outside to see you with a black mustache.

Groucho   Tell him I've already got one.

Of course, the woman didn't mean to imply that the man outside was waiting with (that is, accompanied by) a mustache; she meant to say, "There's a man with a black mustache who is waiting outside. . . ."

A poster advertising a lecture on campus provided this opportunity for humor: "Professor Elizabeth Sewell will discuss the latest appearance of Halley's Comet in room 104." Under the announcement a local wit had scribbled, "Shall we reserve room 105 for the tail?" Or take the case of this startling headline: "Kicking Baby Considered Healthy."

Here are some other examples of misplaced modifiers:

Misplaced   Dilapidated and almost an eyesore, Shirley bought the old house to restore it to its original beauty. [Did the writer mean that Shirley needed a beauty treatment?]

Revised   Shirley bought the old house, which was dilapidated and almost an eyesore, to restore it to its original beauty.

Misplaced   Because she is now thoroughly housebroken, Sarah can take her dog almost anywhere she goes. [Did the writer mean that Sarah once had an embarrassing problem?]

Revised	Because she is now thoroughly housebroken, Sarah's dog can accompany her almost anywhere she goes.
Misplaced	Three family members were found bound and gagged by the grandmother. [Did the writer mean that the grandmother had taken up a life of crime?]
Revised	The grandmother found the three family members who had been bound and gagged.
Misplaced	The lost child was finally found wandering in a frozen farmer's field. [Did the writer mean to say that the farmer was that cold?]
Revised	The lost child was finally found wandering in a farmer's frozen field.

In each of the preceding examples the writer forgot to place the modifying phrase so that it modifies the correct subject. In most cases, a sentence with a misplaced modifier can be corrected easily by moving the word or phrase closer to the word that should be modified.

In some sentences, however, the object of the modifying phrase is missing entirely. Such a phrase is called a "dangling modifier." Most of these errors may be corrected by adding the missing subject. Here are some examples followed by their revisions:

Dangling	Waving farewell, the plane began to roll down the runway. [Did the writer mean the plane was waving farewell?]
Revised	Waving farewell, we watched as the plane began to roll down the runway.
Dangling	After taking hours to plant hundreds of strawberry plants, the gophers came back to the garden and ate every one of them. [Did the writer mean that the gophers had a good meal after putting in such hard work?]
Revised	After Ralph spent hours planting hundreds of strawberry plants, the gophers came back to the garden and ate every one of them.
Dangling	While telling a joke to my roommate, a cockroach walked across my souffle. [Did the writer mean that the cockroach was a comedian?]
Revised	While telling a joke to my roommate, I saw a cockroach walking across my soufflé.

Dangling   Having tucked the children into bed, the cat was put out for the night. [Did the writer mean that the family pet had taken up nanny duties?]

Revised   Having tucked the children into bed, Mother and Father put the cat out for the night.

Misplaced and dangling modifiers frequently occur when you think faster than you write; a careful reading of your rough drafts will help you weed out any confused or unintentionally humorous sentences. (For additional examples of misplaced and dangling modifiers, see pp. 455–456 in Part Four.)

Avoid Mixed Constructions and Faulty Predication

Sometimes you may begin with a sentence pattern in mind and then shift, midsentence, to another pattern—a change that often results in a generally confusing sentence. In many of these cases, you will find that the subject of your sentence simply doesn't fit with the predicate. Look at the following examples and note their corrections:

Faulty   Financial aid is a growing problem for many college students. [Financial aid itself isn't a problem; rather, it's the lack of aid.]

Revised   College students are finding it harder to obtain financial aid.

Faulty   Pregnant cows are required to teach a portion of two courses in Animal Science, AS100 (Breeding of Livestock) and AS200 (Problems in Reproduction of Cattle). [Obviously, the cows will not be the instructors for the classes.]

Revised   The Animal Science Department needs to purchase pregnant cows for use in two courses, AS100 (Breeding of Livestock) and AS200 (Problems in Reproduction of Cattle).

Faulty   Love is when you start rehearsing dinner-date conversation before breakfast. [A thing is never a "when" or a "where"; rewrite all "is when" or "is where" constructions.]

Revised   You're in love if you start rehearsing dinner-date conversation before breakfast.

Many mixed constructions occur because the writer is in too much of a hurry; check your rough drafts carefully to see if you have included sentences in which you started one pattern and switched to another. (For more help on faulty predications and mixed constructions, see pp. 460–461 in Part Four.)

DEVELOPING A CONCISE STYLE

Almost all writing suffers from wordiness—the tendency to use more words than necessary. When useless words weigh down your prose, the meaning is often lost, confused, or hidden. Flabby prose calls for a reducing plan: put those obese sentences on a diet by cutting out unnecessary words, just as you avoid fatty foods to keep yourself trim. Mushy prose is ponderous and boring; crisp, to-the-point writing, on the other hand, is both accessible and pleasing. Beware, however, a temptation to overdiet—you don't want your prose to become so thin or brief that your meaning disappears completely. Therefore, cut out only the *unessential* words and phrases.

Wordy prose is frequently the result of using one or more of the following: (1) deadwood constructions (2) redundancies (3) pretentious diction.

Avoid Deadwood Constructions

Always try to cut empty "deadwood" from your sentences. Having a clear, concise style does not mean limiting your writing to choppy, childish Dick-and-Jane sentences; it only means that all unnecessary words, phrases, and clauses should be deleted. Below are some sentences containing common deadwood constructions and ways they may be pruned:

Poor   The *reason* the starving novelist drove 50 miles to a new restaurant was *because* it was serving his favorite chicken dish, Pullet Surprise. ["The reason . . . was because" is both wordy and ungrammatical. If you have a reason, you don't need a "reason because."]

Revised   The starving novelist drove 50 miles to a new restaurant because it was serving his favorite chicken dish, Pullet Surprise.

Poor   The land settlement *was an example where* my client, Ms. Patti O. Furniture, did not receive fair treatment.

Revised   The land settlement was unfair to my client, Ms. Patti O. Furniture.

Poor   Because *of the fact that* his surfboard business failed after only a month, my brother decided to leave Minnesota.

Revised   Because his surfboard business failed after only a month, my brother decided to leave Minnesota.

Other notorious deadwood constructions include the following:

regardless of the fact that	(use "although")
due to the fact that	(use "because")
the reason is that	(omit)

as to whether or not to	(omit "as to" and "or not")
at this point in time	(use "now" or "today")
it is believed that	(use a specific subject and "believes")
concerning the matter of	(use "about")
by means of	(use "by")
these are the kinds of . . . that	(use "these" plus a specific subject)

Watch a tendency to tack on empty "fillers" that stretch one word into an awkward phrase:

Wordy   Each candidate should be evaluated *on an individual basis.*

Concise   Each candidate should be evaluated *individually.*

Wordy   Television does not portray violence *in a realistic fashion.*

Concise   Television does not portray violence *realistically.*

Wordy   The New York blackout produced a *crisis-type situation.*

Concise   The New York blackout produced a *crisis.*

To retain your reader's interest and improve the flow of your prose, trim all the fat from your sentences.

"There are," "It is."   These introductory phrases are often space wasters. When possible, omit them or replace them with specific subjects, as shown in the following:

Wordy   *There are* ten dental students on Full-Bite Scholarships attending this university.

Revised   Ten dental students on Full-Bite Scholarships attend this university.

Wordy   *It is* true that the County Fair offers many fun contests, including the ever-popular map fold-off.

Revised   The County Fair offers many fun contests, including the ever-popular map fold-off.

"Who" and "which" clauses.   Some "who" and "which" clauses are unnecessary and may be turned into modifiers placed before the noun:

Wordy   The getaway car, *which* was stolen, turned the corner.

Revised   The stolen getaway car turned the corner.

Wordy   The chef, *who was* depressed, ordered his noisy lobsters to simmer down.

Revised   The depressed chef ordered his noisy lobsters to simmer down.

When adjective clauses are necessary, the words "who" and "which" may sometimes be omitted:

Wordy   Ms. Quito, *who is* a local English teacher, was delighted to hear that she had won the annual lottery, *which is* sponsored by the Shirley Jackson Foundation.

Revised   Ms. Quito, a local English teacher, was delighted to hear that she had won the annual lottery, sponsored by the Shirley Jackson Foundation.

"To be." Most "to bes" are unnecessary and ought not to be. Delete them every time you can.

Wordy   She seems *to be* angry.

Revised   She seems angry.

Wordy   Herb's charisma-bypass operation proved *to be* successful.

Revised   Herb's charisma-bypass operation proved successful.

Wordy   The new mayor wanted his archenemy, the local movie critic, *to be* arrested.

Revised   The new mayor wanted his archenemy, the local movie critic, arrested.

"Of" and infinitive phrases. Many "of" and infinitive ("to" plus verb) phrases may be omitted or revised by using possessives, adjectives, and verbs, as shown below:

Wordy   At the *time of registration* students are required *to make* payment *of their library fees.*

Revised   At registration students must pay their library fees.

Wordy   The producer fired the mother *of the director of the movie.*

Revised   The producer fired the movie director's mother.

Including deadwood phrases makes your prose puffy; streamline your sentences to present a simple, direct style.

Avoid Redundancy

Many flabby sentences contain *redundancies* (words that repeat the same idea or whose meanings overlap). Consider the following examples:

> In this day and time, people expect to live at least seventy years. ["Day" and "time" present a similar idea.]

> He repeated the winning bingo number over again. ["Repeated" means "to say again," so there is no need for "over again."]

> The group consensus was that the pizza crust tasted like cardboard. ["Consensus" means "general agreement," so it's unnecessary to add "group."]

Some other common redundancies include:

reverted ~~back~~	~~new~~ innovation
reflected ~~back~~	red ~~in color~~
retreated ~~back~~	burned ~~down~~ up
fell ~~down~~	~~pair of~~ twins/~~two~~ twins
climb ~~up~~	~~resulting~~ effect (or just "result")
a ~~true~~ fact	~~final~~ outcome

Carefully Consider Your Passive Verbs

When the subject of the sentence performs the action, the verb is *active*; when the subject of the sentence is acted on, the verb is *passive*. You can sometimes recognize sentences with passive verbs because they often contain the word "by," telling who performed the action.

Passive   The wedding date *was announced* by the young couple.

Active   The young couple *announced* their wedding date.

Passive   His letter of resignation *was accepted* by the Board of Trustees.

Active   The Board of Trustees *accepted* his letter of resignation.

Passive   The trivia contest *was won* by the ever-popular Boulder team, The Godzillas Must Be Crazy.

Active   The ever-popular Boulder team, The Godzillas Must Be Crazy, *won* the trivia contest.

In addition to being wordy and weak, passive sentences often disguise the performer of the action in question. You might have heard a politician, for example, say something similar to this: "It was decided this year to give all congressmen an increase in salary." The question of *who* decided to raise salaries remains foggy—perhaps purposefully so. But in your own prose, you should strive for clarity and directness; therefore, use active verbs as often as you can except when you wish to stress the person or thing that receives the action, as shown in the following samples:

The baby was born September 30, 1980.

The elderly man was struck by a drunk driver.

Special note: Authorities in some professional and technical fields still prefer the passive construction because they wish to put emphasis on the experiment or process rather than on the people performing the action. If the passive voice is preferred in your field, you should abide by that convention when you are writing reports or papers for your professional colleagues.

Avoid Pretentiousness

Another enemy of clear, concise prose is *pretentiousness.* Pompous, inflated language surrounds us, and because it often sounds learned or official, we may be tempted to use it when we want to impress others with our writing. But as George Orwell, author of *1984,* noted, an inflated style is like "a cuttlefish squirting out ink." If you want your prose easily understood, write as clearly and plainly as possible.

To illustrate how confusing pretentious writing can be, here is a copy of a government memo announcing a blackout order, issued in 1942 during World War II:

Such preparations shall be made as will completely obscure all Federal buildings and non-Federal buildings occupied by the Federal government during an air raid for any period of time from visibility by reason of internal or external illumination.

President Franklin Roosevelt intervened and rewrote the order in plain English, clarifying its message and reducing the number of words by half:

Tell them that in buildings where they have to keep the work going to put something across the windows.

By translating the obscure original memo into easily understandable language, Roosevelt demonstrated that a natural prose style can get necessary information to the reader more quickly and efficiently than bureaucratic jargon. (For more advice on ridding your prose of jargon, see pp. 169–170.)

> ### REMEMBER
>
> In other—shorter—words, to attract and hold your readers' attention, to communicate clearly and quickly, make your sentences as informative, straightforward, specific, and concise as possible.

 PRACTICING WHAT YOU'VE LEARNED

A. Some of the following sentences are vague, "empty," overpacked, or contorted. Rewrite each one so that it is clear and specific, combining or dividing sentences as necessary.

1. Roger was a pretty awesome guy who was really an important part of his company.

2. There's a new detective show on television. It stars Phil Noir and is set in the 1940s.

3. Sarah's room was always a huge disaster.

4. The book *Biofeedback: How to Stop It* is a good one because of all the ideas the writer put into it.

5. Some people think capital punishment should be allowed to exist because it acts as a deterrent to people about to commit crimes or who are even considering them, but other people hold the view that they shouldn't have to pay for feeding and housing them for years after crimes are committed, so they should be executed instead.

6. My junk mail is incredible.

7. I've signed up for a course at my local college. The class is "Cultivating the Mold in Your Refrigerator for Fun and Profit."

8. Reading your horoscope is a fun way to get information about your life, but some people think it's too weird.

9. I'm not sure but I think that Lois is the author of *The Underachiever's Guide to Very Small Business Opportunities* or is she the writer of *Whine Your Way to Success* because I know she's written several books since she's having an autograph party at the campus bookstore either this afternoon or tomorrow.

10. I can't help but wonder whether or not he isn't unwelcome.

B. The sentences below contain misplaced words and phrases as well as other faulty constructions. Revise them so that each sentence is clear.

1. If you are accosted in the subway at night, you should learn to escape harm from the police.

2. Desperation is when you try to lose weight through Pyramid Power.

3. Almost dead for five years now, I miss my dog so much.

4. For sale: unique, handmade gifts for that special hard-to-find person in your life.

5. The reason I finally got my leg operated on over Thanksgiving break is because it had been hanging over my head for years.

6. We need to hire two three-year-old teachers for preschool kids who don't smoke.

7. The story of Rip Van Winkle is one of the dangers endured by those who oversleep.

8. We gave our waterbed to friends we didn't want anymore.

9. People who are allergic to chocolate and children under 6 should not be given the new vaccine.

10. At 7:00 A.M. Brenda starts preparing for another busy day as an executive in her luxurious bathroom.

C. The sentences below are filled with deadwood, redundancies, and passive constructions. Rewrite each one so that it is concise and direct.

1. In point of fact, the main reason he lost the editing job was primarily because of his careless and sloppy proofreading work.

2. It was revealed today that there are some professors in the Prehistoric History department who are incompetent.

3. My brother, who happens to be older than me, can't drive to work this week due to the fact that he was in a wreck in his car at 2:00 A.M. Saturday morning.

4. In this modern world of today, we often criticize or disapprove of advertising that is thought to be damaging to women by representing them in an unfair way.

5. When the prosecution tried to introduce the old antique gun, this was objected to by the attorney defending the two twin brothers.

6. What the poet is trying to get across to the reader in the poem "Now is the Winter of Our Discount Tent" is her feeling of disgust with camping.

7. We very often felt that although we expressed our deepest concerns to our boss, she often just sat there and gave us the real impression that she was taking what we said in a very serious manner although, in our opinion, she did not really and truly care about our concerns.

8. It is a true fact that certainly bears repeating over and over again that learning word processing can help you perform in a more efficient way at work and also can save you lots of time too.

9. Personally, I believe that there are too many people who go to eat out in restaurants who always feel they must continually assert their superior natures by acting in a rude, nasty fashion to the people who are employed to wait on their tables.

10. In order to enhance my opportunities for advancement in the workplace at this point in time, I arrived at the decision to seek the hand of my employer's daughter in the state of matrimony.

 ASSIGNMENT

Write a paragraph of at least five sentences as clearly and concisely as you can. Then rewrite this paragraph, filling it with as many vague words, redundancies, and deadwood constructions as possible. Exchange this rewritten paragraph for a similarly faulty one written by a classmate; give yourselves fifteen minutes to "translate" each other's sentences into effective prose. Compare the translations to the original paragraphs. Which version is clearer? Why?

DEVELOPING A LIVELY STYLE

Good writing demands clarity and conciseness—but that's not all. Good prose must also be lively, forceful, and interesting. It should excite, intrigue, and charm; each line should seduce the reader into the next. Consider, for example, one of the duller textbooks you've read lately. It probably was written clearly, but it may have failed to inform because of its insufferably bland tone; by the time you finished your assignment, most likely your brain was asleep.

You can prevent your readers from succumbing to a similar case of the blahs by developing a vigorous prose style that continually surprises and pleases them. As one writer has pointed out, all subjects—with the possible exceptions of sex and money—are dull until somebody makes them interesting. As you revise your rough drafts, remember: bored readers are not born but made. Therefore, here are some practical suggestions to help you transform ho-hum prose into lively sentences and paragraphs:

Use specific, descriptive verbs. Avoid bland verbs that must be supplemented by modifiers.

Bland   His fist *broke* the window *into many little pieces.*

Better   His fist *shattered* the window.

Bland   Dr. Love *asked* his congregation about donating money to his "love mission" *over and over again.*

Better   Dr. Love *hounded* his congregation into donating money to his "love mission."

Bland   The exhausted runner *walked* up the last hill *very slowly.*

Better   The exhausted runner *staggered* up the last hill.

To cut wordiness that weighs down your prose, try to use active verbs instead of nouns and colorless verbs such as "to be," "to have," "to get," "to do," and "to make":

Wordy   By sunrise the rebels had *made their way* to the capital city.

Better   By sunrise the rebels had *battled* to the capital city.

Wordy   At first the players and managers *had an argument* over the money, but finally they *came to an agreement that got* the contract dispute settled.

Better   At first the players and managers *argued* over the money, but finally they *settled* the contract dispute.

Wordy   The executives *made the decision* to *have* another meeting on Tuesday.

Better   The executives *decided* to *meet* again on Tuesday.

Use specific, precise modifiers that help the reader see, hear, or feel what you are describing. Adjectives such as "good," "bad," "many," "more," "great," "a lot," "important," and "interesting" are too vague to paint the reader a clear picture. Similarly, the adverbs "very," "really," "too," and "quite" are overused and add little to sentence clarity. The following are examples of weak sentences and their revisions:

Imprecise   The potion changed the scientist into a *really old* man.

Better   The potion changed the scientist into a *one hundred-year-old* man.

Imprecise Marcia is a *very interesting* person.

Better Marcia is *witty, intelligent,* and *talented.*

Imprecise The vegetables tasted *funny.*

Better The vegetables tasted *like moss mixed with Krazy Glue.*

(For more advice on using specific, colorful words, see also pp. 166–167 in Chapter 7.)

Emphasize people when possible. Try to focus on persons rather than abstractions whenever you can. Next to our fascinating selves, we most enjoy hearing about other people. Although all the sentences in the first paragraph following are correct, the second one, revised by a class of composition students at Brown University, is clearer and more useful because the jargon has been eliminated and the focus changed from the tuition rules to the students.

Original Tuition regulations currently in effect provide that payment of the annual tuition entitles an undergraduate-degree candidate to full-time enrollment, which is defined as registration for three, four, or five courses per semester. This means that at no time may an undergraduate student's official registration for courses drop below three without a dean's permission for part-time status and that at no time may the official course registration exceed five. (Brown University Course Announcement)

Revised If students pay their tuition, they may enroll in three, four, or five courses per semester. Fewer than three or more than five can be taken only with a dean's permission.

Here's a similar example with a bureaucratic focus rather than a personal one:

Original The salary deflations will most seriously impact the secondary educational profession.

Revised High school teachers will suffer the biggest salary reductions.

Obviously, the revised sentence is the more easily understood of the two because the reader knows exactly who will be affected by the pay cuts. In your own prose, wherever appropriate, try to replace vague abstractions such as "society," "culture," "administrative concerns," "programmatic expectations," and so forth, with the human beings you're thinking about. In other words, remember to talk *to* people *about* people.

Vary your sentence style. The only torture worse than listening to someone's nails scraping across a blackboard is being forced to read a paragraph full of identically constructed sentences. To illustrate this point, below are a few sentences composed in the all-too-common subject + predicate pattern:

Soccer is the most popular sport in the world. Soccer exists in almost every country. Soccer players are sometimes more famous than movie stars. Soccer teams compete every few years for the World Soccer Cup. Soccer fans often riot if their team loses. Soccer fans even commit suicide. Soccer is the only game in the world that makes people so crazy.

Excruciatingly painful, yes? Each of us has a tendency to repeat a particular sentence pattern (though the choppy subject + predicate is by far the most popular); you can often detect your own by reading your prose aloud. To avoid overdosing your readers with the same pattern, vary the length, arrangement, and complexity of your sentences. Of course, this doesn't mean that you should contort your sentences merely for the sake of illustrating variety; just read your rough draft aloud, listening carefully to the rhythm of your prose so you can revise any monotonous passages or disharmonious sounds. (Try, also, to avoid the hiccup syndrome, in which you begin a sentence with the same words that end the preceding sentence: "The first president to install a telephone on his desk was Herbert *Hoover. Hoover* refused to use the telephone booth outside his office.")

Avoid overuse of any one kind of construction in the same sentence. Don't, for example, pile up too many negatives, "who" or "which" clauses, and prepositional or infinitive phrases in one sentence.

He *couldn't* tell whether she *didn't* want him to go or *not.*

I gave the money to my brother, *who* returned it to the bank president, *who* said the decision to prosecute was up to the sheriff, *who* was out of town.

I went to the florist *for* my father *for* a dozen roses *for* his date.

Try also to avoid stockpiling nouns, one on top of another, so that your sentences are difficult to read. Although some nouns may be used as adjectives to modify other nouns ("book mark," "gasoline pump," "food processor"), too many nouns grouped together sound awkward and confuse readers. If you have run too many nouns together, try using prepositional phrases ("an income tax bill discussion" becomes "discussion of an income tax bill") or changing the order or vocabulary of the sentence:

Confusing The legislators are currently considering the *liability insurance multiple-choice premium proposal.*

Clearer The legislators are currently considering the *proposal* that suggests *multiple-choice premiums* for *liability insurance.*

Confusing We're concerned about the low *female labor force participation figures* in our department.

Clearer We're concerned about the low *number of women working* in our department.

Don't change your point of view between or within sentences. If, for example, you begin your essay discussing students as "they," don't switch midway—or midsentence—to "we" or "you."

Inconsistent Students pay tuition, which should entitle *them* to some voice in the university's administration. Therefore, *we* deserve one student on the Board of Regents.

Consistent Students pay tuition, which should entitle *them* to some voice in the university's administration. Therefore, *they* deserve one student on the Board of Regents.

Inconsistent *I* like my photography class because *we* learn how to restore *our* old photos and how to take better color portraits of *your* family.

Consistent *I* like my photography class because *I'm* learning how to restore *my* old photos and how to take better color portraits of *my* family.

Perhaps this is a good place to dispel the myth that the pronoun "I" should never be used in an essay; on the contrary, many of our best essays have been written in the first person. Some of your former teachers may have discouraged the use of "I" for these two reasons: (1) overuse of "I" makes your essay sound like the work of an egomaniac; (2) writing in the first person often results in too many empty phrases such as "I think that" and "I believe that." Nevertheless, if the situation demands a personal point of view, feel free—if you're comfortable doing so—to use the first person, but use it in moderation; make sure that every sentence doesn't begin with "I" plus a verb.

 PRACTICING WHAT YOU'VE LEARNED

A. Replace the underlined words below so that the sentences are clear and vivid. In addition, rephrase any awkward constructions or unnecessarily abstract words you find.

1. Judging from the <u>crazy</u> sound of the reactor, it isn't obvious to me that nuclear power as we know it today isn't a technology with a less than wonderful future.

2. The City Council felt <u>bad</u> because the revised tourist development activities grant fund application form letters were mailed without stamps.

3. To watch Jim Bob eat pork chops was <u>most interesting</u>.

4. For sale: <u>very nice</u> antique bureau suitable for ladies or gentlemen with thick legs and extra-large side handles.

5. The workshop on family relationships we're attending is <u>great</u> because you learn to control your parents through blackmail and guilt.

6. The new diet made me feel <u>awful</u>, and it <u>did many horrible things</u> to my body.

7. After reading "The Looter's Guide to Riot-Prone Cities," Eddie <u>asked to have</u> a transfer really soon.

8. The wild oats soup was <u>fantastic</u>, so we drank <u>a lot of it very fast</u>.

9. When his new cat Chairman Meow won the pet show, owner Warren Peace got <u>pretty excited</u>.

10. My roommate is <u>sort of different</u>, but he's a <u>good</u> guy at heart.

B. Fill in the blanks with colorful words. Make the paragraph as interesting, exciting, or humorous as you can. Avoid clichés and insta-prose (those predictable phrases that first come to mind). Make your responses original and creative.

As midnight approached, Janet and Brad _____ toward the _____ castle to escape the _____ storm. Their _____ car had _____, _____, and finally _____ on the road nearby. The night was _____, and Brad _____ at the shadows with _____ and _____. As they _____ up the _____ steps to the _____ door, the _____ wind was filled with _____ and _____ sounds. Janet _____ on the door, and moments later, it opened to reveal the _____ scientist, clutching a _____· Brad and Janet _____ at each other and then _____ (complete this sentence and then end the paragraph and the story).

ASSIGNMENT

Find a short piece of writing you think is too bland, boring, abstract, or confusing. (Possible sources: your college catalog, a business contract or letter, your student health insurance policy, or a textbook.) In a well-written paragraph of your own, identify the sample's major problems and offer some specific suggestions for improving the writing. (If time permits, read aloud several of the samples and vote to give one the Most Lifeless Prose Award.)

DEVELOPING AN EMPHATIC STYLE

Some words and phrases in your sentences are more important than others and, therefore, need more emphasis. Three ways to vary emphasis are by (1) word order, (2) coordination, and (3) subordination.

Word Order

The arrangement of words in a sentence can determine which ideas receive the most emphasis. To stress a word or phrase, place it at the end of the sentence or at the beginning of the sentence. Accordingly, a word or phrase receives least emphasis when buried in the middle of the sentence. Compare the examples below, in which the word "murder" receives varying degrees of emphasis:

Least emphatic	Colonel Mustard knew *murder* was his only solution.
Emphatic	*Murder* was Colonel Mustard's only solution.
Emphatic	Colonel Mustard knew only one solution: *murder*.

Another use of word order to vary emphasis is *inversion,* taking a word out of its natural or usual position in a sentence and inserting it in an unexpected place.

Usual order	Parents who give their children both roots and wings are *wise*.
Inverted order	*Wise* are the parents who give their children both roots and wings.

Not all your sentences will contain words that need special emphasis; good writing generally contains a mix of some sentences in natural order and others rearranged for special effects.

Coordination

When you have two closely related ideas and want to stress them equally, coordinate them.* In coordination, you join two sentences with a coordinating conjunction. To remember the coordinating conjunctions ("for," "and," "nor," "but," "or," "yet," "so"), think of the acronym FANBOYS; then always join two sentences with a comma and one of the FANBOYS. Here are two samples:

Choppy   The most popular girl's name today is Jennifer.
                    The most popular boy's name today is Michael.

Coordinated   The most popular girl's name today is Jennifer, *and* the most popular boy's name is Michael.

Choppy   Imelda brought home a pair of ruby slippers.
                    Ferdinand made her return them.

Coordinated   Imelda brought home a pair of ruby slippers, *but* Ferdinand made her return them.

You can use coordination to show a relationship between ideas and to add variety to your sentence structures. Be careful, however, to select the right words while linking ideas, unlike the sentence that appeared in a church newsletter: "The ladies of the church have discarded clothing of all kinds, and they have been inspected by the minister." In other words, writers often need to slow down and make sure that their thoughts are not joined in misleading or even unintentionally humorous ways: "For those of you who have children and don't know it, we have a nursery downstairs."

Sometimes when writers are in a hurry, they join ideas that are clearly related in their own minds, but whose relationship is confusing to the reader:

Confusing   My laboratory report isn't finished, and today my sister is leaving for a visit home.

Clear   I'm still working on my laboratory report, so I won't be able to catch a ride home with my sister who's leaving today.

You should also avoid using coordinating conjunctions to string too many ideas together like linked sausages:

Poor   We went inside the famous cave and the guide turned off the lights and we saw the rocks that glowed.

---

*To remember that the term "coordination" refers to equally weighted ideas, think of other words with the prefix "co," such as "copilots," "coauthors," or "cooperation."

Revised   After we went inside the famous cave, the guide turned off the lights so we could see the rocks that glowed.

Subordination

Some sentences contain one main statement and one or more less emphasized elements; the less important ideas are subordinate to, or are dependent on, the sentence's main idea.* Subordinating conjunctions introducing dependent clauses show a variety of relationships between the clauses and the main part of the sentence. Here are four examples of subordinating conjunctions and their uses:

1. To show time

Without subordination   Superman stopped changing his clothes. He realized the phone booth was made of glass.

With subordination   Superman stopped changing his clothes *when* he realized the phone booth was made of glass.

2. To show cause

Without subordination   The country-western singer failed to gain success in Nashville. She sadly returned to Snooker Hollow to work in the sequin mines.

With subordination   *Because* the country-western singer failed to gain success in Nashville, she sadly returned to Snooker Hollow to work in the sequin mines.

3. To show condition

Without subordination   Susan ought to study the art of tattooing. She will work with colorful people.

With subordination   *If* Susan studies the art of tattooing, she will work with colorful people.

4. To show place

Without subordination   Bulldozers are smashing the old movie theater. That's the place I first saw Roy Rogers and Dale Evans ride into the sunset.

---

* To remember that the term "subordination" refers to sentences containing dependent elements, think of words such as "a subordinate" (someone who works for someone else) or a post office "substation" (a branch of the post office less important than the main branch).

With subordination	Bulldozers are smashing the old movie theater *where* I first saw Roy Rogers and Dale Evans ride into the sunset.

Subordination is especially useful in ridding your prose of choppy Dick-and-Jane sentences and those "empty sentences" discussed on page 129. Below are some examples of choppy, weak sentences and their revisions, which contain subordinate clauses:

Choppy   Lew makes bagels on Tuesday. Lines in front of his store are a block long.

Revised   When Lew makes bagels on Tuesday, lines in front of his store are a block long.

Choppy   I have fond memories of Zilker Park. My husband and I met there.

Revised   I have fond memories of Zilker Park because my husband and I met there.

A correctly subordinated sentence is one of the marks of a sophisticated writer because it presents adequate information in one smooth flow instead of in monotonous drips. Subordination, like coordination, also adds variety to your sentence construction.

Generally, when you subordinate one idea, you emphasize another, so to avoid the tail-wagging-the-dog problem, put your important idea in the main clause. Also, don't let your most important idea become buried under an avalanche of subordinate clauses, as in the sentence that follows:

When he was told by his boss, *who* had always treated him fairly, that he was being fired from a job *that* he had held for twenty years at a factory *where* he enjoyed working *because* the pay was good, Henry felt angry and frustrated.

Practice blending choppy sentences by studying the sentence-combining exercise below. In this exercise a description of a popular movie or book has been chopped into simple sentences and then combined into one complex sentence.

1. *Psycho* (1960)
   Norman Bates manages a motel.
   It is remote.
   It is dangerous.
   Norman has a mother.
   She seems overly fond of knives.
   He tries to protect his mom.

In a remote—and dangerous—motel, manager Norman Bates tries to protect his mother, who seems overly fond of knives.

2. *King Kong* (1933)
A showman goes to the jungle.
He captures an ape.
The ape is a giant.
The ape is taken to New York City.
He escapes.
He dies fighting for a young woman.
He loves her.
She is beautiful.

A giant ape, captured in the jungle by a showman, is taken to New York City, where he escapes and dies fighting for the beautiful young woman he loves.

3. *Casablanca* (1942)
Rick is an American.
He is cynical.
He owns a café.
He lives in Casablanca.
He meets an old flame.
She is married.
Her husband is a French resistance leader.
Rick helps the couple.
He regains self-respect.

When Rick, a cynical American café-owner in Casablanca, helps his old flame and her husband, a French resistance leader, he regains his self-respect.

Please note that the sentences in these exercises may be combined effectively in a number of ways. For instance, the description of *King Kong* might be rewritten this way: "After a showman captures him in the jungle, a giant ape escapes in New York City but dies fighting for the love of a beautiful young woman." How might you rewrite the other two sample sentences?

 PRACTICING WHAT YOU'VE LEARNED

A. Revise the sentences that follow so that the underlined words receive more emphasis.

1. A remark attributed to the one-time heavyweight boxing champion <u>Joe Louis</u> is "I don't really like money, but it quiets my nerves."

2. According to recent polls, <u>television</u> is where most Americans get their news.

3. Of all the world's problems, it is <u>hunger</u> that is most urgent.

4. I enjoyed visiting many foreign countries last year, with <u>Greece</u> being my favorite of all of them.

5. The annoying habit of <u>knuckle-cracking</u> is something I can't stand.

B. Combine the pairs of sentences below using coordination or subordination.

1. The guru rejected his dentist's offer of novocaine. He could transcend dental medication.

2. John failed his literature test. John incorrectly identified Harper Lee as the author of the south-of-the-border classic *Tequila Mockingbird*.

3. Dr. Acula recently opened a new office. He specializes in acupuncture in the neck.

4. The police had only a few clues. They suspected Jean and David had strangled each other in a desperate struggle over control of the thermostat.

5. Bubba's favorite movie is *Sorority Babes in the Slimeball Bowl-O-Rama* (1988). A film critic called it "a pinhead chiller."

6. We're going to the new Psychoanalysis Restaurant. Their menu includes banana split personality, repressed duck, shrimp basket case, and self-expresso.

7. Kato lost the junior high spelling bee. He could not spell *DNA*.

8. Colorado hosts an annual BobFest to honor all persons named Bob. Events include playing softbob, bobbing for apples, listening to bob-pipes, and eating bob-e-que.

9. The earthquake shook the city. Louise was practicing primal-scream therapy at the time.

10. In 1789 many Parisians bought a new perfume called "Guillotine." They wanted to be on the cutting edge of fashion.

C. Combine the following simple sentences into one complex sentence. See if you can guess the name of the books or movies described in the sentences. (Answers appear on p. 156.)

1. A boy runs away from home.
   His companion is a runaway slave.
   He lives on a raft.
   The raft is on the Mississippi River.
   He has many adventures.
   The boy learns many lessons.
   Some lessons are about human kindness.
   Some lessons are about friendship.

2. A young man returns from prison.
   He returns to his family.
   His family lives in the Dust Bowl.
   The family decides to move.
   The family expects to find jobs in California.
   The family finds intolerance.
   They also find dishonest employers.

3. A scientist is obsessed.
   He wants to re-create life.
   He creates a monster.
   The monster rebels against the scientist.
   The monster kills his creator.
   The villagers revolt.
   The villagers storm the castle.

 ASSIGNMENT

A. Make up your own sentence-combining exercise by finding or writing one-sentence descriptions of popular or recent movies, books, or television shows. Divide the complex sentences into simple sentences and exchange papers with a classmate. Give yourselves ten minutes to combine sentences and guess the titles.

B. The two paragraphs below are poorly written because of their choppy, wordy, and monotonous sentences. Rewrite each passage so that it is clear, lively, and emphatic.

1. There is a new invention on the market. It is called a "dieter's conscience." It is a small box to be installed in one's refrigerator. When the door of the refrigerator is opened by you, a tape recorder begins to start. A really loud voice yells, "You eating again? No wonder you're getting fat." Then the very loud voice says, "Close the door; it's getting warm." Then the voice laughs a lot in an insane and crazy

fashion. The idea is one that is designed to mock people into a habit of stopping eating.

2. In this modern world of today, man has come up with another new invention. This invention is called the "Talking Tombstone." It is made by the Gone-But-Not-Forgotten Company, which is located in Burbank, California. This company makes a tombstone that has a device in it that makes the tombstone appear to be talking aloud in a realistic fashion when people go close by it. The reason is that the device is really a recording machine that is turned on due to the simple fact of the heat of the bodies of the people who go by. The closer the people get, the louder the sound the tombstone makes. It is this device that individual persons who want to leave messages after death may utilize. A hypochondriac, to cite one example, might leave a recording of a message that says over and over again in a really loud voice, "See, I told you I was sick!" It may be assumed by one and all that this new invention will be a serious aspect of the whole death situation in the foreseeable future.

 ## APPLYING WHAT YOU'VE LEARNED TO **YOUR** WRITING

If you have drafted a piece of writing and are satisfied with your essay's ideas and organization, begin revising your sentences for clarity, conciseness, and emphasis. As you move through your draft, think about your readers. Ask yourself, "Are any of my sentences too vague, overpacked, or contorted for my readers to understand? Can I clarify any of my ideas by using simpler, more specific language or by using less confusing sentence constructions?

If one of your sentences is confusing but, after many tries, you can't seem to untangle it, follow the sentence-combining exercise described on pages 151–152 of this chapter—but in reverse. Instead of combining ideas, break your thought into a series of simpler units. Think about what you want to say and put the person or thing of importance in the subject position at the beginning of the sentence. Then select a verb and a brief phrase to complete the sentence. You will most likely need several of these simpler constructions to communicate the complexity of your original thought. Once you have your thought broken into smaller, simpler units, carefully begin to combine some of them as you strive for clarity and sentence variety.

Remember that it's not enough for you, the writer, to understand what your sentences mean—your readers must be able to follow your ideas, too. When in doubt, always revise your writing so that it is clear, concise, and inviting. (For more help, turn to Chapter 5, on Revision.)

CHAPTER 6 SUMMARY

Here is a brief summary of what you should remember about writing effective sentences:

1. All good writers revise and polish their sentences.

2. You can help clarify your ideas for your readers by writing sentences that are informative, straightforward, and precise.

3. You can communicate your ideas more easily to your readers if you cut out deadwood, redundancies, confusing passives, and pretentious language.

4. You can maintain your readers' interest in your ideas if you cultivate a style that is specific, varied, and emphatic.

Answers to sentence-combining exercise:

1. *Huckleberry Finn*
2. *The Grapes of Wrath*
3. *Frankenstein*

CHAPTER

7

Word Logic

The English language contains over a half million words—quite a selection for you as a writer to choose from. But such a wide choice may make you feel like a starving person confronting a six-page, fancy French menu. Which choice is best? How do I choose? Is the choice so important?

Word choice can make an enormous difference in the quality of your writing for at least one obvious reason: if you substitute an incorrect or vague word for the right one, you take the risk of being totally misunderstood. Ages ago Confucius made the same point: "If language is incorrect, then what is said is not meant. If what is said is not meant, then what ought to be done remains undone." It isn't enough that you know what you mean; you must transfer your ideas onto paper in the proper words so that others understand your exact meaning.

To help you avoid possible paralysis from indecision over word choice, this chapter offers some practical suggestions on selecting words that are not only accurate and appropriate but also memorable and persuasive.

SELECTING THE CORRECT WORDS

Accuracy: Confused Words

Unless I get a bank loan soon, I will be forced to lead an *immortal* life.

Dobermans make good pets if you train them with enough *patients*.

He dreamed of eating *desert* after *desert*.

She had dieted for so long that she had become *emancipated*.

The young man was completely in *ah* of the actress's beauty.

Socrates died from an overdose of *wedlock*.

The preceding sentences share a common problem: each one contains an error in word choice. In each sentence, the *underlined* word is incorrect, causing the sentence to be nonsensical or silly. (Consider a sign recently spotted in a local night spot: "No miners allowed." Did the owner think the lights on their hats would bother the other customers?) To avoid such confusion in word choice, make sure you check words for *accuracy*. Use only those words whose precise meaning, usage, and spelling you know; look in your dictionary to double-check any words whose definitions (or spellings) are fuzzy to you. As Mark Twain noted, the difference between the right word and the wrong one is the difference between lightning and the lightning bug.

Here is a list of words that are often confused in writing. Use your dictionary to determine the meanings or usage of any word unfamiliar to you.

its/it's	lead/led	choose/chose
to/too/two	cite/sight/site	accept/except
there/their/they're	affect/effect	council/counsel
your/you're	good/well	where/wear
complement/compliment	who's/whose	lose/loose
stationary/stationery	lay/lie	precede/proceed
capitol/capital	than/then	illusion/allusion
principal/principle	insure/ensure	farther/further

Accuracy: Idiomatic Phrases

Occasionally you may have an essay returned to you with words marked "awkward diction" or "idiom." In English, as in all languages, we have word groupings that seem governed by no particular logic except the ever-popular "that's-the-way-we-say-it" rule. Many of these idiomatic expressions involve prepositions that beginning writers sometimes confuse or misuse. Some common idiomatic errors and their corrected forms are listed on the next page.

regardless ~~to~~ of
insight ~~of~~ into
similar ~~with~~ to
comply ~~to~~ with
contrast ~~against~~ to

different ~~than to~~ from
must ~~of~~ have known
superior ~~than~~ to
~~to~~ in my opinion
meet ~~to~~ her standards

relate ~~with~~ to
capable ~~to~~ of
aptitude ~~toward~~ for
prior ~~than~~ to
should ~~of~~ have

To avoid idiomatic errors, consult your dictionary and read your essay aloud; often your ears will catch mistakes in usage that your eyes have overlooked.*

Levels of Language

In addition to choosing the correct word, you should also select words whose status is suited to your purpose. For convenience here, language has been classified into three categories or levels of usage: (1) colloquial, (2) informal, and (3) formal.

Colloquial language is the kind of speech you use most often in conversation with your friends, classmates, and family. It may not always be grammatically correct ("it's me"); it may include fragments of speech, contractions, some slang, words identified as nonstandard by the dictionary (such as "yuck" or "lousy"), and shortened or abbreviated words ("grad school," "photos," "TV"). Colloquial speech is everyday language, and although you may use it in some writing (personal letters, journals, memos, and so forth), you should think carefully about using colloquial language in most college essays or in professional letters, reports, or papers because such a choice implies a casual relationship between writer and reader.

Informal language is called for in most college and professional assignments. The tone is more formal than in colloquial writing or speech; no slang or nonstandard words are permissible. Informal writing consistently uses correct grammar; fragments are used for special effect or not at all. Authorities disagree on the use of contractions in informal writing: some say

---

* You may not immediately recognize what's wrong with words your teacher has labeled "diction" or "idiom," as these marks often cover many problems. If you're uncertain about an error, don't hesitate to ask your teacher for clarification; after all, if you don't know what's wrong with your prose, you can't very well avoid making the same mistake again. To illustrate this point, here's a true story: A bright young woman was having trouble with prepositional phrases in her essays, and although her professor repeatedly marked her incorrect expressions with the marginal note "idiom," she never improved. Finally, one day near the end of the term, she approached her teacher in tears and wailed, "Professor Jones, I know I'm not a very good writer, but must you write 'idiot,' 'idiot,' 'idiot' all over my papers?" The moral of this story is simple: it's easy to misunderstand a correction or misread your teacher's writing. Since you can't improve until you know what's wrong, always ask when you're in doubt.

avoid them entirely; others say they're permissible; still others advocate using them only to avoid stilted phrases ("let's go," for example, is preferable to "let us go"). Most, if not all, of your essays in English classes will be written in informal language.

Formal language is found in important documents and in serious, often ceremonial, speeches. Characteristics include an elevated—but not pretentious—tone, no contractions, and correct grammar. Formal writing often uses inverted word order and balanced sentence structure. John F. Kennedy's 1960 Inaugural Address, for example, was written in a formal style ("Ask not what your country can do for you; ask what you can do for your country"). Most people rarely, if ever, need to write formally; if you are called on to do so, however, be careful to avoid formal diction that sounds pretentious, pompous, or phony.

Tone

Tone is a general word that describes writers' attitudes toward their subject matter and audience. There are as many different kinds of tones as there are emotions. Depending on how the writer feels, an essay's "voice" may sound light-hearted, indignant, or solemn, to name but a few of the possible choices. In addition to presenting a specific attitude, a good writer gains credibility by maintaining a tone that is generally reasonable, sincere, and authentic.

Although it is impossible to analyze all the various kinds of tones one finds in essays, it is nevertheless beneficial to discuss some of those that repeatedly give writers trouble. Here are some tones that should be used carefully or avoided altogether:

Invective

Invective is unrestrained anger, usually expressed in the form of violent accusation or denunciation. Let's suppose, for example, you hear a friend argue, "Anyone who votes for Joe Smith is a Fascist pig." If you are considering Smith, you are probably offended by your friend's abusive tone. Raging emotion, after all, does not sway the opinions of intelligent people; they need to hear the facts presented in a calm, clear discussion. Therefore, in your own writing, aim for a reasonable tone. You want your readers to think, "Now here is someone with a good understanding of the situation, who has evaluated it with an unbiased, analytical mind." Keeping a controlled tone doesn't mean you shouldn't feel strongly about your subject—on the contrary, you certainly should—but you should realize that a hysterical or outraged tone defeats your purpose by causing you to sound irrational and therefore untrustworthy. For this reason, you should probably avoid using profanity in your essays; the shock value of an obscenity may not be worth what you might lose in credibility (and besides, is anyone other than your Aunt Fanny really amazed by profanity these days?). The most effective way to get your point across is to persuade, not offend, your reader.

Sarcasm

In most of your writing you'll discover that a little sarcasm—bitter, derisive remarks—goes a long way. Like invective, too much sarcasm can damage the reasonable tone your essay should present. Instead of saying, "You can recognize the supporters of the new tax law by the points on the tops of their heads," give your readers some reasons why you believe the tax bill is flawed. Sarcasm can be effective, but realize that it often backfires by causing the writer to sound like a childish name-caller rather than a judicious commentator.

Irony

Irony is a figure of speech whereby the writer or speaker says the opposite of what is meant; for the irony to be successful, however, the audience must understand the writer's true intent. For example, if you have slopped to school in a rainstorm and your drenched teacher enters the classroom saying, "Ah, nothing like this beautiful sunny weather," you know that your teacher is being ironic. Perhaps one of the most famous cases of irony occurred in 1938, when Sigmund Freud, the famous Viennese psychiatrist, was arrested by the Nazis. After being harassed by the Gestapo, he was released on the condition that he sign a statement swearing he had been treated well by the secret police. Freud signed it, but he added a few words after his signature: "I can heartily recommend the Gestapo to anyone." Looking back, we easily recognize Freud's jab at his captors; the Gestapo, however, apparently overlooked the irony and let him go.

Although irony is often an effective device, it can also cause great confusion, especially when it is written rather than spoken. Unless your readers thoroughly understand your position in the first place, they may become confused by what appears to be a sudden contradiction. Irony that is too subtle, too private, or simply out of context merely complicates the issue. Therefore, you must make certain that your reader has no trouble realizing when your tongue is firmly embedded in your cheek. And unless you are assigned to write an ironic essay (in the same vein, for instance, as Swift's "A Modest Proposal"), don't overuse irony. Like any rhetorical device, its effectiveness is reduced with overkill.

Flippancy or Cuteness

If you sound too flip, hip, or bored in your essay ("People with IQs lower than their sunscreen number will object . . ."), your readers will not take you seriously and, consequently, will disregard whatever you have to say. Writers suffering from cuteness will also antagonize their readers. For example, let's assume you're assigned the topic "Which Person Has Done the Most to Arouse the Laboring Class in Twentieth-Century England?" and you begin your essay with a discussion of the man who invented the alarm clock. Although that joke might be funny in an appropriate situation, it's not likely to impress your reader, who's looking for serious commentary. How much cuteness is too much is often a matter of taste, but if you have any doubts about the quality of your humor, leave it out. Also, omit personal messages or comic asides to your reader (such as "Ha, ha, just kidding!" or "I knew you'd love this part"). Humor is often effective, but remember that the point of any essay is to persuade an audience to accept your thesis, not merely to entertain with freestanding jokes. In other words, if you use humor, make sure it is appropriate to your subject matter and that it works to help you make your point.

Sentimentality

Sentimentality is the excessive show of cheap emotions—"cheap" because they are not deeply felt but evoked by clichés and stock, tear-jerking situations. In the nineteenth century, for example, a typical melodrama played on the sentimentality of the audience by presenting a black-hatted, cold-hearted, mustache-twirling villain tying a golden-haired, pure-hearted "Little Nell" to the railroad tracks after driving her ancient, sickly mother out into a snowdrift. Today, politicians (among others) often appeal to our sentimentality by conjuring up vague images they feel will move us emotionally rather than rationally to take their side: "My friends," says Senator Stereotype, "this fine nation of ours was founded by men like myself, dedicated to the principles of family, flag, and freedom. Vote for me, and let's get back to those precious basics that make life in America so grand." Such gush is hardly convincing; good writers and speakers use evidence and logical reason to persuade their audience. For example, don't allow yourself to become too carried away with emotion, as did this student: "My dog, Cuddles, is the sweetest, cutest, most precious little puppy dog in the whole wide world, and she will always be my best friend because she is so sweet and adorable." In addition to sending the reader into sugar shock, this passage fails to present any specific reasons why anyone should appreciate Cuddles. In other words, be sincere in your writing, but don't lose so much control of your emotions that you become mushy or maudlin.

Preachiness

Even if you are so convinced of the rightness of your position that a burning bush couldn't change your mind, try not to sound smug about it. No one likes to be lectured by someone perched atop the mountain of morality. Instead of preaching, adopt a tone that says, "I believe my position is correct, and I am glad to have this opportunity to explain why." Then give your reasons and meet objections in a positive but not holier-than-thou manner.

Pomposity

The "voice" of your essay should sound as natural as possible; don't strain to sound scholarly, scientific, or sophisticated. If you write "My summer sojourn through the Western states of this grand country was immensely pleasurable" instead of "My vacation last summer in the Rockies was fun," you sound merely phony, not dignified and learned. Select only words you know and can use easily. Never write anything you wouldn't say in an ordinary conversation. (For more information on correcting pretentious writing, see p. 139 and pp. 169–172.)

> To achieve the appropriate tone, be as sincere, forthright, and reasonable as you can. Let the tone of your essay establish a basis of mutual respect between you and your reader.

Connotation and Denotation

A word's *denotation* refers to its literal meaning, the meaning defined by the dictionary; a word's *connotation* refers to the emotional associations surrounding its meaning. For example, "home" and "residence" both may be defined as the place where one lives, but "home" carries connotations of warmth, security, and family that "residence" lacks. Similarly, "old" and "antique" have similar denotative meanings, but "antique" has the more positive connotation because it suggests something that also has value. Reporters and journalists do the same job, but the latter name somehow seems to indicate someone more sophisticated and professional. Because many words with similar denotative meanings do carry different connotations, good writers must be careful with their word choice. *Select only words whose connotations fit your purpose.* If, for example, you want to describe your grandmother in a positive way as someone who stands up for herself, you might refer to her as "assertive" or "feisty"; if you want to present her negatively, you might call her "aggressive" or "pushy."

In addition to selecting words with the appropriate connotations for your purpose, be careful to avoid offending your audience with particular connotations. For instance, if you were trying to persuade a group of politically conservative doctors to accept your stand on a national health-care program, you would not want to refer to your opposition as "right-wingers" or "reactionaries," extremist terms that have negative connotations. Remember, you want to inform and persuade your audience, not antagonize them.

You should also be alert to the use of words with emotionally charged connotations, especially in advertising and propaganda of various kinds. Car manufacturers, for example, have often used names of swift, bold, or graceful animals (Jaguar, Cougar, Impala) to sway prospective buyers; cosmetic manufacturers in recent years have taken advantage of the trend toward lighter makeup by associating words such as "nature," "natural," and "healthy glow" with their products. Diet-conscious Americans are now deluged with "light" and "organic" food products. Politicians, too, are heavy users of connotation; they often drop in emotionally positive, but virtually meaningless, words and phrases such as "defender of the American Way," "friend of the common man," and "visionary" to describe themselves, while tagging their opponents with such negative, emotionally charged labels as "radical," "elitist," and "permissive." Intelligent readers, like intelligent voters and consumers, want more than emotion-laden words; they want facts and logical argument. Therefore, as a good writer, you should use connotation as only one of many persuasive devices to enhance your presentation of evidence; never depend solely on an emotional appeal to convince your audience that your position—or thesis—is correct.

 PRACTICING WHAT YOU'VE LEARNED

A. Some of the underlined words below are used incorrectly; some are correct. Substitute the accurate word wherever necessary.

1. The finances of the chicken ranch are in <u>fowl</u> shape because the hens are <u>lying</u> down on the job.

2. The professor, <u>whose</u> famous for his <u>photogenic</u> memory, graciously <u>excepted</u> a large <u>amount</u> of <u>complements</u>.

3. <u>Its</u> to bad you don't like <u>they're</u> new Popsicle stick sculpture since <u>their</u> giving it <u>to</u> you for Christmas.

4. Vacations of <u>to</u> weeks with <u>to</u> friends are always <u>to</u> short, and while you're <u>to</u> tired <u>to</u> return <u>to</u> work, <u>your</u> <u>to</u> broke not <u>to</u>.

5. Sara June felt she deserved an "A" in math, <u>irregardless</u> of her 59 average in the <u>coarse</u>.

6. Does the pamphlet "Ridding Your Home of Pesky <u>Aunts</u>" belong in the domestic-relations area of the public library?

7. Did the high school <u>principal</u> <u>loose</u> <u>you're</u> heavy <u>medal</u> tape and <u>it's</u> case <u>too</u>?

8. The new city <u>counsel</u> parade ordinance will <u>effect</u> everyone in the <u>capitol</u> city <u>except</u> members of the Lawn Chair Marching Band.

B. The sentences below contain words and phrases that interfere with the sincere, reasonable tone good writers try to create. Rewrite each sentence, replacing sarcasm, sentimentality, cuteness, invective, and pretentiousness with more appropriate language.

1. The last dying rays of day were quickly ebbing in the West as if to signal the feline to begin its lonely vigil.

2. Only a jerk would support the President's Mideast peace plan.

3. I was desirous of acquiring knowledge about members of our lower income brackets.

4. If the bill to legalize marijuana is passed, we can safely assume that the whole country will soon be going to pot (heh, heh!).

5. I just love to look at those little white mice with their itty-bitty red eyes.

C. In each group of words listed below, identify the words with the most pleasing and least positive (or even negative) connotations.

1. dull/drab/quiet/boring/colorless/serene

2. slender/slim/skinny/thin/slight/anorexic

3. famous/notorious/well-known/infamous

4. wealthy/opulent/rich/affluent/privileged

5. teacher/instructor/educator/professor/lecturer

D. Replace the underlined words in the sentences below with words arousing more positive feelings:

1. The stench from Jean's kitchen meant dinner was ready and was about to be served.

2. My neighbor was a fat spinster lady.

3. The coach had rigid rules for all his players.

4. His obsession with his yard pleased the city's beautification committee.

5. The slick car salesman made a pitch to the old geezer who walked in the door.

6. Textbook writers admit to having a few bizarre habits.

7. Carol was a mediocre student.

8. His odd clothes made Mary think he was a bum.

9. The High Priest explained his tribe's <u>superstitions</u>.

10. Many of the board members were amazed to see how Algernon <u>dominated</u> the meeting.

SELECTING THE BEST WORDS

In addition to selecting the correct word and appropriate tone, good writers also choose words that firmly implant their ideas in the minds of their readers. The best prose not only makes cogent points but also states these points memorably. To help you select the best words to express your ideas, the following is a list of do's and don't's covering the most common diction (word choice) problems in students' writing today.

Do make your words as precise as possible. Always choose vigorous, active verbs and colorful, specific nouns and modifiers. "The big tree was hit by lightning," for example, is not as informative or interesting as "Lightning splintered the neighbors' thirty-foot oak." *Don't* use words whose meanings are unclear:

Vague Verbs

Unclear   She is *involved* in a lawsuit. [How?]

Clear   She is suing her dentist for filling the wrong tooth.

Unclear   Tom can *relate* to Jennifer. [What's the relationship?]

Clear   Tom understands Jennifer's financial problem.

Unclear   He won't *deal* with his ex-wife. [In what way?]

Clear   He refuses to speak to his ex-wife.

Unclear   Clyde *participated* in an off-Broadway play. [How?]

Clear   Clyde held the cue cards for the actors.

Vague Nouns

Unclear   The burglar took several valuable *things* from our house.* [What items?]

Clear   The burglar took a *color TV, a VCR,* and a *microwave oven* from our house.

---

* One specific piece of advice: banish the word "thing" from your writing. In nine out of ten cases, it is a lazy substitute for some other word. Unless you mean "an inanimate object," replace "thing" with the specific word it stands for.

Unclear   When I have my car serviced, there is always *trouble*. [What kind?]

Clear   When I have my car serviced, *the mechanics always find additional repairs and never have the car ready when it is promised*.

Unclear   When I have *problems*, I always call my friends for advice. [What problems?]

Clear   *If my girlfriend breaks up with me, my roof needs repairing*, or *my dog needs surgery*, I always call my friends for advice.

Unclear   I like to have *fun* while I'm on vacation. [What sort of activities?]

Clear   I like to *eat in fancy restaurants, fly stunt kites*, and *walk along the beach* when I'm on vacation.

Vague Modifiers

Unclear   His *terrible* explanation left me *very* confused. [Why "terrible"? How confused?]

Clear   His disorganized explanation left me too confused to begin the project.

Unclear   The boxer hit the punching bag *really* hard. [How hard?]

Clear   The boxer hit the punching bag so hard it split open.

Unclear   *Casablanca* is a *good* movie *with something for everyone*. [Why "good" and for everyone?]

Clear   *Casablanca* is a witty, sentimental movie that successfully combines an adventure story and a romance.

Do make your word choices as fresh and original as possible. Instead of saying, "My hometown is very quiet," you might say, "My hometown's definition of an orgy is a light burning after midnight." In other words, if you can make your readers admire and remember your prose, you have a better chance of persuading them to accept your ideas.

Conversely, to avoid ho-hum prose, *don't* fill your sentences with clichés and platitudes—overworked phrases that cause your writing to sound lifeless and trite. Although we use clichés in everyday conversation, good writers avoid them in writing because (1) they are often vague or imprecise (just how pretty is "pretty as a picture?"), (2) they are used so frequently that they rob your prose style of personality and uniqueness ("It was raining cats and dogs"—does that phrase help your reader "see" the particular rainstorm you're trying to describe?).

Novice writers often include trite expressions because they do not recognize them as clichés; therefore, below is a partial list (there are literally thousands more) of phrases to avoid. Instead of using a cliché, try substituting an original phrase to describe what you see or feel. Never try to disguise a cliché by putting it in quotation marks—a baboon in dark glasses and a wig is still a baboon.

crack of dawn	needle in a haystack
a crying shame	bed of roses
white as a sheet	cold as ice
depths of despair	hard as nails
dead of night	white as snow
shadow of a doubt	almighty dollar
hear a pin drop	busy as a bee
blessed event	after all is said and done
first and foremost	to make a long story short

It would be impossible, of course, to memorize all the clichés and trite expressions in our language, but do check your prose for recognizable, overworked phrases so that your words will not be predictable and, consequently, dull. If you aren't sure if a phrase is a cliché—but you've heard it used frequently—your prose will probably be stronger if you substitute an original phrase for the suspected one.

Don't use trendy expressions or slang in your essays. Slang generally consists of commonly used words made up by special groups to communicate among themselves. Slang has many origins, from sports to space travel; for example, surfing gave us the expression "to wipe out" (to fail), the military lent "snafu" (from the first letters of "situation normal—all fouled up"), the astronauts provided "A-OK" (all systems working).

Although slang often gives our speech color and vigor, it is unacceptable in most writing assignments for several reasons. First, slang is often part of a private language understood only by members of a particular professional, social, or age group. Second, slang often presents a vague picture or one that changes meanings from person to person or from context to context. More than likely, each person has a unique definition for a particular slang expression, and although these definitions may overlap, they are not precisely the same. Consequently, your reader could interpret your words in one way whereas you mean them in another, a dilemma that might result in total miscommunication. Too often beginning writers rely on vague, popular clichés ("The party was truly awesome") instead of thinking of specific words to express specific ideas. Moreover, slang becomes dated quickly, and almost nothing sounds worse than yesterday's "in" expressions. (Can you seriously imagine calling a friend "Daddy-O" or telling someone you're "feelin' groovy?")

Try to write so that your prose will be as fresh and pleasing ten years from now as today. Don't allow slang to give your writing a flippant tone that detracts from a serious discussion. Putting slang in quotation marks isn't the solution—omit the slang and use precise words instead.

Do select simple, direct words your readers can easily understand. Don't use pompous or pseudosophisticated language in place of plain speech. Wherever possible, avoid *jargon*—that is, words and phrases that are unnecessarily technical, pretentious, or abstract.

Technical jargon—terms specific to one area of study or specialization—should be omitted or clearly defined in essays directed to a general audience because such language is often inaccessible to anyone outside the writer's particular field. By now most of us are familiar with bureaucratese, journalese, and psychobabble, in addition to gobbledygook from business, politics, advertising, and education. If, for example, you worry that "a self-actualized person such as yourself cannot transcend either your hostile environment or your passive-aggressive behavior to make a commitment to a viable lifestyle and meaningful interpersonal relationships," you are indulging in psychological or sociological jargon; if you "review existing mechanisms of consumer input, thruput, and output via the consumer communications channel module," you are speaking business jargon. Although most professions do have their own terms, you should limit your use of specialized language to writing aimed solely at your professional colleagues; always try to avoid technical jargon in prose directed at a general audience.

Today the term "jargon" also refers to prose containing an abundance of abstract, pretentious, multisyllable words. The use of this kind of jargon often betrays a writer's attempt to sound sophisticated and intellectual; actually, it only confuses meaning and delays communication. Here, for instance, is an excerpt of incomprehensible jargon from a college president who obviously prefers twenty-five-cent words to simple, straightforward nickel ones: "We will divert the force of this fiscal stress into leverage energy and pry important budgetary considerations and control out of our fiscal and administrative procedures." Or look at the thirty-eight-word definition of "exit" written by an Occupational Safety and Health Administration bureaucrat: "That portion of a means of egress which is separated from all spaces of the building or structure by construction or equipment as required in this subpart to provide a protected way of travel to the exit discharge." Such language is not only pretentious and confusing but almost comic in its wordiness.

Jargon is so pervasive these days that even some English teachers are succumbing to its use. A group of high school teachers, for instance, was asked to indicate a preference for one of the following sentences:

> His expression of ideas that are in disagreement with those of others will often result in his rejection by them and his isolation from the life around him.

If he expresses ideas that others disagree with, he will often be rejected by them and isolated from the life around him.

Surprisingly, only nineteen percent chose the more direct second sentence. The others saw the wordy, pompous first statement as "mature" and "educated," revealing that some teachers themselves may be both the victims and perpetrators of doublespeak.

To avoid such verbal litter in your own writing, follow these rules:

1. Always select the plainest, most direct words you know.

Jargon   The editor wanted to halt the proliferation of the product because she discovered an error on the page that terminates the volume.

Revised   The editor wanted to stop publishing the book because she found an error on the last page.

2. Replace nominalizations (nouns that are made from verbs and adjectives, usually by adding endings such as *-tion, -ism, -ness,* or *-al*) with simpler verbs and nouns.

Jargon   The departmental head has come to the recognition that the utilization of verbose verbalization renders informational content inaccessible.

Revised   The head of the department recognizes that wordiness confuses meaning.

3. Avoid adding *-ize* or *-wise* to verbs and adverbs.

Jargon   *Weatherwise,* it looked like a good day to *finalize* her report on wind tunnels.

Revised   The day's clear weather would help her finish her report on wind tunnels.

4. Drop out meaningless tack-on words such as "factor," "aspect," and "situation."

Jargon   The convenience factor of the neighborhood grocery store is one aspect of its success.

Revised   The convenience of the neighborhood grocery store contributes to its success.

Remember that good writing is clear and direct, never wordy, cloudy, or ostentatious. (For more hints on developing a clear style, see pp. 128–134.)

Do call things by their proper names. Don't sugarcoat your terms by substituting euphemisms—words that sound nice or pretty applied to subjects some people find distasteful. For example, you've probably heard someone say, "she passed away" instead of "she died," or "he was under the influence of alcohol" instead of "he was drunk." Airline stewards instruct passengers "in the event of a 'water landing.'" "Senior Citizens" (or worse, the "chronologically advantaged") may receive special discounts. Often euphemisms are used to soften names of jobs: "sanitary engineer" for garbage collector, "field representative" for salesperson, "information processor" for typist, "vehicle appearance specialist" for car washer, and so forth.

Some euphemisms are dated and now seem plain silly: in Victorian times, for example, the word "leg" was considered unmentionable in polite company, so people spoke of "piano limbs" and asked for the "first joint" of a chicken. The phrases "white meat" and "dark meat" were euphemisms some people used to avoid asking for a piece of chicken breast or thigh.

Today, euphemisms still abound. Though our generation is perhaps more direct about sex and death, many current euphemisms gloss over unpleasant or unpopular business, military, and political practices. Some stockbrokers, for example, once referred to an October market crash as "a fourth-quarter equity retreat," and General Motors didn't really shut down one of its plants— the closing was merely a "volume-related production schedule adjustment." Similarly, Chrysler didn't lay off workers; it simply "initiated a career alternative enhancement program." Nuclear power plants no longer have dumps; they have "containment facilities" with radiation "migration" rather than leaks and "inventory discrepancies" rather than thefts of plutonium. Simple products are now complex technology: clocks are "analog temporal displacement monitors," toothbrushes are "home plaque removal instruments," sinks are part of the "hygienic hand-washing media," and pencils are "portable handheld communications inscribers." Vinyl is now "vegetarian leather." Newspaper ads in essay form are disguised as "advertorials."

Euphemisms abound in governments and official agencies as those in charge try to hide or disguise the truth from the public. On the national level, a former budget director gave us "revenue enhancements" instead of new taxes, and a former Secretary of Health, Education, and Welfare once tried to camouflage cuts in social services by calling them "advance downward adjustments." Wiretaps have become "technical collection sources" used by "special investigators units" instead of burglars, and plain lying became on one important occasion merely "plausible deniability."

In a large Southwestern city, people were possibly surprised to learn that there were no potholes in the streets—only "pavement deficiencies." In some jails, a difficult prisoner who once might have been sent to solitary confinement is now placed in the "meditation room" or the "adjustment center." In some hospitals, sick people do not die—they experience "negative patient care outcome"; if they died because of a doctor's mistake, they underwent a "diagnostic misadventure of a high magnitude." (Incidentally, those patients who survive no longer receive greeting cards; instead, they open "social expression products.")

Perhaps the military is the all-time winner of the "substitute-a-euphemism" contest. Over the years the military has used a variety of words such as "neutralization," "pacification," and "liberation" to mean the invasion and destruction of other countries and governments. During the Gulf War with Iraq, for example, bombs that fell on civilians were referred to as "incontinent ordnance," with the dead becoming "collateral damage." Earlier, to avoid publicizing a retreat, the military simply called for "backloading our augmentation personnel." On the less serious side, the Navy changes ocean waves into "climatic disturbances at the air-sea interface," and the Army, not to be outdone, transforms the lowly shovel into a "combat emplacement evacuator."

Although many euphemisms seem funny and harmless, too many of them are not because people—often those with power to shape public opinion—have intentionally designed them to obscure the reality of a particular situation or choice of action. Because euphemisms can be used unscrupulously to manipulate people, you should always avoid them in your own prose and be suspicious of them in the writing of others. As Aldous Huxley, author of *Brave New World,* noted, "An education for freedom is, among other things, an education in the proper uses of language."

In addition to weakening the credibility of one's ideas, euphemisms can make prose unnecessarily abstract, wordy, pretentious, or even silly. For a clear and natural prose style, use terms that are straightforward and simple. In other words, call a spade a spade, not "an implement for use in horticultural environments."

Avoid sexist language. Most people will agree that language helps shape thought. Consequently, writers should avoid using any language that promotes demeaning stereotypes. Sexist language, in particular, often subtly suggests that women are less rational, intelligent, or capable of handling certain tasks or jobs. To make your writing as accurate and unbiased as possible, here are some simple suggestions for ways to write nonsexist prose:

1. Try using plural nouns to eliminate the need for the singular pronouns "he" and "she":

Original Today's *doctor* knows *he* must carry extra malpractice insurance.

Revision Today's *doctors* know *they* must carry extra malpractice insurance.

2. Try substituting gender-neutral occupational titles for those ending in "man" or "woman":

Original   The *fireman* and the *saleslady* watched the *policeman* arrest the *mailman.*

Revision   The *firefighter* and the *sales clerk* watched the *police officer* arrest the *mail carrier.*

3. Don't contribute to stereotyping by assigning particular roles solely to men or women:

Original   *Mothers* concerned about the possibility of Reyes syndrome should avoid giving their sick children aspirin.

Revision   *Parents* concerned about the possibility of Reyes syndrome should avoid giving their sick children aspirin.

4. Try substituting words such as "people," "persons," "one," "voters," "workers," "students," and so on, for "man" or "woman":

Original   Any *man* who wants to become a corporation executive before thirty should buy this book.

Revision   *Anyone* who wants to become a corporation executive before thirty should buy this book.

5. Don't use inappropriate diminutives:

Original   In the annual office picture, the photographer asked the men to stand behind the *girls.*

Revision   In the annual office picture, the photographer asked the men to stand behind the *women.*

6. Consider avoiding words that use "man" to describe the actions or characteristics of a group ("man the barricades") or that refer to people in general.

Original   Rebuilding the space shuttle will call for extra money and *man-power,* but such an endeavor will benefit *mankind* in the generations to come.

Revision   Rebuilding the space shuttle will call for extra money and *employees,* but such an endeavor will benefit future *generations.*

7. Be consistent in your treatment of men's and women's names, marital status, professional titles, and physical appearances:

Original   Neither Herman Melville, the inspired novelist, nor Miss Emily Dickinson, the spinster poetess of Amherst, gained fame or fortune in their lifetimes.

Revision   Neither Herman Melville, the novelist, nor Emily Dickinson, the poet, gained fame or fortune in their lifetimes.

Revising your writing to eliminate certain kinds of gender-specific references does not mean turning clear phrases into awkward or confusing jumbles of "he/she told him/her that the car was his/hers." By following the suggestions above, you should be able to make your prose both clear and inoffensive to all members of your audience.

Do enliven your writing with figurative language, when appropriate. Figurative language produces pictures or images in a reader's mind, often by comparing something unfamiliar to something familiar. The two most common figurative devices are the simile and the metaphor. A *simile* is a comparison between two people, places, feelings, or things, using the word "like" or "as"; a more forceful comparison, omitting the word "like" or "as," is a *metaphor*. Below are two examples:

Simile   George eats his meals like a hog.

Metaphor   George is a hog at mealtime.

In both sentences George, whose eating habits are unfamiliar to the reader, is likened to a hog, whose sloppy manners are generally well known. By comparing George to a hog, the writer gives the reader a clear picture of George at the table. Figurative language not only can help you present your ideas in clear, concrete, economical ways but also can make your prose more memorable—especially if the image or picture you present is a fresh, arresting one. Below are some examples of striking images designed to catch the reader's attention and to clarify the writer's point:

- An hour away from him felt like a month in the country.
- The atmosphere of the meeting room was as tense as a World Series game tied up in the ninth inning.
- The woman's earrings were as big as butter plates.
- The angry accusation flew like a spear: once thrown, it could not be retrieved and it cut deeply.
- Out of the night came the convoy of big trucks, modern-day buffalo thundering single-file across the prairie, eyes on fire.
- Behind her broad polished desk, Matilda was a queen bee with a legion of office drones lined up at her door.
- The factory squatted on the bank of the river like a huge black toad.

Figurative language can spice up your prose, but like any spice, it can be misused, thus spoiling your soup. Therefore, don't overuse figurative language; not every point needs a metaphor or simile for clarity or emphasis. Too many images are confusing. Moreover, don't use stale images. (Clichés—discussed on pp. 167–168—are often tired metaphors or similes: snake in the grass, hot as fire, quiet as a mouse, etc.) If you can't catch your readers' attention with a fresh picture, don't bore them with a stale one.

And finally, don't mix images—this too often results in a confusing or unintentionally comic scene. For example, a former mayor of Denver once responded to a question about city fiscal requirements this way: "I think the proper approach is to go through this Garden of Gethsemane that we're in now, give birth to a budget that will come out of it, and then start putting our ducks in order with an appeal and the backup we would need to get something done at the state level." Or consider the defensive attorney who didn't particularly like his client's plea-bargaining deal but nevertheless announced, "Given the attitude of the normal jury on this type of crime, I feel we would be paddling up a stream behind the eight ball." Perhaps a newspaper columnist wins the prize for confusion with this triple-decker: "The Assemblymen also were miffed at their Senate counterparts because they have refused to bite the bullet that now seems to have grown to the size of a millstone to the Assemblymen whose necks are on the line."

Think of figurative language as you might regard a fine cologne on the person sitting next to you in a crowded theater: just enough is engaging; too much is overpowering.

Do vary your word choice so that your prose does not sound wordy, repetitious, or monotonous. Consider the following sentence:

According to child psychologists, depriving a child of artistic stimulation in the earliest stages of childhood can cause the child brain damage.

Reworded, the sentence below eliminates the tiresome, unnecessary repetition of the word "child":

According to child psychologists, depriving infants of artistic stimulation can cause brain damage.

By omitting or changing repeated words, you can add variety and crispness to your prose. Of course, don't ever change your words or sentence structure to achieve variety at the expense of clarity or precision; at all times your goal is making your prose clear to your readers.

Do remember that wordiness is a major problem for all writers, even the professionals. State your thoughts directly and specifically in as few words as necessary to communicate your meaning clearly. In addition to the advice given here on avoiding wordy or vague jargon, euphemisms, and clichés, you might review the sections on simplicity and conciseness in Chapter 6.

> *THE MOST IMPORTANT KEY TO EFFECTIVE WORD CHOICE IS REVISION.*
>
> As you write your first draft, don't fret about selecting the best words to communicate your ideas; in later drafts one of your main tasks will be replacing the inaccurate or imprecise words with better ones (Dorothy Parker, famous for her witty essays, once lamented, "I can't write five words but that I change seven"). All good writers rewrite, so revise your prose to make each word count.

 PRACTICING WHAT YOU'VE LEARNED

A. Underline the vague nouns, verbs, and modifiers in the sentences that follow. Then rewrite each sentence so that it says something clear and specific.

1. The experiment had very bad results.

2. The speaker came up with some odd items.

3. The house was big, old, and ugly.

4. The man was a nice guy with a good personality.

5. I felt that the whole ordeal was quite an experience.

6. The machine we got was missing a few things.

7. The woman was really something special.

8. The classroom material wasn't interesting.

9. The child made a lot of very loud noises.

10. The cost of the unusual meal was amazing.

B. Rewrite the following sentences, eliminating all the clichés, sexist language, and euphemisms you find.

1. When my mother didn't return from the little girl's room, we decided she was as slow as molasses.

2. According to former-President Jimmy Carter, the aborted rescue of the hostages in Iran was an incomplete success.

3. On election day, all of us over the ripe old age of eighteen should exercise our most sacred democratic privilege.

4. After all is said and done, the range technicians and the agricultural producers will still be the new disadvantaged class.

5. Each officer in the Armed Forces realizes that someday he may be called on to use the peacekeepers to depopulate an emerging nation in a lethal intervention.

6. Although he once regarded her as sweet and innocent, he realized then and there that she was really a wolf in sheep's clothing.

7. Any good cook will be green with envy when she tastes your apple pie.

8. The city councilman was stewing in his juices when he learned that his son had been arrested for fooling around with the funds for the fiscal underachievers' home.

9. After the policemen detained the rebels, some of the newspapermen who had been watching the incident experienced unlawful deprivation of life.

10. The automobile company sent a letter warning that "driving with a failed bearing could . . . adversely affect vehicle control" but also praising the new man-made custom upholstery.

C. Rewrite the following sentences, replacing the jargon, slang, and cloudy language with clear, precise words and phrases.

1. To maintain a state of high-level wellness, one should use a wooden interdental stimulator at least once a day and avoid spending time at fake-bake salons.

2. According to the military, one should not attempt a predawn vertical insertion without an aerodynamic personnel decelerator because it could lead to sudden deceleration trauma upon landing.

3. American Airlines' passengers can now arrive and depart planes on customer conveyance mobile lounges.

4. If you are in the armed services, you should avoid receiving a ballistically induced aperture in the subcutaneous environment that might lead to your being terminated with extreme prejudice.

5. The U.S. Embassy in Budapest warned its employees: "It must be assumed that available casual indigenous female companions work for or cooperate with the Hungarian government security establishment."

6. "I thought the evening would be totally awesome but my blind date turned out to be a double-bagger babe with an attitude so I split," said Wayne, who was somewhat of a geek himself.

7. The employee was outplaced for a lack of interpersonal skills and for failing to optimize productivity.

8. My institute of higher learning announced today that its academic evaluation program had been delayed and in all probability indefinitely postponed due to circumstances relating to financial insolvency.

9. All of us could relate to Mabel's essay on the significant educational factors involved in the revenue enhancement tax-base erosion control program.

10. "We were not micromanaging Grenada intelligencewise until about that time frame," said Admiral Wesley L. McDonald, when asked what was happening on the island just prior to the United States' 1983 rescue mission.

 ASSIGNMENT

A. The recipe below pokes fun at bureaucractic jargon. See if you can translate the bureaucratese into clear, simple instructions. Then look at your writing to make certain that you are not guilty of using similar gobbledygook in your own prose.

Input to output, 35 minutes

For government employees and bureaucrats who have problems with standard recipes, here's one that should make the grade—a classic version of the chocolate-chip cookie translated for easy reading.

Total Lead Time: 35 minutes.

Inputs:
  1 cup packed brown sugar
  ½ cup granulated sugar
  ½ cup softened butter
  ½ cup shortening
  2 eggs
  1½ teaspoons vanilla
  2½ cups all-purpose flour
  1 teaspoon baking soda
  ½ teaspoon salt
  12-ounce package semi-sweet chocolate pieces
  1 cup chopped walnuts or pecans

Guidance:

After procurement actions, decontainerize inputs. Perform measurement tasks on a case-by-case basis. In a mixing type bowl, impact heavily on brown sugar, granulated sugar, softened butter and shortening. Coordinate the interface of eggs and vanilla, avoiding an overrun scenario to the best of your skills and abilities.

At this point in time, leverage flour, baking soda and salt into a bowl and aggregate. Equalize with prior mixture and develop intense and continuous liaison among inputs until well-coordinated. Associate key chocolate and nut subsystems and execute stirring operations.

Within this time frame, take action to prepare the heating environment for throughput by manually setting the oven baking unit by hand to a temperature of 375 degrees Fahrenheit (190 Celsius). Drop mixture in an ongoing fashion from a teaspoon implement onto an ungreased cookie sheet at intervals sufficient enough apart to permit total and permanent separation of throughputs to the maximum extent practicable under operating conditions.

Position cookie sheet in a bake situation and survey for 8 to 10 minutes or until cooking action terminates. Initiate coordination of outputs within the cooling rack function. Containerize, wrap in red tape and disseminate to authorized staff personnel on a timely and expeditious basis.

Output:

Six dozen official government chocolate-chip cookie units.

B. Write two of the following paragraphs and then exchange them with those written by a classmate. Translate faulty prose into crisp, clear sentences.

- A paragraph of clichés and vague language arguing the value of having a particular major in college

- A paragraph of jargon and euphemisms by a politician explaining why he or she abused a congressional privilege

- A paragraph of vague language and clichés persuading your banker to advance you funds to invest in a get-rich-quick scheme

- A paragraph of slang, clichés, and sexist language advising your friends on their approaching marriage

- A paragraph of jargon and vague language praising a product you've invented and are trying to market

APPLYING WHAT YOU'VE LEARNED TO YOUR WRITING

If you have drafted a piece of writing and you are satisfied with the development and organization of your ideas, you may want to begin revising your word choice. First, read your draft for accuracy. Circle and then look up any words you suspect may have been used incorrectly. Then focus your attention on your draft's tone, on the "voice" that your words are creating. Have you selected the right words for your purpose and for your audience? Last, change any words that you feel are vague, bland, or confusing; substitute clear prose for jargon, slang, clichés, or euphemisms. Make each word count: allow your words to clarify, not muddy, your meaning.

 CHAPTER 7 SUMMARY

Here is a brief restatement of what you should remember about word choice:

1. Consult a dictionary if you are in doubt about the meaning or usage of a particular word.
2. Choose words that are appropriate for your purpose and audience.
3. Choose words that are clear, specific, and fresh rather than vague, bland, or clichéd.
4. Avoid language that is sexist, trendy, or that tries to hide truth behind jargon or euphemisms.
5. Work for prose that is concise rather than wordy, precise rather than foggy.

CHAPTER

8

The Reading-Writing Connection

It's hardly surprising that good readers often become good writers themselves. Good readers note effectiveness in the writing of others and use these observations to help clarify their own ideas and rhetorical choices about organization, development, and style. Analogies abound in every skill: singers listen to vocalists they admire, tennis players watch championship matches, actors evaluate their colleagues' award-winning performances, medical students observe famous surgeons, all with an eye to improving their own craft. Therefore, to help you become a better writer, your instructor may ask you to study some of the professional essays included in other sections of this text. Learning to read these essays analytically will help when you face your own writing decisions. To sharpen your reading skills, follow the steps suggested in this chapter. After practicing these steps several times, you should discover that the process is becoming a natural part of your reading experience.

HOW CAN READING WELL HELP ME BECOME A BETTER WRITER?

Close reading of the professional essays in this text should help you become a better writer in several ways. First, understanding the opinions expressed in these essays may spark interesting ideas for your own essays; second, discovering the various ways other writers have organized and explained their material should give you some new ideas about selecting your own strategies and supporting evidence. Familiarizing yourself with the effective stylistic devices and diction of other writers may also encourage you to use language in ways you've never tried before.

Perhaps most important, analyzing the prose of others should make you more aware of the writing process itself. Each writer represented in this text faced a series of decisions regarding organization, development, and style, just as you do when you write. By asking questions (Why did the writer begin the essay this way? Why compare this event to that one? Why use a personal example in that paragraph?), you will begin to see how the writer put the essay together—and that knowledge will help you plan and shape your own essay. Questioning the rhetorical choices of other writers should also help you revise your prose because it promotes the habit of asking yourself questions that consider the reader's point of view. (Does the point in paragraph three need more evidence to convince my reader? Will the reader be confused if I don't add a smoother transition from paragraph four to five? Does the conclusion fall flat?)

In other words, the skills you practice as an analytical reader are those you'll use as a good writer.

HOW CAN I BECOME AN ANALYTICAL READER?

Becoming an analytical reader may, at first, demand more time—and involvement—than you are used to devoting to a reading assignment. Analytical reading requires more than allowing your eyes to pass over the words on the page; it's not like channel-surfing through late-night TV shows, stopping here or there as interest strikes. Analytical reading asks you to understand not only the writer's ideas, but also to consider *how* those ideas were presented, *why* the writer presented them that way, and whether that presentation was *effective*. Consequently, to improve your understanding of the reading-writing connection, you should plan on two readings of the sample essay, some note-taking, and some marking of the text (called *annotating*). This procedure may seem challenging at first, but the benefits to you as both reader and writer will be well worth the extra minutes.

Steps to Reading Well:

1. Before you begin the essay itself, note the *publication information* and *biographical data* on the author in the paragraph that precedes each selection in this text. Where and when was the essay originally published? Was it directed toward a particular or a general audience? Was it written in response to some event or controversy? Is the essay still timely or does it seem out of date? Does the author seem qualified to write about this subject? Does the introduction offer any other information that might help you assess the essay's effectiveness?

2. Next, note the *title* of the essay. Does it draw you into the essay? Does it suggest a particular tone or image?

3. You're now ready to begin your first reading of the essay. Some readers like to read through the essay without stopping; others feel comfortable at this point underlining a few main ideas or making checks in the margins. You may also have to make a dictionary stop if words you don't know are appearing in key places in the essay. Many times you can figure out definitions from context—that is, from the words and ideas surrounding them—but don't miss the point of a major part of an essay because of failure to recognize an important word, especially if that word is repeated or emphasized in some way.

When you finish this reading, write a sentence or two summarizing your general impression of the essay's content or ideas. Consider the author's *purpose:* what do you think the writer was trying to do? Overall, how well did he or she succeed? (A typical response might be "argued for tuition hike—unconvincing, boring—too many confusing statistics.")

Now prepare to take another, closer look at the essay. Make some notes in the margins or in another convenient place as you respond to the questions below. Remember that analytical reading is not a horse race: there are no trophies for finishing quickly! Fight the bad habit of galloping at breakneck speed through an essay; slow down to admire the verbal roses the writer has tried to place in your path.

4. Look at the *title* (again) and at the essay's *introductory paragraph(s)*. Did they effectively set up your expectations? Introduce the essay's topic, main idea, tone? (Would some other title or introductory "hook" have worked better?)

5. Locate the writer's main point or *thesis;* this idea may be stated plainly or it may be clearly implied. If you didn't mark this idea on your first reading, do so now by placing a "T" in the margin so you can refer to the thesis easily. (If the thesis is implied, you may wish to mark places that you think most clearly indicate the writer's stance.)

6. As you reread the essay, look for important statements that support or illustrate the thesis. (As you know, these are often found as *topic sentences* occurring near the beginning or end of the body paragraphs.) Try numbering these supporting points or ideas and jotting a key word by each one in the margin.

7. As you identify each important supporting point, ask yourself how the writer develops, explains, or argues that idea. For example, does the writer develop or support the point by providing examples, testimony, or statistics? By comparing or contrasting one thing to another? By showing a cause-effect relationship? Some other method? A combination of methods? A writer may use one or many methods of development, but each major point in an essay should be explained clearly and logically. Make brief marginal notes to indicate how well you think the writer has succeeded ("convincing example," "generalization without support," "questionable authority cited," "good comparison," etc.).

8. Practice using marginal symbols, such as stars (for especially effective statements, descriptions, arguments) or question marks (for passages you think are weak, untrue, or exaggerated). Make up your own set of symbols to help yourself remember your evaluations of the writer's ideas and techniques.

9. Look back over the essay's general *organization*. Did the writer use one of the expository, descriptive, narrative, or argumentative strategies to structure the essay? Some combination of strategies? Was this choice effective? (Always consider alternate ways: would another choice have allowed the writer to make his or her main point more emphatically? Why or why not?)

10. Does the essay flow logically and coherently? If you are having trouble with *unity* or *coherence* in your own essays, try looking closely at the transition devices used in a few paragraphs; bracketing transition words or phrases in a few of the body paragraphs might show you how the writer achieved a sense of unity and flow.

11. Consider the writer's *style* and the essay's *tone*. Does the writer use figurative language in an arresting way? Specialized diction for a particular purpose? Repetition of words or phrases? Any especially effective sentence patterns? Does the writer's tone of voice come through clearly? Is the essay serious, humorous, angry, consoling, happy, sad, sarcastic, or something else? Is the tone appropriate for the purpose and audience of this essay? Writers use a variety of stylistic devices to create prose that is vivid and memorable; you might mark uses of language you would like to experiment with in essays of your own.

Now is also the time to look up meanings of any words you felt you could skip during your first time through the essay, especially if you sense that these words are important to the writer's tone or use of imagery.

Once you have completed these steps and added any other comments that seem important to the analysis of the essay, review your notes. Is this an effective essay? Is the essay's thesis explained or supported adequately with enough logically developed points and evidence? Is the essay organized as effectively as it could have been? What strengths and weaknesses did you find after this analytical reading? Has your original evaluation of this essay changed in any way? If so, write a new assessment, adding any other notes you want to help you remember your evaluation of this essay.

Finally, after this close reading of the essay, did you discover any new ideas, strategies, or techniques you might incorporate into your current piece of writing?

SAMPLE ANNOTATED ESSAY

Here is a professional essay annotated according to the steps listed on the previous pages.

By closely reading and annotating the professional essays in this text, you can improve your own writing in numerous ways. Once you have practiced analyzing essays by other writers, you may discover that you can assess your own drafts' strengths and weaknesses more easily and with more confidence.

Television and the American Family
Marie Winn (1936–   )

Title announces subject

Marie Winn is the author of eleven books for or about children and many articles for such publications as The New York Times Magazine *and* The Village Voice. *Her book,* Children Without Childhood *(1983), illustrates the changes in attitudes toward children since the 1960s. The essay below is an excerpt from her well-known book* The Plug-In Drug: Television, Children and the Family, *published in 1977.*

Author is widely published

General audience of readers concerned about television's relationship to family

Over 20 years ago. Dated?

1   Home and family life have changed in important ways since the advent of television. The peer group has become television-oriented, and much of the time children spend together is occupied by television viewing. Culture generally has been transformed by television. Therefore it is improper to assign to television the subsidiary role its many apologists (too often members of the television industry) insist it plays. Television is not merely one of a number of important influences upon today's child. Through the changes it has made in family life, television emerges as *the* important influence in children's lives today.

Introduction sets up T.V. as most important influence

The Quality of Family Life

2   Television's contribution to family life has been an (equivocal) one. For while it has, indeed, kept the

having more than one outcome

members of the family from dispersing, it has not served to bring them *together*. By its domination of the time families spend together, it destroys the special quality that distinguishes one family from another, a quality that depends to a great extent on what a family *does,* what special rituals, games, recurrent jokes, familiar songs, and shared activities it accumulates.

3   "Like the sorcerer of old," writes Urie Bronfenbrenner,* "the television set casts its magic spell, freezing speech and action, turning the living into silent statues so long as the enchantment lasts. The primary danger of the television screen lies not so much in the behavior it produces—although there is danger there—as in the behavior it prevents: the talks, the games, the family festivities and arguments through which much of the child's learning takes place and through which his character is formed. Turning on the television set can turn off the process that transforms children into people."

4   Yet parents have accepted a television-dominated family life so completely that they cannot see how the medium is involved in whatever problems they might be having. A first-grade teacher reports:

5   "I have one child in the group who's an only child. I wanted to find out more about her family life because this little girl was quite isolated from the group, didn't make friends, so I talked to her mother. Well, they don't have time to do anything in the evening, the mother said. The parents come home after picking up the child at the baby-sitter's. Then the mother fixes dinner while the child watches TV. Then they have dinner and the child goes to bed. I said to this mother, 'Well, couldn't she help you fix dinner? That would be a nice time for the two of you to talk,' and the mother said, 'Oh, but I'd hate to have her miss "Zoom." It's such a good program!'"

6   Even when families make efforts to control television, too often its very presence counter-balances the positive features of family life. A writer and mother of two boys aged 3 and 7 described her family's television schedule in *The New York Times:*

*Urie Bronfenbrenner was a Professor of Human Development at Cornell University.

Margin annotations:
Thesis: T.V.'s domination of family time destroys "specialness"

supporting testimony

1. Acceptance by parents

Testimony shows T.V. replacing mother–daughter conversation

2. Even "controlled" T.V. disrupts family life

We were in the midst of a full-scale War. Every day was a new battle and every program was a major skirmish. We agreed it was a bad scene all around and were ready to enter diplomatic negotiations. . . . In principle we have agreed on 2½ hours of TV a day, "Sesame Street," "Electric Company" (with dinner gobbled up in between) and two half-hour shows between 7 and 8:30 which enables the grown-ups to eat in peace and prevents the two boys from destroying one another. Their pre-bedtime choice is dreadful, because, as Josh recently admitted, "There's nothing much on I really like." So . . . it's "What's My Line" or "To Tell the Truth." . . . Clearly there is a need for first-rate children's shows at this time. . . .

More testimony shows that watching is all-important

7   Consider the "family life" described here: Presumably the (father) comes home from work during the "Sesame Street"—"Electric Company" stint. The children are either watching television, gobbling their dinner, or both. While the parents eat their dinner in peaceful privacy, the children watch another hour of television. Then there is only a half-hour left before bedtime, just enough time for baths, getting pajamas on, brushing teeth, and so on. The children's evening is regimented with an almost military precision. They watch their favorite programs, and when there is "nothing much on I really like," they watch whatever else is on—because *watching* is the important thing. Their mother does not see anything amiss with watching programs just for the sake of watching; she only wishes there were some first-rate children's shows on at those times.

and mother?

?

3. Better shows not the solution

8   Without conjuring up memories of the Victorian era with family games and long, leisurely meals, and large families, the question arises: isn't there a better family life available than this dismal, mechanized arrangement of children watching television for however long is allowed them, evening after evening?

Contrast to pre-television era

9   Of course, families today still do *special* things together at times: go camping in the summer, go to the zoo on a nice Sunday, take various trips and expeditions. But their *ordinary* daily life together is diminished—

4. T.V. diminishes ordinary life

that sitting around at the dinner table, that spontaneous taking up of an activity, those little games invented by children on the spur of the moment when there is nothing else to do, the scribbling, the chatting, and even the quarreling, all the things that form the fabric of a family, that define a childhood. Instead, the children have their regular schedule of television programs and bedtime, and the parents have their peaceful dinner together.

Gives examples of what's missed

10   The author of the article in the *Times* notes that "keeping a family sane means mediating between the needs of both children and adults." But surely the needs of adults are being better met than the needs of the children, who are effectively shunted away and rendered untroublesome, while their parents enjoy a life as undemanding as that of any childless couple. In reality, it is those very demands that young children make upon a family that lead to growth, and it is the way parents accede to those demands that builds the relationships upon which the future of the family depends. If the family does not accumulate its backlog of shared experiences, shared *everyday* experiences that occur and recur and change and develop, then it is not likely to survive as anything other than a caretaking institution.

5. T.V. keeps peace but prevents family growth

exaggerated?

Conclusion: calls for shared experiences & gives warning

First impression: Winn wants us to see that television is destroying the quality of family life. Several persuasive points show how T.V. replaces family activities, talking.

Notes: Causal analysis essay, developed with good use of examples and testimony to support points. Examples dated but essay still clear.

Final evaluation: Winn is convincing. It's not just violent T.V. that hurts little kids—it's the time spent watching instead of interacting as a family. I agree—when I think of good times with my family, we were doing things together, not watching T.V. (Possible essay topic: the importance of last summer's family camping trip)

PRACTICING WHAT YOU'VE LEARNED

Select one of the professional essays reprinted in this text and annotate it according to the steps described in this chapter. Note at least one strength in this essay that you would like to incorporate into your own writing.

 ASSIGNMENT

Select one of the professional essays in this text to read analytically and annotate. Then choose one of the following:

1. Write a short essay that praises the effectiveness or criticizes the ineffectiveness of the essay you read. Explain two or three major strengths or weaknesses by showing how the writer's rhetorical choices affected the reader.

2. Write a short essay in response to the essay's thesis, in which you argue for or against the writer's position.

 CHAPTER 8 SUMMARY

1. Reading and analyzing essays can improve your writing skills.
2. Learning to recognize and evaluate the strategies and stylistic techniques of other writers may help you plan and shape your own essays.
3. Assessing the effectiveness of other essays can help you become more confident about revising your own essay.
4. Reading analytically takes time and practice, but is well worth the extra effort.

THE BASICS OF THE SHORT ESSAY: PART ONE SUMMARY

Here are ten suggestions to keep in mind while you are working on the rough drafts of your essay:

1. Be confident that you have something important and interesting to say.

2. Identify your particular audience and become determined to communicate effectively with them.

3. Use prewriting techniques to help you focus on one main idea that will become the thesis of your essay.

4. Organize your essay's points logically, in a persuasive and coherent order.

5. Develop each of your ideas with enough evidence and specific details.

6. Cut out any irrelevant material that disrupts the smooth flow from idea to idea.

7. Compose sentences that are clear, concise, and informative; choose accurate, vivid words.

8. Improve your writing by learning to read analytically.

9. Revise your prose.

10. Revise your prose.

PART
Two

PURPOSES, MODES, AND STRATEGIES

Communication may be divided into four types (or "modes" as they are often called): exposition, argumentation, description, and narration. Although each one will be explained in greater detail in this section of the text, the four modes may be defined briefly as follows:

Exposition
the writer intends to explain or inform

Argumentation
the writer intends to convince or persuade

Description
the writer intends to create in words a picture of a person, place, object, or feeling

Narration
the writer intends to tell a story or recount an event.

Although we commonly refer to exposition, argumentation, description, and narration as the basic types of prose, in reality it is difficult to find any one mode in a pure form. In fact, almost all essays are combinations of two or more modes; it would be virtually impossible, for instance, to write a story—narration—without including description or to argue without also giving some information. Nevertheless, by determining a writer's *main* purpose, we can usually identify an essay or prose piece as primarily exposition, argumentation, description, or narration. In other words, an article may include a brief description of a new mousetrap, but if the writer's main intention is to explain how the trap works, then we may designate the essay as exposition. In most cases, the primary mode of any essay will be readily apparent to the reader.

In Part Two of this text, you will study each of the four modes in detail and learn some of the patterns of development, called *strategies,* that will enable you to write the kind of prose most frequently demanded in college and professional work. Mastering the most common prose patterns in their simplest forms now will help you successfully assess and organize any kind of complex writing assignment you may face in the future. Chapter 13 concludes this section by discussing the more complex essay, developed through use of multiple strategies.

CHAPTER

9

Exposition

Exposition refers to prose whose primary purpose is giving information. Some familiar examples of expository writing include encyclopedias, dictionaries, news magazines, and textbooks. In addition, much of your own college work may be classified as exposition: book reports, political analyses, laboratory and business reports, and most essay exams, to cite only a few of the possibilities.

But while all expository writing does present information, a good expository essay is more than a collection of facts, figures, and details. First, each essay should contain a thesis statement announcing the writer's purpose and position. Then the essay should be organized so that the body paragraphs explain and support that thesis. In an expository essay the writer says, in effect, here are the facts *as I see them;* therefore, the writer's main purpose is not only to inform the readers but also to convince them that this essay explains the subject matter in the clearest, most truthful way.

THE STRATEGIES OF EXPOSITION

There are a variety of ways to organize an expository essay, depending on your purpose. The most common strategies, or patterns, of organization include development by *example, process analysis, comparison and contrast, definition, classification,* and *causal analysis.* However, an essay is rarely developed completely by a single strategy (an essay developed by comparison and contrast, for instance, may also contain examples; a classification essay may contain definitions, and so forth); therefore, as in the case of the four modes, we identify the kind of expository essay by its *primary* strategy of development. To help you understand every expository strategy thoroughly before going on to the next, each is presented here separately. Each discussion section follows a similar pattern, which includes explanation of the strategy, advice on developing your essay, a list of essay topics, a topic proposal sheet, a revision checklist, two sample essays (one written by a student and the other by a professional writer), and a progress report.

STRATEGY ONE: DEVELOPMENT BY EXAMPLE

Perhaps you've heard a friend complain lately about a roommate. "Tina is an inconsiderate boor, impossible to live with," she cries. Your natural response might be to question your friend's rather broad accusation: "What makes her so terrible? What does she do that's so bad?" Your friend might then respond with specific examples of Tina's insensitivity: she never washes her dishes, she ties up the telephone for hours, and she plays her radio until three every morning. By citing several examples, your friend clarifies and supports her general criticism of Tina, thus persuading you to accept her point of view.

Examples in an essay work precisely the same way as in the hypothetical story above: they *support, clarify, interest,* and *persuade.*

In your writing assignments, you might want to assert that dorm food is cruel and inhuman punishment, that recycling is a profitable hobby, or that the cost of housing is rising dramatically. But without some carefully chosen examples to show the truth of your statements, these remain unsupported generalities or mere opinions. Your task, then, is to provide enough specific examples to support your general statements, to make them both clear and convincing. Below is a statement offering the reader only hazy generalities:

> Our locally supported TV channel presents a variety of excellent educational shows. The shows are informative on lots of different subjects for both children and adults. The information they offer makes channel 19 well worth the public funds that support it.

Rewritten below, the same paragraph explains its point clearly through the use of specific examples:

> Our locally supported TV channel presents a variety of excellent educational shows. For example, young children can learn their alphabet and

numbers from *Sesame Street;* imaginative older children can be encouraged to create by watching *Kids' Writes,* a show on which four hosts read and act out stories written and sent in by youngsters from eight to fourteen. Adults may enjoy learning about antiques and collectibles from a program called *The Collector;* each week the show features an in-depth look at buying, selling, trading, and displaying collectible items, from Depression glass to teddy bears to Shaker furniture. Those folks wishing to become handy around the home can use information on repairs from plumbing to wiring on *This Old House,* while the nonmusical can learn the difference between scat singing and arias on such programs as *Jazz!* and *Opera Today.* And the money-minded can profit from the tips dropped by stockbrokers who appear on *Wall Street Week.* The information offered makes these and other educational shows on channel 19 well worth the public funds that support the station.

Although the preceding example is based on real shows, you may also use personal experiences, hypothetical situations, anecdotes, research material, facts, testimony, or any combination thereof, to explain or support the points in your essays.

In some cases you may find that a series of short examples fits your purpose, illustrating clearly the idea you are presenting to your reader:

In the earlier years of Hollywood, actors aspiring to become movie stars often adopted new names that they believed sounded more attractive to the public. Frances Ethel Gumm, for instance, decided to change her name to Judy Garland long before she flew over any rainbows, and Alexander Archibald Leach became Cary Grant on his way from England to America. Alexandra Cymboliak and Merle Johnson, Jr., might not have set teenage hearts throbbing in the early 1960s, but Sandra Dee and Troy Donahue certainly did. And while some names were changed to achieve a smoother flow (Frederic Austerlitz to Fred Astaire, for example), some may have also been changed to ensure a good fit on movie theater marquees as well as a place in their audience's memory: the little Turner girl, Julia Jean Mildred Frances, for instance, became just Lana.

Or you may decide that two or three examples, explained in some detail, provide the best support for your topic rather than a series of short examples. In the paragraph that follows, the writer chose to develop two examples to illustrate her point about her unusual dog:

Our family dog Sparky always let us know when he wasn't getting enough attention. For instance, if he thought we were away from home too much, he'd perform his record trick. While we were out, Sparky would push an album out of the record rack and then tap the album cover in just such a way that the record would roll out. Then he would chomp the record! We'd return to find our favorite LP (somehow, always our current favorite) chewed into tiny bits of black vinyl scattered about the room. Another popular Sparky trick was the cat-sit. If the family was peacefully settled on the porch, not playing with him, Sparky would grab the family cat by the ear and drag her over to the steps, whereupon he would sit on top of her until someone paid attention to him. He never hurt the cat; he simply sat on her as one would sit on a fine cushion, with her head poking out under his tail, and a silly grin on his face that said, "See, if you'd play with me, I wouldn't get into such mischief."

You may also find that in some cases, one long, detailed example (called an *extended example*) is more useful than several shorter ones. If you were writing a paragraph urging the traffic department to install a stop sign at a particularly dangerous corner, you probably should cite numerous examples of accidents there. On the other hand, if you were praising a certain kind of local architecture, you might select one representative house and discuss it in detail. In the paragraph below, for instance, the writer might have supported his main point by citing a number of cases in which lives had been saved by seat belts; he chose instead to offer one detailed example, in the form of a personal experience:

Wearing seat belts can protect people from injury, even in serious accidents. I know because seat belts saved me and my Dad two years ago when we were driving to see my grandparents who live in California. Because of the distance, we had to travel late on a rainy, foggy Saturday night. My Dad was driving, but what he didn't know was that there was a car a short way behind us driven by a drunk who was following our car's tail lights in order to keep himself on the road. About midnight, my Dad decided to check the map to make sure we were headed in the right direction, so he signaled, pulled over to the shoulder, and began to come to a stop. Unfortunately for us, the drunk didn't see the signal and moved his car over to the shoulder thinking that the main road must have curved slightly since our car had gone that way. As Dad slowed our car, the other car plowed into us at a speed estimated later by the police as over eighty miles an hour. The car hit us like Babe Ruth's bat hitting a slow pitch; the force of the speeding car slammed us hard into the dashboard, but not through the windshield and out onto the rocky shoulder, because, lucky for us, we were wearing our seat belts. The highway patrolmen, who arrived quickly on the scene, testified later at the other driver's trial that without question my Dad and I would have been seriously injured, if not killed, had it not been for our seat belts restraining us in the front seat.

The story of the accident illustrates the writer's claim that seat belts can save lives; without such an example, the writer's statement would be only an unsupported generalization.

In addition to making general statements specific and thus more convincing, good examples can explain and clarify unfamiliar, abstract, or difficult concepts for the reader. For instance, Newton's law of gravity might be more easily understood once it is explained through the simple, familiar example of an apple falling from a tree.

Moreover, clear examples can add to your prose vivid details that hold the reader's attention while you explain your points. A general statement decrying animal abuse, for instance, may be more effective accompanied by several examples detailing the brutal treatment of one particular laboratory's research animals.

The use of good examples is not, however, limited only to essays primarily developed by example. In actuality, you will probably use examples in every essay you write. You couldn't, for instance, write an essay classifying kinds of popular movies without including examples to help identify your categories. Similarly, you couldn't write essays defining the characteristics of a good teacher or a comparison between two kinds of cars without ample use of specific examples. To illustrate the importance of examples in all patterns of essay development, here are two excerpts from student essays reprinted in other parts of this text. The first excerpt comes from an essay classifying the Native American eras at Mesa Verde National Park (pp. 263–265). In his discussion of a particular time period, the writer uses a dwelling called Balcony House as an example to illustrate his claims about the Native Americans' skills in building construction.

> The third period lasted until A.D. 1300 and saw the innovation of pueblos, or groups of dwellings, instead of single-family units. Nearly eight hundred dwellings show the large number of people who inhabited the complex, tunneled houses, shops, storage rooms, courtyards, and community centers whose masonry walls, often elaborately decorated, were three and four stories high. At the spacious Balcony House pueblo, for example, an adobe court lies beneath another vaulted roof; on three sides stand two-story houses with balconies that lead from one room to the next. In back of the court is a spring, and along the front side is a low wall that kept the children from falling down the seven-hundred-foot cliff to the canyon floor below. Balcony House also contains two *kivas,* circular subterranean ceremonial chambers that show the importance of fellowship and religion to the people of this era.

Another student uses a personal example to help her support a point in her essay that contrasts a local co-op to a big chain grocery store (pp. 232–235). By using her friend's experience as an example, the writer shows the reader how a co-op may assist local producers in the community:

> Direct selling offers two advantages for producers: they get a better price for their wares than by selling them through a middleman, and at the same time they establish an independent reputation for their business, which can be immensely valuable to their success later on. In Fort Collins, for example, Luna tofu (bean curd) stands out as an excellent illustration of this kind of mutual support. Several years ago my friend Carol Jones began making tofu in small batches to sell to the co-op as a way to earn a part-time income as well as to contribute to the co-op. Her enterprise has now grown so well that last year her husband quit his job to go into business with her full time. She currently sells to distributors and independent stores from here to Denver; even Lane Grocer, who earlier would not consider selling her tofu even on a trial basis, is now thinking about changing its policy.

Learning to support, explain, or clarify your assertions by clear, thoughtful examples will help you develop virtually every piece of writing you are assigned, both in school and on the job. Development by example is the most widely used of all the expository strategies and by far the most important.

Developing Your Essay

An essay developed by example is one of the easiest to organize. In most cases, your first paragraph will present your thesis; each body paragraph will contain a topic sentence and as many effectively arranged examples as necessary to explain or support each major point; your last paragraph will conclude your essay in some appropriate way. Although the general organization is fairly simple, you should double-check the examples in your rough draft by asking these questions:

Are all my examples relevant? Each specific example should support, clarify, or explain the general statement it illustrates; each example should provide readers with additional insight into the subject under discussion. Keep the purpose of your paragraphs in mind: don't wander off into an analysis of the causes of crime if you are only supposed to show examples of it in your neighborhood. Keep your audience in mind, too: which examples will provide the kinds of information that your particular readers need to understand your point?

Are my examples well chosen? To persuade your readers to accept your opinion, you should select those examples that are the strongest and most convincing. Let's say you were writing a research paper exposing a government agency's wastefulness. To illustrate your claim, you would pick out those cases that most obviously show gross or ridiculous expenditures rather than asking your readers to consider some unnecessary but minor expenses. And you would try to select cases that represent recent or current examples of wastefulness rather than discussing expenditures too dated to be persuasive. In other words, when you have a number of examples to choose from, evaluate them and then select the best ones to support your point.

Are there enough examples to make each point clear and persuasive? Put yourself in your reader's place: would you be convinced with three brief examples? Five? One extended example? Two? Use your own judgment, but be careful to support or explain your major points adequately. It's better to risk overexplaining than to leave your reader confused or unconvinced.

Problems to Avoid

The most common weakness in essays developed by example is a lack of specific detail. Too often novice writers present a sufficient number of relevant, well-chosen examples, but the illustrations themselves are too general, vague, or brief to be helpful. Examples should be clear, specific, and adequately detailed so that the reader receives the full persuasive impact of each one. For instance, in an essay claiming that college football has become too violent, don't merely say, "Too many players got hurt last year." Such a statement only hints; it lacks enough development to be fully effective. Go into more detail by giving actual examples of jammed fingers, wrenched backs, fractured legs, crushed kneecaps, and broken dreams. Present these examples in specific, vivid language; once your readers begin to "see" that field covered with blood and bruised bodies, you'll have less trouble convincing them that your point of view is accurate.

The second biggest problem in example essays is the lack of coherence. The reader should never sense an interruption in the flow of thought from one example to the next in paragraphs containing more than one example. Each body paragraph of this kind should be more than a topic sentence and a choppy list of examples. You should first arrange the examples in an order that best explains the major point presented by your topic sentence; then carefully check to make sure each example is smoothly connected in thought to the statements preceding and following it. You can avoid a listing effect by using transition devices where necessary to ensure easy movement from example to example and from point to point. A few common transition words often found in essays of example include "for instance," "for example," "to illustrate," "another," and "in addition." (For a list of other transition words and additional help on writing coherent paragraphs, review pp. 76–82 and pp. 86–87.)

ESSAY TOPICS

Try using the topics below to help you discover, narrow, and focus an essay topic of your own design. For additional ideas, turn to the "Suggestions for Writing" section following the professional essay on page 207.

1. Heroes today are merely media creations rather than truly admirable people.

2. First impressions are often the best/worst means of judging people.

3. Failure is a better teacher than success.

4. My fear of flying (or some other fear) prevents me from living a normal life.

5. The willingness to undertake adventure is a necessary part of a happy life.

6. Doing good deeds can backfire.

7. Complaining can produce unforeseen results.

8. Travel can be the best medicine.

9. Consumers are often at the mercy of unscrupulous companies.

10. Visits to the doctor/dentist/veterinarian can prove more traumatic than the illness.

11. Failure to keep my mouth shut (or some other bad habit) leads me into trouble.

12. Participation in (a particular sport, club, hobby, event) teaches valuable lessons.

13. Modern technology can produce more inconvenience than convenience.

14. Job hunting today is a difficult process.

15. Moving frequently has its advantages (or disadvantages).

16. Movies today are unnecessarily violent.

17. Many required courses are/are not relevant to a student's education.

18. High schools do/do not adequately prepare students for college.

19. The most common political attitude among students today is "I'm apathetic, and I don't care."

20. One important event can change the course of a life.

A Topic Proposal for Your Essay

Selecting the right subject matter is important to every writer. To help you clarify your ideas and strengthen your commitment to your topic, here is a proposal sheet that asks you to describe some of your preliminary ideas about your subject before you begin drafting. Although as you draft your ideas may change (they will almost certainly become more refined), thinking through your choice of topic now may help you avoid several false starts.

1. In a few words, note the subject of your essay as you have narrowed and focused it for this assignment. Write a rough statement of your opinion or attitude toward this topic.

2. Why are you interested in this topic? Do you have a personal or professional connection to the subject? State at least one reason for your choice of topic.

3. Is this a significant topic of interest to others? Why? Who specifically might find it interesting, informative, or entertaining?

4. Describe in one or two sentences the primary effect you would like to have on your audience. After they read your essay, what do you want your audience to think, feel, or do? (In other words, what is your purpose in writing this essay?)

5. Writers use examples to explain and clarify their ideas. Briefly list two or three examples you might develop in your essay to support discussion of your chosen topic.

6. What difficulties, if any, might this topic present during your drafting? For example, do you know enough about this topic to illustrate it with specific rather than vague examples? Might the topic still be too broad or unfocused for this assignment? Revise your topic now or make notes for an appropriate plan of action to resolve any difficulties you foresee.

S A M P L E   S T U D E N T   E S S A Y

Study the use of specific examples in the brief student essay that follows. If the writer were to expand this essay, where might he add more examples or details?

RIVER RAFTING TEACHES WORTHWHILE LESSONS

Introduction: A description

Sun-warmed water slaps you in the face, the blazing sun beats down on your shoulders, and canyon walls speed by as you race down rolling waves of water. No experience can equal that of river rafting. In addition to being fun and exciting, rafting has

Thesis

many educational advantages as well, especially for those involved in school-sponsored rafting trips. River trips teach students how to prevent some of the environmental destruction

Essay map

that concerns the park officials, and, in addition, river trips teach students to work together in a way few other experiences can.

Topic sentence one: Trip teaches respect for environment

The most important lesson a rafting trip teaches students is respect for the environment. When students are exposed to the outdoors, they can better learn to appreciate its beauty and feel the need to preserve it. For example, I went on a rafting trip three summers ago with the biology department at my high school. Our trip lasted seven days down the Green River through the isolated Desolation Canyon in Utah. After the first day of rafting, I found myself surrounded by steep canyon walls and saw virtually no evidence of human life. The starkly beautiful, unspoiled atmosphere soon became a major influence on us during the trip.

**Two brief examples illustrating respect:
1. Cleaning up trash
2. Foregoing suds in river**

By the second day I saw classmates, whom I had previously seen fill an entire room with candy wrappers and empty soda cans, voluntarily inspecting our campsite for trash. And when twenty-four high school students sacrifice washing their hair for the sake of a sudless and thus healthier river, some new, better attitudes about the environment have definitely been established.

In addition to the respect for nature a rafting trip encourages, it also teaches the importance of group cooperation. Since school-associated trips put students in command of the raft, the students find that in order to stay in control each member must be reliable, be able to do his or her own part, and be alert to the actions of others. These skills are quickly learned when students see the consequences of noncooperation. Usually this occurs the first day, when the left side of the raft paddles in one direction, and the right the other way, and half the crew ends up seasick from going in circles. An even better illustration is another experience I had on my river trip. Because an upcoming rapid was usually not too rough, our instructor said a few of us could jump out and swim in it. Instead of deciding as a group who should go, though, five eager swimmers bailed out. This left me, an angry instructor, and another student to steer the raft. As it turned out, the rapid was fairly rough, and we soon found ourselves heading straight for a huge hole (a hole is formed from swirling funnel-like currents and can pull a raft under). The combined effort of the three of us was not enough to get the raft completely clear of the hole, and the raft tipped up vertically on its side, spilling us into the river. Luckily, no one was hurt, and the raft did not topple over, but the near loss of our food rations for the next five days, not to mention the raft itself, was enough to make us all more willing to work as a group in the future.

Despite the obvious benefits rafting offers, the number of river permits issued to school groups continues to decline because of financial cutbacks. It is a shame that those in charge of these cutbacks do not realize that in addition to having fun and learning about themselves, students are learning valuable lessons through rafting trips—lessons that may help preserve the rivers for future rafters.

Topic sentence two: Trip teaches cooperation

Two examples of the need for cooperation:

1. Difficulties in paddling raft

2. A near accident

Conclusion: Importance of lessons

P R O F E S S I O N A L   E S S A Y *

So What's So Bad about Being So-So?

Lisa Wilson Strick

Lisa Wilson Strick is a freelance writer who publishes in a variety of women's maga-zines, frequently on the subjects of family and education. This essay first appeared in Woman's Day *in 1984.*

1   The other afternoon I was playing the piano when my seven-year-old walked in. He stopped and listened awhile, then said: "Gee, Mom, you don't play that thing very well, do you?"

2   No, I don't. I am a piano lesson dropout. The fine points of fingering totally escape me. I play everything at half-speed, with many errant notes. My performance would make any serious music student wince, but I don't care. I've enjoyed playing the piano badly for years.

3   I also enjoy singing badly and drawing badly. (I used to enjoy sewing badly, but I've been doing that so long that I finally got pretty good at it.) I'm not ashamed of my incompetence in these areas. I do one or two other things well and that should be enough for anybody. But it gets bor-ing doing the same things over and over. Every now and then it's fun to try something new.

4   Unfortunately, doing things badly has gone out of style. It used to be a mark of class if a lady or a gentleman sang a little, painted a little, played the violin a little. You didn't have to be *good* at it; the point was to be fortunate enough to have the leisure time for such pursuits. But in today's competitive world we have to be "experts"—even in our hobbies. You can't tone up your body by pulling on your sneakers and slogging around the block a couple of times anymore. Why? Because you'll be laughed off the street by the "serious" runners—the ones who log twenty-plus miles a week in their headbands, sixty-dollar running suits and fancy shoes. The shoes are really a big deal. If you say you're think-ing about taking up almost any sport, the first thing the aficionados will ask is what you plan to do about shoes. Leather or canvas? What type of soles? Which brand? This is not the time to mention that the gym shoes you wore in high school are still in pretty good shape. As far as sports enthusiasts are concerned, if you don't have the latest shoes you are hopelessly committed to mediocrity.

5   The runners aren't nearly so snobbish as the dance freaks, however. In case you didn't know, "going dancing" no longer means putting on a pretty dress and doing a few turns around the ballroom with your favorite man on Saturday night. "Dancing" means squeezing into tights

* To help you read this essay analytically, review pages 182–185.

and a leotard and leg warmers, then sweating through six hours of warm-ups and five hours of ballet and four hours of jazz classes. Every week. Never tell anyone that you "like to dance" unless this is the sort of activity you enjoy. (At least the costume isn't so costly, as dancers seem to be cultivating a riches-to-rags look lately.)

6 We used to do these things for fun or simply to relax. Now the competition you face in your hobbies is likely to be worse than anything you run into on the job. "Oh, you've taken up knitting," a friend recently said to me. "Let me show you the adorable cable-knit, popcorn-stitched cardigan with twelve tiny reindeer prancing across the yoke that I made for my daughter. I dyed the yarn myself." Now why did she have to go and do that? I was getting a kick out of watching my yellow stockinette muffler grow a couple of inches a week up till then. And all I wanted was something to keep my hands busy while I watched television anyway.

7 Have you noticed what this is doing to our children? "We don't want that dodo on our soccer team," I overheard a ten-year-old sneer the other day. "He doesn't know a goal kick from a head shot." As it happens, the boy was talking about my son, who did not—like some of his friends—start soccer instruction at age three (along with preschool diving, creative writing and Suzuki clarinet). I'm sorry, Son, I guess I blew it. In *my* day when we played softball on the corner lot, we expected to give a little instruction to the younger kids who didn't know how. It didn't matter if they were terrible; we weren't out to slaughter the other team. Sometimes we didn't even keep score. To us, sports were just a way of having a *good time.* Of course we didn't have some of the nifty things kids have today—such as matching uniforms and professional coaches. All we had was a bunch of kids of various ages who enjoyed each other's company.

8 I don't think kids have as much fun as they used to. Competition keeps getting in the way. The daughter of a neighbor is a nervous wreck worrying about getting into the *best* gymnastics school. "I was a late starter," she told me, "and I only get to practice five or six hours a week, so my technique may not be up to their standards." The child is nine. She doesn't want to *be* a gymnast when she grows up; she wants to be a nurse. I asked what she likes to do for fun in her free time. She seemed to think it was an odd question. "Well, I don't actually *have* a lot of free time," she said. "I mean homework and gymnastics and flute lessons kind of eat it all up. I have flute lessons three times a week now, so I have a good shot at getting into the all-state orchestra."

9 Ambition, drive and the desire to excel are all admirable within limits, but I don't know where the limits are anymore. I know a woman who has always wanted to learn a foreign language. For years she has complained that she hasn't the time to study one. I've pointed out that an evening course in French or Italian would take only a couple of hours a week, but she keeps putting it off. I suspect that what she hasn't got the

time for is to become completely fluent within the year—and that any lesser level of accomplishment would embarrass her. Instead she spends her evenings watching reruns on television and tidying up her closets—occupations at which no particular expertise is expected.

10   I know others who are avoiding activities they might enjoy because they lack the time or the energy to tackle them "seriously." It strikes me as so silly. We are talking about *recreation*. I have nothing against self-improvement. But when I hear a teenager muttering "practice makes perfect" as he grimly makes his four-hundred-and-twenty-seventh try at hooking the basketball into the net left-handed, I wonder if some of us aren't improving ourselves right into the loony bin.

11   I think it's time we put a stop to all this. For sanity's sake, each of us should vow to take up something new this week—and to make sure we never master it completely. Sing along with grand opera. Make peculiar-looking objects out of clay. I can tell you from experience that fallen souf-flés still taste pretty good. The point is to enjoy being a beginner again; to rediscover the joy of creative fooling around. If you find it difficult, ask any two-year-old to teach you. Two-year-olds have a gift for tackling the impossible with zest; repeated failure hardly discourages them at all.

12   As for me, I'm getting a little out of shape so I'm looking into tennis. A lot of people I know enjoy it, and it doesn't look too hard. Given a couple of lessons I should be stumbling gracelessly around the court and playing badly in no time at all.

Questions on Content, Structure, and Style

1. Why does Strick begin her essay with the comment from her son and the list of activities she does badly?

2. What is Strick's thesis? Is it specifically stated or clearly implied?

3. What examples does Strick offer to illustrate her belief that we no longer take up hobbies for fun? Are there enough well-chosen examples to make her position clear?

4. What is the effect, according to Strick, of too much competition on kids? In what ways does she show this effect?

5. Does Strick use enough details in her examples to make them clear, vivid, and persuasive? Point out some of her details to support your answer.

6. What does Strick gain by using dialogue in some of her examples?

7. What solution to the problem does Strick offer? How does she clarify her suggestion?

8. Characterize the tone of Strick's essay. Is it appropriate for her purpose and for her intended audience? Why or why not?

9. Evaluate Strick's conclusion. Does it effectively wrap up the essay?

10. Do you agree or disagree with Strick? What examples could you offer to support your position?

Suggestions for Writing

Try using Lisa Strick's essay "So What's So Bad about Being So-So?" as a stepping stone, moving from one or more of her ideas to a subject for your own essay. For instance, consider writing an essay that illustrates or challenges Strick's view that competition is taking all the fun out of recreation. Perhaps Strick's advice urging her readers to undertake new activities might lead you to an essay about your best or worst "beginner" experience. Look through Strick's essay once more to find other springboard ideas for *your* writing.

Vocabulary*

errant (2)	mediocrity (4)	fluent (9)
incompetence (3)	excel (9)	zest (11)
aficionados (4)		

 A REVISION WORKSHEET

As you write your rough drafts, consult Chapter 5 for guidance through the revision process. In addition, here are a few questions to ask yourself as you revise your example essay:

1. Is the essay's thesis clear to the reader?

2. Do the topic sentences support the thesis?

3. Do the examples in each paragraph effectively illustrate the claim of the topic sentence?

4. Are there enough well-chosen examples to make each point clear and convincing?

5. Is each example developed in enough specific detail? Where could more details be added?

6. If a paragraph contains multiple examples, are they arranged in the most effective order, with a smooth transition from one to another?

* Numbers in parentheses following vocabulary terms refer to paragraphs in the essay.

7. If a paragraph contains an extended example, does the discussion flow logically and with coherence?

After you've revised your essay extensively, you might exchange rough drafts with a classmate and answer these questions for each other, making specific suggestions for improvement wherever appropriate. (For advice on productive participation in classroom workshops, see pp. 117–119.)

Reviewing Your Progress

After you have completed your essay developed by examples, take a moment to measure your progress as a writer by responding to the following questions. Such analysis will help you recognize growth in your writing skills and may enable you to identify areas that are still problematic.

1. What is the best feature of your essay? Why?

2. After considering your essay's supporting examples, which one do you think most effectively explains or illustrates your ideas? Why?

3. What part of your essay gave you the most trouble? How did you overcome the problem?

4. If you had more time to work on this essay, what would receive additional attention? Why?

5. What did you learn about your topic from writing this essay? About yourself as a writer?

STRATEGY TWO: DEVELOPMENT BY PROCESS ANALYSIS

Process analysis identifies and explains what steps must be taken to complete an operation or procedure. There are two kinds of process analysis essays: directional and informative.

A *directional process* tells the reader how to do or make something; in simple words, it gives directions. You are more familiar with directional process than you might think; when you open a telephone book, for example, you see the pages in the front explaining how to make a long-distance call. When you tell friends how to find your house, you're asking them to follow a directional process. The most widely read books in American libraries fall into the how-to-do-it (or how-to-fix-it) category: how to wire a house, how to repair a car, how to play winning poker, how to become a millionaire overnight, and so forth. And almost every home contains at least one cookbook full of recipes providing step-by-step directions for preparing various dishes. (Even Part One of this text is, in detailed fashion, a directional process telling how to write a short essay, beginning with the selection of a topic and concluding with advice on revision.)

An *informative process* tells the reader how something is or was made or done or how something works. Informative process differs from directional process in that it is not designed primarily to tell people how to do it; instead, it describes the steps by which someone other than the reader does or makes something (or how something was made or done in the past). For example, an informative process essay might describe how a television show is produced, how scientists discovered polio vaccine, how the Huns sacked Rome, or how an engine propels a jet. In other words, this type of essay gives information on processes that are not intended to be—or cannot be—duplicated by the individual reader.

Developing Your Essay

Of all the expository essays, students usually agree that the process paper is the easiest to organize, mainly because it is presented in simple, chronological steps. To prepare a well-written process essay, however, you should remember the following advice:

Select an appropriate subject. First, make sure you know your subject thoroughly; one fuzzy step could wreck your entire process. Second, choose a process that is simple and short enough to describe in detail. In a 500- to 800-word essay, for instance, it's better to describe how to build a ship in a bottle than how to construct a life-size replica of Noah's Ark. On the other hand, don't choose a process so simple-minded, mundane, or mechanical that it insults your readers' intelligence. (Some years ago at a major state university it was popular to assign a process essay on "How to Sharpen a Pencil"; with the assignment of such stirring, creative topics, it's a wonder that English department produced any majors at all that year.)

Describe any necessary equipment and define special terms. In some process essays, you will need to indicate what equipment, ingredients, or tools are required. Such information is often provided in a paragraph following the thesis, before the process itself is described; in other cases, the explanation of proper equipment is presented as the need arises in each step of the process. As the writer, you must decide which method is best for your subject. The same is true for any terms that need defining. Don't lose your reader by using terms only you, the specialist, can comprehend. Always remember that you're trying to tell people about a process they don't understand.

State your steps in a logical, chronological order. Obviously, if someone wanted to know it how to bake bread, you wouldn't begin with "Put the prepared dough in the oven." Start at the beginning and carefully follow through, step by step, until the process is completed. Don't omit any steps or directions, no matter how seemingly insignificant. Without complete instructions, for example, the would-be baker might end up with a gob of dough rather than a loaf of bread—simply because the directions didn't say to heat the oven to a certain temperature.

Explain each step clearly, sufficiently, and accurately. If you've ever tried to assemble a child's toy or a piece of furniture, you probably already know how frustrating—and infuriating—it is to work from vague, inadequate directions. Save your readers from tears and tantrums by describing each step in your process as clearly as possible. Use enough specific details to distinguish one step from another. As the readers finish each step, they should know how the subject matter is supposed to look, feel, smell, taste, or sound at that stage of the process. You might also explain why each step is necessary ("Cutting back the young avocado stem is necessary to prevent a spindly plant"; "Senator Snort then had to win over the chair of the Arms Committee to be sure his bill would go to the Senate floor for a vote."). In some cases, especially in directional processes, it's helpful to give warnings ("When you begin tightrope walking, the condition of your shoes is critical; be careful the soles are not slick.") or descriptions of errors and how to rectify them ("If you pass a white church, you've gone a block too far; turn right at the church and circle back on Candle Lane"; "If the sauce appears gray and thick, add one teaspoon more of cornstarch until the gravy is white and bubbly.").

Organize your steps effectively. If you have a few big steps in your process, you probably will devote a paragraph to each one. On the other hand, if you have several small steps, you should organize them into a few manageable units. For example, in the essay "How to Prepare Fresh Fish" the list of small steps on the left has been grouped into three larger units, each of which becomes a body paragraph:

1. scaling	I. Cleaning
2. beheading	A. scaling
3. gutting	B. beheading
4. washing	C. gutting
5. seasoning	II. Cooking
6. breading	A. washing
7. frying	B. seasoning
8. draining	C. breading
9. portioning	D. frying
10. garnishing	III. Serving
	A. draining
	B. portioning
	C. garnishing

In addition, don't forget to use enough transition devices between steps to avoid the effect of a mechanical list. Some frequently used linking words in process essays include the following:

next	first, second, third, etc.
then	at this point
now	following
to begin	when
finally	at last
before	afterward

Vary your transition words sufficiently so that your steps are not linked by a monotonous repetition of "and then" or "next."

Problems to Avoid

Don't forget to include a thesis. You already know, of course, that every essay needs a thesis, but the advice bears repeating here because for some reason some writers often omit the statement in their process essays. Your thesis might be (1) your reason for presenting this process—why you feel it's important or necessary for the readers to know it ("Because rescue squads often arrive too late, every adult should know how to administer CPR to accident victims") or (2) an assertion about the nature of the process itself ("Needlepoint is a simple, restful, fun hobby for both men and women"). Here are some other subjects and sample theses:

- Donating blood is not the painful process one might suspect.

- The raid on Pearl Harbor wasn't altogether unexpected.

- Returning to school as an older-than-average student isn't as difficult as it may look.

- Sponsoring a five-mile run can be a fun way for your club or student organization to raise money for local charities.

- Challenging a speeding ticket is a time-consuming, energy-draining, but financially rewarding endeavor.

- The series of public protests that led to the return of the traditional Coca-Cola was an unparalleled success in the history of American consumerism.

Presenting a thesis and referring to it appropriately gives your essay unity and coherence, as well as ensuring against a monotonous list of steps.

Pay special attention to your conclusion. Don't allow your essay to grind to an abrupt halt after the final step. You might conclude the essay by telling the significance of the completed process or by explaining other uses it may have. Or, if it is appropriate, finish your essay with an amusing story or emphatic comment. However you conclude, leave the reader with a feeling of satisfaction, with a sense of having completed an interesting procedure. (For more information on writing good conclusions, see pp. 94–97.)

 ## ESSAY TOPICS

Below are suggested topics for both directional and informative process essays. Some of the topics may be used in humorous essays, such as "How to Flunk a Test," "How to Remain a Bench Warmer," or "How to Say Nothing in Eight-Hundred Words." For additional ideas, turn to the "Suggestions for Writing" section following the professional essay on page 225.

1. How you arrived at a major decision or solved an important problem

2. How to survive some aspect of your freshman year

3. How to begin a collection or hobby or acquire a skill

4. How to buy a computer, CD player, VCR, or other recreational product

5. How a popular product or fad originated or grew

6. How to meet the person of your dreams (or escape the nightmare when it's over)

7. How something in nature works or was formed

8. How a company makes or sells a product

9. How a piece of equipment or a machine works

10. How to cure a cold or other common ailment

11. How to get in shape/develop physical fitness

12. How to stop smoking (or break some other bad habit)

13. How to select a car (new or used), house, apartment, roommate

14. How to earn money quickly or easily

15. How a famous invention or discovery occurred

16. How to get rid of pests (human or otherwise)

17. How to succeed or fail in a job interview (or in some other important endeavor)

18. How to build or repair some small item

19. How to plan the perfect party, wedding, holiday, birthday, etc.

20. How a historical event occurred

A Topic Proposal for Your Essay

Selecting the right subject matter is important to every writer. To help you clarify your ideas and strengthen your commitment to your topic, here is a proposal sheet that asks you to describe some of your preliminary ideas about your subject before you begin drafting. Although as you draft your ideas may change (they will almost certainly become more refined), thinking through your choice of topic now may help you avoid several false starts.

1. What process will you explain in your essay? Is it a directional or an informative process? Can you address the complexity of this process in a short essay?

2. Why did you select this topic? Are you personally or professionally interested in this process? Cite at least one reason for your choice.

3. Why do you think this topic would be of interest to others? Who might find it especially informative or enjoyable?

4. Describe in one or two sentences the ideal response from your readers. What would you like them to do or know after reading about your topic?

5. List at least three of the larger steps or stages in the process.

6. What difficulties might this topic present during your drafting? Will this topic require any additional research on your part?

S A M P L E   S T U D E N T   E S S A Y

The essay below is a directional process telling readers how to run a successful garage sale. To make the instructions clear and enjoyable, the writer adopted a chronological order and used many specific examples, details, and warnings.

CATCHING GARAGE SALE FEVER

Introduction: A series of questions to hook the reader

Ever need some easy money fast? To repay those incredible overdue library fines you ran up writing your last research paper? Or to raise money for that much-needed vacation to old Mexico you put on credit cards last Spring Break? Or maybe you feel you simply have to clear out some junk before the piles block the remaining sunlight from your windows? Whether the problem is cash flow or trash flow, you can solve it easily by holding what is fast becoming an all-American sport: the weekend garage sale. As a veteran of some half-dozen successful ventures, I can testify that garage sales are the

Thesis

easiest way to make quick money, with a minimum of physical labor and the maximum of fun.

Step one: Taking inventory

Most garage sale "experts" start getting ready at least two weeks before the sale by taking inventory. Look through your closets and junk drawers to see if you actually have enough items to make a sale worthwhile. If all you have is a mass of miscellaneous small items, think about waiting or joining a friend's sale, because you do need at least a couple of larger items (furniture is always a big seller) to draw customers initially. Also, consider whether the season is appropriate for your items: sun dresses and shorts, for example, sell better in the spring and summer; coats and boots in the fall. As you collect your items, don't underestimate the "saleability" of some of your junk—the hideous purple china bulldog Aunt Clara gave you for Christmas five years ago may be perfect for someone's Ugly Mutt Collection.

As you sort through your junk closets, begin thinking about the time and place of your sale. First, decide if you want a one- or two-day sale. If you opt for only one day, Saturdays are generally best because most people are free that day. Plan to start early—by 8 A.M. if possible—because the experienced buyers get up and get going so they can hit more sales that way. Unless you have nothing else to do that day, plan to end your sale by mid-afternoon; most people have run out of buying energy (or money) by 3 P.M. Deciding on the location of your sale depends, of course, on your housing situation, but you still might need to make some choices. For instance, do you want to put your items out in a driveway, a backyard, or actually in the garage (weather might affect this decision)? Or perhaps a side yard gets more passers-by? Wherever you decide, be sure that there are plenty of places for customers to park close by without blocking your neighbors' driveways.

Unless you live in a very small town or on a very busy street, you'll probably want to place an inexpensive ad in the "garage sale" column of your local newspaper that is scheduled to run a day or two before, and the day of, your sale. Your ad should tell the times and place of the sale (give brief directions or mention landmarks if the location is hard to find) as well as a brief list of some of your items. Few people will turn out for "household goods" alone; some popular items include bookcases, antiques, books, fans, jewelry, toys, baby equipment, and name-brand clothes. One other piece of advice about the ad copy: it should include the phrase "no early sales" unless you want to be awakened at 6:30 A.M., as I was one Saturday, by a bunch of semi-pro garage sale buyers milling restlessly around in your yard, looking like zombies out of a George Romero horror movie. In

Step two: Deciding when and where

Step three: Advertising the sale

A warning

addition to your newspaper ad, you may also wish to put up posters in places frequented by lots of people; laundromats and grocery stores often have bulletin boards for such announcements. You can also put up signs on nearby well-traveled streets, but one warning: in some towns it's illegal to post anything on utility poles or traffic signs, so be sure to check your local ordinances first.

Another warning

Tagging your items with their prices is the least fun, and it can take a day or a week depending on how many items you have and how much time each day you can devote to the project. You can buy sheets of little white stickers or use pieces of masking tape to stick on the prices, but if you want to save time, consider grouping some items and selling them all for the same price—all shirts, for example, are 50¢. Be realistic about your prices; the hand-crafted rug from Greece may have been expensive and important to you, but to others, it's a worn doormat. Some experts suggest pricing your articles at about one-fourth their original value, unless you have special reasons not to (an antique or popular collectors' item, for instance, may be more valuable now than when you bought it). Remember that you can always come down on your prices if someone is interested in a particular item.

Step four: Pricing the merchandise

By the day before your sale you should have all your items clean and tagged. One of the beauties of a garage sale is that there's very little equipment to collect. You'll need tables, benches, or boards supported by bricks to display your goods; a rope tied from side to side of your garage can double as a clothes rack. Try to spread out your merchandise rather than dumping articles in deep boxes; customers don't want to feel

Step five: Setting up your sale

A note on equipment

like they're rummaging through a trash barrel. Most important, you'll need a chair and a table to hold some sort of money box, preferably one with a lock. The afternoon before the sale, take a trip to the bank if you need to, to make sure you have enough one-dollar bills and coins to make plenty of change. The evening before the sale, set up your items on your display benches in the garage or indoors near the site of your sale so that you can quickly set things out in the morning. Get a good night's sleep so you can get up to open on time: the early bird does get the sales in this business.

The sale itself is, of course, the real fun. Half the enjoyment is haggling with the customers, so be prepared to joke and visit with the shoppers. Watching the different kinds of people who show up is also a kick—you can get a cross section from college students on a tight budget to harried mothers toting four kids to real eccentrics in fancy cars who will argue about the price of a 75¢ item (if you're a creative writer, don't forget to take notes for your next novel). If the action slows in the afternoon, you can resort to a half-price or two-for-one sale by posting a large sign to that effect; many shoppers can't resist a sale at a sale!

Step six: Running the sale

By late afternoon you should be richer and junk-free, at least to some extent. If you do have items left after the half-price sale, decide whether you want to box them up for the next sale or drop them by a charitable organization such as Goodwill (some organizations will even pick up your donations; others have convenient drop boxes). After you've taken your articles inside, don't forget to take down any signs you've posted in the neighborhood; old, withered garage sale signs fluttering in the breeze are an eyesore. Last, sit down and count your profits, so

Step seven: Closing up

you can go out in the evening to celebrate a successful business venture.

Conclusion: A summary of the benefits and a humorous warning

The money you make is, of course, the biggest incentive for having one or two sales a year. But the combination of money, clean closets, and memories of the characters you met can be irresistible. Garage sales can rapidly get in your blood; once you hold a successful one, you're tempted to have another as soon as the junk starts to mount up. And having sales somehow leads to attending them too, as it becomes fun to see what other folks are selling at bargain prices. So be forewarned: you too can be transformed into a garage sale junkie, traveling with a now-popular car bumper sticker that proudly proclaims to the world: "Caution! I brake for garage sales"!

To Bid the World Farewell

Jessica Mitford

As an investigative reporter, Jessica Mitford wrote many articles and books, including Kind and Unusual Punishment: The Prison Business *(1973),* A Fine Old Conflict *(1977),* Poison Penmanship *(1979), and* The American Way of Birth *(1979). This essay is from her best-selling book* The American Way of Death *(1963), which scrutinizes the funeral industry.*

1   Embalming is indeed a most extraordinary procedure, and one must wonder at the docility of Americans who each year pay hundreds of millions of dollars for its perpetuation, blissfully ignorant of what it is all about, what is done, how it is done. Not one in ten thousand has any idea of what actually takes place. Books on the subject are extremely hard to come by. They are not to be found in most libraries or bookshops.

2   In an era when huge television audiences watch surgical operations in the comfort of their living rooms, when, thanks to the animated cartoon, the geography of the digestive system has become familiar territory even to the nursery school set, and in a land where the satisfaction of curiosity about almost all matters is a national pastime, the secrecy surrounding embalming can, surely, hardly be attributed to the inherent gruesomeness of the subject. Custom in this regard has within this century suffered a complete reversal. In the early days of American embalming, when it was performed in the home of the deceased, it was almost mandatory for some relative to stay by the embalmer's side and witness the procedure. Today, family members who might wish to be in attendance would certainly be dissuaded by the funeral director. All others, except apprentices, are excluded by law from the preparation room.

3   A close look at what does actually take place may explain in large measure the undertaker's intractable reticence concerning a procedure that has become his major *raison d'être*. Is it possible he fears that public information about embalming might lead patrons to wonder if they really want this service? If the funeral men are loath to discuss the subject outside the trade, the reader may, understandably, be equally loath to go on reading at this point. For those who have the stomach for it, let us part the formaldehyde curtain. . . .

4   The body is first laid out in the undertaker's morgue—or rather, Mr. Jones is reposing in the preparation room—to be readied to bid the world farewell.

5   The preparation room in any of the better funeral establishments has the tiled and sterile look of a surgery, and indeed the embalmer-restorative

* To help you read this essay analytically, review pages 182–185.

artist who does his chores there is beginning to adopt the term "derma-surgeon" (appropriately corrupted by some mortician-writers as "demisurgeon") to describe his calling. His equipment, consisting of scalpels, scissors, augers, forceps, clamps, needles, pumps, tubes, bowls and basins, is crudely imitative of the surgeon's as is his technique, acquired in a nine- or twelve-month post-high-school course in an embalming school. He is supplied by an advanced chemical industry with a bewildering array of fluids, sprays, pastes, oils, powders, creams, to fix or soften tissue, shrink or distend it as needed, dry it here, restore the moisture there. There are cosmetics, waxes and paints to fill and cover features, even plaster of Paris to replace entire limbs. There are ingenious aids to prop and stabilize the cadaver: a Vari-Pose Head Rest, the Edwards Arm and Hand Positioner, the Repose Block (to support the shoulders during the embalming), and the Throop Foot Positioner, which resembles an old-fashioned stocks.

6   Mr. John H. Eckels, president of the Eckels College of Mortuary Science, thus describes the first part of the embalming procedure: "In the hands of a skilled practitioner, this work may be done in a comparatively short time and without mutilating the body other than by slight incision—so slight that it scarcely would cause serious inconvenience if made upon a living person. It is necessary to remove the blood, and doing this not only helps in the disinfecting, but removes the principal cause of disfigurement due to discoloration."

7   Another textbook discusses the all-important time element: "The earlier this is done, the better, for every hour that elapses between death and embalming will add to the problems and complications encountered. . . ." Just how soon should one get going on the embalming? The author tells us, "On the basis of such scanty information made available to this profession through its rudimentary and haphazard system of technical research, we must conclude that the best results are to be obtained if the subject is embalmed before life is completely extinct—that is, before cellular death has occurred. In the average case, this would mean within an hour after somatic death." For those who feel that there is something a little rudimentary, not to say haphazard, about this advice, a comforting thought is offered by another writer. Speaking of fears entertained in early days of premature burial, he points out, "One of the effects of embalming by chemical injection, however, has been to dispel fears of live burial." How true; once the blood is removed, chances of live burial are indeed remote.

8   To return to Mr. Jones, the blood is drained out through the veins and replaced by embalming fluid pumped in through the arteries. As noted in *The Principles and Practices of Embalming,* "every operator has a favorite injection and drainage point—a fact which becomes a handicap only if he fails or refuses to forsake his favorites when conditions demand

it." Typical favorites are the carotid artery, femoral artery, jugular vein, subclavian vein. There are various choices of embalming fluid. If Flextone is used, it will produce a "mild flexible rigidity. The skin retains a velvety softness, the tissues are rubbery and pliable. Ideal for women and children." It may be blended with B. and G. Products Company's Lyf-Lyk tint, which is guaranteed to reproduce "nature's own skin texture . . . the velvety appearance of living tissue." Suntone comes in three separate tints: Suntan; Special Cosmetic Tint, a pink shade "especially indicated for young female subjects"; and Regular Cosmetic Tint, moderately pink.

9   About three to six gallons of a dyed and perfumed solution of formaldehyde, glycerin, borax, phenol, alcohol and water is soon circulating through Mr. Jones, whose mouth has been sewn together with a "needle directed upward between the upper lip and gum and brought out through the left nostril," with the corners raised slightly "for a more pleasant expression." If he should be bucktoothed, his teeth are cleaned with Bon Ami and coated with colorless nail polish. His eyes, meanwhile, are closed with flesh-tinted eye caps and eye cement.

10   The next step is to have at Mr. Jones with a thing called a trocar. This is a long, hollow needle attached to a tube. It is jabbed into the abdomen, poked around the entrails and chest cavity, the contents of which are pumped out and replaced with "cavity fluid." This done, and the hole in the abdomen sewn up, Mr. Jones' face is heavily creamed (to protect the skin from burns which may be caused by leakage of the chemicals), and he is covered with a sheet and left unmolested for a while. But not for long—there is more, much more, in store for him. He has been embalmed, but not yet restored, and the best time to start the restorative work is eight to ten hours after embalming, when the tissues have become firm and dry.

11   The object of all this attention to the corpse, it must be remembered, is to make it presentable for viewing in an attitude of healthy repose. "Our customs require the presentation of our dead in the semblance of normality . . . unmarred by the ravages of illness, disease or mutilation," says Mr. J. Sheridan Mayer in his *Restorative Art.* This is rather a large order since few people die in the full bloom of health, unravaged by illness and unmarked by some disfigurement. The funeral industry is equal to the challenge: "In some cases the gruesome appearance of a mutilated or disease-ridden subject may be quite discouraging. The task of restoration may seem impossible and shake the confidence of the embalmer. This is the time for intestinal fortitude and determination. Once the formative work is begun and affected tissues are cleaned or removed, all doubts of success vanish. It is surprising and gratifying to discover the results which may be obtained."

12   The embalmer, having allowed an appropriate interval to elapse, returns to the attack, but now he brings into play the skill and equipment

of sculptor and cosmetician. Is a hand missing? Casting one in plaster of Paris is a simple matter. "For replacement purposes, only a cast of the back of the hand is necessary; this is within the ability of the average operator and is quite adequate." If a lip or two, a nose or an ear should be missing, the embalmer has at hand a variety of restorative waxes with which to model replacements. Pores and skin texture are simulated by stippling with a little brush, and over this cosmetics are laid on. Head off? Decapitation cases are rather routinely handled. Ragged edges are trimmed, and head joined to torso with a series of splints, wires and sutures. It is a good idea to have a little something at the neck—a scarf or high collar—when time for viewing comes. Swollen mouth? Cut out tissue as needed from inside the lips. If too much is removed, the surface contour can easily be restored by padding with cotton. Swollen necks and cheeks are reduced by removing tissue through vertical incisions made down each side of the neck. "When the deceased is casketed, the pillow will hide the suture incisions . . . . as an extra precaution against leakage, the suture may be painted with liquid sealer."

13 The opposite condition is more likely to present itself—that of emaciation. His hypodermic syringe now loaded with massage cream, the embalmer seeks out and fills the hollowed and sunken areas by injection. In this procedure the backs of the hands and fingers and the under-chin area should not be neglected.

14 Positioning the lips is a problem that recurrently challenges the ingenuity of the embalmer. Closed too tightly, they tend to give a stern, even disapproving expression. Ideally, embalmers feel, the lips should give the impression of being ever so slightly parted, the upper lip protruding slightly for a more youthful appearance. This takes some engineering, however, as the lips tend to drift apart. Lip drift can sometimes be remedied by pushing one or two straight pins through the inner margin of the lower lip and then inserting them between the two front teeth. If Mr. Jones happens to have no teeth, the pins can just as easily be anchored in his Armstrong Face Former and Denture Replacer. Another method to maintain lip closure is to dislocate the lower jaw, which is then held in its new position by a wire run through holes which have been drilled through the upper and lower jaws at the midline. As the French are fond of saying, *il faut souffrir pour être belle.**

15 If Mr. Jones has died of jaundice, the embalming fluid will very likely turn him green. Does this deter the embalmer? Not if he has intestinal fortitude. Masking pastes and cosmetics are heavily laid on, burial garments and casket interiors are color-correlated with particular care, and Jones is displayed beneath rose-colored lights. Friends will say, "How *well* he looks." Death by carbon monoxide, on the other hand, can be

---

* "One must suffer to be beautiful."

rather a good thing from the embalmer's viewpoint: "One advantage is the fact that this type of discoloration is an exaggerated form of a natural pink coloration." This is nice because the healthy glow is already present and needs but little attention.

16   The patching and filling completed, Mr. Jones is now shaved, washed and dressed. Cream-based cosmetic, available in pink, flesh, suntan, brunette and blond, is applied to his hands and face, his hair is shampooed and combed (and, in the case of Mrs. Jones, set), his hands manicured. For the horny-handed son of toil special care must be taken; cream should be applied to remove ingrained grime, and the nails cleaned. "If he were not in the habit of having them manicured in life, trimming and shaping is advised for better appearance—never questioned by kin."

17   Jones is now ready for casketing (this is the present participle of the verb "to casket"). In this operation his right shoulder should be depressed slightly "to turn the body a bit to the right and soften the appearance of lying flat on the back." Positioning the hands is a matter of importance, and special rubber positioning blocks may be used. The hands should be cupped slightly for a more lifelike, relaxed appearance. Proper placement of the body requires a delicate sense of balance. It should lie as high as possible in the casket, yet not so high that the lid, when lowered, will hit the nose. On the other hand, we are cautioned, placing the body too low "creates the impression that the body is in a box."

18   Jones is next wheeled into the appointed slumber room where a few last touches may be added—his favorite pipe placed in his hand or, if he was a great reader, a book propped into position. (In the case of little Master Jones a Teddy bear may be clutched.) Here he will hold open house for a few days, visiting hours 10 A.M. to 9 P.M.

Questions on Content, Structure, and Style

1. By studying the first three paragraphs, summarize both Mitford's reason for explaining the embalming process and her attitude toward undertakers who wish to keep their patrons uninformed about this procedure.

2. Identify this process as either directional or informative.

3. Does Mitford use enough specific details to help you visualize each step as it occurs? Point out examples of details that create vivid descriptions by appealing to your sense of sight, smell, or touch.

4. How does the technique of using the hypothetical "Mr. Jones" make the explanation of the process more effective? Why didn't Mitford simply refer to "the corpse" or "a body" throughout her essay?

5. What is Mitford's general attitude toward this procedure? The overall tone of the essay? Study Mitford's choice of words and then identify the tone in each of the following passages:

"The next step is to have at Mr. Jones with a thing called a tro-car." (10)*

"The embalmer, having allowed an appropriate interval to elapse, returns to the attack. . . ." (12)

"Friends will say, 'How *well* he looks.'" (15)

"On the other hand, we are cautioned, placing the body too low 'creates the impression that the body is in a box.'" (17)

"Here he will hold open house for a few days, visiting hours 10 A.M. to 9 P.M." (18)

What other words and passages reveal Mitford's attitude and tone?

6. Why does Mitford repeatedly quote various undertakers and textbooks on the embalming and restorative process ("'needle directed upward between the upper lip and gum and brought out through the left nostril'")? Why is the quotation in paragraph 7 that begins "'On the basis of such scanty information made available to this profession through its rudimentary and haphazard system of technical research'" particularly effective in emphasizing Mitford's attitude toward the funeral industry?

7. What does Mitford gain by quoting euphemisms used by the funeral business, such as "dermasurgeon," "Repose Block," and "slumber room"? What are the connotations of the words "poked," "jabbed," and "left unmolested" in paragraph 10? What effect is Mitford trying to produce with the series of questions (such as "Head off?") in paragraph 12?

8. Does this process flow smoothly from step to step? Identify several transition devices connecting the paragraphs.

9. Evaluate Mitford's last sentence. Does it successfully sum up the author's attitude and conclude the essay?

10. By supplying information about the embalming process, did Mitford change your attitude toward this procedure or toward the funeral industry? Are there advantages Mitford fails to mention?

* Numbers in parentheses following questions and vocabulary words refer to paragraphs in the essay.

Suggestions for Writing

Try using Jessica Mitford's "To Bid the World Farewell" as a stepping stone to your own writing. Mitford's graphic details and disparaging tone upset some readers who feel funerals are necessary for the living. If you agree, consider writing about a service that challenges Mitford's position. Or adopt Mitford's role as an investigative reporter exposing a controversial process. For example, how is toxic waste disposed of at the student health center? What happens to unclaimed animals at your local shelter? Or try a humorous investigation: just how do they prepare that mystery meat in your dorm cafeteria? Use Mitford's vivid essay as a guide as you present your discoveries.

Vocabulary

docility (1)	*raison d'être* (3)	pliable (8)
perpetuation (1)	ingenious (5)	semblance (11)
inherent (2)	cadaver (5)	ravages (11)
mandatory (2)	somatic (7)	stippling (12)
intractable (3)	rudimentary (7)	emaciation (13)
reticence (3)	dispel (7)	

 A REVISION WORKSHEET

As you write your rough drafts, consult Chapter 5 for guidance through the revision process. In addition, here are a few questions to ask yourself as you revise your process essay:

1. Is the essay's purpose clear to the reader?

2. Has the need for any special equipment been noted and explained adequately? Are all terms unfamiliar to the reader defined clearly?

3. Does the essay include all the steps (and warnings, if appropriate) necessary to understanding the process?

4. Is each step described in enough detail to make it understandable to all readers? Where could more detail be effectively added?

5. Are all the steps in the process presented in an easy-to-follow chronological order, with smooth transitions between steps or stages?

6. Are there any steps that should be combined in a paragraph describing a logical stage in the process?

7. Does the essay have a pleasing conclusion?

After you've revised your essay extensively, you might exchange rough drafts with a classmate and answer these questions for each other, making specific suggestions for improvement wherever appropriate. (For advice on productive participation in classroom workshops, see pp. 117–119.)

Reviewing Your Progress

After you have completed your process essay, take a moment to measure your progress as a writer by responding to the following questions. Such analysis will help you recognize growth in your writing skills and may enable you to identify areas that are still problematic.

1. Which part of your essay is most successful? Why?

2. Select two details that contribute significantly to the clarity of your explanation. Why are these details effective?

3. What part of your essay gave you the most trouble? How did you overcome the problem?

4. If you had more time to work on this essay, what would receive additional attention? Why?

5. What did you learn about your topic from writing this essay? About yourself as a writer?

STRATEGY THREE: DEVELOPMENT BY COMPARISON AND CONTRAST

Every day you exercise the mental process of comparison and contrast. When you get up in the morning, for instance, you may contrast two choices of clothing—a short-sleeved shirt versus a long-sleeved one—and then make your decision after hearing the weather forecast. Or you may contrast and choose between Sugar-Coated Plastic Pops and Organic Mullet Kernels for breakfast, between the health advantages of walking to campus and the speed afforded by your car or bicycle. Once on campus, preparing to register, you may first compare both professors and courses; similarly, you probably compared the school you attend now to others before you made your choice. In short, you frequently use the process of comparison and contrast to come to a decision or make a judgment about two or more objects, persons, ideas, or feelings.

When you write a comparison or contrast essay, your opinion about the two elements* in question becomes your thesis statement; the body of the paper then shows why you arrived at that opinion. For example, if your thesis

---

* It is possible to compare or contrast more than two elements. But until you feel confident about the organizational patterns for this kind of essay, you should probably stay with the simpler format.

states that Mom's Kum-On-Back Hamburger Haven is preferable to McPhony's Mystery Burger Stand, your body paragraphs might contrast the two restaurants in terms of food, service, and atmosphere, revealing the superiority of Mom's on all three counts.

Developing Your Essay

There are two principal patterns of organization for comparison or contrast essays. For most short papers you should choose one of the patterns and stick with it throughout the essay. Later, if you are assigned a longer essay, you may want to mix the patterns for variety as some professional writers do, but do so only if you can maintain clarity and logical organization.

Pattern One: Point by Point

This method of organization calls for body paragraphs that compare or contrast the two subjects first on point one, then on point two, then point three, and so on. Study the following example:

Thesis: Mom's Hamburger Haven is a much better restaurant than McPhony's because of its superior food, service, and atmosphere.

Point 1:   Food

      A. Mom's
      B. McPhony's

Point 2:   Service

      A. Mom's
      B. McPhony's

Point 3:   Atmosphere

      A. Mom's
      B. McPhony's

Conclusion

If you select this pattern of organization, you must make a smooth transition from subject "A" to subject "B" in each discussion to avoid a choppy seesaw effect. Be consistent: present the same subject first in each discussion of a major point. In the essay outlined above, for instance, Mom's is always introduced before McPhony's.

Pattern Two: The Block

This method of organization presents body paragraphs in which the writer first discusses subject "A" on points one, two, three, etc., then discusses subject "B" on the same points. The model below illustrates this block pattern:

Thesis: Mom's Hamburger Haven is a better restaurant than McPhony's because of its superior food, service, and atmosphere.

    A. Mom's
        1. Food
        2. Service
        3. Atmosphere
    B. McPhony's
        1. Food
        2. Service
        3. Atmosphere

Conclusion

If you use the block pattern, you should discuss the three points—food, service, atmosphere—in the same order for each subject. In addition, you must include in your discussion of subject "B" specific references to the points you made earlier about subject "A" (see outline). In other words, because your statements about Mom's superior food may be several pages away by the time your comments on McPhony's food appear, the readers may not remember precisely what you said. Gently, unobtrusively, remind them with a specific reference to the earlier discussion. For instance, you might begin your paragraph on McPhony's service like this: "Unlike the friendly, attentive help at Mom's, service at McPhony's features grouchy persons who wait on you as if they consider your presence an intrusion on their privacy." The discussion of atmosphere might begin, "McPhony's atmosphere is as cold, sterile, and plastic as its decor, in contrast to the warm, homey feeling that pervades Mom's." Without such connecting phrases, what should be one unified essay will look more like two distinct mini-essays, forcing readers to do the job of comparing or contrasting for you.

Problems to Avoid

The single most serious error is the "so-what" thesis. Writers of comparison and contrast essays often wish to convince their readers that something—a restaurant, a movie, a product—is better (or worse) than something else: "Mom's Haven is a better place to eat than McPhony's." But not all comparison or contrast essays assert the absolute superiority or inferiority of their subjects. Sometimes writers simply want to point out the similarities or differences in two or more people, places, or objects, and that's fine, too—*as long as the writer avoids the "so-what" thesis problem.*

Too often novice writers will present thesis statements such as "My sister and I are very different" or "Having a blended family with two stepbrothers and stepsisters has advantages and disadvantages for me." To such theses, readers can only respond, "So what? Who cares?" There are many similarities and differences (or advantages and disadvantages) between countless numbers of things—but why should your readers care about those described in your essay? Comparing or contrasting for no apparent reason is a waste of the readers' valuable time; instead, find a purpose that will draw in your audience. You may indeed wish to write an essay contrasting the pros and cons of your blended family, but do it in a way that has a universal appeal or application. For instance, you might revise your thesis to say something like "Although a blended family often does experience petty jealousies and juvenile bickering, the benefits of having stepsiblings as live-in friends far outweigh the problems," and then use your family to show the advantages and disadvantages. In this way, your readers realize they will learn something about the blended family, a common phenomenon today, as well as learning some information about you and your particular family.

Another way to avoid the "so-what" problem is to direct your thesis to a particular audience. For instance, you might say that "Although Stella's Sweatateria and the Fitness Fanatics Gym are similar in their low student-membership prices and excellent instructors, Stella's is the place to go for those seeking a variety of exercise classes rather than hard-core bodybuilding machines." Or your thesis may wish to show a particular relationship between two subjects. Instead of writing "There are many similarities between the movie *Riot of the Killer Snails* and Mary Sheeley's novel *Salt on the Sidewalk*," write "The many similarities in character and plot (the monster, the scientist, and vegetable garden scene) clearly suggest that the movie director was greatly influenced by— if not actually guilty of stealing—parts of Mary Sheeley's novel."

In other words, tell your readers your point and then use comparison or contrast to support that idea; don't just compare or contrast items in a vacuum. Ask yourself, "What is the significant point I want my readers to learn or understand from reading this comparison/contrast essay? Why do they need to know this?"

Describe your subjects clearly and distinctly. To comprehend a difference or a similarity between two things, the reader must first be able to "see" them as you do. Consequently, you should use as many vivid examples and details as possible to describe both your subjects. Beware a tendency to overelaborate on one subject and then grossly skimp on the other, an especially easy trap to fall into in an essay that asserts "X" is preferable to "Y." By giving each side a reasonable treatment, you will do a better job of convincing your reader that you know both sides and have made a valid judgment.

Avoid a choppy essay. Whether you organize your essay by the point-by-point pattern or the block pattern, you need to use enough transition devices to ensure a smooth flow from one subject to another and from one point to the next. Without transitions, your essay may assume the distracting movement of a Ping-Pong game, as you switch back and forth between discussions of your two subjects. Listed below are some appropriate words to link your points:

COMPARISON	**CONTRAST**
also	however
similarly	on the contrary
too	on the other hand
both	in contrast
like	although
not only . . . but also	unlike
have in common	though
share the same	instead of
in the same manner	but

(For a review of other transition devices, see pp. 79–80.)

 ESSAY TOPICS

Here are some topics that may be compared or contrasted. Remember to narrow your subject, formulate a thesis that presents a clear point, and follow one of the two organizational patterns discussed on pages 227–228. For additional ideas, turn to the "Suggestions for Writing" sections following the professional essays on page 238 and page 242.

1. An expectation and its reality

2. A first impression and a later point of view

3. Two views on a current controversial issue (campus, local, national, or international)

4. Two conflicting theories you are studying in another college course

5. A memory of a person or place and a more recent encounter with that person or place

6. Coverage of the same story by two newspapers or magazines (the *National Enquirer* and the *Dallas Morning News,* for example, or *Time* and *Newsweek*)

7. A hero today and yesterday

8. Two pieces of literature or art

9. Two pieces of technology you've owned or operated or two pieces of sports equipment

10. A public or private myth and its reality

11. Two solutions to a problem in your professional field

12. One of today's popular entertainments and one from an earlier era (board or card games, for instance)

13. Two places you've lived or visited

14. Two instructors or coaches whose teaching styles are effective but different

15. Two books; a book and its movie; a movie and its sequel

16. Two jobs or employers (or your current job and the job of your dreams)

17. Two places that are special for you in different ways

18. An opinion you held before coming to college that has changed now that you are in college

19. A relationship to a family member that has changed (Example: your childhood relationship with your younger sister contrasted to your current feelings)

20. Your attitude toward a social custom or political belief and your parents' (or grandparents') attitude toward that belief or custom

A Topic Proposal for Your Essay

Selecting the right subject matter is important to every writer. To help you clarify your ideas and strengthen your commitment to your topic, here is a proposal sheet that asks you to describe some of your preliminary ideas about your subject before you begin drafting. Although as you draft your ideas may change (they will almost certainly become more refined), thinking through your choice of topic now may help you avoid several false starts.

1. What two subjects will your essay discuss? In what ways are these subjects similar? Different?

2. Do you plan to compare or contrast your two subjects?

3. Write one or two sentences describing your attitude toward these two subjects. Are you stating a preference for one or are you making some other significant point?

4. Why are you interested in these subjects? Are they part of your personal, academic, or professional life?

5. Why would other people find this topic interesting and important? Would a particular group of people be more affected by your topic than others?

6. What difficulties might this topic present during your drafting? Do you, for example, know enough about both subjects to offer a balanced picture?

S A M P L E   S T U D E N T   E S S A Y

Note that this writer takes a definite stand—that local food co-ops are superior to chain stores—and then contrasts two local stores, Lane Grocer and the Fort Collins, Colorado, Co-op, to prove her thesis. She selected the point-by-point pattern to organize her essay, contrasting prices, atmosphere, and benefits to local producers. See if you can identify her transition devices as well as some of her uses of detail that make the essay more interesting and convincing.

BRINGING BACK THE JOY OF MARKET DAY

Now that the old family-run corner grocery is almost extinct, many people are banding together to form their own neighborhood stores as food cooperatives. Locally owned by their

Thesis

members, food co-ops such as the one here in Fort Collins are welcome alternatives to the impersonal chain-store markets such as Lane Grocer. In exchange for volunteering a few hours each

Essay map

month, co-op members share savings and a friendly experience while they shop; local producers gain loyal, local support from the members as well as better prices for their goods in return for providing the freshest, purest food possible.

Point one: Prices

Perhaps the most crucial distinction between the two kinds of stores is that while supermarkets are set up to generate profit for their corporations, co-ops are nonprofit groups whose main purpose is to provide their members and the community with good, inexpensive food and basic household needs. At first glance, supermarkets such as Lane Grocer may appear to be cheaper because they offer so many specials, which they emphasize heavily through ads and in-store promotions. These special deals, known as "loss-leaders" in the retail industry, are more than made up for by the extremely high markups on other products. For example, around Thanksgiving Lane Grocer might have a sale on flour and shortening and then set up the displays with utmost care so that as customers reach for the flour they will be drawn to colorful bottles of pie spices, fancy jars of mincemeat, or maybe an inviting bin of fresh-roasted holiday nuts, all of which may be marked up 100% or more—way above what is being lost on the flour and shortening.

    The Fort Collins Co-op rarely bothers with such pricing gimmicks; instead, it tries to have a consistent markup—just enough to meet overhead expenses. The flour at the co-op may cost an extra few cents, but that same fancy spice bottle that costs over $1.00 from the supermarket display can be refilled at the co-op for less than 25¢. The nuts, considered by regular groceries as a seasonal "gourmet" item, are sold at the co-op for about two-thirds the price. Great savings like these are achieved by buying in bulk and having customers bag their own groceries. Recycled containers are used as much as possible, cutting down substantially on overhead. Buying in bulk may seem awkward at first, but the extra time spent bagging and weighing their own food results in welcome savings for co-op members.

    Once people have become accustomed to bringing their own containers and taking part in the work at the co-ops, they often find that it's actually more fun to shop in the friendly, relaxed atmosphere of the co-ops. At Lane Grocer, for example, I often find shopping a battle of tangled metal carts wielded by bored customers who are frequently trying to manage one or more cranky children. The long aisles harshly lit by rows of cold fluorescent lights and the bland commercial music don't make the chore of shopping any easier either. On the other hand, the Fort Collins Co-op may not be as expertly planned, but at least the chaos is carried on in a friendly way. Parents especially

Examples of Lane Grocer's prices contrasted to examples of co-op prices

Point two: Atmosphere

Description of Lane Grocer's atmosphere contrasted to description of the co-op's atmosphere

appreciate that they can safely let their children loose while they shop because in the small, open-spaced co-op even toddlers don't become lost as they do in the aisles of towering supermarket shelves. Moreover, most members are willing to look after the children of other members if necessary. And while they shop, members can choose to listen to the FM radio or simply to enjoy each other's company in relative quiet.

Point three: Benefits to local producers

As well as benefiting member consumers, co-ops also help small local producers by providing a direct market for their goods. Large chain stores may require minimum wholesale quantities far beyond the capacity of an individual producer, and mass markets like Lane Grocer often feel they are "too big" to negotiate with small local producers. But because of their small, independent nature co-ops welcome the chance to buy direct from the grower or producer. Direct selling offers two

No benefits at Lane Grocer contrasted to two benefits at the co-op

advantages for producers: they get a better price for their wares than by selling them through a middleman, and at the same time they establish an independent reputation for their business, which can be immensely valuable to their success later on. In Fort Collins, for example, Luna tofu (bean curd) stands out as an excellent illustration of this kind of mutual support. Several years ago my friend Carol Jones began making tofu in small batches to sell to the co-op as a way to earn a part-time income as well as to contribute to the co-op. Her enterprise has now grown so well that last year her husband quit his job to go into business with her full time. She currently sells to distributors and independent stores from here to Denver; even Lane Grocer, who earlier would not consider selling her tofu even on a trial basis, is now thinking about changing its policy.

Of course, not all co-ops are like the one here in Fort Collins, but that is one of their best features. Each one reflects the personalities of its members, unlike the supermarket chain stores that vary only slightly. Most important, though, while each has a distinctive character, co-ops share common goals of providing members with high-quality, low-cost food in a friendly, cooperative spirit.

Conclusion: Summarizing the advantages of co-ops over chain stores

P R O F E S S I O N A L   E S S A Y S *

Because there are two common ways to develop comparison/contrast essays, this section offers two professional essays to illustrate each pattern.

I. THE BLOCK METHOD

Two Ways of Viewing the River

Samuel Clemens

Samuel Clemens, whose pen name was Mark Twain, is regarded as one of America's most outstanding writers. Well known for his humorous stories and books, Twain was also a pioneer of fictional realism and local color. His most famous novel, The Adventures of Huckleberry Finn *(1884), is often hailed as a masterpiece. This selection is from the autobiographical book* Life on the Mississippi *(1883), which recounts Clemens' job as a riverboat pilot.*

1   Now when I had mastered the language of this water and had come to know every trifling feature that bordered the great river as familiarly as I knew the letters of the alphabet, I had made a valuable acquisition. But I had lost something, too. I had lost something which could never be restored to me while I lived. All the grace, the beauty, the poetry, had gone out of the majestic river! I still kept in mind a certain wonderful sunset which I witnessed when steamboating was new to me. A broad expanse of the river was turned to blood; in the middle distance the red hue brightened into gold, through which a solitary log came floating, black and conspicuous; in one place a long, slanting mark lay sparkling upon the water; in another the surface was broken by boiling, tumbling rings, that were as many-tinted as an opal; where the ruddy flush was faintest, was a smooth spot that was covered with graceful circles and radiating lines, ever so delicately traced; the shore on our left was densely wooded and the somber shadow that fell from this forest was broken in one place by a long, ruffled trail that shone like silver; and high above the forest wall a clean-stemmed dead tree waved a single leafy bough that glowed like a flame in the unobstructed splendor that was flowing from the sun. There were graceful curves, reflected images, woody heights, soft distances, and over the whole scene, far and near, the dissolving lights drifted steadily, enriching it every passing moment with new marvels of coloring.

2   I stood like one bewitched. I drank it in, in a speechless rapture. The world was new to me and I had never seen anything like this at home. But

---

* To help you read these essays analytically, review pages 182–185.

as I have said, a day came when I began to cease from noting the glories and the charms which the moon and the sun and the twilight wrought upon the river's face; another day came when I ceased altogether to note them. Then, if that sunset scene had been repeated, I should have looked upon it without rapture, and should have commented upon it inwardly after this fashion: "This sun means that we are going to have wind tomorrow; that floating log means that the river is rising, small thanks to it; that slanting mark on the water refers to a bluff reef which is going to kill somebody's steamboat one of these nights, if it keeps on stretching out like that; those tumbling 'boils' show a dissolving bar and a changing channel there; the lines and circles in the slick water over yonder are a warning that that troublesome place is shoaling up dangerously; that silver streak in the shadow of the forest is the 'break' from a new snag and he has located himself in the very best place he could have found to fish for steamboats; that tall dead tree, with a single living branch, is not going to last long, and then how is a body ever going to get through this blind place at night without the friendly old landmark?"

3   No, the romance and beauty were all gone from the river. All the value any feature of it had for me now was the amount of usefulness it could furnish toward compassing the safe piloting of a steamboat. Since those days, I have pitied doctors from my heart. What does the lovely flush in a beauty's cheek mean to a doctor but a "break" that ripples above some deadly disease? Are not all her visible charms sown thick with what are to him the signs and symbols of hidden decay? Does he ever see her beauty at all, or doesn't he simply view her professionally and comment upon her unwholesome condition all to himself? And doesn't he sometimes wonder whether he has gained most or lost most by learning his trade?

Questions on Content, Structure, and Style

1. What is Clemens contrasting in this essay? Identify his thesis.

2. What organizational pattern does he choose? Why is this an appropriate choice for his purpose?

3. How does Clemens make a smooth transition to his second view of the river?

4. Why does Clemens refer to doctors in paragraph 3?

5. What is the purpose of the questions in paragraph 3? Why is the last question especially important?

6. Characterize the language Clemens uses in his description in paragraph 1. Is his diction appropriate?

7. Point out several examples of similes in paragraph 1; what do they add to the description of the sunset?

8. How does the language in the description in paragraph 2 differ from the diction in paragraph 1? What aspect of the river is emphasized there?

9. Identify an example of personification in paragraph 2. Why did Clemens add it to his description?

10. Describe the tone of this essay. Does it ever shift?

Suggestions for Writing

Try using Samuel Clemens' "Two Ways of Viewing the River" as a stepping stone to your own writing. Consider, as Clemens did, writing about a subject before and after you experienced it from a more technically informed point of view. Did your appreciation of your grandmother's quilt increase after you realized how much skill went into making it? Did a starry night have a different appeal after your astronomy course? Did your fondness for a story or poem diminish or increase after you studied its craft? Clemens felt a certain loss came with his expertise, but was this the case in your experience?

Vocabulary

trifling (1)	ruddy (1)
acquisition (1)	wrought (2)
conspicuous (1)	compassing (3)

II. THE POINT-BY-POINT METHOD

Grant and Lee: A Study in Contrasts
Bruce Catton

Bruce Catton, an authority on the Civil War, won both the Pulitzer Prize for historical work and the National Book Award in 1955. He wrote numerous books, including Mr. Lincoln's Army *(1951),* A Stillness at Appomattox *(1953),* Never Call Retreat *(1966), and* Gettysburg: The Final Fury *(1974). This essay is a chapter of* The American Story *(1956), a collection of essays by noted historians.*

1   When Ulysses S. Grant and Robert E. Lee met in the parlor of a modest house at Appomattox Court House, Virginia, on April 9, 1865, to work out the terms for the surrender of Lee's Army of Northern Virginia, a great chapter in American life came to a close, and a great new chapter began.

2   These men were bringing the Civil War to its virtual finish. To be sure, other armies had yet to surrender, and for a few days the fugitive Confederate government would struggle desperately and vainly, trying to find some way to go on living now that its chief support was gone. But in effect it was all over when Grant and Lee signed the papers. And the little room where they wrote out the terms was the scene of one of the poignant, dramatic contrasts in American history.

3   They were two strong men, these oddly different generals, and they represented the strengths of two conflicting currents that, through them, had come into final collision.

4   Back of Robert E. Lee was the notion that the old aristocratic concept might somehow survive and be dominant in American life.

5   Lee was tidewater Virginia, and in his background were family, culture, and tradition . . . the age of chivalry transplanted to a New World which was making its own legends and its own myths. He embodied a way of life that had come down through the age of knighthood and the English country squire. America was a land that was beginning all over again, dedicated to nothing much more complicated than the rather hazy belief that all men had equal rights, and should have an equal chance in the world. In such a land Lee stood for the feeling that it was somehow of advantage to human society to have a pronounced inequality in the social structure. There should be a leisure class, backed by ownership of land; in turn, society itself should be keyed to the land as the chief source of wealth and influence. It would bring forth (according to this ideal) a class of men with a strong sense of obligation to the community; men who lived not to gain advantage for themselves, but to meet the solemn obligations which had been laid on them by the very fact that they were privileged. From them the country would get its leadership; to them it could look for the higher values—of thought, of conduct, of personal deportment—to give it strength and virtue.

6   Lee embodied the noblest elements of this aristocratic ideal. Through him, the landed nobility justified itself. For four years, the Southern states had fought a desperate war to uphold the ideals for which Lee stood. In the end, it almost seemed as if the Confederacy fought for Lee; as if he himself was the Confederacy . . . the best thing that the way of life for which the Confederacy stood could ever have to offer. He had passed into legend before Appomattox. Thousands of tired, underfed, poorly clothed Confederate soldiers, long-since past the simple enthusiasm of the early days of the struggle, somehow considered Lee the symbol of everything for which they had been willing to die. But they could not quite put this feeling into words. If the Lost Cause, sanctified by so much heroism and so many deaths, had a living justification, its justification was General Lee.

7 Grant, the son of a tanner on the Western frontier, was everything Lee was not. He had come up the hard way, and embodied nothing in particular except the eternal toughness and sinewy fiber of the men who grew up beyond the mountains. He was one of a body of men who owed reverence and obeisance to no one, who were self-reliant to a fault, who cared hardly anything for the past but who had a sharp eye for the future.

8 These frontier men were the precise opposites of the tidewater aristocrats. Back of them, in the great surge that had taken people over the Alleghenies and into the opening Western country, there was a deep, implicit dissatisfaction with a past that had settled into grooves. They stood for democracy, not from any reasoned conclusion about the proper ordering of human society, but simply because they had grown up in the middle of democracy and knew how it worked. Their society might have privileges, but they would be privileges each man had won for himself. Forms and patterns meant nothing. No man was born to anything, except perhaps to a chance to show how far he could rise. Life was competition.

9 Yet along with this feeling had come a deep sense of belonging to a national community. The Westerner who developed a farm, opened a shop, or set up in business as a trader could hope to prosper only as his own community prospered—and his community ran from the Atlantic to the Pacific and from Canada down to Mexico. If the land was settled, with towns and highways and accessible markets, he could better himself. He saw his fate in terms of the nation's own destiny. As its horizons expanded, so did his. He had, in other words, an acute dollars-and-cents stake in the continued growth and development of his country.

10 And that, perhaps, is where the contrast between Grant and Lee becomes most striking. The Virginia aristocrat, inevitably, saw himself in relation to his own region. He lived in a static society which could endure almost anything except change. Instinctively, his first loyalty would go to the locality in which that society existed. He would fight to the limit of endurance to defend it, because in defending it he was defending everything that gave his own life its deepest meaning.

11 The Westerner, on the other hand, would fight with an equal tenacity for the broader concept of society. He fought so because everything he lived by was tied to growth, expansion, and a constantly widening horizon. What he lived by would survive or fall with the nation itself. He could not possibly stand by unmoved in the face of an attempt to destroy the Union. He would combat it with everything he had, because he could only see it as an effort to cut the ground out from under his feet.

12 So Grant and Lee were in complete contrast, representing two diametrically opposed elements in American life. Grant was the modern man emerging; beyond him, ready to come on the stage, was the great age of steel and machinery, of crowded cities and a restless, burgeoning

vitality. Lee might have ridden down from the old age of chivalry, lance in hand, silken banner fluttering over his head. Each man was the perfect champion of his cause, drawing both his strengths and his weaknesses from the people he led.

13   Yet it was not all contrast, after all. Different as they were—in background, in personality, in underlying aspiration—these two great soldiers had much in common. Under everything else, they were marvelous fighters. Furthermore, their fighting qualities were really very much alike.

14   Each man had, to begin with, the great virtue of utter tenacity and fidelity. Grant fought his way down the Mississippi Valley in spite of acute personal discouragement and profound military handicaps. Lee hung on in the trenches at Petersburg after hope itself had died. In each man there was an indomitable quality . . . the born fighter's refusal to give up as long as he can still remain on his feet and lift his two fists.

15   Daring and resourcefulness they had, too; the ability to think faster and move faster than the enemy. These were the qualities which gave Lee the dazzling campaigns of Second Manassas and Chancellorsville and won Vicksburg for Grant.

16   Lastly, and perhaps greatest of all, there was the ability, at the end, to turn quickly from war to peace once the fighting was over. Out of the way these two men behaved at Appomattox came the possibility of a peace of reconciliation. It was a possibility not wholly realized, in the years to come, but which did, in the end, help the two sections to become one nation again . . . after a war whose bitterness might have seemed to make such a reunion wholly impossible. No part of either man's life became him more than the part he played in their brief meeting in the McLean house at Appomattox. Their behavior there put all succeeding generations of Americans in their debt. Two great Americans, Grant and Lee—very different, yet under everything very much alike. Their encounter at Appomattox was one of the great moments of American history.

Questions on Content, Style, and Structure

1. What is Catton's thesis?

2. According to Catton, how did Lee view society? Summarize the aristocratic ideal that Lee symbolized.

3. Who did Grant represent? How did they view the country's social structure?

4. After carefully studying paragraphs 4 through 16, describe the pattern of organization Catton uses to present his discussion.

5. What new means of development begins in paragraph 13?

6. How does Catton avoid the choppy seesaw effect as he compares and contrasts his subjects? Point out ways in which Catton makes a smooth transition from point to point.

7. Evaluate Catton's ability to write unified, coherent paragraphs with clearly stated topic sentences. Are his paragraphs adequately developed with enough specific detail? Cite evidence to support your answer.

8. What is the advantage or disadvantage of having only one sentence in paragraph 3? In paragraph 4?

9. What is Catton's opinion of these men? Select words and passages to support your answer. How does Catton's attitude affect the tone of this essay? Is his tone appropriate? Why or why not?

10. Instead of including a separate paragraph, Catton presents his concluding remarks in paragraph 16, in which he discusses his last major point about Grant and Lee. Many essays lacking concluding paragraphs end too abruptly or merely trail off; how does Catton avoid these weaknesses?

Suggestions for Writing

Try using Bruce Catton's "Grant and Lee: A Study in Contrasts" as a stepping stone to your writing. Comparing public figures is a familiar activity. People often discuss the styles and merits of various politicians, writers, business leaders, humanitarians, sports celebrities, and media stars. Write your own essay about two public figures who interest you; similar or different, these people could be from contemporary or older times or you might choose two people from different eras: Hilary Rodham Clinton and Nancy Reagan, Churchill and Roosevelt, Hemingway and Fitzgerald, Babe Didrikson Zaharias and Babe Ruth, Clara Barton and Albert Schweitzer, Madonna and Mozart, Amelia Earhart and Charles Lindbergh. The possibilities are endless and thought-provoking; use your essay to make an interesting specific point about the fascinating (and perhaps heretofore unrecognized) differences/similarities between the people you choose.

Vocabulary

chivalry (5)	tenacity (11)	indomitable (14)
deportment (5)	diametrically (12)	reconciliation (16)
embodied (6)	burgeoning (12)	

A REVISION WORKSHEET

As you write your rough drafts, consult Chapter 5 for guidance through the revision process. In addition, here are a few questions to ask yourself as you revise your comparison/contrast essay:

1. Does the essay contain a thesis that makes a significant point instead of a "so-what" thesis?

2. Is the material organized into the best pattern for the subject matter?

3. If the essay is developed by the point-by-point pattern, are there enough transition words used to avoid the see-saw effect?

4. If the essay is developed by the block pattern, are there enough transition devices and references connecting the two subjects to avoid the split-essay problem?

5. Are the points of comparison/contrast presented in a logical, consistent order that the reader can follow easily?

6. Are both subjects given a reasonably balanced treatment?

7. Are both subjects developed in enough specific detail so that the reader clearly understands the comparison or contrast? Where might more detail be added?

After you've revised your essay extensively, you might exchange rough drafts with a classmate and answer these questions for each other, making specific suggestions for improvement wherever appropriate. (For advice on productive participation in classroom workshops, see pp. 117–119.)

Reviewing Your Progress

After you have completed this essay developed by comparison/contrast, take a moment to measure your progress as a writer by responding to the following questions. Such analysis will help you to recognize growth in your writing skills and may enable you to identify areas that are still problematic.

1. Which part of your essay do you like the best? Why?

2. Which point of comparison or contrast do you think is the most successful? Why is it effective?

3. What part of your essay gave you the most trouble? How did you overcome the problem?

4. If you had more time to work on this essay, what would receive additional attention? Why?

5. What did you learn about your topic from writing this essay? About yourself as a writer?

STRATEGY FOUR: DEVELOPMENT BY DEFINITION

Frequently in conversation we must stop to ask, "What do you mean by that?" because in some cases our failure to comprehend just one particular term may lead to total misunderstanding. Suppose, for example, in a discussion with a friend, you refer to a new law as a piece of "liberal legislation"; if you and your friend do not share the same definition of "liberal," your remark may be completely misinterpreted. Take another example: you tell your parents that you're tired of listening to rap music; if they don't know what rap is, they miss the point entirely. In other words, definition of terms or ideas is often essential to meaningful communication.

Sometimes a dictionary definition or a one- or two-sentence explanation is all a term needs (Hemingway, for example, once defined courage as "grace under pressure"). And sometimes a brief, humorous definition can cut right to the heart of the matter (comedian Robin Williams, for instance, once defined "cocaine" as "God's way of saying you're making too much money").*

Frequently, however, you will find it necessary to provide an *extended definition*—that is, a longer, more detailed explanation that thoroughly defines the subject. Essays of extended definitions are quite common; think, for instance, of the articles you've seen lately on "mercy killing" that try to define death or the arguments on abortion that define "life" in a variety of ways. Other recent essays have grappled with such complex concepts as free speech, animal rights, pornography, executive privilege, and affirmative action.

Many national debates have centered on controversial definitions. For example, the conviction of John Hinckley, who attempted to assassinate former-president Ronald Reagan, produced many articles and editorials debating "criminal insanity," and the murder of a popular television actress brought new attention to the need for clearer "stalker laws" to protect people from frequently dangerous, uninvited attention. The testimony of law professor Anita Hill at the 1991 Supreme Court confirmation hearing of Clarence Thomas stirred debate over the meaning of "sexual harassment," and a rash of shootings by teens in recent times has produced argument on both "gun control" and the legal definition of "adult." In the late-1990s terms

---

*Even graffiti employs definition. One bathroom wall favorite: "Death is Nature's way of telling you to slow down." Another, obviously written by an English major: "A double negative is a no-no."

such as "politically correct" and "multiculturism" are still used in a variety of conflicting ways. Today we continue to discuss new and controversial terms that often need clarification before we can make intelligent choices or take appropriate action.

Why Do We Define?

Essays of extended definition are usually written for one or more of the following reasons:

1. To provide an interpretation of a vague, controversial, or often misunderstood term (such as "feminist," "pornoviolence," or "euthanasia")

2. To explain an abstract term or concept (such as "heroic," "success," or "friendship")

3. To define a new or unusual term, often found in slang, dialect, or the jargon of a particular field of study or industry (such as "dweeb," "objective correlative," or "computer virus")

4. To offer an objective definition of an unfamiliar term for a particular audience ("electron microscope," "tie beam," or "Depression glass")

5. To inform by presenting the interesting history, uses, effects, or examples of a common word or expression ("soul food," "vampire movies," or "Zydeco music")

Developing Your Essay

Here are four suggestions to help you prepare your essay of extended definition:

Know your purpose. Sometimes we need to define a term as clearly and objectively as possible. As a laboratory assistant, for instance, you might need to explain a technical measuring instrument to a group of new students. At other times, however, we may wish to persuade as well as inform our readers. People's interpretations of words, especially abstract or controversial terms, can, and often do, differ greatly depending on their point of view. After all, one person's "protest march" can be another person's street riot. Consequently, before you begin writing, decide on your purpose. If your readers need objective information only, make your definition as unbiased as you can; if your goal is to convince them that your point of view is the right or best one, you may adopt a variety of persuasive techniques as well as subjective language. For example, readers of a paper entitled "Doc in the Box" should quickly realize that they are not getting an objective treatment of the new twenty-four-hour emergency-care offices springing up around the country.

Give your readers a reason to read. One way to introduce your subject is to explain the previous use, misuse, or misunderstanding of the term; then present your new or different interpretation of the term or concept. An introduction and thesis defining a slang word, for instance, might state, "Despite the visions of cornbread dressing and cranberries it conjures up for most Americans, the word 'turkey' does not always refer to the Thanksgiving bird. Today, 'turkey' is also a common slang expression designed primarily to tease or even insult someone." Or take this introduction and thesis aimed at a word the writer feels is unclear to many readers: "When the credits roll at the end of a movie, much of the audience may be perplexed to see the job of 'best boy' listed. No, the 'best boy' doesn't stand up with the groom at a wedding of children—he (or she) is, in fact, the key electrician's first assistant, who helps arrange the lights for the movie's director of photography."

Keep your audience in mind to anticipate and avoid problems of clarity. Because you are trying to present a new or improved definition, you must strive above all for clarity. Ask yourself, "Who is my intended audience? What terms or parts of my definition are strange to them?" You don't help your audience, for example, by defining one campus slang expression in terms of other bits of unfamiliar slang. If, in other words, you defined "space cadet" as an "air-head," you're probably confusing your readers more than you are informing them. If your assignment doesn't specify a particular audience, you may find it useful to imagine one. You might pretend, for instance, that you're defining a campus or slang expression for your grandparents or that you're explaining an ambiguous term to a foreign visitor. After all, your definition is effective only if your explanation is clear not just to you but to those unfamiliar with the term or concept under discussion.

Use as many strategies as necessary to clarify your definition. Depending on your subject, you may use any number of the following methods in your essay to define your term:

1. State some examples

2. Describe the parts

3. Compare and contrast to similar terms

4. Explain an operation or process

5. Give some familiar synonyms

6. Define by negation (i.e., tell what the term doesn't mean)

7. Present the history

8. Discuss causes or effects

To illustrate some of the methods suggested above, let's suppose you wanted to write an extended definition of modern country music. You might choose one or more of these methods:

- Describe the parts: music, lyrics, and typical subject matter

- Compare or contrast to other kinds of music, such as bluegrass and Western swing

- Give some examples of famous country songs

- Trace its historical development from traditional country music to its present state

In the paper on country music or in any definition essay, you should, of course, use only those methods that will best define your term. Never include methods purely for the sake of exhibiting a variety of techniques. You, the writer, must decide which method or methods work best, which should receive the most emphasis, and in which order the chosen methods of definition should appear.

Problems to Avoid

Here is a list of "don'ts" for the writer of extended definition essays:

Don't present an incomplete definition. An inadequate definition is often the result of choosing a subject too broad or complex for your essay. You probably can't, for instance, do a good job of defining "twentieth-century modern art" in all its varieties in a short essay; you might, however, acquaint your reader with some specific school of modern art, such as impressionism, cubism, expressionism, surrealism, or pop. Therefore, narrow your subject to a manageable size and then define it as thoroughly as possible.

Don't begin every definition essay by quoting Webster. If you must include a standard definition of your term, try to find a unique way of blending it into your discussion, perhaps as a point of contrast to your explanation of the word's meaning. Dictionary definitions are generally so overused as opening sentences that they often drive composition teachers to seek more interesting jobs, such as measuring spaghetti in a pasta factory. Don't bore your audience to death; it's a terrible way to go.

Don't define vaguely or by using generalities. As always, use specific, vivid details to explain your subject. If, for example, you define a Shaker chair as "something with four legs," you have also described a dog, cat, horse, and cow, none of which is remotely akin to your subject. Consequently, you must select details that will make your subject distinct from any other. Including concrete examples is frequently useful in any essay but especially so when you are defining an abstract term such as "pride," "faith," or "prejudice." To make your definition both interesting and clear, always add as many precise details as possible. (For a review of using specific, colorful language, see pp. 129–130, 142–144, and 166–168.)

Don't offer circular definitions. To identify a poet as "one who writes poetry" or the American dream as "the dream most Americans hold dear" is about as helpful as a doctor telling a patient, "Your illness is primarily a lack of good health." Explain your subject; don't just rename it.

 ESSAY TOPICS

Below are several suggestions for terms whose meanings are often unclear. Narrow any topic that seems too broad for your assignment, and decide before writing whether your definition will be objective or subjective. (Student writers, by the way, often note that abstract concepts are harder to define than the more concrete subjects, so proceed at your own risk, and remember to use plenty of specific detail in your essay.) For additional ideas, turn to the "Suggestions for Writing" section following the professional essay on pages 256–257.

1. Any current slang, campus, or local expression

2. A term from your field of study

3. A slob (or some other undesirable kind of roommate or friend)

4. Success or failure

5. A good/bad teacher, clerk, coach, friend, parent, date, or spouse

6. Heroism or cowardice

7. A term from environmental issues

8. Any kind of music, painting, architecture, or dance

9. A feminist or some other political label

10. Any current fad or style

11. A rebel or conformist

12. Iridology or channeling (or some other counterculture activity)

13. A good/bad restaurant, store, movie theater, nightspot, class

14. Self-respect

15. Prejudice or discrimination

16. A freshman or senior

17. A controversial political idea or historical movement

18. A term from a hobby

19. A medical term or condition

20. A term from a sport or popular entertainment

A Topic Proposal for Your Essay

Selecting the right subject matter is important to every writer. To help you clarify your ideas and strengthen your commitment to your topic, here is a proposal sheet that asks you to describe some of your preliminary ideas about your subject before you begin drafting. Although as you draft your ideas may change (they will almost certainly become more refined), thinking through your choice of topic now may help you avoid several false starts.

1. What subject will your essay define? Will you define this subject objectively or subjectively? Why?

2. Why are you interested in this topic? Do you have a personal or professional connection to the subject? State at least one reason for your choice of topic.

3. Is this a significant topic of interest to others? Why? Who specifically might find it interesting, informative, or entertaining?

4. Is your subject a controversial, ambiguous, or new term? What will readers gain by understanding this term as defined from your point of view?

5. Writers use a variety of techniques to define terms. At this point, list two techniques you think you might use to help readers understand your topic.

6. What difficulties, if any, can you foresee during the drafting of this essay? For example, do you need to do any additional reading or interviewing to collect information for your definition?

S A M P L E   S T U D E N T   E S S A Y

A student with an interest in running wrote the following essay defining "runner's high." Note that he uses several methods to define his subject, one that is difficult to explain to those who have not experienced it firsthand.

BLIND PACES

Introduction: An example and a general definition of the term

      After running the Mile-Hi ten kilometer race in my hometown, I spoke with several of the leading runners about their experiences in the race. While most of them agreed that the course, which passed through a beautifully wooded yet overly hilly country area, was difficult, they also agreed that it was one of the best races of their running careers. They could not, however, explain why it was such a wonderful race but could rather only mumble something about the tall trees, cool air, and sandy path. When pressed, most of them didn't even remember specific details about the course, except the start and finish, and ended their descriptions with a blank—but content—stare. This self-satisfied, yet almost indescribable, feeling is often the result of an experienced runner running, a feeling often called, because of its similarities to other euphoric experiences, "runner's high."

Definition by negation, contrast

      Because this experience is seemingly impossible to define, perhaps a description of what runner's high is *not* might, by contrast, lead to a better understanding of what it is. I clearly remember—about five years ago—when I first took up running. My first day, I donned my tennis shorts, ragged t-shirt, and white discount-store tennis shoes somewhat ashamedly, knowing that they were symbolic of my novice status. I plodded around my block—just over ½ mile—in a little more than four minutes, feeling and regretting every painful step. My shins and thighs revolted at every jarring move, and my lungs wheezed uncontrollably, gasping for air, yet denied that basic necessity. Worst of all, I was conscious of every aspect of my existence—from the swinging of my arms to the slap of my feet on the road,and from the sweat dripping into my eyes and ears and mouth, to the frantic inhaling and exhaling of my lungs. I kept my eyes carefully peeled on the horizon or the next turn in the road, judging how far away it was, how long it would take me to get there, and how much torture was left before I reached home. These first few runs were, of course, the worst—as far from any euphoria or "high" as possible. They did, however, slowly get easier as my body became accustomed to running.

After a few months, in fact, I felt serious enough about this new pursuit that I decided to invest in a pair of real running shoes and shorts. Admittedly, these changes added to the comfort of my endeavor, but it wasn't until two full years later that the biggest change occurred—and I experienced my first real "high." It was a fall day. The air was a cool sixty-five degrees, the sun was shining intently, the sky was a clear, crisp blue, and a few dead leaves were scattered across the browning lawn. I stepped out onto the road and headed north towards a nearby park for my routine six-mile jog. The next thing I remember, however, was not my run through the park, but rather my return, some forty-two minutes and six miles later, to my house. I woke, as if out of a dream, just as I slowed to a walk, warming down from my run. The only memory I had of my run was a feeling of floating on air—as if my real self was somewhere above and detached from my body, looking down on my physical

Effects of the "high"

self as it went through its blind paces. At first, I felt scared—what if I had run out in front of a car? Would I have even known it? I felt as if I had been asleep or out of control, that my brain had, in some real sense, been turned off.

Now, after five years of running and hundreds of such mystical experiences, I realize that I had never lost control while in this euphoric state—and that my brain hadn't been turned off, or, at least, not completely. But what does happen is hard to prove. George Sheehan, in a column for <u>Runner's World</u>, suggests that "altered states," such as runner's high, result from the loss of conscious control, from the temporary cessation of left-brain messages and the dominance of right-brain activity (the left hemisphere being the seat of reason and rationality; the right, of emotions and inherited archetypal feelings) (14). Another explanation comes from Dr. Jerry Lynch, who argues, in his book <u>The Total Runner</u>, that the "high" results from the secretion of natural opiates, called beta endorphins, in the brain (213). My own explanation draws on both these medical explanations and is perhaps slightly more mystical. It's just possible that indeed natural opiates do go to work and consequently our brains lose track of the ins and outs of everyday activities—of jobs and classes and responsibilities. And because of this relaxed, drugged state, we are able to reach down into something more fundamental, something that ties us not only to each other but to all creation, here and gone. We rejoin nature, rediscovering the thread that links us to the universe.

My explanation is, of course, unscientific and therefore suspect. But I found myself, that day of the Mile-Hi Ten K run, eagerly trying to discuss my experience with the other runners:

Possible causes of the feeling: Two authorities

The writer's explanation

Conclusion: An incomplete understanding doesn't hamper enjoyment

I wanted desperately to discover where I had been and what I had been doing during the race for which I received my first trophy. I didn't discover the answer from my fellow runners that day, but it didn't matter. I'm still running and still feeling the glow—whatever it is.

WORKS CITED

Lynch, Jerry. <u>The Total Runner: A Complete Mind-Body Guide to Optimal Performance</u>. Englewood Cliffs, NJ: Prentice Hall, 1987.

Sheehan, George. "Altered States." <u>Runner's World</u>. Aug. 1988: 14.

P R O F E S S I O N A L   E S S A Y *

The Munchausen Mystery

Don R. Lipsitt

As a professor of psychiatry at Harvard Medical School and chief of psychiatry at Mount Auburn Hospital in Cambridge, Massachusetts, Don R. Lipsitt co-edited the Handbook of Studies on General Hospital Psychiatry *(1991). He published this article in* Psychology Today *in 1983.*

1   In Thomas Mann's *Confessions of Felix Krull, Confidence Man,* young Felix fabricates an illness and convinces both his mother and the family doctor that he is sick. Felix describes the intense pleasure that his performance brings him. "I was delirious with the alternate tension and relaxation necessary to give reality, in my own eyes and others, to a condition that did not exist."

2   I estimate that in any given year in the United States, every general hospital with 100 or more beds admits an average of two patients who deliberately mimic symptoms of disease so convincingly that they deceive reasonably competent physicians. The patients' ages range from 11 to 60, but most are men in their 20s and 30s. Often these strange imposters wander from hospital to hospital, but even if we count only one patient per hospital, we are left with the staggering figure of approximately 4,000 people each year who devote their energies to fooling medical practitioners. If each incurs a cost of $1,000 to $10,000—bills that are not unusual, and that are rarely paid—the annual drain on health services alone is between $4 million and $40 million.

3   What do these people hope to gain? Nothing more, experience and research suggest, than the opportunity to assume the role of patient—in some cases, all the way to the operating table.

4   Unlike hypochondriacs, who really believe that they are ill, these people intentionally use varied and often sophisticated deceptions to duplicate medical problems. These deceptions include: blood "spit up" from a rubber pouch concealed in the mouth; genital bleeding deliberately caused by sharp objects; hypoglycemia (low blood sugar) induced by insulin injections; and skin infections or abscesses caused by injecting oneself with feces, sputum, or laboratory cultures of bacteria. A patient who called himself "the Duncan Hines of American hospitals" logged about 400 admissions in 25 years. Another patient, dubbed the "Indiana cyclone," was hospitalized in at least 12 states and two countries. The dramatic fabrication and extensive wandering often observed in such individuals prompted the late British physician Richard Asher

* To help you read this essay analytically, review pages 182–185.

in 1951 to label their "condition" the Munchausen Syndrome, after a flamboyant 18-century teller of tall tales fictionalized in *The Adventures of Baron von Munchausen,* by Rudolph Erich Raspe. But as Asher himself came to realize, the name is somewhat misleading. While stories of the Baron's escapades are always palpably absurd, the accounts of patients whose condition bears his name are generally quite feasible. "Indeed," says Asher, "it is the credibility of their stories that makes these patients such a perpetual and tedious problem."

5   For obvious reasons, Munchausen patients have been difficult to study—they usually flee once their fictions are exposed. But research to this point provides a minimal portrait. In addition to being primarily men in their 20s and 30s, most have high IQs (as their imaginative inventions indicate), often abuse but are not necessarily addicted to drugs, come from a background in which a doctor was an important figure, are employed in health care, and are productive citizens between episodes.

6   What produces their medical madness? There are three main explanations:

7   The psychoanalytic interpretation draws attention to the unconscious. The Munchausen patient, by feigning illness, presents himself simultaneously as victim and victimizer, and compulsively re-enacts unresolved conflicts: The weak child/patient is challenging and even defying the strong father/surgeon. Paradoxically, the weak patient controls the surgeon/parent—and risks death!—by "making" the doctor perform needless surgery. The psychoanalytic view also sees in the syndrome an attempt to continue into adulthood the game of "doctor," which characterizes a phase of childhood development.

8   A second explanation locates the source of Munchausen behavior in a personality trait known as borderline character disorder. According to Otto Kernberg, a psychoanalyst at Cornell who has most fully researched this trait, the core problems are untamed (often unconscious) rage and chronic feelings of boredom, two emotions that work against each other. The Munchausen character, for example, presents himself as a "sick" patient, a condition that should appeal to a dedicated physician—yet no accepting relationship can grow between a deceptive patient and a suspecting physician who is alternately idealized and despised.

9   The third explanation looks to excessive stress as the trigger that starts Munchausen patients on their medical odyssey. Many of them began their "wandering" and symptom mimicry in response to cumulative major disappointments, losses, or damage to self-image. One patient first sought surgery for questionable persistent stomach pains after being jilted by a medical-student lover, beginning a long string of lies and hospitalizations.

10　　We are beginning to identify the reasons for the behavior of Munchausen patients, but we are still far from knowing how to free them of their remarkably creative compulsion for self-destructive behavior.

Questions on Content, Structure, and Style

1. Why does Lipsitt begin his essay with reference to Thomas Mann's character in *Confessions of Felix Krull, Confidence Man?*

2. What effect does the essay's title have on readers? Why didn't Lipsitt simply call this essay "Munchausen Disease"?

3. Why does Lipsitt feel this syndrome is important to understand? How does this problem affect the health care system?

4. Why explain the origin of the syndrome's name?

5. Why does Lipsitt use specific examples of "deceptions" to develop his extended definition?

6. Similarly, why does Lipsitt offer examples of actual patients? Would additional examples be helpful?

7. How does Lipsitt use contrast as a technique of definition in paragraph 4?

8. What other strategy of definition does Lipsitt employ in paragraphs 6–9? Why might readers interested in understanding this syndrome want such discussion?

9. Evaluate the essay's conclusion. Is it an effective choice for this essay?

10. After reading Lipsitt's descriptive details, examples, and analysis, do you feel you now have a general understanding of a new term? If the writer were to expand his definition, what might he add to make your understanding even more complete? More statistics? Case studies? Testimony from doctors or patients themselves?

Suggestions for Writing

Try using Don Lipsitt's "The Munchausen Mystery" as a stepping stone to your essay. Select a puzzling or "mysterious" subject from a field of study or interest you have explored (or would like to explore). Write an extended definition, as Lipsitt did, that explains this mystery for your readers. As appropriate, include information about its characteristics, parts, history, possible causes, effects, solutions, benefits or dangers. Some examples of mysteries include black holes in space, Stonehenge, the Bermuda Triangle, the Loch Ness monster, the Marfa lights, King Tut's "curse," Big Foot, and even the Roswell "aliens." Remember your definition essay should offer indepth explanation, not just description.

Vocabulary

fabricates (1)
mimic (2)
incurs (2)
hypochondriacs (4)

sputum (4)
palpably (4)
feasible (4)
psychoanalytic (7)

paradoxically (7)
odyssey (9)

 A REVISION WORKSHEET

As you write your rough drafts, consult Chapter 5 for guidance through the revision process. In addition, here are a few questions to ask yourself as you revise your extended definition essay:

1. Is the subject narrowed to manageable size, and is the purpose of the definition clear to the readers?

2. If the definition is objective, is the language as neutral as possible?

3. If the definition is subjective, is the point of view obvious to the readers?

4. Are all the words and parts of the definition itself clear to the essay's particular audience?

5. Are there enough explanatory methods (examples, descriptions, history, causes, effects, etc.) used to make the definition clear and convincing?

6. Have the various methods been organized and ordered in an effective way?

7. Does the essay contain enough specific details to make the definition clear and distinct rather than vague or circular? Where could additional details be added?

After you've revised your essay extensively, you might exchange rough drafts with a classmate and answer these questions for each other, making specific suggestions for improvement wherever appropriate. (For advice on productive participation in classroom workshops, see pp. 117–119.)

Reviewing Your Progress

After you have completed your essay developed by definition, take a moment to measure your progress as a writer by responding to the following questions. Such analysis will help you recognize growth in your writing skills and may enable you to identify areas that are still problematic.

1. What do you like best about your essay? Why?

2. After considering the various methods of definition you used in your essay, which one do you think offered the clearest or most persuasive explanation of your topic? Why was that particular technique effective in this essay?

3. What part of your essay gave you the most trouble? How did you overcome the problem?

4. If you had more time to work on this essay, what would receive additional attention? Why?

5. What did you learn about your topic from writing this essay? About yourself as a writer?

STRATEGY FIVE: DEVELOPMENT BY DIVISION AND CLASSIFICATION

To make large or complex subjects easier to comprehend, we frequently apply the principles of *division* or *classification.*

Division

Division is the act of separating something into its component parts so that it may be better understood or used by the reader. For example, consider a complex subject such as the national budget. Perhaps you have seen a picture on television or in the newspaper of the budget represented by a circle or a pie that has been divided into parts and labeled: a certain percentage or "slice" of the budget for military spending, a certain amount designated for social services, another for education, and so on. By studying the budget after it has been divided into its parts, taxpayers may have a better sense of how their money is being spent.

As a student, you see division in action in many of your college courses. A literature teacher, for instance, might approach a particular drama by dividing its plot into stages such as exposition, rising action, climax, falling action, and dénouement. Or your chemistry lab instructor may ask you to break down a substance into its components to learn how the parts interact to form the chemical. Even this textbook is divided into chapters to make it easier for you to use. When you think of *division,* then, think of dividing, separating, or breaking apart one subject (often a large or complex or unfamiliar one) into its parts to help people understand it more easily.

Classification

While the principle of division calls for separating one thing into its parts, *classification* systematically groups a number of things into categories to make the information easier to grasp. Without some sort of imposed system of order, a body of information can be a jumble of facts and figures. For example, at some point you've probably turned to the classified ads in the newspaper; if the ads were not classified into categories such as "houses to rent," "cars for sale," and "help wanted," you would have to search through countless ads to find the service or item you needed.

Classification occurs everywhere around you. As a student, you may be classified as a freshman, sophomore, junior, or senior; you may also be classified by your major. If you vote, you may be categorized as a Democrat, Republican, Socialist, or something else; if you attend religious services, you may be classified as Baptist, Methodist, Catholic, Jewish, and so on. The books you buy may be grouped and shelved by the bookstore into "mysteries," "Westerns," "biographies," "adventure stories," and other categories; the movies you see have already been typed as "G," "PG," "PG-13," "R," "NC-17," or "X." Professionals classify almost every kind of knowledge: ornithologists classify birds; etymologists classify words by origins; botanists classify plants; zoologists classify animals. Remember that *classification* differs from division in that it sorts and organizes *many* things into appropriate groups, types, kinds, or categories. *Division* begins with *one* thing and separates it into its parts.

Developing Your Essay

A classification or division paper is generally easy to develop. Each part or category is identified and described in a major part of the body of the essay. Frequently, one body paragraph will be devoted to each category. Here are three additional hints for writing your essay:

Select one principle of classification or division and stick to it. If you are classifying students by major, for instance, don't suddenly switch to classification by college: French, economics, psychology, *arts and sciences,* math, and chemistry. A similar error occurs in this classification of dogs by breeds because it includes a physical characteristic: spaniels, terriers, *long-haired,* hounds, and retrievers. Decide on what basis of division you will classify or divide your subject and then be consistent throughout your essay.

Make the purpose of your division or classification clear to your audience. Don't just announce that "There are four kinds of 'X'" or that "'Z' has three important parts." Why does your particular audience need this information? Consider these sample thesis statements:

> By recognizing the three kinds of poisonous snakes in this area, campers and backpackers may be able to take the proper medical steps if they are bitten.

> Knowing the four types of spinning reels will enable novice fishermen to purchase the equipment best suited to their needs.

> Although karate has become a popular form of exercise as well as of self-defense, few people know what the six levels of achievement—or "belts" as they are called—actually stand for.

Organize your material for a particular purpose and then explain to your readers what that purpose is.

Account for all the parts in your division or classification. Don't, for instance, claim to classify all the evergreen trees native to your hometown and then leave out one or more species. For a short essay, narrow your ruling principle rather than omit categories. You couldn't, for instance, classify all the architectural styles in America in a short paper, but you could discuss the *major* styles on your campus. In the same manner, the enormous task of classifying all types of mental illness could be narrowed to the most common forms of childhood schizophrenia. However you narrow your topic, remember that in a formal classification, all the parts must be accounted for.

Like most rules, the one above has an exception. If your instructor permits, you can also write a satirical or humorous classification. In this sort of essay, you make up your own categories as well as your thesis. One writer, for example, recently wrote about the kinds of moviegoers who spoil the show for everyone else, such as "the babbling idiot," "the laughing hyena," and "the wandering dawdler." Another female student described blind dates to avoid, including "Mr. Neanderthal," "Timothy Timid," "Red, the Raging Rebel," and "Frat-Rat Freddie," among others. Still another student classified the various kinds of people who frequent the school library at 2 A.M. In this kind of informal essay, the thesis rule still holds true: though you start by making a humorous or satirical point about your subject, your classification must be more than mere silliness. Effective humor should ultimately make good sense, not nonsense.

Problems to Avoid

Avoid underdeveloped categories. A classification or division essay is not a mechanical list; each category should contain enough specific details to make it clearly recognizable and interesting. To present each category or part, you may draw on the methods of development you already know, such as example, comparison and contrast, and definition. Try to use the same techniques in each category so that no one category or part of your essay seems underdeveloped or unclear.

Avoid indistinct categories. Each category should be a separate unit; there should be no overlap among categories. For example, in a classification of shirts by fabric, the inclusion of flannel with silk, nylon, and cotton is an overlap because flannel is a kind of cotton. Similarly, in a classification of soft drinks by flavor, to include sugar-free with cola, root beer, orange, grape, and so on, is misleading because sugar-free drinks come in many different flavors. In other words, make each category unique.

Avoid too few or too many categories. A classification essay should have at least three categories, avoiding the either-or dichotomy. On the other hand, too many categories give a short essay the appearance of a list rather than a discussion. Whatever the number, don't forget to use transition devices for an easy movement from category to category.

 ESSAY TOPICS

Narrow and focus your subject by selecting an appropriate principle of division or classification. Some of the suggestions are for humorous essays ("The Three Best Breeds of Cats for Antisocial People"). For additional ideas, see the "Suggestions for Writing" section following the professional essay on page 268.

1. Friends or relatives
2. Freshmen
3. Heroes in a particular field
4. Movies popular today
5. Attitudes toward a current controversy
6. Ingredients in a popular cosmetic or household product
7. Specializations in your field of study
8. Approaches to studying a subject
9. Classmates, roommates, or dates
10. Dogs, cats, birds, etc.
11. Sports fans or amateur athletes
12. Chronic moochers or borrowers

13. People who accost you on campus or in airports

14. Ways of accomplishing a task (such as three ways to conduct an experiment, four ways to introduce a bill into Congress, etc.)

15. People who play video games (or some other kind of game)

16. Kinds of tools or equipment for a particular task in your field of study

17. Theories explaining "X" (the disappearance of the dinosaurs, for example)

18. Diets or exercise programs

19. Reasons people participate in some activity (or excuses for not participating)

20. Vegetarians or Breatharians (or some other special-interest group)

A Topic Proposal for Your Essay

Selecting the right subject matter is important to every writer. To help you clarify your ideas and strengthen your commitment to your topic, here is a proposal sheet that asks you to describe some of your preliminary ideas about your subject before you begin drafting. Although as you draft your ideas may change (they will almost certainly become more refined), thinking through your choice of topic now may help you avoid several false starts.

1. What is the subject of your essay? Will you write an essay of classification or division?

2. What principle of classification or division will you employ? Why is this a useful or informative principle for your particular topic and readers?

3. Why are you interested in this topic? Do you have a personal or professional connection to the subject? State at least one reason for your choice of topic.

4. Is this a significant topic of interest to others? Why? Who specifically might find it interesting, informative, or entertaining?

5. List at least three categories you are considering for development in your essay.

6. What difficulties, if any, might arise from this topic during the drafting of your essay? For example, do you know enough about your topic to offer details that will make each of your categories clear and distinct to your readers?

SAMPLE STUDENT ESSAY

In the essay below, the student writer divided the Mesa Verde Indian Era into three time periods that correspond to changes in the people's domestic skills, crafts, and housing. Note the writer's use of description and examples to help the reader distinguish one time period from another.

THE INDIAN ERA AT MESA VERDE

Visiting Mesa Verde National Park is a trip back in time to two-and-a-half centuries before Columbus. The park, located in southwestern Colorado, is the setting of a silent stone city, ten ruins built into protective seven-hundred-foot cliffs that housed hundreds of people from the pre-Columbian era to the end of the thirteenth century. If you visit the park, you'll enjoy its architecture and history more if you know a little about the various people who lived there. The Indian Era may be divided into three time periods that show growing sophistication in such activities as crafts, hunting, trade, and housing: Basket Maker (A.D. 1–450), Modified Basket Maker (A.D. 450–750), and Pueblo (A.D. 750–1300).*

The earliest Mesa Verdeans, the Basket Makers, whose ancestors had been nomads, sought shelter from the dry plains in the cliff caves and became farmers. During growing seasons they climbed up toeholds cut in the cliffs and grew beans and squash on the green mesa above. Settling down also meant more time for crafts. They didn't make pottery yet but instead wove intricate baskets that held water. Instead of depending on

Introduction: Establishing a reason for knowing the classification

Principle of division of the Indian Era

Time period one: Early cliff life

_____
* Last summer I worked at Mesa Verde as a student-guide for the Parks Service; the information in this paper is based on the tour I gave three times a week to hundreds of visitors to the park.

raw meats and vegetables, they could now cook food in these baskets by dropping heated rocks into the water. Because the Basket Makers hadn't discovered the bow and arrow yet, they had to rely on the inaccurate spear, which meant little fresh meat and few animal skins. Consequently, they wore little clothing but liked bone, seed, and stone ornaments.

Time period two: New crafts, trade, and housing

The second period, A.D. 450–750, saw the invention of pottery, the bow and arrow, and houses. Pottery was apparently learned from other tribes. From crude clay baked in the sun, the Mesa Verdeans advanced to clay mixed with straw and sand and baked in kilns. Paints were concocted from plants and minerals, and the tribe produced a variety of beautifully decorated mugs, bowls, jars, pitchers, and canteens. Such pots meant that water could be stored for longer periods, and perhaps a water supply encouraged more trade with neighboring tribes. These Mesa Verdeans also acquired the bow and arrow, a weapon that improved their hunting skills, and enlarged their wardrobes to include animal skins and feather blankets. Their individual living quarters, called pithouses, consisted of twenty-foot-wide holes in the ground with log, grasses, and earthen framework over them.

Time period three: Expanded community living and trade

The third period lasted until A.D. 1300 and saw the innovation of pueblos, or groups of dwellings, instead of single-family units. Nearly eight hundred dwellings show the large number of people who inhabited the complex tunneled houses, shops, storage rooms, courtyards, and community centers whose masonry walls, often elaborately decorated, were three and four stories high. At the spacious Balcony House pueblo, for example, an adobe court lies beneath another vaulted roof; on three sides stand two-story houses with balconies that lead from one room to the next. In back of the court is a spring, and along the front side is a low wall that kept the children from falling down the seven-hundred-foot cliff to the canyon floor below. Balcony House also contains two *kivas*, circular subterranean ceremonial chambers that show the importance of fellowship and religion to the people of this era. During this period the Mesa Verdeans were still farmers and potters, but cotton cloth and other nonnative products found at the ruins suggest a healthy trade with the south. But despite the trade goods, sophisticated pottery, and such innovations in clothing as the "disposable" juniper-bark diapers of babies, life was still simple; the Mesa Verdeans had no system of writing, no wheel, and no metal.

Near the end of the thirteenth century, the cliff dwellings became ghost towns. Archaeologists don't know for certain why the Mesa Verdeans left their elaborate homes, but they speculate that a drought that lasted some twenty years may have driven them south into New Mexico and Arizona, where strikingly similar crafts and tools have been found. Regardless of their reason for leaving, they left an amazing architectural and cultural legacy. Learning about the people who lived in Mesa Verde centuries ago provides an even deeper appreciation of the cliff palaces that awe thousands of national park visitors every year.

Conclusion: The importance of Mesa Verde's people

The Plot Against People

Russell Baker

Russell Baker has been a journalist and social commentator for over forty years. His "Observer" columns, written for The New York Times *and syndicated throughout the country, won him both the George Polk Award for Distinguished Commentary and a Pulitzer Prize for journalism. He has written several books, including* Growing Up *(1982), an autobiography that won him a second Pulitzer Prize,* The Good Times *(1989), and* Russell Baker's Book of American Humor *(1993). This essay originally appeared in* The New York Times *in 1968.*

1   Inanimate objects are classified into three major categories—those that don't work, those that break down and those that get lost.

2   The goal of all inanimate objects is to resist man and ultimately to defeat him, and the three major classifications are based on the method each object uses to achieve its purpose. As a general rule, any object capable of breaking down at the moment when it is most needed will do so. The automobile is typical of the category.

3   With the cunning typical of its breed, the automobile never breaks down while entering a filling station with a large staff of idle mechanics. It waits until it reaches a downtown intersection in the middle of the rush hour, or until it is fully loaded with family and luggage on the Ohio Turnpike.

4   Thus it creates maximum misery, inconvenience, frustration and irritability among its human cargo, thereby reducing its owner's life span.

5   Washing machines, garbage disposals, lawn mowers, light bulbs, automatic laundry dryers, water pipes, furnaces, electrical fuses, television tubes, hose nozzles, tape recorders, slide projectors—all are in league with the automobile to take their turn at breaking down whenever life threatens to flow smoothly for their human enemies.

6   Many inanimate objects, of course, find it extremely difficult to break down. Pliers, for example, and gloves and keys are almost totally incapable of breaking down. Therefore, they have had to evolve a different technique for resisting man.

7   They get lost. Science has still not solved the mystery of how they do it, and no man has ever caught one of them in the act of getting lost. The most plausible theory is that they have developed a secret method of locomotion which they are able to conceal the instant a human eye falls upon them.

8   It is not uncommon for a pair of pliers to climb all the way from the cellar to the attic in its single-minded determination to raise its owner's

* To help you read this essay analytically, review pages 182–185.

blood pressure. Keys have been know to burrow three feet under mattresses. Women's purses, despite their great weight, frequently travel through six or seven rooms to find hiding space under a couch.

9   Scientists have been struck by the fact that things that break down virtually never get lost, while things that get lost hardly ever break down.

10   A furnace, for example, will invariably break down at the depth of the first winter cold wave, but it will never get lost. A woman's purse, which after all does have some inherent capacity for breaking down, hardly ever does; it almost invariably chooses to get lost.

11   Some persons believe this constitutes evidence that inanimate objects are not entirely hostile to man, and that a negotiated peace is possible. After all, they point out, a furnace could infuriate a man even more thoroughly by getting lost than by breaking down, just as a glove could upset him far more by breaking down than by getting lost.

12   Not everyone agrees, however, that this indicates a conciliatory attitude among inanimate objects. Many say it merely proves that furnaces, gloves, and pliers are incredibly stupid.

13   The third class of objects—those that don't work—is the most curious of all. These include such objects as barometers, car clocks, cigarette lighters, flashlights and toy-train locomotives. It is inaccurate, of course, to say that they never work. They work once, usually for the first few hours after being brought home, and then quit. Thereafter, they never work again.

14   In fact, it is widely assumed that they are built for the purpose of not working. Some people have reached advanced ages without ever seeing some of these objects—barometers, for example—in working order.

15   Science is utterly baffled by the entire category. There are many theories about it. The most interesting holds that the things that don't work have attained the highest state possible for an inanimate object, the state to which things that break down and things that get lost can still only aspire.

16   They have truly defeated man by conditioning him never to expect anything of them, and in return they have given man the only peace he receives from inanimate society. He does not expect his barometer to work, his electric locomotive to run, his cigarette lighter to light or his flashlight to illuminate, and when they don't, it does not raise his blood pressure.

17   He cannot attain that peace with furnaces and keys and cars and women's purses as long as he demands that they work for their keep.

Questions on Content, Structure, and Style

1. What is Baker's purpose in writing this classification? What reaction do you think Baker wants to evoke from his reading audience?

2. Where is Baker's thesis statement? Would his essay be more effective if his thesis were preceded by a fully developed lead-in? Why or why not?

3. Identify Baker's categories and principle of classification. What do these categories have in common?

4. Why does Baker give examples of items that belong to each category? Does this strengthen his essay? Why or why not?

5. Of the categories of inanimate objects discussed in the essay, which one is most effectively developed? List some examples of details.

6. Consider Baker's use of personification as he talks about inanimate objects. Give some examples of descriptions that give human qualities to these items. What effect does this have on tone and style?

7. How does Baker's word choice affect his tone? Would it be possible to write an effective essay about this subject from a more serious, informative standpoint? Why or why not?

8. What does Baker's title contribute to his tone and his readers' understanding of his classifying principle?

9. Evaluate Baker's conclusion. Is it effective or too abrupt?

10. What other categories of inanimate objects might you add to this essay? What items could you include under these new classifications?

Suggestions for Writing

Try using Russell Baker's "The Plot Against People" as a stepping stone to your writing. To parallel Russell's criticisms of objects that inflict misery, think about kinds of people or forces that you feel are secretly conspiring to destroy your peace of mind. Consider, for example, kinds of crazed drivers who are contributing to road rage today. Annoying telephone solicitors? Obnoxious waiters or clerks? Grocery shoppers in the check-out line in front of you? Or consider the kinds of rules that govern your life. Inane parking regulations that ensure you will never find a space anywhere near campus? Financial aid red tape only an accounting genius could cut through? Your essay might be humorous, like Russell's, or quite serious, as you expose still another "plot" against humankind.

Vocabulary

inanimate (1)	locomotion (7)	conciliatory (12)
cunning (3)	virtually (9)	barometer (13, 14)
league (5)	inherent (10)	
evolve (6)	constitutes (11)	

A REVISION WORKSHEET

As you write your rough drafts, consult Chapter 5 for guidance through the revision process. In addition, here are a few questions to ask yourself as you revise your classification essay:

1. Is the purpose of the essay clear to the reader?

2. Is the principle of classification or division maintained consistently throughout the essay?

3. If the essay presents a formal division or classification, has the subject been narrowed so that all the parts of the subject are accounted for?

4. If the essay presents an informal or humorous division or classification, does the paper nevertheless make a significant or entertaining point?

5. Is each category developed with enough specific detail? Where might more details be effectively added?

6. Is each class distinct, with no overlap among categories?

7. Is the essay organized logically and coherently with smooth transitions between the discussions of the categories?

After you've revised your essay extensively, you might exchange rough drafts with a classmate and answer these questions for each other, making specific suggestions for improvement wherever appropriate. (For advice on productive participation in classroom workshops, see pp. 117–119.)

Reviewing Your Progress

After you have completed your essay developed by classification or division, take a moment to measure your progress as a writer by responding to the following questions. Such analysis will help you recognize growth in your writing skills and may enable you to identify areas that are still problematic.

1. What is the best feature of your essay? Why?

2. Which category do you think is the clearest or most persuasive in your essay? Why does that one stand above the others?

3. What part of your essay gave you the most trouble? How did you overcome the problem?

4. If you had more time to work on this essay, what would receive additional attention? Why?

5. What did you learn about your topic from writing this essay? About yourself as a writer?

STRATEGY SIX: DEVELOPMENT BY CAUSAL ANALYSIS

Causal analysis explains the cause-and-effect relationship between two (or more) elements. When you discuss the condition producing something, you are analyzing *cause;* when you discuss the result produced by something, you are analyzing *effect.* To find examples of causal analysis, you need only look around you. If your car stops running on the way to class, for example, you may discover the cause was an empty gas tank. On campus, in your history class, you may study the causes of the Civil War; in your economics class, the effects of teenage spending on the cosmetics market; and in your biology class, both the causes and effects of heart disease. Over dinner you may discuss the effects of some crisis in the Middle East on American foreign policy, and, as you drift to sleep, you may ponder the effects of your studying—or *not* studying—for your math test tomorrow.

To express it most simply, *cause* asks:

why did "X" happen?

or, why does "X" happen?

or, why will "X" happen?

Effect, on the other hand, asks:

what did "Y" produce?

or, what does "Y" produce?

or, what will "Y" produce?

Some essays of causal analysis focus on the cause(s) of something; others analyze only the effect(s); still others discuss both causes and effects. If, for example, you wanted to concentrate on the major causes of the Wall Street crash of 1929, you might begin by briefly describing the effects of the crash on the economy, then devote your thesis and the rest of your essay to analyzing the major causes, perhaps allotting one major section (or one paragraph, depending on the complexity of the reasons) to each cause. Conversely, an effect paper might briefly describe the causes of the crash and then detail the most important effects. An essay covering both the causes and effects of something usually demands a longer paper so that each part will be clear. (Your assignment will frequently indicate which kind of causal analysis to write. However, if the choice is yours, let your interest in the subject be your guide.)

Developing Your Essay

Whether you are writing an essay that primarily discusses either causes or effects, or one that focuses on both, you should follow these rules:

Present a reasonable thesis statement. If your thesis makes dogmatic, unsupportable claims ("Medicare will lead to a complete collapse of quality medical treatment") or overly broad assertions ("Peer pressure causes alcoholism among students"), you won't convince your reader. Limit or qualify your thesis whenever necessary by using such phrases as "may be," "a contributing factor," "one of the main reasons," "two important factors," and so on ("Peer pressure is *one of the major causes* of alcoholism among students").

Limit your essay to a discussion of recent, major causes or effects. In a short paper you generally don't have space to discuss minor or remote causes or effects. If, for example, you analyzed your car wreck, you might decide that the three major causes were defective brakes, a hidden yield sign, and bad weather. A minor, or remote, cause might include being tired because of too little sleep, too little sleep because of staying out late the night before, staying out late because of an out-of-town visitor, and so on—back to the womb. In some cases you may want to mention a few of the indirect causes or effects, but do be reasonable. Concentrate on the most immediate, most important factors. Often, a writer of a 500- to 800-word essay will discuss no more than two, three, or four major causes or effects of something; trying to cover more frequently results in an underdeveloped essay that is not convincing.

Organize your essay clearly. Organization of your causal analysis essay will vary, of course, depending on whether you are focusing on the causes of something or the effects, or both. To avoid becoming tangled in causes and effects, you might try sketching out a drawing of your thesis and essay map before you begin your first draft. Here, for instance, are a couple of sketches for essays you might write on your recent traffic accident:

Thesis Emphasizing the Causes:

Cause (defective brakes)
Cause (hidden yield sign)   produced   Effect (my car wreck)
Cause (bad weather)

Thesis Emphasizing the Effects:

Cause (my car wreck)   produced

Effect (loss of car)
Effect (doctor bills)
Effect (higher insurance rates)

Sometimes you may discover that you can't isolate "the three main causes/effects of 'X'"; some essays do in fact demand a narrative explaining a chain reaction of causes and effects. For example, a paper on the rebellion of the American colonies might show how one unjust British law or restriction after another led to the war for independence. In this kind of causal analysis essay, be careful to limit your subject so that you'll have the space necessary to show your readers how each step in the chain led to the next. Here's a sketch of a slightly different car-wreck paper presented in a narrative or chain-reaction format:

Cause ⟶ 1st Effect —causes→ 2nd Effect —causes→ 3rd Effect
(bad weather)   (wet brakes)   (car wreck)   (doctor bills)

Sometimes the plan for organizing your causal analysis paper will be suggested by your subject matter; often, however, you'll have to devote some of your prewriting time to deciding, first, whether you want to emphasize causes or effects and, then, in what arrangement you will present your analysis.

Convince your reader that a causal relationship exists by showing how the relationship works. Let's suppose you are writing an essay in which you want to discuss the three major changes you've undergone since coming to college. Don't just state the changes and describe them; your job is to show the reader how college has *brought about* these changes. If, for instance, your study habits have improved, you must show the reader how the academic demands of your college courses caused you to change your habits; a simple description of your new study techniques is not enough. Remember that a causal analysis essay should stress *how* (and sometimes *why*) "X" caused "Y," rather than merely describing "Y" as it now exists.

Problems to Avoid

Don't oversimplify by assigning one all-encompassing cause to some effect. Most complex subjects have more than one cause (or effect), so make your analysis as complete and objective as you can, especially when dealing with your own problems or beliefs. For example, was that car wreck really caused only by the bad weather—or also because of your carelessness? Did your friend do poorly in math only because the instructor didn't like her? Before judging a situation too quickly, investigate your own biases. Then provide a thoughtful, thorough analysis, effectively organized to convince your readers of the validity of your viewpoint.

Avoid the *post hoc* fallacy. This error in logic (from the Latin phrase *post hoc, ergo propter hoc,* meaning "after this, therefore because of this") results when we mistake a temporal connection for a causal relationship—or in other words, when we assume that because one event follows another in time, the first event caused the second. Most of our superstitions are *post hoc* fallacies; we now realize that bad luck after walking under a ladder is a matter of coincidence, not cause and effect. The *post hoc* fallacy provided the basis for a rather popular joke in the 1960s' debates over decriminalizing marijuana. Those against argued that marijuana led to heroin because most users of the hard drug had first smoked grass. The proponents retorted that milk, then, was the real culprit, because both marijuana and heroin users had drunk milk as babies. The point is this: in any causal analysis, you must be able to offer proof or reasoned logic to show that one event *caused* another, not just that it preceded it in time.

Avoid circular logic. Often causal essays seem to chase their own tails when they include such circular statements as "There aren't enough parking spaces for students on campus because there are too many cars." Such a statement merely presents a second half that restates what is already implied in the first half. A revision might say, "There aren't enough parking spaces for students on campus because the parking permits are not distributed fairly." This kind of assertion can be argued specifically and effectively; the other is a dead end.

 ESSAY TOPICS

The subjects below may be developed into essays emphasizing cause or effect, or both. For additional ideas, turn to the "Suggestions for Writing" section following the professional essay on page 281.

1. A pet peeve or bad habit

2. A change of mind about some important issue or belief

3. An accident, misadventure, or crime

4. A family tradition, ritual, or story

5. Travel or vacation experience

6. Ownership of a particular possession

7. A radical change in your appearance

8. A hobby, sport, or job

9. The best (or worst) advice you ever followed

10. An important decision or action

11. An act of heroism or sacrifice

12. An important idea, event, or discovery in your field of study

13. A superstition or irrational fear

14. A place that is special to you

15. A disappointment or a success

16. Racism or sexism or some other kind of discrimination or prejudice

17. A friendship or influential person

18. A political action (campus, local, state, national), historical event, or social movement

19. Stress or an addiction or an illness

20. Your favorite academic class

A Topic Proposal for Your Essay

Selecting the right subject matter is important to every writer. To help you clarify your ideas and strengthen your commitment to your topic, here is a proposal sheet that asks you to describe some of your preliminary ideas about your subject before you begin drafting. Although as you draft your ideas may change (they will almost certainly become more refined), thinking through your choice of topic now may help you avoid several false starts.

1. What is the subject of your causal analysis essay? Is this subject appropriately narrowed and focused for a discussion of major causes or effects?

2. Will you develop your essay to show the effects or the causes of your topic? Or a causal chain?

3. Why are you interested in this topic? Do you have a personal or professional connection to the subject? State at least one reason for your choice of topic.

4. Is this a significant topic of interest to others? Why? Who specifically might find it interesting, informative, or entertaining?

5. List at least two major causes or effects that you might develop in the discussion of your topic.

6. What difficulties, if any, might arise during your drafting on this topic? For example, how might you convince a skeptical reader that your causal relationship is not merely a temporal one?

SAMPLE STUDENT ESSAY

In the following essay, a student explains why working in a local motel damaged her self-esteem, despite her attempts to do a good job. Note that the writer uses many vivid examples and specific details to show the reader how she was treated and, consequently, how such treatment made her feel.

IT'S SIMPLY NOT WORTH IT

It's hard to get a job these days, and with our town's unemployment rate reaching as high as ten percent, most people feel obligated to "take what they can get." But after working as a maid at a local motel for almost a year and a half, I decided no job is worth keeping if it causes a person to doubt his or her worth. My hard work rarely received recognition or appreciation, I was underpaid, and I was required to perform some of the most disgusting cleaning tasks imaginable. These factors caused me to devalue myself as a person and ultimately motivated me to return to school in hope of regaining my self-respect.

It may be obvious to say, but I believe that when a maid's hours of meticulous cleaning are met only with harsh words and complaints, she begins to lose her sense of self-esteem. I recall the care I took in making the motel's beds, imagining them as globs of clay and molding them into impeccable pieces of art. I would teeter from one side of a bed to the other, over and over again, until I smoothed out every intruding wrinkle or tuck. And the mirrors—I would vigorously massage the glass, erasing any toothpaste splotches or oil smudges that might draw my customer's disapproval. I would scrutinize the mirror first from the left side, then I'd move to the right side, once more to the left until every possible angle ensured an unclouded reflection. And so

Introduction: Her job as a motel maid

Thesis and map: Causes of her poor self-esteem

Cause one: Lack of appreciation

my efforts went, room after room. But, without fail, each day more than one customer would approach me, not with praise for my tidy beds or spotless mirrors, but with nitpicking complaints that undermined my efforts: "Young lady, I just checked into room 143 and it only has one ashtray. Surely for $69.95 a night you people can afford more ashtrays in the rooms."

If it wasn't a guest complaining about ashtrays, it was an impatient customer demanding extra towels or a fussy stay-over insisting his room be cleaned by the time he returned from breakfast at 8:00 A.M. "Can't you come to work early to do it?" he would urge thoughtlessly. Day after day, my spotless rooms went unnoticed, with no spoken rewards for my efforts from either guests or management. Eventually, the ruthless complaints and thankless work began wearing me down. In my mind, I became a servant undeserving of gratitude.

Cause two:
Low pay

The lack of spoken rewards was compounded by the lack of financial rewards. The $5.50/hour appraisal of my worth was simply not enough to support my financial needs or my self-esteem. The measly $1.80 I earned for cleaning one room took a lot of rooms to add up, and by the end of the month I was barely able to pay my bills and buy some food. (My mainstay became sixty-two cent, generic macaroni and cheese dinners.) Because the flow of travelers kept the motel full for only a few months of the year, during some weeks I could only work half time, making a mere $440.00 a month. As a result, one month I was forced to request an extension on my rent payment. Unsympathetically, my landlord threatened to evict me if I didn't pay. Embarrassed, yet desperate, I went to a friend and borrowed money. I felt uneasy and awkward and regretted having to beg a friend for money. I felt like a mooch and a bum; I felt degraded. And the constant reminder from management that there were hundreds of people standing in lines who would be more than willing to work for $4.25 an hour only aided in demeaning me further.

In addition to the thankless work and the inadequate salary, I was required to clean some of the most sickening messes. Frequently, conventions for high school clubs booked the motel. Once I opened the door of a conventioneer's room one morning and almost gagged at the odor. I immediately beheld a trail of vomit that began at the bedside and ended just short of the bathroom door. At that moment I cursed the inventor of shag carpet, for I knew it would take hours to comb this mess out of the fibers. On another day I spent thirty minutes dislodging the bed linen from the toilet where it had been stuffed. And I spent what seemed like hours removing from one of my spotless mirrors the lipstick-drawn message that read, "Yorktown Tigers are number one." But these inconsiderate acts were relaying another message, a message I took personally: "Lady, you're not worth the consideration—you're a maid and you're not worth respecting."

Cause three: Repulsive duties

I've never been afraid to work hard or do jobs that weren't particularly "fun." But the line must be drawn when a person's view of herself becomes clouded with feelings of worthlessness. The thankless efforts, the inadequate wage, and the disgusting work were just parts of a total message that degraded my character and caused me to question my worth. Therefore, I felt compelled to leave this demeaning job in search of a way to rebuild my self-confidence. Returning to school has done just that for me. As my teachers and fellow students take time to listen to my ideas and compliment my responses, I feel once again like a vital, valued, and worthwhile person. I feel human once more.

Conclusion: Review of the problem and a brief explanation of the solution she chose

Mystery!

Nicholas Meyer

Nicholas Meyer is a novelist, screenwriter, and movie director. Many of his novels are mysteries devoted to further adventures of Sherlock Holmes; two of these mysteries, The Seven-Per-Cent Solution *(1974) and* The West End Horror *(1976), were made into successful movies. His latest mystery is* Canary Trainer: From the Memoirs of John H. Watson *(1995). Meyer has recently worked on a variety of science fiction projects, including direction of the movie* Star Trek II: The Wrath of Khan.

1   Reading mysteries is a bedtime recreation for all segments of society—high, low and middle brow. It is the *divertissement*† of prime ministers and plumbers. Mysteries, whether they are on television, paper or movie screens, delight almost all of us. Everyone likes to "curl up" with a good mystery, and that makes this particular kind of literature unique in its ubiquitous appeal. No other genre so transcends what might otherwise appear to be significant differences in the social, educational and economic backgrounds of its audience.

2   Why, for heaven's sake? What is there about mystery and detective stories that fascinate so many of us, regardless of age, sex, color and national origin?

3   On the surface, it seems highly improbable that detective novels should provide such broad-based satisfaction. Their jacket blurbs and ad copy contain plenty of violent, even gory, references: "The body lay inert, the limbs dangling at unnatural angles, the head bashed in, clearly the result of a blunt instrument . . ." Who wants to read this stuff? Even assuming that there is a certain segment of society that delights in sadistic imagery and rejoices in thrills and chills and things that go bump in the night, it is hard to imagine that these sensibilities are in the majority.

4   As the Great Detective‡ himself might have observed, "It is a singular business, Watson, and on the surface, most unlikely." Yet as Holmes was wont to remark, evidence that appears to point in one unerring direction may, if viewed from a slightly altered perspective, admit of precisely the opposite interpretation. People do, in fact, like to "curl up" with a good mystery. They take the corpses and the murderers to bed with them as favorite nighttime reading. One could hardly imagine a more intimate conjunction!

---

* To help you read this essay analytically, review pages 182–185.
† A French word for diversion or entertainment.
‡ Sherlock Holmes

5   But the phrase "curling up" does not connote danger; say rather the reverse. It conjures up snug, warm, secure feelings. Curling up with a good mystery is not exciting or thrilling; it is in fact oddly restful. It is reassuring.

6   Now why should this be? How is it possible that detective stories, with all the murder and blackmail and mayhem and mystery that pervades them, should provide us with feelings of security, coziness and comfort?

7   Well, detective stories have other things in them besides violence and blood. They have solutions, for one thing. Almost invariably, the murderer is caught, or at the very least identified. *As sure as God made little green apples, it all adds up to something.* If it doesn't, we aren't happy with the piece. A good detective story ties up all the loose ends; we resent motives and clues left unconnected.

8   Yes, detective stories have solutions. But life does not. On the contrary, life is an anarchic proposition in which meaningless events conspire daily to alter our destiny without rhyme or reason. Your plane crashes, or the one you were booked on crashes but you missed it; a flat tire, a missed phone call, an open manhole, a misunderstanding—these are the chaotic commonplaces of everyday existence. But they have no place in the mystery novel. In detective novels, nothing happens without a reason. Detective literature, though it may superficially resemble life, in fact has effected at least one profound alteration: mystery stories *organize* life and provide it with meaning and answers. The kind of confusion in which real people are forced to exist doesn't occur in detective stories. Whatever the various people's problems, the only serious difficulty confronting them in detective stories is the fact that they are suspected of committing the crime involved. Once cleared of that lowering cloud, they are free to pursue their lives with, presumably, successful results.

9   So we see that the coziness of detective and mystery stories is not entirely incomprehensible or inappropriate, after all. If we like to take such literature to bed with us and cuddle up with it, what we are really cuddling up to is a highly stylized literary formula, which is remarkably consistent in delivering to us that reassuring picture we all crave of an ordered world.

10   Sherlock Holmes, Philip Marlowe, Miss Marple or Columbo—the stories in which these characters appear all manage to delight us by reassuring us. The victim is usually only slightly known or not very well liked. The world seems better off without him, or else he is so sorely missed that tracking his (or her) murderer will be, in Oscar Wilde's* words, more than a duty, it will be a pleasure.

11   And pleasurable indeed is the process of watching the tracking. There are some highfalutin apologists of the detective genre who would

---

* Oscar Wilde (1854–1900): a famous English wit and author.

have us believe it is the intellectual exercise of following the clues along with the detective—the reader's or viewer's participation in a kind of mental puzzle—that provides the satisfaction associated with detective stories. I believe such participation is largely illusory. We don't really ever have all the pieces at our disposal and most of us are not inclined to work with them very thoroughly, even in those rare cases when the author has been scrupulously "fair" in giving them to us. We enjoy the *illusion* of participation without really doing any of the mental legwork beyond the normal wondering "Whodunit?"

12   In any event, such a theory to justify the fascination exerted by detective and mystery stories is elitist and falsely elitist into the bargain. It distracts our attention with a pretentious and tenuous explanation in place of a much more interesting and persuasive one; namely, that detective stories are appealing because they depict life not as it is but in some sense as it ought to be.

Questions on Content, Structure, and Style

1. In this essay Meyer tries to solve a mystery himself. He is trying to find the cause of our enjoyment of what activity?

2. Why does Meyer begin his essay wondering about the popularity and appeal of this activity? Is this an effective way to begin this essay?

3. What is the purpose of paragraph 6?

4. What is Meyer's thesis? Where does it first become clear?

5. How do mystery stories differ from life? What examples does Meyer provide to help the reader see the contrast?

6. Meyer plays on the cliché of "curling up with a good mystery" several times in this essay; in his opinion, what are we really cuddling up to when we take a good mystery to bed?

7. According to Meyer and Oscar Wilde, mysteries provide another, secondary, source of pleasure. What is that?

8. What other explanation for the mystery's popularity does Meyer reject? Why does he reject this explanation?

9. Meyer often uses informal diction like "stuff" (3) and "highfalutin" (11), and clichés such as "thrills and chills and things that go bump in the night" (3) and "as sure as God made little green apples" (7). Are these choices effective? Why/why not?

10. How does Meyer conclude his essay? Does the ending successfully wrap up his causal analysis? Why/why not?

Suggestions for Writing

Try using Nicholas Meyer's "Mystery!" as a stepping stone to your essay. Think about other kinds of popular culture (movies, television shows, dances, clothing styles, video games, etc.) enjoying favor at this time. Can you account for people's interest in a particular activity or style? For example, in the 1950s movie-goers thrilled to a profusion of monsters, often created through scientific misdeeds or nuclear accidents—giant ants, carnivorous spiders, resurrected pterodactyls, outer-space blobs, and even radiation-crazed rabbits! Clearly, Hollywood was tapping into America's post-atomic bomb fears, which were happily comforted by each monster's destruction at the film's end. Think about popular culture in your lifetime: why did teen-slasher movies become box office hits? Why did the ancient art of tattooing become popular? Why so much interest in space aliens? Become a social scientist and persuasively explain the popularity of some trend or style. (Or, if you prefer, account for the enormous success of a particular movie, television show, author, etc.)

Vocabulary

ubiquitous (1)	anarchic (8)	pretentious (12)
genre (1)	scrupulously (11)	tenuous (12)
mayhem (6)	elitist (12)	

 A REVISION WORKSHEET

As you write your rough drafts, consult Chapter 5 for guidance through the revision process. In addition, here are a few questions to ask yourself as you revise your causal analysis essay:

1. Is the thesis limited to a reasonable claim that can be supported in the essay?

2. Is the organization clear and consistent so that the reader can understand the purpose of the analysis?

3. Does the essay focus on the most important causes and/or effects?

4. If the essay has a narrative form, is each step in the chain reaction clearly connected to the next?

5. Does the essay convincingly show the reader how or why relationships between the causes and effects exist, instead of merely naming and describing them?

6. Does the essay provide enough evidence to show the connections between causes and effects? Where could additional details be added to make the relationships clearer?

7. Has the essay avoided the problems of oversimplification, circular logic, and the *post hoc* fallacy?

After you've revised your essay extensively, you might exchange rough drafts with a classmate and answer these questions for each other, making specific suggestions for improvement wherever appropriate. (For advice on productive participation in classroom workshops, see pp. 117–119.)

Reviewing Your Progress

After you have completed your essay developed by causal analysis, take a moment to measure your progress as a writer by responding to the following questions. Such analysis will help you recognize growth in your writing skills and may enable you to identify areas that are still problematic.

1. What do you like best about your essay? Why?

2. After considering your essay's presentation of the major causes or effects, which part of your analysis do you think readers will find the most convincing? Why?

3. What part of your essay gave you the most trouble? How did you overcome the problem?

4. If you had more time to work on this essay, what would receive additional attention? Why?

5. What did you learn about your topic from writing this essay? About yourself as a writer?

CHAPTER

10

Argumentation

Almost without exception, each of us, every day, argues for or against something with somebody. The discussions may be short and friendly ("Let's go to this restaurant rather than that one") or long and complex ("Mandatory seatbelt laws are an intrusion on civil rights"). Because we do argue our viewpoints so often, most of us realized long ago that shifting into high whine did not always get us what we wanted. On the contrary, we've learned that we usually have a much better chance at winning a dispute or having our plan adopted or changing someone's mind if we present our side of an issue in a calm, logical fashion, giving sound reasons for our position. This approach is just what a good argumentative essay does: it presents logical reasoning and solid evidence that will persuade your readers to accept your point of view.

Some argumentative essays declare the best solution to a problem ("Raising the drinking age will decrease traffic accidents"); others argue a certain way of looking at an issue ("Beauty pageants degrade women"); still others may urge adoption of a specific plan of action ("Voters should pass ordinance 10 to fund the new ice rink"). Whatever your exact purpose, your argument essay should be composed of a clear thesis and body paragraphs that offer enough sensible reasons and persuasive evidence to convince your readers to agree with you.

Developing Your Essay

Here are some suggestions for developing and organizing an effective argumentative essay:

Choose an appropriate topic. Selecting a good topic for any essay is important. Choosing a focused, appropriate topic for your argument essay will save you enormous time and energy even before you begin prewriting. Some subjects are simply too large and complex to be adequately treated in a five-page argumentative essay; selecting such a subject might produce a rough draft of generalities that will not be persuasive. If you have an interest in a subject that is too general or complex for the length of your assignment, see if you can find a more focused, specific issue within it to argue. For example, the large, controversial (and rather overdone) subject "capital punishment" might be narrowed and focused to a paper advocating time limits for the death-row appeal process. A general opinion on "unfair college grading" might become a more interesting persuasive essay in which the writer takes a stand on the use of pluses and minuses (A–, B+, B–, etc.) on transcript grades. Your general annoyance with smokers might move from "All smoking should be outlawed forever" to an essay focused on the controversial smoking bans in open-air sports stadiums. In other words, while we certainly do debate large issues in our lives, in a short piece of writing it may be more effective, and often more interesting, to choose a focused topic that will allow for more depth in the arguments. You must ultimately decide whether your choice of subject is appropriate for your assignment, but taking a close, second look at your choice now may save you frustration later.

Know why you hold your views. We human beings, being opinionated creatures, frequently voice beliefs that we, when pressed, can't always support effectively. Sometimes we hold an opinion simply because on the surface it seems to make good sense to us or because it fits comfortably with our other social, ethical, or political beliefs. Or we may have inherited some of our beliefs from our families or friends, or perhaps we borrowed ideas from well-known people we admire. In some cases, we may have held an opinion for so long that we can't remember why we adopted it in the first place. We may also have a purely sentimental or emotional attachment to some idea or position. Whatever the original causes of our beliefs, we need to examine the real reasons for thinking what we do before we can effectively convince others.

Once you've selected a topic for your argument essay, try writing down a list of the reasons or points that support your opinion on that subject. Then study the list—are your points logical and persuasive? Which aren't, and why not? After this bit of prewriting, you may discover that although you believe something strongly, you really don't have the kinds of factual evidence or reasoned arguments you need to support your opinion. In some cases, depending on your topic, you may wish to talk to others who share your position or to research your subject (for help with research, see Chapter 14); in other cases, you may just need to think longer and harder about your topic and your reasons for maintaining your attitude toward it. With or without formal research, the better you know your subject, the more confident you will be about writing your argumentative essay.

Anticipate opposing views. An argument assumes that there is more than one side to an issue. To be convincing, you must be aware of your opposition's views on the subject and then organize your essay to answer or counter those views. If you don't have a good idea of the opposing arguments, you can't effectively persuade your readers to dismiss their objections and see matters your way. Therefore, before you begin your first rough draft, write down all the opposing views you can think of and an answer to each of them so that you will know your subject thoroughly. (For the sake of clarity throughout this chapter, your act of responding to those arguments against your position will be called *refuting the opposition;* "to refute" means "to prove false or wrong," and that's what you will try to do to some of the arguments of those who disagree with you.)

Know and remember your audience. Although it's important to think about your readers' needs and expectations whenever you write, it is essential to consider carefully the audience of your argumentative essay both before and as you write your rough drafts. Because you are trying to persuade people to adopt some new point of view or perhaps to take some action, you need to decide what kinds of supporting evidence will be most convincing to your particular readers. Try to analyze your audience by asking yourself a series of questions. What do they already know about your topic? What information or terms do they need to know to understand your point of view? What biases might they already have for or against your position? What special concerns might your readers have that influence their receptiveness? To be convincing, you should consider these questions and others by carefully reviewing the discussion of audience on pages 20–24 *before* you begin your drafts.

Decide which points of argument to include. Once you have a good sense of your audience and of your own position and your opposition's strongest arguments, try making a Pro-and-Con Sheet to help you sort out which points you will discuss in your essay.

Let's suppose you want to write an editorial on the sale-of-class-notes controversy at your school. Should professional note-takers be allowed to sit in on a course and then sell their notes to class members? After reviewing the evidence on both sides, you have decided to argue that your school should prohibit professional note-taking services from attending large lecture classes and selling notes. To help yourself begin planning your essay, you list all the pro-and-con arguments you can think of concerning the controversy:

MY SIDE: AGAINST THE SALE OF CLASS NOTES

1. Unfair advantage for some students in some classes

2. Note-taking is a skill students need to develop

3. Rich students can afford and poor can't

4. Prevents students from learning to organize for themselves

5. Encourages class cutting

6. Missing class means no chance to ask questions, participate in discussions

7. Notes taken by others are often inaccurate

8. Some professors don't like strangers in classroom

9. Students need to think for themselves

MY OPPOSITION'S SIDE: FOR THE SALE OF CLASS NOTES

1. Helps students to get better test, course grades

2. Helps students to learn, organize material

3. Helps if you're sick and can't attend class

4. Shows students good models for taking notes and outlining them

5. Other study guides are on the market, why not these?

6. Gives starving graduate students jobs

7. No laws against sale of notes, free country

After making your Pro-and-Con Sheet, look over the list and decide which of your strongest points you want to argue in your paper and also which of your opposition's claims you want to refute. At this point you may also see some arguments on your list that might be combined and some that might be deleted because they're irrelevant or unconvincing. (Be careful not to select more arguments or counterarguments to discuss than the length of your writing assignment will allow. It's far better to present a persuasive analysis of a few points than it is to give an underdeveloped, shallow treatment of a host of reasons.)

Let's say you want to cover the following points in your essay:

• Professional note-taking services keep students from developing own thinking and organizational skills (combination of 4 and 9)

• Professional note-taking services discourage class attendance and participation (5 and 6)

• Unfair advantages to some students (1 and 3).

Your assignment calls for an essay of 750 to 1,000 words, so you figure you'll only have space to refute your opposition's strongest claim. You decide to refute this claim:

- Helps students to learn and organize material (2).

The next step is to formulate a working thesis. At this stage you may find it helpful to put your working thesis in an "although-because" format so you can clearly see both your opposition's arguments and your own. An "although-because" statement for the note-taking essay might look something like this:

> *Although* some students maintain that using professional note-taking services helps them learn more, such services should be banned from our campus *because* they prevent students from developing their own thinking and organizational skills, they discourage class attendance, and they give unfair advantages to some students.

Frequently your "although-because" thesis will be too long and awkward to use in the later drafts of your essay. But for now, it can serve as a guide, allowing you to see your overall position before the writing of the first draft begins.

Organize your essay clearly. Although there is no set model of organization for argumentative essays, here are some common patterns that you might use or that you might combine in some effective way.

Important note: For the sake of simplicity, the first two outlines present two of the writer's points and two opposing ideas. Naturally, your essay may contain any number of points and refuted points, depending on the complexity of your subject and the assigned length of your essay.

In Pattern A you devote the first few body paragraphs to arguing points on your side and then turn to refute or answer the opposition's claims.

Pattern A: Thesis

Body paragraph 1: you present your first point and its supporting evidence

Body paragraph 2: you present your second point and its supporting evidence

Body paragraph 3: you refute your opposition's first point

Body paragraph 4: you refute your opposition's second point

Conclusion

Sometimes you may wish to clear away the opposition's claims before you present the arguments for your side. To do so, you might select Pattern B:

Pattern B: Thesis

Body paragraph 1: you refute your opposition's first point

Body paragraph 2: you refute your opposition's second point

Body paragraph 3: you present your first point and its supporting evidence

Body paragraph 4: you present your second point and its supporting evidence

Conclusion

In some cases you may find that the main arguments you want to present are the very same ones that will refute or answer your opposition's primary claims. If so, try Pattern C, which allows each of your argumentative points to refute one of your opposition's claims in the same paragraph:

Pattern C: Thesis

Body paragraph 1: you present your first point and its supporting evidence, which also refutes one of your opposition's claims

Body paragraph 2: you present a second point and its supporting evidence, which also refutes a second opposition claim

Body paragraph 3: you present a third point and its supporting evidence, which also refutes a third opposition claim

Conclusion

Now you might be thinking, "What if my position on a topic as yet has no opposition?" Remember that almost all issues have more than one side, so try to anticipate objections and then answer them. For example, you might first present a thesis that calls for a new traffic signal at a dangerous intersection in your town and then address hypothetical counter-arguments, such as "The City Council may say that a stop light at Lemay and Columbia will cost too much, but the cost in lives will be much greater" or "Commuters may complain that a traffic light there will slow the continuous flow of north-south traffic, but it is precisely the uninterrupted nature of this road that encourages motorists to speed." By answering hypothetical objections, you impress your readers by showing them you've thought through your position thoroughly before you asked them to consider your point of view.

You might also be thinking, "What if my opposition actually has a valid objection, a legitimate point of criticism? Should I ignore it?" Hoping that an obviously strong opposing point will just go away is like hoping the IRS will cancel income taxes this year—a nice thought but hardly likely. Don't ignore your opposition's good point; instead, acknowledge it, but then go on quickly to show your readers why that reason, though valid, isn't compelling enough by itself to motivate people to adopt your opposition's entire position. Or you might concede that one point while simultaneously showing why your position isn't really in conflict with that criticism, but rather with other, more important, parts of your opponent's viewpoint. By admitting that you see some validity in your opposition's argument, you can again show your readers that you are both fair-minded and informed about all aspects of the controversy.

If you are feeling confident about your ability to organize an argumentative essay, you might try some combination of patterns, if your material allows such a treatment. For example, you might have a strong point to argue, another point that simultaneously answers one of your opposition's strongest claims, and another opposition point you want to refute. Your essay organization might look like this:

Combination: Thesis

Body paragraph 1: A point for your side

Body paragraph 2: One of your points, which also refutes an opposition claim

Body paragraph 3: Your refutation of another opposition claim

In other words, you can organize your essay in a variety of ways as long as your paper is logical and clear. Study your Pro-and-Con Sheet and then decide which organization best presents the arguments and counterarguments you want to include. Try sketching out your essay following each of the patterns; look carefully to see which pattern (or variation of one of the patterns) seems to put forward your particular material most persuasively, with the least repetition or confusion. Sometimes your essay's material will clearly fall into a particular pattern of organization, so your choice will be easy. More often, however, you will have to arrange and rearrange your ideas and counter-arguments until you see the best approach. Don't be discouraged if you decide to change patterns after you've begun a rough draft; what matters is finding the most effective way to persuade the reader to your side.

If no organizational pattern seems to fit at first, ask yourself which of your points or counter-arguments is the strongest or most important. Try putting that point in one of the two most emphatic places: either first or last. Sometimes your most important discussion will lead the way to your other points and consequently should be introduced first; perhaps more often, effective writers and speakers build up to their strongest point, presenting it last as the climax of their argument. Again, the choice depends on your material itself, though it's rare that you would want to bury your strongest point in the middle of your essay.

Now let's return to the essay on note-taking first discussed on page 285. After selecting the most important arguments and counter-arguments (p. 286), let's say that you decide that your main point concerns the development of students' learning skills. Since your opposition claims the contrary, that their service does promote learning, you see that you can make your main point as you refute theirs. But you also wish to include a couple of other points for your side. After trying several patterns, you decide to put the "thinking skills" rebuttal last for emphasis and present your other points first. Consequently, Pattern A best fits your plan. A sketchy outline might look like this:

- *Revised working thesis and essay map:* Professional note-taking services should be banned from our campus. Not only do they give some students unfair advantages and discourage class attendance, they prevent students from developing and practicing good thinking skills.

- *Body paragraph 1 (a first point for the writer's side):* Services penalize some students—those who haven't enough money or take other sections or enroll in classes without notes.

- *Body paragraph 2 (another point for the writer's side):* The service encourages cutting class and so students miss opportunities to ask questions, participate in discussion, talk to instructor, see visual aids, etc.

- *Body paragraph 3 (rebuttal of the opposition's strongest claim):* Services claim they help students learn more, but they don't because they're doing the work students ought to be doing themselves. Students must learn to think and organize for themselves.

Once you have a general notion of where your essay is going, plan to spend some more time thinking about ways to make each of your points clear, logical, and persuasive to your particular audience. (If you wish to see how one student actually developed an essay based on the preceding outline, turn to the sample student paper on pp. 301–304.)

Argue your ideas logically. To convince your readers, you must provide sufficient reasons for your position. You must give more than mere opinion— you must offer logical arguments to back up your assertions. Some of the possible ways of supporting your ideas should already be familiar to you from writing expository essays; listed below are several methods and illustrations:

1. Give examples (real or hypothetical): "Cutting class because you have access to professional notes can be harmful; for instance, you might

miss seeing some slides or graphics essential to your understanding of the lecture."

2. **Present a comparison or contrast:** "In contrast to reading 'canned' notes, outlining your own notes helps you remember the material."

3. **Show a cause-and-effect relationship:** "Dependence on professional notes may mean that some students will never learn to organize their own responses to classroom discussions."

4. **Argue by definition:** "Passively reading through professional notes isn't a learning experience in which one's mind is engaged."

The well-thought-out arguments you choose to support your case may be called *logical appeals* because they appeal to, and depend on, your readers' ability to reason and to recognize good sense when they see it. But there is another kind of appeal often used today: the *emotional appeal.*

Emotional appeals are designed to persuade people by playing on their feelings rather than appealing to their intellect. Rather than using thoughtful, logical reasoning to support their claims, writers and speakers using *only* emotional appeals often try to accomplish their goals by misleading their audiences. Frequently, emotional appeals are characterized by language that plays on people's fears, material desires, prejudices, or sympathies; such language often triggers highly favorable or unfavorable responses to a subject. For instance, emotional appeals are used constantly in advertising, where feel-good images, music, and slogans ("Come to Marlboro Country"; "The Heartbeat of America Is Today's Chevy Truck") are designed to sway potential customers to a product without them thinking about it too much. Some politicians also rely heavily on emotional appeals, often using scare tactics to disguise a situation or to lead people away from questioning the logic of a particular issue.

But in some cases, emotional appeals can be used for legitimate purposes. Good writers should always be aware of their audience's needs, values, and states of mind, and they may be more persuasive in some cases if they can frame their arguments in ways that appeal to both their readers' logic and their emotions. For example, when Martin Luther King, Jr., delivered his famous "I Have A Dream" speech to the crowds gathered in Washington in 1963 and described his vision of little children of different races walking hand-in-hand, being judged not "by the color of their skin but by the content of their character," he certainly spoke with passion that was aimed at the hearts of his listeners. But King was not using an emotional appeal to keep his audience from thinking about his message; on the contrary, he presented powerful emotional images that he hoped would inspire people to act on what they already thought and felt, their deepest convictions about equality and justice.

Appeals to emotions are tricky: you can use them effectively in conjunction with appeals to logic and with solid evidence, but only if you use them ethically. And too many appeals to the emotions are overwhelming; readers tire quickly from too many tugs on the heartstrings. To prevent your readers from suspecting deception, support your assertions with as many logical arguments as you can muster and use emotional appeals only when they legitimately advance your cause.

Offer evidence that effectively supports your claims. In addition to presenting thoughtful, logical reasoning, you may wish to incorporate a variety of convincing evidence to persuade your readers to your side. Your essay might profit from including, where appropriate, some of the following kinds of supporting evidence:

- Personal experiences
- The experiences or testimony of others whose opinions are pertinent to the topic
- Factual information you've gathered from research
- Statistics from current, reliable sources
- Charts, graphs, or diagrams
- Testimony from authorities and experts

You'll need to spend quite a bit of your prewriting time thinking about the best kinds of evidence to support your case. Remember that not all personal experiences or research materials are persuasive. For instance, the experiences we've had (or that our friends have had) may not be representative of a universal experience and consequently may lead to unconvincing generalizations. Even testimony from an authority may not be convincing if the person is not speaking on a topic from his or her field of expertise; famous football players, for instance, don't necessarily know any more about panty hose or soft drinks than anyone else. Always put yourself in the skeptical reader's place and ask, "Does this point convince me? If not, why not?" (For more information on incorporating research material into your essays, see Chapter 14. For more advice on the selection of evidence, see the section on critical thinking in Chapter 5.)

Find the appropriate tone. Sometimes when we argue, it's easy to get carried away. Remember that your goal is to persuade and perhaps change your readers, not alienate them. Instead of laying on insults or sarcasm, present your ideas in a moderate let-us-reason-together spirit. Such a tone will persuade your readers that you are sincere in your attempts to argue as truthfully and fairly as possible. If your readers do not respect you as a reasonable person, they certainly won't be swayed to your side of an issue. Don't preach or pontificate either; no one likes—or respects—a writer with a superior attitude. Write in your natural "voice"; don't adopt a pseudointellectual tone. In short, to argue effectively you should sound logical, sincere, and informed. (For additional comments on tone, review pp. 160–164.)

Consider using Rogerian techniques, if they are appropriate. In some cases, especially those involving tense situations or highly sensitive issues, you may wish to incorporate some techniques of the noted psychologist Carl Rogers, who developed a procedure for presenting what he calls the non-threatening argument. Rogers believes that people involved in a debate should strive for clear, honest communication so that the problem under discussion can be resolved. Instead of going on the defensive and trying to "win" the argument, each side should try to recognize common ground and then develop a solution that will address the needs of both parties.

A Rogerian argument uses these techniques:

1. A clear, objective statement of the problem or issue

2. A clear, objective summary of the opposition's position that shows you understand its point of view and goals

3. A clear, objective summary of your point of view, stated in nonthreatening language

4. A discussion that emphasizes the beliefs, values, and goals that you and your opposition have in common

5. A description of any of your points that you are willing to concede or compromise

6. An explanation of a plan or proposed solution that meets the needs of both sides.

By showing your opposition that you thoroughly understand its position and that you are sincerely trying to effect a solution that is in everyone's—not just your—best interests, you may succeed in some situations that might otherwise be hopeless because of their highly emotional nature. Remember, too, that you can use some of these Rogerian techniques in any kind of argument paper you are writing, if you think they would be effective.

Problems to Avoid

Writers of argumentative essays must appear logical or their readers will reject their point of view. Here is a short list of some of the most common *logical fallacies*—that is, errors in reasoning. Check your rough drafts carefully to avoid these problems.

Students sometimes ask, "If a logical fallacy works, why not use it? Isn't all fair in love, war, and argumentative essays?" The honest answer is "maybe." It's quite true that speakers and writers do use faulty logic and irrational emotional appeals to persuade people every day (one needs only to look at television or a newspaper to see example after example). But the cost of the risk is high: if you do try to slide one by your readers and they see through your trick, you will lose your credibility instantly. On the whole, it's far more effective to use logical reasoning and strong evidence to convince your readers to accept your point of view.

COMMON LOGICAL FALLACIES

Hasty generalization: The writer bases the argument on insufficient or unrepresentative evidence. Suppose, for example, you have owned two poodles and they have both attacked you. If you declare that all poodles are vicious dogs, you are making a hasty generalization. There are, of course, thousands of poodles who have not attacked anyone. Similarly, you're in error if you interview only campus athletes and then declare, "University students favor a new stadium." What about the opinions of the students who aren't athletes? In other words, when the generalization is drawn from a sample that is too small or select, your conclusion isn't valid.

***Non sequitur* ("it doesn't follow"): The writer's conclusion is not necessarily a logical result of the facts.** An example of a *non sequitur* occurs when you conclude, "Professor Smith is a famous historian, so he will be a brilliant history teacher." As you may have realized by now, just because someone knows a subject well does not automatically mean that he or she can communicate the information clearly; hence, the conclusion is not necessarily valid.

Begging the question: The writer presents as truth what is supposed to be proven by the argument. For example, in the statement "All useless laws such as Reform Bill 13 should be repealed," the writer has already assumed the bill is useless without assuming responsibility for proving that accusation. Similarly, the statement "Dangerous pornography should be banned" begs the question (that is, tries like a beggar to get something for nothing from the reader) because the writer gives no evidence for what must first be argued, not merely asserted—that pornography is dangerous.

Red herring: The writer introduces an irrelevant point to divert the readers' attention from the main issue. This term originates from the old tactic used by escaped prisoners, of dragging a smoked herring, a strong-smelling fish, across their trail to confuse tracking dogs by making them follow the wrong scent. For example, roommate A might be criticizing roommate B for his repeated failure to do the dishes when it was his turn. To escape facing the charges, roommate B brings up times in the past when the other roommate failed to repay some money he borrowed. Although roommate A may indeed have a problem with remembering his debts, that discussion isn't relevant to the original argument about sharing the responsibility for the dishes. (By the way, you might have run across a particular newspaper photograph of a California ecology group demonstrating for more protection of dolphins, whales, and other marine life; look closely to see, over in the left corner, almost hidden by the host of placards and banners, a fellow slyly holding up a sign that reads "Save the Red Herring!" Now, who says rhetoricians don't have a good sense of humor?)

Post hoc, ergo propter hoc. See page 273.

Argument *ad hominem* ("to the man"): The writer attacks the opponent's character rather than the opponent's argument. The statement "Dr. Bloom can't be a competent marriage counselor because she's been divorced twice" may not be valid. Bloom's advice to her clients may be excellent regardless of her own marital status.

Faulty use of authority. See page 292 and pages 372–373.

Argument *ad populum* ("to the people"): The writer evades the issues by appealing to readers' emotional reactions to certain subjects. For example, instead of arguing the facts of an issue, a writer might play on the readers' negative response to such words as "communism," "fascism," or "radical" and their positive response to words like "God," "country," or "liberty." In the statement "If you are a true American, you will vote against the referendum on busing," the writer avoids any discussion of the merits or weaknesses of the bill and merely substitutes an emotional appeal. (Advertisers, of course, play on consumers' emotions by filling their ads with pictures of babies, animals, status objects, and sexually attractive men and women.)

Circular thinking. See page 273.

Either/or: The writer tries to convince the readers that there are only two sides to an issue—one right, one wrong. The statement "If you don't go to war against Iceland, you don't love your country" is irrational because it doesn't consider the other possibilities, such as patriotic people's right to oppose war as an expression of love for their country. A classic example of this sort of oversimplification was illustrated in the 1960s' bumper sticker that was popular during the debate over the Vietnam War: "America: Love It or Leave It." Obviously, there are other choices ("Change It or Lose It," for instance, to quote another either/or bumper sticker).

Hypostatization: The writer uses an abstract concept as if it were a concrete reality. Always be suspicious of a writer who frequently uses statements beginning "History has taught us . . ." or "Science has proven . . ." or "Research has discovered. . . ." The implication in each case is that history or science (or any other discipline) has only one voice, one opinion. On the contrary, "history" is written by a multitude of historians who hold a variety of opinions; doctors and scientists also frequently disagree. Instead of generalizing about a particular field, quote a respected authority or simply qualify your statement by referring to "many" or "some" scientists, historians, or other professionals.

Bandwagon appeal: The writer tries to validate a point by intimating that "everyone else believes in this." Such a tactic evades discussion of the issue itself. Advertising often uses this technique: "Everyone who demands real taste smokes Phooey cigarettes"; "Discriminating women use Smacky-Mouth lipstick." (The ultimate in "bandwagon" humor may have appeared on a recent Colorado bumper sticker: "Eat lamb—could 1000s of coyotes be wrong?")

Straw man: The writer selects the opposition's weakest or most insignificant point to argue against, to divert the readers' attention from the real issues. Instead of addressing the opposition's best arguments and defeating them, the writer "sets up a straw man"—that is, the writer picks out a trivial (or irrelevant) argument against his or her own position and easily knocks it down, just as one might easily push over a figure made of straw. Perhaps the most famous example of the "straw man" occurred in 1952 when, during his vice-presidential campaign, Richard Nixon was accused of misappropriating campaign funds for his personal use. Addressing the nation on television, Nixon described how his six-year-old daughter, Tricia, had received a little cocker spaniel named Checkers from a Texas supporter. Nixon went on about how much his children loved the dog and how, regardless of what anyone thought, by gosh, he was going to keep that cute dog for little Tricia. Of course, no one was asking Nixon to return the dog; they were asking about the $18,000 in missing campaign funds. But Nixon's canine gift was much easier for him to defend, and the "Checkers'" speech is now famous as one of the most notorious "straw man" diversions.

Faulty analogy: The writer uses an extended comparison as proof of a point. Look closely at all extended comparisons and metaphors to see if the two things being compared are really similar. For example, in a recent editorial a woman protested the new laws requiring parents to use car seats for small children, arguing that if the state could require the seats they could just as easily require mothers to breastfeed instead of using formula. Are the two situations alike? Car accidents are the leading cause of death of children under four; is formula dangerous? Or perhaps you've read that putting teenagers in sex education classes is like taking an alcoholic to a bar. Is it? If the opinion isn't supported by evidence, the analogy may not be persuasive. Moreover, remember that even though a compelling analogy might suggest similarities, it alone cannot *prove* anything.

Quick fix: The writer leans too heavily on catchy phrases or empty slogans. A clever turn-of-phrase may grab one's attention, but it may lose its persuasiveness when scrutinized closely. For instance, a banner at a recent rally to protest a piece of antigun legislation read, "When guns are outlawed, only outlaws will have guns." Although the sentence had nice balance, it oversimplified the issue. The legislation in question was not trying to outlaw all guns, just the sale of the infamous Saturday Night Specials, most often used in crimes and domestic violence; the sale of guns for sport, such as hunting rifles, would remain legal. Other slogans sound good but are simply irrelevant: a particular soft drink, for example, may be "the real thing," but what drink isn't? Look closely at clever lines substituted for reasoned argument; always demand clear terms and logical explanations.*

 PRACTICING WHAT YOU'VE LEARNED

Errors in reasoning can cause your reader to doubt your credibility. In the following mock essay, for example, the writer includes a variety of fallacies that undermine his argument; see if you can identify all his errors.

BAN THOSE BOOKS!

A serious problem faces America today, a problem of such grave importance that our very existence as a nation is threatened. We must either cleanse our schools of evilminded books, or we must reconcile ourselves to seeing our children become welfare moochers and homeless bums.

History has shown time and time again that placement of immoral books in our schools is part of an insidious plot designed to weaken the moral fiber of our youth from coast

---

*Sometimes advertisers get more for their slogans than they bargained for. According to one news source, a popular soft-drink company had to spend millions to revise its slogan after introducing its product into parts of China. Apparently the slogan "Come alive! Join the Blah-Blah-Cola Generation!" translated into some dialects as "Blah-Blah Cola Brings Your Ancestors Back from the Dead"!

to coast. In Wettuckett, Ohio, for example, the year after books by Mark Twain such as *Tom Sawyer* and *Huckleberry Finn* were introduced into the school library by liberal free-thinkers and radicals, the number of students cutting classes rose by six percent. And in that same year the number of high school seniors going on to college dropped from thirty to twenty-two.

The reason for this could either be a natural decline in intelligence and morals or the influence of those dirty books that teach our beloved children disrespect and irresponsibility. Since there is no evidence to suggest a natural decline, the conclusion is inescapable: once our children read about Twain's characters skipping school and running away from home, they had to do likewise. If they hadn't read about such undesirable characters as Huckleberry Finn, our innocent children would never have behaved in those ways.

Now, I am a simple man, a plain old farm boy—the pseudo-intellectuals call me redneck just like they call you folks. But I can assure you that, redneck or not, I've got the guts to fight moral decay everywhere I find it, and I urge you to do the same. For this reason I want all you good folks to come to the ban-the-books rally this Friday so we can talk it over. I promise you all your right-thinking neighbors will be there.

 ASSIGNMENT

Search for the following:

1. Two examples of advertisements that illustrate one or more of the fallacies or appeals discussed on pages 294–297;

2. One example of illogical or fallacious reasoning in a piece of writing (you might try looking at the editorial page or letters-to-the-editor section of your local or campus newspaper);

3. One example of a logical, persuasive point in a piece of writing.

Be prepared to explain your analyses of your samples, but do not write any sort of identifying label or evaluation on the samples themselves. Bring your ads and pieces of writing to class and exchange them with those of a classmate. After ten minutes, compare notes. Do you and your classmate agree on the evaluation of each sample? Why or why not?

ESSAY TOPICS

Write a convincing argument attacking or defending one of the following statements, or use them to help you think of your own topic. Remember to narrow and focus topic as necessary. (Note that essays on some of the topics presented below would profit from library research material; see Chapter 14 for help.) For additional ideas, see the "Suggestions for Writing" section following the professional essays.

1. Students should/should not work their way through college.

2. To prepare students for a highly technical world, high schools should/should not extend their academic year.

3. Sixteen-year-olds should/should not be issued limited-privilege driver's licenses.

4. Mandatory on-the-job drug tests should/should not be allowed.

5. Birth parents should/should not be allowed to reclaim babies after children have been released for adoption.

6. The advertising of alcohol should/should not be limited to the print media, as are cigarette ads.

7. Students who do poorly in their academic courses should/should not be allowed to participate in athletic programs.

8. Violence in the movies does/does not contribute to crimes by teens.

9. Televised instant replays should/should not be used to call plays in football and other sports.

10. The parking system (computer center, food service, language lab, etc.) at this college should/should not be reorganized.

11. Internet pornography should/should not be regulated.

12. Previously convicted child molesters should/should not be required to register with local police.

13. Students should/should not serve in a youth corps for two years following high school.

14. Organ donors should/should not be allowed to receive financial compensation.

15. Student evaluations should/should not be a major consideration in the rehiring or promotion of a teacher.

16. The Ku Klux Klan (or any controversial organization) should/should not be allowed to speak on campus.

17. State-supported colleges should/should not be allowed to enroll exclusively male or female students.

18. Vitamin C (or herbal healing or any kind of nontraditional treatment) can/cannot help relieve illness.

19. To avoid problems of sexual harassment, men and women in the military should/should not be trained in separate units.

20. Controversial names or symbols of athletic teams ("Redskins," the Confederate flag, the tomahawk chop) should/should not be changed.

A Topic Proposal for Your Essay

Selecting the right subject matter is important to every writer. To help you clarify your ideas and strengthen your commitment to your topic, here is a proposal sheet that asks you to describe some of your preliminary ideas about your subject before you begin drafting. Although as you draft your ideas may change (they will almost certainly become more refined), thinking through your choice of topic now may help you avoid several false starts.

1. What is the subject of your argumentative essay? Is it controversial? Debatable? Write a rough statement of your opinion about this subject.

2. Why are you interested in this topic? Is it important to your personal, civic, or professional life? State at least one reason for your choice of topic.

3. Is this a significant topic of interest to others? Why? Is there a particular audience you would like to address?

4. At this point can you list at least two reasons that support your opinion of your topic?

5. Who opposes your opinion? Can you state clearly at least one of your opposition's major criticisms of your position?

6. What difficulties, if any, might arise during drafting? For example, might you need to collect any additional evidence through reading, research, or interviewing to support your points or to refute your opposition?

S A M P L E   S T U D E N T   E S S A Y

The student who wrote the essay below followed the steps for writing an argumentative paper discussed in this chapter. His intended audience were the readers of his school newspaper, primarily fellow students but instructors as well. To argue his case, he chose Pattern A, presenting two of his own points and then concluding with a rebuttal of an important opposing view. Notice that this writer uses a variety of methods to convince his readers, including hypothetical examples, causal analysis, analogy, and testimony. Does the writer persuade you to his point of view? Which are his strongest and weakest arguments? What might you change to make his essay even more persuasive?

STUDENTS, TAKE NOTE!

A walk across campus this week will reveal students, professors, and administrators arguing about class notes like never before. But they're not engaged in intellectual debates over chemical formulas or literary images. No, they're fighting over the taking of the notes themselves, as professional note-taking services in town are applying for permission to sit in on large, lecture courses and then sell their notes to the students in those classes. Although the prospect of having "canned" notes looks inviting to many students, our administration should nevertheless ban these services from campus. Not only do such businesses give certain students unfair advantages and discourage class attendance, but they also prohibit the development of students' important learning skills, despite the services' claims to the contrary.

What is bothered for many of us about the professional-notes option is our sense of fair play. Let's face it: like it or not, school is, among other things, a place of competition, as students vie for the best academic records to send to prospective employers,

Introduction: Presenting the controversy

Thesis

Essay map

A point for the writer's position: Note-taking services are unfair to some students

graduate and professional schools, and in some cases, paying parents. In today's classes all students have an equal opportunity to come to class, take notes, study, and pass or fail on their own merits. But the expensive professional notes, already organized and outlined, may give those with plenty of money some advantages that poorer students—those on scholarships or with families, for example—just can't afford. In addition, the notes may be available only to those students who take certain sections of a course and not others, thus giving some students an extra option. The same is true for students who satisfy a requirement by taking one course that has notes available rather than another which has not. Knowing that you're doing your own work may make you feel morally superior to a classmate who isn't, but frankly, on some other level, it just plain feels irritating and unfair, sort of like watching your roommate getting away with plagiarizing his paper for a class after you spent weeks researching yours.

Another point for the writer's position: Professional notes discourage students from attending and participating in class

In addition to being a potential source of conflict among students, the professional-note services aren't winning many friends among the faculty either. Several instructors have complained that the availability of notes will encourage many students, especially the weaker ones, to cut classes, assuming that they have all the material necessary for understanding the lecture, discussion, or lab. But anyone who has ever had to use borrowed notes knows something vital is not there. Someone else's interpretations of the information is often hard or impossible to follow, especially if you must understand complex relationships and problems. Moreover, skipping class may mean missed opportunities for students to ask questions or to participate in experiments or in group discussions, all of which often help clarify concepts under study. Not seeing visual aids or diagrams in person can also result in problems understanding the material. And, last, missing class can mean failure to become comfortably acquainted with the teacher, which, in turn, may discourage a student from asking for individual help when it's needed. All these possibilities are real; even Jeff Allridge, owner of the Quotable Notes service, has admitted to a campus reporter, "There *is* an incentive to skip class."

Despite the admission that professional note-taking encourages class-cutting, the services still promote themselves by claiming that students using their notes learn more. They support this claim by arguing that their notes offer students clearly organized information and, according to one advertising brochure, "good models" for students to follow in other classes. But such arguments miss the larger point: students should be learning how to develop their own note-taking, organizing, and thinking skills rather than swallowing the material whole as neatly packaged and delivered. Memorizing class material as outlined can be important, but it's not really as valuable in the long run as learning how to think about the material and use it to solve problems or come up with new ideas later. Taking your own notes teaches you how to listen and how to spot the important concepts; organizing your own notes teaches you how to pull ideas together in a logical way, all skills students will need in other classes, on jobs, and in life in general. Having memorized the outlines but not really mastered the thinking skills won't help the medical student whose patient's symptoms vary from the textbook description or the engineer whose

Presentation and rebuttal of the opposition's claim that students learn more using professional notes airplane wings suddenly fail the stress test for no apparent reason.

Conclusion: Restatement of thesis, ending on pun to emphasize the main idea

By appealing to students who believe professional notes will help them accomplish their educational goals easier and quicker, a variety of note-taking services now have franchises across the country. But our campus shouldn't allow them to move in. Students need to recognize that the difference between the services' definition of "learning" and the real learning experiences college can provide is of notable importance.

PROFESSIONAL ESSAYS*

The following essays were first published together in *USA Today* in a 1998 "Today's Debate" column. The first essay represents the views of the newspaper's editorial board; the second essay was written by Monty Neill, acting executive director of the National Center for Fair and Open Testing.

Although you may already hold an opinion on "grade retention," try to remain objective as you analyze the strengths and weaknesses of both essays. Which points are most and least persuasive, and why?

USA TODAY'S VIEW:

Free Pass Fails Kids

1   Schools finally are ending an educational practice they never should have started—promoting even the students who fail.

2   The mistaken theory behind these "social promotions" is that children who are held back in school suffer damaging blows to their self-esteem. But this feel-good teaching practice ignores basic truths about the learning process. Chiefly, most knowledge is sequential. And a child who can't master material one year isn't likely to grasp more advanced lessons the next.

3   Embarrassed by high school graduates who can't read or write, several school systems are questioning policies allowing the mass promotion of failing students. And governors from California to Texas this month joined President Clinton in calls to abolish the social promotion of students who aren't making the grade. Their doubts make sense. Ignoring academic problems won't make them disappear. And giving students a free pass maintains schools' mediocrity by absolving students and teachers of their failings.

4   Yet bans on social promotions alone won't help the nation's troubled schools or their students. Turning academic failures into success stories is more complicated than telling kids, "Sorry. Try again."

5   There is scant research supporting the notion that students who repeat classes will improve their academic achievement. What's more, dropout rates balloon 20-30% among students who are held back.

6   The debate over dealing with lagging learners requires more than a pass-fail choice. Instead, school systems need better ways of identifying struggling students early on and providing them with intensive tutoring and customized learning plans.

---

*For help reading these essays analytically, review pages 182–185.

7   That's the solution adopted in Long Beach, Calif., where educators have set up academic "checkpoints" in grades 3 and 8. Students missing needed skills are sent to summer school. Similarly, 42,000 Chicago students were required to take summer "bridge" classes last year because of their low test scores. By September, 15,000 had improved enough to be promoted.

8   Weekend classes, tutoring and summer school are costly. But targeted help is no more expensive than the average $5,500 per pupil states pay when students repeat a grade.

9   Replacing the social promotion of failing students with early, effective help teaches kids an important life lesson: Competence counts. And for students, personally, it is more rewarding than a free pass.

OPPOSING VIEW:

Retaining Kids No Answer

Monty Neill

1   Opposition to "social promotion" is another "magic bullet" which offers a false solution to the real problems of students who are not learning.

2   Yes, students who need help should get it. They should not be passed along automatically. But grade retention does not improve learning.

3   Basing promotion decisions on test scores is unfair to many students and undermines educational quality. In Chicago, for example, students who score low on a multiple-choice test are held back. This violates the measurement profession's standards for proper test use, which say schools should not make important decisions based solely on test scores.

4   This is because every test has measurement error. For example, on the SAT, used for college admissions, to know if two students really are different, their scores need to be about 140 points apart on a 1,200-point scale. This imprecision means that some students who should be promoted will be retained (or not graduate), while others who really need help will not get it.

5   What happens to students who are retained? Educational research clearly shows that retention is not helpful. A student who is not doing well in third grade and is held back will, when finally promoted, usually still be at the bottom of the class in fifth grade. However, students who are retained are far more likely to drop out, and repeating grades wastes a lot of taxpayers' money.

6   Meanwhile, to try to raise test scores, many schools reduce the curriculum to test coaching. As a result, many important things are not taught, depriving students of a good education. The "drill and kill" instruction fostered by teaching to the test also causes many young people to dislike school. Summer schools set up to help students pass the test

often focus on students who are close to passing, while ignoring students with even greater needs.

7   No one wins from grade retention. There needs to be a better solution to real educational problems, starting with providing each student a powerful, engaging education. The nation does not need another misfired magic bullet.

Questions on Content, Structure, and Style

1. What is *USA Today's* position on the educational practice of "social promotions"?

2. What are, according to this editorial, the main reasons to oppose promotion of failing students? Ultimately, what "important life lesson" do they wish students to learn?

3. What arguments supporting social promotions are acknowledged by the editorial writers? Why do they mention these opposition arguments?

4. What solution to the pass-fail problem do the writers suggest? Why do they mention Long Beach and Chicago schools? How do they anticipate an objection to their proposed solution?

5. Evaluate the editorial's arguments. Which are the most and least effective? Why? How might you strengthen his arguments?

6. What is Monty Neill's opinion of test-based promotion decisions? What reasons does he give for his position?

7. What, according to Neill, happens to students who are retained?

8. What problems for students may arise from schools' attempts to raise scores by "teaching to the test"?

9. Evaluate Neill's arguments. Which are his most and least effective points? Why? How might you strengthen his arguments?

10. Overall, which of these two essays do you find the more persuasive? Do you think students who fail should be retained? Should promotion be based on test scores? Should summer school be "required" of those who fail? If you were to write your own response to this complex problem, what position would you take and what arguments might you include to support your view?

Suggestions for Writing

Try using the *USA Today* and Neill debate as a stepping stone to your essay. Think of a controversial rule, regulation, or requirement that has greatly impacted your education. Perhaps you have been affected—positively or negatively—by the outcome of a placement or exit exam. What problems are such exams designed to address and are they successful? Would some other policy work better? Or consider a particular college entrance or graduation requirement that you support or think unreasonable. Thoroughly investigate the reasons for and against the academic policy you choose before you formulate your thesis. If appropriate, consider interviewing administrators, teachers, and other students to understand your subject from multiple points of view. Use the information that you gather to help you shape your best arguments and confront your opposition.

Vocabulary

USA Today's editorial:

        sequential (2)   scant (5)
        mediocrity (3)   competence (9)
        absolving (3)

M. Neill's response:

    retention (2)   imprecision (4)   fostered (6)

PRO-AND-CON ADVERTISEMENTS: GUN CONTROL

The National Rifle Association has published a series of advertisements to tell people about the organization. According to the NRA, one of their purposes is to protect Second Amendment rights. However, after the attempted assassination of President Ronald Reagan and the shooting of his Press Secretary James Brady, many ads appeared calling for new gun-control legislation. Many of these ads featured Sarah Brady, who, following her husband's shooting, became a strong advocate of the controversial 1994 "Brady Bill," which requires registration and a waiting period before the sale of some types of handguns. Sarah Brady is now chair of the Center to Prevent Handgun Violence, the organization that sponsored the 1995 ad reprinted here.

Study the two ads on the following pages to determine which appeals they use to persuade readers to their side. Which appeals do you find the most and least persuasive and why?

REP. ALBERTO GUTMAN: Florida Legislator, Businessman,
Husband, Member of the National Rifle Association.

"Being from a country that was once a democracy and
turned communist, I really feel I know what the right to bear arms
is all about. In Cuba, where I was born, the first thing the
communist government did was take away everybody's firearms, leaving
them defenseless and intimidated with fear. That's why our
constitutional right to bear arms is so important to our country's survival.

"As a legislator I have to deal with reality. And the reality
is that gun control does not work. It actually eliminates the rights of the
law-abiding citizen, not the criminal. Criminals will always have
guns, and they won't follow gun control laws anyway. I would like to see tougher
laws on criminals as opposed to tougher laws on legitimate gun
owners. We need to attack the problem of crime at its roots, instead of blaming
crime on gun ownership and citizens who use them lawfully.

"It's a big responsibility that we face retaining the right to bear arms.
That's why I joined the NRA. The NRA is instrumental in
protecting these freedoms. It helps train and educate people, supporting
legislation that benefits not only those who bear arms
but all citizens of the United States. The
NRA helps keep America free." **I'm the NRA.**

The NRA's lobbying organization, the Institute for Legislative Action, is the
nation's largest and most influential protector of the constitutional right to keep and bear arms.
At every level of government and through local grassroots efforts, the Institute
guards against infringement upon the freedoms of law-abiding gun owners. If you would like to
join the NRA or want more information about our programs and benefits, write
J. Warren Cassidy, Executive Vice President, P.O. Box 37484, Dept. AG-15, Washington, D.C. 20013.

Paid for by the members of the National Rifle Association of America. Copyright 1986.

Reprinted with permission of the National Rifle Association.

IS THIS THE "WELL REGULATED MILITIA" PROTECTED BY THE SECOND AMENDMENT?

"A well regulated Militia, being necessary to the security of a free State, the right of the people to keep and bear Arms, shall not be infringed."

—*Second Amendment to the U.S. Constitution*

For years, the National Rifle Association has spread the myth that gun control laws violate the Second Amendment. Now self-styled "citizen militias" invoke the Second Amendment as they stockpile weapons and train for warfare against what they perceive as a "tyrannical" federal government. The NRA declares that the paramilitary activity of these groups is an exercise of their "right to keep and bear arms." Echoing the extremist rhetoric of the "militias," an NRA official has called the Second Amendment "a loaded gun...held to the head of government." This is a perversion of our Constitution.

When our Founding Fathers wrote the Second Amendment more than 200 years ago, the "well regulated militia" was not a privately organized army formed to resist the government of the United States. It was the military arm of state government, formed to maintain public order.

The Supreme Court has ruled that the "obvious purpose" of the Second Amendment was to protect the "militia which the States were expected to maintain and train," and that "the National Guard is the modern militia."

Because laws regulating firearms do not interfere with the modern militia, no gun control law has ever been overturned by the federal courts on Second Amendment grounds. That's why former Supreme Court Chief Justice Warren Burger has called the NRA's Second Amendment propaganda a "fraud on the American public."

The Second Amendment is not a barrier to reasonable gun control laws. Nor is it a license for those who disagree with government policies to resist them by force of arms. It's time for the NRA to stop its Second Amendment fraud.

The Second Amendment protects the National Guard, not private armies preparing to take the law into their own hands.

Sarah Brady, Chair of the Center to Prevent Handgun Violence

Dear Sarah, I want to support your national education campaign to fight the NRA's Second Amendment fraud. Enclosed is my contribution for:

☐ $15   ☐ $25   ☐ $50   ☐ Other _____

NAME _____

ADDRESS _____

CITY, STATE, ZIP _____

E-MAIL _____

Return to: Center to Prevent Handgun Violence, 1225 Eye Street, NW, Room 1100, Washington, DC 20005

Contributions to the Center to Prevent Handgun Violence are tax-deductible.

☐ **I'd like more information on the Second Amendment and the Center to Prevent Handgun Violence.**

NAME _____

ADDRESS _____

CITY, STATE, ZIP _____

Return to: Center to Prevent Handgun Violence
1225 Eye Street, NW, Room 1100
Washington, DC 20005

Brought to you by the Center to Prevent Handgun Violence, Sarah Brady, Chair

COMPETING ADVERTISEMENTS: ENERGY

The advertisement for nuclear energy that follows (p. 312) is part of a series sponsored by the U.S. Council for Energy Awareness to promote the building of more nuclear energy plants. The advertisement presented by the Metropolitan Energy Council (reprinted on p. 313) argues for the use of oil as a source of heating. Study the appeals used in both ads. Which techniques are the most and least successful? Do they appeal to the same audience? Overall, which ad do you think is the most persuasive, and why?

If you were hired to design an advertisement that argues against the use of nuclear energy (or for/against some other energy source such as oil, gas, or solar power), what would your ad say? What photograph or drawing would you select to accompany your argument? What audience would your ad target and why?

 A REVISION WORKSHEET

As you write your rough drafts, consult Chapter 5 for guidance through the revision process. In addition, here are a few questions to ask yourself as you revise your argumentative essay:

1. Does this essay present a clear thesis limited to fit the assigned length of this paper?

2. Does this essay contain a number of strong, persuasive points in support of its thesis?

3. Is the essay organized in an easy-to-follow pattern that avoids repetition or confusion?

4. Does the essay present enough supporting evidence to make each of its points convincing? Where could additional examples, factual information, testimony, or other kinds of supporting material be added to make the arguments even more effective?

5. Will all the supporting evidence be clear to the essay's particular audience? Do any terms or examples need additional explanation or special definition?

6. Have the major opposing arguments been refuted?

7. Does the essay avoid any logical fallacies or problems in tone?

After you've revised your essay extensively, you might exchange rough drafts with a classmate and answer these questions for each other, making specific suggestions for improvement wherever appropriate. (For advice on productive participation in classroom workshops, see pp. 117–119.)

SOME ARGUMENTS FOR NUCLEAR ENERGY ARE SMALLER THAN OTHERS.

Around the nuclear electric plant on Florida's Hutchinson Island, endangered wildlife have a safe haven. The baby sea turtles hatching on nearby beaches are more evidence of the truth about nuclear energy: it peacefully coexists with the environment.

America's 110 operating nuclear plants don't pollute the air, because they don't burn anything to generate electricity. Nor do they eat up valuable natural resources such as oil and natural gas.

Still, more plants are needed—to help satisfy the nation's growing need for electricity without sacrificing the quality of our environment. For a free booklet on nuclear energy, write to the U.S. Council for Energy Awareness, P.O. Box 66080, Dept. TR01, Washington, D.C. 20035.

NUCLEAR ENERGY MEANS CLEANER AIR.

© 1992 USCEA

As seen in April 1992 issues of The Washington Post, FORTUNE, and National Journal; May 1992 issues of TIME, Newsweek, Washington Post National Weekly and Congressional Quarterly; June 1992 issues of National Geographic, Smithsonian, New Choices and Christian Science Monitor; July 1992 issue of Forbes; August 1992 issue of World Monitor; September 1992 issue of Ladies' Home Journal and Natural History; October 1992 issues of Good Housekeeping, Atlantic and American Heritage; and November 1992 issue of Reader's Digest.

This advertisement is provided courtesy of the United States Council for Energy Awareness, Washington, D.C.

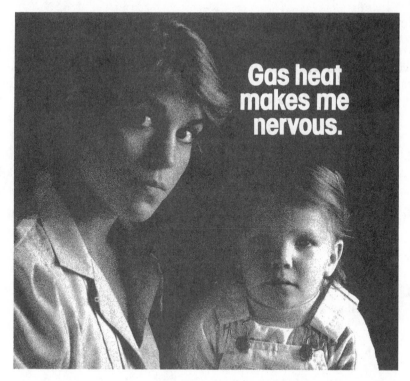

Gas comes from the big utility.
They don't know my name.
They don't know my family.

If you need prompt service from them,
you have to say, "I smell gas."

That's what scares me most. I think gas heat
is dangerous . . . too dangerous
for my home, my kids.

I heat with oil.

Oil heat...The Intelligent Choice

Metropolitan Energy Council, Inc.

66 Morris Ave., P.O. Box 359, Springfield, NJ 07081 • (201) 379-1100

Reviewing Your Progress

After you have completed your argument essay, take a moment to measure your progress as a writer by responding to the following questions. Such analysis will help you recognize growth in your writing skills and may enable you to identify areas that are still problematic.

1. Which part of your essay do you like best? Why?

2. After analyzing your essay's reasoning and evidence, which particular argument or point do you consider the strongest? What makes it so convincing?

3. What part of your essay gave you the most trouble? How did you overcome the problem?

4. If you had more time to work on this essay, what would receive additional attention? Why?

5. What did you learn about your topic from writing this essay? About yourself as a writer?

CHAPTER
11 Description

The writer of description creates a word-picture of persons, places, objects, and emotions, using a careful selection of details to make an impression on the reader. If you have already written expository or argumentative essays in your composition course, you almost certainly have written some descriptive prose. Nearly every essay, after all, calls for some kind of description; for example, in the student comparison/contrast essay (pp. 232–235), the writer describes two kinds of stores; in the professional process essay (pp. 219–224), the writer describes the embalming procedure in great detail. To help you write better description in your other essays, however, you may want to practice writing descriptive paragraphs or a short descriptive essay.

HOW TO WRITE EFFECTIVE DESCRIPTION

When descriptive prose is called for in your writing, consider these four basic suggestions:

Recognize your purpose. Description is not free-floating; it appears in your writing for a particular reason—to help you inform, explain, persuade, or create a mood. In some essays you will want your description as *objective*—without personal impressions—as you can make it; for example, you might describe a scientific experiment or a business transaction in straight factual detail. Other times, however, you will want to convey a particular attitude toward your subject; this approach to description is called *subjective* or *impressionistic*. Note the differences between the following two descriptions of a tall, thin boy: the objective writer sticks to the facts by saying, "The eighteen-year-old boy was 6'1" and weighed 125 pounds," whereas the subjective writer gives an impressionistic description, "The young boy was as tall and scrawny as a birch tree in winter." Before you begin describing anything, you must first decide your purpose and then whether it calls for objective or subjective reporting.

Describe clearly, using specific details. To make any description clear to your reader, you must include a sufficient number of details that are specific rather than fuzzy or vague. If, for example, your family dog had become lost, you wouldn't call the animal shelter and ask if they'd seen a "big brown dog with a short tail"—naturally, you'd mention every distinguishing detail about your pet you could think of: size, color, breed, cut of ears, and special markings. Similarly, if your car was stolen, you'd give the police as clear and as complete a description of your vehicle as possible.

Look at the two paragraphs below. Which more fully tells what a vaulting horse is?

A vaulting horse is a thing usually found in gyms that has four legs and a beam and is used by gymnasts making jumps.

If you didn't already know what a vaulting horse was, you might have trouble picking it out in a gymnasium crowded with equipment. A description with additional details would help you locate it:

A vaulting horse is a piece of equipment used by gymnasts during competition to help propel them into the air when they perform any of a variety of leaps known as vaults. The gymnasts usually approach the vaulting horse from a running start and then place their hands on the horse for support or for a push off as they perform their vaults. The horse itself resembles a carpenter's sawhorse, but the main beam is made of padded leather rather than wood. The rectangular beam is approximately 5 feet, 3 inches long and 13½ inches wide. Supported by four legs usually made of steel, the padded leather beam is approximately 4 feet, ½ inch above the floor in men's competitions and 3 feet, 7 inches in women's competitions. The padded leather beam has two white lines marking off three sections on top: the croup, the saddle, and the neck. The two end sections—the croup and the neck—are each 15½ inches long. Gymnasts place their hands on the neck or croup, depending on the type of vault they are attempting.

Moreover, the reader cannot imagine your subject clearly if your description is couched in vague generalities. The following sentence, for example, presents only a hazy picture:

Larry is a sloppy dresser.

Revised, the picture is now sharply in focus:

Larry wears dirty, baggy pants, shirts too small to stay tucked in, socks that fail to match his pants or each other, and a stained coat the Salvation Army rejected as a donation.

Specific details can turn cloudy prose into crisp, clear images that can be reproduced in the mind like photographs.

Select only appropriate details. In any description the choice of details depends largely on the writer's purpose and audience. However, many descriptions—especially the more subjective ones—will present a *dominant impression;* that is, the writer selects only those details that communicate a particular mood or feeling to the reader. The dominant impression is the controlling focus of a description; for example, if you wrote a description of your grandmother to show her thoughtfulness, you would select only those details that convey an impression of a sweet, kindly old lady. Below are two brief descriptions illustrating the concept of dominant impression. The first writer tries to create a mood of mystery:

Down a black winding road stands the abandoned old mansion, silhouetted against the cloud-shrouded moon, creaking and moaning in the wet chill wind.

The second writer tries to present a feeling of joy and innocence.

A dozen kites filled the spring air, and around the bright picnic tables spread with hot dogs, hamburgers, and slices of watermelon, Tom and Annie played away the warm April day.

In the description of the deserted mansion, the writer would have violated the impression of mystery had the sentence read,

Down the black winding road stands the abandoned old mansion, surrounded by bright, multicolored tulips in early bloom.

Including the cheerful flowers as a detail in the description destroys the dominant mood of bleakness and mystery. Similarly, the second example would be spoiled had the writer ended it this way:

Tom and Annie played away the warm April day until Tom got so sunburned he became ill and had to go home.

Therefore, remember to select only those details that advance your descriptive purpose. Omit any details you consider unimportant or distracting.

See if you can determine the dominant impression of each description below:

The wind had curled up to sleep in the distant mountains. Leaves hung limp and motionless from the silent trees, while birds perched on the branches like little statues. As I sat on the edge of the clearing, holding my breath, I could hear a squirrel scampering through the underbrush. Somewhere far away a dog barked twice, and then the woods were hushed once more.

This poor thing has seen better days, but one should expect the sofa in a fraternity house den to be well worn. The large, plump, brown corduroy pillows strewn lazily on the floor and propped comfortably against the threadbare arms bear the pencil-point scars of frustrated students and foam-bleeding cuts of multiple pillow wars. No less than four pairs of rotting Nikes stand twenty-four-hour guard at the corners of its carefully mended frame. Obviously the relaxed, inviting appearance masks the permanent odors of cheap cigars and Michelob from Thursday night poker parties; at least two or three guests each weekend sift through the popcorn kernels and Doritos crumbs, sprawl face down, and pass out for the duration. However, frequent inhabitants have learned to avoid the dark stains courtesy of the house pup and the red-punch designs of the chapter klutz. Habitually, they strategically lunge over the back of the sofa to an unsoiled area easily identifiable in flight by the large depression left by previous regulars. The quiet *hmmph* of the cushions and harmonious squeal of the exhausted springs signal a perfect landing and utter a warm greeting from an old and faithful friend.

Make your descriptions vivid. By using clear, precise words, you can improve any kind of writing. Chapters 7 (on words) and 6 (on sentences) offer a variety of tips on clarifying your prose style. In addition to the advice given there, here are two other ways to enliven your descriptions, particularly those that call for a subjective approach:

Use sensory details. If it's appropriate, try using images that appeal to your readers' five senses. If, for example, you are describing your broken leg and the ensuing stay in a hospital, tell your readers how the place smelled, how it looked, what your cast felt like, how your pills tasted, and what noises you heard. Below are some specific examples using sensory details:

Sight	The clean white corridors of the hospital resembled the set of a sci-fi movie, with everyone scurrying around in identical starched uniforms.
Hearing	At night, the only sounds I heard were the quiet squeakings of sensible white shoes as the nurses made their rounds.
Smell	The green beans on the hospital cafeteria tray smelled stale and waxy, like crayons.
Touch	The hospital bed sheet felt as rough and heavy as a feed sack.
Taste	Every four hours they gave me an enormous gray pill whose aftertaste reminded me of the stale licorice my grandmother kept in candy dishes around her house.

By appealing to the readers' senses, you better enable them to identify with and imagine the subject you are describing. Joseph Conrad, the famous nineteenth-century novelist, agreed, believing that all art "appeals primarily to the senses, and the artistic aim when expressing itself in written words must also make its appeal through the senses, if its highest desire is to reach the secret spring of responsive emotions." In other words, to make your readers feel, first make them "see."

Use figurative language when appropriate. As you may recall from Chapter 7, figurative language produces images or pictures in the readers' minds, helping them to understand unfamiliar or abstract subjects. Here are some devices you might use to clarify or spice up your prose:

1. Simile: a comparison between two things using the words "like" or "as" (see also pp. 174–175)

Example Seeing exactly the shirt he wanted, he moved as quickly as a starving teenager spotting pie in a refrigerator full of leftover vegetables.

2. Metaphor: a direct comparison between two things that does not use "like" or "as" (see also pp. 174–175)

Example After the holidays her body resembled the "before" shots in every diet ad she'd ever seen.

3. Personification: the attribution of human characteristics and emotions to inanimate objects, animals, or abstract ideas

Example The old teddy bear sat in a corner, dozing serenely before the fireplace.

4. Hyperbole: intentional exaggeration or overstatement

Example "Bring me a steak cooked so rare it's still mooing," roared the cowboy.

5. Understatement: intentional representation of a subject as less important than the facts would warrant (see also irony, p. 161)

Example "The reports of my death are greatly exaggerated."—Mark Twain

6. Synecdoche: a part of something used to represent the whole

Example A hundred tired feet hit the dance floor for one last jitterbug. [Here "feet" stand for the dancing couples themselves.]

Using figures of speech in appropriate places can make your descriptions clear, lively, and memorable.

Problems to Avoid

Keep in mind these three pieces of advice to solve problems that frequently arise in description:

Remember your audience. Sometimes the object of our description is so clear in our minds we forget that our readers haven't seen it, too. Consequently, the description we write turns out to be vague, bland, or skimpy. Ask yourself about your audience: what do they need to know to see this sight as clearly as I do? Then fill in your description with ample, precise details that reveal the best picture possible. Don't forget to define or explain any terms you use that may be puzzling to your audience.

Avoid an erratic organization of details. Too often descriptions are a hodgepodge of details, jotted down randomly. When you write a lengthy description, you should select a plan that will arrange your details in an orderly fashion. Depending on your subject matter and your purpose, you might adopt a plan calling for a description of something from top to bottom, left to right, front to back, and so on. For example, a description of a woman might begin at the head and move to the feet; furniture in a room might be described as your eyes move from one side of the room to another. A second plan for arranging details presents the subject's outstanding characteristics first and then fills in the lesser information; a child's red hair, for example, might be his most striking feature and therefore would be described first. A third plan presents details in the order you see them approaching: dust, then a car, then details about the car, its occupants, and so on. Or you might describe a subject as it unfolds chronologically, as in some kind of a process or operation. Regardless of which plan of organization you choose, the reader should feel a sense of order in your description.

Avoid any sudden change in perspective. If, for example, you are describing the White House from the outside, don't suddenly include details that could be seen only from inside. Similarly, if you are describing a car from a distance, you might be able to tell the car's model, year, and color, but you could hardly describe the upholstery or reveal the mileage. It is, of course, possible for you—or your observer—to approach or move around the subject of your description, but the reader must be aware of this movement. Any shift in point of view must be presented clearly and logically, with no sudden, confusing leaps from a front to a back view, from outside to inside, and so on.

 ESSAY TOPICS

Here are some suggestions for a descriptive essay or paragraph; narrow your topic to fit your assignment. Don't forget that every description, whether objective or subjective, has a purpose and that every detail should support that purpose. For additional ideas, see "Suggestions for Writing" following the professional essay on page 330.

1. A campus character

2. A childhood photograph or a picture of an ancestor

3. A piece of equipment important to your major, a hobby, or favorite sport

4. A building or place you're fond of

5. One dish or foodstuff that should be forever banned

6. A family pet

7. Your most precious material possession

8. The ugliest/most beautiful building on your campus or in town

9. A typical family dinner or ritual in your home

10. Your first or worst car or apartment

11. A piece of clothing that reveals the real "you"

12. A strange-but-wonderful friend or relative

13. An act of heroism or personal success

14. A favorite painting, sculpture, photograph, or art object

15. Your most unforgettable character

16. An event or critter in nature

17. A doctor's waiting room or some other crowded public place

18. A historical figure or event important to you

19. A special time in your life (birthday, holiday, graduation, etc.)

20. The inside of your refrigerator, closet, or some other equally loathsome place in your home

A Topic Proposal for Your Essay

Selecting the right subject matter is important to every writer. To help you clarify your ideas and strengthen your commitment to your topic, here is a proposal sheet that asks you to describe some of your preliminary ideas about your subject before you begin drafting. Although as you draft your ideas may change (they will almost certainly become more refined), thinking through your choice of topic now may help you avoid several false starts.

1. What subject will your essay describe? Will you describe this subject objectively or subjectively? Why?

2. Why are you interested in this topic? Do you have a personal or professional connection to the subject? State at least one reason for your choice of topic.

3. Is this a significant topic of interest to others? Why? Who specifically might find it interesting, informative, or entertaining?

4. In one or two sentences describe the major effect you'd like your descriptive essay to have on your readers. What would you like for them to understand or "see" about your subject?

5. List at least three details that you think will help clarify your subject for your readers.

6. What difficulties, if any, might arise during drafting? For example, what organizational strategy might you think about now that would allow you to guide your readers through your description in a coherent way?

S A M P L E   S T U D E N T   E S S A Y

In her descriptive essay, this student writer recalls her childhood days at the home of her grandparents to make a point about growing up. Notice that the writer uses both figurative language and contrasting images to help her readers understand her point of view.

TREECLIMBING

It was Mike's eighteenth birthday and he was having a little bit of a breakdown. "When was the last time you made cloud pictures?" he asked me absently as he stared up at the ceiling before class started. Before I could answer, he continued, "Did you know that by the time you're an adult, you've lost 85 percent of your imagination?" He paused. "I don't want to grow up." Although I doubted the authenticity of his facts, I understood that Mike—the hopeless romantic with his long ponytail, sullen black clothes, and glinting dark eyes—was caught in a Peter Pan complex. He drew those eyes from the ceiling and focused on me. "There are two types of children. Tree children and dirt children. Kids playing will either climb trees or play in the dirt. Tree children are the dreamers—the hopeful, creative dreamers. Dirt children, they just stay on the ground. Stick to the rules," he trailed off, and then picked up again. "I'm a tree child. I want to make cloud pictures and climb trees. And I don't ever want to come down." Mike's story reminded me of my own days as a tree child, and of the inevitable fall from the tree to the ground.

My childhood was a playground for imagination. Summers were spent surrounded by family at my grandparents' house in Milwaukee, Wisconsin. The rambling Lannonstone bungalow was located on North 46th Street at Burleigh, a block away from center-city Milwaukee, two blocks from Schuster's department store and the Pfister hotel. In the winter, all the houses looked alike, rigid and militant, like white-bearded old generals with icicles hanging from their moustaches. One European-styled house after the other lined the streets in strict parallel formation, block after block.

Introduction: The conversation that triggers her memory

The grandparents' neighborhood remembered in military images and sensory details

But in the summer it was different . . . softer. No subzero winds blew lonely down the back alley. Instead, kids played stickball in it. I had elegant, grass-stained tea parties with a neighborhood girl named Shelly, while my grandfather worked in his thriving vegetable garden among the honeybees, and watched things grow. An ever-present warming smell of yeast filtered down every street as the nearby breweries pumped a constant flow of fresh beer. Looking up, the summer sky looked like an Easter egg God had dipped in blue dye.

Those summer trips to Milwaukee were greatly anticipated events back then. My brother and I itched with repressed energy throughout the long plane ride from the West Coast. We couldn't wait to see Grandma and Papa. We couldn't wait to see what presents Papa had for us. We couldn't wait to slide down the steep, blue- carpeted staircase on our bottoms, and then on our stomachs. Most of all, we couldn't wait to go down to the basement.

The basement was better than a toy store. Yes, the old-fashioned milk chute in the kitchen wall was enchanting, and the laundry chute was fun because it was big enough to throw down Ernie, my stuffed dog companion, so my brother could catch him below in the laundry room, as our voices echoed up and down the chute. But the basement was better than all of these, better even than sliding down those stairs on rug-burned bottoms.

It was always deliciously cool down in the basement. Since the house was built in the '30s, there was no air conditioning. Upstairs, we slept in hot, heavy rooms. My lace-edged nightgown stuck to the sheets, and I would lie awake in the dusky room, listening to crickets, inhaling the beer-sweet smell of the summer

The basement in contrast to other parts of the house

night, hoping for a cool breeze. Nights were forgotten, however, as my brother and I spent hours every day in the basement. There were seven rooms in the basement; some darker rooms I had waited years to explore. There was always a jumbled heap of toys in the middle room, most of which were leftovers from my father's own basement days. It was a child's safe haven; it was a sacred place.

The times spent in the basement were times of a gloriously secure childhood. Empires were created in a day with faded colored building blocks. New territories were annexed when either my brother or I got the courage to venture into one of those Other Rooms—the dark, musty ones without windows— and then scamper back to report of any sightings of monsters or other horrific childhood creatures. In those basement days everything seemed safe and wholesome and secure, with my family surrounding me, protecting me. Like childhood itself, entering the basement was like entering another dimension.

Adventures in the basement

Last summer I returned to Milwaukee to help my grandparents pack to move into an apartment. I went back at 17 to find the house—my kingdom—up for sale. I found another cycle coming to a close, and I found myself separated from what I had once known. I looked at the house. It was old; it was crumbling; it needed paint. I looked down the back alley and saw nothing but trash and bums. I walked to the corner and saw smoke-choked, dirty streets and thick bars in shop windows, nothing more than another worn-out midwestern factory city. I went back to the house and down to the basement, alone.

The house and neighborhood years later

It was gray and dark. Dust filtered through a single feeble sunbeam hitting a cracked window pane. It was empty and

The basement years later

barren. The toys were gone, either packed or thrown away. The silence was unbearable as I walked in and out of rooms. My footsteps echoed as the quietness filled my ears. There was an undeniable musty smell, and in the back of my head the sounds of childhood laughter and chatter played like an old recording.

The dark rooms were filled not with monsters but with remnants of my grandfather's business. A neon sign was propped against the wall in a corner: Ben Strauss Plumbing. Piles of heavy pipes and metal machine parts lay scattered about on shelves. A dusty purple ribbon was thumbtacked to a door. It said SHOOT THE WORKS in white letters. I gently took it down. The ribbon hangs on my door at home now, and out of context it somehow is not quite so awe-inspiring and mystifying as it once was, amidst the dust and the memories and the aspirations. However, it does serve its purpose.

Conclusion: A return to the introduction's images and some advice

All children are tree children, I believe. The basement used to be my tree, the place I could dream in. That last summer I found myself, much to Mike's disappointment, quite mature, quite adult. Maybe Mike fell from his tree and got bruised. Climbing down from that tree doesn't have to be something to be afraid of. One needn't hide in the tree for fear of touching the ground and forgetting how to climb back up when necessary. I think there is a way to balance the two extremes. Climb down gracefully as you grow up, and if you fall, don't land in quicksand. I like to think I'm more of a shrubbery child: not so low as to get stuck in the mud and just high enough to look at the sky and make cloud pictures.

P R O F E S S I O N A L   E S S A Y *

The Discus Thrower

Richard Selzer

Richard Selzer has taught surgery at Yale Medical School and has contributed to a number of magazines. He has published collections of both fiction and essays, including Mortal Lessons *(1977),* Confessions of a Knife *(1979),* Letters to a Young Doctor *(1982),* Taking the World in for Repairs *(1986), and* Down from Troy: A Doctor Comes of Age *(1992). His most recent works include* Raising the Dead *(1994),* Imagine A Woman *(1996),* The Doctor Stories *(1998), and* A Question of Mercy *(1998), a play with David Rabe. This essay was published in* Harper's *in 1977.*

1   I spy on my patients. Ought not a doctor to observe his patients by any means and from any stance, that he might the more fully assemble evidence? So I stand in the doorways of hospital rooms and gaze. Oh, it is not all that furtive an act. Those in bed need only look up to discover me. But they never do.

2   From the doorway of Room 542 the man in the bed seems deeply tanned. Blue eyes and close-cropped white hair give him the appearance of vigor and good health. But I know that his skin is not brown from the sun. It is rusted, rather, in the last stage of containing the vile repose within. And the blue eyes are frosted, looking inward like the windows of a snowbound cottage. This man is blind. This man is also legless—the right leg missing from midthigh down, the left from just below the knee. It gives him the look of a bonsai, roots and branches pruned into the dwarfed facsimile of a great tree.

3   Propped on pillows, he cups his right thigh in both hands. Now and then he shakes his head as though acknowledging the intensity of his suffering. In all of this he makes no sound. Is he mute as well as blind?

4   The room in which he dwells is empty of all possessions—no get-well cards, small, private caches of food, day-old flowers, slippers, all the usual kickshaws of the sickroom. There is only the bed, a chair, a nightstand, and a tray on wheels that can be swung across his lap for meals.

5   "What time is it?" he asks.
"Three o'clock."
"Morning or afternoon?"
"Afternoon."
He is silent. There is nothing else he wants to know.
10   "How are you?" I say.
"Who is it?" he asks.
"It's the doctor. How do you feel?"

---

* To help you read this essay analytically, review pages 182–185.

He does not answer right away.

"Feel?" he says.

15 "I hope you feel better," I say.

I press the button at the side of the bed.

"Down you go," I say.

"Yes, down," he says.

He falls back upon the bed awkwardly. His stumps, unweighted by legs and feet, rise in the air, presenting themselves. I unwrap the bandages from the stumps, and begin to cut away the black scabs and the dead, glazed fat with scissors and forceps. A shard of white bone comes loose. I pick it away. I wash the wounds with disinfectant and redress the stumps. All this while, he does not speak. What is he thinking behind those lids that do not blink? Is he remembering a time when he was whole? Does he dream of feet? Of when his body was not a rotting log?

20 He lies solid and inert. In spite of everything, he remains impressive, as though he were a sailor standing athwart a slanting deck.

"Anything more I can do for you?" I ask.

For a long moment he is silent.

"Yes," he says at last and without the least irony. "You can bring me a pair of shoes."

In the corridor, the head nurse is waiting for me.

25 "We have to do something about him," she says. "Every morning he orders scrambled eggs for breakfast, and, instead of eating them, he picks up the plate and throws it against the wall."

"Throws his plate?"

"Nasty. That's what he is. No wonder his family doesn't come to visit. They probably can't stand him any more than we can."

She is waiting for me to do something.

"Well?"

30 "We'll see," I say.

The next morning I am waiting in the corridor when the kitchen delivers his breakfast. I watch the aide place the tray on the stand and swing it across his lap. She presses the button to raise the head of the bed. Then she leaves.

In time the man reaches to find the rim of the tray, then on to find the dome of the covered dish. He lifts off the cover and places it on the stand. He fingers across the plate until he probes the eggs. He lifts the plate in both hands, sets it on the palm of his right hand, centers it, balances it. He hefts it up and down slightly, getting the feel of it. Abruptly, he draws back his right arm as far as he can.

There is the crack of the plate breaking against the wall at the foot of his bed and the small wet sound of the scrambled eggs dropping to the floor.

And then he laughs. It is a sound you have never heard. It is something new under the sun. It could cure cancer.

35 Out in the corridor, the eyes of the head nurse narrow.

"Laughed, did he?"

She writes something down on her clipboard.

A second aide arrives, brings a second breakfast tray, puts it on the nightstand, out of his reach. She looks over at me shaking her head and making her mouth go. I see that we are to be accomplices.

"I've got to feed you," she says to the man.

40 "Oh, no you don't," the man says.

"Oh, yes I do," the aide says, "after the way you just did. Nurse says so."

"Get me my shoes," the man says.

"Here's oatmeal," the aide says. "Open." And she touches the spoon to his lower lip.

"I ordered scrambled eggs," says the man.

45 "That's right," the aide says.

I step forward.

"Is there anything I can do?" I say.

"Who are you?" the man asks.

In the evening I go once more to that ward to make my rounds. The head nurse reports to me that Room 542 is deceased. She has discovered this quite by accident, she says. No, there had been no sound. Nothing. It's a blessing, she says.

50 I go into his room, a spy looking for secrets. He is still there in his bed. His face is relaxed, grave, dignified. After a while, I turn to leave. My gaze sweeps the wall at the foot of the bed, and I see the place where it has been repeatedly washed, where the wall looks very clean and very white.

Questions on Content, Structure, and Style

1. This essay presents several scenes in a hospital. From whose point of view do we see these scenes? How is this point of view introduced?

2. Does this essay contain objective or subjective description or both? Are there enough clear, specific details to make the descriptions vivid to the reader? Cite some details to support your answer.

3. What does Selzer's description of the hospital room itself suggest about the patient?

4. The title of this essay alludes to or reminds readers of a famous statue of a young Greek athlete. Why is Selzer's choice of titles ironic? What does the patient's use of his eggs and his call for shoes reveal about his attitude toward his illness?

5. What is Selzer's attitude toward his patient? How do you know? What is the attitude of the head nurse?

6. What is Selzer's purpose in describing this patient and his actions? Why doesn't he "do something" about the patient, as the nurse wants?

7. Point out several examples of metaphor and simile in this essay. What do these add to the effectiveness of Selzer's descriptions?

8. Why does Selzer use dialogue on some occasions instead of describing what is taking place?

9. Why does Selzer end his essay by referring to the clean wall? Is this an effective conclusion? Why or why not?

10. Selzer's subtitle for this essay was "Do Not Go Gentle," a reference to a well-known poem by Dylan Thomas. In the poem Thomas tells his dying father "Do not go gentle into that good night/Rage, rage against the dying of the light." Why is Selzer's subtitle an appropriate complement to this essay?

Suggestions for Writing

Try using Richard Selzer's "The Discus Thrower" as a stepping stone to your essay. Imitate Selzer's technique by observing someone several times and then writing a vivid description that captures, as Selzer's essay did, the state of mind or attitude of that person. For example, what does a multiple observation of a campus cafeteria worker, a security guard, a librarian, or a custodian tell you about their attitude toward their jobs? In additional to generous use of descriptive details, consider employing metaphors, similes, and dialogue, as Selzer did, if they contribute to your reader's understanding of this person. Can you think of a title (or subtitle) with an allusion that also reveals something important about the subject of your essay?

Vocabulary

furtive (1)	caches (4)	inert (20)
vile (2)	kickshaws (4)	athwart (20)
repose (2)	shard (19)	irony (23)
facsimile (2)		

 A REVISION WORKSHEET

As you write your rough drafts, consult Chapter 5 for guidance through the revision process. In addition, here are a few questions to ask yourself as you revise your description:

1. Is the descriptive essay's purpose clear to the reader?

2. Are there enough specific details in the description to make the subject matter distinct to readers who are unfamiliar with the scene, person, or object? Where might more detail be added?

3. Are the details arranged in an order that's easy to follow?

4. If the assignment called for an objective description, are the details as "neutral" as possible?

5. If the assignment called for a subjective description, does the writer's particular attitude come through clearly with a consistent use of well-chosen details or imagery?

6. Could any sensory details or figurative language be added to help the reader "see" the subject matter?

7. Does this essay end with an appropriate conclusion or does description merely stop?

After you've revised your essay extensively, you might exchange rough drafts with a classmate and answer these questions for each other, making specific suggestions for improvement wherever appropriate. (For advice on productive participation in classroom workshops, see pp. 117–119.)

Reviewing Your Progress

After you have completed your descriptive essay, take a moment to measure your progress as a writer by responding to the following questions. Such analysis will help you recognize growth in your writing skills and may enable you to identify areas that are still problematic.

1. What is the best part of your essay? Why?

2. Which one descriptive detail or image do you think is the clearest or most vivid in your essay? Why does that one stand above the others?

3. What part of your essay gave you the most trouble? How did you overcome the problem?

4. If you had more time to work on this essay, what would receive additional attention? Why?

5. What did you learn about your topic from writing this essay? About yourself as a writer?

CHAPTER

12 Narration

When many people hear the word "narrative," they think of a made-up story. But not all stories are fiction. In this chapter we are not concerned with writing literary short stories—that's a skill you may work on in a creative writing class—but rather with nonfiction expository *narratives,* stories that are used to explain or prove a point. We most often use two kinds of these stories:

1. the *extended narrative*—a long episode that by itself illustrates or supports an essay's thesis

2. the *brief narrative*—a shorter incident that is often used in a body paragraph to support or illustrate a particular point in an essay.

Let's suppose, for example, you wanted to write an essay showing how confusing the registration system is at your school. To illustrate the problems vividly, you might devote your entire essay to the retelling of a friend's seven-hour experience signing up for classes last fall, thus making use of extended narration. Or take another example: in an argumentative essay advocating the nationwide use of automobile air bags, you might use a brief narrative about a car wreck to support a paragraph's point about air bags' ability to save lives. Regardless of which type of narrative best fits your purpose, the telling of a story or incident can be an interesting, persuasive means of informing your readers.

WRITING THE EFFECTIVE NARRATIVE ESSAY

Know your purpose. What are you trying to accomplish by writing this narrative essay? Are you, for example, offering an *objective* retelling of a historical event (the dropping of the atomic bomb) to inform your readers who may not be acquainted with this story? Or are you presenting a *subjective* narrative, which persuasively tells a story (Susan B. Anthony's arrest for voting) from a clearly defined point of view? Perhaps your narrative is a personal story, whose point you wish readers to share. Whatever your choice—an objective, factual retelling or a subjective interpretation—your narrative's purpose should be clear to your readers, who should never reach the end of the story wondering, "What was that all about?" Knowing your purpose will help you select your essay's point of view (objective third-person reporter? subjective first-person story-teller?), kinds of details, and tone.

Make your main point clear. To ensure that readers understand their purpose, many writers of subjective narration present a thesis statement; others, however, choose to imply a main point or distinct point of view through the unfolding action and choice of descriptive details. An implied thesis is always riskier than a stated one, so unless you are absolutely convinced that your readers cannot fail to see your point, work on finding a smooth way of incorporating a statement of your main idea into your essay.

Follow a logical time sequence. Many narrative essays—and virtually all brief stories used in other kinds of essays—follow a chronological order, presenting events as they naturally occur in the story. Occasionally, however, a writer will use the flashback technique, which takes the readers back in time to reveal an incident that occurred before the present scene of the story. If you decide to use shifts in time, use transition phrases or other signals to ensure that your readers don't become confused or lost.

Use details to present the setting. Most extended narratives are set in particular times and places. If the setting plays an important role in your story, you must describe it in vivid terms so that your readers can imagine it easily. For example, let's suppose you are pointing out the necessity of life preservers on sailboats by telling the story of how you spent a stormy night in the lake, clinging to your capsized boat. To convince your readers, let them "feel" the stinging rain and the icy current trying to drag you under; let them "see" the black waves and the dark menacing sky; let them "hear" the howling wind and the gradual splitting apart of the boat. Effective narration often depends on effective description, and effective description depends on vivid, specific detail. (For more help on writing description, see Chapter 11.)

Make your characters believable. Again, the use of detail is crucial. Your readers should be able to visualize the people in your narrative clearly; if your important characters are drawn too thinly or if they seem phony or stereotyped, your readers will not fully grasp the intensity of your story, and thus its meaning will be lost. Show your readers a picture of the major characters (as you see them) by commenting unobtrusively on their appearances, speech, and actions. In addition, a successful narrative depends on the reader's understanding of people's motives—why they act the way they do in certain situations. A narrative about your hometown's grouchiest miser who suddenly donated a large sum of money to a poor family isn't very believable unless we know the motive behind the action. In other words, let your readers know what is happening to whom by explaining or showing why.

Use dialogue realistically. Writers often use dialogue, their characters' spoken words, to reveal action or personality traits of the speakers. By presenting conversations, writers show rather than tell, often creating emphasis or a more dramatic effect. Dialogue often helps readers identify with or feel closer to the characters or action by creating a sense of "you-are-there." If your narrative would profit from dialogue, be certain the word choice and the manner of speaking are in keeping with each character's education, background, age, location, and so forth. Don't, for example, put a sophisticated philosophical treatise into the mouth of a ten-year-old boy or the latest campus slang into the speech of an auto mechanic from Two Egg, Florida. Also, make sure that your dialogue doesn't sound "wooden" or phony. The right dialogue can help make your characters more realistic and interesting, provided that the conversations are essential to the narrative and are not merely padding the plot. (To see excellent use of dialogue throughout an essay, read "The Discus Thrower," pp. 327–329, or "Sister Flowers," pp. 342–346, in this chapter. For help in punctuating dialogue, see pp. 474–476 in Part Four.)

Problems to Avoid

Weak, boring narratives are often the result of problems with subject matter or poor pacing; therefore, you should keep in mind the following advice:

Choose your subject carefully. Most of the best narrative essays come from personal experience or study, and the reason is fairly obvious: it's difficult to write convincingly about something you've never seen or done or read about. You probably couldn't, for instance, write a realistic account of a bullfight unless you'd seen one or at least had studied the subject in great detail. The simplest, easiest, most interesting nonfiction narrative you can write is likely to be about an event with which you are personally familiar. This doesn't mean that you can't improvise many details or create a hypothetical story to illustrate a point. Even so, you will probably still have more success basing your narrative—real or hypothetical—on something or someone you know well.

Limit your scope. When you wish to use an extended narrative to illustrate a thesis, don't select an event or series of actions whose retelling will be too long or complex for your assignment. In general, it's better to select one episode and flesh it out with many specific details so that your readers may clearly see your point. For instance, you may have had many rewarding experiences during the summer you worked as a lifeguard, but you can't tell them all. Instead, you might focus on one experience that captures the essence of your attitude toward your job—say, the time you saved a child from drowning—and present the story so vividly that the readers can easily understand your point of view.

Don't let your story lag or wander. At some time you've probably listened to a storyteller who became stuck on some insignificant detail ("Was it Friday or Saturday the letter came? Let's see now. . . ." "Then Joe said to me—no, it was Sally—no, wait, it was. . . ."). And you've probably also heard bores who insist on making a short story long by including too many unimportant details or digressions. These mistakes ruin the *pacing* of their stories; in other words, the story's tempo or movement becomes bogged down until the readers are bored witless. To avoid putting your readers to sleep, dismiss all unessential information and focus your attention—and use of detail—on the important events, people, and places. Skip uneventful periods of time by using such phrases as "A week went by before Mr. Smith called . . ." or "Later that evening, around nine o'clock. . . . " In short, keep the story moving quickly enough to hold the readers' interest. Moreover, use a variety of transition devices to move the readers from one action to another; don't rely continuously on the "and then . . . and then . . ." method.

 ESSAY TOPICS

Use one of the topics below to suggest an essay that is developed by narration. Remember that each essay must have a clear purpose. For additional ideas, see the "Suggestions for Writing" section following the professional essay on page 347.

1. An act of courage or cowardice

2. An event of historical, medical, or scientific importance

3. The worst mix-up of your life

4. Your best holiday, trip, or special occasion

5. A family story passed down through the generations

6. Your worst accident or brush with danger

7. Your most frightening or wonderful childhood experience

8. A memorable event governed by nature

9. A time you gained self-confidence or changed your self-image

10. An event that changed your thinking on a particular subject

11. Challenging an authority or asking for help

12. An event that led to an important decision

13. Your experience with prejudice or with an act of charity or friendship

14. Giving in to or resisting peer pressure

15. A gain or loss of something or someone important

16. A risk that paid off (or a triumph against the odds)

17. A nonacademic lesson learned at school or on a job

18. A special first or last day

19. A bad habit that got you into (or out of) trouble

20. An episode marking your passage from one stage of your life to another

A Topic Proposal for Your Essay

Selecting the right subject matter is important to every writer. To help you clarify your ideas and strengthen your commitment to your topic, here is a proposal sheet that asks you to describe some of your preliminary ideas about your subject before you begin drafting. Although as you draft your ideas may change (they will almost certainly become more refined), thinking through your choice of topic now may help you avoid several false starts.

1. In a sentence or two, briefly tell the subject of your narrative. Did you or someone you know participate in this story?

2. Why did you select this narrative? Does it have importance for you personally, academically, or professionally? In some other way? Explain your reason for picking this story to tell.

3. Will others be informed or entertained by this story? Who might be especially interested in hearing your narrative?

4. What is the primary effect you would like your narrative to have on your readers? What would you like them to feel or think about after they read your story? Why?

5. What is the critical moment in your story? At what point, in other words, does the action reach its peak? Summarize this moment in a few descriptive words.

6. What difficulties, if any, might this narrative present as you are drafting? For example, if the story you want to tell is long or complex, how might you focus on the main action and pace it appropriately?

S A M P L E   S T U D E N T   E S S A Y

In this narrative a student uses a story about a sick but fierce dog to show how she learned a valuable lesson in her job as a veterinarian's assistant. Notice the student's good use of vivid details that makes this well-paced story both clear and interesting.

NEVER UNDERESTIMATE THE LITTLE THINGS

When I went to work as a veterinarian's assistant for Dr. Sam Holt and Dr. Jack Gunn last summer, I was under the false impression that the hardest part of veterinary surgery would be the actual performance of an operation. The small chores demanded before this feat didn't occur to me as being of any importance. As it happened, I had been in the veterinary clinic only a total of four hours before I met a little animal who convinced me that the operation itself was probably the easiest part of treatment. This animal, to whom I owe thanks for so enlightening me, was a chocolate-colored chihuahua of tiny size and immense perversity named Smokey.

Smokey could have very easily passed for some creature from another planet. It wasn't so much his gaunt little frame and overly large head, or his bony paws with nearly saberlike claws, as it was his grossly infected eyes. Those once-shining eyes were now distorted and swollen into grotesque balls of septic, sightless flesh. The only vague similarity they had to what we'd normally think of as the organs of vision was a slightly upraised dot, all that was left of the pupil, in the center of a pink and purply marble. As if that were not enough, Smokey had a temper to match his ugly sight. He also had surprisingly good aim, considering his largely diminished vision, toward any moving object that happened to place itself unwisely before his ever-inquisitive nose, and with sudden and

Introduction: A misconception

Thesis

Description of the main character: His appearance

His personality

wholly vicious intent he would snap and snarl at whatever blocked the little light that could filter through his swollen and ruptured blood vessels. Truly, in many respects, Smokey was a fearful dog to behold.

The difficulty of moving the dog to the surgery room

Such an appearance and personality did nothing to encourage my already flagging confidence in my capabilities as a vet's assistant. How was I supposed to get that little demon out of his cage? Jack had casually requested that I bring Smokey to the surgery room, but did he really expect me to put my hands into the mouth of the cage of that devil dog? I suppose it must have been my anxious expression that saved me, for as I turned uncertainly toward the kennel, Jack chuckled nonchalantly and accompanied me to demonstrate how professionals in his line of work dealt with professionals in Smokey's. He took a small rope about four feet long with a slipnoose at one end and began to unlatch Smokey's cage. Then cautiously he reached in and dangled the noose before the dog's snarling jaws. Since Smokey could only barely see what he was biting at, his attacks were directed haphazardly in a semicircle around his body. The tiny area of his cage led to his capture, for during one of Smokey's forward lunges, Jack dropped the noose over his head and dragged the struggling creature out onto the floor. The fight had only just begun for Smokey, however, and he braced his feet against the slippery linoleum tiling and forced us to drag him, like a little pull toy on a string, to the surgery.

In the surgery room: The difficulty of moving the dog to the table

Once in the surgery, however, the question that hung before our eyes like a veritable presence was how to get the dog from the floor to table. Simply picking him up and plopping him down was out of the question. One glance at the quivering little figure emitting ominous and throaty warnings was enough to assure us of that. Realizing that the game was over, Jack grimly handed me the rope and reached for a muzzle. It was a doomed attempt from the start: the closer Jack dangled the tiny leather cup to the dog's nose, the more violent did Smokey's contortions and rage-filled cries become and the more frantic our efforts became to try to keep our feet and fingers clear of the angry jaws. Deciding that a firmer method had to be used, Jack instructed me to raise the rope up high enough so that Smokey'd have to stand on his hind legs. This greatly reduced his maneuverability but served to increase his tenacity, for at this the little dog nearly went into paroxysms of frustration and rage. In his struggles, however, Smokey caught his forepaw on his swollen eye, and the blood that had been building up pressure behind the fragile cornea burst out and dripped to the floor. In the midst of our surprise and the twinge of panic startling the three of us, Jack saw his chance and swiftly muzzled the animal and lifted him to the operating table.

Even at that point it wasn't easy to put the now terrified dog to sleep. He fought even the local anesthesia and caused Jack to curse as he was forced to give Smokey far more of the drug than should have been necessary for such a small beast. After what seemed an eternity, Smokey lay prone on the table, breathing deeply and emitting soft snores and gentle whines. We also breathed deeply in relief, and I relaxed to watch fascinated, while Jack performed a very delicate operation quite smoothly and without mishap.

The difficulty of putting the dog to sleep before the surgery

Such was my harrowing induction into the life of a veterinary surgeon. But Smokey did teach me a valuable lesson that has proven its importance to me many times since: wherever animals are concerned, even the smallest detail should never be taken for granted.

Conclusion: The lesson she learned

Sister Flowers

Maya Angelou

Maya Angelou is an American author, actress, civil-rights activist, poet, and professor. She has written multiple volumes of poetry and a series of popular autobiographical works, including Wouldn't Take Nothing for My Journey Now *(1993). This essay is a chapter from her first autobiographical volume,* I Know Why the Caged Bird Sings *(1969). Her most recent books are* Even the Stars Look Lonesome *(1997) and* All God's Children Need Traveling Shoes *(1997).*

1   For nearly a year, I sopped around the house, the Store, the school and the church, like an old biscuit, dirty and inedible. Then I met, or rather got to know, the lady who threw me my first life line.

2   Mrs. Bertha Flowers was the aristocrat of Black Stamps. She had the grace of control to appear warm in the coldest weather, and on the Arkansas summer days it seemed she had a private breeze which swirled around, cooling her. She was thin without the taut look of wiry people, and her printed voile dresses and flowered hats were as right for her as denim overalls for a farmer. She was our side's answer to the richest white woman in town.

3   Her skin was a rich black that would have peeled like a plum if snagged, but then no one would have thought of getting close enough to Mrs. Flowers to ruffle her dress, let alone snag her skin. She didn't encourage familiarity. She wore gloves too.

4   I don't think I ever saw Mrs. Flowers laugh, but she smiled often. A slow widening of her thin black lips to show even, small white teeth, then the slow effortless closing. When she chose to smile on me, I always wanted to thank her. The action was so graceful and inclusively benign.

5   She was one of the few gentlewomen I have ever known, and has remained throughout my life the measure of what a human being can be.

6   Momma[†] had a strange relationship with her. Most often when she passed on the road in front of the Store, she spoke to Momma in that soft yet carrying voice, "Good day, Mrs. Henderson." Momma responded with "How you, Sister Flowers?"

7   Mrs. Flowers didn't belong to our church, nor was she Momma's familiar. Why on earth did she insist on calling her Sister Flowers? Shame made me want to hide my face. Mrs. Flowers deserved better than to be called Sister. Then, Momma left out the verb. Why not ask, "How *are*

---

* To help you read this essay analytically, review pages 182–185.

† "Momma" was the grandmother who raised Angelou and her brother in Stamps, Arkansas; she was the respected owner of a general store.

you, *Mrs.* Flowers?" With the unbalanced passion of the young, I hated her for showing her ignorance to Mrs. Flowers. It didn't occur to me for many years that they were as alike as sisters, separated only by formal education.

8   Although I was upset, neither of the women was in the least shaken by what I thought an unceremonious greeting. Mrs. Flowers would continue her easy gait up the hill to her little bungalow, and Momma kept on shelling peas or doing whatever had brought her to the front porch.

9   Occasionally, though, Mrs. Flowers would drift off the road and down to the Store and Momma would say to me, "Sister, you go on and play." As she left I would hear the beginning of an intimate conversation. Momma persistently using the wrong verb, or none at all.

10   "Brother and Sister Wilcox is sho'ly the meanest—" "Is," Momma? "Is"? Oh, please, not "is," Momma, for two or more. But they talked, and from the side of the building where I waited for the ground to open up and swallow me, I heard the soft-voiced Mrs. Flowers and the textured voice of my grandmother merging and melting. They were interrupted from time to time by giggles that must have come from Mrs. Flowers (Momma never giggled in her life). Then she was gone.

11   She appealed to me because she was like people I had never met personally. Like women in English novels who walked the moors (whatever they were) with their loyal dogs racing at a respectful distance. Like the women who sat in front of roaring fireplaces, drinking tea incessantly from silver trays full of scones and crumpets. Women who walked over the "heath" and read morocco-bound books and had two last names divided by a hyphen. It would be safe to say that she made me proud to be Negro, just by being herself.

12   She acted just as refined as whitefolks in the movies and books and she was more beautiful, for none of them could have come near that warm color without looking gray by comparison.

13   I was fortunate that I never saw her in the company of po-whitefolks. For since they tend to think of their whiteness as an evenizer, I'm certain that I would have had to hear her spoken to commonly as Bertha, and my image of her would have been shattered like the unmendable Humpty-Dumpty.

14   One summer afternoon, sweet-milk fresh in my memory, she stopped at the Store to buy provisions. Another Negro woman of her health and age would have been expected to carry the paper sacks home in one hand, but Momma said, "Sister Flowers, I'll send Bailey* up to your house with these things."

15   She smiled that slow dragging smile, "Thank you, Mrs. Henderson. I'd prefer Marguerite, though." My name was beautiful when she said it.

---

* Angelou's brother.

"I've been meaning to talk to her, anyway." They gave each other age-group looks.

16   Momma said, "Well, that's all right then. Sister, go and change your dress. You going to Sister Flowers's."

17   The chifforobe was a maze. What on earth did one put on to go to Mrs. Flowers' house? I knew I shouldn't put on a Sunday dress. It might be sacrilegious. Certainly not a house dress, since I was already wearing a fresh one. I chose a school dress, naturally. It was formal without suggesting that going to Mrs. Flowers' house was equivalent to attending church.

18   I trusted myself back into the Store.

19   "Now, don't you look nice." I had chosen the right thing, for once. . . .

20   There was a little path beside the rocky road, and Mrs. Flowers walked in front swinging her arms and picking her way over the stones.

21   She said, without turning her head, to me, "I hear you're doing very good school work, Marguerite, but that it's all written. The teachers report that they have trouble getting you to talk in class." We passed the triangular farm on our left and the path widened to allow us to walk together. I hung back in the separate unasked and unanswerable questions.

22   "Come and walk along with me, Marguerite." I couldn't have refused even if I wanted to. She pronounced my name so nicely. Or more correctly, she spoke each word with such clarity that I was certain a foreigner who didn't understand English could have understood her.

23   "Now no one is going to make you talk—possibly no one can. But bear in mind, language is man's way of communicating with his fellow man and it is language alone which separates him from the lower animals." That was a totally new idea to me, and I would need time to think about it.

24   "Your grandmother says you read a lot. Every chance you get. That's good, but not good enough. Words mean more than what is set down on paper. It takes the human voice to infuse them with the shades of deeper meaning."

25   I memorized the part about the human voice infusing words. It seemed so valid and poetic.

26   She said she was going to give me some books and that I not only must read them, I must read them aloud. She suggested that I try to make a sentence sound in as many different ways as possible.

27   "I'll accept no excuse if you return a book to me that has been badly handled." My imagination boggled at the punishment I would deserve if in fact I did abuse a book of Mrs. Flowers's. Death would be too kind and brief.

28   The odors in the house surprised me. Somehow I had never connected Mrs. Flowers with food or eating or any other common experience of common people. There must have been an outhouse, too, but my mind never recorded it.

29   The sweet scent of vanilla had met us as she opened the door.

30   "I made tea cookies this morning. You see, I had planned to invite you for cookies and lemonade so we could have this little chat. The lemonade is in the icebox."

31   It followed that Mrs. Flowers would have ice on an ordinary day, when most families in our town bought ice late on Saturdays only a few times during the summer to be used in the wooden ice-cream freezers.

32   She took the bags from me and disappeared through the kitchen door. I looked around the room that I had never in my wildest fantasies imagined I would see. Browned photographs leered or threatened from the walls and the white, freshly done curtains pushed against themselves and against the wind. I wanted to gobble up the room entire and take it to Bailey, who would help me analyze and enjoy it.

33   "Have a seat, Marguerite. Over there by the table." She carried a platter covered with a tea towel. Although she warned that she hadn't tried her hand at baking sweets for some time, I was certain that like everything else about her the cookies would be perfect.

34   They were flat round wafers, slightly browned on the edges and butter-yellow in the center. With the cold lemonade they were sufficient for childhood's lifelong diet. Remembering my manners, I took nice little lady-like bites off the edges. She said she had made them expressly for me and that she had a few in the kitchen that I could take home to my brother. So I jammed one whole cake in my mouth and the rough crumbs scratched the insides of my jaws, and if I hadn't had to swallow, it would have been a dream come true.

35   As I ate she began the first of what we later called "my lessons in living." She said that I must always be intolerant of ignorance but understanding of illiteracy. That some people, unable to go to school, were more educated and even more intelligent than college professors. She encouraged me to listen carefully to what country people called mother wit. That in those homely sayings was couched the collective wisdom of generations.

36   When I finished the cookies she brushed off the table and brought a thick, small book from the bookcase. I had read *A Tale of Two Cities* and found it up to my standards as a romantic novel. She opened the first page and I heard poetry for the first time in my life.

37   "It was the best of times and the worst of times . . ." Her voice slid in and curved down through and over the words. She was nearly singing. I wanted to look at the pages. Were they the same that I had read? Or were there notes, music, lined on the pages, as in a hymn book? Her sounds began cascading gently. I knew from listening to a thousand preachers that she was nearing the end of her reading, and I hadn't really heard, heard to understand, a single word.

38   "How do you like that?"

39   It occurred to me that she expected a response. The sweet vanilla flavor was still on my tongue and her reading was a wonder in my ears. I had to speak.

40   I said, "Yes, ma'am." It was the least I could do, but it was the most also.

41   "There's one more thing. Take this book of poems and memorize one for me. Next time you pay me a visit, I want you to recite."

42   I have tried often to search behind the sophistication of years for the enchantment I so easily found in those gifts. The essence escapes but its aura remains. To be allowed, no, invited, into the private lives of strangers, and to share their joys and fears, was a chance to exchange the Southern bitter wormwood for a cup of mead with Beowulf or a hot cup of tea and milk with Oliver Twist. When I said aloud, "It is a far, far better thing that I do, than I have ever done . . ." tears of love filled my eyes at my selflessness.

43   On that first day, I ran down the hill and into the road (few cars ever came along it) and had the good sense to stop running before I reached the Store.

44   I was liked, and what a difference it made. I was respected not as Mrs. Henderson's grandchild or Bailey's sister but for just being Marguerite Johnson.

45   Childhood's logic never asks to be proved (all conclusions are absolute). I didn't question why Mrs. Flowers had singled me out for attention, nor did it occur to me that Momma might have asked her to give me a little talking to. All I cared about was that she had made tea cookies for *me* and read to *me* from her favorite book. It was enough to prove that she liked me.

Questions on Content, Structure, and Style

1. What is Angelou's main purpose in this narrative? What does she want to show about Sister Flowers' effect on her?

2. How does Angelou use sensory details and imagery in paragraphs 2–4 to introduce Mrs. Flowers' character?

3. Why does Angelou emphasize the embarrassment she felt when Momma talked to Mrs. Flowers? What do these conversations reveal about Angelou's attitude toward her grandmother at this time?

4. As an adult, what does Angelou suspect about her grandmother's relationship to Mrs. Flowers that she didn't see as a child?

5. Why was Angelou impressed by Mrs. Flowers? To what kinds of women is she compared? Why is Angelou glad she had never seen Mrs. Flowers spoken to by white people?

6. What sort of young girl was Angelou before she became friends with Mrs. Flowers? Cite some evidence from the essay that supports your view of her character.

7. How does the description of Mrs. Flowers' house and possessions help communicate Angelou's childhood reverence for this woman? Why were the cookies and lemonade so important?

8. Why does Angelou choose to use dialogue in paragraphs 37–41 instead of just describing the scene?

9. Does Angelou use enough vivid details to make her narrative seem believable and her characters realistic? Cite two or three examples of descriptive language that you think are particularly effective.

10. Why does Angelou include paragraphs 42, 44, and 45 at the end of her essay? Would the extent of Mrs. Flowers' impact on the author be as complete without them?

Suggestions for Writing

Try using Maya Angelou's "Sister Flowers" as a stepping stone to your writing. Think of an adult who helped or guided you when you were a child: how did this person make a difference in your life? This person might be a relative, a teacher, a neighbor, a coach, a friend's parent. Tell a story that captures an important moment in your relationship with this person: your first meeting, a crucial event, an incident that crystallized this person's influence on you. Or perhaps you have played an important role in a child's life. In either case, what insight about the value of intergenerational relationships might your narrative offer?

Vocabulary

voile (2)	chifforobe (17)	homely (35)
benign (4)	infuse (24)	aura (42)
gait (8)	boggled (27)	wormwood (42)
morocco-bound (11)	leered (32)	mead (42)

 A REVISION WORKSHEET

As you write your rough drafts, consult Chapter 5 for guidance through the revision process. In addition, here are a few questions to ask yourself as you revise your narrative:

1. Is the narrative essay's purpose clear to the reader?

2. Is the thesis plainly stated or at least clearly implied?

3. Does the narrative convincingly support or illustrate its intended point? If not, how might the story be changed?

4. Does the story maintain a logical point of view and an understandable order of action?

5. Are the characters, actions, and settings presented in enough vivid detail to make them clear and believable? Where could more detail be effectively added?

6. Is the story coherent and well paced or does it wander or bog down in places because of irrelevant or repetitious details? What might be condensed or cut?

7. Does the essay end in a satisfying way or does the action stop too abruptly?

After you've revised your essay extensively, you might exchange rough drafts with a classmate and answer these questions for each other, making specific suggestions for improvement wherever appropriate. (For advice on productive participation in classroom workshops, see pp. 117–119.)

Reviewing Your Progress

After you have completed your narrative essay, take a moment to measure your progress as a writer by responding to the following questions. Such analysis will help you recognize growth in your writing skills and may enable you to identify areas that are still problematic.

1. What do you like best about your narrative essay? Why?

2. After reading through your essay, select the description, detail, or piece of dialogue that you think best characterizes a major figure or most effectively advances the action in your story. Explain the reason for your choice in one or two sentences.

3. What part of your essay gave you the most trouble? How did you overcome the problem?

4. If you had more time to work on this essay, what would receive additional attention? Why?

5. What did you learn about your topic from writing this essay? About yourself as a writer?

CHAPTER

13

Writing Essays Using Multiple Strategies

In Part Two of this text, you have been studying essays developed primarily by a single mode or expository strategy. You may have, for example, written essays primarily developed by multiple examples, process analysis, or comparison/contrast techniques. Concentrating on a single strategy in your essays has allowed you to practice, in a focused way, each of the patterns of development most often used in writing tasks. Although practicing each strategy in isolation this way is somewhat artificial, it is the easiest, simplest way to master the common organizational patterns. Consider the parallels to learning almost any skill: before you attempt a complex dive with spins and flips, you first practice each maneuver separately. Having understood and mastered the individual strategies of development, you should feel confident about facing any writing situation, including those that would most profit from incorporating multiple strategies to accomplish their goal.

Most essays *do* call upon multiple strategies of development to achieve their purpose, a reality you have probably discovered for yourself as you wrote and studied various essays in this text. In fact, you may have found it difficult—or impossible—to avoid combining modes and strategies in your own essays. As noted in the introduction to Part Two, writers virtually always blend strategies, using examples in their comparisons, description in their definitions, examples in their arguments, and so on. Therein is the heart of the matter: the single patterns of development you have been practicing are *thinking* strategies—ways of considering a subject and generating ideas—as well as organizing tools. In most writing situations, writers study their tasks and choose the strategies that will *most effectively* accomplish their purpose.

In addition, some writing tasks, often the longer ones, will clearly profit from combining multiple strategies in distinct ways to thoroughly address the essay's subject, purpose, and audience. Suppose, for example, you are given a problem-solving assignment in a business class: selling the City Council on a plan to build a low-income housing project in a particular neighborhood. You might call upon your writing resources and use multiple strategies to

- Describe the project
- Explain the causes (the need for such a project)
- Argue its strengthens, deflect opposition arguments
- Contrast it to other housing options
- Cite similar examples in other towns
- Explain its long-term beneficial effects on tenants, neighbors, businesses, etc.

Or perhaps you are investigating recent disciplinary action taken against Colorado high school seniors for decorating their graduation gowns. Your essay might combine three strategies: first presenting examples of the controversy, then contrasting arguments among administrators and students, and concluding with a step-by-step process for avoiding future problems.

As a writer who now knows how to use a variety of thinking and organizational methods, you can assess any writing situation and select the strategy—or strategies—that will work best for your topic, purpose, and audience.

Choosing the Best Strategies

To help you choose the best means of development for your essay, here is a brief review of the modes and strategies accompanied by some pertinent questions:

1. **Example:** Would real or hypothetical illustrations make my subject more easily understood?

2. **Process:** Would a step-by-step procedural analysis clarify my subject?

3. Comparison/Contrast: Would aligning or juxtaposing my subject to something else be helpful?

4. Definition: Would my subject profit from an extended explanation of its meaning?

5. Division/Classification: Would separating my subject into its component parts or grouping its parts into categories be useful?

6. Causal Analysis: Would explaining causes or effects add important information?

7. Argument: Would my position be advanced by offering logical reasons and/or addressing objections?

8. Description: Would vivid details, sensory images, or figurative language help readers visualize my subject?

9. Narrative: Would a story best illustrate some idea or aspect of my subject?

Try using these questions as prompts to help you generate ideas and select those strategies that best accomplish your purpose.

Problems to Avoid

Avoid overkill. Being prepared to use any of the writing strategies is akin to carrying many tools in your carpenter's bag. But just because you own many tools doesn't mean you must use all of them in one project—rather, you select only the ones you need for the specific job at hand. If you do decide to use multiple strategies in a particular essay, avoid a hodgepodge of information that runs in too many directions. Sometimes your essay's prescribed length means you cannot present all you know; again, let your main purpose guide you to including the best or most important ideas.

Organize logically. If you decide that multiple strategies will work best, you must find an appropriate order and coherent flow for your essay. In the hypothetical problem-solving essay on the housing project mentioned earlier, for instance, the writer must decide whether the long-term effects of the project should be discussed earlier or later in the paper. In the student essay that follows, the writer struggled with the question of putting kinds of vegetarians before or after discussion of reasons for adopting vegetarianism. There are no easy answers to such questions—each writer must experiment with outlines and rough drafts to find the most successful arrangement, one that will offer the most effective response to the particular material, the essay's purpose, and the audience's needs. Be patient as you try various ways of combining strategies into a coherent rather than choppy paper.

SAMPLE STUDENT ESSAY

In the essay that follows, the student writer responds to an assignment that asked her to write about an important belief or distinguishing aspect of her life. The purpose, audience, and development of her essay were left to her; the length was designated at 750 to 1000 words. As a confirmed vegetarian for well over a decade, she often found herself questioned about her beliefs. After deciding to clarify (and encourage) vegetarianism for an audience of interested but often puzzled fellow students, she developed her essay by drawing on many strategies, including causal analysis, example, classification, contrast, argument, and process analysis. Because her rough draft was too long, the writer edited out an extended narrative telling the story of her own "conversion" to vegetarianism, viewing that section as less central to her essay's main purpose than the other parts.

PASS THE BROCCOLI—PLEASE!

Introduction: 1   What do Benjamin Franklin, Charles Darwin, Leonardo da Vinci,
famous
examples   Percy Bysshe Shelley, Mohandas Gandhi, Albert Einstein, and I have

in common? In addition to being great thinkers, of course, we are

all vegetarians, people who have rejected the practice of eating

animals. Vegetarianism is growing rapidly in America today, but

some people continue to see it as a strange choice. If you are

Thesis,   thinking of making this decision yourself or are merely curious,
purpose,
audience   taking time to learn about vegetarianism is worthwhile.

     2   In a land where hamburgers, pepperoni pizza, and fried

chicken are among our favorite foods, just why do Americans

Contrast to   become vegetarians anyway? Worldwide, vegetarianism is often
other parts
of the world   part of religious faith, especially to Buddhists, Hindus, and others

whose spiritual beliefs emphasize nonviolence, karma, and

reincarnation. But in this country the reasons for becoming

vegetarian are more diverse. Some people cite ecological reasons,

Causal   arguing that vegetarianism is best for our planet because it takes
analysis: 3
reasons   less land and food to raise vegetables and grain than livestock.

Others choose vegetarianism because of health reasons. Repeated studies by groups such as the American Heart Association and the American Medical Association show that diets lower in animal fats and higher in fiber decrease the risk of heart disease, cancer, diabetes, hypertension, and osteoporosis.

3   Still other people's ethical beliefs bring them to vegetarianism. These people object to the ways that some animals, such as cows and chickens, are confined and are often fed various chemicals, such as growth hormones, antibiotics, and tranquilizers. They object to the procedures of slaughterhouses. They object to killing animals for consumption or for their decorative body parts (hides, fur, skins, tusks, feathers, etc.) and for using them for science or cosmetic experiments. These vegetarians believe that animals feel fear and pain and that it is morally wrong for one species to inflict unnecessary suffering on another. I count myself among this group; consequently, my vegetarian choices extend to wearing no leather or fur and I do not use household or cosmetic products tested on animals.

Personal example

4   Regardless of reasons for our choice, all vegetarians reject eating meat. However, there are actually several kinds of vegetarians, with the majority falling into three categories:

1. Ovo-lacto vegetarians eat milk, cheese, eggs, and honey;
2. Lacto vegetarians do not eat eggs but may keep other dairy products in their diet;
3. Vegans do not eat dairy products or any animal by-products whatsoever.

Classification: 3 types

Many people, including myself, begin as ovo-lacto vegetarians but eventually become vegans, considered the most complete or pure type.

5   Perhaps the most common objection to any type of vegetarianism comes from a misconception about deficiencies in

Argument: refutation, evidence, examples

the diet, particularly protein. But it is a mistake to think only meat offers us protein. Vegetarians who eat dairy products, grains, vegetables, beans, and nuts receive more than enough nutrients, including protein. In fact, according to the cookbook *The Higher Taste,* cheese, peanuts, and lentils contain more protein per ounce than hamburger, pork, or a porterhouse steak. Many medical experts think that Americans actually eat too much protein, as seen in the revised food pyramid that now calls for an increase in vegetables, fruits, and grains over meat and diary products. A vegetarian diet will not make someone a limp weakling. Kevin Newbanks, *Tonight Show* band leader, is, for example, not only a busy musician but also a weightlifter. Some members of the Denver Broncos football team, according to their manager, no longer eat red meat at their training table.

6   For those who would like to give vegetarianism a try, here are a few suggestions for getting started:

Process:
4 steps to
begin

1. Explore your motives. If you are only becoming a vegetarian to please a friend, for example, you won't stick with it. Be honest with yourself: the reasons behind your choice have a lot to do with your commitment.

2. Read more. The library can provide you with answers to your questions and concerns. There are hundred of books full of ecological, medical, and ethical arguments for vegetarianism.

(More
argument and
examples)

3. Eat! Another popular misconception is that vegetarianism means a life of eating tasteless grass; nothing could be less true. Visit a vegetarian restaurant several times to see how many delicious dishes are available. Even grocery stores now carry a variety of vegetarian entrees. Or try one of the many vegetarian cookbooks on the market today. You may

be surprised to discover that tofu enchiladas, soy burgers, and stuffed eggplant taste better than you could ever imagine.

4. Start slowly. You don't have to become a vegan overnight if it doesn't feel right. Some people begin by excluding just red meat from their diets. Feeling good as time goes by can direct your choices. Books, such as *The Beginning Vegetarian*, and magazines, such as *Vegetarian Times*, can offer encouragement.

7   It's never too late to change your lifestyle. Nobel Prize-winning author Isaac Bashevis Singer became a vegetarian at age 58. Making this choice now may allow you to live longer and feel better. In fifty years you may be like playwright George Bernard Shaw, who at 25 was warned against a vegetarian diet. As a vigorous old man, Shaw wanted to tell all those people they were wrong, but noted he couldn't: "They all passed away years ago"!

Conclusion: Additional famous examples, witty quotation

Don't Let Stereotypes Warp Your Judgments
Robert L. Heilbroner

Robert L. Heilbroner is a former professor of economics at the New School for Social Research in New York. His books include The Worldly Philosophers *(1954),* The Future as History *(1960), and* The Nature and Logic of Capitalism *(1985). This essay, published in* Readers Digest, *uses multiple strategies to expose a social problem, explain its causes and effects, and offer some practical suggestions for change.*

1   Is a girl called Gloria apt to be better-looking than one called Bertha? Are criminals more likely to be dark than blond? Can you tell a good deal about someone's personality from hearing his voice briefly over the phone? Can a person's nationality be pretty accurately guessed from his photograph? Does the fact that someone wears glasses imply that he is intelligent?

2   The answer to all these questions is obviously, "No."

3   Yet, from all the evidence at hand, most of us believe these things. Ask any college boy if he'd rather take his chances with a Gloria or a Bertha, or ask a college girl if she'd rather blind-date a Richard or a Cuthbert. In fact, you don't have to ask: college students in questionnaires have revealed that names conjure up the same images in their minds as they do in yours—and for as little reason.

4   Look into the favorite suspects of persons who report "suspicious characters" and you will find a large percentage of them to be "swarthy" or "dark and foreign-looking"—despite the testimony of criminologists that criminals do *not* tend to be dark, foreign or "wild-eyed." Delve into the main asset of a telephone stock swindler and you will find it to be a marvelously confidence-inspiring telephone "personality." And whereas we all think we know what an Italian or a Swede looks like, it is the sad fact that when a group of Nebraska students sought to match faces and nationalities of 15 European countries, they were scored wrong in 93 percent of their identifications. Finally, for all the fact that horn-rimmed glasses have now become the standard television sign of an "intellectual," optometrists know that the main thing that distinguishes people with glasses is just bad eyes.

5   Stereotypes are a kind of gossip about the world, a gossip that makes us prejudge people before we ever lay eyes on them. Hence it is not surprising that stereotypes have something to do with the dark world of prejudice. Explore most prejudices (note that the word means prejudgment) and you will find a cruel stereotype at the core of each one.

* For help reading this essay analytically, review pages 182–185.

6   For it is the extraordinary fact that once we have typecast the world, we tend to see people in terms of our standardized pictures. In another demonstration of the power of stereotypes to affect our vision, a number of Columbia and Barnard students were shown 30 photographs of pretty but unidentified girls, and asked to rate each in terms of "general liking," "intelligence," "beauty" and so on. Two months later, the same group were shown the same photographs, this time with fictitious Irish, Italian, Jewish and "American" names attached to the pictures. Right away the ratings changed. Faces which were now seen as representing a national group went down in looks and still farther down in likability, while the "American" girls suddenly looked decidedly prettier and nicer.

7   Why is it that we stereotype the world in such irrational and harmful fashion? In part, we begin to type-cast people in our childhood years. Early in life, as every parent whose child has watched a TV Western knows, we learn to spot the Good Guys from the Bad Guys. Some years ago, a social psychologist showed very clearly how powerful these stereotypes of childhood vision are. He secretly asked the most popular youngsters in an elementary school to make errors in their morning gym exercises. Afterwards, he asked the class if anyone had noticed any mistakes during gym period. Oh, yes, said the children. But it was the *unpopular* members of the class—the "bad guys"—they remembered as being out of step.

8   We not only grow up with standardized pictures forming inside of us, but as grown-ups we are constantly having them thrust upon us. Some of them, like the half-joking, half-serious stereotypes of mothers-in-law, or country yokels, or psychiatrists, are dinned into us by the stock jokes we hear and repeat. In fact, without such stereotypes, there would be a lot fewer jokes. Still other stereotypes are perpetuated by the advertisements we read, the movies we see, the books we read.

9   And finally, we tend to stereotype because it helps us make sense out of a highly confusing world, a world which William James* once described as "one great, blooming, buzzing confusion." It is a curious fact that if we don't *know* what we're looking at, we are often quite literally unable to *see* what we're looking at. People who recover their sight after a lifetime of blindness actually cannot at first tell a triangle from a square. A visitor to a factory sees only noisy chaos where the superintendent sees a perfectly synchronized flow of work. As Walter Lippmann† has said, "For the most part we do not first see, and then define; we define first, and then we see."

10   Stereotypes are one way in which we "define" the world in order to see it. They classify the infinite variety of human beings into a convenient

---

* William James (1842–1910) was an American philosopher and psychologist.
† Walter Lippmann was a twentieth-century American journalist.

handful of "types" towards whom we learn to act in stereotyped fashion. Life would be a wearing process if we had to start from scratch with each and every human contact. Stereotypes economize on our mental effort by covering up the blooming, buzzing confusion with big recognizable cutouts. They save us the "trouble" of finding out what the world is like—they give it its accustomed look.

11   Thus the trouble is that stereotypes make us mentally lazy. As S. I. Hayakawa, the authority on semantics, has written: "The danger of stereotypes lies not in their existence, but in the fact that they become for all people some of the time, and for some people all the time, *substitutes for observation.*" Worse yet, stereotypes get in the way of our judgment, even when we do observe the world. Someone who has formed rigid preconceptions of all Latins as "excitable," or all teenagers as "wild," doesn't alter his point of view when he meets a calm and deliberate Genoese,* or a serious-minded high school student. He brushes them aside as "exceptions that prove the rule." And, of course, if he meets someone true to type, he stands triumphantly vindicated. "They're all like that," he proclaims, having encountered an excited Latin, an ill-behaved adolescent.

12   Hence, quite aside from the injustice which stereotypes do to others, they impoverish ourselves. A person who lumps the world into simple categories, who type-casts all labor leaders as "racketeers," all businessmen as "reactionaries," all Harvard men as "snobs," and all Frenchmen as "sexy," is in danger of becoming a stereotype himself. He loses his capacity to be himself—which is to say, to see the world in his own absolutely unique, inimitable and independent fashion.

13   Instead, he votes for the man who fits his standardized picture of what a candidate "should" look like or sound like, buys the goods that someone in his "situation" in life "should" own, lives the life that others define for him. The mark of the stereotype person is that he never surprises us, that we do indeed have him "typed." And no one fits this straitjacket so perfectly as someone whose opinions about *other people* are fixed and inflexible.

14   Impoverishing as they are, stereotypes are not easy to get rid of. The world we type-cast may be no better than a Grade B movie, but at least we know what to expect of our stock characters. When we let them act for themselves in the strangely unpredictable way that people do act, who knows but that many of our fondest convictions will be proved wrong?

15   Nor do we suddenly drop our standardized pictures for a blinding vision of the Truth. Sharp swings of ideas about people often just substitute one stereotype for another. The true process of change is a slow one that adds bits and pieces of reality to the pictures in our heads, until gradually they take on some of the blurriness of life itself. Little by little,

---

* Genoese refers to a citizen of Genoa, Italy.

we learn not that Jews and Negroes and Catholics and Puerto Ricans are "just like everybody else"—for that, too, is a stereotype—but that each and every one of them is unique, special, different and individual. Often we do not even know that we have let a stereotype lapse until we hear someone saying, "all so-and-so's are like such-and-such," and we hear ourselves saying, "Well—maybe."

16   Can we speed the process along? Of course we can.

17   First, we can become *aware* of the standardized pictures in our heads, in other peoples' heads, in the world around us.

18   Second, we can become suspicious of all judgments that we allow exceptions to "prove." There is no more chastening thought than that in the vast intellectual adventure of science, it takes but one tiny exception to topple a whole edifice of ideas.

19   Third, we can learn to be chary of generalizations about people. As F. Scott Fitzgerald* once wrote: "Begin with an individual, and before you know it you have created a type; begin with a type, and you find you have created—nothing."

20   Most of the time, when we type-cast the world, we are not in fact generalizing about people at all. We are only revealing the embarrassing facts about the pictures that hang in the gallery of stereotypes in our own heads.

Questions on Content, Structure, and Style

1. Why does Heilbroner begin his essay with a series of questions, references to criminal reports, and the Nebraska study? How does this introduction set up Heilbroner's thesis?

2. How does Heilbroner define stereotypes in paragraph 5? What do the studies at Barnard and Columbia University and at the elementary school (paragraph 7) illustrate about prejudice?

3. Why does Heilbroner use "we" and "us" so often in this essay instead of referring to "people who stereotype"? Is his choice a good one?

4. What explanation of causes does Heilbroner offer? How do stereotypes contribute to the ways we try to "define" the world?

5. In addition to the injustice inflicted on others, what negative effects does stereotyping have on those who employ it?

6. Throughout his essay, Heilbroner uses vivid, specific examples, both real and hypothetical. Cite and explain some of his most effective uses of this strategy.

*F. Scott Fitzgerald (1896–1940) was an American writer, best known for his novel *The Great Gatsby*.

7. Why does Heilbroner include a three-step process near the end of his essay?

8. Why does Heilbroner quote the words of well-known figures such as William James, S. I. Hayakawa, Walter Lippmann, and F. Scott Fitzgerald in various places in his essay? What purposes do their words serve?

9. Evaluate this essay's conclusion. How does Heilbroner use figurative language to make a memorable last impression on his readers?

10. List the main strategies Heilbroner uses to develop his essay. Which do you find the most effective? If Heilbroner were to extend his essay, what other strategies might he incorporate in his exploration of stereotyping?

Suggestions for Writing

Try using Robert Heilbroner's "Don't Let Stereotypes Warp Your Judgments" as a stepping stone to an essay of your own. Have you ever been the victim of someone's irrational or harmful standardized picture? Or have you yourself been guilty of misjudging someone else? Remember that not all stereotypes are racial or ethnic; typecasting surrounds economic status (the "welfare moocher"), gender (the "dumb blonde"), locations (the redneck Texan), and professions (the mousey accountant), to name only a few areas. Write an essay that explores the topic of stereotyping or prejudice; use any of the modes or strategies you find helpful. You might, for example, describe an incident, explain causes, analyze effects on you and/or the other person involved, argue for other approaches to solving the problem, or outline specific steps you once took to escape "the gallery of stereotypes" in your head.

Vocabulary

swarthy (4)	semantics (11)	edifice (18)
dinned (8)	vindicated (11)	chary (19)
perpetuated (8)	impoverish (12)	
synchronized (9)	chastening (18)	

 A REVISION WORKSHEET

As you write your rough drafts, consult Chapter 5 for guidance through the revision process. In addition, here are a few questions to ask yourself before and during the early stages of your writing:

1. What is my main purpose in writing this particular essay?

2. Does my assignment or the subject itself suggest a primary method of development or would combining several strategies be more effective?

3. If no one strategy seems adequate, have I considered my subject from multiple directions, as suggested by the questions on pages 350–351?

4. Have I selected the best strategies to accomplish my purpose and develop my topic to meet the needs of my particular audience?

5. Would the addition of other strategies help my readers understand my topic and my essay's purpose? Or, am I trying to include too many approaches, move in too many directions, resulting in an essay that seems too scattered?

6. Have I considered an effective order for the strategies I've chosen? Do the parts of my essay flow smoothly together?

7. Have I avoided common weaknesses such as vague examples, fuzzy directions, circular definitions, overlapping categories, or logical fallacies, as discussed in the "Problems to Avoid" sections of Chapters 9–12?

After you've revised your essay extensively, you might exchange rough drafts with a classmate and answer these questions for each other, making specific suggestions for improvement wherever appropriate. (For advice on productive participation in classroom workshops, see pages 117–119.)

Reviewing Your Progress

After you have completed your essay, take a moment to measure your progress as a writer by responding to the following questions. Such analysis will help you recognize growth in your writing skills and may enable you to identify areas that are still problematic.

1. What do you like best about your essay? Why?

2. After considering the multiple strategies of development used in your essay, which one do you find most effective and why?

3. What part of your essay gave you the most trouble? How did you overcome the problem?

4. If you had more time to work on this essay, what would receive additional attention? Why?

5. What did you learn about your topic from writing this essay? About yourself as a writer?

PART
Three

SPECIAL ASSIGNMENTS

The third section of this text addresses three kinds of assignments frequently included in many—but not all—composition classes. Chapter 14 will first explain ways to conduct formal research on a topic and then show you how to best incorporate your research into your essay. Chapter 15, "Writing about Literature," illustrates several uses of poetry and short stories in the composition classroom and provides some guidelines for both close reading and analytical thinking. "Writing In-Class Assignments," Chapter 16, confronts the anxiety that writing under pressure may bring by helping you respond quickly but effectively to a variety of timed essays and exams.

If you have worked through Parts One and Two of this book, you have already practiced many of the skills demanded by these special assignments. Information in the next three chapters will build on what you already know about writing good essays.

CHAPTER

14

Writing a Paper Using Research

Although the words *research paper* have been known to produce anxiety worse than that caused by the sound of a dentist's drill, you should try to relax. A research paper is similar to the kinds of expository and argumentative essays described in the earlier parts of this book, the difference being the use of documented source material to support, illustrate, or explain your ideas. Research papers still call for thesis statements, logical sequences of paragraphs, well-developed supporting evidence, smooth conclusions—or in other words, all the skills you've been practicing throughout this book. By citing sources in your essays or reports, you merely show your readers that you have investigated your ideas and found support for them. In addition, using sources affords your readers the opportunity to look into your subject further if they so desire, consulting your references for additional readings.

The process described in the next few pages should help you write a paper using research that is carefully and effectively documented. This chapter also contains sample documentation forms for a variety of research sources and a sample student essay using MLA style.

FOCUSING YOUR TOPIC

In some cases, you will be assigned your topic, and you will be able to begin your research right away. In other cases, however, you may be encouraged to select your own subject, or you may be given a general subject ("health care reform," "recycling," "U.S. immigration policies") that you must narrow and then focus into a specific, manageable topic. If the topic is your choice, you need to do some preliminary thinking about what interests you; as in any assignment, you should make the essay a learning experience from which both you and your readers will profit. Therefore, you may want to brainstorm for a while on your general subject before you go to the library, asking yourself questions about what you already know and don't know. Some of the most interesting papers are argumentative essays in which writers set about to find an answer to a controversy or to find support for a solution they suspect might work. Other papers, sometimes called "research reports," expose, explain, or summarize a situation or a problem for their audience.

Throughout this chapter we will track the research and writing process of Amy Lawrence, a composition student whose writing assignment called for an essay presenting her view of a controversy in her major field of study. As a history major, Amy is particularly interested in the Russian Revolution of 1918, when the Romanov family, the last ruling family of Russia, was assassinated by the Bolsheviks, the Communist revolutionaries led by Lenin. The long-standing controversy surrounding this assassination focuses on the question of whether the two youngest Romanov children, the beautiful Anastasia and the sickly Alexei, escaped execution. New forensic and historical research concerning this controversy was making headlines at the time of Amy's assignment, so she chose the Romanov assassination as her topic. Because she already had some general knowledge of the controversy, Amy was able to think about her topic in terms of some specific *research questions:* What would research tell her about the possibility of the Romanov children's escape? Would the new evidence support the theory of an escape—or would it put such a claim to rest forever? (Amy's completed essay appears on pp. 399–406.)

BEGINNING YOUR LIBRARY RESEARCH

Once you have a general topic (and perhaps have some research questions in mind), your next step is familiarizing yourself with the school or public library where you will do your research. Most libraries have handouts, maps, or librarians who will help you locate the important parts of the library; do not be shy about asking for such information *before* you start your search.

After you become comfortable in the library, you can begin to compile a *working bibliography,* that is, a list of possible sources for your topic. You may find it useful to start by investigating one or more of the following reference room tools:

Computer Catalogs of Library Holdings/The Card Catalog

In libraries across the country, card catalogs are being replaced by computers as the primary guide to a library's holdings. During this time of transition, you may find libraries that no longer have any card catalogs, some that blend computer and card catalog use, and a few that have not yet installed any computer databases. No two libraries are exactly alike, and technological resources vary from place to place. As a result, consulting a librarian about the system(s) currently in use at your school or public library may be essential as you begin your research. Never be afraid to ask for help!

The *card catalog* is usually a series of cabinets containing alphabetized index cards; in some libraries, the card catalog is divided into three parts so that you may look up information under "subject," "author," and "title."

Subject Card from Card Catalog:

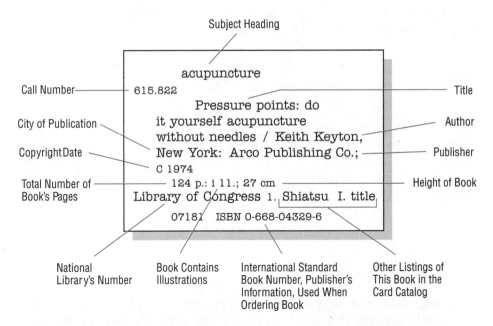

Computer catalogs offer these same three divisions as well as on-screen prompts to guide you through the process of searching under each catalog. Unless you are already familiar with authorities or their books on your subject, you will most likely begin with the "subject" catalog. If your subject is "acupuncture," you might find a catalog subject card that looks like the sample above. Most computer catalogs use a similar format to ease the researcher's transition from card catalog to computer. If you look under the subject heading "acupuncture" in a computer catalog, you will find on-screen data similar to the sample on page 368. For both card catalogs and computer catalogs, you may have to look under several headings in the subject catalog to find the one your library uses for your topic. If you can't find your subject under the headings that first come to your mind, ask your librarian for the *Library of Congress Subject Headings,* a common reference book that will suggest other names for your topic. Once you have a call number, consult a library map to determine the book's location on the shelves.

Subject Screen from Computer Catalog:

```
Title:     Complete Guide to Acupuncture and Acupressure
Author:    Toguchi, Masaru

       Pub.
#      Date     Call Number                      Status of Item
1      1985     AN 615.89-Toguchi, Masaru            Available
```

For more detailed information about this book, the researcher would use on-screen prompts to bring up the following data:

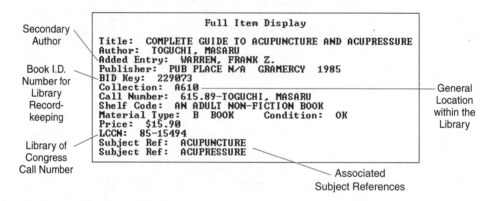

Secondary Author

Book I.D. Number for Library Record-keeping

Library of Congress Call Number

```
                  Full Item Display
Title:  COMPLETE GUIDE TO ACUPUNCTURE AND ACUPRESSURE
Author:  TOGUCHI, MASARU
Added Entry:  WARREN, FRANK Z.
Publisher:  PUB PLACE N/A   GRAMERCY   1985
BID Key:  229073
Collection:  A610
Call Number:  615.89-TOGUCHI, MASARU
Shelf Code:  AN ADULT NON-FICTION BOOK
Material Type:  B  BOOK     Condition:  OK
Price:  $15.90
LCCN:  85-15494
Subject Ref:  ACUPUNCTURE
Subject Ref:  ACUPRESSURE
```

General Location within the Library

Associated Subject References

Periodical Indexes

Periodical indexes list magazines and journals that contain articles you may wish to consult. Most of these indexes are now available on computer databases; you will probably find the most up-to-date information there. However, if computer time is not available to you when you need your research, you can always turn to the print versions. Most libraries will have desk copies of specialized indexes such as the *Business Periodicals Index,* the *Humanities Index,* the *Applied Science and Technology Index,* the *Social Sciences Index,* and others. *The Readers' Guide to Periodical Literature* lists magazines of general interest, such as *Time* and *Newsweek.* Print indexes may be used only at the library.

Electronic Sources

A computer database, in brief, is any block of information that can be accessed with a computer. A database search allows you to use a computer to scan electronic indexes that list thousands of bibliographic sources, abstracts, and texts.

Sometimes, perhaps as you begin your research process, you may wish to use one or more of the many CD-ROMS (compact discs of stored information) in your library. Commonly available CD-ROM titles include *NewsBank* (indexes and full texts of U.S. newspaper articles), *ABI* (indexes and abstracts of articles from hundreds of business publications), and *Encarta* (an encyclopedia); many other CD-ROM titles are available and may be especially useful in the early or background stages of your research.

Other sources, often more specialized or field-specific, are available online today. Most libraries subscribe to information services that will lead you to an appropriate database for your subject. Libraries subscribe to different services, however, so you may need to consult your librarian. You might, for example, use *Infotrac* or *ProQuest* for indexes, abstracts, and some articles from general-interest periodicals; other indexes are focused on specialized topics (health, business, law, education, etc.). These online databases are updated frequently and may provide you with the most reliable, current information on your essay topic.

If you have never used a database before, enlist the help of a librarian. A piece of advice: your librarian will be most helpful to a prepared researcher. Compile ahead of time a list of key words, known as *descriptors,* that you might search under to find your topic. For example, composition student Amy Lawrence began her research by searching *Encarta,* the CD-ROM encyclopedia published by Microsoft. Some of the descriptors she used were "Romanov," "Nicholas II," "Anastasia Romanov," and "Alexei Romanov." While there were no entries under the last two terms, she found potentially useful information under "Romanov" and "Nicholas II." You will find it saves time and energy to narrow your search by combining descriptors whenever possible. Later in her research, Amy consulted an index of *The Denver Post* newspaper (one of the two largest newspapers in her state), using the combined descriptors "Romanov DNA testing" to begin a search that yielded four articles, one of which was very useful. If Amy had used the more general descriptor "DNA testing," she would have had to scan too many articles irrelevant to her topic.

Once you have found useful information through electronic sources, libraries today usually have printers available to print out the on-screen data you wish to keep; you may have to pay a small fee for this (or other) copying, so it's probably a good rule to never go to your library without a bit of cash. And once again, the very best advice bears repeating: never hesitate to ask your library staff for help!

Special Note to Internet Users

The most effective approach to discovering useful material on the Internet is by accessing search engines. Several of the most popular include Exite, AltaVista, Yahoo!, HotBot, and Infoseek; each has its own search methods and directions for its use that will appear on your screen. Because the Internet contains more information and sources than you could ever read in this decade, it is essential that to save yourself time and frustration, you narrow your search through use of your key words, as described in the previous section. A special warning for Internet users, too: be sure to evaluate carefully any information you obtain. Opinions abound on the Internet, but often they are just that—opinions—unsupported, often biased, casual chat. Not all Web sites (information sites created by specific individuals or groups on specific topics) are reliable sources.

Special Collections

Your library may contain special collections that will help you research your subject. Some libraries, for example, have extensive collections of government documents or educational materials or newspapers from foreign cities. Other libraries may have invested in manuscripts from famous authors or in a series of works on a particular subject, such as your state's history, a Vietnam War collection, or studies on human rights in post-World War II Latin America. Remember, too, that some libraries contain collections of early films, rare recordings, or unique photographs. Consult your librarian or the handouts describing your library's special holdings.

PREPARING A WORKING BIBLIOGRAPHY

Looking through computer databases and various indexes will take time, but seeing what's been published on your subject may help you focus on a specific topic. You may also find it useful at this point to skim a number of articles on your subject, so that eventually you reach the specific idea you want to research and write about. (And don't underestimate the value of browsing—sometimes the most interesting book on your subject is on the shelf next to the book you were looking for.)

Once you have a narrowed focus, prepare a *working bibliography,* a list of the most promising sources for your paper. To compile a working bibliography, you should copy on an index card (or print out) the following information for each book: author's name, full title of the book, publisher, date, and city of publication, page numbers of the material you're interested in, and library call number. If the source is a magazine or journal, record the author's name, journal's name, article's name, volume number, issue number, date of issue, and page numbers of the article within the journal. If you are using an electronic

Article in Magazine

Elliot, Dorinda
"The Legacy of the Last Czar"
<u>Newsweek</u> pp. 60–61
Sept. 21, 1992

Book

Radzinsky, Edvard; translated by Marian Schwartz
<u>The Last Tsar: The Life and Death of Nicholas II</u>
Doubleday Publishers
New York, New York 1992 (English edition)
pp. 8–10, 315–434
call number: AN947.083

Electronic Source

John Varoli
"Nemtsov: Bury Tsar in St. Petersburg July 17"
<u>The St. Petersburg Times</u>
St. Petersburg, Russia
Feb. 9–15 1998
<http://www.spb.ru/times/336–337/nemtsov.html>
Internet   (date access: 3/24/98)

source, write down (or print out) as much information as is available. Information from a nonperiodical CD-ROM database, for example, is cited similarly to information noted about a book, but you also list the medium, the distributor, and the place and date of the electronic publication. Online sources might also include the publication medium (Online), name of computer service (CompuServe) or network (Internet), electronic address, and the date of posting or your access.

Three entries from a working bibliography appear on the previous page.

CHOOSING AND EVALUATING YOUR SOURCES

After you have found a number of promising sources, take a closer look at them. The strength and credibility of your research paper will depend directly on the strength and credibility of your sources. In short, a research paper built on shaky, unreliable sources will not convince a thoughtful reading audience.

To help you choose your sources, ask yourself the following questions as you try to decide which facts, figures, and testimonies will best support or illustrate your ideas.

What do I know about the author? Does this writer have any expertise or particular knowledge about the subject matter? If the author of an article about nuclear fusion is a physics professor at a respected university, her views will be more informed than those of a journalist who never took a physics course. Although authors of full-length books generally cite their own qualifications, the credentials of journalists and other writers for periodicals may be harder to evaluate. Internet sources, as mentioned earlier, may be highly suspect. In these cases, in which the background of a writer is unknown, you should examine the writer's use of his or her own sources. Are verifiable sources for specific data or opinions given? Read these articles, books, or Web sites carefully, looking for authorities and sources cited. Be aware that for all your sources, the objectivity of the author must be considered: some authorities stand to gain economically or politically from taking a particular point of view. The president of a tobacco company, for instance, might insist that secondary smoke from the cigarettes of others will not harm nonsmokers, but does he or she have an objective opinion? Try to present testimony from those authorities whose views will sway your readers.

What do I know about the publisher? Who published your sources? Major, well-known publishing houses can be one indication of a book's credibility. If you are unfamiliar with a particular publisher, consult a librarian or professor in that field. Often, books on technical issues are published by firms specializing in that area (there are publishers, for example, who only produce books about computer-related topics). Be aware that there are many publishers who only publish books supporting a specific cause or viewpoint; the bias in such books may limit their usefulness to your research.

For periodicals, consider the nature of the journal, magazine, or newspaper. Who is its intended audience? A highly technical paper on sickle cell anemia, for example, might be weakened by citing a very general discussion of the disease from *Reader's Digest;* an article from *The Journal of the American Medical Association,* however, might be valuable. Is it a publication known to be fairly objective (*The New York Times*) or does it have a particular cause to support (animal rights or gun control issues)? Looking at the masthead of a journal or other publication will often tell you whether articles are subjected to stringent review before acceptance for publication. In general, articles published in "open" or nonselective publications should be examined closely for credibility. In a recent case, the newsletter for MENSA—a well-known international society for individuals who have documented IQs in the top 2 percent of the population—created a furor when articles appeared recommending the euthanasia of the mentally and physically disabled, the homeless, and other so-called "nonproductive" members of society. The newsletter editor's explanation was that all articles submitted for publication are generally accepted.

Is my research reasonably balanced? Your treatment of your subject—especially if it is a controversial one—should show your readers that you investigated all sides of the issue before reaching a conclusion. If your sources are drawn only from authorities well-known for voicing one position, your readers will tend to become skeptical about the quality of your research. For instance, if in a paper on support for public broadcasting, you refer only to the opinions of William F. Buckley, Newt Gingrich, and Jesse Helms, all well-known conservatives, you may antagonize the reader who wants a thorough analysis of all sides of the question. Do use sources that support your position, but don't overload your argument with obviously biased sources.

Are my sources reporting valid research? Is your source the original researcher or is he or she reporting someone else's study?* If the information is being reported secondhand, has your source been accurate and clear? Is the original source named or footnoted in some way so that the information could be checked?

A thorough researcher will note the names of authorities frequently cited by other writers or researchers and will obtain the original works by those authorities. This tip was useful for Amy Lawrence as she found frequent mention

---

* Interviews, surveys, studies, and experiments conducted firsthand are referred to as *primary sources;* reports and studies written by someone other than the original researcher are called *secondary sources.*

of the Russian researcher Edvard Radzinsky in newspaper and magazine articles. Once she obtained a copy of his often-quoted book, she had a wealth of valuable information to consider for her paper.

Look too at the way information in your source was obtained in the first place. Did the original researchers themselves draw the logical conclusions from their evidence? Did they run their study or project in a fair, impartial way? For example, a survey of people whose names were obtained from the rolls of the Democratic party will hardly constitute a representative sampling of voters' opinions on an upcoming election.

Moreover, be especially careful with statistics because they can be manipulated quite easily to give a distorted picture. A recent survey, for instance, asked a large sample of people to rate a number of American cities based on questions dealing with quality of life. Pittsburgh—a lovely city to be sure—came out the winner, but only if one agrees that all the questions should be weighted equally; that is, the figures gave Pittsburgh the highest score only if one rates "weather" as equally important as "educational opportunities," "amount of crime," "cultural opportunities," and other factors. In short, always evaluate the quality of your sources' research and the validity of their conclusions before you decide to incorporate their findings into your own paper. (And don't forget Mark Twain's reference to "lies, damned lies, and statistics.")

Are my sources still current? Although some famous experiments or studies have withstood the years, many controversial topics demand research as current as possible. What was written ten, or even two, years ago may have been disproved or surpassed since, especially in our rapidly changing political world and ever-expanding fields of technology. A paper on the status of the U.S. space program, for example, demands recent sources, and research on personal computer use in the United States would be severely weakened by the use of a text published as recently as 1996 for "current" statistics.

If they're appropriate, journals and other periodicals may contain more up-to-date reports than books printed several years ago; computer searches can often provide the most current information (Amy Lawrence, for example, was able to read about the latest findings of the Russian special commission during the week they were officially announced.). Readers usually appreciate hearing the most recent word on the topic under examination, though you certainly shouldn't ignore a "classic" study on your subject, especially if it is the one against which all the other studies are measured. A student researching the life of Abraham Lincoln, for instance, might find Carl Sandburg's multivolume biography of over 60 years ago as valuable as more recent works.

(For more advice to help you think critically about your sources, see Chapter 5.)

PREPARING AN ANNOTATED BIBLIOGRAPHY

While you are gathering and assessing your sources, you may be asked to compile an annotated bibliography—a description of each important source that includes the basic bibliographic facts as well as a brief summary of each entry's content. Annotated bibliographies are formatted and ordered in the same manner as a working bibliography. Here's one of Amy Lawrence's annotated bibliography entries:

> Elliott, Dorinda. "The Legacy of the Last Czar." <u>Newsweek</u> 21 Sept. 1992: 60–61.
>
> Elliot offers the results of early forensic analysis of the Romanov grave site and a brief description of the events surrounding the executions. The article quotes forensic experts and historians as well as including the views of Russian citizens on the significance of finding and identifying the remains of the Romanov family.

Compiling an annotated bibliography will give you a clear sense of how strong and balanced your sources are in supporting your research; it may indicate which sources will be most valuable as you write your paper and which sources should be used sparingly or not at all. Later, your annotated bibliography may also provide a useful reference for readers interested in obtaining any of your sources for further reading.

TAKING NOTES

After you have evaluated your sources and have selected those that will be most useful for your research, review each source and take notes on *content cards*. Most researchers recommend that you take notes on index cards rather than on notebook paper because the cards can be shuffled around more easily later when you are organizing your paper. In addition, you may find it helpful to use cards of a different color or size from the bibliography cards, just for ease of sorting.

When you find a useful book or magazine, be sure you have a bibliography card for it. Plan to use several content cards for each book or article because you may wish to divide your notes into categories of ideas that will later help you organize your paragraphs. Write on one side of the content cards only, to avoid having some material out of sight and mind while you're organizing your notes for your first rough draft. Always note the page numbers from which you are collecting information.

Your notes will probably be of four kinds:

1. *Direct quotations.* When you lift material word for word,* you must al-ways use quotation marks and note the precise page number of the quotation. If the quoted material runs from one page onto another, use some sort of signal to yourself such as a slash bar (child/abuse) or arrow (→ p. 162) at the break so if you use only part of the quoted material in your paper, you will know on which page it appeared. If the quoted material contains odd, archaic, or incor-rect spelling, punctuation marks, or grammar, insert the word [*sic*] in brackets next to the item in question; [sic] means "this is the way I found it in the origi-nal text," and such a symbol will remind you later that you did not miscopy the quotation. Otherwise, always double-check to make sure you did copy the ma-terial accurately and completely to avoid having to come back to the source as you prepare your essay. If the material you want to quote is lengthy, you will find it easier—though not cheaper—to photocopy (or print out) the material rather than transcribe it (almost all libraries have one or more photocopy ma-chines, but be prepared to bring your own bag of correct change).

2. *Paraphrase.* You paraphrase when you put into your own words what someone else has written or said. Please note: *paraphrased ideas are borrowed ideas, not your original thoughts, and consequently they must be attributed to their owner just as direct quotations are.*

To remind yourself that certain information on your note cards is para-phrased, always leave space in the left-hand margin for some sort of notation, such as a circled ℗. Quotation marks will always tell you what you borrowed directly, but sometimes when writers take notes one week and write their first draft a week or two later, they cannot remember if a note was paraphrased or if it was original thinking. Writers occasionally plagiarize unintentionally be-cause they believe only direct quotations and statistics must be attributed to their proper sources, so make your notes as clear as possible (for more infor-mation on avoiding plagiarism, see pp. 381–383).

3. *Summary.* You may wish to condense a piece of writing so you may offer it as support for your own ideas. Using your own words, you should pre-sent in shorter form the writer's thesis and supporting ideas. You may find it helpful to include a few direct quotations in your summary to retain the flavor of the original work. Of course, you will tell your readers what you are sum-marizing and by whom it was written. Remember to make a note in the margin of your content card to indicate summarized, rather than original, material.

4. *Your own ideas.* Your note cards may also contain your personal com-ments (judgments, flashes of brilliance, notions of how to use something you've just read, notes to yourself about connections between sources, questions, and so forth) that will aid you in the writing of your paper. It might be helpful

---

*All tables, graphs, and charts that you copy must also be directly attributed to their sources, though you do not enclose graphics in quotation marks.

to jot these down in a different-colored pen or put them in brackets that you've initialed, so that you will recognize them later as your own responses when your note cards are cold.

Distinguishing Paraphrase from Summary

Because novice writers sometimes have a hard time telling the difference between paraphrase and summary, here is an explanation and a sample of each. The original paragraph that appears was taken from a magazine article describing an important 1984 study still frequently cited.

> Another successful approach to the prevention of criminality has been to target very young children in a school setting before problems arise. The Perry Preschool Program, started 22 years ago in a low socioeconomic area of Ypsilanti, Michigan, has offered some of the most solid evidence to date that early intervention through a high-quality preschool program can significantly alter a child's life. A study released this fall tells what happened to 123 disadvantaged children from preschool age to present. The detention and arrest rates for the 58 children who had attended the preschool program was 31 percent, compared to 51 percent for the 65 who did not. Similarly, those in the preschool program were more likely to have graduated from high school, have enrolled in postsecondary education programs and be employed, and less likely to have become pregnant as teenagers.
>
> —from "Arresting Delinquency," Dan Hurley, <u>Psychology Today</u>, March 1985, p. 66

Paraphrase

A *paraphrase* puts the information in the researcher's own words, but it does follow the order of the original text, and it does include the important details.

Quality preschooling for high-risk children may help stop crime before it starts. A 1984 study from the Perry Preschool Program located in a poor area of Ypsilanti, Michigan, shows that of 123 socially and economically disadvantaged children, the 58 who attended preschool had an arrest rate of 31 percent compared to 51 percent for those 65 who did not attend. The adults with preschool experience had also graduated from high school in larger numbers; in addition, more of them had attended postsecondary education programs, were employed, and had avoided teenage pregnancy (Hurley 66).

Summary

A *summary* is generally much shorter than the original; the researcher picks out the key ideas but often omits many of the supporting details.

A 1984 study from the Perry Preschool Program in Michigan suggests that disadvantaged children who attend preschool are less likely to be arrested as adults. Those in this study with preschool experience also chose more education, had better employment records, and avoided teenage pregnancy more often than those without preschool (Hurley 66).

REMEMBER:

Both paraphrased and summarized ideas must be attributed to their sources, even if you do not reproduce exact words or figures.

INCORPORATING YOUR SOURCE MATERIAL

Be aware that a research paper is not a massive collection of quotations and paraphrased or summarized ideas glued together with a few transitional phrases. It is, instead, an essay in which you offer *your* thesis and ideas based on and supported by your research. Consequently, you will need to incorporate and blend in your reference material in a variety of smooth, persuasive ways. Here are some suggestions:

Use your sources in a clear, logical way. Make certain that you understand your source material well enough to use it in support of your own thoughts. Once you have selected the best references to use, be as convincing as possible. Ask yourself if you're using enough evidence and if the information you're offering really does clearly support your point. As in any essay, you need to avoid oversimplification, hasty generalizations, *non sequiturs,* and other problems in logic (for a review of common logical fallacies, see pp. 294–297). Resist the temptation to add quotations, facts, or statistics that are interesting but not really relevant to your paper.

Don't overuse direct quotations. It's best to use a direct quotation *only* when it expresses a point in a far more impressive, emphatic, or concise way than you could say it yourself. Suppose, for instance, you were analyzing the films of a particular director and wanted to include a sample of critical reviews.

As one movie critic wrote, "This film is really terrible, and people should ignore it" (Dennison 14).

The direct quotation above isn't remarkable and could be easily paraphrased.

As one movie critic wrote, "This film's plot is so idiotic that the director must have intended it for people who move their lips not only when they read but also when they watch TV" (Dennison 14).

You might be tempted to quote the line above to show your readers an emphatically negative review of this movie.

When you do decide to use direct quotations, don't merely drop them in next to your prose. Instead, lead into them smoothly so that they obviously support or clarify what you are saying.

Dropped in   Scientists have been studying the ill effects of nitrites on test animals since 1961. "Nitrites produced malignant tumors in 62 percent of the test animals within six months" (Smith 109).

Better   Scientists have been studying the ill effects of nitrites on test animals since 1961. According to Dr. William Smith, head of the Farrell Institute of Research, "Nitrites produced malignant tumors in 62 percent of the test animals within six months" (109).

Vary your sentence pattern when you present your quotations. Here are some sample phrases for quotations:

In his introduction to The Great Gatsby, Professor William Smith points out that "Fitzgerald wrote about himself and produced a narcissistic masterpiece" (5).

William Smith, author of Impact, summarized the situation this way: "Eighty-eight percent of the sales force threaten a walkout" (21).

"Only the President controls the black box," according to the White House Press Secretary (Smith 129).

As drama critic William Smith observed last year in The Saturday Review, the play was "a rousing failure" (212).

Perhaps the well-known poet William Smith expressed the idea best when he wrote, "Love is a spider waiting to entangle its victims" (14).

Congressman William Smith presented the opposing view when he claimed, "Employment figures are down three percent from last year" (32).

In other words, don't simply repeat "William Smith said," "John Jones said," "Mary Brown said."

Punctuate your quotations correctly. The proper punctuation will help your reader understand who said what. For information on the appropriate uses of quotation marks surrounding direct quotations, see pages 474–475 in Part Four. If you are incorporating a long quoted passage into your essay, one that appears as more than four typed lines in your manuscript, you should present it in block form without quotation marks, as described on page 386. To omit words in a quoted passage, use ellipses marks, explained on page 482.

Make certain your support is in the paper, not still in your head or back in the original source. Sometimes when you've read a number of persuasive facts in an article or book, it's easy to forget that your reader doesn't know them as you do now. For instance, the writer of the paragraph below isn't as persuasive as she might be because she hides the support for her controversial point in the reference to the article, forgetting that the reader needs to know what the article actually said:

> An organ transplant from one human to another is becoming an everyday occurrence, an operation that is generally applauded by everyone as a life-saving effort. But people are overlooking many of the serious problems that come with the increase in transplant surgery. Studies show that a growing problem today in Asia is the traffic in organs on the Black Market. Cases recorded recently have risen to an alarming number and are very disturbing (Wood 35).

For the reader to be persuaded, he or she needs to know what the writer learned from the article: what studies? what is "disturbing" about these cases? who has recorded these? is the source reliable? Instead of offering the necessary support in the essay, the writer merely points to the article as proof. Few readers will take the time to look up the article to find the information they need to understand or believe your point. Therefore, when you use source material, always be sure that you have remembered to put your support on the page, *in the essay itself,* for the reader to see. Don't let the essence of your point remain hidden, especially when the claim is controversial (as in the example above about Black Market organs).

Don't let reference material dominate your essay. Remember that your reader is interested in *your* thesis and *your* conclusions, not just in a string of references. Use your researched material wisely whenever your statements need clarification, support, or amplification. But don't use quotations, paraphrased, or summarized material at every turn, just to show that you've done your homework.

AVOIDING PLAGIARISM

Unfortunately, most discussions of research must include a brief word about plagiarism. Novice writers often unintentionally plagiarize, as noted before, because they fail to recognize the necessity of attributing paraphrased, summarized, and borrowed ideas to their original owners. And indeed it is difficult sometimes after days of research to know exactly what one has read repeatedly and what one originally thought. Also, there's frequently a thin line between general or common knowledge ("Henry Ford was the father of the automobile industry in America") that does not have to be documented and those ideas and statements that do ("USX reported an operating loss of four million in its last quarter"). As a rule of thumb, ask yourself whether the majority of your readers would recognize the fact or opinion you're expressing or if it's repeatedly found in commonly used sources; if so, you may not need to document it. For example, most people would acknowledge that the Wall Street crash of 1929 ushered in the Great Depression of the 1930s, but the exact number of bank foreclosures in 1933 is not common knowledge and needs documenting. Similarly, a well-known quotation from the Bible or Mother Goose or even the Declaration of Independence might pass without documentation, but a line from the vice-president's latest speech needs a reference to its source. When in doubt, the best choice is to document anything that you feel may be in question.

To help you understand the difference between plagiarism and proper documentation, here is an original passage and both incorrect and correct ways to use it in a paper of your own:

Original   It is a familiar nightmare: a person suffers a heart attack, and as the ambulance fights heavy traffic, the patient dies. In fact, 350,000 American heart-attack victims each year die without ever reaching a hospital. The killer in many cases is ventricular fibrillation, uncoordinated contraction of the heart muscle. Last week a team of Dutch physicians reported in *The New England Journal of Medicine* that these early deaths can often be prevented by administration of a common heart drug called lidocaine, injected into the patient's shoulder muscle by ambulance paramedics as soon as they arrive on the scene.

—from "First Aid for Heart Attacks,"
<u>Newsweek</u>, November 11, 1985,
page 88

Plagiarized   It is a common nightmare: a person with a heart attack dies as the ambulance sits in heavy traffic, often a victim of ventricular fibrillation, uncoordinated contraction of the heart muscle. Today, however, these early deaths can often be prevented by an injection into the patient's shoulder of a common heart drug called lidocaine, which may be administered by paramedics on the scene.

This writer has changed some of the words and sentences, but the passage has obviously been borrowed and must be attributed to its source.

Also plagiarized   According to <u>Newsweek</u>, 350,000 American heart attack victims die before reaching help in hospitals ("First Aid for Heart Attacks" 88). However, a common heart drug called lidocaine, which may be injected into the patient by paramedics on the scene of the attack, may save many victims who die en route to doctors and sophisticated life-saving equipment.

This writer did attribute the statistic to its source, but the remainder of the paragraph is still borrowed and must be documented.

Properly documented   Ambulance paramedics can, and often do, play a vital life-saving role today. They are frequently the first medical assistance available, especially to those patients or accident victims far away from hospitals. Moreover, according to a <u>Newsweek</u> report, paramedics are now being trained to administer powerful drugs to help the sick survive until they reach doctors and medical equipment. For instance, paramedics can inject the common heart drug lidocaine into heart attack victims on the scene, an act that may save many of the 350,000 Americans who die of heart attacks before ever reaching a hospital ("First Aid for Heart Attacks" 88).

This writer used the properly documented information to support her own point about paramedics and has not tried to pass off any of the article as her own.

Although plagiarism is often unintentional, it's your job to be as honest and careful as possible. If you're in doubt about your use of a particular idea, consult your instructor for a second opinion.

Here's a suggestion that might help you avoid plagiarizing by accident. When you are drafting your essay and come to a spot in which you want to incorporate the ideas of someone else, think of the borrowed material as if it were in a window.* Always frame the window at the top with some sort of introduction that identifies the author (or source) and frame the window on the bottom with a reference to the location of the material:

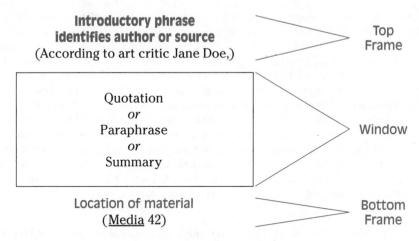

A sample might look like this:

Introductory phrase identifies author

As humorist Mike McGrady once said of housekeeping, "Any job that requires six hours to do and can be undone in six minutes by one small child carrying a plate of crackers and a Monopoly set—this is not a job that will long capture my interest" (13).

Window

Location

In a later draft, you'll probably want to vary your style so that all your borrowed material doesn't appear in exactly the same "window" format (see p. 379 for suggestions). But until you get the habit of *always* documenting your sources, you might try using the "window" technique in your early drafts.

PRACTICING WHAT YOU'VE LEARNED

As Amy Lawrence researched the Romanov execution, she found the following information about one of the earlier Romanov czars. To practice some of the

---

*I am indebted to Professor John Clark Pratt of Colorado State University for this useful suggestion. Professor Pratt is the author of *Writing from Scratch: The Essay* (1987) published by Hamilton Press, and the editor of the *Writing from Scratch* series.

skills you've learned so far, read the following passage on Alexander II of Russia (1855–1881) and do the tasks that are listed after it.

Alexander's greatest single achievement was his emancipation of some forty million Russian serfs, a deed which won him the title of "Tsar Liberator." To visit a rural Russian community in the earlier nineteenth century was like stepping back into the Middle Ages. Nine-tenths of the land was held by something less than one hundred thousand noble families. The serfs, attached to the soil, could be sold with the estates to new landlords, conscripted into the nobleman's household to work as domestic servants, or even sent to the factories in the towns for their master's profit. Though some nobles exercised their authority in a kindly and paternal fashion, others overworked their serfs, flogged them cruelly for slight faults, and interfered insolently in their private affairs and family relations. A serf could not marry without his master's consent, could not leave the estate without permission, and might be pursued, brought back, and punished if he sought to escape. He lived at the mercy of his master's caprice.

1. The book from which the above passage was taken contains the information listed below. Select the appropriate information and prepare a working bibliography card.

   A Survey of European Civilization Part Two, Since 1660

   Third Edition
   Houghton Mifflin Company, Publishers
   Boston
   First edition, 1936
   853.21
   1012 pages
   Authors:
   Wallace K. Ferguson, The University of Western Ontario
   Geoffrey Brun, Formerly Visiting Professor of History, Cornell University
   Indexes: general, list of maps
   Picture Acknowledgments, xxvii
   copyright 1962
   p. 716
   44 chapters

2. Paraphrase the passage.

3. Summarize the passage, but do not quote from it.

4. Select an important idea from the passage to quote directly and lead into the quotation with a smooth acknowledgment of its source.

5. Select an idea or a quotation from the passage and use it as support for a point of your own, being careful not to plagiarize the borrowed material.

 ASSIGNMENT

In your school or local library, look up a newspaper from any city or state and find the issue published on the day of your birth. Prepare a bibliography card for the issue you chose. Then summarize the most important or "lead" article on the front page. (Don't forget to acknowledge the source of your summary.)

CHOOSING THE DOCUMENTATION STYLE FOR YOUR ESSAY

Once you begin to write your paper incorporating your source material, you need to know how to show your readers where your material came from. You may have already learned a documentation system in a previous writing class, but since today's researchers and scholars use a number of different documentation styles, it's important that you know which style is appropriate for your current essay. In some cases your instructors (or the audience for whom you are writing) will designate a particular style; at other times, the choice will be yours. In this chapter, we will look at three widely used systems:

A. MLA style

B. Traditional footnotes with bibliography

C. APA style

A. MLA Style

Most instructors in the humanities assign the documentation form prescribed by the Modern Language Association of America (MLA). Since 1984, the MLA has recommended a form of documentation that no longer uses traditional footnotes or endnotes to show references.* The current form calls for *parenthetical documentation,* most often consisting of the author's last name and the appropriate page number(s) in parentheses immediately following the

---

*If you wish a more detailed description of the current MLA form, you should ask your local bookstore for the *MLA Handbook for Writers of Research Papers,* 4th ed. (New York: MLA, 1995) and also the *MLA Style Manual and Guide to Scholarly Publishing,* 2nd ed. (New York: MLA, 1998). The most up-to-date documentation forms may be found on the MLA Web site <http://www.MLA.org>.

source material in your paper. The information in the parentheses is then keyed to a "Works Cited" page at the end of your discussion, a list of the sources used in your essay.

MLA Citations in Your Essay

Here are some guidelines for using the MLA parenthetical reference form within your paper:

1. If you use a source by one author, place the author's name and page number right after the quoted, paraphrased, or summarized material. Note that the parentheses go *before* the end punctuation, and there is no punctuation between the author's name and the page number.

Example Although pop art often resembles the comic strip, it owes a debt to such painters as Magritte, Matisse, and de Kooning (Rose 184).

2. If you use a source by one author and give credit to that author by name in your paper, you need only give the page number in the parentheses.

Example According to art critic Barbara Rose, pop art owes a large debt to such painters as Magritte, Matisse, and de Kooning (184).

3. If you are directly quoting material of more than four typed lines, indent the material one inch (ten spaces) from the left margin, double-space, and do not use quotation marks. Do not change the right margin. Note that in this case, the parentheses appears *after* the punctuation that ends the quoted material.

Example   In addition to causing tragedy for others, Crane's characters

who are motivated by a desire to appear heroic to their peers

may also cause themselves serious trouble. For example,

Collins, another Civil War private, almost causes his own

death because of his vain desire to act bravely in front of his

fellow soldiers.   (Hall 16)

4. If you are citing more than one work by the same author, include a short title in the parentheses.

Example Within 50 years the Inca and Aztec civilizations were defeated and overthrown by outside invaders (Thomas, Lost Cultures 198).

5. If you are citing a work by two or three authors, use all last names and the page number.

Examples Prisons today are overcrowded to the point of emergency; conditions could not be worse, and the state budget for prison reforms is at an all-time low (Smith and Jones 72).

Human infants grow quickly, with most babies doubling their birth weight in the first six months of life and tripling their weight by their first birthday (Pantell, Fries, and Vickery 52).

6. For more than three authors, use all the names or use the name of the first author plus *et al.* (Latin for "and others") and the page number.

Example Casualties of World War II during 1940–45 amounted to more than twenty-five million soldiers and civilians (Blum et al. 779).

7. If you cite a work that has no named author, use the work's title and the page number.

Example Each year 350,000 Americans will die of a heart attack before reaching a hospital ("First Aid for Heart Attacks" 88).

8. If the work you are citing appears in a series, include the volume and page number with the author's name.

Example The most common view camera format is 4″ by 5″, though many sizes are available on today's market (Pursell 1:29).

9. If the material you are citing comes from an electronic source that has no page numbers, use the author's last name. If the author's name is unavailable, use a short reference to the work's title.

Example The Chinese in Indonesia account for only 4% of the population but control 70% of the economy (Thompson).

Note: Some instructors may ask you to include the paragraph number or the page number of the reference within the electronic source's total number of pages, especially if the document is lengthy. The example that follows shows how a reader could quickly find the information in the sixth paragraph of the document instead of searching through the entire ten.

Example The Chinese in Indonesia account for only 4% of the population but control 70% of the economy (Thompson par. 6 of 10).

10. If the material you are citing contains a passage quoted from another source, indicate the use of the quotation in the parentheses.

Example According to George Orwell, "Good writing is like a window-pane" (qtd. in Murray 142).

Compiling a Works Cited List

If you are using the MLA format, at the end of your essay you should include a *Works Cited* page—a formal listing of the sources you used in your essay. (If you wish to show all the sources you consulted, but did not cite, add a Works Consulted page.) Arrange the entries alphabetically by the authors' last names; if no name is given, arrange your sources by the first important word of the title. Double-space each entry, and double-space after each one. If an entry takes more than one line, indent the subsequent lines one-half inch (five spaces). New MLA guidelines indicate one space following punctuation marks. (Some instructors still prefer the traditional two spaces, however, so you might check with your teacher on this issue.) See the sample entries that follow.

Sample Entries: MLA Style

Here are some sample entries to help you prepare a Works Cited page according to the MLA guidelines. Please note that MLA style recommends shortened forms of publishers' names: Holt for Holt, Rinehart & Winston; Harcourt for Harcourt Brace College Publishers; UP for University Press; and so forth. Also, omit business descriptions, such as Inc., Co., Press, or House.

Remember, too, when you type your paper, the titles of books and journals should be underlined even though you may see them printed in books or magazines in italics. The titles of articles, essays, and chapters should be enclosed in quotation marks.

Books
* Book with one author

  Keillor, Garrison. <u>WLT: A Radio Romance</u>. New York: Viking, 1991.

* Two books by the same author

  Keillor, Garrison. <u>Leaving Home</u>. New York: Viking, 1987.

  ---. <u>WLT: A Radio Romance</u>. New York: Viking, 1991.

* Book with two or three authors

  Pizzo, Stephen, and Paul Muolo. <u>Profiting from the Bank and Savings and Loan Crisis</u>. New York: Harper, 1993.

- Book with more than three authors

  Guerin, Wilfred L., et al. <u>A Handbook of Critical Approaches to Literature</u>. New
  York: Harper, 1979.

You may use *et al.* for the other names or you may give all names in full in the
order they appear on the book's title page.

- Book with author and editor

  Chaucer, Geoffrey. <u>The Tales of Canterbury</u>. Ed. Robert Pratt. Boston:
  Houghton, 1974.

- Book with corporate authorship

  United States Council on Fire Prevention. <u>Stopping Arson Before It Starts</u>.
  Washington: Edmondson, 1982.

- Book with an editor

  Knappman, Edward W., ed. <u>Great American Trials: From Salem Witchcraft to
  Rodney King</u>. Detroit: Visible Ink, 1994.

- Selection or chapter from an anthology or collection with an editor

  Chopin, Kate. "La Belle Zoraide." <u>Classic American Women Writers</u>. Ed. Cynthia
  Griffin Wolff. New York: Harper, 1980. 250–273.

- Work in more than one volume

  Piepkorn, Arthur C. <u>Profiles in Belief: The Religious Bodies of the United
  States and Canada</u>. 2 vols. New York: Harper, 1977, 1978.

- Work in a series

  Berg, Barbara L. <u>The Remembered Gate: Origins of American Feminism</u>. Urban
  Life in America Series. New York: Oxford UP, 1978.

- Translation

  Radzinsky, Edvard. <u>The Last Tsar: The Life and Death of Nicholas II</u>. Trans.
  Marian Schwartz. New York: Doubleday, 1992.

- Reprint

  Thaxter, Celia. <u>Among the Isles of Shoals</u>. 1873. Hampton, NH: Heritage, 1978.

Magazines and Periodicals

- Signed article in magazine

  Kaminer, Wendy. "Feminism's Identity Crisis." <u>The Atlantic</u> Oct. 1993: 51–68.

- Unsigned article in magazine

  "A Path Paved With Palms." <u>Southern Living</u> Feb. 1994: 4–6.

- Signed article in periodical

  Lockwood, Thomas. "Divided Attention in <u>Persuasion</u>." <u>Nineteenth-Century</u>
  <u>Fiction</u> 33 (1978): 309–23.

- A review

  Spudis, Paul. Rev. of <u>To a Rocky Moon: A Geologist's History of Lunar</u>
  <u>Exploration</u>, by Don E. Wilhelms. <u>Natural History</u> Jan. 1994: 66–69.

Newspapers

- Signed article in newspaper

  Friedman, Thomas. "World Answer to Jobs: Schooling." <u>Denver Post</u> 16 Mar.
  1994: 9A.

- Unsigned article in newspaper

  "Blackhawks Shut Down Gretsky, Kings, 4–0." <u>Washington Post</u> 11 Mar. 1994:
  C4.

- Unsigned editorial

  "Give Life after Death." Editorial. <u>Coloradoan</u> [Ft. Collins, CO] 23 Dec. 1985: A4.

If the newspaper's city of publication is not clear from the title, put the location in brackets following the paper's name, as shown above.

- A letter to the newspaper

  Franklin, Charles. Letter. <u>Denver Post</u> 10 Sept. 1985: B10.

Encyclopedias, Pamphlets, Dissertations

- Signed article in an encyclopedia

  Collins, Dean R. "Light Amplifier." <u>McGraw-Hill Encyclopedia of Science and</u>
  <u>Technology</u>. 1987 ed.

- Unsigned article in an encyclopedia

  "Sailfish." <u>The International Wildlife Encyclopedia</u>. 1970.

- A pamphlet

  Young, Leslie. <u>Baby Care Essentials for the New Mother</u>. Austin: Hall, 1985.

- A government document

  Department of Health. National Institute on Drug Abuse. <u>Drug Abuse</u>
      <u>Prevention</u>. Washington: GPO, 1980.

- Unpublished dissertations and theses

  Harmon, Gail A. "Poor Writing Skills at the College Level: A Program for
      Correction." Diss. U of Colorado, 1992.

Films, Television, Radio, Performances, Recordings
- A film

  <u>Schindler's List</u>. Dir. Steven Spielberg. Perf. Liam Neeson and Ben Kingsley.
      Universal, 1994.

If you are referring to the contribution of a particular individual, such as the director, writer, actor, or composer, begin with that person's name:

  Spielberg, Steven, Dir. <u>Schindler's List</u>. Perf. Liam Neeson and Ben Kingsley.
      Universal, 1994.

- A television or radio show

  <u>Innovation</u>. WNET, Newark. 12 Oct. 1985.

If your reference is to a particular episode or person associated with the show, cite that name first, before the show's name:

  "General Stonewall Jackson." <u>Civil War Journal</u>. Arts and Entertainment
      Network. 10 June 1992.

  Moyers, Bill, writ. and narr. <u>Bill Moyers' Journal</u>. PBS. WABC, Denver. 30 Sept.
      1980.

- Performances (plays, concerts, ballets, operas)

  <u>Julius Caesar</u>. By William Shakespeare. Perf. Royal Shakespeare Company.
      Booth Theater, New York. 13 Oct. 1982.

If you are referring to the contribution of a particular person associated with the performance, put that person's name first:

  Shao, En, cond. Colorado Symphony Orch. Concert. Boettcher Concert Hall,
      Denver. 18 Mar. 1994.

- A recording

  Marsalis, Wynton. "Oh, But on the Third Day." Rec. 27–28 Oct. 1988. <u>The</u>
      <u>Majesty of the Blues</u>. Columbia, 1989.

Letters, Lectures, and Speeches

- A letter

> Steinbeck, John. Letter to Elizabeth R. Otis. 11 Nov. 1944. Steinbeck
>
> Collection. Stanford U Lib., Stanford, CA.

- A lecture or speech

Give the speaker's name and the title of the talk first, before the sponsoring organization (or occasion) and location. If there is no title, substitute the appropriate label, such as "lecture" or "speech."

> Dippity, Sarah N. "The Importance of Prewriting." CLAS Convention. Colorado
>
> Springs. 15 Feb. 1992.

Interviews

- A published interview

Cite the person interviewed first. Use the word "Interview" if the interview has no title:

> Mailer, Norman. "Dialogue with Mailer." With Andrew Gordon. <u>Berkeley Times</u>
>
> 15 Jan. 1969.

- A personal interview

> Adkins, Camille. Personal interview. 4 Sept. 1992.
>
> Clay, Marilyn. Telephone interview. 13 April 1992.

Electronic Sources

Many entries for electronic sources are similar to those for printed material: they begin with the author's name (if given), name of the material (in quotation marks), title of original source and its publication date (if printed previously), and page numbers. They may also include the title of the database (underlined), publication medium (edition or version, if relevant), and the name of the computer service/network. If page or paragraph numbers are not available, some instructors will request the phrase *n. pag.* (no pagination) or ask you to include a figure indicating the document's number of paragraphs. The last date in these entries is the "date of access"—that is, the date on which you, the researcher, retrieved the document. Some instructors may also ask you to include the electronic address you used to access the material; angle brackets should enclose this address.

It's important to remember that in the last decade forms of electronic sources have changed dramatically—and continue to do so. As technology expands, new ways of documenting electronic sources are also being created to help people access material in the clearest, quickest ways. Consequently, you may wish to consult the most up-to-the-minute documentation guide available in your library or online if you need help beyond the sample entries offered here.

CD-ROMs

Jenkins, Robert N. "Czarist Artifacts Coming to the Heartland." <u>Denver Post</u> 28 May 1995: T1. <u>Denver Post NewsBank</u>. CD-ROM. NewsBank. Dec. 1995.

"Nicholas II." <u>Encarta</u>. CD-ROM. Redmond: Microsoft. 10 Oct. 1997.

Online Databases

Carpenter, Dudley. "Romanov Bones Will Finally Rest." <u>New York Times</u> 2 February 1998: A2. <u>New York Times Online</u>. 25 Feb. 1998. Nexis.

Web Sites

Wright, Robert. "The Evolution of Despair." <u>Time</u> 28 Aug. 1995: n. pag. 14 Sept. 1995 <http://www.pathfinder.com/Time/index.html>.

Footnote/Bibliography Form

In case your assignment calls for traditional footnotes with a bibliography page, rather than for the MLA format, here is a brief description of that form.

Each idea you borrow and each quotation you include must be attributed to its author(s) in a footnote that appears at the bottom of the appropriate page.* Number your footnotes consecutively throughout the essay (do not start over with "1" on each new page), and place the number in the text to the right of and slightly above the end of the passage, whether it is a direction quotation, a paraphrase, or a summary. Place the corresponding number, indented (five spaces) and slightly raised, before the footnote at the bottom of the page. Double-space each entry, and double-space after each footnote if more than one appears on the same page. (See p. 394 for sample footnote entries.)

Once you have provided a first full reference, subsequent footnotes for that source may only include the author's last name and page number. However, some authorities still require the use of Latin abbreviations such as *ibid.* ("in the same place") and *op. cit.* ("in the work cited"); if your assignment does require these Latin abbreviations, use *ibid.* immediately after the original footnote to substitute for the author's name, the title, and the publication information; add

---

*Some writing situations permit the use of endnotes that appear in a list on a page following the essay before the bibliography. Consult your teacher or the person (or publication) for whom you are writing to see if endnotes are permissible or even preferred.

a page number only if it differs from the one in the original footnote. Use *op. cit.* with the author's name to substitute for the title in later references.

At the end of your essay, list your sources by author in alphabetical order on a page entitled Bibliography.

First footnote reference	[5]Garrison Keillor, <u>Leaving Home</u> (New York: Viking, 1987) 23.
Next footnote	[6]Keillor 79.
Later reference	[12]Keillor 135.
Bibliographical entry	Keillor, Garrison. <u>Leaving Home</u>. New York: Viking Penguin, Inc., 1987.

APA Style

The American Psychological Association (APA) recommends a documentation style for research papers in the social sciences.* Your instructors in psychology and sociology classes, for example, may prefer that you use the APA form when you write essays for them.

The APA style is similar to the MLA style in that it calls for parenthetical documentation within the essay itself, although the information cited in the parentheses differs slightly from that presented according to the MLA format. For example, you will note that in the APA style the date of publication follows the author's last name and precedes the page number in the parentheses. Another important difference concerns capitalization of book and article titles: in the MLA style, all important words are capitalized, but in the APA style, only proper names, the first word of titles, and any words appearing after a colon are capitalized. Instead of a "Works Cited" page, the APA style uses a "References" page at the end of the essay to list those sources cited in the text. A "Bibliography" page lists all works that were consulted.

APA Citations in Your Essay

Here are some guidelines for using the APA parenthetical form within your paper:

1. If you use a source by one author, place the author's name, the date of publication, and the page number in parentheses right after the quoted,

---

* If you wish a more detailed description of the APA style, you might order a copy of the *Publication Manual of the American Psychological Association,* 4th ed. (Washington, DC: Psychological Association, 1994).

paraphrased, or summarized material. Note that in APA style, you use commas between the items in the parentheses, and you do include the "p." abbreviation for page (these are omitted in MLA style). The entire parentheses goes before the end punctuation of your sentence.

Example   One crucial step in developing a so-called "deviant" personality may, in fact, be the experience of being caught in some act and consequently being publicly labeled as a deviant (Becker, 1983, p. 31).

2. If you use a source by one author and give credit to that author by name within your paper, you need give only the date and the page number. Note that the publication date follows directly after the name of the author.

Example   According to Green (1994), gang members from upper-class families are rarely convicted for their crimes and almost never labeled as delinquent (p. 101).

3. If you are citing a work with more than two authors, but fewer than six, list all last names in the first reference; in subsequent references, use only the first author's last name and *et al.* (which means "and others"). For six or more authors, use only the last name of the first author followed by *et al.* for all citations, including the first.

Example   *First reference:* After divorce, men's standard of living generally rises some 75% whereas women's falls to approximately 35% of what it once was (Bird, Gordon, & Smith, 1992, p. 203).

Subsequent references: Almost half of all the poor households in America today are headed by single women, most of whom are supporting a number of children (Bird et al., 1992, p. 285).

4. If you cite a work that has a corporate author, cite the group responsible for producing the work.

Example   In contrast, the State Highway Research Commission (1989) argues, "The return to the sixty-five-mile-an-hour speed limit on some of our state's highways has resulted in an increase in traffic fatalities" (p. 3).

Compiling a List of References

If you are using the APA style, at the end of your essay you should include a page labeled References—a formal listing of the sources you cited in your essay. Arrange the entries alphabetically by the authors' last names; use initials for the authors' first and middle names. If there are two or more works by one author, list them chronologically, beginning with the earliest publication date. If an author published two or more works in the same year, the first reference is designated *a,* the second *b,* and so on (Feinstein 1989a; Feinstein 1989b).

Remember that in APA style, you underline books and journals but you do not put the names of articles in quotation marks. Although you do capitalize the major words in the titles of magazines, newspapers, and periodicals, you do not capitalize any words in the titles of books or articles except the first word in each title, the first word following a colon, and all proper names.

APA now requires paragraph-style indentation of entries on manuscript reference lists. The hanging indentation used in the past (in which every line *except* the first is indented) may still be used if requested by your instructor.

Study the form of the examples below.

Sample Entries: APA Style

Books

- Book with one author

    Gould, S. J. (1985). <u>The flamingo's smile</u>. New York: W. W. Norton and Co.

- Book with two or more authors

    Forst, M. L. & Blomquist, M. (1991). <u>Missing children: Rhetoric and reality</u>. New York: Lexington Books.

- Books by one author published in the same year

    Hall, S. L. (1980a). <u>Attention deficit disorder</u>. Denver: Bald Mountain Press.

    Hall, S. L. (1980b). <u>Taming your adolescent</u>. Detroit: Morrison Books.

- Book with an editor

    Banks, A. S. (Ed.). (1988). <u>Political handbook of the world</u>. Binghampton, NY: CSA Publications.

- Selection or chapter from collection with an editor

    Newcomb, T. M. (1958). Attitude development as a function of reference groups: The Bennington study. In E. Maccoby, T. M. Newcomb, & E. L. Hartley (Eds.), <u>Readings in social psychology</u> (pp. 10–12). New York: Holt, Rinehart and Winston.

- A book with a corporate author

    Population Reference Bureau. (1985). <u>1985 world population data</u>. Washington, DC: U.S. Government Printing Office.

Articles

Use p. or pp. with page numbers in newspapers but not in magazines or periodicals.

- An article in a magazine

    Langer, E. T. (1989, May). The mindset of health. <u>Psychology Today</u>, 1138–1241.

- An article in a periodical

    Nyden, P. W. (1985). Democratizing organizations: A case study of a union reform movement. <u>American Journal of Sociology</u>, <u>90</u>, 1119–1203.

Note that when a volume number appears, it is also underlined.

- An article in a newspaper

    Noble, K. B. (1986, September 1). For ex-Hormel workers, no forgive and forget. <u>New York Times</u>, p. A5.

Electronic Databases
- CD-ROM

    Miller, B. C. (1994, June 6). Increasing your comfort on international flights. <u>Business Traveller's World</u> [CD-ROM]. Available: InfoServe.

The "available" statement indicates the vendor of the CD-ROM.

- Online Databases

    Levy, R. P. (1993, March). Limitations of micro-management theory in small businesses. <u>Small Business Quarterly</u> [Online]. Available: ComNet.

The "available" statement indicates the online service where the database can be found.

Interviews
- A published interview

    Backus, R. (1985). [Interview with Lorena Smith.] In Frank Reagon (Ed.), <u>Today's sociology studies</u> (pp. 32–45). Washington: Scientific Library.

- An unpublished interview

    O'Connor, L. (1995, Feb. 15). [Personal interview].

USING SUPPLEMENTARY NOTES

Sometimes when writers of research papers wish to give their readers additional information about their topic or about a particular piece of source material, they include *supplementary notes.* If you are using the MLA or APA format, these notes should be indicated by using a raised number in your text (The study seemed incomplete at the time of its publication.[2]); the explanations appear on a page called "Notes" (MLA) or "Footnotes" (APA) that immediately follows the end of your essay. If you are using traditional footnote form, simply include the supplementary notes in your list of footnotes at the bottom of the page or in the list of endnotes following your essay's conclusion.

Supplementary notes can offer a wide variety of additional information.

Examples

[1]For a different interpretation of this imagery, see Spiller 1021–1023.

[2]Simon and Brown have also contributed to this area of investigation. For a description of their results, see <u>Report on the Star Wars Project</u>, 98–102.

[3]It is important to note here that Brown's study followed Smith's by at least six months.

[4]Later in his report Carducci himself contradicts his earlier evaluation by saying, "Our experiment was contaminated from the beginning" (319).

Don't overdo supplementary notes; use them only when you think the additional information would be truly valuable to your readers. Obviously, information critical to your essay's points should go in the appropriate body paragraphs.

S A M P L E   S T U D E N T   P A P E R
U S I N G   M L A   S T Y L E

Here is the result of Amy Lawrence's research into the recent forensic and historical discoveries concerning the 1918 Romanov assassination. As you read her essay, ask yourself how effectively she uses research material to explain and support her view of the controversy surrounding the assassination and possible escape. Do you find her essay informative? Interesting? Convincing? Point out major strengths and weaknesses that you see. Does her method of structuring her essay—the step-by-step revelation of the new "clues"—add to the sense of mystery?

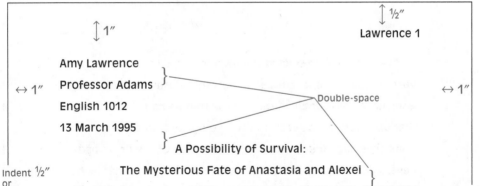

↕ ½"

Lawrence 1

↕ 1"

Amy Lawrence

Professor Adams

English 1012

13 March 1995

↔ 1"

↔ 1"

Double-space

A Possibility of Survival:

The Mysterious Fate of Anastasia and Alexei

Indent ½"
or
5 spaces →

The mystery has raged for over seventy-five years. According to the history books, in 1918 Bolshevik revolutionaries brutally executed all seven members of the Russian royal family, the Romanovs. Immediately following the murders, however, rumors appeared claiming that one, or perhaps two, of the Romanov children had escaped the assassination. Is there any evidence to support even the possibility that seventeen-year-old Anastasia and/or thirteen-year-old Alexei were somehow secreted away from the murder scene? Or is this merely a romantic story that has been repeated generation after generation?

Introduction: History of the controversy and the research questions

Over the years, many people have come forth to claim their identities as either Anastasia or Alexei. Movies, plays, and even a ballet have repeatedly captured the public's fascination with this story that just won't die.[1] Until recently, many dismissed the story entirely as pure fiction. However, the recent political changes in the Soviet Union have produced a government that is more open to research into the haunting Romanov mystery. Today, historical information and improved forensic research have provided exciting evidence that points to a new conclusion based on facts, not rumors. It is indeed possible that Anastasia and Alexei survived the execution designed to end the Romanov dynasty forever.

Thesis

↕ 1"

Lawrence 2

Release of
evidence: The
grave site

The first break in solving the mystery came in 1989 when the Russian government released important information about the Romanovs' mass grave. Although the rumors had always insisted that discovery of the secret grave would confirm that two Romanovs had indeed escaped, the location of the grave had never been revealed. In 1976 a Soviet writer claimed that he had uncovered the common grave in woods near the murder site, but its location was kept secret by the Communist government (Kurth 100). The 1989 revelation of this grave site was important to Romanov scholars because it did support the often-retold escape stories: although <u>eleven</u> people were reported executed (seven Romanov family members and four attendants), only <u>nine</u> bodies were found in the grave (Trimble 23). But was this really the Romanov grave?

More
historical
information
uncovered:
The "Yurovsky
note"

The next important historical information came in 1992 from Edward Radzinsky, a Russian playwright whose research on the Romanovs could now be published. Radzinsky had spent two decades studying the Central State Archives in Moscow, discovering the unread diaries of the murdered Czar Nicholas II and Czarina Alexandra and, even more important, the previously secret "Yurovsky note." Yakov Yurovsky was the leader of the execution squad and his statement contained not only his description of the horrible night but also testimony from other guards at the scene (Radzinsky 373). The "Yurovsky note" clearly emphasized the chaos of the execution and contributed to the possible explanation surrounding the persistent rumors of two survivals.

According to Yurovsky, in the early hours of July 17, 1918, the Romanov family—the Czar, the Czarina, four daughters, and

Lawrence 3

son—were taken with their personal physician and three servants into the cellar in the house where they had been held prisoners by the revolutionaries.[2] During the executions, the room filled with smoke and noise, and the bullets seemed to be oddly ricocheting, "jumping around the room like hail" (quoted in Radzinsky 389). Although many bullets were fired at close range, Yurovsky mentions that the deaths of all five children were strangely hard to accomplish. Finally, as the guards hurriedly prepared to load the bodies onto a waiting truck, one of the guards heard a daughter cry out and then it was discovered that, amazingly, all the daughters were still alive (391). The daughters were then supposedly murdered by a drunken guard with a bayonet, who again experienced difficulty: "the point would not go through [the] corset" (qtd. in Radzinsky 391).

What the guards did NOT know until much later (at the grave site) was that at least three of the daughters, and possibly all the children, were wearing "corsets made of a solid mass of diamonds" (373). The hidden Romanov jewels had acted like bullet-proof vests and were the reason the bullets and bayonet were deflected (373). Radzinsky argues that the chaos of the dark night, the drunken state of nervous, hurried guards, and the protective corsets cast serious doubt on the success of all the murder attempts (392).

The trip to the grave site was not smooth either. The truck broke down twice, and it was hard to move the bodies from the truck through the woods to the actual grave site. Yurovsky wrote that to lighten the load two bodies were cremated, supposedly the Czarina and her son, but he also claims that by mistake the family maid was confused with Czarina Alexandra

Lawrence 4

(410). Although the cremation story would account for the two bodies missing in the common grave, no remains or sign of a cremation site have ever been found. Consequently, many Romanov researchers have another explanation. They argue that the two youngest Romanovs, wounded but still alive thanks to their protective corsets of jewels, were secretly removed from the truck during a break-down by guards who regretted their part in the killing of the Romanov children (Smith 5D). After all, why stop to burn only two bodies? Why just two and not all? Wouldn't such a cremation have taken valuable time and attracted attention? Why choose the boy and not Nicholas, the hated Czar? Could Yurovsky have been covering up the fact that by the time they reached the grave site two bodies were missing—the boy and a female? (Radzinsky 416).

New forensic research:
1. DNA analysis

Although the newly recovered historical evidence added important pieces, it did not solve the puzzle. However, forensic research, using techniques not available until 1993, has now shed light on the decades-old controversy. An international team of geneticists conducted DNA analysis on the nine recovered skeletons. Through mitochondrial-DNA sequencing, a process that analyzes DNA strains, and comparison to DNA samples donated by living relatives of the Romanovs, the team concluded in July 1993 that the skeletons were indeed the remains of five members of the Romanov family and four members of their household staff (Dricks A1). Yurovsky's story about the cremation of the maid was therefore not true—two Romanovs were missing!

2. Computer modeling

Taking the next step, scientists used computer modeling to superimpose facial photographs onto the skulls to determine

Lawrence 5

structural matches that would tell which family members the skeletons actually were. The computer technology plus other tests positively identified the Czar and Czarina as two of the bodies. Then more news: all of the remaining Romanov skeletons were of young females (Elliot 61). Alexei, the heir to the throne, was one of the missing—just as the rumors have always claimed.

To discover if the missing daughter was in fact Anastasia, the scientists compared the size and age of the girls to the skeletons. According to Dr. William Maples, leader of the American forensics team, the skeletons are too tall to be Anastasia: "The bones we have show completed growth which indicated more mature individuals" (qtd. in Toufexis 65). According to the American scientists, Anastasia was definitely not in the Romanov grave.

3. Skeletal measurements

Six more years of sophisticated experiments by Russian and British scientists followed these initial studies; DNA tests were replicated and results confirmed (Little). Finally, in February 1998, a special federal commission chaired by First Deputy Prime Minister Boris Nemtsov officially announced its findings to Russian President Boris Yeltsin and the world: the bones are, beyond a shadow of scientific doubt, those of the Romanovs— but the bodies of Alexei and Anastasia remain unaccounted for (Varoli).[3]

More tests lead to official announcement

The stories throughout the years have always focused on the survival of the beautiful Anastasia and her sweet, sickly brother, often describing a devoted guard smuggling them out through dark woods or secret passages. Doubters have always said that the story was a fairy tale not worth serious investigation. The

Lawrence 6

Conclusion:
The search
should
continue

most recent historical and forensic research, however, tells us this much: the real fate of Anastasia and Alexei is still unknown. Therefore, their survival of the execution is still a possibility. Now, at last, there is a scientific basis for continuing the search for the missing Romanovs. Someday, the mystery of their fate will be solved.

Lawrence 7

Notes

[1] The most well-known story was told by Anna Anderson, a woman found in Berlin in 1920 who convinced many people throughout the world that she was indeed Anastasia. In 1956 her story was made into a popular movie starring Ingrid Bergman (Smith 5D). The most recent treatment is the 1997 animated Fox film <u>Anastasia</u>, in which the young girl is saved by a servant boy, loses her memory, but is ultimately restored to her true identity (Addiego C1).

[2] The Russian revolutionaries wanted to be rid of Czar Nicholas II and the entire Romanov family, which had ruled Russia since 1613. The Bolsheviks had held the family captive, charging Nicholas II with responsibility for Russia's poverty and social problems during World War I ("Romanov").

[3] The bones will be officially buried in July 1998 in the Peter and Paul Fortress in St. Petersburg, resting place of all the Romanov czars since Peter the Great. The date marks the 80th anniversary of the Romanov execution (Harding).

↑ ½"

↑ 1"

Double-space

Works Cited

Indent ½"
or
5 spaces →

Addiego, Walter. "The Princess & the Pretender." <u>San Francisco</u>
<u>Examiner</u> 21 Nov. 1997: C1.

Dricks, Victor. "Part of Royal Murder Mystery May Be Solved—in
Scottsdale." <u>Phoenix Gazette</u> 1 Oct. 1993: A1.

Elliott, Dorinda. "The Legacy of the Last Czar." <u>Newsweek</u> 21 Sept.
1992: 60–61.

Harding, Andrew. "Russia to Rebury Czar Nicholas." <u>BBC News</u> 27
Feb. 1998: n. pag. 28 Feb. 1998 <http://news.bbc.co.UK/
newsid _60000/60720.stm>.

Kurth, Peter. "The Mystery of the Romanov Bones." <u>Vanity Fair</u>
Jan. 1993: 96–103; 117–125.

Little, Alan. "Romanov Remains to Be Buried." <u>BBC News</u> 27 Jan.
1998: n. pag. 28 Jan. 1998 <http://news.bbc.co.UK/
newsid_51000/51142.stm>.

Radzinsky, Edvard. <u>The Last Tsar: The Life and Death of Nicholas</u>
<u>II</u>. Trans. Marian Schwartz. New York: Doubleday, 1992.

"Romanov." <u>Encarta.</u> 1993 ed. CD-ROM. Redmond: Microsoft, 1993.

Smith, Lucinda. "Was She Anastasia or a World-Class Imposter?"
<u>The Denver Post</u> 18 July 1993: 5D.

↔ 1"

Toufexia, Anastasia. "It's the Czar All Right, But Where's
Anastasia?" <u>Time</u> 14 Sept. 1992: 65.

↔ 1"

Trimble, Jack. "Bones of Contention." <u>US News and World Report</u>
6 July 1992: 23.

Varoli, John. "Bury Tsar in St. Petersburg July 17." <u>St. Petersburg</u>
<u>Times</u> 9–16 Feb. 1998: n. pag. 3 Mar. 1998 <http://
www.spb.ru/times/336-337/nemtsov.html>.

↑ 1"

CHAPTER

15

Writing about Literature

People read literature for many, many reasons, including amusement, comfort, escape, new ideas, exploration of values, intellectual challenge, and on and on. Similarly, people write about literature to accomplish a variety of purposes. Literary essays may inform readers about the ideas in a work, analyze its craft, or focus on the work's relationship to the time or culture in which it was written. Other essays might explore biographical, psychological, archetypal, or personal readings of a work.

Although approaches to literature are diverse and may be studied in depth in other English courses, writing essays about literature is worthwhile in the composition classroom as well. Writing about literature offers an opportunity to practice the important skills of close reading, critical thinking, and effective expression of ideas.

USING LITERATURE IN THE COMPOSITION CLASSROOM

Teachers of writing most often use literature in their courses in two ways: as "prompts" to inspire personal essay topics and as subjects of interpretative essays.

1. *Prompts:* You might be asked to read a poem or short story and then use some aspect of it—its ideas or characters, for example—as a springboard to discover an essay topic of your own. For instance, after reading John Updike's "A & P," a story about a rather naive young man who receives a real-world lesson, you might write about a coming-of-age experience you had. Or your teacher might assign Shirley Jackson's "The Lottery" and ask you to agree or disagree with the author's views on unexamined conformity to tradition.

2. *Literary Analysis:* Rather than responding to a piece of literature in a personal essay, you might be assigned a literary analysis, asking you to study a piece of literature and then offer your interpretation—that is, your insight into the work (or some important part of it). Your insight becomes your thesis; the body of your essay explains this reading, supported by textual evidence (material from the work) to help your reader understand your view and perhaps gain greater pleasure in, and appreciation of, the work itself.

Literary analysis assignments may be focused in different ways, as well. Some common examples include essays whose main purpose is to show:

- how the various parts or elements of a piece of literature work together to present the main ideas (for example, how the choices of narrator, stanza form, and figurative language in a poem effectively complement each other);

- how one element fits into the complex whole (for example, how setting contributes to a story);

- how two works or two elements may be profitably read together (two poems with similar ideas but different forms; two characters from one story);

- how one interpretation is more insightful than another reading;

- how a work's value has been overlooked or misunderstood.

There are as many possibilities for essay topics as there are readers!

Regardless of the exact assignment, you should feel confident about writing an essay of literary analysis. Working through Part Two of this text, you have already practiced many of the strategies required. For example, to present a particular reading of a poem, you may organize your discussion by *dividing* it into its major literary elements: point of view, setting, structure, language, and so on. Your essay may offer specific lines or images from the work as *examples* illustrating your reading. Working with more than one piece of literature or literary element calls for *comparison and contrast* techniques.

And every paper—whether it is a personal response or literary analysis—uses the skills you learned in Part One of this text: a clear thesis, adequate development of ideas, coherent organization, and effective use of language.

SUGGESTIONS FOR CLOSE READING OF LITERATURE

Writing about literature begins with careful reading—and, yes, rereading. The steps suggested below are certainly not exhaustive; one can ask literally hundreds, thousands, of questions about a complex piece of literature. Rather, these questions are intended to give you a start: practicing close reading and annotation should help you generate ideas and lead you to additional questions of your own.

Our discussion in this chapter is limited to poems and short stories because composition courses frequently do not have the time to include novels and plays (or long narrative poems, for that matter). However, many of the suggestions for reading short stories and poems may be applied to the reading of longer fiction and drama.

Before you begin reading the suggestions that follow, let's dispel the myth about "hidden meanings." A work of literature is not a trick or puzzle box wherein the author has hidden a message for readers to discover if they can just uncover the right clues. Literary works are open to discussion and interpretation; that's part of their appeal. They contain ideas and images that the author thought important, and some ideas or elements the writer may not have consciously been aware of. You, as the reader, will have insights into a poem or story that your classmates don't. It's your job as the writer of your literary analysis to explain not only *WHAT* you see but also *WHY* and *HOW*, supporting your interpretation in ways that seem reasonable, persuasive, and satisfying to your readers.

STEPS TO READING STORIES

If possible, read with a pen in hand. Prepare to make notes, underline important lines, circle revealing words or images, and put stars, question marks, or your own symbols in the margins.

1. Before you begin the piece, read any biographical information that may precede the story. Knowing information about the author and when the story was written or published may offer some insight. Also, note the title. Does it offer intriguing hints about the story's content?

2. Read through the story at least once to clearly acquaint yourself with its *plot,* the series of actions and events that make up the narrative. In other words, what happened and to whom? Is there a conflict of some sort? Is it resolved or is the story left open-ended?

3. Many times you'll see words in a story you don't know. Sometimes you can figure them out from their context, but if you find unknown words that might indeed have a critical bearing on your understanding of a character, for example, look these up now.

4. Jot a few notes describing your initial reactions to the story's main idea(s) or major *theme(s).* (If it's helpful, think of the story in terms of its "about-ness." What do you as reader think this story is about? Loss of innocence? The bitterness of revenge? The power of sympathy? Tragic lack of communication? The wonder of first love?) In other words, what comments or observations does this story make about the human condition?

5. As you review the story, begin to think about its parts, always asking yourself "why?": why did the author choose to do it this way? What is gained (or lost) by writing it this way? What does "X" contribute to my understanding of the story? You might begin noting *point of view—* that is, who is narrating this story? Is a character telling this story or is it told by an all-knowing (omniscient) narrator? A narrator who is partially omniscient, seeing into the thoughts of only some characters? What is gained through the story's choice of narration?

6. Is the story *structured* in chronological order or does the writer shift time sequences through flashbacks or multiple points of view? Does the story contain foreshadowing, early indications in the plot that signal later developments? Again, think about the author's choices in terms of communicating the story's ideas.

7. Think about the *characters,* their personalities, beliefs, motivations. How do they interact? Do any of them change—refuse or fail to change? Look closely at their descriptions, thoughts, and dialogue. Sometimes names are important, too.

8. What is the relationship between the *setting* of the story and its action and/or characters? Remember that setting can include place, time of year, hour of day or night, weather or climate, terrain, culture, and so on. Settings can create mood and even function symbolically to reveal character or foreshadow a coming event.

9. Look closely at the *language* of the story, paying attention to revealing images, metaphors, and similes (for help identifying these, see pp. 174–175). Note any use of *symbols*—persons, places, or things

that bear a significant meaning beyond their usual meaning. Would you characterize the story's *style* as realistic or something else? What is the *tone* of the story? Serious? Humorous? Does irony, the discrepancy between appearance and reality, play a part?

10. After you've looked at these and any other important elements of the reading, review your initial reactions. How would you now describe the main ideas or major themes of this story? How do the parts of the story work together to clarify those themes?

Remember to add your own questions to this list, ones that address your specific story in a meaningful way.

ANNOTATED STORY

Using these guidelines, here is how one student annotated the story that follows. Some of the notes she made on imagery became the basis for her short essay, which appears on pp. 414–417. Before you read the story, however, cover the marginal notes with a sheet of paper. Then read the story, making your own notes. Now uncover the student's notes and reread the story. Compare your reactions to those of the student writer. What new or different insights did you have?

The Story of an Hour

Kate Chopin

Kate Chopin was a nineteenth-century American writer whose stories appeared in such magazines as The Atlantic Monthly, Century, *and* Saturday Evening Post. *She published two collections of short stories and two novels; one of her novels,* The Awakening *(1899), was considered so shocking in its story of a married woman who desired a life of her own that it was removed from some library shelves. "The Story of an Hour" was first published in* Vogue *in 1894.*

similar theme

1 Knowing that Mrs. Mallard was afflicted with a heart trouble, great care was taken to break to her as gently as possible the news of her husband's death.

foreshadowing

2 It was her sister Josephine who told her, in broken sentences, veiled hints that revealed in half concealing. Her husband's friend Richards was there, too, near her. It was he who had been in the newspaper

office when intelligence of the railroad disaster was received, with Brently Mallard's name leading the list of "killed." He had only taken the time to assure himself of its truth by a second telegram, and had hastened to forestall any less careful, less tender friend in bearing the sad message.

3   She did not hear the story as many women have heard the same, with a paralyzed inability to accept its significance. She wept at once, with sudden, wild abandonment, in her sister's arms. When the storm of grief had spent itself she went away to her room alone. She would have no one follow her.

storm imagery

4   There stood, facing the open window, a comfortable, roomy armchair. Into this she sank, pressed down by a physical exhaustion that haunted her body and seemed to reach into her soul.

5   She could see in the open square before her house the tops of trees that were all aquiver with the new spring life. The delicious breath of rain was in the air. In the street below a peddler was crying his wares. The notes of a distant song which some one was singing reached her faintly, and countless sparrows were twittering in the eaves.

Setting: closed room but open window
—spring
—trees, air
—songs
—blue sky

6   There were patches of blue sky showing here and there through the clouds that had met and piled each above the other in the west facing her window.

7   She sat with her head thrown back upon the cushion of the chair quite motionless, except when a sob came up into her throat and shook her, as a child who has cried itself to sleep continues to sob in its dreams.

8   She was young, with a fair, calm face, whose lines bespoke repression and even a certain strength. But now there was a dull stare in her eyes, whose gaze was fixed away off yonder on one of those patches of blue sky. It was not a glance of reflection, but rather indicated a suspension of intelligent thought.

Mrs. M.: repression and strength

9   There was something coming to her and she was waiting for it, fearfully. What was it? She did not know; it was too subtle and elusive to name. But she felt it, creeping out of the sky, reaching toward her through the sounds, the scents, the color that filled the air.

3rd person narrator —readers know her thoughts, feelings

new insight from spring sky

10   Now her bosom rose and fell tumultuously. She was beginning to recognize this thing that was approaching to possess her, and she was striving to beat

she resists—conflict within herself

it back with her will—as powerless as her two white slender hands would have been.

11 When she abandoned herself a little whispered word escaped her slightly parted lips. She said it over and over under her breath: "Free, free, free!" The vacant stare and the look of terror that had followed it went from her eyes. They stayed keen and bright. Her pulses beat fast, and the coursing blood warmed and relaxed every inch of her body.

Revelation: freedom

images of vitality

12 She did not stop to ask if it were not a monstrous joy that held her. A clear and exalted perception enabled her to dismiss the suggestion as trivial.

13 She knew that she would weep again when she saw the kind, tender hands folded in death; the face that had never looked save with love upon her, fixed and gray and dead. But she saw beyond that bitter moment a long procession of years to come that would belong to her absolutely. And she opened and spread her arms out to them in welcome.

more "open" imagery

14 There would be no one to live for during those coming years; she would live for herself. There would be no powerful will bending her in that blind persistence with which men and women believe they have a right to impose a private will upon a fellow creature. A kind intention or a cruel intention made the act seem no less a crime as she looked upon it in that brief moment of illumination.

**self-assertion, wants to control her own life*

15 And yet she had loved him—sometimes. Often she had not. What did it matter! What could love, the unsolved mystery, count for in face of this possession of self-assertion which she suddenly recognized as the strongest impulse of her being.

16 "Free! Body and soul free!" she kept whispering.

17 Josephine was kneeling before the closed door with her lips to the keyhole, imploring for admission. "Louise, open the door! I beg; open the door—you will make yourself ill. What are you doing, Louise? For heaven's sake open the door."

closed door, illness imagery vs "elixir of life" (potion that cures all), open window

18 "Go away. I am not making myself ill." No; she was drinking in a very elixir of life through that open window.

19 Her fancy was running riot along those days ahead of her. Spring days, and summer days, and all sorts of days that would be her own. She breathed a quick

future: seasons of life, growth

prayer that life might be long. It was only yesterday she had thought with a shudder that life might be long.

20   She arose at length and opened the door to her sister's importunities. There was a feverish triumph in her eyes, and she carried herself unwittingly like a goddess of Victory. She clasped her sister's waist, and together they descended the stairs. Richards stood waiting for them at the bottom.

victory imagery

21   Some one was opening the front door with a latchkey. It was Brently Mallard who entered, a little travel-stained, composedly carrying his gripsack and umbrella. He had been far from the scene of accident, and did not even know there had been one. He stood amazed at Josephine's piercing cry; at Richards' quick motion to screen him from the view of his wife.

Is he associated with rain?

22   But Richards was too late.

23   When the doctors came they said she had died of heart disease—of joy that kills.

Irony: She may die from a "broken" heart all right, but readers know it's not from joy.

Initial Reactions: Mrs. Mallard is sad about her husband's death, though I'm not sure she really loved him all that much. He wasn't a bad guy—she just wants to be a "free" woman, back when women had few rights, little control over their lives. She dies—of shock?—when he turns up alive.

After Re-Reading: I think Chopin wanted readers to see how confined some 19th Century women felt in their traditional roles. I felt sorry for Mrs. Mallard, whose realization that life will not be hers after all is so traumatic for her that it kills her.

Open window—lets in scenes, colors, sounds of new life—symbol of future possibilities.

Question: Why is she named "Mallard"—a duck?

SAMPLE STUDENT ESSAY: ANALYSIS OF FICTION

After studying Chopin's story, this student writer decided to focus her essay on an important element in the work, the life-death imagery, to show how contrasting images reveal the main character's changes in attitude. Numbers in parenthesis following direct quotations refer to the paragraphs in the story.

A BREATH OF FRESH AIR

In Kate Chopin's 1894 story "The Story of an Hour" a young wife grieves over news of her husband's accidental death but soon discovers herself elated at the prospect of a life under her own control. The story ends tragically when the husband's sudden reappearance causes her weak heart to fail—not from joy—but from the devastating realization that her new-found freedom is lost. To help readers understand Mrs. Mallard's all-too-brief transformation to a hopeful "free" woman, Chopin contrasts images of illness and lifelessness with positive images of vitality and victory.

In the first line of the story, Mrs. Mallard is associated with illness because of her "heart trouble" (1). Following a "storm of grief" (3) on hearing of her husband's death, she isolates herself in her room, lifeless and numb behind a closed door. Chopin describes Mrs. Mallard as feeling "pressed down" (4) and "haunted" (4), exhausted in body and soul; she sits "motionless" (7) with a "dull stare" (8), except for an occasional sob. The lines in her strong, fair face "bespoke repression" (8) and indeed Mrs. Mallard is a young woman who, only the day before, hopelessly shuddered to think "that life might be long"(19).

In direct contrast with these images of lifelessness and emotional repression, Chopin introduces images of rebirth and hope. Mrs. Mallard's room has an open window, which becomes the key symbol in the description of Mrs. Mallard's transformation. Chopin uses the open window to provide Mrs. Mallard with both a view of new life and with fresh air, paralleling the new hopeful feelings that come to her. Through this "open window" (4) Mrs. Mallard sees beyond her house to

Introduction: title and author identified; brief summary of plot and theme

Thesis

Images of illness and lifelessness, supported by examples from the story

Contrasting images of rebirth, supported by examples

an "open square" (5) with "trees that were all aquiver with the new spring life" (5). The repetition of the word "open," the budding trees, and the spring season all emphasize the contrast between the world of possibilities and new life and Mrs. Mallard's enclosed room and enclosed spirit. The air after a life-giving spring rain has a "delicious breath" (5), and both people and birds are now singing. "Patches of blue sky" (6) are symbolically breaking through the clouds, but, as yet, Mrs. Mallard can only stare vacantly at the blue sky rather than respond to it.

Soon, however, Mrs. Mallard realizes that something—she's not sure what—is "creeping out of the sky, reaching toward her through the sounds, the scents, the color that filled the air" (9). She resists at first but ultimately allows herself the glorious revelation that she is free to live a new life as she, not others, wants it to be. The imagery associated with this revelation shows Mrs. Mallard becoming energized and healthy, in direct contrast to the imagery of lifelessness that characterized her before. The "vacant stare" (11) is replaced by eyes that are "keen and bright" (11). No longer beaten down, "her pulses beat fast, and the coursing blood warmed and relaxed every inch of her body" (11). In contrast to her previous hopeless view of the future, Mrs. Mallard joyfully thinks of the future years and "opened and spread her arms out to them in welcome" (13). This open gesture aligns her with the open window and open square, with their images of rebirth and hope.

Chopin emphasizes the transformation even further by contrasting Mrs. Mallard's description to her sister Josephine's image of her. Symbolically placed on the opposite side of the

Contrasting images of vitality, supported by examples and comparison

closed door from the open window and spring sky, her sister
tells Mrs. Mallard that "you will make yourself ill" (17). But the
images associated with the transformed Mrs. Mallard are not of
illness but of health and victory. Through the open window, she
is drinking in a "very elixir of life" (18), a potion that restores the
sick to health, as she thinks of spring and summer, seasons of
fertility and growth. She finally emerges from her room with
"triumph in her eyes" (20) carrying herself "like a goddess of
Victory" (20).

 Mrs. Mallard's victory is cut short, however, as the return of
Mr. Mallard destroys her hopes for her future life. The image of
illness once again prevails, as doctors wrongly attribute her
death to "heart disease—of joy that kills" (23). With this ironic
last line echoing the story's first line, Chopin's imagery
describing her character comes full circle, from illness to life and
back to death, to emphasize for her readers the tragedy of Mrs.
Mallard's momentary gain and then the crushing defeat of her
spiritual triumph.

Marginal notes:

Contrast of illness imagery to images of health, victory

Conclusion: Restatement of thesis showing purpose of the imagery

STEPS TO READING A POEM

Close reading of a poem is similar to reading a story in many ways. Again, try to read with pen in hand so you can take notes, circle important words, and make comments in the margins.

1. Pay attention to any biographical information on the author and the date of publication, which may give you insight into the poem. Also note the title, as it may introduce the poem's main idea or tone.

2. Read through the poem at least twice. Poetry does differ from prose in that poets often compress or turn sentence structure in unusual ways, to create new images and fit rhyme and rhythm patterns. You might find it helpful to try to paraphrase (put into your own words) the lines of shorter poems (or summarize distinct parts) so that you have a clear understanding of the basic content. If you're lost in several lines, try to locate the subject, the verb, and objects of the action or description. And, always, before you begin to analyze a poem, be sure you know the meaning of all the words. Looking up unfamiliar words is critical here—short poems are compact so every word counts.

3. Some poems are *narratives* and contain a plot; others, often referred to as *lyrics,* capture a scene, a series of images, an emotion, or a thought that has universal appeal. At this point, what action, situation, or ideas do you see presented in this poem? Is there a dominant tone or point of view expressed? Make some notes about your initial reactions to the poem's issues, themes, or ideas. As in fiction, poets often offer comments on the human condition or social values.

4. Now begin to analyze the elements of the poem. Identifying the speaker (or narrator) of the poem is a good place to start. Is it someone with recognizable characteristics or personality traits? Someone involved in the action of the poem? Young or old? Male or female? Mother, father, lover, friend? Tone of voice (angry, pleading, sad, joyful, etc.)? Remember that a speaker using "I" is not necessarily the poet but rather a persona or role the poet has assumed. Or is the speaker unidentified as she or he unfolds the poem for the reader? And to whom is the poem addressed? A specific person, a group of people, any readers?

5. What is the *setting* or *occasion* of the poem? Is the place, time, season, climate, or historical context important to understanding the poem? Why/why not?

6. What *characters,* if any, appear in the poem? What is the relationship between the speaker and others in the poem? What values, opinions, and motivations do these characters present? What conflicts or changes occur?

7. Look carefully at the poem's *diction* (choice of words). Most poems contain description and figurative language to create imagery, the vivid pictures that create meaning in the reader's mind. Look for similes and metaphors, as defined on p. 174, that make abstract or unfamiliar images clear through comparisons, as well as personification and synecdoche (p. 319). Poets often use patterns or groups of *images* to present a dominant impression and concrete objects as *symbols* to represent abstract ideas within the poem (cold rain as death, a spring flower as rebirth). They also use *allusions,* brief references to other well-known persons, places, things, and literary works that shed light on their subject by comparison (a reference to Romeo and Juliet might suggest ill-fated lovers). Underline or circle those words and images that you find most effective in communicating ideas or emotions.

8. How is the poem *structured?* There are too many poetic forms to define each one here (ballads, sonnets, odes, villainelles, etc.) so you might consult a more detailed handbook to help you identify the characteristics of each one. However, to help you begin, here is a brief introduction. Some poems are written in patterns called "fixed" or "closed" form. They often appear in stanzas, recognizable units often containing the same number of lines and the same rhyme and rhythm pattern in those lines. They often present one main idea per unit and have a space between each one. Some poems are not divided into stanzas but nevertheless have well-known fixed forms, such as the Shakespearean sonnet, which traditionally challenges the poet to write within 14 lines, in a predictable line rhythm and rhyme scheme.

   Other poems are written in free verse (or "open" form), with no set line length nor regular rhyme pattern; these poems may rely on imagery, line lengths, repetition, or sound devices to maintain unity and show progression of ideas.

   Study your poem and try to identify its form. How does its structure help communicate its ideas? Why might have the poet chosen this particular structure?

9. *Sound devices* may help unify a poem, establish tone, emphasize a description, and communicate theme. There are many kinds of rhyme (end, internal, slant, etc.), which often help unify or link ideas and parts of poems. For example, stanzas often have set patterns of end

rhyme that pull a unit together: a quatrain (four line stanza), for example, might rhyme *abab,* as shown below:

... free,   a
... sky,   b
... sea,   a
... fly.   b

Four other common sound devices include:

- *Alliteration:* repetition of consonant sounds at the beginning of words ("The Soul selects her own Society") often used to link and emphasize a relationship among words;
- *Assonance:* repetition of vowel sounds ("child bride of time") to link and underscore a relationship among the words;
- *Onomatopoeia:* a word whose sound echoes, and thus emphasizes, its meaning (buzz, rustle, hiss, boom, sigh);
- *Repetition:* repeating the same words, phrases, or lines for unity, emphasis, or musical effect ("Sing on, spring! Sing on, lovers!").

Sound devices not only unify poems; they also add to their communication of images and meaning. Harsh-sounding, monosyllabic words ("the cold stone tomb") may slow a line and create a very different tone in a poem than multisyllabic words with soft, flowing sounds. Poets pick their words carefully for their sounds as well as their connotations and denotations. Ask yourself: what sound devices appear in the poem I'm reading, and why?

10. *Rhythm,* the repetition of stresses and pauses, may also play an important part in the creation of tone and meaning. A poem about a square dance, for example, might echo the content by having a number of quick stresses to imitate the music and the caller's voice. You can discover patterns of rhythm in lines of poetry by marking the accented (´) and unaccented (˘) syllables:

My mistress' eyes are nothing like the sun

Many poems demand a prescribed rhythm as part of their fixed form; lines from a Shakespearean sonnet, as illustrated above, contain an often-used pattern called *iambic pentameter:* five units (called feet) of an unaccented syllable followed by an accented syllable.

Another device that contributes to the rhythm of a line is the *caesura,* a heavy pause in a line of poetry. Caesuras (indicated by a ‖ mark) may be used to isolate and thus emphasize words or slow the pace. Sometimes they are used to show strong contrasts, as in the line below:

Before, a joy proposed; ‖ behind, a dream.

Caesuras may follow punctuation marks such as commas, semi-colons, or periods, marks that say "slow down" to the reader.

After you have looked at the various elements of a poem (and there are many others in addition to the ones mentioned here), reassess your initial reaction. Do you understand the poem in a different or better way? Remember that the elements of an effective poem work together, so be sensitive to the poet's choices of point of view, language, structure, and so on. All these choices help communicate the tone and underscore the ideas of the poem. Ask yourself: What is gained through the poet's choice? What might be different— or lost—if the poet had chosen something else?

A N N O T A T E D   P O E M

Using the suggestions of this chapter, a student responded to the Walt Whitman poem on page 422. The student essay on pp. 422–425 presents an analysis developed from some of the notes shown here.

When I Heard the Learn'd Astronomer
Educated   *someone who studies the stars, sky*   *used here too*

Walt Whitman

Walt Whitman was a nineteenth-century American poet whose free-verse poems often broke with conventional style and subject matter. Some of his most famous poems, including "Song of Myself," "Crossing Brooklyn Ferry," and "Passage to India," extoll the virtues of the common people and stress their unity with a universal spirit. This poem was published in 1865.

settings: inside lecture hall

When I heard the learn'd astronomer;
When the proofs, the figures, were ranged in columns
   before me;
When I was shown the charts and the diagrams, to
   add, divide, and measure them;
When I, sitting, heard the astronomer, where he
   lectured with much applause in the lecture-room.

speaker: "I" in audience
8 lines: 2 parts

scientific images, repetition, long lines, slow pace

outside at night

5 How soon, unaccountable, I became tired and sick;
Till rising and gliding out, I wander'd off by myself,
In the mystical moist night-air, and from time to time,
Look'd up in perfect silence at the stars.

Contrast to 4 lines above: quicker, smoother sounds; nature imagery; appeals to senses not brain

assonance   *alliteration*

Initial Reaction: The speaker of the poem (a student?) is listening to an astronomer's lecture—lots of facts and figures. He gets tired (bored?) and goes outside and looks at the nice night himself.

After re-reading: I see two ways of looking at the sky here. You can learn second-hand or you can use your own senses. I think Whitman prefers the natural experience because the language and images are much more positive in the last lines of the poem when the speaker is looking at nature for himself.
The poem shows the contrast between the two ways by using two different styles and tones. Cold vs. warm. Passive vs. active. Facts vs. mystical experience.

S A M P L E   S T U D E N T   E S S A Y

After studying the Whitman poem, the student writer wrote this essay to show how many poetic elements work together to present the main idea. Do you agree with his analysis? Which of his claims seems the most or least persuasive, and why? What different interpretation(s) might you suggest?

TWO WAYS OF KNOWING

In the poem "When I Heard the Learn'd Astronomer" nineteenth-century American poet Walt Whitman contrasts two ways people may study the world around them. They can approach the world through lectures and teachers, and they can experience nature first-hand through their own senses. Through the use of contrasting structures, imagery, diction, and sound devices in this poem, Whitman expresses a strong preference for personal experience.

The poem's structure clearly presents the contrast between the two ways of experiencing the world, or in this specific case, two ways of studying the heavens. The eight-line, free verse poem breaks into two parts, with the first four lines describing an indoor academic setting, followed by a one-line transition to three concluding lines describing an outdoor night scene. The two parts are unified by a first-person narrator who describes and reacts to both scenes.

In the first four lines the narrator is sitting in "a lecture-room" (l. 4) as part of an audience listening to an astronomer's talk. The dominant imagery of lines 2–3 is scientific and mathematical: "proofs," "figures," "charts," and "diagrams" are presented so that the audience "may add, divide, and measure them" (l. 3). The words, mostly nouns, appear without any colorful modifiers; the facts and figures are carefully arranged "in columns" (l. 2) for objective analysis. This approach to learning is clearly logical and systematic.

The structure and word choice of the first four lines of the poem also subtly reveal the narrator's attitude toward the lecture, which he finds dry and boring. To emphasize the

Introduction: title, author, brief overview of content

Thesis

Two-part structure

Part 1: Inside lecture hall

narrator's emotional uninvolvement with the material, Whitman presents him passively "sitting" (l. 4), the object of the passive verb "was shown" (l. 3). Lines 2, 3, and 4, which describe the lecture, are much longer than the lines in the second section, with many caesuras, commas, and semi-colons that slow the rhythm and pace (for example, l. 3: "When I was shown the charts and diagrams, to add, divide, and measure them;"). The slow, heavy pace of the lines, coupled with the four repetitions of the introductory "when" phrases, emphasizes the narrator's view of the lecture as long, drawn out, and repetitious. Even though the rest of the audience seems to appreciate the astronomer, giving him "much applause" (l. 4), the narrator becomes restless, "tired and sick" (l. 5), and leaves the lecture hall.

Part 2: Outside under stars

In the last three lines of the poem, the language and sound devices change dramatically, creating positive images of serenity, wonder, and beauty. The narrator leaves the hall by "rising and gliding out" (l. 6), a light, floating, almost spirit-like

"mystical" imagery

image that connects him with the "mystical" (l. 7) nature of the heavens. Whitman also uses assonance (repetition of the "i" sound) to strengthen the connection between the "rising and gliding" narrator and the "mystical . . . night-air" (l. 7). In the lecture hall, the narrator was bored, passive, and removed from nature, but now he is spiritually part of the experience himself.

contrasting diction, flowing lines, smooth sounds

Alone outside in the night, away from the noisy lecture hall, the narrator quietly contemplates the wonder of the sky, using his own senses of sight, touch, and hearing to observe the stars and feel the air. Positive words such as "mystical" (l. 7) and "perfect" (1.8) describe the scene, whose beauty is immediately accessible rather than filtered through the astronomer's cold "proofs" and "diagrams." Examples of alliteration tie together flowing images of natural beauty and serenity: "mystical moist night-air" (l. 7), "from time to time" (l. 7), "silence at the stars" (l. 8). Whitman's choice of the soft "m" and "s" sounds here also adds to the pleasing fluid rhythm, which stands in direct, positive contrast to the harsher, choppier sounds ("charts," "add," "divide") and slow, heavy pauses found in the poem's first four lines.

Through careful selection and juxtaposition of language, sound, and structure in the two parts of this short poem, Whitman contrasts distinct ways of studying the natural world. One may learn as a student of facts and figures or choose instead to give oneself over to the wonders of the immediate experience itself. Within the context of this poem, it's no contest: first-hand natural experience wins easily over logic and lectures. Stars, 1; astronomers, 0.

Conclusion: Restatement of thesis and poem's main idea

SOME GUIDELINES FOR WRITING YOUR ESSAYS

Here are some suggestions that will improve any essay of literary analysis:

1. **Select a workable topic.** If the choice of subject matter is yours, you must decide if you will approach a work through discussion of several elements or if you will focus on some specific part of it as it relates to the whole work. You must also select a topic that is interesting and meaningful for your readers. If your topic is too obvious or insignificant, your readers will be bored. In other words, your essay should inform your readers and increase their appreciation of the work.

2. **Present a clear thesis.** Remember that your purpose is to provide new insight to your readers. Consequently, they need to know exactly what you see in the work. Don't just announce your topic ("This poem is about love"); rather, put forth your argumentative thesis clearly and specifically ("Through its repeated use of sewing imagery, the story emphasizes the tragedy of a tailor's wasted potential as an artist"). And don't waltz around vaguely talking about something readers may not have seen the first time through ("At first the warehouse scene doesn't look that important but after reading it a few times you see that it really does contain some of the meaningful ideas in the story"). Get on with it! cries your impatient reader. Tell me what you see!

3. **Follow literary conventions.** Essays of literary analysis have some customs you should follow, unless instructed otherwise. Always include the full name of the author and the work in your introductory paragraph; author's last name is fine after that. Titles of short poems and stories are enclosed in quotation marks. Most literary essays are written in present tense (the poet presents an image of a withered tree), from third-person point of view rather than the more informal first-person "I." So that your readers may easily follow your discussion, include a copy of the work or at least indicate publication information describing the location of the work (the name of volume, publisher, date, pages, and so forth).

   Within your essay, it's also helpful to include a poem's line number following a direct quotation: "the silent schoolyard" (l. 10). Some instructors also request paragraph or page numbers in essays on fiction.

4. **Organize effectively.** Your method of organization may depend heavily on your subject matter. A poem, for example, might be best discussed by devoting a paragraph to each stanza; on the other hand, another work might profit from a paragraph on imagery, another on

point of view, another on setting, and so on. You must decide what arrangement makes the best sense for your readers. Experiment by moving your ideas around in your prewriting outlines and drafts.

5. **Use ample evidence.** Remember that you are, in essence, arguing your interpretation—you are saying to your reader, "Understand this work the way I do." Therefore, it is absolutely essential that you offer your reader convincing evidence, based on reasonable readings of words in the work itself. The acceptance of your views depends on your making yourself clear and convincing. To do so, include plenty of references to the work through direct quotation and paraphrase. Don't assume that your reader sees what you see—or sees it in the way you do. You must *fight* for your interpretation by offering reasonable readings substantiated with references to the work.

> *Unsupported claim:* Robert feels sorry for himself throughout the story.
>
> *Claim supported with text:* Robert's self-pity is evident throughout the story as he repeatedly thinks to himself, "No one on this earth cares about me" (p. 4) and "There isn't a soul I can turn to" (p. 5).

Ask yourself as you work through your drafts, am I offering enough clear, specific, convincing evidence here to persuade my reader to accept my reading?

6. **Find a pleasing conclusion.** At the end of your literary analysis, readers should feel they have gained new knowledge or understanding of a work or some important part of it. You might choose to wrap up your discussion with a creative restatement of your reading, its relation to the writer's craft, or even your assessment of the work's significance within the author's larger body of writing. However you conclude, the readers should feel intellectually and emotionally satisfied with your discussion.

Problems to Avoid

Don't assign meanings. By far the most common problem in essays of literary analysis involves interpretation without clear explanation of supporting evidence. Remember that your readers may not see what you see in a particular line or paragraph; in fact, they may see something quite different. The burden is on you to show cause—how you derived your reading and why it is a good one. Don't represent claims as truth even if they ever-so-conveniently fit your thesis: "It is clear that the moon is used here as a symbol of her family's loss." Clear to whom? If it helps, each time you make an interpretative claim, imagine a classmate who immediately says, "Uh, sorry, but I don't get it. Show me how you see that?" Or imagine a hostile reader with a completely different reading who sneers, "Oh yeah, says who? Convince me."

Use quoted material effectively. Many times your supporting evidence will come from quotations from the text you're analyzing. But don't just drop a quoted line onto your page, as if it were pushed from the roof of a tall building. You run the risk of your readers reading the quoted material and still not seeing in it what you do. Blend the quoted material smoothly into your prose, in a way that illustrates or supports your clearly stated point:

Dropped in: Miranda is twenty-four years old. "After working for three years on a morning newspaper she had an illusion of maturity and experience" (p. 280). [What exact point do you want your reader to understand?]

Point Clarified: Although Miranda is twenty-four and has worked on a newspaper for three years, she is not as worldly-wise as she thinks she is, having acquired only the "illusion of maturity and experience" (p. 280).

Review pages 378–380 for some ways to blend your quotations into your prose. Always double-check to ensure you are quoting accurately; refer to page 386 and pages 474–476 for help with proper punctuation and block indention of longer quoted material.

Analysis is not plot summary. Sometimes you may want to offer your readers a brief overview of the work before you begin your in-depth analysis. And certainly there will be times in the body of your essay, especially if you are writing about fiction, you will need to paraphrase actions or descriptions rather than quote long passages directly. Paraphrasing can indeed provide effective support, but do beware a tendency to fall into unproductive plot-telling. Remember that the purpose of your paper is providing insight into the work's ideas and craft—not merely presenting a rehash of the plot. Keep your eye on each of your claims and pull out or paraphrase only those particular lines or important passages that illustrate and support your points. Use your editing pen as a sharp stick to beat back plot summary if it begins taking over your paragraphs.

 PRACTICING WHAT YOU'VE LEARNED

Read the poem that follows several times and then use the suggestions on pages 418–421 to help you analyze the work. What happens to Richard Cory and why is his action surprising?

Richard Cory

Edwin Arlington Robinson

Edwin Arlington Robinson is perhaps best known for his character studies, explorations of human psychology in painstakingly crafted poems. Born in Maine in 1869, he often used small New England towns as settings in his earlier poems; later, longer narratives focused on the Arthurian legends and on the themes of responsibility and regeneration in modern life. Three of his volumes, including his first Collected Poems *(1921), won the Pulitzer Prize. This poem first appeared in 1897.*

> Whenever Richard Cory went down town,
> We people on the pavement looked at him:
> He was a gentleman from sole to crown,
> Clean favored, and imperially slim.
>
> 5 And he was always quietly arrayed,
> And he was always human when he talked;
> But still he fluttered pulses when he said,
> "Good-morning," and he glittered when he walked.
>
> And he was rich—yes, richer than a king—
> 10 And admirably schooled in every grace:
> In fine, we thought that he was everything
> To make us wish that we were in his place.
>
> So on we worked, and waited for the light,
> And went without the meat, and cursed the bread;
> 15 And Richard Cory, one calm summer night,
> Went home and put a bullet through his head.

Suggestions for Writing

The story and two poems reprinted in this chapter may be used as the basis for your own essays. Some suggestions:

1. Use one of the works as a "prompt" for your own personal essay. For example, have you, like Mrs. Mallard in "The Story of an Hour," ever reacted to a situation in a way that was grossly misunderstood by those close to you? Or, have you ever misread someone else, as did the people in Richard Cory's town? Perhaps the Whitman poem reminded you of a time when you learned something through hands-on experience rather than study? Or perhaps the opposite was true: you didn't fully appreciate an experience until you had studied or analyzed it?

2. Write an essay that presents your interpretation of "Richard Cory." Or, if you see similarities in subject matter, compare and contrast the poem to Chopin's story.

3. Argue your own reading of Whitman's poem or Chopin's story, one that improves on the interpretations presented in the student essays.

4. Write an essay analyzing some other important element(s) in "The Story of an Hour." For example, consider the other people in the story, including Mr. Mallard: how are they characterized, and why?

5. Find a poem or story that you admire and, using this chapter as a guide, write your own essay of literary analysis. Be sure your readers have access to a copy of the work you choose.

CHAPTER
16

Writing In-Class Assignments

In-class writing assignments call for good writing skills, analytical reading skills, and confidence. When you write essays out of class, you have the luxury of time: you can mull over your ideas, talk about them with friends or classmates, prewrite, plan, revise, or even start over if you wish. Because essay assignments written in class must be planned and composed on the spot under the pressure of a time limit, they may induce anxiety in some students. (One composition-class student characterized his feelings of terror this way: "I felt like a slug caught in a sudden salt storm!")

Never fear! Hope reigns! By remembering what you already know about writing the short essay and by learning to analyze quickly the demands of the task you face, you can substantially reduce your anxiety level. With practice, you may discover that in-class writing assignments are not nearly as threatening as you once thought.

STEPS TO WRITING WELL UNDER PRESSURE

1. After you are assigned in-class writing, your first step is to **clarify for yourself the kind of task you face.** Sometimes your instructor will tell you about the assignment's format or general design in advance. Other times, however, figuring out the demands of the assignment on the spot and following the instructions carefully will be part of the task itself. Understanding the kind of exam or essay question you face will help you prepare your response and boost your confidence. Here are some common formats for in-class assignments that call for your writing skills:

- **Short-answer exam questions**

  Your instructor might give an exam that asks you to write a well-developed paragraph or two to identify, define, or explain a term or idea. For example, a political science instructor might ask for paragraphs explaining the importance of certain treaties or laws; a literature teacher might ask for paragraphs that explain the significance of certain lines, characters, or symbols in a particular work; a science instructor might ask for extended definitions of important biological terms, and so on. The paragraph skills you learned in Chapter 3—focus, development, unity, and coherence—are all relevant here.

- **Essay exam questions**

  Frequently, questions appear on exams that call for more detailed discussion of specific material studied in a course. An essay question on a history exam might ask you to "Explain the major causes of the Civil War." Or in biology you might be asked to "Trace a drop of blood on its circulatory journey from the human heart throughout the body." You would be expected to shape your answer into a multiparagraphed essay developed clearly in an easy-to-follow organizational pattern.

- **Personal opinion essays**

  Perhaps the most common in-class assignment in composition classes asks students to respond thoughtfully to some *prompt*—that is, students are asked to give their own opinion about a specific topic presented in a written passage or question, such as "Do you think teenage consumers are too influenced by television?" Other times, students will be asked to read a quotation or proverb ("All that glitters is not gold") and then directed to respond in a personal essay. Other prompts include a statement of a current controversy (students should/should not be assessed a special fee for athletics on this campus) or the description of a hypothetical problem (the developer of large shopping centers has applied for a building permit on the edge of a wildlife preserve). Each student is responsible for explaining and supporting his or her position on the topic presented by the prompt.

- **Summary-and-response essays**

  Some in-class essays ask students to do more than voice their opinions in response to a short prompt. One common assignment is known as the summary-and-response essay. Students first read an essay by a professional writer (the reading may be done either in or out of class, depending on the instructor's preference). Once in class, students write an essay that begins with a clear summary of the essay they have just read (an activity that demonstrates analytical reading abilities), and then they present a reasoned argument that agrees or disagrees with the professional essay's thesis. Summary-and-response essays are often used as entrance or exit exams for composition classes at many schools throughout the country because they allow students to display both reading and writing skills.

There are numerous kinds and combinations of essay exams and in-class writing assignments. You can best prepare yourself mentally if you know in advance the purpose and format of the writing task you will face. If possible, ask your instructor to clarify the nature of your assignment before you come to class to write. (Also, some instructors allow students to bring dictionaries, outlines, or notes to class, but others don't. Ask your instructor for his or her preference.)

2. Once you are in class ready to write, **read the assignment with great care.** First, underline *key words* that are important to the subject matter of your essay; then circle the *directional words* that give you clues to the method of development you might use to organize your response.

Example Explain the (effects) of the Triangle Shirtwaist Factory fire on child-labor laws in America from 1912 to 1915.

Example In *The Grapes of Wrath* John Steinbeck criticizes the unfair treatment of the farm workers by the wealthy California land owners. Illustrate this criticism with at least three (examples) from the novel.

To help you identify some of the frequently used directional words and understand the approaches they suggest, study the chart on page 434.

Note that essay questions may demand more than one pattern of development:

(Explain the meaning) of the term "hospice" and (show the differences) between the Hospice Movement in Great Britain and that of the United States. [definition and contrast]

(Discuss) Weber's three (types) of authority, giving (examples) of societies that illustrate each type. [classification and example]

(Explain) President Truman's (reasons) for bombing Japan during World War II and then (defend or attack) Truman's decision. [causal analysis and argument]

Directional Word or Phrase	Suggested Method of Development
Illustrate . . . Provide examples of . . . Show a number of . . . Support with references to . . .	Example
Explain the steps . . . Explain the procedure . . . Outline the sequence of . . . Trace the events . . . Review the series of . . . Give the history of . . .	Process or Narration
Discuss the effects of . . . Show the consequences of . . . Give the reasons for . . . Explain why . . . Discuss the causes of . . . Relate X to Y . . . Show the influence of . . .	Causal Analysis
Compare the following . . .* Show the differences between . . . Discuss the advantages and disadvantages . . . Show the similarities among . . .	Comparison/Contrast
Describe the following . . . Recreate the scene . . . Discuss in detail . . . Explain the features of . . .	Description
Agree or disagree . . . Defend or attack . . . Offer proof . . . Present evidence . . . Criticize . . . Evaluate . . . State reasons for . . . Justify your answer . . . What if . . .	Argument
Discuss the types of . . . Show the kinds of . . . Analyze the parts of . . . Classify the following . . .	Classification
Define . . . Explain the meaning of . . . Identify the following . . . Give the origins of the term . . .	Definition

*Remember that the directional word "compare" may indicate a discussion of both similarities and differences; the directional word "contrast" focuses only on the differences.

Learning to recognize quickly key directional words will point you in the right direction as you begin to focus your essay. Always read the assignment at least twice and ask your instructor for clarification if some part of the assignment seems confusing to you.

3. Once you have read and fully understood the purpose and direction of your assignment, **prepare to write.** The following advice may be helpful:

- Think positively: remind yourself that the task you face is not unknown to you. You are being asked to write—yes, quickly—the same kind of essay that you have been practicing in your composition class. You *CAN* do this!

- If you are writing an in-class essay, take the first few minutes to think and plan. Many times it's helpful to formulate a thesis in a direct rephrasing of the exam question or "prompt" you have been assigned. For example:

  Assignment: After reading "Our Youth Should Serve," write an essay agreeing/disagreeing with Steven Muller's position on the creation of a voluntary youth corps.

  Thesis: The voluntary youth corps described by Steven Muller in his essay "Our Youth Should Serve" is an excellent program that should be implemented as soon as possible.

  Assignment: Discuss Weber's three types of authority, giving examples to clarify your answer.

  Thesis: Weber's three types of authority are traditional authority, charismatic authority, and legal authority. The three types may be exemplified, respectively, by the 19th-century absolute monarchs of Europe, by a variety of religious groups, and by the constitutional government of the United States.

- After deciding on your thesis, jot down on scratch paper a brief plan or outline that sketches out the main points that will appear in the body of your essay. You might scribble a few key words to remind yourself of the supporting evidence or important details you will use. Don't get too bogged down in detailed outlining—just use enough words to help you stay on track.

- You might also budget your time now—thinking "by 2:30 I should be done with two points in my discussion." While such figuring is approximate at best, having a general schedule in mind might keep you from drifting as you write the first parts of your essay. In most cases, you should not assume you will be able to write a rough draft of your essay and then have the time to massively reorganize as you re-copy it.

4. As you **begin writing,** remember what you have learned about para-graphing, topic sentences, and supporting evidence. If you have been given multiple tasks, be sure that you are responding to all parts of the assignment. If the assignment asks you to present your own opinion, focus your answer ac-cordingly. In timed-writing situations, you can't take on the world, but you can offer intelligent commentary on selected ideas. If you only have an hour or less to complete your essay, consider aiming for three well-developed points of discussion. You may be writing the traditional five-paragraph essay, but fre-quently such a clear pattern of organization works best when nervous writers are under pressure and time is short.

Two more suggestions:

- It may be a good idea to write on one side of your paper only, leaving wide margins on both sides; consider, too, leaving extra lines between paragraphs. If you discover that you have time after finishing your essay, you might wish to add additional information to your exam an-swer or perhaps another persuasive example to a body paragraph. Leaving plenty of blank spaces will allow you to insert information neatly, instead of jamming in handwriting too small for your instructor to decipher.

- If you are writing an essay, do try to conclude in a satisfactory way. Your conclusion may be brief, but even a few sentences are better than an abrupt mid-sentence halt when time runs out.

5. In the time remaining after writing the complete draft of your essay, **read what you have written.** Aim for sufficient, appropriate content and clear organization. Insert, delete, or make changes neatly. Once you are rea-sonably satisfied with the essay's content and flow, take a few minutes to proofread and edit. While most instructors do not expect an in-class essay to be as polished as one written out of class, you are responsible for the best spelling, grammar, and punctuation you can muster under the circum-stances. Take care to apply what you know to sentence problems, especially the run-ons, comma splices, and twisted predicates that tend to surface when writers are composing in a hurry. After all, information too deeply hid-den in a contorted sentence is information that may not be counted in your favor.

- Before you turn in your work, be sure your name is on your essay so your instructor will know who to praise for a job well done.

Problems to Avoid

Misreading the assignment. Always read the directions and the assignment completely and carefully before you start prewriting. Mark key and directional words. Do you have multiple tasks? Consider numbering the tasks to avoid overlooking any parts. Important choices to make? Neatly put a line through the options you don't want. Grossly misreading your assignment may give you as much chance at success as a pig at a barbecue.

Incomplete essay/exam. Don't begin writing without a plan, even if you are excited about the topic and want to dive right in. Having a plan and budgeting your time accordingly will avoid the common problem of not finishing all parts of the exam or essay, which, in the end, may cost you dearly. Don't allow yourself to ramble off on a tangent in one part of the assignment. Stay focused on your plan and complete the entire essay or exam. If you have left blank space as described previously, you can return to a part of the essay to add more information if time permits. Wear a watch and consult it regularly! Don't depend on a classmate or your instructor to advise you of the time remaining. (While we're on the subject of time: although this advice seems obvious, always bring adequate supplies with you to the exam. Rustling around to borrow extra paper or a pen when yours inevitably runs dry costs you valuable minutes and is also disturbing to others.)

Composition amnesia. Writing essays under time pressure causes some students suddenly to forget everything they ever knew about essay organization. This memory loss often wreaks havoc on paragraphing skills, resulting in a half-dozen one-and-two sentence string-bean paragraphs without adequate development; at other times, it results in one long super-paragraph that stretches for pages before the eye like the Mohave Desert, no relief nor rest stop in sight. Emphasize your good ideas by presenting them in a recognizable organizational structure, just as you would do in an out-of-class assignment.

Gorilla generalizations. Perhaps the biggest problem instructors find is the lack of adequate, specific evidence to explain or support shaggy, gorilla-sized generalities roaming aimlessly through students' essays. If, for example, you argue, "Team sports are good for kids because they build character," *why* do you believe this? What particular character traits do you mean? Can you offer a personal example or a well-known study to clarify and support your claim? Remember what you learned in Chapter 3 about using evidence—examples, details, testimony—to illustrate or back up any general claims you are making. Your goal is to be as clear and persuasive as you can be—*show* what you know!

PRACTICING WHAT YOU'VE LEARNED

A. Underline the key words and circle the directional words or phrases in the following assignments. What pattern(s) of development are suggested in each assignment?

1. Discuss three examples of flower imagery as they clarify the major theme of Toni Morrison's novel *The Bluest Eye*.

2. Trace the events that led to the Bay of Pigs invasion of Cuba.

3. Discuss Louis B. Mayer's major influences on the American film industry during the "Golden Age of Moviemaking."

4. Agree or disagree with the following statement: "The 1957 launching of the Russian satellite Sputnik caused important changes in the American educational system."

5. Consider the similarities and differences between the surrealistic techniques of the Russian-American painter Peter Blume and those of Spanish painter Salvador Dali. Illustrate your answer with references to important works of both artists.

B. Use one of the quotations on pp. 47–48 in Chapter 2 as a "prompt" for an in-class assignment asking for a personal opinion essay. Allow yourself 10–15 minutes to write a working thesis and a sketch outline for your in-class essay.

 ASSIGNMENT

Practice timed writing by composing a summary-and-response essay out of class. Read one of the professional essays in this book and then give yourself 50 minutes to (1) summarize* its thesis and main points, (2) plan and write a personal response that either agrees or disagrees with the author's position. After time runs out, evaluate the strengths and weaknesses of your effort. Did you follow your organizational plan? Develop your points adequately? Complete the essay? What part of your response needs extra practice in preparation for your next in-class essay assignment?

---

* If you need to review advice on writing a summary, see pages 376–378.

CHAPTER 16 SUMMARY

1. In-class assignments require good writing skills, careful reading habits, and self-confidence.

2. Prepare for your in-class writing task by first ascertaining the purpose and format of your assignment, in advance if possible.

3. Read assignment instructions carefully, underlining key words and circling directional words that may suggest appropriate patterns of organization and development.

4. Before you begin writing an in-class essay, always take a few minutes to plan your response and generally schedule your time.

5. Try to relax and remember what you have learned from your composition class about writing the short essay. Gain confidence by knowing that the skills demanded by in-class writing assignments are the ones you have practiced in your out-of-class essays.

PART
Four

A CONCISE HANDBOOK

In this section you will learn to recognize and correct the most common errors in grammar, punctuation, and mechanics. Each error will be explained as simply as possible, with a minimum of technical language. Beside each rule you will find the mark many teachers use to indicate that error in your essays.

17 Major Errors in Grammar

ERRORS WITH VERBS

Faulty Agreement   S-V Agr

Make your verb agree in number with its subject; a singular subject takes a singular verb, and a plural subject takes a plural verb.

Incorrect   *Lester Peabody,* principal of the Kung Fu School of Grammar, *don't* agree that gum chewing should be banned in the classroom.

Correct   *Lester Peabody,* principal of the Kung Fu School of Grammar, *doesn't* agree that gum chewing should be banned in the classroom.

Incorrect   The *actions* of the new senator *hasn't* been consistent with his campaign promises.

Correct   The *actions* of the new senator *haven't* been consistent with his campaign promises.

A compound subject takes a plural verb, unless the subject refers to a single person or a single unit.

Examples *Bean sprouts* and *tofu are* dishes Jim Bob won't consider eating. ["Bean Sprouts" and "tofu" are two elements in a compound subject; therefore, use a plural verb.]

The *winner* and new *champion refuses* to give up the microphone at the news conference. ["Winner" and "champion" refer to single person; therefore, use a singular verb.]

Listed below are some of the most confusing subject-verb agreement problems:

1. With a collective noun: a singular noun referring to a collection of elements as a unit generally takes a singular verb.

Incorrect During boring parts of the Transcendental Vegetation lecture, the *class* often *chant* dirty mantras.

Correct During boring parts of the Transcendental Vegetation lecture, the *class* often *chants* dirty mantras.

Incorrect The *army* of the new nation *want* shoes, bullets, and weekend passes.

Correct The *army* of the new nation *wants* shoes, bullets, and weekend passes.

2. With a relative pronoun ("that," "which," and "who") used as a subject: the verb agrees with its antecedent, the word being described.

Incorrect The boss rejected a shipment of *shirts, which was* torn.

Correct The boss rejected a shipment of *shirts, which were* torn.

3. With "each," "none," "everyone," and "neither" as the subject: use a singular verb even when followed by a plural construction.

Incorrect *Each* of the children *think* Mom and Dad are automatic teller machines.

Correct *Each* of the children *thinks* Mom and Dad are automatic teller machines.

Incorrect All the students saw the teacher pull out his hair, but *none know* why he did it.

Correct All the students saw the teacher pull out his hair, but *none knows* why he did it.

Incorrect *Neither have* a dime left by the second of the month.

Correct *Neither has* a dime left by the second of the month.

4. With "either . . . or" and "neither . . . nor": the verb agrees with the nearer item.

Incorrect	Neither rain nor dogs nor *gloom of night keep* the mail carrier from delivering bills.
Correct	Neither rain nor dogs nor *gloom of night keeps* the mail carrier from delivering bills.
Incorrect	Either Betty or her *neighbors is* hosting a come-as-you-are breakfast.
Correct	Either Betty or her *neighbors are* hosting a come-as-you-are breakfast.

5. With "here is (are)" and "there is (are)": the verb agrees with the number indicated by the subject following the verb.

Incorrect	*There is* only two good *reasons* for missing this law class: death and jury duty.
Correct	*There are* only two good *reasons* for missing this law class: death and jury duty.
Incorrect	To help you do your shopping quickly, Mr. Scrooge, *here are* a *list* of gifts under a dollar.
Correct	To help you do your shopping quickly, Mr. Scrooge, *here is* a *list* of gifts under a dollar.

6. With plural nouns intervening between subject and verb: the verb still agrees with the subject.

Incorrect	The *jungle,* with its poisonous plants, wild animals, and biting insects, *make* Herman long for the sidewalks of Topeka.
Correct	The *jungle,* with its poisonous plants, wild animals, and biting insects, *makes* Herman long for the sidewalks of Topeka.

7. With nouns plural in form but singular in meaning: a singular verb is usually correct.

Examples	*News travels* slowly if it comes through the post office.
	Charades is the exhibitionist's game of choice.
	Politics is often the rich person's hobby.

Subjunctive   V Sub

When you make a wish or a statement that is contrary to fact, use the subjunctive verb form "were."

Incorrect   I wish I *was* queen so I could levy a tax on men who spit.

Correct   I wish I *were* queen so I could levy a tax on men who spit. [This expresses a wish.]

Incorrect   If "Fightin' Henry" *was* a foot taller and thirty pounds heavier, we would all be in trouble.

Correct   If "Fightin' Henry" *were* a foot taller and thirty pounds heavier, we would all be in trouble. [This proposes a statement contrary to fact.]

Tense Shift   T

In most cases the first verb in a sentence establishes the tense of any later verb. Keep your verbs within the same time frame.

Incorrect   Big Joe *saw* the police car coming up behind, so he *turns* into the next alley.

Correct   Big Joe *saw* the police car coming up behind, so he *turned* into the next alley.

Incorrect   Horace *uses* an artificial sweetener in his coffee all day, so he *felt* a pizza and a hot-fudge sundae *were* fine for dinner.

Correct   Horace *uses* an artificial sweetener in his coffee all day, so he *feels* a pizza and a hot-fudge sundae *are* fine for dinner.

Incorrect   Rex the Wonder Horse *was* obviously very smart because he *taps* out the telephone numbers of the stars with his hoof.

Correct   Rex the Wonder Horse *was* obviously very smart because he *tapped* out the telephone numbers of the stars with his hoof.

Split Infinitive   Sp I

Many authorities insist that you never separate *to* from its verb; today, however, some grammarians allow the split infinitive except in the most formal kinds of writing. Nevertheless, because it offends some readers, it is probably best to avoid the construction unless clarity or emphasis is clearly served by its use.

Traditional   A swift kick is needed to *start* the machine properly.

Untraditional   A swift kick is needed *to* properly *start* the machine.

Traditional   The teacher wanted Lori *to communicate* her ideas clearly.

Untraditional The teacher wanted Lori *to* clearly *communicate* her ideas.

Double Negatives   D Neg

Don't use a negative verb and a negative qualifier together.

Incorrect I *can't hardly* wait until Jim Bob gets his jaw out of traction, so I can challenge him to a bubble gum blowing contest again.

Correct I *can hardly* wait until Jim Bob gets his jaw out of traction, so I can challenge him to a bubble gum blowing contest again.

Incorrect Even when he flew his helicopter upside-down over her house, she *wouldn't scarcely* look at him.

Correct Even when he flew his helicopter upside-down over her house, she *would scarcely* look at him.

Passive Voice   Pass

For the most part, your prose style will improve if you choose strong, active-voice verbs over wordy or unclear passive constructions.

Wordy passive construction   It was assumed by David that Jean had used his computer because there was correction fluid on the screen.

Active verb   David assumed Jean had used his computer because there was correction fluid on the screen.

Wordy passive construction   After the successful nose-transplant operation, the surgeon and his staff were given a round of applause by the malpractice lawyers in attendance.

Active verb   After the successful nose-transplant operation, the malpractice lawyers in attendance applauded the surgeon and his staff.

Unclear passive construction   Much protest is being voiced over the new electric fireworks. [Who is protesting?]

Active verb   Members of the Fuse Lighters Association are protesting the new electric fireworks.

(For more examples of active and passive voice verbs, see pp. 138–139.)

PRACTICING WHAT YOU'VE LEARNED

Errors with Verbs

A. The following sentences contain subject–verb agreement errors. Correct the problems by changing the verbs. Some sentences contain more than one error.

1. A recent report on Cuban land crabs show they can run faster than horses.

2. The team from Snooker Hollow High School are considering switching from basketball to basket weaving because passing athletics are now required for graduation.

3. None of the students know that both mystery writer Agatha Christie and inventor Thomas Edison was dyslexic.

4. Each of the twins have read about Joseph Priestley's contribution to the understanding of oxygen, but neither were aware that he also invented the pencil eraser.

5. Clarity in speech and writing are absolutely essential in the business world today.

6. Some scholars believe that the world's first money, in the form of coins, were made in Lydia, a country that is now part of Turkey.

7. Bananas, rich in vitamins and low in fats, is rated the most popular fruit in America.

8. There is many children in this country who appreciate a big plate of hot grits, but none of the Hall kids like this Southern dish.

9. Either the cocker spaniel or the poodle hold the honor of being the most popular breed of dogs in the United States, say the American Kennel Club.

10. Many people considers Johnny Appleseed a mythical figure, but now two local historians, authors of a well-known book on the subject, argues he was a real person named John Chapman.

B. The following sentences contain incorrect verb forms, tense shifts, and double negatives. Correct any problems you see, and rewrite any sentences whose clarity or conciseness would be improved by using active rather than passive verbs.

1. She couldn't hardly wait to hear Johnny Cash sing his version of her favorite song, "I've Been Flushed from the Bathroom of Your Heart."

2. "If you was in Wyoming and couldn't hear the wind blowing, what would people call you?" asked Jethro. "Dead," replies his buddy Herman.

3. It was believed by Aztec ruler Montezuma that chocolate had magical powers and can act as an aphrodisiac.

4. Tammy's favorite band is Opie Gone Bad so she always was buying their new album every six months or so.

5. Suspicions of arson are being raised by the Fire Department following the burning of the new Chip and Dale Furniture Factory.

ERRORS WITH NOUNS   N

Possessive with "-ing" Nouns

When the emphasis is on the action, use the possessive pronoun plus the "-ing" noun.

Example   He hated *my* singing around the house, so I made him live in the garage. [The emphasis is on *singing.*]

When the emphasis is not on the action, you may use a noun or pronoun plus the "-ing" noun.

Example   He hated *me* singing around the house, so I made him live in the garage. [The emphasis is on the person singing—me—not the action; he might have liked someone else singing.]

Misuse of Nouns as Adjectives

Some nouns may be used as adjectives modifying other nouns: "horse show," "movie star," or "theater seats." But some nouns used as adjectives sound awkward or like jargon. To avoid such awkwardness, you may need to change the noun to an appropriate adjective or reword the sentence.

Awkward   The group decided to work on local *environment* problems.

Better   The group decided to work on local *environmental* problems.

Jargon   The executive began a *cost estimation comparison study* of the two products.

Better   The executive began to *study a comparison* of the two products' costs.

(For more information on ridding your prose of multiple nouns, see pp. 145–146.)

ERRORS WITH PRONOUNS

Faulty Agreement   Pro Agr

A pronoun should agree in number and gender with its antecedent (that is, the word the pronoun stands for).

Incorrect   To get a temperamental *actress* to sign a contract, the director would lock *them* in their dressing room.

Correct   To get a temperamental *actress* to sign a contract, the director would lock *her* in her dressing room.

Use the singular pronoun with "everyone," "anyone," and "each."

Incorrect   When the belly dancer asked for a volunteer partner, *everyone* in the men's gym class raised *their* hand.

Correct   When the belly dancer asked for a volunteer partner, *everyone* in the men's gym class raised *his* hand.

Incorrect   *Each* of the new wives decided to keep *their* own name.

Correct   *Each* of the new wives decided to keep *her* own name.

In the past, writers have traditionally used the masculine pronoun "he" when the gender of the antecedent is unknown, as in the following: "If a *spy* refuses to answer questions, *he* should be forced to watch James Bond movies until *he* cracks." Today, however, many authorities prefer the nonsexist "she/he" even though the construction can be awkward when maintained over a stretch of prose. Perhaps the best solution is to use the impersonal "one" when possible or simply rewrite the sentence in the plural: "If *spies* refuse to answer questions, *they* should be forced to watch James Bond movies until *they* crack." (For more examples, see pp. 172–173.)

Vague Reference   Ref

Your pronoun references should be clear.

Vague   If the trained seal won't eat its dinner, throw *it* into the lion's cage. [What goes into the lion's cage?]

Clear   If the trained seal won't eat its dinner, throw *the food* into the lion's cage.

Vague   After the dog bit Harry, *he* raised such a fuss at the police station that the sergeant finally had *him* impounded. [Who raised the fuss? Who was impounded?]

Clear   After being bitten, Harry raised such a fuss at the police station that the sergeant finally had the *dog* impounded.

Sometimes you must add a word or rewrite the sentence to make the pronoun reference clear:

Vague   I'm a lab instructor in the biology department and am also taking a statistics course. *This* has always been difficult for me. [What is difficult?]

Clear   I'm a lab instructor in the biology department and am also taking statistics, a *course* that has always been difficult for me.

Also clear   I'm a lab instructor in the biology department and am also taking a statistics course. Being a teacher and a student at the same time is difficult for me.

Shift in Pronouns   P Sh

Be consistent in your use of pronouns; don't shift from one person to another.

Incorrect   *One* shouldn't eat pudding with *your* fingers.

Correct   *One* shouldn't eat pudding with *one's* fingers.

Correct   *You* shouldn't eat pudding with *your* fingers.

Incorrect   *We* left-handed people are at a disadvantage because most of the time *you* can't rent left-handed golf clubs or bowling balls.

Correct   *We* left-handed people are at a disadvantage because most of the time *we* can't rent left-handed golf clubs or bowling balls.

(For additional examples, see p. 146.)

Incorrect Case   Ca

The case of a pronoun is determined by its function. If the pronoun is a subject, use the nominative case: "I," "he," "she," "we," and "they"; if the pronoun is an object, use the objective case: "me," "him," "her," "us," and "them." To check your usage, all you need to do in most cases is isolate the pronoun in the manner shown here and see if it makes sense alone.

Incorrect Give the treasure map to Frankie and *I*.

Isolated Give the treasure map to *I*.

Correct Give the treasure map to Frankie and *me*.

Incorrect Bertram and *her* suspect that the moon is hollow.

Isolated *Her* suspects that the moon is hollow.

Correct Bertram and *she* suspect that the moon is hollow.

In other cases, to determine the correct pronoun, you will need to add implied but unstated sentence elements:

Examples Mother always liked Dickie more than *me*. [Mother liked Dickie more than *she liked* me.]

She is younger than *I* by three days. [She is younger than I *am* by three days.]

To solve the confusing *who/whom* pronoun problem, first determine the case of the pronoun in its own clause in each sentence.

1. If the pronoun is the subject of a clause, use "who" or "whoever."

Examples I don't know *who* spread the peanut butter on my English paper. ["Who" is the subject of the verb "spread" in the clause "who spread the peanut butter on my English paper."]

Rachel is a librarian who only likes books with pictures. ["Who" is the subject of the verb "likes" in the clause "who only likes books with pictures."]

He will sell secrets to *whoever* offers the largest sum of money. ["Whoever" is the subject of the verb "offers" in the clause "whoever offers the largest sum of money."]

2. If the pronoun is the object of a verb, use "whom" or "whomever."

Examples *Whom* am I kicking? ["Whom" is the direct object of the verb "kicking."]

Sid is a man *whom* I distrust. ["Whom" is the direct object of the verb "distrust."]

Whomever he kicked will probably be angry. ["Whomever" is the direct object of the verb "kicked."]

3. If the pronoun occurs as the object of a preposition, use "whom," especially when the preposition immediately precedes the pronoun.

Examples *With whom* am I speaking?

To whom does the credit belong for spreading peanut butter on my English paper?

Do not ask *for whom* the bell tolls.

 PRACTICING WHAT YOU'VE LEARNED

Errors with Nouns and Pronouns

Correct the sentences below. Skip any correct sentences.

1. The executive knew she was in trouble when her salary underwent a modification reduction adjustment of fifty percent.

2. Of whom did Oscar Wilde once say, "He hasn't a single redeeming vice"?

3. It was a surprise to both Mary and I to learn that Switzerland didn't give women the right to vote until 1971.

4. Each of the young women in the Family Life class decided not to marry after they read that couples today have 2.3 children.

5. Jim Bob explained to Frankie that the best way for him to avoid his recurring nosebleeds was to stay out of his cousin's marital arguments.

6. Those of us who'd had the flu agreed that one can always get your doctor to return your call quicker if you get in the shower.

7. The stranger gave the free movie tickets to Louise and I after he saw people standing in line to leave the theater.

8. The personnel director told each of the employees, most of who opposed him, to signify their "no" vote by saying, "I resign."

9. Clarence and me have an uncle who is so mean he writes the name of the murderer on the first page of mystery novels that are passed around the family.

10. One of the first movies to gross over one million dollars was *Tarzan of the Apes* (1932) starring Johnny Weismuller, a former Olympic star who became an actor. This didn't happen often in the movie industry at that time.

ERRORS WITH ADVERBS AND ADJECTIVES

Incorrect Usage   Adv   Adj

Incorrect use of adverbs and adjectives often occurs when you confuse the two modifiers. Adverbs qualify the meanings of verbs, adjectives, and other adverbs; they frequently end in "-ly," and they often answer the question "how?"

Incorrect   After Kay argued with the mechanic, her car began running *bad*.

Correct   After Kay argued with the mechanic, her car began running *badly*.

Adjectives, on the other hand, describe or qualify the meanings of nouns only.

Example   The *angry* mechanic neglected to put oil into Kay's car.

One of the most confusing pairs of modifiers is "well" and "good." We often use "good" as an adjective modifying a noun and "well" as an adverb modifying a verb.

Examples   *A Sap's Fables* is a *good* book for children, although it is not *well* organized.

Bubba was such a *good* liar his wife had to call in the children at suppertime.

After eating the Rocky Mountain oysters, Susie did not feel *well*.

Did you do *well* on your math test?

If you cannot determine whether a word is an adverb or adjective, consult your dictionary.

Faulty Comparison   Comp

When you compare two elements to a higher or lower degree, you often add "-er" or "-r" to the adjective.

Incorrect   Of the two sisters, Sarah is the *loudest*.

Correct   Of the two sisters, Sarah is the *louder*.

When you compare more than two elements, you often add "-est" to the adjective.

Example   Sarah is the loudest of the four children in the family.

Other adjectives use the words "more," "most," "less," and "least" to indicate comparison.

Examples   Bela Lugosi is *more* handsome than Lon Chaney but *less* handsome than Vincent Price.

Boris Karloff is the *most* handsome, and Christopher Lee is the *least* handsome of all the horror film stars.

ERRORS IN MODIFYING PHRASES

Dangling Modifiers   DM

A modifying—or descriptive—phrase must have a logical relationship to some specific words in the sentence. When those words are omitted, the phrase "dangles" without anything to modify. Dangling modifiers frequently occur at the beginnings of sentences and often may be corrected by adding the proper subjects to the main clauses.

Dangling   Not knowing how to swim, buying scuba gear was foolish.

Correct   Not knowing how to swim, *we* decided that buying scuba gear was foolish.

Dangling   Feeling too sick to ski, her vacation to the mountains was postponed.

Correct   Feeling too sick to ski, *Laura* postponed her vacation to the mountains.

(For additional examples, see pp. 133–134.)

Misplaced Modifiers   MM

When modifying words, phrases, or clauses are not placed near the word they describe, confusion or unintentional humor often results.

Misplaced   Teddy swatted the fly still dressed in his pajamas.

Correct   Still dressed in his pajamas, Teddy swatted the fly.

Misplaced   Visitors may leave notes for the minister hanging on the front door.

Correct   Visitors may leave notes hanging on the front door for the minister.

(For additional examples, see pp. 132–133.)

 PRACTICING WHAT YOU'VE LEARNED

Errors with Adverbs, Adjectives, and Modifying Phrases
Correct the errors in the sentences below.

1. Squeezing the can, it was hard to tell if the tomatoes were ripe.

2. Although liver is probably the worse food in the world, buttermilk is hardly more better.

3. After the optometrist pulled her eye tooth, Hortense didn't behave very (good/well) in the waiting room.

4. He didn't think the car would make it over the mountains, being eight years old.

5. The James brothers decided to have their cattle engraved instead of branded, since they were so rich.

6. In the Death Valley Swim Meet, Maria could use the backstroke or sidestroke in the first race, whichever was best for her.

7. I didn't do (good/well) on my nature project because my bonsai sequoia tree grew real bad in its small container.

8. After boarding Hard Luck Airways, the meals we were offered convinced us to return by ship.

9. I've read that a number of modern sailors, like Thor Heyerdahl, have sailed primitive vessels across the ocean in a book from the public library.

10. We are enclosing with this letter the new telephone number for notifying the fire department of any fires that may be attached to your telephone.

ERRORS IN SENTENCES

Fragments   Frag

A complete sentence must contain a subject and a verb. A fragment is an incomplete sentence; it is often a participial phrase or dependent clause that belongs to the preceding sentence. To check for fragments, try reading your prose, one sentence at a time, starting at the *end* of your essay. If you find a "sentence" that makes no sense alone, it's probably a fragment that should either be rewritten or connected to another sentence.

Incorrect   Bubba's parents refuse to send him to a psychiatrist. Although they both know he eats shoelaces and light bulbs.

Correct   Bubba's parents refuse to send him to a psychiatrist although they both know he eats shoelaces and light bulbs.

Incorrect   This tape recording of the symphony's latest concert is so clear you can hear every sound. Including the coughs and whispers of the audience.

Correct   This tape recording of the symphony's latest concert is so clear you can hear every sound, including the coughs and whispers of the audience.

Incorrect   At Liz's most recent wedding, the photographer used an instant camera. Because her marriages break up so fast.

Correct   At Liz's most recent wedding, the photographer used an instant camera because her marriages break up so fast.

You can also try this test to see if a group of words is a fragment: say the phrase "It is true that" in front of the words in question. A complete sentence will still make sense, but a fragment won't.

Example   At Liz's most recent wedding, the photographer used an instant camera. Because her marriages break up so fast.

Which is a fragment?

It is true that *at Liz's most recent wedding the photographer used an instant camera.* [This sentence makes sense, so it's not a fragment.]

It is true that *because her marriages break up so fast.* [Yes, this is a fragment.]

PRACTICING WHAT YOU'VE LEARNED

Fragment Sentence Errors

Rewrite the sentences below so that there are no fragments. Try using the "It is true that" test if you are unsure which group of words is a fragment.

1. The idea of a credit card first appeared in 1887. According to Lawrence M. Ausbel, author of "Credit Cards," in *The McGraw-Hill Encyclopedia of Economics.*

2. Originally an imaginary concept in a futurist novel by Edward Bellamy. The card allowed characters to charge against future earnings.

3. Around the turn of the century some American stores issued paper or metal "shoppers' plates." Although they were only used by retailers to identify their credit customers.

4. The first real credit card was issued in 1947 by a New York bank and was a success. Despite the fact that customers could only charge purchases in a two-block area in Brooklyn.

5. Travel and entertainment cards soon appeared that allowed customers to charge items and services across the country. For example, the American Express card in 1958 and Carte Blanche in 1959.

Comma Splice   CS

A comma splice occurs when two sentences are linked with a comma. To correct this error, you can (1) separate the two sentences with a period, (2) separate the two sentences with a semicolon, (3) insert a coordinating conjunction (such as "and," "or," "nor," "so," "yet") after the comma, (4) subordinate one clause.

Incorrect	Grover won a stuffed gila monster at the church raffle, his mother threw it away the next day while he was in school.
Correct	Grover won a stuffed gila monster at the church raffle. His mother threw it away the next day while he was in school.
Correct	Grover won a stuffed gila monster at the church raffle; his mother threw it away the next day while he was in school.
Correct	Grover won a stuffed gila monster at the church raffle, but his mother threw it away the next day while he was in school.
Correct	Although Grover won a stuffed gila monster at the church raffle, his mother threw it away the next day while he was in school.

(For more help on correcting comma splices, see pp. 465–466; coordination and subordination are discussed in detail on pp. 149–151.)

Run-On Sentence   R-O

Don't run two sentences together without any punctuation. Use a period, a semicolon, a comma plus a coordinating conjunction (if appropriate), or subordinate one clause.

Incorrect   The indicted police chief submitted his resignation the mayor accepted it gratefully.

Correct   The indicted police chief submitted his resignation. The mayor accepted it gratefully.

Correct   The indicted police chief submitted his resignation; the mayor accepted it gratefully.

Correct   The indicted police chief submitted his resignation, and the mayor accepted it gratefully.

Correct   When the indicted police chief submitted his resignation, the mayor accepted it gratefully.

 PRACTICING WHAT YOU'VE LEARNED

Comma Splice and Run-On Sentence Errors
Correct the sentences below. Skip any correct sentences you find.

1. My mother is very politically conservative, she's written in George III for president in the last two elections.

2. Mary Lou decided not to eat the alphabet soup the letters spelled out "botulism."

3. A friend of mine offers a good definition of nasty theater critics on opening night, according to him, they're the people who can't wait to stone the first cast.

4. Opportunists who came to the South after the Civil War were often called "carpetbaggers," they carried their belongings in cheaply produced travel bags made of Belgian carpet.

5. A dried gourd containing seeds probably functioned as the first baby rattle, ancient Egyptian wall paintings show babies with such gourds clutched in their fingers.

6. When English scientist James Smithson died in 1829, he willed his entire fortune to the United States to establish a foundation for knowledge, that's how the Smithsonian Institute was started.

7. The word "jack-o'-lantern" may have come from the legend of Irish Jack, a mean old man in life, he was condemned after death to wander the earth carrying a hollow turnip with a lump of burning coal inside.

8. Americans forget how large the blue whale is it has a heart as large as a Volkswagen Beetle and can hold an elephant on its tongue.

9. According to a study by the Fish and Wildlife Service, American's favorite animals are dogs, horses, swans, robins, and butterflies; their least favorites are cockroaches, mosquitos, rats, wasps, and rattlesnakes.

10. The famous Eiffel Tower, built for the 1889 Paris Exposition, has inspired many crazy stunts, for example, in 1891 Silvain Dornon climbed the 363 steps on stilts.

Faulty Parallelism   //

Parallel thoughts should be expressed in similar constructions.

Awkward Boa constrictors like *to lie* in the sun, *to hang* from limbs, and *swallowing* small animals.

Better Boa constrictors like *to lie* in the sun, *to hang* from limbs, and *to swallow* small animals.

Awkward Whether *working* on his greasy car, *fistfighting* at the hamburger stand, or in bed, my brother always kept his hair combed.

Better Whether *working* on his greasy car, *fistfighting* at the hamburger stand, or *lounging* in bed, my brother always kept his hair combed.

False Predication   Pred

This error occurs when the predicate (that part of the sentence that says something about the subject) doesn't fit properly with the subject. Illogical constructions result.

Incorrect The meaning of the sermon deals with love. [A "meaning" cannot deal with anything; the author, speaker, or work itself can, however.]

Correct The sermon deals with love.

Incorrect	Energy is one of the world's biggest problems. ["Energy" itself is not a problem.]
Correct	The lack of fuel for energy is one of the world's biggest problems.
Incorrect	True failure is when you make an error and don't learn anything from it. [Avoid all "is when" and "is where" constructions. The subject does not denote a time, so the predicate is faulty.]
Correct	You have truly failed only when you make an error and don't learn anything from it.
Incorrect	Her first comment after winning the lottery was exciting. [Her comment wasn't exciting; her feeling was.]
Correct	Her first comment after winning the lottery expressed her excitement.

(For other examples of faulty predication, see p. 134.)

Mixed Structure   Mix S

"Mixed structure" is a catchall term that applies to a variety of sentence construction errors. Usually, the term refers to a sentence in which the writer begins with one kind of structure and then shifts to another in midsentence. Such a shift often occurs when the writer is in a hurry, and the mind has already jumped ahead to the next thought.

Confused	By the time one litter of cats is given away seems to bring a new one.
Clear	Giving away one litter of cats seems to tell the mother cat that it's time to produce a new batch.
Confused	The bank robber realized that in his crime spree how very little fun he was having.
Clear	The bank robber realized that he was having very little fun in his crime spree.
Confused	The novel is too confusing for what the author meant.
Clear	The novel is too confused for me to understand what the author meant.
Confused	Children with messages from their parents will be stapled to the bulletin board.

Clear   Children will find messages from their parents stapled to the bulletin board.

(For other examples of mixed structure, see p. 134.)

 PRACTICING WHAT YOU'VE LEARNED

Errors of Faulty Parallelism, False Predication, and Mixed Structure

Rewrite the sentences below so that each one is clear and coherent. When appropriate, rephrase parts of sentences so that parallel ideas are expressed in similar grammatical constructions.

1. Is it true that Superman could leap tall buildings, run faster than a locomotive, and that bullets would bounce off his skin?

2. An example of his intelligence is when he brought home a twenty-pound block of ice after ice fishing all day.

3. We attended the Texas Spamarama Festival to participate in the spambalaya cook-off, the spam-can toss, the spam jam jazz session, and always enjoying dancing to such favorites as "Twist and Snout."

4. My Aunt Clara swears she has seen Elvis snacking at the deli, browsing at the supermarket, munching at the pizza parlor, and in the cook book section of a local book store.

5. According to my husband, summer air in Louisiana is one part oxygen, nine parts water, and the rest is mosquitos, about ninety percent.

CHAPTER

18

A Concise Guide to Punctuation

Punctuation marks do not exist, as one student recently complained, to make your life complicated. They are used to clarify your written thoughts so that the reader understands your meaning. Just as traffic signs and signals tell a driver to slow down, stop, or go, so punctuation is intended to guide the reader through your prose. Look, for example, at the confusion in the sentences below when the necessary punctuation marks are omitted:

Confusing   Has the tiger been fed Bill? [Bill was the tiger's dinner?]

Clear   Has the tiger been fed, Bill?

Confusing   After we had finished raking the dog jumped into the pile of leaves. [Raking the dog?]

Clear   After we had finished raking, the dog jumped into the pile of leaves.

Confusing   The coach called the swimmers names. [Was the coach fired for verbally abusing the swimmers?]

Clear   The coach called the swimmers' names.

Because punctuation helps you communicate clearly with your reader, you should familiarize yourself with the following rules.

THE PERIOD (.)   P

1. Use a period to end a sentence.

Examples Employees at that company are not allowed to go on coffee breaks. It takes too long to retrain them.

2. Use a period after initials and many abbreviations.

Examples W. B. Yeats, 12 A.M., Dr., etc., M.A.

3. Only one period is necessary if the sentence ends with an abbreviation.

Examples The elephant was delivered C.O.D.

To find a good job, you should obtain a B.S. or B.A.

THE QUESTION MARK (?)   P

1. Use a question mark after every direct question.

Examples May I borrow your galoshes?

Is the sandstorm over now?

2. No question mark is necessary after an indirect question.

Examples Jean asked why no one makes a paper milk carton that opens without tearing.

Dave wondered how the television detective always found a parking place next to the scene of the crime.

THE EXCLAMATION POINT (!)   P

The exclamation point follows words, phrases, or sentences to show strong feelings.

Examples Fire! Call the rescue squad!

The Broncos finally won the Super Bowl!

THE COMMA (,)   P

1. Use a comma to separate two independent clauses* joined by a coordinating conjunction. To remember the coordinating conjunctions, think of the acronym FANBOYS: "for," "and," "nor," "but," "or," "yet," and "so." Always use one of the FANBOYS and a comma when you join two independent clauses.

Examples You can bury your savings in the backyard, *but* don't expect Mother Nature to pay interest.

I'm going home tomorrow, *and* I'm never coming back.

After six weeks Louie's diet was making him feel lonely and depressed, *so* he had a bumper sticker printed that said, "Honk if you love groceries."

Do *not* join two sentences with a comma only; such an error is called a comma splice. Use a comma plus one of the coordinating conjunctions listed previously, a period, a semicolon, or subordination.

Comma splice Beatrice washes and grooms the chickens, Samantha feeds the spiders.

Correct Beatrice washes and grooms the chickens, and Samantha feeds the spiders.

Correct Beatrice washes and grooms the chickens. Samantha feeds the spiders.

Correct Beatrice washes and grooms the chickens; Samantha feeds the spiders.

Correct When Beatrice washes and grooms the chickens, Samantha feeds the spiders.

Comma splice Jack doesn't like singing groups, he won't go with us to hear Fed Up with People.

Correct Jack doesn't like singing groups, so he won't go with us to hear Fed Up with People.

Correct Jack doesn't like singing groups. He won't go with us to hear Fed Up with People.

Correct Jack doesn't like singing groups; he won't go with us to hear Fed Up with People.

---

*An independent clause looks like a complete sentence; it contains a subject and a verb, and it makes sense by itself.

Correct Because Jack doesn't like singing groups, he won't go with us to hear Fed Up with People.

(For additional help, see p. 458.)

2. Conjunctive adverbs, such as "however," "moreover," "thus," "consequently," and "therefore," are used to show continuity and are frequently set off by commas when they appear in midsentence.

Examples She soon discovered, *however,* that he had stolen her monogrammed towels in addition to her pet avocado plant.

She felt, *consequently,* that he was not trustworthy.

When a conjunctive adverb occurs at the beginning of a sentence, it may be followed by a comma, especially if a pause is intended. If no pause is intended, you may omit the comma, but inserting the comma is never wrong.

Examples *Thus,* she resolved never to speak to him again.

Thus she resolved never to speak to him again.

Therefore, he resolved never to speak to her again.

Therefore he resolved never to speak to her again.

Please note that "however" can never, never be used as a coordinating conjunction joining two independent clauses. Incorrect use of "however" most often results in a comma splice.

Comma splice The police arrested the thief, *however,* they had to release him because the plant wouldn't talk.

Correct The police arrested the thief; *however,* they had to release him because the plant wouldn't talk.

Also correct The police arrested the thief. *However,* they had to release him because the plant wouldn't talk.

3. Set off with a comma an introductory phrase or clause.

Examples After we had finished our laundry, we discovered one sock was missing.

According to the owner of the laundromat, customers have conflicting theories about missing laundry.

For example, one man claims his socks make a break for freedom when no one is watching the dryers.

4. Set off nonessential phrases and clauses. If the information can be omitted without changing the meaning of the main clause, then the phrase or clause is nonessential. Do *not* set off clauses or phrases that are essential to the meaning of the main clause.

Essential

He looked worse than my friend *who gets his clothes from the "lost and found" at the bus station.* [The "who" clause is essential to explain which friend.]

The storm *that destroyed Mr. Peartree's outhouse* left him speechless with anger. [The "that" clause is essential to explain why the storm angered Mr. Peartree.]

The movie *showing now at the Ritz* is very obscene and very popular. [The participial phrase is essential to identify the movie.]

Nonessential

Joe Medusa, *who won the jalapeno-eating contest last year,* is this year's champion cow-chip tosser. [The "who" clause is nonessential because it only supplies additional information to the main clause.]

Black widow spiders, *which eat their spouses after mating,* are easily identifiable by the orange hourglass design on their abdomens. [The "which" clause is nonessential because it only supplies additional information.]

The juke box, *now reappearing in local honky-tonks,* first gained popularity during the 1920s. [The participial phrase is nonessential because it only supplies additional information.]

5. Use commas to separate items in a series of words, phrases, or clauses.

Examples

Julio collects coins, stamps, bottle caps, erasers, and pocket lint.

Mrs. Jones chased the burglar out the window, around the ledge, down the fire escape, and into the busy street.

Although journalists and some grammarians permit the omission of the last comma before the "and," many authorities believe the comma is necessary for clarity. For example, how many pints of ice cream are listed in the sentence below?

Please buy the following pints of ice cream: strawberry, peach, coffee, vanilla and chocolate swirl.

Four or five pints? Without a comma before the "and," the reader doesn't know if vanilla and chocolate swirl are (is?) one item or two. By inserting the last comma, you clarify the sentence:

> Please buy the following pints of ice cream: strawberry, peach, coffee, vanilla, and chocolate swirl.

6. Use commas to separate adjectives of equal emphasis that modify the same noun. To determine if a comma should be used, see if you can insert the word "and" between the adjectives; if the phrase still makes proper sense with the substituted "and," use a comma.

Examples   She finally moved out of her cold, dark apartment.

She finally moved out of her cold and dark apartment.

I have a sweet, handsome husband.

I have a sweet and handsome husband.

He called from a convenient telephone booth.

But not: He called from a convenient and telephone booth. ["Convenient" modifies the unit "telephone booth," so there is no comma.]

Hand me some of that homemade pecan pie.

But not: Hand me some of that homemade and pecan pie. ["Homemade" modifies the unit "pecan pie," so there is no comma.]

7. Set off a direct address with commas.

Examples   Gentlemen, keep your seats.

Car fifty-four, where are you?

Not now, Eleanor, I'm busy.

8. Use commas to set off items in addresses and dates.

Examples   The sheriff followed me from Austin, Texas, to question me about my uncle.

He found me on February 2, 1978, when I stopped for gas in Fairbanks, Alaska.

9. Use commas to set off a degree or title following a name.

Examples   John Dough, M.D., was audited when he reported only $5.68 in taxable income last year.

The Neanderthal Award went to Samuel Lyle, Ph.D.

10. Use commas to set off dialogue from the speaker.

Examples Alexander announced, "I don't think I want a second helping of possum."

"Eat hearty," said Marie, "because this is the last of the food."

11. Use commas to set off "yes," "no," "well," and other weak exclamations.

Examples Yes, I am in the cat condo business.

No, all the units with decks are sold.

Well, perhaps one with a pool will do.

12. Set off interrupters or parenthetical elements appearing in the midst of a sentence. A parenthetical element is additional information placed as explanation or comment within an already complete sentence. This element may be a word (such as "certainly" or "fortunately"), a phrase ("for example" or "in fact"), or a clause ("I believe" or "you know"). The word, phrase, or clause is parenthetical if the sentence parts before and after it fit together and make sense.

Examples Jack is, *I think,* still a compulsive gambler.

Harvey, *my brother,* sometimes has breakfast with him.

Jack cannot, *for example,* resist shuffling the toast or dealing the pancakes.

 PRACTICING WHAT YOU'VE LEARNED

Comma Errors

A. Study the comma rules numbered 1–4 on the previous pages. Correct any comma errors you see in the following sentences.

1. In 1886 temperance leader Harvey Wilcox left Kansas, he purchased 120 acres near Los Angeles to develop a new town.

2. Although there were no holly trees growing in that part of California Mrs. Wilcox named the area Hollywood.

3. Mrs. Wilcox may have named the place after a friend's summer home, that was located in Illinois.

4. During the early years settlers who shared the Wilcoxs' values moved to the area and banned the recreational drinking of alcoholic beverages, however, some alcohol consumption was allowed for medicinal purposes.

5. Nevertheless by 1910 the first film studio open its doors inside a tavern on Sunset Boulevard, within seven short years the quiet community started by the Wilcoxs had vanished.

B. Study the comma rules 5–12 on the previous pages. Correct any comma errors you see in the following sentences.

1. Yes Hortense in the 1920s young women did indeed cut their hair raise their hemlines dab perfume behind their knees and dance the Charleston.

2. In 1873 Cornell University cancelled the school's first intercollegiate football game with Michigan when the president announced "I will not permit 30 men to travel 400 miles merely to agitate a bag of wind."

3. Jane Marian Donna Ann and Cissy graduated from high school on June 5 1964 in Texarkana Texas in the old Walnut Street Auditorium.

4. "I may be a man of few opinions" said Henry "but I insist that I am neither for nor against apathy."

5. Did you know for instance that early American settlers once thought the tomato was so poisonous they only used the plant for decoration?

C. The sentences below contain many kinds of comma errors, including the comma splice. Correct any errors you see by adding, deleting or changing the commas as needed.

1. The father decided to recapture his youth, he took his son's car keys away.

2. Although ice cream didn't appear in America until the 1700s our country now leads the world in ice-cream consumption, Australia is second I think.

3. Last summer the large friendly family that lives next door flew Discount Airlines and visited three cities on their vacation, however, their suitcases visited five.

4. Researchers in Balboa, Panama have discovered that the poisonous, yellow-belly, sea snake which descended from the cobra, is the most deadly serpent in the world.

5. Lulu Belle, my cousin, spend the week of Sept. 1–7, 1986 in the woods near Dimebox, Texas looking for additions to her extinct, butterfly collection, however she wasn't at all successful in her search.

For additional practice correcting comma splice errors, see p. 458 in Chapter 17.

THE SEMICOLON (;)   P

1. Use a semicolon to link two closely related independent clauses.

Examples   Jean has been cooking Cajun-style for years without realizing it; her specialty is blackened eggs.

Kate's mother does not have to begin a jogging program; she gets all the exercise she needs by worrying in place.

2. Use a semicolon to avoid a comma splice when connecting two independent clauses with words like "however," "moreover," "thus," "therefore," and "consequently."

Examples   Vincent Van Gogh sold only one painting in his entire life; however, in 1987 his *Sunflowers* sold for almost $40 million.

All Esmeralda's plants die shortly after she gets them home from the store; consequently, she has the best compost heap in town.

This town is not big enough for both of us; therefore, I suggest we expand the city limits.

3. Use a semicolon in a series between items that already contain internal punctuation.

Examples   Last year the Wildcats suffered enough injuries to keep them from winning the pennant, as Jake Pritchett, third baseman, broke his arm in a fight; Hugh Rosenbloom, starting pitcher, sprained his back on a trampoline; and Boris Baker, star outfielder, ate rotten clams and nearly died.

Her children were born a year apart: Moe, 1936; Curley, 1937; and Larry, 1938.

THE COLON (:)   P

1. Use a colon to introduce a long or formal list, but do not use one after "to be" verbs.

Correct   Please pick up these items at the store: garlic, wolfbane, mirrors, a prayer book, a hammer, and a wooden stake.

Incorrect   Jean is such a bad cook that she thinks the four basic food groups are: canned, frozen, ready-to-mix, and take-out.

Correct   Jean is such a bad cook that she thinks the four basic food groups are canned, frozen, ready-to-mix, and take-out.

Avoid needless colons.

Incorrect   At the store I couldn't find: wolfbane or a wooden stake.

Correct   At the store I couldn't find wolfbane or a wooden stake.

2. A colon may be used to introduce a quotation or definition.

Examples   Ninteenth-century writer Ambrose Bierce offers this definition of a bore: "A person who talks when you wish him to listen."

Critic Dorothy Parker was unambiguous in her review of the novel: "This is not a book that should be tossed aside lightly; it should be thrown with great force."

In singer Jimmy Buffett's Margaritaville shop and cafe in Key West, a sign warns: "Shoplifters will be forced to listen to Barry Manilow."

3. Use a colon to introduce a word, phrase, or sentence that emphatically explains, summarizes, or amplifies the preceding sentence.

Examples   Harriet knew the one ingredient that would improve any diet dinner: chocolate.

Zsa Zsa Gabor's advice for becoming a marvelous housekeeper is simple: every time you leave a relationship, keep the house.

Horace made a big mistake at the office party: he kissed his boss's wife hello and his job goodbye.

 PRACTICING WHAT YOU'VE LEARNED

Errors with Semicolons and Colons

Correct the semicolon and colon errors below by adding, deleting, or substituting an appropriate mark of punctuation. Skip any correct sentences.

1. My doctor failed in his career as a kidnapper, no one could read his ransom notes.

2. Some of the cars manufactured between 1907 and 1912 that didn't achieve the popularity of the Model T were: the Black Crow, the Swallow, the Bugmobile, and the Carnation.

3. The highest point in the United States is Mt. McKinley at 20,320 feet, in contrast, the lowest point is Death Valley at 282 feet below sea level.

4. There's only one thing that can make our lawn look as good as our neighbor's; snow.

5. In a Thurmont, Maryland, cemetery can be found this epitaph "Here lies an Atheist, all dressed up, and no place to go."

6. According to an 1863 book of etiquette, the perfect hostess will see to it that the works of male and female authors are properly separated on her bookshelves, however, if the authors happen to be married, their proximity may be tolerated.

7. Some inventors who named weapons after themselves include Samuel Colt, the Colt revolver, Henry Deringer, Jr., the derringer pistol, Dr. Richard J. Gatling, the crank machine gun, Col. John T. Thompson, the submachine or "tommy" gun, and Oliver F. Winchester, the repeating rifle.

8. George Bernard Shaw, the famous playwright, claimed he wanted the following epitaph on his tombstone: "I knew if I stayed around long enough, something like this would happen."

9. As we drove down the highway we saw a sign that said "See the World's Largest Prairie Dog Turn Right at this Exit," therefore we stopped to look.

10. The next billboard read "See Live Rattlesnakes Pet Baby Pigs"; making us want to stop again.

THE APOSTROPHE (')   AP

1. Use an apostrophe to indicate a contraction.

Examples   *It's* too bad your car burned.*

              Wouldn't the insurance company believe your story?

2. Add an apostrophe plus "s" to a noun to show possession.

Examples   *Jack's* dog ate the *cat's* dinner.

              The *veterinarian's* assistant later doctored the *puppy's* wounds.

3. Add only an apostrophe to a plural noun ending in "s" to show possession.

---

*Don't confuse the contraction "it's" (for "it is") with the possessive pronoun "its," which never takes an apostrophe. (The car was old, but *its* coat of paint was new.)

Examples   Goldilocks invaded the *bears'* house.

She ignored her *parents'* warning about breaking and entering.

4. In some cases you may add an apostrophe plus "s" to a singular word ending in "s," especially when the word is a proper name.

Examples   Bill Jones's car

Doris's chair

the class's project

5. To avoid confusion, you may use an apostrophe plus "s" to form the plurals of letters, figures, and words discussed as words; no apostrophe is also acceptable.

Examples   He made four *"C's"* last fall. [or *"Cs"*]

The right to resist the draft was a major issue in the *1960's*. [or *1960s*]

You use too many *"and's"* in your sentence. [or *"ands"*]

QUOTATION MARKS (" " AND ' ')   P

1. Use quotation marks to enclose someone's spoken or written words.

Examples   The daughter wrote, "Remember, Daddy, when you pass on you can't take your money with you."

"But I've already bought a fireproof money belt," answered her father.

2. Use quotation marks around the titles of essays,* articles, chapter headings, short stories, short poems, and songs.

Examples   "How to Paint Ceramic Ashtrays"

"The Fall of the House of Usher"

"Stopping by Woods on a Snowy Evening"

"Yankee Doodle"

---

*Do *not,* however, put quotation marks around your own essay's title on either the title page or the first page of your paper.

3. You may either underline or place quotation marks around a word, phrase, or letter used as the subject of discussion.

Examples   Never use "however" as a coordinating conjunction.

The word "bigwig," meaning an important person, is derived from the large wigs worn by seventeenth-century British judges.

Is your middle initial "X" or "Y"?

Her use of such adjectives as "drab," "bleak," and "musty" gives the poem a somber tone.

4. Place quotation marks around uncommon nicknames and words used ironically. Do not, however, try to apologize for slang or clichés by enclosing them in quotation marks; instead, substitute specific words.

Examples   "Scat-cat" Malone takes candy from babies.

Her "friend" was an old scarecrow in an abandoned barn.

Slang   After work Chuck liked to "simple out" in front of the television.

Specific   After work Chuck liked to relax by watching old movies on television.

5. The period and the comma go inside quotation marks; the semicolon and the colon go outside. If the quoted material is a question, the question mark goes inside; if the quoted material is a part of a whole sentence that is a question, the mark goes outside. The same is true for exclamation points.

Examples   According to cartoonist Matt Groening, "Love is a snowmobile racing across the tundra; suddenly it flips over, pins you underneath, and at night the ice weasels come."

"Love is a snowmobile racing across the tundra; suddenly it flips over, pins you underneath, and at night the ice weasels come," says cartoonist Matt Groening.

According to cartoonist Matt Groening, "Love is a snowmobile . . . suddenly it flips over, pins you underneath, and at night the ice weasels come"; Groening also advises that bored friends are one of the first signs that you're in love.

Did he really say, "At night the ice weasels come"?

Sally asked, "Do you think you're in love or just in a snowmobile?"

6. Use single quotation marks to enclose a quotation (or words requiring quotation marks) within a quotation.

Examples   Professor Hall asked his class, "Do you agree with Samuel Johnson, who once said that a second marriage represents 'the triumph of hope over experience'?"

"One of my favorite songs is 'In My Life' by the Beatles," said Jane.

"I'm so proud of the 'A' on my grammar test," Sue told her parents.

 PRACTICING WHAT YOU'VE LEARNED

Errors with Apostrophes and Quotation Marks
A. Correct the apostrophe errors you see in the phrases below.

1. A horses' pajamas

2. The queens throne

3. The tree lost its' leaves

4. Ten students grades

5. The Depression of the 1930s'

6. That dress of hers'

7. The childrens' toys

8. Both twins dinner

9. Its unfortunate but true

10. The young lass' smile

B. Correct the errors below by adding, changing, or deleting apostrophes and quotation marks.

1. Its true that when famous wit Dorothy Parker was told that President Coolidge, also known as Silent Cal, was dead, she exclaimed, How can they tell?

2. When a woman seated next to Coolidge at a dinner party once told him she had made a bet with a friend that she could get more than two words out of him, he replied You lose.

3. Twenty-one of Elvis Presleys albums have sold over a million copies; twenty of the Beatles albums have also done so.

4. Cinderellas stepmother wasn't pleased that her daughter received an F in her creative writing class on her poem Seven Guys and a Gal, which she had plagiarized from her two friend's Snow White and Dopey.

5. Wasn't it Mae West who said, When choosing between two evils, I always like to try the one I've never tried before? asked Olivia.

6. Horace said Believe me, its to everybodies' advantage to sing the popular song You Stole My Heart and Stomped That Sucker Flat, if thats what the holdup man wants.

7. A scholars research has revealed that the five most commonly used words in written English are the, of, and, a, and to.

8. The triplets mother said that while its' hard for her to choose, O. Henrys famous short story The Ransom of Red Chief is probably her favorite.

9. Despite both her lawyers advice, she used the words terrifying, hideous, and unforgettable to describe her latest flight on Golden Fleece Airways, piloted by Jack One-Eye Marcus.

10. Its clear that Bubba didnt know if the Christmas' tree thrown in the neighbors yard was ours, theirs', or your's.

PARENTHESES ( )   P

1. Use parentheses to set off words, dates, or statements that give additional information, explain, or qualify the main thought.

Examples To encourage sales, some automobile manufacturers name their cars after fast or sleek animals (Impala, Mustang, and Thunderbird, for example).

Popular American author Mark Twain (Samuel Clemens) described many of his childhood experiences in *Tom Sawyer* (1876).

The Ford Motor Company once rejected the name Utopian Turtletop for one of its new cars, choosing instead to call it the Edsel (that name obviously didn't help sales either).

2. The period comes inside the close parenthesis if a complete sentence is enclosed; it occurs after the close parenthesis when the enclosed matter comes at the end of the main sentence and is only a part of the main sentence.

Examples The Colorado winters of 1978 and 1979 broke records for low temperatures. (See pp. 72–73 for temperature charts.)

Jean hates Colorado winters and would prefer a warmer environment (such as Alaska, the North Pole, or a meat locker in Philadelphia).

3. If you are confused trying to distinguish whether information should be set off by commas, parentheses, or dashes, here are three general guidelines:

a. Use commas to set off information closely related to the rest of the sentence.

Example   When Billy Clyde married Maybelle, his brother's young widow, the family was shocked. [The information identifies Maybelle and tells why the family was shocked.]

b. Use parentheses to set off information loosely related to the rest of the sentence or material that would disturb the grammatical structure of the main sentence.

Examples   Billy Clyde married Maybelle (his fourth marriage, her second) in Las Vegas on Friday. [The information is merely additional comment not closely related to the meaning of the sentence.]

Billy Clyde married Maybelle (she was previously married to his brother) in Las Vegas on Friday. [The information is an additional comment that would also disturb the grammatical structure of the main sentence were it not enclosed in parentheses.]

c. Use dashes to set off information dramatically or emphatically.

Example   Billy Clyde eloped with Maybelle—only three days after her husband's funeral—without saying a word to anyone in the family.

BRACKETS [ ]   P

1. Use brackets to set off editorial explanations in quoted material.

Examples   According to the old letter, the treasure map could be found "in the library taped to the back of the portrait [of Gertrude the Great] that faces north."

The country singer ended the interview by saying, "My biggest hit so far is 'You're the Reason Our Kids Are Ugly' [original version by Lola Jean Dillon]."

2. Use brackets to set off editorial corrections in quoted material. By placing the bracketed word "sic" (meaning "thus") next to an error, you indicate that the mistake appeared in the original text and that *you* are not misquoting or misspelling.

Examples The student wrote, "I think it's unfair for teachers to count off for speling [sic]."

"Sic" in brackets indicates that the student who is quoted misspelled the word "spelling."

The highway advertisement read as follows: "For great stakes [sic], eat at Joe's, located right behind Daisy's Glue Factory."

Here, "sic" in brackets indicates an error in word choice; the restaurant owner incorrectly advertised "stakes" instead of "steaks."

THE DASH (—)*   P

1. Use a dash to indicate a strong or sudden shift in thought.

Examples Now, let's be reasonable—wait, put down that ice pick!

"It's not athlete's foot—it's deadly coreopsis!" cried Dr. Mitty.

2. Use dashes to set off parenthetical matter that deserves more emphasis than parentheses denote.

Examples Wanda's newest guru—the one who practiced catatonic hedonism—taught her to rest and play at the same time.

He was amazed to learn his test score—a pitiful 43.

(To clear up any confusion over the uses of dashes, commas, and parentheses, see the guidelines on p. 478.)

3. Use a dash before a statement that summarizes or amplifies the preceding thought. (Dashes can also be used to introduce a humorous or ironic twist on the first idea in the sentence.)

Examples Aged wine, delicious food, someone else picking up the check—the dinner was perfect.

Not everyone agrees with football coach Vince Lombardi, who said, "Winning isn't everything—it's the only thing."

According to Hollywood star Cher, "The trouble with some women is that they get all excited about nothing—and then marry him."

* Please note that in a typed work, a dash is indicated by *two* bar marks ("—"); one bar mark ("-") indicates a hyphen.

THE HYPHEN (-)   P

1. Use a hyphen to join words into a single adjective before a noun.

Examples a wind-blown wig

the mud-caked sneakers

a made-for-television movie

a well-written essay

a five-year-old boy

Do *not* use a hyphen when the modifier ends in "ly."

Examples a highly regarded worker

a beautifully landscaped yard

2. Writers who create original compound adjectives join the words with hyphens.

Examples Compulsive shoppers suffer from stuff-lust syndrome.

She prefers novels with they-lived-wretchedly-ever-after endings.

3. Some compound words use a hyphen; always check your dictionary when you're in doubt.

Examples mother-in-law

president-elect

runner-up

good-for-nothing

twenty-one

4. Some words with prefixes use a hyphen; again, check your dictionary if necessary.

Examples all-American

ex-wife

self-esteem

non-English

5. Use a hyphen to mark the separation of syllables when you divide a word at the end of a line. Do not divide one-syllable words; do not leave one or two letters at the end of a line. (In most dictionaries, dots are used to indicate the division of syllables. Example: va • ca • tion.)

Examples In your essays you should avoid using frag-ment sentences.

Did your father try to help you with your home-work?

UNDERLINING* (_____) P

1. Underline or place quotation marks around a word, phrase, or letter used as the subject of discussion. Whether you underline or use quotation marks, always be consistent. (See also p. 475.)

Examples No matter how I spell offered, it always looks wrong.

Is your middle initial X or Y?

Her use of such words as drab, bleak, and musty give the poem a somber tone.

2. Underline the title of books, magazines, newspapers, movies, works of art, television programs (but use quotation marks for individual episodes), airplanes, trains, and ships.

Examples Moby Dick

The Reader's Digest

Texarkana Gazette

Gone with the Wind

Mona Lisa

Sixty Minutes

Spirit of St. Louis

Queen Mary

Exceptions: Do not underline the Bible or the titles of legal documents, including the United States Constitution, or the name of your own essay when it appears on your title page. Do not underline the city in a newspaper title unless the city's name is actually part of the newspaper's title.

---

*In some printed matter, words that might otherwise be underlined are presented in italics: she had just finished reading *The Great Gatsby*.

3. Underline foreign words that are not commonly regarded as part of the English language.

Examples   He shrugged and said, "C'est la vie."

Under the "For Sale" sign on the old rusty truck, the farmer had written the words "caveat emptor," meaning "let the buyer beware."

4. Use underlining sparingly to show emphasis.

Examples   Everyone was surprised to discover that the butler didn't do it.

"Do you realize that your son just ate a piece of my priceless sculpture?" the artist screamed at the museum director.

THE ELLIPSIS MARK (. . . OR . . . .)   P

1. To show an omission in quoted material within a sentence, use three periods, with spaces before and after each one.

Example   Every time my father tells the children about having to trudge barefooted to school in the snow, the walk gets longer and the snow gets deeper.

Every time my father tells the children about having to trudge barefooted to school . . . the snow gets deeper.

2. Three periods with spaces may be used to show an incomplete or interrupted thought.

Example   My wife is an intelligent, beautiful woman who wants me to live a long time. On the other hand, Harry's wife . . .

3. If you omit any words at the end of a quotation and you are also ending your sentence, use three dots plus a fourth to indicate your period. Do not add space before the first dot.

Example   Lincoln wrote, "Four score and seven years ago our fathers brought forth upon this continent, a new nation. . . ."

4. If the omission of one or more sentences occurs at the end of a quoted sentence, use four periods with no space before the first dot.

Example   "The Lord is my shepherd; I shall not want. . . . he leadeth me in the paths of righteousness for his name's sake."

PRACTICING WHAT YOU'VE LEARNED

Errors with Parentheses, Brackets, Dashes, Hyphens,
Underlining, and Ellipses

Correct the errors below by adding, changing, or deleting parentheses, brackets, dashes, hyphens, underlining, and ellipses.

1. Many moviegoers know that the ape in King Kong the original 1933 version, not the re-make was only an eighteen inch tall animated figure, but not everyone realizes that the Red Sea Moses parted in the 1923 movie of The Ten Commandments was a quivering slab of Jell O sliced down-the-middle.

2. We recall the last words of General John B. Sedwick at the Battle of Spotsylvania in 1864: "They couldn't hit an elephant at this dist   ."

3. In a person to person telephone call the twenty five year old starlet promised the hard working gossip columnist that she would "tell the truth . . . and nothing but the truth" about her highly-publicized feud with her exhusband, editor in chief of Meat Eaters Digest.

4. While sailing across the Atlantic on board the celebrity filled yacht Titanic II, Dottie Mae Haskell she's the author of the popular new self help book Finding Wolves to Raise Your Children confided that until recently she thought chutzpah was an Italian side dish.

5. During their twenty four hour sit in at the melt down site, the anti nuclear protestors began to sing, "Oh, say can you see . . . "

6. Few people know that James Arness later Matt Dillon in the long running television series Gunsmoke got his start by playing the vegetable creature in the postwar monster movie The Thing 1951.

7. Similarly, the well known TV star Michael Landon he died of cancer in 1991 played the leading role in the 1957 classic I Was a Teenage Werewolf.

8. A French chemist named Georges Claude invented the first neon sign in 1910. For additional information on his unsuccessful attempts to use seawater to generate electricity, see pp. 200–205.

9. When Lucille Ball, star of I Love Lucy, became pregnant with her first child, the network executives decided that the word expecting could be used on the air to refer to her condition, but not the word pregnant.

10. In mystery stories the detective often advises the police to cherchez la femme. Editor's note: Cherchez la femme means "look for the woman."

19

A Concise Guide to Mechanics

CAPITALIZATION   CAP

1. Capitalize the first word of every sentence.

Example   The lazy horse leans against a tree all day.

2. Capitalize proper nouns—the specific names of people, places, and products—and also the adjectives formed from proper nouns.

Examples   John Doe

Austin, Texas

First National Bank

the Eiffel Tower

Chevrolets

Japanese cameras

Spanish class

an English major

3. Always capitalize the days of the week, the names of the months, and holidays.

Examples   Saturday, December 14

Tuesday's meeting

Halloween parties

Special events are often capitalized: Superbowl, World Series, Festival of Lights.

4. Capitalize titles when they are accompanied by proper names.

Examples President Jones, Major Smith, Governor Brown, Judge Wheeler, Professor Plum, Queen Elizabeth

5. Capitalize all the principal words in titles of books, articles, stories, plays, movies, and poems. Prepositions, articles, and conjunctions are not capitalized unless they begin the title or contain more than four letters.

Examples "The Face on the Barroom Floor"

A Short History of the War Between the States

For Whom the Bell Tolls

6. Capitalize the first word of a direct quotation.

Examples Shocked at actor John Barrymore's use of profanity, the woman said, "Sir, I'll have you know I'm a lady!"

Barrymore replied, "Your secret is safe with me."

7. Capitalize "east," "west," "north," and "south" when they refer to particular sections of the country but not when they merely indicate direction.

Examples The South has produced many excellent writers, including William Faulkner and Flannery O'Connor. ["South" here refers to a section of the country.]

If you travel south for ten miles, you'll see the papier-mâché replica of the world's largest hamburger. [In this case, "south" is a direction.]

8. Capitalize a title when referring to a particular person;* do not capitalize a title if a pronoun precedes it.

Examples The President announced a new national holiday honoring Frank H. Fleer, inventor of bubble gum.

The new car Dad bought is guaranteed for 10,000 miles or until something goes wrong.

My mother told us about a Hollywood party during which Zelda and F. Scott Fitzgerald collected and boiled all the women's purses.

---

* Some authorities disagree; others consider such capitalization optional.

ABBREVIATIONS   AB

1. Abbreviate the titles "Mr.," "Mrs.," "Ms.," "St.," and "Dr." when they precede names.

Examples Dr. Scott, Ms. Steinham, Mrs. White, St. Jude

2. Abbreviate titles and degrees when they follow names.

Examples Charles Byrd, Jr.; David Hall, Ph.D.; Dudley Carpenter, D.D.S.

3. You may abbreviate the following in even the most formal writing: A.M. (*ante meridiem,* before noon), P.M. (*post meridiem,* after noon), A.D. (*anno Domini,* in the year of our Lord), B.C. (before Christ), etc. (*et cetera,* and others), i.e. (*id est,* that is), and e.g. (*exempli gratia,* for example).

4. In formal writing do *not* abbreviate the names of days, months, centuries, states, countries, or units of measure. Do *not* use an ampersand ("&") unless it is an official part of a title.

Incorrect in formal writing	Tues., Sept., 18th century, Ark., Mex., lbs.
Correct	Tuesday, September, eighteenth century, Arkansas, Mexico, pounds
Incorrect	Tony & Gus went to the store to buy ginseng root.
Correct	Tony *and* Gus went to the A & P to buy ginseng root. [The "&" in "A & P" is correct because it is part of the store's official name.]

5. Do *not* abbreviate the words for page, chapter, volume, and so forth, except in footnotes and bibliographies, which have prescribed rules of abbreviation. (For additional information on proper abbreviation, consult your dictionary.)

NUMBERS   NUM

1. Use figures for dates, street numbers, page numbers, telephone numbers, and hours with A.M. and P.M.*

Examples April 22, 1946

710 West 14th Street

page 242

---

* 8:00 A.M. but eight o'clock.

476–1423

10:00 A.M.

2. Some authorities say spell out numbers that can be expressed in one or two words; others say spell out numbers under one hundred.

Examples Ten thousand dollars or $10,000

Twenty-four hours

Thirty-nine years

Five partridges

$12.99 per pair

1,294 essays

3. When several numbers are used in a short passage, use figures.

Examples On the punctuation test, Jennifer made 82, Juan made 91, Pete made 86, and I made 60.

According to the U.S. Census Bureau, on an average day 11,000 babies are born, 6,000 people die, 7,000 couples marry, and 3,000 couples divorce.

4. Never begin a sentence with a figure.

Incorrect 50 spectators turned out to watch the surfing exhibition at Niagara Falls.

Correct Fifty spectators turned out to watch the surfing exhibition at Niagara Falls.

 PRACTICING WHAT YOU'VE LEARNED

Errors with Capitalization, Abbreviations, and Numbers

A. Correct the errors in capitalization in the following phrases.

1. delicious chinese food

2. memorial day memories

3. fiery southwestern salsa

4. his latest novel, *the story of a prince among thieves*

5. my son's Wedding at the baptist church

6. count Dracula's castle in transylvania

7. african-american heritage

8. a dodge van driven across the golden gate bridge

9. sunday morning newspapers

10. the british daughter-in-law of senator Snort

B. Correct the errors below by adding, deleting, or changing capitals, abbreviations, and numbers. Skip any correct words, letters, or numbers you may find.

1. Speaking to students at Gallaudet university, Marian Wright Edelman, Founder and president of the Children's Defense Fund, noted that an american child is born into poverty every thirty seconds, is born to a teen mother every 60 seconds, is abused or neglected every 26 seconds, is arrested for a violent crime every five minutes, and is killed by a gun every two hours.

2. My sister, who lives in the east, was amazed to read studies by Thomas Radecki, MD, showing that 12-year-olds commit 300 percent more murders than did the same age group 30 years ago.

3. In sixty-seven A.D. the roman emperor Nero entered the chariot race at the olympic games, and although he failed to finish the race, the judges unanimously declared him the Winner.

4. According to John Alcock, a Behavioral Ecologist at Arizona State University, in the U.S.A. the chances of being poisoned by a snake is 20 times less than that of being hit by lightning and 300 times less than the risk of being murdered by a fellow American.

5. The official chinese news agency, located in the city of xinhua, estimates that there are ten million guitar players in their country today, an amazing number considering that the instrument had been banned during the cultural revolution that lasted 10 years, from nineteen sixty-six to nineteen seventy-six.

6. 231 electoral votes were cast for James Monroe but only 1 for John Quincy Adams in the 1820 Presidential race.

7. The british soldier T. E. Lawrence, better known as "lawrence of arabia," stood less than 5 ft. 6 in. tall.

8. Drinking a glass of french wine makes me giddy before my 10 a.m. english class, held in wrigley field every other friday except on New Year's day.

9. When a political opponent once called him "two-faced," president Lincoln retorted, "if I had another face, do you think I would wear this one?"

10. Alexander Graham Bell, inventor of the telephone, died in nova scotia on aug. 2, 1922; 2 days later, on the day of his burial, for 1 minute no telephone in north america was allowed to ring.

SPELLING   SP

For some folks, learning to spell correctly is harder than trying to herd cats. Entire books have been written to teach people to become better spellers, and some of these are probably available at your local book store (and, no, not listed under witchcraft, either). Here, however, are a few suggestions that seem to work for a number of students:

1. Keep a list of the little beasties you misspell. After a few weeks you may notice that you tend to misspell the same words again and again or that the words you misspell tend to fit a pattern—that is, you can't remember when the *i* goes before the *e* or when to change the *y* to *i* before *ed*. Try to memorize the words you repeatedly misspell, or at least keep the list somewhere handy so you can refer to it when you're editing your last draft (listing the words on the inside cover of your dictionary makes sense).

2. Become aware of a few rules that govern some of our spelling in English. For example, many people know the rule in the jingle "*I* before *E* except after *C* or when it sounds like *A* as in *neighbor* and *weigh*." Not everyone, however, knows the follow-up line, which contains most of the exceptions to that jingle: "Neither the weird financier nor the foreigner seizes leisure at its height."

3. Here are some other rules, without jingles, for adding suffixes, a common plague for poor spellers:

- Change final *y* to *i* if the *y* follows a consonant.

    bury = buried
    marry = marries

- But if the suffix is -*ing,* keep the *y*.

    marry + ing = marrying
    worry + ing = worrying

- If the word ends in a single consonant after a single vowel and the accent is on the last syllable, double the consonant before adding the suffix.

occur = occurred
cut = cutting
swim = swimmer

• If a word ends in a silent *e,* drop the *e* before adding *-able* or *-ing*.

love + able = lovable
believe + able = believable

4. And here's an easy rule governing the doubling of letters with the addition of prefixes: most of the time, you simply add all the letters you've got when you mix the word and the prefix.

mis + spell = misspell

un + natural = unnatural

re + entry = reentry

5. Teach yourself to spell the words that you miss often by making up your own silly rules or jingles. For instance:

dessert (one *s* or two?): I always want two helpings so I double the *s.*

apparently (apparantly?): Apparently, my *parent* knows the whole story.

separate (seperate?): I'd be *a rat* to sep*arate* from you.

a lot (or alot?): A cot (not *acot*) provides *a lot* of comfort.

And so on.

6. Don't forget to proofread your papers carefully. Anything that looks misspelled probably is, and deserves to be looked up in your dictionary. Reading your paper one sentence at a time from the end helps, too, because you tend to start thinking about your ideas when you read from the beginning of your paper. (And if you are writing on a word processor that has a spell program, don't forget to run it!)

Although these few suggestions won't completely cure your spelling problems, they may make a dramatic improvement in the quality of your papers and give you the confidence to continue learning and practicing other rules that govern the spelling of our language. Good luck!

PART
Five

ADDITIONAL
READINGS

CHAPTER 20

Exposition: Development by Example

Darkness at Noon

Harold Krents

Harold Krents was a Washington, D.C., attorney and activist for the rights of the disabled. Before his death in 1987, Krents served on the President's Committee on Employment of the Handicapped and was a member of the Vera Institute of Justice and Mainstream, Incorporated. His autobiography To Race the Wind *was published in 1972; his life was the inspiration for the Broadway play and popular movie* Butterflies Are Free. *This essay originally appeared in* The New York Times *in 1976.*

1   Blind from birth, I have never had the opportunity to see myself and have been completely dependent on the image I create in the eye of the observer. To date it has not been narcissistic.

2   There are those who assume that since I can't see, I obviously also cannot hear. Very often people will converse with me at the top of their lungs, enunciating each word very carefully. Conversely, people will also often whisper, assuming that since my eyes don't work, my ears don't either.

3   For example, when I go to the airport and ask the ticket agent for assistance to the plane, he or she will invariably pick up the phone, call a ground hostess and whisper: "Hi, Jane, we've got a 76 here." I have concluded that the word "blind" is not used for one of two reasons: Either they fear that if the dread word is spoken, the ticket agent's retina will immediately detach, or they are reluctant to inform me of my condition of which I may not have been previously aware.

4   On the other hand, others know that of course I can hear, but believe that I can't talk. Often, therefore, when my wife and I go out to dinner, a waiter or waitress will ask Kit if "*he* would like a drink" to which I respond that "indeed *he* would."

5   This point was graphically driven home to me while we were in England. I had been given a year's leave of absence from my Washington law firm to study for a diploma in law degree at Oxford University. During the year I became ill and was hospitalized. Immediately after admission, I was wheeled down to the X-ray room. Just at the door sat an elderly woman—elderly I would judge from the sound of her voice. "What is his name?" the woman asked the orderly who had been wheeling me.

6   "What's your name?" the orderly repeated to me.

7   "Harold Krents," I replied.

8   "Harold Krents," he repeated.

9   "When was he born?"

10   "When were you born?"

11   "November 5, 1944," I responded.

12   "November 5, 1944," the orderly intoned.

13   This procedure continued for approximately five minutes at which point even my saint-like disposition deserted me. "Look," I finally blurted out, "this is absolutely ridiculous. Okay, granted I can't see, but it's got to have become pretty clear to both of you that I don't need an interpreter."

14   "He says he doesn't need an interpreter," the orderly reported to the woman.

15   The toughest misconception of all is the view that because I can't see, I can't work. I was turned down by over forty law firms because of my blindness, even though my qualifications included a cum laude degree from Harvard College and a good ranking in my Harvard Law School class.

16   The attempt to find employment, the continuous frustration of being told that it was impossible for a blind person to practice law, the rejection letters, not based on my lack of ability but rather on my disability, will always remain one of the most disillusioning experiences of my life.

17   Fortunately, this view of limitation and exclusion is beginning to change. On April 16 [1976], the Department of Labor issued regulations that mandate equal-employment opportunities for the handicapped. By and large, the business community's response to offering employment to the disabled has been enthusiastic.

18   I therefore look forward to the day, with the expectation that it is certain to come, when employers will view their handicapped workers as a little child did me years ago when my family still lived in Scarsdale.

19   I was playing basketball with my father in our backyard according to procedures we had developed. My father would stand beneath the hoop, shout, and I would shoot over his head at the basket attached to our garage. Our next-door neighbor, aged five, wandered over into our yard with a playmate. "He's blind," our neighbor whispered to her friend in a voice that could be heard distinctly by Dad and me. Dad shot and missed; I did the same. Dad hit the rim; I missed entirely; Dad shot and missed the garage entirely. "Which one is blind?" whispered back the little friend.

20   I would hope that in the near future when a plant manager is touring the factory with the foreman and comes upon a handicapped and non-handicapped person working together, his comment after watching them work will be, "Which one is disabled?"

Black Men and Public Space

Brent Staples

Brent Staples has written articles and editorials for a number of newspapers and journals, including the Chicago Sun-Times, The New York Times Magazine, *and* Harper's. *He has served on the editorial board of* The New York Times, *and his memoir* Parallel Time: Growing Up in Black and White *was published in 1994. This selection originally appeared in* Ms. *magazine in 1986.*

1   My first victim was a woman—white, well dressed, probably in her late twenties. I came upon her late one evening on a deserted street in Hyde Park, a relatively affluent neighborhood in an otherwise mean, impoverished section of Chicago. As I swung onto the avenue behind her, there seemed to be a discreet, uninflammatory distance between us. Not so. She cast back a worried glance. To her, the youngish black man—a broad six feet two inches with a beard and billowing hair, both hands shoved into the pockets of a bulky military jacket—seemed menacingly close. After a few more quick glimpses, she picked up her pace and was soon running in earnest. Within seconds she disappeared into a cross street.

2   That was more than a decade ago, I was twenty-two years old, a graduate student newly arrived at the University of Chicago. It was in the echo of that terrified woman's footfalls that I first began to know the unwieldy inheritance I'd come into—the ability to alter public space in ugly ways. It was clear that she thought herself the quarry of a mugger, a rapist, or worse. Suffering a bout of insomnia, however, I was stalking sleep, not defenseless wayfarers. As a softy who is scarcely able to take

a knife to a raw chicken—let alone hold one to a person's throat—I was surprised, embarrassed, and dismayed all at once. Her flight made me feel like an accomplice in tyranny. It also made it clear that I was indistinguishable from the muggers who occasionally seeped into the area from the surrounding ghetto. That first encounter, and those that followed, signified that a vast, unnerving gulf lay between nighttime pedestrians—particularly women—and me. And I soon gathered that being perceived as dangerous is a hazard in itself. I only needed to turn a corner into a dicey situation, or crowd some frightened, armed person in a foyer somewhere, or make an errant move after being pulled over by a policeman. Where fear and weapons meet—and they often do in urban America—there is always the possibility of death.

3   In that first year, my first away from my hometown, I was to become thoroughly familiar with the language of fear. At dark, shadowy intersections, I could cross in front of a car stopped at a traffic light and elicit the *thunk, thunk, thunk, thunk* of the driver—black, white, male, or female—hammering down the door locks. On less traveled streets after dark, I grew accustomed to but never comfortable with people crossing to the other side of the street rather than pass me. Then there were the standard unpleasantries with policemen, doormen, bouncers, cabdrivers, and others whose business it is to screen out troublesome individuals *before* there is any nastiness.

4   I moved to New York nearly two years ago and I have remained an avid night walker. In central Manhattan, the near-constant crowd cover minimizes tense one-on-one street encounters. Elsewhere—in SoHo, for example, where sidewalks are narrow and tightly spaced buildings shut out the sky—things can get very taut indeed.

5   After dark, on the warrenlike streets of Brooklyn where I live, I often see women who fear the worst from me. They seem to have set their faces on neutral, and with their purse straps strung across their chests bandolier-style, they forge ahead as though bracing themselves against being tackled. I understand, of course, that the danger they perceive is not a hallucination. Women are particularly vulnerable to street violence, and young black males are drastically overrepresented among the perpetrators of that violence. Yet these truths are no solace against the kind of alienation that comes of being ever the suspect, a fearsome entity with whom pedestrians avoid making eye contact.

6   It is not altogether clear to me how I reached the ripe old age of twenty-two without being conscious of the lethality nighttime pedestrians attributed to me. Perhaps it was because in Chester, Pennsylvania, the small, angry industrial town where I came of age in the 1960s, I was scarcely noticeable against a backdrop of gang warfare, street knifings, and murders. I grew up one of the good boys, had perhaps a half-dozen fistfights. In retrospect, my shyness of combat has clear sources.

7   As a boy, I saw countless tough guys locked away; I have since buried several, too. They were babies, really—a teenage cousin, a brother of twenty-two, a childhood friend in his mid-twenties—all gone down in episodes of bravado played out in the streets. I came to doubt the virtues of intimidation early on. I chose, perhaps unconsciously, to remain a shadow—timid, but a survivor.

8   The fearsomeness mistakenly attributed to me in public places often has a perilous flavor. The most frightening of these confusions occurred in the late 1970s and early 1980s, when I worked as a journalist in Chicago. One day, rushing into the office of a magazine I was writing for with a deadline story in hand, I was mistaken for a burgular. The office manager called security and, with an ad hoc posse, pursued me through the labyrinthine halls, nearly to my editor's door. I had no way of proving who I was. I could only move briskly toward the company of someone who knew me.

9   Another time I was on assignment for a local paper and killing time before an interview. I entered a jewelry store on the city's affluent Near North Side. The proprietor excused herself and returned with an enormous red Doberman pinscher straining at the end of a leash. She stood, the dog extended toward me, silent to my questions, her eyes bulging nearly out of her head. I took a cursory look around, nodded, and bade her good night.

10   Relatively speaking, however, I never fared as badly as another black male journalist. He went to nearby Waukegan, Illinois, a couple of summers ago to work on a story about a murderer who was born there. Mistaking the reporter for the killer, police officers hauled him from his car at gunpoint and but for his press credentials would probably have tried to book him. Such episodes are not uncommon. Black men trade tales like this all the time.

11   Over the years, I learned to smother the rage I felt at so often being taken for a criminal. Not to do so would surely have led to madness. I now take precautions to make myself less threatening. I move about with care, particularly late in the evening. I give a wide berth to nervous people on subway platforms during the wee hours, particularly when I have exchanged business clothes for jeans. If I happen to be entering a building behind some people who appear skittish, I may walk by, letting them clear the lobby before I return, so as not to seem to be following them. I have been calm and extremely congenial on those rare occasions when I've been pulled over by the police.

12   And on late-evening constitutionals I employ what has proved to be an excellent tension-reducing measure: I whistle melodies from Beethoven and Vivaldi and the more popular classical composers. Even steely New Yorkers hunching toward nighttime destinations seem to relax, and occasionally they even join in the tune. Virtually everybody seems to sense

that a mugger wouldn't be warbling bright, sunny selections from Vivaldi's *Four Seasons.* It is my equivalent of the cowbell that hikers wear when they know they are in bear country.

Rambos of the Road

Martin Gottfried

Martin Gottfried was first a music critic for the Village Voice *and then became established as a drama critic for* The New York Post *and* Saturday Review. *He is the author of* Broadway Musicals *(1979),* In-Person: The Great Entertainers *(1985),* All His Jazz: The Life and Death of Bob Fosse *(1990), and* George Burns and the Hundred Year Dash *(1996). This essay was first published in* Newsweek *in 1986.*

1   The car pulled up and its driver glared at us with such sullen intensity, such hatred, that I was truly afraid for our lives. Except for the Mohawk haircut he didn't have, he looked like Robert DeNiro in "Taxi Driver," the sort of young man who, delirious for notoriety, might kill a president.

2   He was glaring because we had passed him and for that affront he pursued us to the next stoplight so as to express his indignation and affirm his masculinity. I was with two women and, believe it, was afraid for all three of us. It was nearly midnight and we were in a small, sleeping town with no other cars on the road.

3   When the light turned green, I raced ahead, knowing it was foolish and that I was not in a movie. He didn't merely follow, he chased, and with his headlights turned off. No matter what sudden turn I took, he followed. My passengers were silent. I knew they were alarmed, and I prayed that I wouldn't be called upon to protect them. In that cheerful frame of mind, I turned off my own lights so I couldn't be followed. It was lunacy. I was responding to a crazy *as* a crazy.

4   "I'll just drive to the police station," I finally said, and as if those were the magic words, he disappeared.

5   It seems to me that there has recently been an epidemic of auto macho—a competition perceived and expressed in driving. People fight it out over parking spaces. They bully into line at the gas pump. A toll booth becomes a signal for elbowing fenders. And beetle-eyed drivers hunch over their steering wheels, squeezing the rims, glowering, preparing the excuse of not having seen you as they muscle you off the road. Approaching a highway on an entrance ramp recently, I was strong-armed by a trailer truck, so immense that its driver all but blew me away by blasting his horn. The behemoth was just inches from my hopelessly mismatched coupe when I fled for the safety of the shoulder.

6   And this is happening on city streets, too. A New York taxi driver told me that "intimidation is the name of the game. Drive as if you're deaf and blind. You don't hear the other guy's horn and you sure as hell don't see him."

7   The odd thing is that long before I was even able to drive, it seemed to me that people were at their finest and most civilized when in their cars. They seemed so orderly and considerate, so reasonable, staying in the right-hand lane unless passing, signaling all intentions. In those days you really eased into highway traffic, and the long, neat rows of cars seemed mobile testimony to the sanity of most people. Perhaps memory fails, perhaps there were always testy drivers, perhaps—but everyone didn't give you the finger.

8   A most amazing example of driver rage occurred recently at the Manhattan end of the Lincoln Tunnel. We were four cars abreast, stopped at a traffic light. And there was no moving even when the light had changed. A bus had stopped in the cross traffic, blocking our paths: it was a normal-for-New-York-City gridlock. Perhaps impatient, perhaps late for important appointments, three of us nonetheless accepted what, after all, we could not alter. One, however, would not. He would not be helpless. He would go where he was going even if he couldn't get there. A Wall Street type in suit and tie, he got out of his car and strode toward the bus, rapping smartly on its doors. When they opened, he exchanged words with the driver. The doors folded shut. He then stepped in front of the bus, took hold of one of its large windshield wipers and broke it.

9   The bus doors reopened and the driver appeared, apparently giving the fellow a good piece of his mind. If so, the lecture was wasted, for the man started his car and proceeded to drive directly *into the bus.* He rammed it. Even though the point at which he struck the bus, the folding doors, was its most vulnerable point, ramming the side of a bus with your car has to rank very high on a futility index. My first thought was that it had to be a rented car.

10   To tell the truth, I could not believe my eyes. The bus driver opened his doors as much as they could be opened and he stepped directly onto the hood of the attacking car, jumping up and down with both his feet. He then retreated into the bus, closing the doors behind him. Obviously a man of action, the car driver backed up and rammed the bus again. How this exercise in absurdity would have been resolved none of us will ever know for at that point the traffic unclogged and the bus moved on. And the rest of us, we passives of the world, proceeded, our cars crossing a field of battle as if nothing untoward had happened.

11   It is tempting to blame such belligerent, uncivil and even neurotic behavior on the nuts of the world, but in our cars we all become a little crazy. How many of us speed up when a driver signals his intention of

pulling in front of us? Are we resentful and anxious to pass him? How many of us try to squeeze in, or race along the shoulder of a lane merger? We may not jump on hoods, but driving the gantlet, we seethe, cursing not so silently in the safety of our steel bodies on wheels—fortresses for cowards.

12   What is it within us that gives birth to such antisocial behavior and why, all of a sudden, have so many drivers gone around the bend? My friend Joel Katz, a Manhattan psychiatrist, calls it, "a Rambo pattern. People are running around thinking the American way is to take the law into your own hands when anyone does anything wrong. And what constitutes 'wrong'? Anything that cramps your style."

13   It seems to me that it is a new America we see on the road now. It has the mentality of a hoodlum and the backbone of a coward. The car is its weapon and hiding place, and it is still a symbol even in this. Road Rambos no longer bespeak a self-reliant, civil people tooling around in family cruisers. In fact, there aren't families in these machines that charge headlong with their brights on in broad daylight, demanding we get out of their way. Bullies are loners, and they have perverted our liberty of the open road into drivers' license. They represent an America that derides the values of decency and good manners, then roam the highways riding shotgun and shrieking freedom. By allowing this to happen, the rest of us approve.

CHAPTER
21

Exposition: Process Analysis

Attitude

Garrison Keillor

Garrison Keillor is a writer, storyteller, and humorist. He may be best known as the host of National Public Radio's long-running A Prairie Home Companion, *which presents the mythical town of Lake Wobegon, where "all the women are strong, all the men are good-looking, and all the children are above average." Keillor is the author of many books including* Lake Wobegon Days *(1985),* We Are Still Married *(1989),* WLT: A Radio Romance *(1991), and* Wobegon Boy *(1997). The following essay is from* Happy to Be Here *(1982), a collection of* New Yorker *articles.*

1   Long ago I passed the point in life when major-league ballplayers begin to be younger than yourself. Now all of them are, except for a few aging trigenarians and a couple of quadros who don't get around on the fastball as well as they used to and who sit out the second games of doubleheaders. However, despite my age (thirty-nine), I am still active and have a lot of interests. One of them is slow-pitch softball, a game that lets me go through the motions of baseball without getting beaned or having to run too hard. I play

on a pretty casual team, one that drinks beer on the bench and substitutes freely. If a player's wife or girlfriend wants to play, we give her a glove and send her out to right field, no questions asked, and if she lets a pop fly drop six feet in front of her, nobody agonizes over it.

2   Except me. This year. For the first time in my life, just as I am entering the dark twilight of my slow-pitch career, I find myself taking the game seriously. It isn't the bonehead play that bothers me especially— the pop fly that drops untouched, the slow roller juggled and the ball then heaved ten feet over the first baseman's head and into the next diamond, the routine singles that go through outfielders' legs for doubles and triples with gloves flung after them. No, it isn't our stone-glove fielding or pussyfoot base-running or limp-wristed hitting that gives me fits, though these have put us on the short end of some mighty ridiculous scores this summer. It's our attitude.

3   Bottom of the ninth, down 18–3, two outs, a man on first and a woman on third, and our third baseman strikes out. *Strikes out!* In slow-pitch, not even your grandmother strikes out, but this guy does, and after his third strike—a wild swing at a ball that bounces on the plate— he topples over in the dirt and lies flat on his back, laughing. *Laughing!*

4   Same game, earlier. They have the bases loaded. A weak grounder is hit toward our second baseperson. The runners are running. She picks up the ball, and she looks at them. She looks at first, at second, at home. We yell, "Throw it! Throw it!" and she throws it, underhand, at the pitcher, who has turned and run to back up the catcher. The ball rolls across the third-base line and under the bench. Three runs score. The batter, a fatso, chugs into second. The other team hoots and hollers, and what does she do? She shrugs and smiles ("Oh, silly me"); after all, it's only a game. Like the aforementioned strikeout artist, she treats her error as a joke. They have forgiven themselves instantly, which is unforgivable. It is *we* who should forgive them, who can say, "It's all right, it's only a game." They are supposed to throw up their hands and kick the dirt and hang their heads, as if this boner, even if it is their sixteenth of the afternoon—*this* is the one that really and truly breaks their hearts.

5   That attitude sweetens the game for everyone. The sinner feels sweet remorse. The fatso feels some sense of accomplishment; this is no bunch of rumdums he forced into an error but a team with some class. We, the sinner's teammates, feel momentary anger at her—dumb! dumb play!— but then, seeing her grief, we sympathize with her in our hearts (any one of us might have made that mistake or one worse), and we yell encouragement, including the shortstop, who, moments before, dropped an easy throw for a force at second. "That's all right! Come on! We got 'em!" we yell. "Shake it off! These turkeys can't hit!" This makes us all feel good, even though the turkeys now lead us by ten runs. We're getting clobbered, but we have a winning attitude.

6   Let me say this about attitude: Each player is responsible for his or her own attitude, and to a considerable degree you can *create* a good attitude by doing certain little things on the field. These are certain little things that ballplayers do in the Bigs, and we ought to be doing them in the Slows.

7   1. When going up to bat, don't step right into the batter's box as if it were an elevator. The box is your turf, your stage. Take possession of it slowly and deliberately, starting with a lot of back-bending, knee-stretching, and torso-revolving in the on-deck circle. Then, approaching the box, stop outside it and tap the dirt off your spikes with your bat. You don't have spikes, you have sneakers, of course, but the significance of the tapping is the same. Then, upon entering the box, spit on the ground. It's a way of saying, "This here is mine. This is where I get my hits."

8   2. Spit frequently. Spit at all crucial moments. Spit correctly. Spit should be *blown,* not ptuied weakly with the lips, which often results in dribble. Spitting should convey forcefulness of purpose, concentration, pride. Spit down, not in the direction of others. Spit in the glove and on the fingers, especially after making a real knucklehead play; it's a way of saying, "I dropped the ball because my glove was dry."

9   3. At bat and in the field, pick up dirt. Rub dirt in the fingers (especially after spitting on them). Toss dirt, as if testing the wind for velocity and direction. Smooth the dirt. Be involved with dirt. If no dirt is available (e.g., in the outfield), pluck tufts of grass. Fielders should be grooming their areas constantly between plays, flicking away tiny sticks and bits of gravel.

10   4. Take your time. Tie your laces. Confer with your teammates about possible situations that may arise and conceivable options in dealing with them. Extend the game. Three errors on three consecutive plays can be humiliating if the plays occur within the space of a couple of minutes, but if each error is separated from the next by extensive conferences on the mound, lace-tying, glove adjustments, and arguing close calls (if any), the effect on morale is minimized.

11   5. Talk. Not just an occasional "Let's get a hit now" but continuous rhythmic chatter, a flow of syllables: "Hey babe hey babe c'mon babe good stick now hey babe long tater take him downtown babe . . . hey good eye good eye."

12   Infield chatter is harder to maintain. Since the slow-pitch pitch is required to be a soft underhand lob, infielders hesitate to say, "Smoke him babe hey low heat hey throw it on the black babe chuck it in there back him up babe no hit no hit." Say it anyway.

13   6. One final rule, perhaps the most important of all: When your team is up and has made the third out, the batter and the players who were left

on base do not come back to the bench for their gloves. *They remain on the field, and their teammates bring their gloves out to them.* This requires some organization and discipline, but it pays off big in morale. It says, "Although we're getting our pants knocked off, still we must conserve our energy."

14   Imagine that you have bobbled two fly balls in this rout and now you have just tried to stretch a single into a double and have been easily thrown out sliding into second base, where the base runner ahead of you had stopped. It was the third out and a dumb play, and your opponents smirk at you as they run off the field. You are the goat, a lonely and tragic figure sitting in the dirt. You curse yourself, jerking your head sharply forward. You stand up and kick the base. How miserable! How degrading! Your utter shame, though brief, bears silent testimony to the worthiness of your teammates, whom you have let down, and they appreciate it. They call out to you now as they take the field, and as the second base-man runs to his position he says, "Let's get 'em now," and tosses you your glove. Lowering your head, you trot slowly out to right. There you do some deep knee bends. You pick grass. You find a pebble and fling it into foul territory. As the first batter comes to the plate, you check the sun. You get set in your stance, poised to fly. Feet spread, hands on hips, you bend slightly at the waist and spit the expert spit of a veteran ballplayer—a player who has known the agony of defeat but who always bounces back, a player who has lost a stride on the base paths but can still make the big play.

15   This is *ball,* ladies and gentlemen. This is what it's all about.

Ditch Diving
Tom Bodett

Tom Bodett has been a logger, sailor, builder, and the voice of popular radio commercials. He has broadcast a radio show from Alaska and is known for his humorous appearances on National Public Radio. Bodett has published several collections of essays, including As Far as You Can Go Without a Passport *(1985),* The End of the Road *(1989),* The Big Garage on Clear Shot *(1990), and* Small Comforts *(1987), from which this essay was taken. His most recent work is* America's Historic Trails, with Tom Bodett *(1997), the companion book to a 13-part PBS television series.*

1 The graceful winter sports of skiing, skating and dog-sledding get a lot of attention around Alaska, but there's another winter activity that nobody seems to appreciate for the art that it actually is—ditch diving. We all become practitioners of this art at one time or another, but none of us

seems to hold proper appreciation of what we're doing, perhaps because its aesthetics have never been fully defined for us. Allow me.

2 To dive you need a road, a ditch, some snow on the ground, and any licensed highway vehicle or its equivalent. Nothing else is required, but a good freezing rain will speed up the process.

3 The art of the dive is in the elegance with which you perform three distinct actions. The first one, of course, is that you and your car *leave the roadway.* Not so fast there, hotshot—remember, this is an art. The manner and theme of your dive are weighed heavily in this maneuver.

4 For instance, the "I wasn't looking and drove into the ditch" dive will gain you nothing with the critics. The "He wasn't looking and drove me into the ditch" dive is slightly better, but lacks character. The "It sucked me into the ditch" dive shows real imagination, and the "We spun around three times, hit the ditch going backwards, and thought we were all going to die" dive will earn you credits for sheer drama. The "I drove in the ditch rather than slide past the school bus" dive might win the humanitarian award, but only if you can explain to the police why you were going that fast in the first place.

5 Okay, so now you've left the road. Your second challenge is to *place the vehicle.* Any dumbbell can put a car in a ditch, but it takes an artist to put one there with panache. The overall appeal of your installation is gauged by how much the traffic slows down to gawk at it.

6 Nosed-in within ten degrees of level won't even turn a head. Burrowed into a snowbank with one door buried shut is better, and if you're actually caught in the act of climbing out a window, you're really getting somewhere. Letting your car sit overnight so the snowplows can bury it is a good way of gaining points with the morning commuter traffic. Any wheel left visibly off the ground is good for fifty points each, with a hundred-point bonus for all four. Caution: Only master-class ditch divers should endeavor to achieve this bonus positioning.

7 All right, there you are, nicely featured alongside your favorite roadway. The third part of your mission is to *ask for assistance.* Simply walking to a phone and calling a tow truck will prove you a piker and not an artist at all. Hit the showers, friend. The grace and creativity you display getting back on the road must at least equal those you employed while leaving it.

8 Let's say you were forced into the ditch and are neatly enshrined with one rear wheel off the ground and the hood buried in the berm. Wait until any truck bigger than your bathroom happens along and start walking in that direction with a pronounced limp. Look angry but not defeated, as if you'd walk all night to find the guy who ran you off the road. Look the driver in the eye like it would have been him if he'd been there sooner. This is a risky move, but it's been proven effective. If the truck

has personalized license plates and lights mounted all over it, you're in good shape. Those guys love to show how hard their trucks can pull on things.

9   I prefer, however, to rely on the softer side of human nature. Addle-brained people hold a special place in our hearts, and I like to play on these protective instincts. If my car is buried beyond hope, I'll display my tongue in the corner of my mouth and begin frantically digging at the snow drift with my hands until someone stops to talk me out of it. If my hands get cold and still nobody's stopped, I'll crawl head-first into the hole I've dug and flail my legs around like I was thrown clear of the wreck. This works every time and has won me many a ditch-diving exhibition over the years.

10   I certainly hope I've enlarged your appreciation of this undervalued creative medium. I warn against exercising this art to excess, but when the opportunity arises, remember: Hit 'er hard, sink 'er deep, get 'er out, and please, dive carefully.

The Jeaning of America

Carin C. Quinn

Carin C. Quinn is an essayist who received her Master's degree in American Studies from California State University at Los Angeles in 1976. "The Jeaning of America—and the World," was first published in American Heritage *magazine in 1978.*

1   This is the story of a sturdy American symbol which has now spread throughout most of the world. The symbol is not the dollar. It is not even Coca-Cola. It is a simple pair of pants called blue jeans, and what the pants symbolize is what Alexis de Tocqueville called "a manly and legitimate passion for equality. . . ." Blue jeans are favored equally by bureaucrats and cowboys; bankers and deadbeats; fashion designers and beer drinkers. They draw no distinctions and recognize no classes; they are merely American. Yet they are sought after almost everywhere in the world—including Russia, where authorities recently broke up a teen-aged gang that was selling them on the black market for two hundred dollars a pair. They have been around for a long time, and it seems likely that they will outlive even the necktie.

2   This ubiquitous American symbol was the invention of a Bavarian-born Jew. His name was Levi Strauss.

3   He was born in Bad Ocheim, Germany, in 1829, and during the European political turmoil of 1848 decided to take his chances in New York, to which his two brothers already had emigrated. Upon arrival, Levi soon found that his two brothers had exaggerated their tales of an easy life in the land of the main chance. They were landowners, they had told him;

instead, he found them pushing needles, thread, pots, pans, ribbons, yarn, scissors, and buttons to housewives. For two years he was a lowly peddler, hauling some 180 pounds of sundries door-to-door to eke out a marginal living. When a married sister in San Francisco offered to pay his way West in 1850, he jumped at the opportunity, taking with him bolts of canvas he hoped to sell for tenting.

4   It was the wrong kind of canvas for that purpose, but while talking with a miner down from the mother lode, he learned that pants—sturdy pants that would stand up to the rigors of the digging—were almost impossible to find. Opportunity beckoned. On the spot, Strauss measured the man's girth and inseam with a piece of string and, for six dollars in gold dust, had [the canvas] tailored into a pair of stiff but rugged pants. The miner was delighted with the result, word got around about "those pants of Levi's," and Strauss was in business. The company has been in business ever since.

5   When Strauss ran out of canvas, he wrote his two brothers to send more. He received instead a tough, brown cotton cloth made in Nîmes, France—called *serge de Nîmes* and swiftly shortened to "denim" (the word "jeans" derives from Génes, the French word for Genoa, where a similar cloth was produced). Almost from the first, Strauss had his cloth dyed the distinctive indigo that gave blue jeans their name, but it was not until the 1870s that he added the copper rivets which have long since become a company trademark. The rivets were the idea of a Virginia City, Nevada, tailor, Jacob W. Davis, who added them to pacify a mean-tempered miner called Alkali Ike. Alkali, the story goes, complained that the pockets of his jeans always tore when he stuffed them with ore samples and demanded that Davis do something about it. As a kind of joke, Davis took the pants to a blacksmith and had the pockets riveted; once again, the idea worked so well that word got around; in 1873 Strauss appropriated and patented the gimmick—and hired Davis as a regional manager.

6   By this time, Strauss had taken both his brothers and two brothers-in-law into the company and was ready for his third San Francisco store. Over the ensuing years the company prospered locally, and by the time of his death in 1902, Strauss had become a man of prominence in California. For three decades thereafter the business remained profitable though small, with sales largely confined to the working people of the West— cowboys, lumberjacks, railroad workers, and the like. Levi's jeans were first introduced to the East, apparently, during the dude-ranch craze of the 1930s, when vacationing Easterners returned and spread the word about the wonderful pants with rivets. Another boost came in World War II, when blue jeans were declared an essential commodity and were sold only to people engaged in defense work. From a company with fifteen salespeople, two plants, and almost no business east of the Mississippi in 1946, the organization grew in thirty years to include a sales force of

more than twenty-two thousand, with fifty plants and offices in thirty-five countries. Each year, more than 250,000,000 items of Levi's clothing are sold—including more than 83,000,000 pairs of riveted blue jeans. They have become, through marketing, word of mouth, and demonstrable reliability, the common pants of America. They can be purchased pre-washed, pre-faded, and pre-shrunk for the suitably proletarian look. They adapt themselves to any sort of idiosyncratic use; women slit them at the inseams and convert them into long skirts, men chop them off above the knees and turn them into something to be worn while challenging the surf. Decorations and ornamentations abound.

7   The pants have become a tradition, and along the way have acquired a history of their own—so much so that the company has opened a museum in San Francisco. There was, for example, the turn-of-the-century trainman who replaced a faulty coupling with a pair of jeans; the Wyoming man who used his jeans as a towrope to haul his car out of a ditch; the Californian who found several pairs in an abandoned mine, wore them, then discovered they were sixty-three years old and still as good as new and turned them over to the Smithsonian as a tribute to their toughness. And then there is the particularly terrifying story of the careless construction worker who dangled fifty-two stories above the street until rescued, his sole support the Levi's belt loop through which his rope was hooked.

CHAPTER 22

Exposition: Comparison/Contrast

Columbus and the Moon

Tom Wolfe

Tom Wolfe is a journalist, novelist, and essayist, who often writes about American popular culture. Wolfe received a Ph.D. in American Studies from Yale and spent several years as a newspaper reporter and magazine writer before publishing his first book, The Kandy-Kolored Tangerine-Flake Streamline Baby *in 1964. Some of his other works include* The Electric Kool-Aid Acid Test *(1968),* The Right Stuff *(1979),* The Bonfire of the Vanities *(1985),* Ambush at Fort Bragg *(1996), and* A Man in Full *(1998). This essay was first published in* The New York Times *in 1979.*

1 The National Aeronautics and Space Administration's moon landing 10 years ago today was a Government project, but then so was Columbus's voyage to America in 1492. The Government, in Columbus's case, was the Spanish Court of Ferdinand and Isabella. Spain was engaged in a sea race with Portugal in much the same way that the United States would be caught up in a space race with the Soviet Union four and a half centuries later.

2   The race in 1492 was to create the first shipping lane to Asia. The Portuguese expeditions had always sailed east, around the southern tip of Africa. Columbus decided to head due west, across open ocean, a scheme that was feasible only thanks to a recent invention—the magnetic ship's compass. Until then ships had stayed close to the great land masses even for the longest voyages. Likewise, it was only thanks to an invention of the 1940s and early 1950s, the high-speed electronic computer, that NASA would even consider propelling astronauts out of the Earth's orbit and toward the moon.

3   But NASA and Columbus made not one but a series of voyages. NASA landed men on six different parts of the moon. Columbus made four voyages to different parts of what he remained convinced was the east coast of Asia. As a result both NASA and Columbus had to keep coming back to the Government with their hands out, pleading for refinancing. In each case the reply of the Government became, after a few years: "This is all very impressive, but what earthly good is it to anyone back home?"

4   Columbus was reduced to making the most desperate claims. When he first reached land in 1492 at San Salvador, off Cuba, he expected to find gold, or at least spices. The Arawak Indians were awed by the strangers and their ships, which they believed had descended from the sky, and they presented them with their most prized possessions, live parrots and balls of cotton. Columbus soon set them digging for gold, which didn't exist. So he brought back reports of fabulous riches in the form of manpower; which is to say, slaves. He was not speaking of the Arawaks, however. With the exception of criminals and prisoners of war, he was supposed to civilize all natives and convert them to Christianity. He was talking about the Carib Indians, who were cannibals and therefore qualified as criminals. The Caribs would fight down to the last unbroken bone rather than endure captivity, and few ever survived the voyages back to Spain. By the end of Columbus's second voyage, in 1496, the Government was becoming testy. A great deal of wealth was going into voyages to Asia, and very little was coming back. Columbus made his men swear to return to Spain saying that they had not only reached the Asian mainland, they had heard Japanese spoken.

5   Likewise by the early 1970s, it was clear that the moon was in economic terms pretty much what it looked like from Earth, a gray rock. NASA, in the quest for appropriations, was reduced to publicizing the "spinoffs" of the space program. These included Teflon-coated frying pans, a ballpoint pen that would write in a weightless environment, and a computerized biosensor system that would enable doctors to treat heart patients without making house calls. On the whole, not a giant step for mankind.

6   In 1493, after his first voyage, Columbus had ridden through Barcelona on the side of King Ferdinand in the position once occupied by

Ferdinand's late son, Juan. By 1500, the bad-mouthing of Columbus had reached the point where he was put in chains at the conclusion of his third voyage and returned to Spain in disgrace. NASA suffered no such ignominy, of course, but by July 20, 1974, the fifth anniversary of the landing of Apollo 11, things were grim enough. The public had become gloriously bored by space exploration. The fifth anniversary celebration consisted mainly of about 200 souls, mostly NASA people, sitting on folding chairs underneath a camp meeting canopy on the marble prairie outside the old Smithsonian Air Museum in Washington listening to speeches by Neil Armstrong, Michael Collins, and Buzz Aldrin and watching the caloric waves ripple.

7   Extraordinary rumors had begun to circulate about the astronauts. The most lurid said that trips to the moon, and even into earth orbit, had so traumatized the men, they had fallen victim to religious and spiritualist manias or plain madness. (Of the total 73 astronauts chosen, one, Aldrin, is known to have suffered from depression, rooted, as his own memoir makes clear, in matters that had nothing to do with space flight. Two teamed up in an evangelical organization, and one set up a foundation for the scientific study of psychic phenomena—interests the three of them had developed long before they flew in space.) The NASA budget, meanwhile, had been reduced to the light-bill level.

8   Columbus died in 1509, nearly broke and stripped of most of his honors as Spain's Admiral of the Ocean, a title he preferred. It was only later that history began to look upon him not as an adventurer who had tried and failed to bring home gold—but as a man with a supernatural sense of destiny, whose true glory was his willingness to plunge into the unknown, including the remotest parts of the universe he could hope to reach.

9   NASA still lives, albeit in reduced circumstances, and whether or not history will treat NASA like the admiral is hard to say.

10   The idea that the exploration of the rest of the universe is its own reward is not very popular, and NASA is forced to keep talking about things such as bigger communications satellites that will enable live television transmission of European soccer games at a fraction of the current cost. Such notions as "building a bridge to the stars for mankind" do not light up the sky today—but may yet.

My Real Car

Bailey White

Georgia-born Bailey White has published stories and essays in many magazines, but she is perhaps best known as a story teller on National Public Radio. Her essays and sketches have been collected in Mama Makes Up Her Mind and Other Dangers of

Southern Living *(1993) and* Sleeping at the Starlight Motel *(1995); her first novel is* Quite a Year for Plums *(1998). This selection was originally published in the* Smithsonian *magazine in 1991.*

1   It really makes you feel your age when you get a letter from your insurance agent telling you that the car you bought, only slightly used, the year you got out of college is now an antique. "Beginning with your next payment, your premiums will reflect this change in classification," the letter said.

2   I went out and looked at the car. I thought back over the years. I could almost her my uncle's disapproving voice. "You should never buy a used car," he had told me the day I brought it home. Ten years later I drove that used car to his funeral. I drove my sister to the hospital in that car to have her first baby, and I drove to Atlanta in that car when the baby graduated from Georgia Tech with a degree in physics.

3   "When are you going to get a new car?" my friends asked me.

4   "I don't need a new car," I said. "This car runs fine."

5   I changed the oil often, and I kept good tires on it. It always got me where I wanted to go. But the stuffing came out of the backseat and the springs poked through, and the dashboard disintegrated. At 300,000 miles the odometer quit turning, but I didn't really care to know how far I had driven. A hole wore in the floor where my heel rested in front of the accelerator, and the insulation all peeled off the fire wall. "Old piece of junk," my friends whispered. The seat-belt catch finally wore out, and I tied on a huge bronze hook with a fireman's knot.

6   Then one day on my way to work, the car coughed, sputtered and stopped. "This is it," I thought, and I gave it a pat. "It's been a good car."

7   The mechanic laughed at me. "You know what's wrong with that car?" he asked. "That car is out of gas." So I slopped some gas in the tank and drove ten more years.

8   The fuel gauge never worked again after that, but I got to where I could tell when the gas was low by the smell. I think it was the smell of the bottom of the tank. There was also a little smell of brake fluid, a little smell of exhaust, a little smell of oil and, after all the years, a little smell of me. Car smells.

9   And sounds. The wonderful sound when the engine finally catches on a cold day, and an ominous *tick tick* in July when the radiatior is working too hard. The windshield wipers said "Gracie Allen Gracie Allen Gracie Allen." I didn't like a lot of conversation in the car, because I had to keep listening for a little skip that meant I needed to jump out and adjust the carburetor. I kept a screwdriver close at hand, and a pint of brake fluid

and a new rotor, just in case. "She's strange," my friends whispered. "And she drives so slow."

10   I don't know how fast I drove. The speedometer had quit working years ago. But when I would look down through the hole in the floor and see the pavement, a gray blur, whizzing by just inches away from my feet, and feel the tremendous heat from the internal-combustion engine pouring back through the fire wall into my lap, and hear each barely contained explosion, just as a heart attack victim is able to hear her own heartbeat, it didn't feel like slow to me. A whiff of brake fluid would remind me just what a tiny thing I was relying on to stop myself from hurtling along the surface of the Earth at an unnatural speed. When I arrived at my destination, I would slump back, unfasten the seat-belt hook with trembling hands and stagger out. I would gather up my things and give the car a last look. "Thank you, sir," I would say. "We got here one more time."

11   But after I received that letter I began thinking about buying a new car. I read the newspaper every night. Finally I found one that sounded good. It was the same make as my car, but almost new. "Call Steve," the ad said. I went to see the car. It was parked in Steve's driveway. It was a fashionable wheat color. There was carpet on the floor and the seats were covered with soft, velvety-feeling stuff. It smelled like acrylic, and vinyl, and Steve. I turned a knob. Mozart's Concerto for Flute and Harp poured out of four speakers. "But how can you listen to the engine with music playing?" I asked Steve.

12   I turned the key. The car started instantly. I fastened my seat belt. Nothing but a click. Steve got in the passenger seat, and we went for a test drive. We floated down the road. I couldn't hear a sound, but I decided it must be time to shift gears. I stomped around on the floor and grabbed Steve's knee before I remembered the car had automatic transmission.

13   "You mean you just put it in 'Drive' and drive?" I asked. Steve scrunched himself against his door and clamped his knees together. He tested his seat belt. "Have you ever driven before?" he asked.

14   I bought it. I rolled all the windows up by mashing a button beside my elbow, set the air-conditioning on "Recirc" and listened to Vivaldi all the way home.

15   So now I have two cars. I call them my new car and my real car. Most of the time I drive my new car. But on some days I go out to the barn and get in my real car. I shoo the rats out of the backseat and crank up the engine. Even without daily practice my hands and feet know just what to do. My ears perk up, and I sniff the air. I add a little brake fluid, a little water. I sniff again. It'll need gas next week, and an oil change. I back it out and we roll down the road. People stop and look. They smile. "Neat car!" they say.

Life in a Bundle of Letters

Ellen Goodman

Ellen Goodman has written for Newsweek, *the* Detroit Free Press, *and the* Boston Globe. *Her popular newspaper column, "At Large," has been syndicated since 1976. She has won praise as a radio and television commentator, and in 1980 she won the Pulitzer Prize for distinguished commentary. Her essays have been collected in* Close to Home *(1979),* At Large *(1980),* Keeping in Touch *(1985),* Making Sense *(1989), and* Value Judgments *(1993). The following essay was first published in 1985.*

1   Somewhere, in the boxes that I have moved from one address to another, are small packages of summers past. Letters from my parents. Letters from school friends. Love letters. Private history wrapped neatly in rubber bands.

2   Most of them are, by now, more than 20 summers old. The datelines remind me of camp, college, trips. They also remind me of my father's humor, the rhythms of my mother's daily life, the code words of adolescent friendships—S.W.A.K., sealed with a kiss—the intimacy of the young.

3   My friends, my family and I rarely mail our thoughts anymore. The mailman brings more catalogues than correspondence to our homes. The letters that come through our mail slot are mostly addressed in robotype. The stamps we buy are to go on bills.

4   We direct-dial now. Spoiled by the instant gratification and the ease of the phone, we talk. The telephone call has replaced the letter in our lives nearly as completely as the car has replaced the cart.

5   When we were kids, I remember, long distance was reserved for announcements. The operator was almost an evil omen. If we had called from camp or campus our parents would have answered the phone with "What's wrong?" Today, our own children, the products of Sesame Street numbers and telephone-company technology, have grown up knowing area codes before they knew addition. They bounce intercontinental calls off satellites . . . just to say "Hello."

6   I am not railing against this progress. A Frequent Dialer with the bills to prove it, I often choose the give and take, the immediacy of the phone. I accept charges from children with an uneconomical glee. A friend and I, separated by hundreds of miles, have declared our phone bills "cheaper than therapy." It's good to hear a voice. But it isn't the same.

7   Sometimes I think that the telephone call is as earthbound as daily dialogue, while a letter is an exchange of gifts. On the telephone you talk; in a letter you tell. There is a pace to letter writing and reading that doesn't come from the telephone company but from our own inner rhythm.

8   We live mostly in the high-tech, reach-out-and-touch-someone modern world. Communication is an industry. It makes demands of us. We are expected to respond as quickly as computers. A voice asks a question across the ocean in a split second and we are supposed to formulate an answer at this high-speed rate of exchange.

9   But we cannot, blessedly, "interface" by mail. There is leisure and emotional luxury in letter-writing. There are no obvious silences to anxiously fill. There are no interruptions to brook. There are no nuances and tones of voice to distract.

10   A letter doesn't take us by surprise in the middle of dinner, or intrude when we are with other people, or ambush us in the midst of other thoughts. It waits. There is a private space between the give and the take for thinking.

11   I have known lovers, parents and children, husbands and wives, who send each other letters from one room to another simply for the chance to complete a story of events, thoughts, feelings. I have known people who could not "hear" what they could read.

12   There is this advantage to slowing down the pace of communications. The phone demands a kind of simultaneous satisfaction that is as elusive in words as in sex. It's letters that let us take turns, let us sit and mull and say exactly what we mean.

13   Today we are supposed to travel light, to live in the moment. The past is, we are told, excess baggage. There is no question that the phone is the tool of these times. As fine and as ephemeral as a good meal.

14   But you cannot hold a call in your hands. You cannot put it in a bundle. You cannot show it to your family. Indeed there is nothing to show for it. It doesn't leave a trace. Tell me, how can you wrap a lifetime of phone calls in a rubber band for a summer's night when you want to remember?

CHAPTER

23

Exposition: Definition

The Heroes Among Us

Stephen M. Wolf

Stephen M. Wolf has been the Chairman and Chief Executive Officer of U.S. Airways Group, Inc., since 1996. Previously, he was the chairman and CEO of United Airlines. This essay was first published in Hemispheres *magazine in 1993.*

1   Especially in today's world, our children need heroes. And we need to help them discover the kind of people who show us through their lives that the world is better than the headlines make us believe. Somewhere along the way, we seem to have confused celebrities with heroes. So we can hardly blame our children when the people they most admire do not live a life that is, as Webster defines it, "noted for courageous acts or nobility of purpose."

2   Historian Daniel Boorstin made the distinction between the hero and the celebrity clearly. "The hero was distinguished by his achievement; the celebrity by his image or trademark," he wrote. "The hero created himself; the celebrity is created by the media. The hero was a big man; the celebrity is a big name." Too often, the media manufactures celebrities and packages them as

heroes. We learn little of their contributions to society and more than we need to about their fashions or love affairs. That is not to say some celebrities are not heroes. In fact, more than a few athletes, actors, and artists have broken barriers and dedicated themselves to important humanitarian causes. Unfortunately, those actions command less attention than the latest scandal.

3   Television distorts reality and, in the process, obscures fundamental values. Children are often shown that wealth and beauty are the keys to happiness. They do not see people working hard for that wealth because that does not make for an exciting broadcast. And they rarely see programs featuring those whose beauty goes much deeper than the surface. Such programming offers children a world of shallow values, instant gratification, and quick fixes, with heroes who are always attractive and never work for what they have or want.

4   Instead of allowing children simply to focus on television or the movies in their search for heroes, we should encourage them to look closer to home. Extraordinary acts of courage and selflessness abound in communities everywhere. These stories deserve more than a few sentences buried in the back of Saturday's newspaper. Local heroes make up the fiber of a community's life; they provide its vitality, its strength. These people struggle to make their neighborhoods better places to live, to teach children after others have given up, to ensure the safety of those in violence-plagued communities.

5   I read an interesting article in *The Seattle Times,* about true heroes, individuals whom columnist Dale Turner described as people who "do not moan about how bad the world is, but they work for the good it was intended to be. They lift our society and do not lean upon it. Instead of cursing their genes, their parents, their circumstances or their luck, they buck the negatives and assume responsibility for their own lives and try to be helpful in the lives of others." Whether it is a teacher, a firefighter, a social worker, or an entrepreneur who fits that description, their courage and "nobility of purpose" is much more real—and important for children to see—than any celluloid cowboy or special effect could ever be.

6   We have the power and the means to expose more heroes and to address their human failures candidly, without dissecting every last flaw. No one is perfect, no matter how much we might wish them to be. Perhaps this is the most important lesson taught by the men and women who are true heroes. They show us how to be people of courage despite the odds, and to be people of grace, kindness, and nobility despite our humanity.

Excerpt from *Slouching Towards Bethlehem*

Joan Didion

Joan Didion is a novelist and a screen writer, but she is perhaps best known for her insightful essays on American culture and values. Her novels include Play It As It Lays *(1971),* A Book of Common Prayer *(1977),* Democracy *(1984), and* The Last Thing He Wanted *(1996). Her nonfiction collections include* Slouching Towards Bethlehem *(1968), from which this selection is taken,* The White Album *(1979),* Salvador *(1983),* Miami *(1987), and* After Henry *(1992).*

1   There is something uneasy in the Los Angeles air this afternoon, some unnatural stillness, some tension. What it means is that tonight a Santa Ana will begin to blow, a hot wind from the northeast whining down through the Cajon and San Gorgonio Passes, blowing up sandstorms out along Route 66, drying the hills and the nerves to the flash point. For a few days now we will see smoke back in the canyons, and hear sirens in the night. I have neither heard nor read that a Santa Ana is due, but I know it, and almost everyone I have seen today knows it too. We know it because we feel it. The baby frets. The maid sulks. I rekindle a waning argument with the telephone company, then cut my losses and lie down, given over to whatever it is in the air. To live with the Santa Ana is to accept, consciously or unconsciously, a deeply mechanistic view of human behavior.

2   I recall being told, when I first moved to Los Angeles and was living on an isolated beach, that the Indians would throw themselves into the sea when the bad wind blew. I could see why. The Pacific turned ominously glossy during a Santa Ana period, and one woke in the night troubled not only by the peacocks screaming in the olive trees but by the eerie absence of surf. The heat was surreal. The sky had a yellow cast, the kind of light sometimes called "earthquake weather." My only neighbor would not come out of her house for days, and there were no lights at night, and her husband roamed the place with a machete. One day he would tell me that he had heard a trespasser, the next a rattlesnake.

3   "On nights like that," Raymond Chandler once wrote about the Santa Ana, "every booze party ends in a fight. Meek little wives feel the edge of the carving knife and study their husbands' necks. Anything can happen." That was the kind of wind it was. I did not know then that there was any basis for the effect it had on all of us, but it turns out to be another of those cases in which science bears out folk wisdom. The Santa Ana, which is named for one of the canyons it rushes through, is a *foehn* wind, like the *foehn* of Austria and Switzerland and the *hamsin* of Israel. There are a number of persistent malevolent winds, perhaps the best known of which are the mistral of France and the Mediterranean sirocco, but a *foehn* wind has distinct characteristics: it occurs on the leeward slope of

a mountain range and, although the air begins as a cold mass, it is warmed as it comes down the mountain and appears finally as a hot dry wind. Whenever and wherever a *foehn* blows, doctors hear about headaches and nausea and allergies, about "nervousness," about "depression." In Los Angeles some teachers do not attempt to conduct formal classes during a Santa Ana, because the children become unmanageable. In Switzerland the suicide rate goes up during the *foehn*, and in the courts of some Swiss cantons the wind is considered a mitigating circumstance for crime. Surgeons are said to watch the wind, because blood does not clot normally during a *foehn*. A few years ago an Israeli physicist discovered that not only during such winds, but for the ten or twelve hours which precede them, the air carries an unusually high ratio of positive to negative ions. No one seems to know exactly why that should be; some talk about friction and others suggest solar disturbances. In any case the positive ions are there, and what an excess of positive ions does, in the simplest terms, is make people unhappy. One cannot get much more mechanistic than that.

4   Easterns commonly complain that there is no "weather" at all in Southern California, that the days and the seasons slip by relentlessly, numbingly bland. That is quite misleading. In fact the climate is characterized by infrequent but violent extremes: two periods of torrential subtropical rains which continue for weeks and wash out the hills and send subdivisions sliding toward the sea; about twenty scattered days a year of the Santa Ana, which, with its incendiary dryness, invariably means fire. At the first prediction of a Santa Ana, the Forest Service flies men and equipment from northern California into the southern forests, and the Los Angeles Fire Department cancels its ordinary nonfirefighting routines. The Santa Ana caused Malibu to burn the way it did in 1956, and Bel Air in 1961, and Santa Barbara in 1964. In the winter of 1966–67 eleven men were killed fighting a Santa Ana fire that spread through the San Gabriel Mountains.

5   Just to watch the front-page news out of Los Angeles during a Santa Ana is to get very close to what it is about the place. The longest single Santa Ana period in recent years was in 1957, and it lasted not the usual three or four days but fourteen days, from November 21 until December 4. On the first day 25,000 acres of the San Gabriel Mountains were burning, with gusts reaching 100 miles an hour. In town, the wind reached Force 12, or hurricane force, on the Beaufort Scale; oil derricks were toppled and people ordered off the downtown streets to avoid injury from flying objects. On November 22 the fire in the San Gabriels was out of control. On November 24 six people were killed in automobile accidents, and by the end of the week the Los Angeles *Times* was keeping a box score of traffic deaths. On November 26 a prominent Pasadena attorney, depressed about money, shot and killed his wife, their two sons, and himself. On November 27 a South Gate divorcee, twenty-two, was murdered

and thrown from a moving car. On November 30 the San Gabriel fire was still out of control, and the wind in town was blowing eighty miles an hour. On the first day of December four people died violently, and on the third the wind began to break.

6   It is hard for people who have not lived in Los Angeles to realize how radically the Santa Ana figures in the local imagination. The city burning is Los Angeles's deepest image of itself: Nathanael West perceived that, in *The Day of the Locust;* and at the time of the 1965 Watts riots what struck the imagination most indelibly were the fires. For days one could drive the Harbor Freeway and see the city on fire, just as we had always known it would be in the end. Los Angeles weather is the weather of catastrophe, of apocalypse, and, just as the reliably long and bitter winters of New England determine the way life is lived there, so the violence and the unpredictability of the Santa Ana affect the entire quality of life in Los Angeles, accentuate its impermanence, its unreliability. The wind shows us how close to the edge we are.

What Is Poverty?

Jo Goodwin Parker

When George Henderson, a professor at the University of Oklahoma, was writing his 1971 book, America's Other Children: Public Schools Outside Suburbia, *he received the following essay in the mail. It was signed "Jo Goodwin Parker" and had been mailed from West Virginia. No further information was ever discovered about the essay or its source. Whether the author of this essay was in reality a woman describing her own painful experiences or a sympathetic writer who had adopted her persona, Jo Goodwin Parker remains a mystery.*

1   You ask me what is poverty? Listen to me. Here I am, dirty, smelly, and with no "proper" underwear on and with the stench of my rotting teeth near you. I will tell you. Listen to me. Listen without pity. I cannot use your pity. Listen with understanding. Put yourself in my dirty, worn out, ill-fitting shoes, and hear me.

2   Poverty is getting up every morning from a dirt- and illness-stained mattress. The sheets have long since been used for diapers. Poverty is living with a smell that never leaves. This is a smell of urine, sour milk, and spoiling food sometimes joined with the strong smell of long-cooked onions. Onions are cheap. If you have smelled this smell, you did not know how it came. It is the smell of the outdoor privy. It is the smell of young children who cannot walk the long dark way in the night. It is the smell of the mattresses where years of "accidents" have happened. It is the smell of the milk which has gone sour because the refrigerator long has not worked, and it costs money to get it fixed. It is the smell of rotting garbage. I could bury it, but where is the shovel? Shovels cost money.

3   Poverty is being tired. I have always been tired. They told me at the hospital when the last baby came that I had chronic anemia caused from poor diet, a bad case of worms, and that I needed a corrective operation. I listened politely—the poor are always polite. The poor always listen. They don't say that there is no money for iron pills, or better food, or worm medicine. The idea of an operation is frightening and costs so much that, if I had dared, I would have laughed. Who takes care of my children? Recovery from an operation takes a long time. I have three children. When I left them with "Granny" the last time I had a job, I came home to find the baby covered with fly specks, and a diaper that had not been changed since I left. When the dried diaper came off, bits of my baby's flesh came with it. My other child was playing with a sharp bit of broken glass, and my oldest was playing alone at the edge of a lake. I made twenty-two dollars a week, and a good nursery school costs twenty dollars a week for three children. I quit my job.

4   Poverty is dirt. You say in your clean clothes coming from your clean house, "Anybody can be clean." Let me explain about housekeeping with no money. For breakfast I give my children grits with no oleo or cornbread without eggs and oleo. This does not use up many dishes. What dishes there are, I wash in cold water and with no soap. Even the cheapest soap has to be saved for the baby's diapers. Look at my hands, so cracked and red. Once I saved for two months to buy a jar of Vaseline for my hands and the baby's diaper rash. When I had saved enough, I went to buy it and the price had gone up two cents. The baby and I suffered on. I have to decide every day if I can bear to put my cracked, sore hands into the cold water and strong soap. But you ask, why not hot water? Fuel costs money. If you have a wood fire it costs money. If you burn electricity, it costs money. Hot water is a luxury. I do not have luxuries. I know you will be surprised when I tell you how young I am. I look so much older. My back has been bent over the wash tubs for so long, I cannot remember when I ever did anything else. Every night I wash every stitch my school age child has on and just hope her clothes will be dry by morning.

5   Poverty is staying up all night on cold nights to watch the fire, knowing one spark on the newspaper covering the walls means your sleeping children die in flames. In summer poverty is watching gnats and flies devour your baby's tears when he cries. The screens are torn and you pay so little rent you know they will never be fixed. Poverty means insects in your food, in your nose, in your eyes, and crawling over you when you sleep. Poverty is hoping it never rains because diapers won't dry when it rains and soon you are using newspapers. Poverty is seeing your children forever with runny noses. Paper handkerchiefs cost money and all your rags you need for other things. Even more costly are antihistamines. Poverty is cooking without food and cleaning without soap.

6   Poverty is asking for help. Have you ever had to ask for help, knowing your children will suffer unless you get it? Think about asking for a loan

from a relative, if this is the only way you can imagine asking for help. I will tell you how it feels. You find out where the office is that you are supposed to visit. You circle that block four or five times. Thinking of your children, you go in. Everyone is very busy. Finally, someone comes out and you tell her that you need help. That never is the person you need to see. You go see another person, and after spilling the whole shame of your poverty all over the desk between you, you find that this isn't the right office after all—you must repeat the whole process, and it never is any easier at the next place.

7   You have asked for help, and after all it has a cost. You are again told to wait. You are told why, but you don't really hear because of the red cloud of shame and the rising black cloud of despair.

8   Poverty is remembering. It is remembering quitting school in junior high because "nice" children had been so cruel about my clothes and my smell. The attendance officer came. My mother told him I was pregnant. I wasn't but she thought that I could get a job and help out. I had jobs off and on, but never long enough to learn anything. Mostly I remember being married. I was so young then. I am still young. For a time, we had all the things you have. There was a little house in another town, with hot water and everything. Then my husband lost his job. There was unemployment insurance for a while and what few jobs I could get. Soon, all our nice things were repossessed and we moved back here. I was pregnant then. This house didn't look so bad when we first moved in. Every week it gets worse. Nothing is ever fixed. We now had no money. There were a few odd jobs for my husband, but everything went for food then, as it does now. I don't know how we lived through three years and three babies, but we did. I'll tell you something, after the last baby I destroyed my marriage. It had been a good one, but could you keep on bringing children in this dirt? Did you ever think how much it costs for any kind of birth control? I knew my husband was leaving the day he left, but there were no good-byes between us. I hope he has been able to climb out of this mess somewhere. He never could hope with us to drag him down.

9   That's when I asked for help. When I got it, you know how much it was? It was, and is, seventy-eight dollars a month for the four of us; that is all I ever can get. Now you know why there is no soap, no needles and thread, no hot water, no aspirin, no worm medicine, no hand cream, no shampoo. None of these things forever and ever and ever. So that you can see clearly, I pay twenty dollars a month rent, and most of the rest goes for food. For grits and cornmeal, and rice and milk and beans. I try my best to use only the minimum electricity. If I use more, there is that much less for food.

10   Poverty is looking into a black future. Your children won't play with my boys. They will turn to other boys who steal to get what they want. I can already see them behind the bars of their prison instead of behind the bars of my poverty. Or they will turn to the freedom of alcohol or

drugs, and find themselves enslaved. And my daughter? At best, there is for her a life like mine.

11   But you say to me, there are schools. Yes, there are schools. My children have no extra books, no magazines, no extra pencils, or crayons, or paper and the most important of all, they do not have health. They have worms, they have infections, they have pinkeye all summer. They do not sleep well on the floor, or with me in my one bed. They do not suffer from hunger, my seventy-eight dollars keeps us alive, but they do suffer from malnutrition. Oh yes, I do remember what I was taught about health in school. It doesn't do much good. In some places there is a surplus commodities program. Not here. The county said it cost too much. There is a school lunch program. But I have two children who will already be damaged by the time they get to school.

12   But, you say to me, there are health clinics. Yes, there are health clinics and they are in the towns. I live out here eight miles from town. I can walk that far (even if it is sixteen miles both ways), but can my little children? My neighbor will take me when he goes; but he expects to get paid, *one way or another.* I bet you know my neighbor. He is that large man who spends his time at the gas station, the barbershop, and the corner store complaining about the government spending money on the immoral mothers of illegitimate children.

13   Poverty is an acid that drips on pride until all pride is worn away. Poverty is a chisel that chips on honor until honor is worn away. Some of you say that you would do *something* in my situation, and maybe you would, for the first week or the first month, but for year after year after year?

14   Even the poor can dream. A dream of a time when there is money. Money for the right kinds of food, for worm medicine, for iron pills, for toothbrushes, for hand cream, for a hammer and nails and a bit of screening, for a shovel, for a bit of paint, for some sheeting, for needles and thread. Money to pay *in money* for a trip to town. And, oh, money for hot water and money for soap. A dream of when asking for help does not eat away the last bit of pride. When the office you visit is as nice as the offices of other governmental agencies, when there are enough workers to help you quickly, when workers do not quit in defeat and despair. When you have to tell your story to only one person, and that person can send you for other help and you don't have to prove your poverty over and over and over again.

15   I have come out of my despair to tell you this. Remember I did not come from another place or another time. Others like me are all around you. Look at us with an angry heart, anger that will help you help me. Anger that will let you tell of me. The poor are always silent. Can you be silent too?

CHAPTER 24

Exposition: Division/Classification

A Brush with Reality: Surprises in the Tube

David Bodanis

David Bodanis did his undergraduate and graduate work in math, biology, and genetics at the University of Chicago before becoming a journalist. His four books, offering his readers revealing insights into their bodies and homes, include The Body Book: A Fantastic Voyage to the World Within *(1984);* The Secret Garden: Dawn to Dusk in the Astonishing Hidden World of the Garden *(1992);* The Secret Family: Twenty-four Hours Inside the Mysterious World of Our Minds and Bodies *(1997); and* The Secret House *(1986), from which this excerpt is taken.*

1 Into the bathroom goes our male resident, and after the most pressing need is satisfied it's time to brush the teeth. The tube of toothpaste is squeezed, its pinched metal seams are splayed, pressure waves are generated inside, and the paste begins to flow. But what's in this toothpaste, so carefully being extruded out?

2 Water mostly, 30 to 45 percent in most brands: ordinary, everyday simple tap water. It's there because people like to have a big

gob of toothpaste to spread on the brush, and water is the cheapest stuff there is when it comes to making big gobs. Dripping a bit from the tap onto your brush would cost virtually nothing; whipped in with the rest of the toothpaste the manufacturers can sell it at a neat and accountant-pleasing $2 per pound equivalent. Toothpaste manufacture is a very lucrative occupation.

3   Second to water in quantity is chalk: exactly the same material that schoolteachers use to write on blackboards. It is collected from the crushed remains of long-dead ocean creatures. In the Cretaceous seas chalk particles served as part of the wickedly sharp outer skeleton that these creatures had to wrap around themselves to keep from getting chomped by all the slightly larger other ocean creatures they met. Their massed graves are our present chalk deposits.

4   The individual chalk particles—the size of the smallest mud particles in your garden—have kept their toughness over the aeons, and now on the toothbrush they'll need it. The enamel outer coating of the tooth they'll have to face is the hardest substance in the body—tougher than skull, or bone, or nail. Only the chalk particles in toothpaste can successfully grind into the teeth during brushing, ripping off the surface layers like an abrading wheel grinding down a boulder in a quarry.

5   The craters, slashes, and channels that the chalk tears into the teeth will also remove a certain amount of build-up yellow in the carnage, and it is for that polishing function that it's there. A certain amount of unduly enlarged extra-abrasive chalk fragments tear such cavernous pits into the teeth that future decay bacteria will be able to bunker down there and thrive; the quality control people find it almost impossible to screen out these errant super-chalk pieces, and government regulations allow them to stay in.

6   In case even the gouging doesn't get all the yellow off, another substance is worked into the toothpaste cream. This is titanium dioxide. It comes in tiny spheres, and it's the stuff bobbing around in white wall paint to make it come out white. Splashed around onto your teeth during the brushing it coats much of the yellow that remains. Being water soluble it leaks off in the next few hours and is swallowed, but at least for the quick glance up in the mirror after finishing it will make the user think his teeth are truly white. Some manufacturers add optical whitening dyes—the stuff more commonly found in washing machine bleach—to make extra sure that that glance in the mirror shows reassuring white.

7   These ingredients alone would not make a very attractive concoction. They would stick in the tube like a sloppy white plastic lump, hard to squeeze out as well as revolting to the touch. Few consumers would savor rubbing in a mixture of water, ground-up blackboard chalk, and the whitener from latex paint first thing in the morning. To get around

that finicky distaste the manufacturers have mixed in a host of other goodies.

8   To keep the glop from drying out, a mixture including glycerine glycol—related to the most common car antifreeze ingredient—is whipped in with the chalk and water, and to give *that* concoction a bit of substance (all we really have so far is wet colored chalk) a large helping is added of gummy molecules from the seaweed *Chondrus Crispus*. This seaweed ooze spreads in among the chalk, paint, and antifreeze, then stretches itself in all directions to hold the whole mass together. A bit of paraffin oil (the fuel that flickers in camping lamps) is pumped in with it to help the moss ooze keep the whole substance smooth.

9   With the glycol, ooze, and paraffin we're almost there. Only two major chemicals are left to make the refreshing, cleansing substance we know as toothpaste. The ingredients so far are fine for cleaning, but they wouldn't make much of the satisfying foam we have come to expect in the morning brushing.

10   To remedy that, every toothpaste on the market has a big dollop of detergent added too. You've seen the suds detergent will make in a washing machine. The same substance added here will duplicate that inside the mouth. It's not particularly necessary, but it sells.

11   The only problem is that by itself this ingredient tastes, well, too like detergent. It's horribly bitter and harsh. The chalk put in toothpaste is pretty foul-tasting too for that matter. It's to get around that gustatory discomfort that the manufacturers put in the ingredient they tout perhaps the most of all. This is the flavoring, and it has to be strong. Double rectified peppermint oil is used—a flavorer so powerful that chemists know better than to sniff it in the raw state in the laboratory. Menthol crystals and saccharin or other sugar simulators are added to complete the camouflage operation.

12   Is that it? Chalk, water, paint, seaweed, antifreeze, paraffin oil, detergent, and peppermint? Not quite. A mix like that would be irresistible to the hundreds of thousands of individual bacteria lying on the surface of even an immaculately cleaned bathroom sink. They would get in, float in the water bubbles, ingest the ooze and paraffin, maybe even spray out enzymes to break down the chalk. The result would be an uninviting mess. The way manufacturers avoid that final obstacle is by putting something in to kill the bacteria. Something good and strong is needed, something that will zap any accidentally intrudant bacteria into oblivion. And that something is formaldehyde—the disinfectant used in anatomy labs.

13   So it's chalk, water, paint, seaweed, antifreeze, paraffin oil, detergent, peppermint, formaldehyde, and fluoride (which can go some way towards preserving children's teeth)—that's the usual mixture raised to the mouth on the toothbrush for a fresh morning's clean. If it sounds too

unfortunate, take heart. Studies show that thorough brushing with just plain water will often do as good a job.

Party Manners

Richard Grossman

Richard Grossman has served as director of the Center for Health in Medicine at Montefiore Hospital and Medical Center in the Bronx, New York, and has been a contributing editor to Family Health *magazine. He is the author of* Choosing and Changing: A Guide to Self-Reliance *(1978),* Natural First Aid *(1981),* Other Medicines *(1985),* Fear at Work *(1990),* The Alphabet Man *(1993), and* The Book of Lazarus *(1997). This 1983 article first appeared in* Health, *in Grossman's column called "Richard's Almanac."*

1   The Romans had their Colosseum, the Elizabethans their village promenades and their Globe Theater. For centuries the French and Germans had their spectacular court balls. Queens and Presidents have their state dinners, complete with chamber music. And we ordinary moderns? We have *parties.*

2   From college "mixers" to suburban cocktail "standarounds," from children's ice-cream splattered birthday celebrations to retirement dinners, from political fund-raisers to bridal showers, the party has become as ubiquitous an institution as the Internal Revenue Service. And familiar though it is, the party has a psychologically transforming effect on many of us. Somehow our attendance at a gathering called a "party" causes us to behave in ways we never do elsewhere, as though we were players in a drama meant to reveal some of the hidden parts of our personalities. The party setting seems to provide a license to unveil attitudes that we would never display at the office or the family dinner table. And though party behavior may not be a reliable guide to all our psychological tics, it is nevertheless a place to see how we "go public" with some of our unresolved problems. Consider this cast of characters, for example:

The Cartoonist

3   Here's the person who has no other arena in his life in which to be a vocal social critic, who sees every party as an opportunity to be the local Andy Rooney. No dancing or merrymaking for this one, but rather a steady stream of mini-lectures on the foibles and deficiencies of all the other guests. The Cartoonist is someone who does not want to be part of the crowd, but needs to keep his distance and act the reporting observer, drawing verbal caricatures of "them" as though he were sending communiqués back to Mars on the tribal rituals of the "Earthlings." What's really going on, of course, is that the fear of spontaneity and the

relaxation of conventions is just too threatening, so the only safe stance is to play the part of the uninvolved expert.

The Spotter

4   This character is the familiar shopper for greener pastures. She is talking to you, but is looking over your shoulder the whole time, ever alert to someone just a little more interesting or a little more important who may be on the other side of the room. This person is usually the inside-dopester, the one who craves the latest information, who drops the trendiest names, who goes to the hottest events. The Spotter has the attention span of an alcoholic mayfly and cannot wait to move on, fearful that she is missing out on something better. The usual result, of course, is that she has a terrible time at parties and can't understand why all those other folks are laughing.

The Performer

5   He's often known as "the life of the party" and is the one for whom every party is the high school play in which he didn't get a part. Parties for this type are only an opportunity to grab the spotlight that he wants desperately but is being denied elsewhere. There are variations, of course: The Practical Joker, The Bathroom Comedian, The Barroom Baritone, The Poor Man's Rich Little*—but all are revealing only one sad fact: They are yearning for notoriety and attention.

The Wallflower

6   Here you have the reverse image of The Performer: The person who gains attention by a silent, martyred withdrawal from the center of the party. Sooner or later, someone will spot her standing in a corner with a rueful smile on her face, just waiting to be asked if something is wrong. If you should inquire, you'll hear that she "just isn't good in crowds," or "hates all that noise," or "never could learn to disco." Do not be deceived into thinking that you've discovered an authentically shy or lonely person. This routine is simply a device to get attention with a passive strategy. (The *really* shy one didn't come to the party.)

The Swashbuckler

7   Also known as "The Last of the Big Benders," this is a person who may be in real trouble. Something has gone drastically wrong somewhere in his life, and he is frightened or even desperate about the outcome. If he is not working on the problem in another corner of life or getting the help he really needs, then the only place for that terrified energy to go is into uncharacteristically heavy drinking and raucous, high-pitched haranguing. There are usually very real and troubling issues underlying

---

* A comedian known for his impersonation of famous celebrities.

this kind of behavior, and the party can, unfortunately, provide a convenient setting for acting out.

The Scarlet Pimpernel

8   She's the person who sees every party invitation as an opportunity to project her romantic fantasy. Feeling frustrated by a humdrum, uneventful existence, such a person mentally writes out a script for Meryl Streep or Julie Christie and goes off to the party prepared to try out the new role, altering the voice to sound sultry or provocative, speaking in cryptic or poetic language, gliding around the room like a visitor from the Court of St. James. Sometimes this is just playfulness or harmless flirtatiousness, but usually the pseudo-romantic is simply saying through her behavior that the rest of her life is dull and gray, and needs spicing up.

9   Now, a certain amount of nervousness and unease about going to a party is clearly normal, and it would be simple-minded to claim that even the types described above are necessarily displaying secret pathology. But if parties regularly call up odd or extraordinary behavior in you, or become a theater for exposing subterranean needs, it might be a good idea to look at the usual, non-partying areas of your life and see what's troubling you. Some parties are boring, to be sure, and a dose of silly, unplanned frolicking may liven them up. But we should remember that parties are usually designed as a means to gather in a friendly, open, genuine way; as a chance to enjoy the warmth and closeness of other human beings. If those are not reasons enough for going, if we need parties to ventilate other feelings, perhaps we should consider group therapy instead.

College Pressures

William Zinsser

As a faculty member at Yale, William Zinsser designed and taught the first course in nonfiction writing offered at that University. Drawing on his experiences as a freelance writer and as a teacher, he has written On Writing Well: An Informal Guide to Writing Nonfiction *(1976),* Writing with a Word Processor *(1982), and* Writing to Learn: How to Write and Think Clearly About Any Subject at All *(1988). He is also the editor of a series of books that offer advice to writers of biography, children's literature, religion, and travel. The most recent of these is* Inventing the Truth: The Art and Craft of Memoir *(1998). This essay was originally published in* Country Journal *in 1979.*

1   *Dear Carlos: I desperately need a dean's excuse for my chem midterm which will begin in about 1 hour. All I can say is that I totally blew it this week. I've fallen incredibly, inconceivably behind.*

2   *Carlos: Help! I'm anxious to hear from you. I'll be in my room and won't leave it until I hear from you. Tomorrow is the last day for . . .*

3   *Carlos: I left town because I started bugging out again. I stayed up all night to finish a take home make-up exam & am typing it to hand in on the 10th. It was due on the 5th. P.S. I'm going to the dentist. Pain is pretty bad.*

4   *Carlos: Probably by Friday I'll be able to get back to my studies. Right now I'm going to take a long walk. This whole thing has taken a lot out of me.*

5   *Carlos: I'm really up the proverbial creek. The problem is I really bombed the history final. Since I need that course for my major . . .*

6   *Carlos: Here follows a tale of woe. I went home this weekend, had to help my Mom, & caught a fever so didn't have much time to study. My professor . . .*

7   *Carlos: Aargh! Nothing original but everything's piling up at once. To be brief, my job interview . . .*

8   *Hey Carlos, good news! I've got mononucleosis.*

9   Who are these wretched supplicants, scribbling notes so laden with anxiety, seeking such miracles of postponement and balm? They are men and women who belong to Branford College, one of the twelve residential colleges at Yale University, and the messages are just a few of the hundreds that they left for their dean, Carlos Hortas—often slipped under his door at 4 A.M.—last year.

10   But students like the ones who wrote those notes can also be found on campuses from coast to coast—especially in New England and at many other private colleges across the country that have high academic standards and highly motivated students. Nobody could doubt that the notes are real. In their urgency and their gallows humor they are authentic voices of a generation that is panicky to succeed.

11   My own connection with the message writers is that I am master of Branford College. I live in its Gothic quadrangle and know the students well. (We have 485 of them.) I am privy to their hopes and fears—and also to their stereo music and their piercing cries in the dead of night ("Does anybody *ca-a-are?*"). If they went to Carlos to ask how to get through tomorrow, they come to me to ask how to get through the rest of their lives.

12   Mainly I try to remind them that the road ahead is a long one and that it will have more unexpected turns than they think. There will be plenty of time to change jobs, change careers, change whole attitudes and approaches. They don't want to hear such liberating news. They want a map—right now—that they can follow unswervingly to career security, financial security, Social Security and, presumably, a prepaid grave.

13   What I wish for all students is some release from the clammy grip of the future. I wish them a chance to savor each segment of their education as an experience in itself and not as a grim preparation for the next step. I wish them the right to experiment, to trip and fall, to learn that defeat is as instructive as victory and is not the end of the world.

14   My wish, of course, is naive. One of the few rights that America does not proclaim is the right to fail. Achievement is the national god, venerated in our media—the million-dollar athlete, the wealthy executive— and glorified in our praise of possessions. In the presence of such a potent state religion, the young are growing up old.

15   I see four kinds of pressure working on college students today: economic pressure, parental pressure, peer pressure, and self-induced pressure. It is easy to look around for villains—to blame the colleges for charging too much money, the professors for assigning too much work, the parents for pushing their children too far, the students for driving themselves too hard. But there are no villains; only victims.

16   "In the late 1960s," one dean told me, "the typical question that I got from students was 'Why is there so much suffering in the world?' or 'How can I make a contribution?' Today it's 'Do you think it would look better for getting into law school if I did a double major in history and political science, or just majored in one of them?'" Many other deans confirmed this pattern. One said "They're trying to find an edge—the intangible something that will look better on paper if two students are about equal."

17   Note the emphasis on looking better. The transcript has become a sacred document, the passport to security. How one appears on paper is more important than how one appears in person. *A* is for Admirable and *B* is for Borderline, even though, in Yale's official system of grading, *A* means "excellent" and *B* means "very good." Today, looking very good is no longer good enough, especially for students who hope to go on to law school or medical school. They know that entrance into the better schools will be an entrance into the better law firms and better medical practices where they will make a lot of money. They also know that the odds are harsh. Yale Law School, for instance, matriculates 170 students from an applicant pool of 3,700; Harvard enrolls 550 from a pool of 7,000.

18   It's all very well for those of us who write letters of recommendation for our students to stress the qualities of humanity that will make them good lawyers or doctors. And it's nice to think that admission officers are really reading our letters and looking for the extra dimension of commitment or concern. Still, it would be hard for a student not to visualize these officers shuffling so many transcripts studded with *A*s that they regard a *B* as positively shameful.

19   The pressure is almost as heavy on students who just want to graduate and get a job. Long gone are the days of the "gentleman's C," when students journeyed through college with a certain relaxation, sampling a

wide variety of courses—music, art, philosophy, classics, anthropology, poetry, religion—that would send them out as liberally educated men and women. If I were an employer I would rather employ graduates who have this range and curiosity than those who narrowly pursued safe subjects and high grades. I know countless students whose inquiring minds exhilarate me. I like to hear the play of their ideas. I don't know if they are getting *As* or *Cs,* and I don't care. I also like them as people. The country needs them, and they will find satisfying jobs. I tell them to relax. They can't.

20   Nor can I blame them. They live in a brutal economy. Tuition, room, and board at most private colleges now comes to at least $7,000, not counting books and fees. This might seem to suggest that the colleges are getting rich. But they are equally battered by inflation. Tuition covers only 60 percent of what it costs to educate a student, and ordinarily the remainder comes from what colleges receive in endowments, grants, and gifts. Now the remainder keeps being swallowed by the cruel costs—higher every year—of just opening the doors. Heating oil is up. Insurance is up. Postage is up. Health-premium costs are up. Everything is up. Deficits are up. We are witnessing in America the creation of a brotherhood of paupers—colleges, parents, and students, joined by the common bond of debt.

21   Today it is not unusual for a student, even if he works part time at college and full time during the summer, to accrue $5,000 in loans after four years—loans that he must start to repay within one year after graduation. Exhorted at commencement to go forth into the world, he is already behind as he goes forth. How could he not feel under pressure throughout college to prepare for this day of reckoning? I have used "he," incidentally, only for brevity. Women at Yale are under no less pressure to justify their expensive education to themselves, their parents, and society. In fact, they are probably under more pressure. For although they leave college superbly equipped to bring fresh leadership to traditionally male jobs, society hasn't yet caught up with this fact.

22   Along with economic pressure goes parental pressure. Inevitably, the two are deeply intertwined.

23   I see many students taking pre-medical courses with joyless tenacity. They go off to their labs as if they were going to the dentist. It saddens me because I know them in other corners of their life as cheerful people.

24   "Do you want to go to medical school?" I ask them.

25   "I guess so," they say, without conviction, or "Not really."

26   "Then why are you going?"

27   "Well, my parents want me to be a doctor. They're paying all this money and . . ."

28   Poor students, poor parents. They are caught in one of the oldest webs of love and duty and guilt. The parents mean well: they are trying

to steer their sons and daughters toward a secure future. But the sons and daughters want to major in history or classics or philosophy—subjects with no "practical" value. Where's the payoff on the humanities? It's not easy to persuade such loving parents that the humanities do indeed pay off. The intellectual faculties developed by studying subjects like history and classics—an ability to synthesize and relate, to weigh cause and effect, to see events in perspective—are just the faculties that make creative leaders in business or almost any general field. Still, many fathers would rather put their money on courses that point toward a specific profession—courses that are pre-law, pre-medical, pre-business, or, as I sometimes heard it put, "pre-rich."

29   But the pressure on students is severe. They are truly torn. One part of them feels obligated to fulfill their parents' expectations; after all, their parents are older and presumably wiser. Another part tells them that the expectations that are right for their parents are not right for them.

30   I know a student who wants to be an artist. She is very obviously an artist and will be a good one—she has already had several modest local exhibits. Meanwhile she is growing as a well-rounded person and taking humanistic subjects that will enrich the inner resources out of which her art will grow. But her father is strongly opposed. He thinks that an artist is a "dumb" thing to be. The student vacillates and tries to please everybody. She keeps up with her art somewhat furtively and takes some of the "dumb" courses her father wants her to take—at least they are dumb courses for her. She is a free spirit on a campus of tense students—no small achievement in itself—and she deserves to follow her muse.

31   Peer pressure and self-induced pressure are also intertwined, and they begin almost at the beginning of freshman year.

32   "I had a freshman student I'll call Linda," one dean told me, "who came in and said she was under terrible pressure because her roommate, Barbara, was much brighter and studied all the time. I couldn't tell her that Barbara had come in two hours earlier to say the same thing about Linda."

33   The story is almost funny—except that it's not. It's symptomatic of all the pressures put together. When every student thinks every other student is working harder and doing better, the only solution is to study harder still. I see students going off to the library every night after dinner and coming back when it closes at midnight. I wish they could sometimes forget about their peers and go to a movie. I hear the clacking of typewriters in the hours before dawn. I see the tension in their eyes when exams are approaching and papers are due: *"Will I get everything done?"*

34   Probably they won't. They will get sick. They will get "blocked." They will sleep. They will oversleep. They will bug out. *Hey Carlos, help!*

35   Part of the problem is that they do more than they are expected to do. A professor will assign five-page papers. Several students will start

writing ten-page papers to impress him. Then more students will write ten-page papers, and a few will raise the ante to fifteen. Pity the poor student who is still just doing the assignment.

36 "Once you have twenty or thirty percent of the student population deliberately overexerting," one dean points out, "it's bad for everybody. When a teacher gets more and more effort from his class, the student who is doing normal work can be perceived as not doing well. The tactic works, psychologically."

37 Why can't the professor just cut back and not accept longer papers? He can, and he probably will. But by then the term will be half over and the damage done. Grade fever is highly contagious and not easily reversed. Besides, the professor's main concern is with his course. He knows his students only in relation to the course and doesn't know that they are also overexerting in their other courses. Nor is it really his business. He didn't sign up for dealing with the student as a whole person and with all the emotional baggage the student brought along from home. That's what deans, masters, chaplains, and psychiatrists are for.

38 To some extent this is nothing new: a certain number of professors have always been self-contained islands of scholarship and shyness, more comfortable with books than with people. But the new pauperism has widened the gap still further, for professors who actually like to spend time with students don't have as much time to spend. They also are overexerting. If they are young, they are busy trying to publish in order not to perish, hanging by their fingernails onto a shrinking profession. If they are old and tenured, they are buried under the duties of administering departments—as departmental chairmen or members of committees—that have been thinned out by the budgetary axe.

39 Ultimately it will be the students' own business to break the circles in which they are trapped. They are too young to be prisoners of their parents' dreams and their classmates' fears. They must be jolted into believing in themselves as unique men and women who have the power to shape their own future.

40 "Violence is being done to the undergraduate experience," says Carlos Hortas. "College should be open-ended: at the end it should open many, many roads. Instead, students are choosing their goal in advance, and their choices narrow as they go along. It's almost as if they think that the country has been codified in the type of jobs that exist—that they've got to fit into certain slots. Therefore, fit into the best-paying slot.

41 "They ought to take chances. Not taking chances will lead to a life of colorless mediocrity. They'll be comfortable. But something in the spirit will be missing."

42 I have painted too drab a portrait of today's students, making them seem a solemn lot. That is only half of their story; if they were so dreary I wouldn't so thoroughly enjoy their company. The other half is that they

are easy to like. They are quick to laugh and to offer friendship. They are not introverts. They are usually kind and are more considerate of one another than any student generation I have known.

43 Nor are they so obsessed with their studies that they avoid sports and extracurricular activities. On the contrary, they juggle their crowded hours to play on a variety of teams, perform with musical and dramatic groups, and write for campus publications. But this in turn is one more cause of anxiety. There are too many choices. Academically, they have 1,300 courses to select from; outside class they have to decide how much spare time they can spare and how to spend it.

44 This means that they engage in fewer extracurricular pursuits than their predecessors did. If they want to row on the crew and play in the symphony they will eliminate one; in the '60s they would have done both. They also tend to choose activities that are self-limiting. Drama, for instance, is flourishing in all twelve of Yale's residential colleges as it never has before. Students hurl themselves into these productions—as actors, directors, carpenters, and technicians—with a dedication to create the best possible play, knowing that the day will come when the run will end and they can get back to their studies.

45 They also can't afford to be the willing slave of organizations like the *Yale Daily News.* Last spring at the one-hundredth anniversary banquet of that paper—whose past chairmen include such once and future kings as Potter Stewart, Kingman Brewster, and William F. Buckley, Jr.—much was made of the fact that the editorial staff used to be small and totally committed and that "newsies" routinely worked fifty hours a week. In effect they belonged to a club; newsies is how they defined themselves at Yale. Today's student will write one or two articles a week, when he can, and he defines himself as a student. I've never heard the word newsie except at the banquet.

46 If I have described the modern undergraduate primarily as a driven creature who is largely ignoring the blithe spirit inside who keeps trying to come out and play, it's because that's where the crunch is, not only at Yale but throughout American education. It's why I think we should all be worried about the values that are nurturing a generation so fearful of risk and so goal-obsessed at such an early age.

47 I tell students that there is no one "right" way to get ahead—that each of them is a different person, starting from a different point and bound for a different destination. I tell them that change is a tonic and that all the slots are not codified nor the frontiers closed. One of my ways of telling them is to invite men and women who have achieved success outside the academic world to come and talk informally with my students during the year. They are heads of companies or ad agencies, editors of magazines, politicians, public officials, television magnates, labor leaders, business

executives, Broadway producers, artists, writers, economists, photographers, scientists, historians—a mixed bag of achievers.

48   I ask them to say a few words about how they got started. The students assume that they started in their present profession and knew all along that it was what they wanted to do. Luckily for me, most of them got into their field by a circuitous route, to their surprise, after many detours. The students are startled. They can hardly conceive of a career that was not pre-planned. They can hardly imagine allowing the hand of God or chance to nudge them down some unforeseen trail.

CHAPTER

25

Exposition:
Causal Analysis

Kids in the Mall

William Severini Kowinski

William Severini Kowinski is a writer of poetry, fiction, and nonfiction. He has published articles in a number of magazines, such as Esquire, New Times, *and* The New York Times Magazine. *This selection is taken from his book-length study,* The Malling of America: An Inside Look at the Great Consumer Paradise *(1985), which investigates the effects of shopping malls on the lives of modern Americans.*

1 From his sister at Swarthmore, I'd heard about a kid in Florida whose mother picked him up after school every day, drove him straight to the mall, and left him there until it closed—all at his insistence. I'd heard about a boy in Washington who, when his family moved from one suburb to another, pedaled his bicycle five miles every day to get back to his old mall, where he once belonged.

2   These stories aren't unusual. The mall is a common experience for the majority of American youth; they have probably been going there all their lives. Some ran within their first large open space, saw their first

fountain, bought their first toy, and read their first book in a mall. They may have smoked their first cigarette or first joint or turned them down, had their first kiss or lost their virginity in the mall parking lot. Teenagers in America now spend more time in the mall than anywhere else but home and school. Mostly it is their choice, but some of that mall time is put in as the result of two-paycheck and single-parent households, and the lack of other viable alternatives. But are these kids being harmed by the mall?

3   I wondered first of all what difference it makes for adolescents to experience so many important moments in the mall. They are, after all, at play in the fields of its little world and they learn its ways; they adapt to it and make it adapt to them. It's here that these kids get their street sense, only it's mall sense. They are learning the ways of a large-scale artificial environment: its subtleties and flexibilities, its particular pleasures and resonances, and the attitudes it fosters.

4   The presence of so many teenagers for so much time was not something mall developers planned on. In fact, it came as a big surprise. But kids became a fact of mall life very early, and the International Council of Shopping Centers found it necessary to commission a study, which they published along with a guide to mall managers on how to handle the teenage incursion.

5   The study found that "teenagers in suburban centers are bored and come to the shopping centers mainly as a place to go. Teenagers in suburban centers spent more time fighting, drinking, littering, and walking than did their urban counterparts, but presented fewer overall problems." The report observed that "adolescents congregated in groups of two to four and predominantly at locations selected by them rather than management." This probably had something to do with the decision to install game arcades, which allow management to channel these restless adolescents into naturally contained areas away from major traffic points of adult shoppers.

6   The guide concluded that mall management should tolerate and even encourage the teenage presence because, in the words of the report, "The vast majority support the same set of values as does shopping center management." *The same set of values* means simply that mall kids are already preprogrammed to be consumers and that the mall can put the finishing touches to them as hard-core, lifelong shoppers just like everybody else. That, after all, is what the mall is about. So it shouldn't be surprising that in spending a lot of time there, adolescents find little that challenges the assumption that the goal of life is to make money and buy products, or that just about everything else in life is to be used to serve those ends.

7   Growing up in a high-consumption society already adds inestimable pressure to kids' lives. Clothes consciousness has invaded the grade

schools, and popularity is linked with having the best, newest clothes in the currently acceptable styles. Even what they read has been affected. "Miss [Nancy] Drew wasn't obsessed with her wardrobe," noted *The Wall Street Journal.* "But today the mystery in teen fiction for girls is what outfit the heroine will wear next." Shopping has become a survival skill and there is certainly no better place to learn it than the mall, where its importance is powerfully reinforced and certainly never questioned.

8   The mall as a university of suburban materialism, where Valley Girls and Boys from coast to coast are educated in consumption, has its other lessons in this era of change in family life and sexual mores and their economic and social ramifications. The plethora of products in the mall, plus the pressure on teens to buy them, may contribute to the phenomenon that psychologist David Elkin calls "the hurried child": kids who are exposed to too much of the adult world too quickly, and must respond with a sophistication that belies their still-tender emotional development. Certainly the adult products marketed for children—formfitting designer jeans, sexy tops for preteen girls—add to the social pressure to look like an adult, along with the homegrown need to understand adult finances (why mothers must work) and adult emotions (when parents divorce).

9   Kids spend so much time at the mall partly because their parents allow it and even encourage it. The mall is safe, it doesn't seem to harbor any unsavory activities, and there is adult supervision; it is, after all, a controlled environment. So the temptation, especially for working parents, is to let the mall be their babysitter. At least the kids aren't watching TV. But the mall's role as a surrogate mother may be more extensive and more profound.

10   Karen Lansky, a writer living in Los Angeles, has looked into the subject and she told me some of her conclusions about the effects on its teenaged denizens of the mall's controlled and controlling environment. "Structure is the dominant idea, since true 'mall rats' lack just that in their home lives," she said, "and adolescents about to make the big leap into growing up crave more structure than our modern society cares to acknowledge." Karen pointed out some of the elements malls supply that kids used to get from their families, like warmth (Strawberry Shortcake dolls and similar cute and cuddly merchandise), old-fashioned mothering ("We do it all for you," the fast-food slogan), and even home cooking (the "homemade" treats at the food court).

11   The problem in all this, as Karen Lansky sees it, is that while families nurture children by encouraging growth through the assumption of responsibility and then by letting them rest in the bosom of the family from the rigors of growing up, the mall as a structural mother encourages passivity and consumption, as long as the kid doesn't make trouble. Therefore all they learn about becoming adults is how to act and how to consume.

12   Kids are in the mall not only in the passive role of shoppers—they also work there, especially as fast-food outlets infiltrate the mall's enclosure. There they learn how to hold a job and take responsibility, but still within the same value context. When *CBS Reports* went to Oak Park Mall in suburban Kansas City, Kansas, to tape part of their hour-long consideration of malls, "After the Dream Comes True," they interviewed a teenaged girl who worked in a fast-food outlet there. In a sequence that didn't make the final program, she described the major goal of her present life, which was to perfect the curl on top of the ice-cream cones that were her store's specialty. If she could do that, she would be moved from the lowly soft-drink dispenser to the more prestigious ice-cream division, the curl on top of the status ladder at her restaurant. These are the achievements that are important at the mall.

13   Other benefits of such jobs may also be overrated, according to Laurence D. Steinberg of the University of California at Irvine's social ecology department, who did a study on teenage employment. Their jobs, he found, are generally simple, mindlessly repetitive, and boring. They don't really learn anything, and the jobs don't lead anywhere. Teenagers also work primarily with other teenagers; even their supervisors are often just a little older than they are. "Kids need to spend time with adults," Steinberg told me. "Although they get benefits from peer relationships, without parents and other adults it's one-sided socialization. They hang out with each other, have age-segregated jobs, and watch TV."

14   Perhaps much of this is not so terrible or even so terribly different. Now that they have so much more to contend with in their lives, adolescents probably need more time to spend with other adolescents without adult impositions, just to sort things out. Though it is more concentrated in the mall (and therefore perhaps a clearer target), the value system there is really the dominant one of the whole society. Attitudes about curiosity, initiative, self-expression, empathy, and disinterested learning aren't necessarily made in the mall; they are mirrored there, perhaps a bit more intensely—as through a glass brightly.

15   Besides, the mall is not without its educational opportunities. There are bookstores, where there is at least a short shelf of classics at great prices, and other books from which it is possible to learn more than how to do sit-ups. There are tools, from hammers to VCRs, and products, from clothes to records, that can help the young find and express themselves. There are older people with stories, and places to be alone or to talk one-on-one with a kindred spirit. And there is always the passing show.

16   The mall itself may very well be an education about the future. I was struck with the realization, as early as my first forays into Greengate [Mall], that the mall is only one of a number of enclosed and controlled environments that are part of the lives of today's young. The mall is just

an extension, say of those large suburban schools—only there's Karmelkorn instead of chem lab, the ice rink instead of the gym: It's high school without the impertinence of classes.

17   Growing up, moving from home to school to the mall—from enclosure to enclosure, transported in cars—is a curiously continuous process, without much in the way of contrast or contact with unenclosed reality. Places must tend to blur into one another. But whatever differences and dangers there are in this, the skills these adolescents are learning may turn out to be useful in their later lives. For we seem to be moving inexorably into an age of preplanned and regulated environments, and this is the world they will inherit.

18   Still, it might be better if they had more of a choice. One teenaged girl confessed to *CBS Reports* that she sometimes felt she was missing something by hanging out at the mall so much. "But I'm here," she said, "and this is what I have."

The Best Years of My Life
Betty Rollin

Betty Rollin is a journalist and editor who has worked on both television and magazines such as Look *and* Vogue. *Her best-known book is* First, You Cry *(1976), a personal account of her fight against breast cancer. Other books include* Last Wish *(1985) and* Unheeded Cry *(1990). This essay was first published in* The New York Times Magazine *in 1980.*

1   I am about to celebrate an anniversary. Not that there will be a party with funny hats. Nor do I expect any greetings in the mail. Hallmark, with its infinite variety of occasions about which to fashion a 50-cent card, has skipped this one. This, you see, is my cancer anniversary. Five years ago tomorrow, at Beth Israel Hospital in New York City, a malignant tumor was removed from my left breast and, along with the tumor, my left breast. To be alive five years later means something in cancer circles. There is nothing intrinsically magical about the figure five, but the numbers show that if you have survived that many years after cancer has been diagnosed, you have an 80 percent shot at living out a normal life span.

2   Still, you probably think Hallmark is right not to sell a card, and that it's weird to "celebrate" such a terrible thing as cancer. It's even weirder than you imagine. Because not only do I feel good about (probably) having escaped a recurrence of cancer, I also feel good about having gotten cancer in the first place. Here is the paradox: although cancer was the worst thing that ever happened to me, it was also the best. Cancer (the kind I had, with no spread and no need of chemotherapy, with its often

harrowing side effects) enriched my life, made me wiser, made me happier. Another paradox: although I would do everything possible to avoid getting cancer again, I am glad I had it.

3   There is a theory about people who have had a life-and-death scare that goes something like this: for about six months after surviving the scare, you feel shaken and grateful. Armed with a keen sense of what was almost The End, you begin to live your life differently. You pause during the race to notice the foliage, you pay more attention to the people you love—maybe you even move to Vermont. You have gained, as they say, a "new perspective." But then, according to this theory, when the six months are over, the "introperspective" fades, you sell the house in Vermont and go back to the same craziness that was your life before the car crash or whatever it was. What has happened is that you've stopped feeling afraid. The crash is in the past. The it-can't-happen-to-me feelings that were dashed by the accident re-emerge after six months, as it-can't-happen-to-me-*again*.

4   It's different for people whose crash is cancer. You can stay off the freeways, but you can't do much about preventing whatever went wrong in your own body from going wrong again. Unless your head is buried deep in the sand, you know damn well it *can* happen again. Even though, in my case the doctors say it isn't likely, the possibility of recurrence is very real to me. Passing the five-year mark is reassuring, but I know I will be a little bit afraid for the rest of my life. But—ready for another paradox?—certain poisons are medicinal in small doses. To be a little bit afraid of dying can do wonders for your life. It has done wonders for mine. That's because, unlike the way many people feel, my sense of death is not an intellectual concept. It's a lively presence in my gut. It affects me daily—for the better.

5   First, when you're even slightly afraid of death, you're less afraid of other things—e.g., bosses, spouses, plumbers, rape, bankruptcy, failure, not being liked, the flu, aging. Next to the Grim Reaper, how ferocious can even the most ferocious boss be? How dire the direst household calamity? In my own professional life, I have lost not only some big fears, but most of the small ones. I used to be nervous in front of television cameras. That kind of nervousness was a fear of not being thought attractive, smart and winning. It still pleases me greatly if someone besides my husband and mother thinks I'm attractive, smart and winning; but I am no longer afraid that someone won't. Cancer made me less worried about what people think of me, both professionally and socially. I am less concerned about where my career is going. I don't know where it's going. I don't think about that. I think about where I am and what I'm doing and whether I like it. The result is that these days I continually seem to be doing what I like. And probably I'm more successful than when I aimed to please.

6   My book *First, You Cry,* which has given me more pleasure than any-thing else in my professional life, is a good example of this. As a career move, leaving television for six months to write a book about a cancer op-eration seemed less than sensible. But as soon as I got cancer, I stopped being "sensible." I wanted to write the book. And, just in case I croaked, I wanted to write it the way that was right for me, not necessarily for the market. So I turned down the publisher who wanted it to be a "how-to" book. I like to think I would have done that, cancer or not, but had it not been for cancer, I probably wouldn't have written a book at all, because I would have been too afraid to drop out of television even for six months. And if I had written a book, I doubt that I would have been so open about my life and honest about my less-than-heroic feelings. But, as I wrote, I remember thinking, "I might die, so what does it matter what anyone thinks of me?" A lot of people write honestly and openly without having had a disease, but I don't think I would have. I hadn't done it before.

7   A touch of cancer turns you into a hypochondriac. You get a sore throat and you think you've got cancer of the throat; you get a corn from a pair of shoes that are too tight and you're sure it's a malignant tumor. But—here's the bright side—cancer hypochondria is so compelling it never occurs to you that you could get anything *else.* And, when you do, you're so glad it's not cancer that you feel like celebrating. "Goody, it's the flu!" I heard myself say to myself a couple of weeks ago.

8   Some physicians are more sensitive than others to cancer anxiety. My gynecologist prattled on once about some menstrual irregularity without noticing that, as he spoke, I had turned to stone. "Is it cancer?" I finally whispered. He looked dumbfounded and said, "Of course not!" As if to say, "How could you think such a thing?" But an orthopedist I saw about a knee problem took an X-ray and, before saying a word about what it was (a torn cartilage), told me what it wasn't. I limped home joyously.

9   I never went to Vermont because I can't stand that much fresh air; but in my own fashion, I sop up pleasure where and when I can, some-times at the risk of professional advancement and sometimes at the risk of bankruptcy. An exaggeration, perhaps, but there's no question about it: since cancer, I spend more money than I used to. (True, I have more to spend, but that's mostly because of the book, which is also thanks to cancer.) I had always been parsimonious—some would say cheap—and I'm not anymore. The thinking is, "Just in case I do get a recurrence, won't I feel like a fool for having flown coach to Seattle?" (I like to think I'm more generous with others as well. It seems to me that, since having cancer, I give better presents.)

10   Cancer kills guilt. You not only take a vacation now because next year you might be dead, but you take a *better* vacation because, even if you don't die soon, after what you've been through, you feel you de-serve it. In my own case, I wouldn't have expected that feeling to

survive six months because, once those months passed, I realized that, compared to some people, I had not been through much at all. But my hedonism continues to flourish. Maybe it was just a question of changing a habit.

11   My girlish masochism didn't resurface, either. Most women I know go through at least a phase of needing punishment from men. Not physical punishment, just all the rest: indifference, harshness, coldness, rudeness or some neat combination. In the past, my own appetite for this sort of treatment was voracious. Conversely, if I happened to connect with a man who was nice to me, I felt like that song: "This can't be love because I feel so well." The difference was that, in the song, it really *was* love, and with me, it really *wasn't.* Only when I was miserable did I know I really cared.

12   The minute I got cancer, my taste in men improved. It's not that my first husband was a beast. I'm fond of him, but even he would admit he was very hard on me. Maybe I asked for it. Well, once you've been deftly kicked in the pants by God (or whoever distributes cancer), you stop wanting kicks from mortals. Everyone who knows the man I married a year ago thinks I'm lucky—even my mother!—and I do, too. But I know it wasn't only luck. It was that cancer made me want someone wonderful. I wasn't ready for him before. I was so struck by this apparent change in me that I checked it out with a psychoanalyst, who assured me that I was not imagining things—that the damage to my body had, indeed, done wonders for my head.

13   Happiness is probably something that shouldn't be talked about too much, but I can't help it. Anyway, I find the more I carry on about it, the better it gets. A big part of happiness is noticing it. It's trite to say, but if you've never been ill, you don't notice—or enjoy—not being ill. I even notice my husband's good health. (He doesn't, but how could he?)

14   I haven't mentioned losing that breast, have I? That's because, in spite of the fuss I made about it five years ago, that loss now seems almost not worth mentioning. Five years ago, I felt sorry for myself that I could no longer keep a strapless dress up. Today I feel that losing a breast saved my life, and wasn't I lucky. And when I think of all the other good things that have come from that loss, I just look at that flat place on my body and think: small price.

15   Most of my friends who are past 40 shudder on their birthdays. Not me. They feel a year closer to death, I suppose. I feel a year further from it.

16   O.K., what if I get a recurrence? I'm not so jolly all the time that I haven't given this some serious thought. If it happens, I'm sure I won't be a good sport about it—especially if my life is cut short. But even if it is, I will look back at the years since the surgery and know I got the best from them. And I will be forced to admit that the disease that is ending my life is the very thing that made it so good.

The Teacher Who Changed My Life

Nicholas Gage

Born in Greece in 1939, journalist and author Nicholas Gage is best known for Eleni *(1983), the story of his mother's life and execution in 1948 during the Greek civil war. The story of this murder and Gage's subsequent search for her killers was made into a well-received movie in 1985. The story of Gage's family,* A Place for Us: Eleni's Children in America *(1989), contains a version of the following essay, which also appeared in* Parade Magazine.

1   The person who set the course of my life in the new land I entered as a young war refugee—who, in fact, nearly dragged me onto the path that would bring all the blessings I've received in America—was a salty-tongued, no-nonsense schoolteacher named Marjorie Hurd. When I entered her classroom in 1953, I had been to six schools in five years, starting in the Greek village where I was born in 1939.

2   When I stepped off a ship in New York Harbor on a gray March day in 1949, I was an undersized nine-year-old in short pants who had lost his mother and was coming to live with the father he didn't know. My mother, Eleni Gatzoyiannis, had been imprisoned, tortured, and shot by Communist guerrillas for sending me and three of my four sisters to freedom. She died so that her children could go to their father in the United States.

3   The portly, bald, well-dressed man who met me and my sisters seemed a foreign, authoritarian figure. I secretly resented him for not getting the whole family out of Greece early enough to save my mother. Ultimately, I would grow to love him and appreciate how he dealt with becoming a single parent at the age of fifty-six, but at first our relationship was prickly, full of hostility.

4   As Father drove us to our new home—a tenement in Worcester, Mass.—and pointed out the huge brick building that would be our first school in America, I clutched my Greek notebooks from the refugee camp, hoping that my few years of schooling would impress my teachers in this cold, crowded country. They didn't. When my father led me and my eleven-year-old sister to Greendale Elementary School, the grim-faced Yankee principal put the two of us in a class for the mentally retarded. There was no facility in those days for non-English-speaking children.

5   By the time I met Marjorie Hurd four years later, I had learned English, been placed in a normal, graded class and had even been chosen for the college preparatory track in the Worcester public school system. I was thirteen years old when our father moved us yet again, and I entered Chandler Junior High shortly after the beginning of seventh grade. I found myself surrounded by richer, smarter, and better-dressed classmates who

looked askance at my strange clothes and heavy accent. Shortly after I arrived, we were told to select a hobby to pursue during "club hour" on Fridays. The idea of hobbies and clubs made no sense to my immigrant ears, but I decided to follow the prettiest girl in my class—the blue-eyed daughter of the local Lutheran minister. She led me through the door marked "Newspaper Club" and into the presence of Miss Hurd, the newspaper adviser and English teacher who would become my mentor and my muse.

6   A formidable, solidly built woman with salt-and-pepper hair, a steely eye, and a flat Boston accent, Miss Hurd had no patience with layabouts. "What are all you goof-offs doing here?" she bellowed at the would-be journalists. "This is the Newspaper Club! We're going to put out a *newspaper.* So if there's anybody in this room who doesn't like work, I suggest you go across to the Glee Club now, because you're going to work your tails off here!"

7   I was soon under Miss Hurd's spell. She did indeed teach us to put out a newspaper, skills I honed during my next twenty-five years as a journalist. Soon I asked the principal to transfer me to her English class as well. There, she drilled us on grammar until I finally began to understand the logic and structure of the English language. She assigned stories for us to read and discuss; not tales of heroes, like the Greek myths I knew, but stories of underdogs—poor people, even immigrants, who seemed ordinary until a crisis drove them to do something extraordinary. She also introduced us to the literary wealth of Greece—giving me a new perspective on my war-ravaged, impoverished homeland. I began to be proud of my origins.

8   One day, after discussing how writers should write about what they know, she assigned us to compose an essay from our own experience. Fixing me with a stern look, she added, "Nick, I want you to write about what happened to your family in Greece." I had been trying to put those painful memories behind me and left the assignment until the last moment. Then, on a warm spring afternoon, I sat in my room with a yellow pad and pencil and stared out the window at the buds on the trees. I wrote that the coming of spring always reminded me of the last time I said goodbye to my mother on a green and gold day in 1948.

9   I kept writing, one line after another, telling how the Communist guerrillas occupied our village, took our home and food, how my mother started planning our escape when she learned that children were to be sent to re-education camps behind the Iron Curtain, and how, at the last moment, she couldn't escape with us because the guerrillas sent her with a group of women to thresh wheat in a distant village. She promised she would try to get away on her own, she told me to be brave and hung a silver cross around my neck, and then she kissed me. I watched the line of women being led down into the ravine and up the other side, until they

disappeared around the bend—my mother a tiny brown figure at the end who stopped for an instant to raise her hand in one last farewell.

10   I wrote about our nighttime escape down the mountain, across the minefields, and into the lines of the Nationalist soldiers, who sent us to a refugee camp. It was there that we learned of our mother's execution. I felt very lucky to have come to America, I concluded, but every year, the coming of spring made me feel sad because it reminded me of the last time I saw my mother.

11   I handed in the essay, hoping never to see it again, but Miss Hurd had it published in the school paper. This mortified me at first, until I saw that my classmates reacted with sympathy and tact to my family's story. Without telling me, Miss Hurd also submitted the essay to a contest sponsored by the Freedoms Foundation at Valley Forge, and it won a medal. The Worcester paper wrote about the award and quoted my essay at length. My father, by then a "five-and-dime-store chef," as the paper described him, was ecstatic with pride, and the Worcester Greek community celebrated the honor to one of its own.

12   For the first time, I began to understand the power of the written word. A secret ambition took root in me. One day, I vowed, I would go back to Greece, find out the details of my mother's death, and write about her life, so her grandchildren would know of her courage. Perhaps I would even track down the men who killed her and write of their crimes. Fulfilling that ambition would take me thirty years.

13   Meanwhile, I followed the literary path that Miss Hurd had so forcefully set me on. After junior high, I became the editor of my school paper at Classical High School and got a part-time job at the Worcester *Telegram and Gazette.* Although my father could only give me $50 and encouragement toward a college education, I managed to finance four years at Boston University with scholarships and part-time jobs in journalism. During my last year of college, an article I wrote about a friend who had died in the Philippines—the first person to lose his life working for the Peace Corps—led to my winning the Hearst Award for College Journalism. And the plaque was given to me in the White House by President John F. Kennedy.

14   For a refugee who had never seen a motorized vehicle or indoor plumbing until he was nine, this was an unimaginable honor. When the Worcester paper ran a picture of me standing next to President Kennedy, my father rushed out to buy a new suit in order to be properly dressed to receive the congratulations of the Worcester Greeks. He clipped out the photograph, had it laminated in plastic, and carried it in his breast pocket for the rest of his life to show everyone he met. I found the much-worn photo in his pocket on the day he died twenty years later.

15   In our isolated Greek village, my mother had bribed a cousin to teach her to read, for girls were not supposed to attend school beyond a certain

age. She had always dreamed of her children receiving an education. She couldn't be there when I graduated from Boston University, but the person who came with my father and shared our joy was my former teacher, Marjorie Hurd. We celebrated not only my bachelor's degree but also the scholarships that paid my way to Columbia's Graduate School of Journalism. There, I met the woman who would eventually become my wife. At our wedding and at the baptisms of our three children, Marjorie Hurd was always there, dancing alongside the Greeks.

16   By then, she was Mrs. Rabidou, for she had married a widower when she was in her early forties. That didn't distract her from her vocation of introducing young minds to English literature, however. She taught for a total of forty-one years and continually would make a "project" of some balky student in whom she spied a spark of potential. Often these were students from the most troubled homes, yet she would alternately bully and charm each one with her own special brand of tough love until the spark caught fire. She retired in 1981 at the age of sixty-two but still avidly follows the lives and careers of former students while overseeing her adult stepchildren and driving her husband on camping trips to New Hampshire.

17   Miss Hurd was one of the first to call me on December 10, 1987, when President Reagan, in his television address after the summit meeting with Gorbachev, told the nation that Eleni Gatzoyiannis's dying cry, "My children!" had helped inspire him to seek an arms agreement "for all the children of the world."

18   "I can't imagine a better monument for your mother," Miss Hurd said with an uncharacteristic catch in her voice.

19   Although a bad hip makes it impossible for her to join in the Greek dancing, Marjorie Hurd Rabidou is still an honored and enthusiastic guest at all our family celebrations, including my fiftieth birthday picnic last summer, where the shish kebab was cooked on spits, clarinets and *bouzoukis* wailed, and costumed dancers led the guests in a serpentine line around our Colonial farmhouse, only twenty minutes from my first home in Worcester.

20   My sisters and I felt an aching void because my father was not there to lead the line, balancing a glass of wine on his head while he danced, the way he did at every celebration during his ninety-two years. But Miss Hurd was there, surveying the scene with quiet satisfaction. Although my parents are gone, her presence was a consolation, because I owe her so much.

21   This is truly the land of opportunity, and I would have enjoyed its bounty even if I hadn't walked into Miss Hurd's classroom in 1953. But she was the one who directed my grief and pain into writing, and if it weren't for her I wouldn't have become an investigative reporter and foreign correspondent, recorded the story of my mother's life and death in

Eleni and now my father's story in *A Place for Us,* which is also a testament to the country that took us in. She was the catalyst that sent me into journalism and indirectly caused all the good things that came after. But Miss Hurd would probably deny this emphatically.

22   A few years ago, I answered the telephone and heard my former teacher's voice telling me, in that won't-take-no-for-an-answer tone of hers, that she had decided I was to write and deliver the eulogy at her funeral. I agreed (she didn't leave me any choice), but that's one assignment I never want to do. I hope, Miss Hurd, that you'll accept this remembrance instead.

CHAPTER
26

Argumentation

PRO/CON ARGUMENT: THE EXTENDED SCHOOL YEAR

U.S. Kids Need More School Time
Ellen Goodman

Ellen Goodman has written for Newsweek, *the* Detroit Free Press, *and the* Boston Globe. *Her popular newspaper column, "At Large," has been syndicated since 1976. She has won praise as a radio and television commentator, and in 1980 she won the Pulitzer Prize for distinguished commentary. Her essays have been collected in* Close to Home *(1979),* At Large *(1980),* Keeping in Touch *(1985),* Making Sense *(1989), and* Value Judgments *(1993). The following essay was published in 1988.*

1 The kids are hanging out. I pass small bands of once-and-future students, on my way to work these mornings. They have become a familiar part of the summer landscape.

2 These kids are not old enough for jobs. Nor are they rich enough for camp. They are school children without school. The calendar called the school year ran out on them a few weeks ago. Once supervised by teachers and principals, they now appear to be in "self care." Like others who fall through the cracks of their parents' makeshift plans—a week with relatives, a day at the playground—they hang out.

3   Passing them is like passing through a time zone. For much of our history, after all, Americans framed the school year around the needs of work and family. In 19th century cities, schools were open seven or eight hours a day, 11 months a year. In rural America, the year was arranged around the growing season. Now, only 3 percent of families follow the agricultural model, but nearly all schools are scheduled as if our children went home early to milk cows and took months off to work the crops. Now, three-quarters of the mothers of school-age children work, but the calendar is written as if they were home waiting for the school bus.

4   The six-hour day, the 180-day school year is regarded as somehow sacrosanct. But when parents work an eight-hour day and a 240-day year, it means something different. It means that many kids go home to empty houses. It means that, in the summer, they hang out.

5   "We have a huge mismatch between the school calendar and the realities of family life," says Dr. Ernest Boyer, head of the Carnegie Foundation for the Advancement of Teaching.

6   Dr. Boyer is one of many who believe that a radical revision of the school calendar is inevitable. "School, whether we like it or not, is custodial and educational. It always has been."

7   His is not a popular idea. Schools are routinely burdened with the job of solving all our social problems. Can they be asked now to synchronize our work and family lives?

8   It may be easier to promote a longer school year on its educational merits and, indeed, the educational case is compelling. Despite the complaints and studies about our kids' lack of learning, the United States still has a shorter school year than any industrial nation. In most of Europe, the school year is 220 days. In Japan, it is 240 days long. While classroom time alone doesn't produce a well-educated child, learning takes time and more learning takes more time. The long summers of forgetting take a toll.

9   The opposition to a longer school year comes from families that want to and can provide other experiences for their children. It comes from teachers. It comes from tradition. And surely from kids. But the crux of the conflict has been over money.

10   But we can, as Boyer suggests, begin to turn the hands of the school clock forward. The first step is to extend an optional after-school program of education and recreation to every district. The second step is a summer program with its own staff, paid for by fees for those who can pay and vouchers for those who can't.

11   The third step will be the hardest: a true overhaul of the school year. Once, school was carefully calibrated to arrange children's schedules around the edges of family needs. Now, working parents, especially mothers, even teachers, try and blend their work lives around the edges of the school day.

12   So it's back to the future. Today there are too many school doors locked and too many kids hanging out. It's time to get our calendars updated.

The School Year Needs to Be Better, Not Longer
Colman McCarthy

Colman McCarthy is a journalist, teacher, social activist, and columnist for The Washington Post. *In 1982 he founded the Center for Teaching Peace, which teaches courses on nonviolence. He is the author of* Involvements: One Journalist's Place in the World *(1984) and* All of One Peace: Essays on Nonviolence *(1994). His work as a volunteer teacher in Maryland high school English classes influenced this essay, which first appeared in* The Washington Post *in 1990.*

1   In eight years of teaching high school students in both private and public schools, I've learned that on the subject of education their ideas are often sounder and their opinions sharper than what's coming from the on-high experts and theorists. Two of them, in particular.

2   Thomas A. Shannon, director of the National School Boards Association, is pushing for a 12-month academic year. No summer idleness, either for students or school buildings. In Massachusetts, Michael Barrett, a state senator, has introduced a bill to extend the school year from 180 to 220 days.

3   Both of these time-savers are fretting that compared with other countries the United States is encouraging laziness and ignorance by its short school year. Students in Japan, West Germany, South Korea, Israel and Luxembourg all have a minimum of 210 calendar days of class. No slackers there.

Longer Year Theory

4   Barrett, as if scratching his fingernails on the blackboard to make us dolts understand, writes in the *Atlantic:*

5   "First, compared with their peers in Asian and European countries, American students stand out for how little they work. Second, compared with Asians and Europeans, American students stand out for how poorly they do." Barrett believes a school year of 220 days is an essential reform—"a superstructure under which other changes can be made."

6   The unsuper arguments from Shannon and Barrett have been regularly thrown into the education hopper since the late 1940s—and just as regularly rejected. The longer-is-better theorists—Barrett spent a day teaching seventh-graders, so his experiential knowledge is vast—are like teachers who begin each class, "Let's get started; we have a lot of

ground to cover." This is the track coach method, substituting pages in a book for yardage.

7   Teachers intent on covering ground won't be any better at their craft with 220 days than at 180. An inspired teacher can change a student's life—rouse the imagination, stir once-hidden powers of the intellect—in a day, week or month. Extra teaching talent, not extra time, is needed.

Keep Students Enthusiastic

8   This theme ran through the papers I asked my students at Bethesda-Chevy Chase High School to write. A young man offered this:

9   "The problem does not lie in the number of days students attend class but in keeping students enthusiastic about learning. . . . Instead of being followers of Japan, South Korea and Taiwan, why doesn't America use its innovative spirit and reconstruct its educational program, not by adding days but by adding stimulation to the classroom."

10   On the issue that the young waste their time in June, July and August, a senior woman wrote: "Nothing is like experiencing life firsthand by spending a few months in nature, in another country, living with another culture or working at an office or in Congress. I learned more about myself this summer when I traveled with the circus than in four years of high school."

11   A third student asked: "If people are so concerned about education, why don't they increase the amount of money available for teacher salaries? It is hard to attract good educators to teach when they earn little money."

More Funding

12   Students are right to resist the call for a longer academic year. They know it means more time in custody, not just in class. The issue is more money, not more schooling. With 70 percent of federal research-and-development funds going into military programs and less than 2 percent to education, the message is obvious: Soldiers are more valued than students, weapons over wisdom.

13   Despite the generosity of a few corporations, private money to schools is niggardly. Robert Reich reports in the winter 1991 issue of *The American Prospect* that corporate largess is seldom showered upon public primary or secondary schools: "Of the $2.6 billion contributed to education in 1989, only $156 million went to support the public schools (about 6 percent); the rest went to colleges and universities (especially the nation's most prestigious, which the firms' CEOs were likely to have attended), and to private preparatory schools (ditto)." Public schools received only 1.8 percent of all corporate donations.

14   Calls for a longer school year are like parents lengthening the time for the family's dinner. If there's little or nothing to eat, why bother?

Schools are famished for money. I've never had a student who didn't know that.

How about Low-Cost Drugs for Addicts?

Louis Nizer

Louis Nizer was an attorney, perhaps best known for defending country humorist John Henry Faulk in a case that defeated the practice of "blacklisting" radio, television, and movie stars during the Communist witch-hunts of the McCarthy Era in the 1950s. He was the author of nine books about his life as a trial lawyer, including My Life In Court *(1983). This article was written as an editorial for* The New York Times *in 1986.*

1   We are losing the war against drug addiction. Our strategy is wrong. I propose a different approach.

2   The Government should create clinics, manned by psychiatrists, that would provide drugs for nominal charges or even free to addicts under controlled regulations. It would cost the Government only 20 cents for a heroin shot, for which the addicts must now pay the mob more than $100, and there are similar price discrepancies in cocaine, crack and other such substances.

3   Such a service, which would also include the staff support of psychiatrists and doctors, would cost a fraction of what the nation now spends to maintain the land, sea and air apparatus necessary to interdict illegal imports of drugs. There would also be a savings of hundreds of millions of dollars from the elimination of the prosecutorial procedures that stifle our courts and overcrowd our prisons.

4   We see in our newspapers the triumphant announcements by Government agents that they have intercepted huge caches of cocaine, the street prices of which are in the tens of millions of dollars. Should we be gratified? Will this achievement reduce the number of addicts by one? All it will do is increase the cost to the addict of his illegal supply.

5   Many addicts who are caught committing a crime admit that they have mugged or stolen as many as six or seven times a day to accumulate the $100 needed for a fix. Since many of them need two or three fixes a day, particularly for crack, one can understand the terror in our streets and homes. It is estimated that there are in New York City alone 200,000 addicts, and this is typical of cities across the nation. Even if we were to assume that only a modest percentage of a city's addicts engage in criminal conduct to obtain the money for the habit, requiring multiple muggings and thefts each day, we could nevertheless account for many of the tens of thousands of crimes each day in New York City alone.

6   Not long ago, a Justice Department division issued a report stating that more than half the perpetrators of murder and other serious crimes

were under the influence of drugs. This symbolizes the new domestic terror in our nation. This is why our citizens are unsafe in broad daylight on
the most traveled thoroughfares. This is why typewriters and television
sets are stolen from offices and homes and sold for a pittance. This is
why parks are closed to the public and why murders are committed. This
is why homes need multiple locks, and burglary systems, and why store
windows, even in the most fashionable areas, require iron gates.

7   The benefits of the new strategy to control this terrorism would be
immediate and profound.

8   First, the mob would lose the main source of its income. It could not
compete against a free supply for which previously it exacted tribute
estimated to be hundreds of millions of dollars, perhaps billions, from
hopeless victims.

9   Second, pushers would be put out of business. There would be no
purpose in creating addicts who would be driven by desperate compulsion to steal and kill for the money necessary to maintain their habit.
Children would not be enticed. The mob's macabre public-relations program is to tempt children with free drugs in order to create customers
for the future. The wave of street crimes in broad daylight would diminish to a trickle. Homes and stores would not have to be fortresses. Our
recreational areas could again be used. Neighborhoods would not be
scandalized by sordid street centers where addicts gather to obtain their
supply from slimy merchants.

10   Third, police and other law-enforcement authorities, domestic or foreign, would be freed to deal with traditional nondrug crimes.

11   There are several objections that might be raised against such a salu-
tary solution.

12   First, it could be argued that by providing free drugs to the addict we
would consign him to permanent addiction. The answer is that medical
and psychiatric help at the source would be more effective in controlling
the addict's descent than the extremely limited remedies available to the
victim today. I am not arguing that the new strategy will cure everything.
But I do not see many addicts being freed from their bonds under the present system.

13   In addition, as between the addict's predicament and the safety of
our innocent citizens, which deserves our primary concern? Drug-induced
crime has become so common that almost every citizen knows someone
in his immediate family or among his friends who has been mugged. It is
these citizens who should be our chief concern.

14   Another possible objection is that addicts will cheat the system by
obtaining more than the allowable free shot. Without discounting the resourcefulness of the bedeviled addict, it should be possible to have Government cards issued that would be punched so as to limit the free
supply in accord with medical authorization.

15   Yet all objections become trivial when matched against the crisis itself. What we are witnessing is the demoralization of a great society: the ruination of its school children, athletes and executives, the corrosion of the workforce in general.

16   Many thoughtful sociologists consider the rapidly spreading drug use the greatest problem that our nation faces—greater and more real and urgent than nuclear bombs or economic reversal. In China, a similar crisis drove the authorities to apply capital punishment to those who trafficked in opium—an extreme solution that arose from the deepest reaches of frustration.

17   Free drugs will win the war against the domestic terrorism caused by illicit drugs. As a strategy, it is at once resourceful, sensible and simple. We are getting nowhere in our efforts to hold back the ocean of supply. The answer is to dry up demand.

A Scientist: "I Am the Enemy"
Ron Kline

Ron Kline is a pediatric oncologist and bone marrow specialist involved in immunological research at the University of California at San Francisco. In 1989 Kline published the following essay, arguing the necessity of animals in medical research experiments, in Newsweek *magazine's "My Turn" section, a column of opinion written by readers of the magazine.*

1   I am the enemy! One of those vilified, inhumane physician-scientists involved in animal research. How strange, for I have never thought of myself as an evil person. I became a pediatrician because of my love for children and my desire to keep them healthy. During medical school and residency, however, I saw many children die of leukemia, prematurity and traumatic injury—circumstances against which medicine has made tremendous progress, but still has far to go. More important, I also saw children, alive and healthy, thanks to advances in medical science such as infant respirators, potent antibiotics, new surgical techniques and the entire field of organ transplantation. My desire to tip the scales in favor of the healthy, happy children drew me to medical research.

2   My accusers claim that I inflict torture on animals for the sole purpose of career advancement. My experiments supposedly have no relevance to medicine and are easily replaced by computer simulation. Meanwhile, an apathetic public barely watches, convinced that the issue has no significance, and publicity-conscious politicians increasingly give way to the demands of the activists.

3   We in medical research have also been unconscionably apathetic. We have allowed the most extreme animal-rights protesters to seize the

initiative and frame the issue as one of "animal fraud." We have been complacent in our belief that a knowledgeable public would sense the importance of animal research to the public health. Perhaps we have been mistaken in not responding to the emotional tone of the argument created by those sad posters of animals by waving equally sad posters of children dying of leukemia or cystic fibrosis.

4   Much is made of the pain inflicted on these animals in the name of medical science. The animal-rights activists contend that this is evidence of our malevolent and sadistic nature. A more reasonable argument, however, can be advanced in our defense. Life is often cruel, both to animals and human beings. Teenagers get thrown from the back of a pickup truck and suffer severe head injuries. Toddlers, barely able to walk, find themselves at the bottom of a swimming pool while a parent checks the mail. Physicians hoping to alleviate the pain and suffering these tragedies cause have but three choices: create an animal model of the injury or disease and use that model to understand the process and test new therapies; experiment on human beings—some experiments will succeed, most will fail—or finally, leave medical knowledge static, hoping that accidental discoveries will lead us to the advances.

5   Some animal-rights activists would suggest a fourth choice, claiming that computer models can simulate animal experiments, thus making the actual experiments unnecessary. Computers can simulate, reasonably well, the effects of well-understood principles on complex systems, as in the application of the laws of physics to airplane and automobile design. However, when the principles themselves are in question, as is the case with the complex biological systems under study, computer modeling alone is of little value.

6   One of the terrifying effects of the effort to restrict the use of animals in medical research is that the impact will not be felt for years and decades: drugs that might have been discovered will not be; surgical techniques that might have been developed will not be, and fundamental biological processes that might have been understood will remain mysteries. There is the danger that politically expedient solutions will be found to placate a vocal minority, while the consequences of those decisions will not be apparent until long after the decisions are made and the decision makers forgotten.

7   Fortunately, most of us enjoy good health, and the trauma of watching one's child die has become a rare experience. Yet our good fortune should not make us unappreciative of the health we enjoy or the advances that make it possible. Vaccines, antibiotics, insulin and drugs to treat heart disease, hypertension and stroke are all based on animal research. Most complex surgical procedures, such as coronary-artery by-pass and organ transplantation, are initially developed in animals. Presently undergoing animal studies are techniques to insert genes in

humans in order to replace the defective ones found to be the cause of so much disease. These studies will effectively end if animal research is severely restricted.

8   In America today, death has become an event isolated from our daily existence—out of the sight and thoughts of most of us. As a doctor who has watched many children die, and their parents grieve, I am particularly angered by people capable of so much compassion for a dog or a cat, but with seemingly so little for a dying human being. These people seem so insulated from the reality of human life and death and what it means.

9   Make no mistake, however: I am not advocating the needlessly cruel treatment of animals. To the extent that the animal-rights movement has made us more aware of the needs of these animals, and made us search harder for suitable alternatives, they have made a significant contribution. But if the more radical members of this movement are successful in limiting further research, their efforts will bring about a tragedy that will cost many lives. The real question is whether an apathetic majority can be aroused to protect its future against a vocal, but misdirected, minority.

CHAPTER
27

Description

Ode to Thanksgiving

Michael J. Arlen

Michael J. Arlen is a journalist, critic, and former staff writer for The New Yorker. *He won the Screen Directors' Guild Award for television criticism in 1968 and the National Book Award for contemporary affairs in 1976. Arlen is the author of numerous books, including* Living-Room War *(1969),* Passage to Ararat *(1975), and* The View from Highway 1 *(1976). This essay is from* The Camera Age *(1981), a collection of his* New Yorker *articles.*

1   It is time, at last, to speak the truth about Thanksgiving, and the truth is this. Thanksgiving is really not such a terrific holiday. Consider the traditional symbols of the event: Dried cornhusks hanging on the door! Terrible wine! Cranberry jelly in little bowls of extremely doubtful provenance which everyone is required to handle with the greatest of care! Consider the participants, the merrymakers: men and women (also children) who have survived passably well throughout the years, mainly as a result of living at considerable distances from their dear parents and beloved siblings, who on this feast of feasts must apparently forgather (as if beckoned by an aberrant Fairy Godmother), usually by circuitous

routes, through heavy traffic, at a common meeting place, where the very moods, distempers, and obtrusive personal habits that have kept them all happily apart since adulthood are then and there encouraged to slowly ferment beneath the cornhusks, and gradually rise with the aid of the terrible wine, and finally burst forth out of control under the stimulus of the cranberry jelly! No, it is a mockery of a holiday. For instance: *Thank you, O Lord, for what we are about to receive.* This is surely not a gala concept. There are no presents, unless one counts Aunt Bertha's sweet rolls a present, which no one does. There is precious little in the way of costumery: miniature plastic turkeys and those witless Pilgrim hats. There is no sex. Indeed, Thanksgiving is the one day of the year (a fact known to everybody) when all thoughts of sex completely vanish, evaporating from apartments, houses, condominiums, and mobile homes like steam from a bathroom mirror.

2   Consider also the nowhereness of the time of year: the last week or so in November. It is obviously not yet winter: winter, with its death-dealing blizzards and its girls in tiny skirts pirouetting on the ice. On the other hand, it is certainly not much use to anyone as fall: no golden leaves or Oktoberfests, and so forth. Instead, it is a no-man's-land between the seasons. In the cold and sobersided northern half of the country, it is a vaguely unsettling interregnum of long, mournful walks beneath leafless trees: the long, mournful walks following the midday repast with the dread inevitability of pie following turkey, and the leafless trees looming or standing about like eyesores, and the ground either as hard as iron or slightly mushy, and the light snow always beginning to fall when one is halfway to the old green gate—flecks of cold, watery stuff plopping between neck and collar, for the reason that, it being not yet winter, one has forgotten or not chosen to bring along a muffler. It is a corollary to the long, mournful Thanksgiving walk that the absence of this muffler is quickly noticed and that four weeks or so later, at Christmastime, instead of the Sony Betamax one had secretly hoped the children might have chipped in to purchase, one receives another muffler: by then the thirty-third. Thirty-three mufflers! Some walk! Of course, things are more fun in the warm and loony southern part of the country. No snow there of any kind. No need of mufflers. Also, no long, mournful walks, because in the warm and loony southern part of the country everybody drives. So everybody drives over to Uncle Jasper's house to watch the Cougars play the Gators, a not entirely unimportant conflict which will determine whether the Gators get a Bowl bid or must take another post-season exhibition tour of North Korea. But no sooner do the Cougars kick off (an astonishing end-over-end squiggly thing that floats lazily above the arena before plummeting down toward K. C. McCoy and catching him on the helmet) than Auntie Em starts hustling

turkey. Soon Cousin May is slamming around the bowls and platters, and Cousin Bernice is oohing and ahing about "all the fixin's," and Uncle Bob is making low, insincere sounds of appreciation: "Yummy, yummy, Auntie Em, I'll have me some more of these delicious yams!" Delicious yams? Uncle Bob's eyes roll wildly in his head. Billy Joe Quaglino throws his long bomb in the middle of Grandpa Morris saying grace, Grandpa Morris speaking so low nobody can hear him, which is just as well, since he is reciting what he can remember of his last union contract. And then, just as J. B. (Speedy) Snood begins his ninety-two-yard punt return, Auntie Em starts dealing everyone second helpings of her famous stuffing, as if she were pushing a controlled substance, which it well might be, since there are no easily recognizable ingredients visible to the naked eye.

3   Consider for a moment the Thanksgiving meal itself. It has become a sort of refuge for endangered species of starch: cauliflower, turnips, pumpkin, mince (whatever "mince" is), those blessed yams. Bowls of luridly colored yams, with no taste at all, lying torpid under a lava flow of marshmallow! And then the sacred turkey. One might as well try to construct a holiday repast around a fish—say, a nice piece of boiled haddock. After all, turkey tastes very similar to haddock: same consistency, same quite remarkable absence of flavor. But then, if the Thanksgiving *pièce de résistance* were a nice piece of boiled haddock instead of turkey, there wouldn't be all that fun for Dad when Mom hands him the sterling-silver, bone-handled carving set (a wedding present from her parents and not sharpened since) and then everyone sits around pretending not to watch while he saws and tears away at the bird as if he were trying to burrow his way into or out of some grotesque, fowl-like prison.

4   What of the good side to Thanksgiving, you ask. There is always a good side to everything. Not to Thanksgiving. There is only a bad side and then a worse side. For instance, Grandmother's best linen tablecloth is a bad side: the fact that it is produced each year, in the manner of a red flag being produced before a bull, and then is always spilled upon by whichever child is doing poorest at school that term and so is in need of greatest reassurance. Thus: "Oh, my God, *Veronica,* you just spilled grape juice [or plum wine or tar] on Grandmother's best linen tablecloth!" But now comes worse. For at this point Cousin Bill, the one who lost all Cousin Edwina's money on the car dealership three years ago and has apparently been drinking steadily since Halloween, bizarrely chooses to say: "Seems to me those old glasses are always falling over." To which Auntie Meg is heard to add: "Somehow I don't remember receivin' any of those old glasses." To which Uncle Fred replies: "That's because you and George decided to go on vacation to Hawaii the summer Grandpa Sam was dying." Now Grandmother is sobbing, though not so uncontrollably that she can refrain from murmuring: "I think that volcano

painting I threw away by mistake got sent me from Hawaii, heaven knows why." But the gods are merciful, even the Pilgrim-hatted god of cornhusks and soggy stuffing, and there is an end to everything, even to Thanksgiving. Indeed, there is a grandeur to the feelings of finality and doom which usually settle on a house after the Thanksgiving celebration is over, for with the completion of Thanksgiving Day the year itself has been properly terminated: shot through the cranium with a high-velocity candied yam. At this calendrical nadir, all energy on the planet has gone, all fun has fled, all the terrible wine has been drunk.

5   But then, overnight, life once again begins to stir, emerging, even by the next morning, in the form of Japanese window displays and Taiwanese Christmas lighting, from the primeval ooze of the nation's department stores. Thus, a new year dawns, bringing with it immediate and cheering possibilities of extended consumer debt, office-party flirtations, good— or, at least, mediocre—wine, and visions of Supersaver excursion fares to Montego Bay. It is worth noting, perhaps, that this true new year always starts with the same mute, powerful mythic ceremony: the surreptitious tossing out, in the early morning, of all those horrid aluminum-foil packages of yams and cauliflower and stuffing and red, gummy cranberry substance which have been squeezed into the refrigerator as if a reenactment of the siege of Paris were shortly expected. Soon afterward, the phoenix of Christmas can be observed as it slowly rises, beating its drumsticks, once again goggle-eyed with hope and unrealistic expectations.

Hush, Timmy—This Is Like a Church
Kurt Anderson

Kurt Anderson is a writer and painter, whose books include Idiot's Pursuit *(1985) and* Turn of the Century *(1998). He wrote this essay on the Vietnam Veterans Memorial for* Time *magazine in 1985, describing the site, its history of controversy, its visitors, and its power.*

1 The veteran and his wife had already stared hard at four particular names. Now the couple walked slowly down the incline in front of the wall, looking at rows of hundreds, thousands more, amazed at the roster of the dead. "All the names," she said quietly, sniffling in the early-spring chill. "It's unreal, how many names." He said nothing. "You have to see it to believe it," she said.

2   Just so. In person, close up, the Viet Nam Veterans Memorial—two skinny black granite triangles wedged onto a mound of Washington sod—is some kind of sanctum, beautiful and terrible. "We didn't plan that," says John Wheeler, chairman of the veterans' group that raised the money and built it. "I had a picture of seven-year-olds throwing a Frisbee

around on the grass in front. But it's treated as a spiritual place." When Wheeler's colleague Jan Scruggs decided there ought to be a monument, he had only vague notions of what it might be like. "You don't set out and *build* a national shrine," Scruggs says. "It *becomes* one."

3   Washington is thick with monuments, several of them quite affecting. But as the Viet Nam War was singular and strange, the dark, dreamy, re-demptive memorial to its American veterans is like no other. "It's more solemn," says National Park Service Ranger Sarah Page, who has also worked at the memorials honoring Lincoln, Washington and Jefferson. "People give it more respect." Lately it has been the most visited monu-ment in the capital: 2.3 million saw it in 1984, about 45,000 a week, but it is currently drawing 100,000 a week. Where does it get its power—to con-sole, and also to make people sob?

4   The men who set up the Viet Nam Veterans Memorial Fund wanted something that would include the name of every American killed in Viet Nam, and would be contemplative and apolitical. They conducted an open design competition that drew 1,421 entries, all submitted anony-mously. The winner, Maya Ying Lin, was a Chinese-American undergrad-uate at Yale: to memorialize men killed in a war in Asia, an Asian female studying at an old antiwar hotbed.

5   Opposition to Lin's design was intense. The opponents wanted some-thing gleaming and grand. To them, the low-slung black wall would send the same old defeatist, elitist messages that had lost the war in the '60s and then stigmatized the veterans in the '70s. "Creating the memorial triggered a lot of old angers and rage among vets about the war," recalls Wheeler, a captain in Viet Nam and now a Yale-trained government lawyer. "It got white hot."

6   In the end, Lin's sublime and stirring wall was built, 58,022 names in-scribed. As a compromise with opponents, however, a more conven-tional figurative sculpture was added to the site last fall (at a cost of $400,000). It does not spoil the memorial, as the art mandarins had warned. The three U.S. soldiers, cast in bronze, stand a bit larger than life, carry automatic weapons and wear fatigues, but the pose is not John Wayne-heroic: these American boys are spectral and wary, even slightly bewildered as they gaze southeast toward the wall. While he was plan-ning the figures, sculptor Frederick Hart spent time watching vets at the memorial. Hart now grants that "no modernist monument of its kind has been as successful as that wall. The sculpture and the wall interact beau-tifully. Everybody won." Nor does Lin, his erstwhile artistic antagonist, still feel that Hart's stature is so awfully trite. "It captures the mood," says Lin. "Their faces have a lost look." Out at the memorial last week, one veteran looked at the new addition and nodded: "That's us."

7   But it is the wall that vets approach as if it were a force field. It is at the wall that families of the dead cry and leave flowers and mementos

and messages, much as Jews leave notes for God in the cracks of Jerusalem's Western Wall. Around the statue, people talk louder and breathe easier, snap vacation photos unselfconsciously, eat Eskimo Pies and Fritos. But near the wall, a young Boston father tells his rambunctious son, "Hush, Timmy—this is like a church." The visitors' processionals do seem to have a ritual, even liturgical quality. Going slowly down toward the vertex, looking at the names, they chat less and less, then fall silent where the names of the first men killed (July 1959) and the last (May 1975) appear. The talk begins again, softly, as they follow the path up out of the little valley of the shadow of death.

8   For veterans, the memorial was a touchstone from the beginning, and the 1982 dedication ceremony a delayed national embrace. "The actual act of being at the memorial is healing for the guy or woman who went to Viet Nam," says Wheeler, who visits at least monthly. "It has to do with the felt presence of comrades." He pauses. "I always look at Tommy Hayes' name. Tommy's up on panel 50 east, line 29." Hayes, Wheeler's West Point pal, was killed 17 years ago this month. "I know guys," Wheeler says, "who are still waiting to go, whose wives have told me, 'He hasn't been able to do it yet.'" For those who go, catharsis is common. As Lin says of the names, chronologically ordered, "Veterans can look at the wall, find a name, and in a sense put themselves back in that time." The war has left some residual pathologies that the memorial cannot leach away. One veteran killed himself on the amphitheatrical green near the wall. A second, ex-Marine Randolph Taylor, tried and failed in January. "I regret what I did," he said. "I feel like I desecrated a holy place."

9   The memorial has become a totem, so much so that its tiniest imperfections make news. Last fall somebody noticed a few minute cracks at the seams between several of the granite panels. The cause of the hairlines is still unknown, and the builders are a little worried.

10   Probably no one is more determined than Wheeler to see the memorial's face made perfect, for he savors the startlingly faithful reflections the walls give off: he loves seeing the crowds of visitors looking simultaneously at the names and themselves. "Look!" he said the other day, gesturing at panel 4 east. "You see that plane taking off? You see the blue sky? No one expected that."

The Man in the Water

Roger Rosenblatt

During the 1970s Roger Rosenblatt served as director of expository writing at Harvard University. He has also been an editor for The New Republic, The Washington Post, *and* U.S. News & World Report. *He has published* Black Fiction *(1974),* Children of War

(1983), Witness: The World Since Hiroshima *(1985),* Life Itself: Abortion in the Mind of America *(1992), and* Coming Apart: A Memoir of the Harvard Wars of 1969 *(1997).* *As a senior writer for* Time *magazine, he first published this selection in 1982, following the crash of an Air Florida plane into the freezing waters of the Potomac River in Washington, DC. It was republished in* Man in the Water: Essays and Stories *(1994).*

1   As disasters go, this one was terrible, but not unique, certainly not among the worst on the roster of U.S. air crashes. There was the unusual element of the bridge, of course, and the fact that the plane clipped it at a moment of high traffic, one routine thus intersecting another and disrupting both. Then, too, there was the location of the event. Washington, the city of form and regulations, turned chaotic, deregulated, by a blast of real winter and a single slap of metal on metal. The jets from Washington National Airport that normally swoop around the presidential monuments like famished gulls are, for the moment, emblemized by the one that fell; so there is that detail. And there was the aesthetic clash as well—blue-and-green Air Florida, the name a flying garden, sunk down among gray chunks in a black river. All that was worth noticing, to be sure. Still, there was nothing very special in any of it, except death, which, while always special, does not necessarily bring millions to tears or to attention. Why, then, the shock here?

2   Perhaps because the nation saw in this disaster something more than a mechanical failure. Perhaps because people saw in it no failure at all, but rather something successful about their makeup. Here, after all, were two forms of nature in collision: the elements and human character. Last Wednesday, the elements, indifferent as ever, brought down Flight 90. And on that same afternoon, human nature—groping and flailing in mysteries of its own—rose to the occasion.

3   Of the four acknowledged heroes of the event, three are able to account for their behavior. Donald Usher and Eugene Windsor, a park police helicopter team, risked their lives every time they dipped the skids into the water to pick up survivors. On television, side by side in bright blue jumpsuits, they described their courage as all in the line of duty. Lenny Skutnik, a 28-year-old employee of the Congressional Budget Office, said: "It's something I never thought I would do"—referring to his jumping into the water to drag an injured woman to shore. Skutnik added that "somebody had to go in the water," delivering every hero's line that is no less admirable for its repetitions. In fact, nobody had to go into the water. That somebody actually did so is part of the reason this particular tragedy sticks in the mind.

4   But the person most responsible for the emotional impact of the disaster is the one known at first simply as "the man in the water." (Balding, probably in his 50s, an extravagant mustache.) He was seen clinging with five other survivors to the tail section of the airplane. This man

was described by Usher and Windsor as appearing alert and in control. Every time they lowered a lifeline and flotation ring to him, he passed it on to another of the passengers. "In a mass casualty, you'll find people like him," said Windsor. "But I've never seen one with that commitment." When the helicopter came back for him, the man had gone under. His selflessness was one reason the story held national attention; his anonymity another. The fact that he went unidentified invested him with a universal character. For a while he was Everyman, and thus proof (as if one needed it) that no man is ordinary.

5   Still, he could never have imagined such a capacity in himself. Only minutes before his character was tested, he was sitting in the ordinary plane among the ordinary passengers, dutifully listening to the stewardess telling him to fasten his seat belt and saying something about the "no smoking sign." So our man relaxed with the others, some of whom would owe their lives to him. Perhaps he started to read, or to doze, or to regret some harsh remark made in the office that morning. Then suddenly he knew that the trip would not be ordinary. Like every other person on that flight, he was desperate to live, which makes his final act so stunning.

6   For at some moment in the water he must have realized that he would not live if he continued to hand over the rope and ring to others. He *had* to know it, no matter how gradual the effect of the cold. In his judgment he had no choice. When the helicopter took off with what was to be the last survivor, he watched everything in the world move away from him, and he deliberately let it happen.

7   Yet there was something else about the man that kept our thoughts on him, and which keeps our thoughts on him still. He was *there,* in the essential, classic circumstance. Man in nature. The man in the water. For its part, nature cared nothing about the five passengers. Our man, on the other hand, cared totally. So the timeless battle commenced in the Potomac. For as long as that man could last, they went at each other, nature and man; the one making no distinctions of good and evil, acting on no principles, offering no lifelines; the other acting wholly on distinctions, principles and, one supposes, on faith.

8   Since it was he who lost the fight, we ought to come again to the conclusion that people are powerless in the world. In reality, we believe the reverse, and it takes the act of the man in the water to remind us of our true feelings in this matter. It is not to say that everyone would have acted as he did, or as Usher, Windsor and Skutnik. Yet whatever moved these men to challenge death on behalf of their fellows is not peculiar to them. Everyone feels the possibility in himself. That is the abiding wonder of the story. That is why we would not let go of it. If the man in the water gave a lifeline to the people gasping for survival, he was likewise giving a lifeline to those who observed him.

9   The odd thing is that we do not even really believe that the man in the water lost his fight. "Everything in Nature contains all the powers of Nature," said Emerson. Exactly. So the man in the water had his own natural powers. He could not make ice storms, or freeze the water until it froze the blood. But he could hand life over to a stranger, and that is a power of nature too. The man in the water pitted himself against an implacable, impersonal enemy; he fought it with charity; and he held it to a standoff. He was the best we can do.

CHAPTER

28 Narration

38 Who Saw Murder Didn't Call the Police

Martin Gansberg

Martin Gansberg was a reporter and editor for The New York Times *for over 40 years, until his retirement in 1985. He also wrote for such magazines as* Diplomat, Catholic Digest, *and* Facts. *This article was published in* The New York Times *in 1964, shortly after the murder of Kitty Genovese.*

1   For more than half an hour 38 respectable, law-abiding citizens in Queens watched a killer stalk and stab a woman in three separate attacks in Kew Gardens.

2   Twice the sound of their voices and the sudden glow of their bedroom lights interrupted him and frightened him off. Each time he returned, sought her out and stabbed her again. Not one person telephoned the police during the assault; one witness called after the woman was dead.

3   That was two weeks ago today. But Assistant Chief Inspector Frederick M. Lussen, in charge of the borough's detectives and a veteran of 25 years of homicide investigations, is still shocked.

4   He can give a matter-of-fact recitation of many murders. But the Kew Gardens slaying baffles him—not because it is a murder, but because the "good people" failed to call the police.

5   "As we have reconstructed the crime," he said, "the assailant had three chances to kill this woman during a 35-minute period. He returned twice to complete the job. If we had been called when he first attacked, the woman might not be dead now."

6   This is what the police say happened beginning at 3:20 A.M. in the staid, middle-class, tree-lined Austin Street area:

7   Twenty-eight-year-old Catherine Genovese, who was called Kitty by almost everyone in the neighborhood, was returning home from her job as manager of a bar in Hollis. She parked her red Fiat in a lot adjacent to the Kew Gardens Long Island Rail Road Station, facing Mowbray Place. Like many residents of the neighborhood, she had parked there day after day since her arrival from Connecticut a year ago, although the railroad frowns on the practice.

8   She turned off the lights of her car, locked the door and started to walk the 100 feet to the entrance of her apartment at 82–70 Austin Street, which is in a Tudor building, with stores on the first floor and apartments on the second.

9   The entrance to the apartment is in the rear of the building because the front is rented to retail stores. At night the quiet neighborhood is shrouded in the slumbering darkness that marks most residential areas.

10   Miss Genovese noticed a man at the far end of the lot, near a seven-story apartment house at 82–40 Austin Street. She halted. Then, nervously, she headed up Austin Street toward Lefferts Boulevard, where there is a call box to the 102nd Police Precinct in nearby Richmond Hill.

"He Stabbed Me"

11   She got as far as a street light in front of a bookstore before the man grabbed her. She screamed. Lights went on in the 10-story apartment house at 82–67 Austin Street, which faces the bookstore. Windows slid open and voices punctuated the early-morning stillness.

12   Miss Genovese screamed: "Oh, my God, he stabbed me! Please help me! Please help me!"

13   From one of the upper windows in the apartment house, a man called down: "Let that girl alone!"

14   The assailant looked up at him, shrugged and walked down Austin Street toward a white sedan parked a short distance away. Miss Genovese struggled to her feet.

15   Lights went out. The killer returned to Miss Genovese, now trying to make her way around the side of the building by the parking lot to get to her apartment. The assailant stabbed her again.

16   "I'm dying!" she shrieked. "I'm dying!"

A City Bus Passed

17   Windows were opened again, and lights went on in many apartments. The assailant got into his car and drove away. Miss Genovese staggered to her feet. A city bus, Q-10, the Lefferts Boulevard line to Kennedy International Airport, passed. It was 3:35 A.M.

18   The assailant returned. By then, Miss Genovese had crawled to the back of the building, where the freshly painted brown doors to the apartment house held out hope of safety. The killer tried the first door; she wasn't there. At the second door, 82–62 Austin Street, he saw her slumped on the floor at the foot of the stairs. He stabbed her a third time—fatally.

19   It was 3:50 by the time the police received their first call, from a man who was a neighbor of Miss Genovese. In two minutes they were at the scene. The neighbor, a 70-year-old woman and another woman were the only persons on the street. Nobody else came forward.

20   The man explained that he had called the police after much deliberation. He had phoned a friend in Nassau County for advice and then he had crossed the roof of the building to the apartment of the elderly woman to get her to make the call.

21   "I didn't want to get involved," he sheepishly told the police.

Suspect Is Arrested

22   Six days later, the police arrested Winston Moseley, a 29-year-old business-machine operator, and charged him with homicide. Moseley had no previous record. He is married, has two children and owns a home at 133-19 Sutter Avenue, South Ozone Park, Queens. On Wednesday, a court committed him to Kings County Hospital for psychiatric observation.

23   When questioned by the police, Moseley also said that he had slain Mrs. Annie May Johnson, 24, of 146–12 133d Avenue, Jamaica, on Feb. 29 and Barbara Kralik, 15, of 174–17 140th Avenue, Springfield Gardens, last July. In the Kralik case, the police are holding Alvin L. Mitchell, who is said to have confessed that slaying.

24   The police stressed how simple it would have been to have gotten in touch with them. "A phone call," said one of the detectives, "would have done it." The police may be reached by dialing "O" for operator or SPring 7-3100. . . .

25   Today witnesses from the neighborhood, which is made up of one-family homes in the $35,000 to $60,000 range with the exception of the two apartment houses near the railroad station, find it difficult to explain why they didn't call the police. . . .

26   A housewife, knowingly if quite casually, said, "We thought it was a lover's quarrel." A husband and wife both said, "Frankly, we were afraid." They seemed aware of the fact that events might have been different. A

distraught woman, wiping her hands in her apron, said, "I didn't want my husband to get involved."

27   One couple, now willing to talk about that night, said they heard the first screams. The husband looked thoughtfully at the bookstore where the killer first grabbed Miss Genovese.

28   "We went to the window to see what was happening," he said, "but the light from our bedroom made it difficult to see the street." The wife, still apprehensive, added: "I put out the light and we were able to see better."

29   Asked why they hadn't called the police, she shrugged and replied: "I don't know."

30   A man peeked out from a slight opening in the doorway to his apartment and rattled off an account of the killer's second attack. Why hadn't he called the police at the time? "I was tired," he said without emotion. "I went back to bed."

31   It was 4:25 A.M. when the ambulance arrived to take the body of Miss Genovese. It drove off. "Then," a solemn police detective said, "the people came out."

The Talkies

James Lileks

Humorist James Lileks is a columnist for the Minneapolis Star Tribune *and a contributor to* The Washington Post. *In addition to hosting a radio talk show, Lileks has written two novels,* Falling Up the Stairs *(1988) and* Mr. Obvious *(1995), and has published two collections of essays,* Notes of a Nervous Man *(1991), from which this excerpt is taken, and* Fresh Lies *(1995).*

1   I am a tolerant man. Especially at the movies. I do not complain when the seats are as plush as a Baptist pew, or the buttered popcorn tastes like packing material with a drizzle of melted crayon. I don't mind that I have to cash a bond to buy a box of Dots, and if I have to use solvents to free my feet from the floor at the end of the film, that's acceptable. I'm not happy when the man with the big yellow hat from the Curious George books sits directly in front of me and blocks my view, but accept it as the price you pay for a communal experience.

2   But people who talk in movies make me turn eight shades of mad. Plunk two talkers behind me and I start to pine for a decent billy club. Something well weighted with a comfortable grip. As I see it, there are two excuses for talking during movies: (*a*) you are on the screen; or (*b*) you have a rare neurological disease that causes you to blurt out statements like "I CAN'T BELIEVE SISKEL AND EBERT GAVE THIS TWO THUMBS UP!" at inappropriate times—and so you go to movie theaters where your affliction seems less bizarre.

3   Mind you, I am not discussing those who lean to their partner and whisper a few words or observations. Most of you whisper, or keep it to yourselves. The people to whom I refer are those who speak at a volume just a few decibels shy of the level you would use to warn someone in a crowd of a falling piano. The people who seem to expect their names to be listed in the credits under "Additional Dialogue."

4   Last week I went to see *Mississippi Burning*. I use the word "see" with precision, for I heard not a line of the dialogue. The entire row behind me talked all through the trailers.* That's fine. That's what trailers are for. Go on, get it out of your system. They also talked during the opening credits, but that was acceptable; they'd arrived late—I know this because one of them hit me in the head with her purse—and they were still flush with the excitement that comes with leaving the house three minutes before the film starts.

5   But as the film progressed, it became obvious that the row behind us was a group from the Institute for Pointing Out the Obvious, off on a field trip. The first image of the film, an early '60s-model car cresting a hill, prompted the gentleman behind me to note, "That's an old car." The appearance of several more cars of the same period gave the man an empirical Epiphany, and he could not help but burst out with his conclusion:

6   "This must be set in the past."

7   There was a period of silence, during which he may or may not have whispered, "Note how reflective and rectangular the screen is," to his partner. The slack was taken up by a group to his right, who were attempting to recall what this film was about, perhaps on the assumption that the plot, due to malicious filmmakers anxious for financial ruin, would remain inscrutable for the next two hours.

8   These folk soon shut up—after my buddy had turned around, locked eyes, and given his best I-taught-Manson-all-he-knows look. But the ones behind me were just beginning.

9   Nothing escaped comment. The streets in the rural Mississippi town were unpaved? Lo, hear them discuss the volume of dust raised by a passing car. The sheriff was fat? Lend an ear to "Looka that gut," and other biting witticisms (such as, "I mean it, how can he be that fat? I'll never get that fat."). Woe to any screen characters who fail to heed their judgments, and prolonged approval of those who do.

10   Often I was treated to a critical evaluation in process. At one point, Gene Hackman drives up to the house of a woman who knows something but isn't telling the Feds. This prompts the following speech:

11   "Oh, it's broad daylight, he'd better not go up to that house. People would talk and her husband would hear about it, don't you think?"

12   "I imagine so."

*A "trailer" is a preview of a forthcoming movie.

13   "Well, everyone knows that's his car."

14   "See, he's leaving."

15   "Yeah, he's turning around."

16   "Good. 'Cause he'd have gotten in trouble, and so would she."

17   Turning around and shouting "SHUT UP! SHUT UP AND REMAIN IN A STATE OF SHUTUPEDNESS!" would have done no good. I had spent the previous hour turning around and glaring, but they apparently took this to mean I was angry that they were speaking too softly, and hence depriving me of their views. For a while I was turning around, glaring and turning away with a heavy sigh, but given the classical decor of the theater, they probably interpreted this as a nostalgic sigh of regret for an idealized world long passed. Nothing worked. When the man issued a few racking coughs interspersed with words, I considered lighting up a cigarette and letting the smoke waft his way, but smoking, of course, is considered discourteous to others.

18   For a while I attempted to use telekinesis to loose a piece of plaster on the ceiling directly above them, but this did not work.

19   I finally turned around and said, "Quiet!" They nodded, as though I was describing an attribute of the theater. I might as well have said "Dark!" or "Chairs in rows!" They embarked anew on another discussion of whether or not that actor was in that Jack Nicholson film.

20   Actors, incidentally, were not allowed to have roles. When they discussed the motivations of Gene Hackman's character, they addressed him as Gene Hackman. "See, Gene Hackman wants to do it his way, that's the problem." This helped all of us within hearing range maintain our suspension of disbelief. Willem Dafoe, late of *Platoon,* was known only as "the guy in the glasses." They would occasionally bring out the depth in his character by asking, "Why is he always wearing a suit? It looks so warm, doesn't he sweat?"

21   If I seem to be exaggerating, I assure you I am not. These people babbled without cease, as though the fountain at the concession stand had added sodium pentothal to their beverages. I could not move, as there was not a decent seat to be had in the theater. I could barely concentrate on the film, as I was always steeled for another pronouncement. All I could do was entertain the idea of following them home, standing in the corner of their bedroom, and saying things like, "Oh, see, he has his arm around her shoulder, he likes her. Okay, well, she's getting ready for bed now, that's a nice set of sheets, I have ones like those at home. Say, that's quite a mole, I'd get that checked out if I had a mole like that," and so forth.

22   It would only be fair.

23   So, friends, if you're in a movie house, and you have something to say, ask yourself this: Do you, in the course of your day, constantly have to shout over the sound of a jackhammer, and should you now adjust

your voice accordingly? Is what you have to say really necessary? Is the gentleman in front of you waving a flag on which is printed the nautical symbol for PUT A LID ON IT?

24 If you feel you still have to speak, ask yourself this: If this was World War II, and I was behind German lines with Nazis everywhere, could the Nazis hear me if I spoke at this level, and subsequently submit me to horrible torture? If the answer is yes, tone it down. Or write it out and hand it to your partner, with the instructions to swallow it immediately.

25 Or, go on talking. Go ahead. You paid your money. Gab it up. And make sure you kick the seat in front of you when you cross your legs. You're only conforming to ancient tradition, after all. Movies are nothing more than modern versions of cavemen telling tales around the fire, and back then there were always a couple who talked all through the story.

26 We know this because of drawings on the walls of caves where they buried the talkers.

Beauty: When the Other Dancer Is the Self

Alice Walker

A poet, essayist, and novelist, Alice Walker is best known for The Color Purple, *which won both the Pulitzer Prize and the American Book Award in 1982. Some of her other works include* The Temple of My Familiar *(1989),* Her Blue Body Everything We Know: Earthling Poems 1965–1990 *(1991),* Possessing the Secret of Joy *(1992), and* Anything We Love Can Be Saved *(1997). The following selection comes from her 1983 collection of essays,* In Search of Our Mothers' Gardens.

1 It is a bright summer day in 1947. My father, a fat, funny man with beautiful eyes and a subversive wit, is trying to decide which of his eight children he will take with him to the county fair. My mother, of course, will not go. She is knocked out from getting most of us ready: I hold my neck stiff against the pressure of her knuckles as she hastily completes the braiding and then beribboning of my hair.

2 My father is the driver for the rich old white lady up the road. Her name is Miss Mey. She owns all the land for miles around, as well as the house in which we live. All I remember about her is that she once offered to pay my mother thirty-five cents for cleaning her house, raking up piles of her magnolia leaves, and washing her family's clothes, and that my mother—she of no money, eight children, and a chronic earache—refused it. But I do not think of this in 1947. I am two and a half years old. I want to go everywhere my daddy goes. I am excited at the prospect of riding in a car. Someone has told me fairs are fun. That there is room in the car for only three of us doesn't faze me at all. Whirling happily in my starchy frock, showing off my biscuit-polished patent-leather shoes and

lavender socks, tossing my head in a way that makes my ribbons bounce, I stand, hands on hips, before my father. "Take me, Daddy," I say with assurance: "I'm the prettiest!"

3   Later, it does not surprise me to find myself in Miss Mey's shiny black car, sharing the back seat with the other lucky ones. Does not surprise me that I thoroughly enjoy the fair. At home that night I tell the unlucky ones all I can remember about the merry-go-round, the man who eats live chickens, and the teddy bears, until they say: that's enough, baby Alice. Shut up now, and go to sleep.

4   It is Easter Sunday, 1950. I am dressed in a green, flocked, scalloped-hem dress (handmade by my adoring sister, Ruth) that has its own smooth satin petticoat and tiny hot-pink roses tucked into each scallop. My shoes, new T-strap patent leather, again highly biscuit-polished. I am six years old and have learned one of the longest Easter speeches to be heard that day, totally unlike the speech I said when I was two: "Easter lilies / pure and white / blossom in / the morning light." When I rise to give my speech I do so on a great wave of love and pride and expectation. People in the church stop rustling their new crinolines. They seem to hold their breath. I can tell they admire my dress, but it is my spirit, bordering on sassiness (womanishness), they secretly applaud.

5   "That girl's a little *mess*," they whisper to each other, pleased.

6   Naturally I say my speech without stammer or pause, unlike those who stutter, stammer, or, worst of all, forget. This is before the word "beautiful" exists in people's vocabulary, but "Oh, isn't she the *cutest* thing!" frequently floats my way. "And got so much sense!" they gratefully add . . . for which thoughtful addition I thank them to this day.

7   *It was great fun being cute. But then, one day, it ended.*

8   I am eight years old and a tomboy. I have a cowboy hat, cowboy boots, checkered shirt and pants, all red. My playmates are my brothers, two and four years older than I. Their colors are black and green, the only difference in the way we are dressed. On Saturday nights we all go to the picture show, even my mother; Westerns are her favorite kind of movie. Back home, "on the ranch," we pretend we are Tom Mix, Hopalong Cassidy, Lash LaRue (we've even named one of our dogs Lash LaRue); we chase each other for hours rustling cattle, being outlaws, delivering damsels from distress. Then my parents decide to buy my brothers guns. These are not "real" guns. They shoot "BBs," copper pellets my brothers say will kill birds. Because I am a girl, I do not get a gun. Instantly I am relegated to the position of Indian. Now there appears a great distance between us. They shoot and shoot at everything with their new guns. I try to keep up with my bow and arrows.

9 One day while I am standing on top of our makeshift "garage"—pieces of tin nailed across some poles—holding my bow and arrow and looking out toward the fields, I feel an incredible blow in my right eye. I look down just in time to see my brother lower his gun.

10 Both brothers rush to my side. My eye stings, and I cover it with my hand. "If you tell," they say, "we will get a whipping. You don't want that to happen, do you?" I do not. "Here is a piece of wire," says the older brother, picking it up from the roof; "say you stepped on one end of it and the other flew up and hit you." The pain is beginning to start. "Yes," I say. "Yes, I will say that is what happened." If I do not say this is what happened, I know my brothers will find ways to make me wish I had. But now I will say anything that gets me to my mother.

11 Confronted by our parents we stick to the lie agreed upon. They place me on a bench on the porch and I close my left eye while they examine the right. There is a tree growing from underneath the porch that climbs past the railing to the roof. It is the last thing my right eye sees. I watch as its trunk, its branches, and then its leaves are blotted out by the rising blood.

12 I am in shock. First there is intense fever, which my father tries to break using lily leaves bound around my head. Then there are chills: my mother tries to get me to eat soup. Eventually, I do not know how, my parents learn what has happened. A week after the "accident" they take me to see a doctor. "Why did you wait so long to come?" he asks, looking into my eye and shaking his head. "Eyes are sympathetic," he says. "If one is blind, the other will likely become blind too."

13 This comment of the doctor's terrifies me. But it is really how I look that bothers me most. Where the BB pellet struck there is a glob of whitish scar tissue, a hideous cataract, on my eye. Now when I stare at people—a favorite pastime, up to now—they will stare back. Not at the "cute" little girl, but at her scar. For six years I do not stare at anyone, because I do not raise my head.

14 Years later, in the throes of a mid-life crisis, I ask my mother and sister whether I changed after the "accident." "No," they say, puzzled. "What do you mean?"

15 *What do I mean?*

16 I am eight, and, for the first time, doing poorly in school, where I have been something of a whiz since I was four. We have just moved to the place where the "accident" occurred. We do not know any of the people around us because this is a different county. The only time I see the friends I knew is when we go back to our old church. The new school is the former state penitentiary. It is a large stone building, cold and drafty, crammed to overflowing with boisterous, ill-disciplined children. On the

third floor there is a huge circular imprint of some partition that has been torn out.

17   "What used to be here?" I ask a sullen girl next to me on our way past it to lunch.

18   "The electric chair," says she.

19   At night I have nightmares about the electric chair, and about all the people reputedly "fried" in it. I am afraid of the school, where all the students seem to be budding criminals.

20   "What's the matter with your eye?" they ask, critically.

21   When I don't answer (I cannot decide whether it was an "accident" or not), they shove me, insist on a fight.

22   My brother, the one who created the story about the wire, comes to my rescue. But then brags so much about "protecting" me, I become sick.

23   After months of torture at the school, my parents decide to send me back to our old community, to my old school. I live with my grandparents and the teacher they board. But there is no room for Phoebe, my cat. By the time my grandparents decide there *is* room, and I ask for my cat, she cannot be found. Miss Yarborough, the boarding teacher, takes me under her wing, and begins to teach me to play the piano. But soon she marries an African—a "prince," she says—and is whisked away to his continent.

24   At my old school there is at least one teacher who loves me. She is the teacher who "knew me before I was born" and bought my first baby clothes. It is she who makes life bearable. It is her presence that finally helps me turn on the one child at the school who continually calls me "one-eyed bitch." One day I simply grab him by his coat and beat him until I am satisfied. It is my teacher who tells me my mother is ill.

25   My mother is lying in bed in the middle of the day, something I have never seen. She is in too much pain to speak. She has an abscess in her ear. I stand looking down on her, knowing that if she dies, I cannot live. She is being treated with warm oils and hot bricks held against her cheek. Finally a doctor comes. But I must go back to my grandparents' house. The weeks pass but I am hardly aware of it. All I know is that my mother might die, my father is not so jolly, my brothers still have their guns, and I am the one sent away from home.

26   "You did not change," they say.

27   *Did I imagine the anguish of never looking up?*

28   I am twelve. When relatives come to visit I hide in my room. My cousin Brenda, just my age, whose father works in the post office and whose mother is a nurse, comes to find me. "Hello," she says. And then she asks, looking at my recent school picture, which I did not want taken,

and on which the "glob," as I think of it, is clearly visible. "You still can't see out of that eye?"

29   "No," I say, and flop back on the bed over my book.

30   That night, as I do almost every night, I abuse my eye. I rant and rave at it, in front of the mirror. I plead with it to clear up before morning. I tell it I hate and despise it. I do not pray for sight. I pray for beauty.

31   "You did not change," they say.

32   I am fourteen and baby-sitting for my brother Bill, who lives in Boston. He is my favorite brother and there is a strong bond between us. Understanding my feelings of shame and ugliness he and his wife take me to a local hospital, where the "glob" is removed by a doctor named O. Henry. There is still a small bluish crater where the scar tissue was, but the ugly white stuff is gone. Almost immediately I become a different person from the girl who does not raise her head. Or so I think. Now that I've raised my head I win the boyfriend of my dreams. Now that I've raised my head I have plenty of friends. Now that I've raised my head classwork comes from my lips as faultlessly as Easter speeches did, and I leave high school as valedictorian, most popular student, and *queen,* hardly believing my luck. Ironically, the girl who was voted most beautiful in our class (and was) was later shot twice through the chest by a male companion, using a "real" gun, while she was pregnant. But that's another story in itself. Or is it?

33   "You did not change," they say.

34   It is now thirty years since the "accident." A beautiful journalist comes to visit and to interview me. She is going to write a cover story for her magazine that focuses on my latest book. "Decide how you want to look on the cover," she says. "Glamorous, or whatever."

35   Never mind "glamorous," it is the "whatever" that I hear. Suddenly all I can think of is whether I will get enough sleep the night before the photography session: if I don't, my eye will be tired and wander, as blind eyes will.

36   At night in bed with my lover I think up reasons why I should not appear on the cover of a magazine. "My meanest critics will say I've sold out," I say. "My family will now realize I write scandalous books."

37   "But what's the real reason you don't want to do this?" he asks.

38   "Because in all probability," I say in a rush, "my eye won't be straight."

39   "It will be straight enough," he says. Then, "Besides, I thought you'd made your peace with that."

40   And I suddenly remember that I have.

41   *I remember:*

42   I am talking to my brother Jimmy, asking if he remembers anything unusual about the day I was shot. He does not know I consider that day the last time my father, with his sweet home remedy of cool lily leaves, chose me, and that I suffered and raged inside because of this. "Well," he says, "all I remember is standing by the side of the highway with Daddy, trying to flag down a car. A white man stopped, but when Daddy said he needed somebody to take his little girl to the doctor, he drove off."

43   *I remember:*

44   I am in the desert for the first time. I fall totally in love with it. I am so overwhelmed by its beauty, I confront for the first time, consciously, the meaning of the doctor's words years ago: "Eyes are sympathetic. If one is blind, the other will likely become blind too." I realize I have dashed about the world madly, looking at that, storing up images against the fading of the light. *But I might have missed seeing the desert!* The shock of that possibility—and gratitude for over twenty-five years of sight—sends me literally to my knees. Poem after poem comes—which is perhaps how poets pray.

On Sight

I am so thankful I have seen
The Desert
And the creatures in the desert
And the desert itself.

The desert has its own moon
Which I have seen
With my own eye.

There is no flag on it.

Trees of the desert have arms
All of which are always up
That is because the moon is up
The sun is up
Also the sky
The stars
Clouds
None with flags.

If there *were* flags, I doubt
the trees would point.
Would you?

45   *But mostly, I remember this:*

46   I am twenty-seven, and my baby daughter is almost three. Since her birth, I have worried about her discovery that her mother's eyes are

different from other people's. Will she be embarrassed? I think. What will she say? Every day she watches a television program called "Big Blue Marble." It begins with a picture of the earth as it appears from the moon. It is bluish, a little battered-looking, but full of light, with whitish clouds swirling around it. Every time I see it I weep with love, as if it is a picture of Grandma's house. One day when I am putting Rebecca down for her nap, she suddenly focuses on my eye. Something inside me cringes, gets ready to try to protect myself. All children are cruel about physical differences, I know from experience, and that they don't always mean to be is another matter. I assume Rebecca will be the same.

47   But no-o-o-o. She studies my face intently as we stand, her inside and me outside her crib. She even holds my face maternally between her dimpled little hands. Then, looking every bit as serious and lawyerlike as her father, she says, as if it may just possibly have slipped my attention: "Mommy, there's a *world* in your eye." (As in, "Don't be alarmed, or do anything crazy.") And then, gently, but with great interest: "Mommy, where did you *get* that world in your eye?"

48   For the most part, the pain left then. (So what, if my brothers grew up to buy even more powerful pellet guns for their sons and to carry real guns themselves. So what, if a young "Morehouse man" once nearly fell off the steps of Trevos Arnett Library because he thought my eyes were blue.) Crying and laughing I ran to the bathroom, while Rebecca mumbled and sang herself off to sleep. Yes indeed, I realized, looking into the mirror. There *was* a world in my eye. And I saw that it was possible to love it: that in fact, for all it had taught me of shame and anger and inner vision, I *did* love it. Even to see it drifting out of orbit in boredom, or rolling up out of fatigue, not to mention floating back at attention in excitement (bearing witness, a friend has called it), deeply suitable to my personality, and even characteristic of me.

49   That night I dream I am dancing to Stevie Wonder's song "Always" (the name of the song is really "As," but I hear it as "Always"). As I dance, whirling and joyous, happier than I've ever been in my life, another bright-faced dancer joins me. We dance and kiss each other and hold each other through the night. The other dancer has obviously come through all right, as I have done. She is beautiful, whole and free. And she is also me.

CHAPTER

29

Essays for Further Analysis: Multiple Strategies and Styles

I Have a Dream

Martin Luther King, Jr.

The Rev. Martin Luther King, Jr., president of the Southern Christian Leadership Conference, was the most well-known leader of the civil rights movement of the 1960s and the recipient of the 1964 Nobel Peace Prize. He was assassinated in 1968. King delivered this speech in 1963 at a celebration of the Emancipation Proclamation, before a crowd of thousands who had marched to the Lincoln Memorial in Washington, D.C.

1   Five score years ago, a great American, in whose symbolic shadow we stand, signed the Emancipation Proclamation. This momentous decree came as a great beacon light of hope to millions of Negro slaves who had been seared in the flames of withering injustice. It came as a joyous daybreak to end the long night of captivity.

2   But one hundred years later, we must face the tragic fact that the Negro is still not free. One hundred years later, the life of the Negro is still sadly crippled by the manacles of segregation and the chains of

discrimination. One hundred years later, the Negro lives on a lonely island of poverty in the midst of a vast ocean of material prosperity. One
hundred years later, the Negro is still languishing in the corners of American society and finds himself an exile in his own land. So we have come
here today to dramatize an appalling condition.

3   In a sense we have come to our nation's capital to cash a check.
When the architects of our republic wrote the magnificent words of the
Constitution and the Declaration of Independence, they were signing a
promissory note to which every American was to fall heir. This note was
a promise that all men would be guaranteed the unalienable rights of life,
liberty, and the pursuit of happiness.

4   It is obvious today that America has defaulted on this promissory
note insofar as her citizens of color are concerned. Instead of honoring
this sacred obligation, America has given the Negro people a bad check;
a check which has come back marked "insufficient funds." But we refuse
to believe that the bank of justice is bankrupt. We refuse to believe that
there are insufficient funds in the great vaults of opportunity of this nation. So we have come to cash this check—a check that will give us upon
demand the riches of freedom and the security of justice. We have also
come to this hallowed spot to remind America of the fierce urgency of
now. This is no time to engage in the luxury of cooling off or to take the
tranquilizing drugs of gradualism. *Now* is the time to make real the
promises of Democracy. *Now* is the time to rise from the dark and deso-
late valley of segregation to the sunlit path of racial justice. *Now* is the
time to open the doors of opportunity to all of God's children. *Now* is
the time to lift our nation from the quicksands of racial injustice to the
solid rock of brotherhood.

5   It would be fatal for the nation to overlook the urgency of the moment
and to underestimate the determination of the Negro. This sweltering
summer of the Negro's legitimate discontent will not pass until there is
an invigorating autumn of freedom and equality. Nineteen sixty-three is
not an end, but a beginning. Those who hope that the Negro needed to
blow off steam and will now be content will have a rude awakening if the
nation returns to business as usual. There will be neither rest nor tran-
quillity in America until the Negro is granted his citizenship rights. The
whirl-winds of revolt will continue to shake the foundations of our nation
until the bright day of justice emerges.

6   But there is something that I must say to my people who stand on the
warm threshold which leads into the palace of justice. In the process of
gaining our rightful place we must not be guilty of wrongful deeds. Let us
not seek to satisfy our thirst for freedom by drinking from the cup of
bitterness and hatred. We must forever conduct our struggle on the
high plane of dignity and discipline. We must not allow our creative
protest to degenerate into physical violence. Again and again we must

rise to the majestic heights of meeting physical force with soul force. The marvelous new militancy which has engulfed the Negro community must not lead us to a distrust of all white people, for many of our white brothers, as evidenced by their presence here today, have come to realize that their destiny is tied up with our destiny and their freedom is inextricably bound to our freedom. We cannot walk alone.

7   And as we walk, we must make the pledge that we shall march ahead. We cannot turn back. There are those who are asking the devotees of civil rights, "When will you be satisfied?" We can never be satisfied as long as the Negro is the victim of the unspeakable horrors of police brutality. We can never be satisfied as long as our bodies, heavy with the fatigue of travel, cannot gain lodging in the motels of the highways and the hotels of the cities. We cannot be satisfied as long as the Negro's basic mobility is from a smaller ghetto to a larger one. We can never be satisfied as long as a Negro in Mississippi cannot vote and a Negro in New York believes he has nothing for which to vote. No, no, we are not satisfied, and we will not be satisfied until justice rolls down like waters and righteousness like a mighty stream.

8   I am not unmindful that some of you have come here out of great trials and tribulations. Some of you have come fresh from narrow jail cells. Some of you have come from areas where your quest for freedom left you battered by the storms of persecution and staggered by the winds of police brutality. You have been the veterans of creative suffering. Continue to work with the faith that unearned suffering is redemptive.

9   Go back to Mississippi, go back to Alabama, go back to South Carolina, go back to Georgia, go back to Louisiana, go back to the slums and ghettos of our northern cities, knowing that somehow this situation can and will be changed. Let us not wallow in the valley of despair.

10   I say to you today, my friends, that in spite of the difficulties and frustrations of the moment I still have a dream. It is a dream deeply rooted in the American dream.

11   I have a dream that one day this nation will rise up and live out the true meaning of its creed: "We hold these truths to be self-evident; that all men are created equal."

12   I have a dream that one day on the red hills of Georgia the sons of former slaves and the sons of former slaveowners will be able to sit down together at the table of brotherhood.

13   I have a dream that one day even the state of Mississippi, a desert state sweltering with the heat of injustice and oppression, will be transformed into an oasis of freedom and justice.

14   I have a dream that my four little children will one day live in a nation where they will not be judged by the color of their skin but by the content of their character.

15   I have a dream today.

16   I have a dream that one day the state of Alabama, whose governor's lips are presently dripping with the words of interposition and nullification, will be transformed into a situation where little black boys and black girls will be able to join hands with little white boys and white girls and walk together as sisters and brothers.

17   I have a dream today.

18   I have a dream that one day every valley shall be exalted, every hill and mountain shall be made low, the rough places will be made plain, and the crooked places will be made straight, and the glory of the Lord shall be revealed, and all flesh shall see it together.

19   This is our hope. This is the faith with which I return to the South. With this faith we will be able to hew out of the mountain of despair a stone of hope. With this faith we will be able to transform the jangling discords of our nation into a beautiful symphony of brotherhood. With this faith we will be able to work together, to pray together, to struggle together, to go to jail together, to stand up for freedom together, knowing that we will be free one day.

20   This will be the day when all of God's children will be able to sing with new meaning

> My country, 'tis of thee,
> Sweet land of liberty,
>   Of thee I sing:
> Land where my fathers died,
> Land of the pilgrims' pride,
> From every mountain-side
>   Let freedom ring.

21   And if America is to be a great nation this must become true. So let freedom ring from the prodigious hilltops of New Hampshire. Let freedom ring from the mighty mountains of New York. Let freedom ring from the heightening Alleghenies of Pennsylvania!

22   Let freedom ring from the snowcapped Rockies of Colorado!

23   Let freedom ring from the curvaceous peaks of California!

24   But not only that; let freedom ring from Stone Mountain of Georgia!

25   Let freedom ring from Lookout Mountain of Tennessee!

26   Let freedom ring from every hill and molehill of Mississippi. From every mountainside, let freedom ring.

27   When we let freedom ring, when we let it ring from every village and every hamlet, from every state and every city, we will be able to speed up that day when all of God's children, black men and white men, Jews and Gentiles, Protestants and Catholics, will be able to join hands and sing in the words of the old Negro spiritual, "Free at last! free at last! thank God almighty, we are free at last!"

Politics and the English Language

George Orwell

George Orwell is the pseudonym of Eric Arthur Blair, a British novelist and essayist. Some of his best-known works include Down and Out in Paris and London *(1933) and the novels* Animal Farm *(1945) and* 1984 *(1949). This famous essay, which explores the relationship among language, thought, and politics, first appeared in the collection* Shooting an Elephant and Other Essays *(1950).*

1   Most people who bother with the matter at all would admit that the English language is in a bad way, but it is generally assumed that we cannot by conscious action do anything about it. Our civilization is decadent and our language—so the argument runs—must inevitably share in the general collapse. It follows that any struggle against the abuse of language is a sentimental archaism, like preferring candles to electric light or hansom cabs to aeroplanes. Underneath this lies the half-conscious belief that language is a natural growth and not an instrument which we shape for our own purpose.

2   Now, it is clear that the decline of a language must ultimately have political and economic causes: it is not due simply to the bad influence of this or that individual writer. But an effect can become a cause, reinforcing the original cause and producing the same effect in an intensified form, and so on indefinitely. A man may take to drink because he feels himself to be a failure, and then fail all the more completely because he drinks. It is rather the same thing that is happening to the English language. It becomes ugly and inaccurate because our thoughts are foolish, but the slovenliness of our language makes it easier for us to have foolish thoughts. The point is that the process is reversible. Modern English, especially written English, is full of bad habits which spread by imitation and which can be avoided if one is willing to take the necessary trouble. If one gets rid of these habits one can think more clearly, and to think clearly is a necessary first step toward political regeneration: so that the fight against bad English is not frivolous and is not the exclusive concern of professional writers. I will come back to this presently, and I hope that by that time the meaning of what I have said here will have become clearer. Meanwhile, here are five specimens of the English language as it is now habitually written.

3   These five passages have not been picked out because they are especially bad—I could have quoted far worse if I had chosen—but because they illustrate various of the mental vices from which we now suffer. They are a little below the average, but are fairly representative samples. I number them so that I can refer back to them when necessary:

> (1) I am not, indeed, sure whether it is not true to say that the Milton who once seemed not unlike a seventeenth-century Shelley had not become, out

of an experience ever more bitter in each year, more alien [*sic*] to the founder of that Jesuit sect which nothing could induce him to tolerate.

Professor Harold Laski (Essay in *Freedom of Expression*)

(2) Above all, we cannot play ducks and drakes with a native battery of idioms which prescribes such egregious collocations of vocables as the Basic *put up with* for *tolerate* or *put at a loss* for *bewilder*.

Professor Lancelot Hogben *(Interglossa)*

(3) On the one side we have the free personality: by definition it is not neurotic, for it has neither conflict nor dream. Its desires, such as they are, are transparent, for they are just what institutional approval keeps in the forefront of consciousness; another institutional pattern would alter their number and intensity; there is little in them that is natural, irreducible, or culturally dangerous. But *on the other side,* the social bond itself is nothing but the mutual reflection of these self-secure integrities. Recall the definition of love. Is not this the very picture of a small academic? Where is there a place in this hall of mirrors for either personality or fraternity?

Essay on psychology in *Politics* (New York)

(4) All the "best people" from the gentlemen's clubs, and all the frantic fascist captains, united in common hatred of Socialism and bestial horror of the rising tide of the mass revolutionary movement, have turned to acts of provocation, to foul incendiarism, to medieval legends of poisoned wells, to legalize their own destruction of proletarian organizations, and rouse the agitated petty-bourgeoisie to chauvinistic fervor on behalf of the fight against the revolutionary way out of the crisis.

Communist pamphlet

(5) If a new spirit *is* to be infused into this old country, there is one thorny and contentious reform which must be tackled, and that is the humanization and galvanization of the B.B.C. Timidity here will bespeak cancer and atrophy of the soul. The heart of Britain may be sound and of strong beat, for instance, but the British lion's roar at present is like that of Bottom in Shakespeare's *Midsummer Night's Dream*—as gentle as any sucking dove. A virile new Britain cannot continue indefinitely to be traduced in the eyes or rather ears, of the world by the effete languors of Langham Place, brazenly masquerading as "standard English." When the Voice of Britain is heard at nine o'clock, better far and infinitely less ludicrous to hear aitches honestly dropped than the present priggish, inflated, inhibited, school-ma'amish arch braying of blameless bashful mewing maidens!

Letter in *Tribune*

4   Each of these passages has faults of its own, but, quite apart from avoidable ugliness, two qualities are common to all of them. The first is staleness of imagery; the other is lack of precision. The writer either has

a meaning and cannot express it, or he inadvertently says something else, or he is almost indifferent as to whether his words mean anything or not. The mixture of vagueness and sheer incompetence is the most marked characteristic of modern English prose, and especially of any kind of political writing. As soon as certain topics are raised, the concrete melts into the abstract and no one seems to think of turns of speech that are not hackneyed: prose consists less and less of *words* chosen for the sake of their meaning, and more and more of *phrases* tacked together like the sections of a prefabricated henhouse. I listed below, with notes and examples, various of the tricks by means of which the work of prose-construction is habitually dodged:

Dying Metaphors

5   A newly invented metaphor assists thought by evoking a visual image, while on the other hand a metaphor which is technically "dead" (e.g., *iron resolution*) has in effect reverted to being an ordinary word and can generally be used without loss of vividness. But in between these two classes there is a huge dump of worn-out metaphors which have lost all evocative power and are merely used because they save people the trouble of inventing phrases for themselves. Examples are: *ring the changes on, take up the cudgels for, toe the line, ride roughshod over, stand shoulder to shoulder with, play into the hands of, no axe to grind, grist to the mill, fishing in troubled waters, rift within the lute, on the order of the day, Achilles' heel, swan song, hotbed.* Many of these are used without knowledge of their meaning (what is a "rift," for instance?), and incompatible metaphors are frequently mixed, a sure sign that the writer is not interested in what he is saying. Some metaphors now current have been twisted out of their original meaning without those who use them even being aware of the fact. For example, *toe the line* is sometimes written *tow the line.* Another example is *the hammer and the anvil,* now always used with the implication that the anvil gets the worst of it. In real life it is always the anvil that breaks the hammer, never the other way about: a writer who stopped to think what he was saying would be aware of this, and would avoid perverting the original phrase.

Operators or Verbal False Limbs

6   These save the trouble of picking out appropriate verbs and nouns, and at the same time pad each sentence with extra syllables which give it an appearance of symmetry. Characteristic phrases are: *render inoperative, militate against, make contact with, be subjected to, give rise to, give grounds for, have the effect of, play a leading part (role) in, make itself felt, take effect, exhibit a tendency to, serve the purpose of, etc., etc.* The keynote is the elimination of simple verbs. Instead of being a single word, such as *break, stop, spoil, mend, kill,* a verb becomes a *phrase,* made up

of a noun or adjective tacked on to some general-purpose verb such as *prove, serve, form, play, render.* In addition, the passive voice is wherever possible used in preference to the active, and noun constructions are used instead of gerunds (*by examination of* instead of *by examining*). The range of verbs is further cut down by means of the *-ize* and *de-* formation, and the banal statements are given an appearance of profundity by means of the *not un-* formation. Simple conjunctions and prepositions are replaced by such phrases as *with respect to, having regard to, the fact that, by dint of, in view of, in the interests of, on the hypothesis that;* and the ends of sentences are saved from anticlimax by such resounding commonplaces as *greatly to be desired, cannot be left out of account, a development to be expected in the near future, deserving of serious consideration, brought to a satisfactory conclusion,* and so on and so forth.

Pretentious Diction

7   Words like *phenomenon, element, individual* (as noun), *objective, categorical, effective, virtual, basic, primary, promote, constitute, exhibit, exploit, utilize, eliminate, liquidate,* are used to dress up simple statements and give an air of scientific impartiality to biased judgments. Adjectives like *epoch-making, epic, historic, unforgettable, triumphant, age-old, inexorable, inevitable, veritable,* are used to dignify the sordid processes of international politics, while writing that aims at glorifying war usually takes on an archaic color, its characteristic words being: *realm, throne, chariot, mailed fist, trident, sword, shield, buckler, banner, jackboot, clarion.* Foreign words and expressions such as *cul de sac, ancien régime, deus ex machina, mutatis mutandis, status quo, gleich-shaltung, weltanschauung,* are used to give an air of culture and elegance. Except for the useful abbreviations *i.e., e.g.,* and *etc.,* there is no real need for any of the hundreds of foreign phrases now current in English. Bad writers, and especially scientific, political and sociological writers, are nearly always haunted by the notion that Latin or Greek words are grander than Saxon ones, and unnecessary words like *expedite, ameliorate, predict, extraneous, deracinated, clandestine, subaqueous* and hundreds of others constantly gain ground from their Anglo-Saxon opposite numbers.* The jargon peculiar to Marxist writing (*hyena, hangman, cannibal, petty bourgeois, these gentry, lacquey, flunkey, mad dog, White Guard,* etc.) consists largely of words and phrases translated from Russian, German, or French; but the normal way of coining a new word is to use a Latin or

---

*An interesting illustration of this is the way in which the English flower names which were in use till very recently are being ousted by Greek ones, *snapdragon* becoming *antirrhinum, forget-me-not* becoming *myosotis,* etc. It is hard to see any practical reason for this change of fashion: it is probably due to an instinctive turning-away from the more homely word and a vague feeling that the Greek word is scientific. [Orwell's note]

Greek root with the appropriate affix and, where necessary, the *-ize* formation. It is often easier to make up words of this kind (*deregionalize, impermissible, extramarital, nonfragmentatory* and so forth) than to think up the English words that will cover one's meaning. The result, in general, is an increase in slovenliness and vagueness.

Meaningless Words

8   In certain kinds of writing, particularly in art criticism and literary criticism, it is normal to come across long passages which are almost completely lacking in meaning.* Words like *romantic, plastic, values, human, dead, sentimental, natural, vitality,* as used in art criticism, are strictly meaningless in the sense that they not only do not point to any discoverable object, but are hardly ever expected to do so by the reader. When one critic writes, "The outstanding feature of Mr. X's work is its living quality," while another writes, "The immediately striking thing about Mr. X's work is its peculiar deadness," the reader accepts this as a simple difference of opinion. If words like *black* and *white* were involved, instead of the jargon words *dead* and *living,* he would see at once that language was being used in an improper way. Many political words are similarly abused. The word *Fascism* has now no meaning except in so far as it signifies "something not desirable." The words *democracy, socialism, freedom, patriotic, realistic, justice,* have each of them several different meanings which cannot be reconciled with one another. In the case of a word like *democracy,* not only is there no agreed definition, but the attempt to make one is resisted from all sides. It is almost universally felt that when we call a country democratic we are praising it: consequently the defenders of every kind of régime claim that it is a democracy, and fear that they might have to stop using the word if it were tied down to any one meaning. Words of this kind are often used in a consciously dishonest way. That is, the person who uses them has his own private definition, but allows his hearer to think he means something quite different. Statements like *Marshall Pétain was a true patriot, The Soviet Press is the freest in the world, The Catholic Church is opposed to persecution,* are almost always made with intent to deceive. Other words used in variable meanings, in most cases more or less dishonestly, are: *class, totalitarian, science, progressive, reactionary, bourgeois, equality.*

9   Now that I have made this catalogue of swindles and perversions, let me give another example of the kind of writing that they lead to. This

---

*Example: "Comfort's catholicity of perception and image, strangely Whitmanesque in range, almost the exact opposite in aesthetic compulsion, continues to evoke that trembling atmospheric accumulative hinting at a cruel, an inexorably serene timelessness ... Wrey Gardiner scores by aiming at simple bull's-eyes with precision. Only they are not so simple, and through this contended sadness runs more than the surface bitter-sweet of resignation." *(Poetry Quarterly).* [Orwell's note] time it must of its nature be an imaginary one. I am going to translate a passage of good English into modern English of the worst sort. Here is a well-known verse from *Ecclesiastes:*

> I returned and saw under the sun, that the race is not to the swift, nor the battle to the strong, neither yet bread to the wise, nor yet riches to men of understanding, nor yet favour to men of skill; but time and chance happeneth to them all.

Here it is in modern English:

> Objective consideration of contemporary phenomena compels the conclusion that success or failure in competitive activities exhibits no tendency to be commensurate with innate capacity, but that a considerable element of the unpredictable must invariably be taken into account.

10   This is a parody, but not a very gross one. Exhibit (3), above, for instance, contains several patches of the same kind of English. It will be seen that I have not made a full translation. The beginning and ending of the sentence follow the original meaning fairly closely, but in the middle the concrete illustrations—race, battle, bread—dissolve into the vague phrase "success or failure in competitive activities." This had to be so, because no modern writer of the kind I am discussing—no one capable of using phrases like "objective consideration of contemporary phenomena"—would ever tabulate his thoughts in that precise and detailed way. The whole tendency of modern prose is away from concreteness. Now analyze these two sentences a little more closely. The first contains forty-nine words but only sixty syllables, and all its words are those of everyday life. The second contains thirty-eight words of ninety syllables: eighteen of its words are from Latin roots, and one from Greek. The first sentence contains six vivid images, and only one phrase ("time and chance") that could be called vague. The second contains not a single fresh, arresting phrase, and in spite of its ninety syllables it gives only a shortened version of the meaning contained in the first. Yet without a doubt it is the second kind of sentence that is gaining ground in modern English. I do not want to exaggerate. This kind of writing is not yet universal; and outcrops of simplicity will occur here and there in the worst-written page. Still, if you or I were told to write a few lines on the uncertainty of human fortunes, we should probably come much nearer to my imaginary sentence than to the one from *Ecclesiastes.*

11   As I have tried to show, modern writing at its worst does not consist in picking out words for the sake of their meaning and inventing images in order to make the meaning clearer. It consists in gumming together long strips of words which have already been set in order by someone

else, and making the results presentable by sheer humbug. The attraction of this way of writing is that it is easy. It is easier—even quicker once you have the habit—to say *In my opinion it is a not unjustifiable assumption that* than to say *I think*. If you use ready-made phrases, you not only don't have to hunt about for words; you also don't have to bother with the rhythms of your sentences, since these phrases are generally so arranged as to be more or less euphonious. When you are composing in a hurry—when you are dictating to a stenographer, for instance, or making a public speech—it is natural to fall into a pretentious, Latinized style. Tags like *a consideration which we should do well to bear in mind* or *a conclusion to which all of us would readily assent* will save many a sentence from coming down with a bump. By using stale metaphors, similes and idioms, you save much mental effort, at the cost of leaving your meaning vague, not only for your reader but for yourself. This is the significance of mixed metaphors. The sole aim of a metaphor is to call up a visual image. When these images clash—as in *The Fascist octopus has sung its swan song, the jackboot is thrown into the melting pot*—it can be taken as certain that the writer is not seeing a mental image of the objects he is naming; in other words he is not really thinking. Look again at the examples I gave at the beginning of this essay. Professor Laski (1) uses five negatives in fifty-three words. One of these is superfluous, making nonsense of the whole passage, and in addition there is the slip *alien* for *akin,* making further nonsense, and several avoidable pieces of clumsiness which increase the general vagueness. Professor Hogben (2) plays ducks and drakes with a battery which is able to write prescriptions, and, while disapproving of the everyday phrase *put up with,* is unwilling to look *egregious* up in the dictionary and see what it means. (3), if one takes an uncharitable attitude towards it, is simply meaningless. Probably one could work out its intended meaning by reading the whole of the article in which it occurs. In (4), the writer knows more or less what he wants to say, but an accumulation of stale phrases chokes him like tea leaves blocking a sink. In (5), words and meaning have almost parted company. People who write in this manner usually have a general emotional meaning—they dislike one thing and want to express solidarity with another—but they are not interested in the detail of what they are saying. A scrupulous writer, in every sentence that he writes, will ask himself at least four questions, thus: What am I trying to say? What words will express it? What image or idiom will make it clearer? Is this image fresh enough to have an effect? And he will probably ask himself two more: Could I put it more shortly? Have I said anything that is avoidably ugly? But you are not obliged to go to all this trouble. You can shirk it by simply throwing your mind open and letting the ready-made phrases come crowding in. They will construct your sentences for you—even think your thoughts for you, to a certain extent—and at need they will perform the important service of partially concealing your meaning even from yourself. It is at this point that the special connection between politics and the debasement of language becomes clear.

12   In our times it is broadly true that political writing is bad writing. Where it is not true, it will generally be found that the writer is some kind of rebel, expressing his private opinions and not a "party line." Orthodoxy, of whatever color, seems to demand a lifeless, imitative style. The political dialects to be found in pamphlets, leading articles, manifestos, White Papers and the speeches of under-secretaries do, of course, vary from party to party, but they are all alike in that one almost never finds in them a fresh, vivid, home-made turn of speech. When one watches some tired hack on the platform mechanically repeating the familiar phrases—*bestial atrocities, iron heel, bloodstained tyranny, free peoples of the world, stand shoulder to shoulder*—one often has a curious feeling that one is not watching a live human being but some kind of dummy, a feeling which suddenly becomes stronger at moments when the light catches the speaker's spectacles and turns them into blank discs which seem to have no eyes behind them. And this is not altogether fanciful. A speaker who uses that kind of phraseology has gone some distance towards turning himself into a machine. The appropriate noises are coming out of his larynx, but his brain is not involved as it would be if he were choosing his words from himself. If the speech he is making is one that he is accustomed to make over and over again, he may be almost unconscious of what he is saying, as one is when one utters the responses in church. And this reduced state of consciousness, if not indispensable, is at any rate favorable to political conformity.

13   In our time, political speech and writing are largely the defense of the indefensible. Things like the continuance of British rule in India, the Russian purges and deportations, the dropping of the atom bomb on Japan, can indeed be defended, but only by arguments which are too brutal for most people to face, and which do not square with the professed aims of political parties. Thus political language has to consist largely of euphemism, question-begging and sheer cloudy vagueness. Defenseless villages are bombarded from the air, the inhabitants driven out into the countryside, the cattle machine-gunned, the huts set on fire with incendiary bullets: this is called *pacification*. Millions of peasants are robbed of their farms and sent trudging along the roads with no more than they can carry: this is called *transfer of population* or *rectification of frontiers*. People are imprisoned for years without trial, or shot in the back of the neck or sent to die of scurvy in Arctic lumber camps: this is called *elimination of unreliable elements*. Such phraseology is needed if one wants to name things without calling up mental pictures of them. Consider for instance some comfortable English professor defending Russian totalitarianism. He cannot say outright, "I believe in killing off your opponents

when you can get good results by doing so." Probably, therefore, he will
say something like this:

14 "While freely conceding that the Soviet régime exhibits certain features which the humanitarian may be inclined to deplore, we must, I
think, agree that a certain curtailment of the right to political opposition
is an unavoidable concomitant of transitional periods, and that the rigors
which the Russian people have been called upon to undergo have been
amply justified in the sphere of concrete achievement."

15 The inflated style is itself a kind of euphemism. A mass of Latin
words falls upon the facts like soft snow, blurring the outlines and covering up all the details. The great enemy of clear language is insincerity.
When there is a gap between one's real and one's declared aims, one
turns as it were instinctively to long words and exhausted idioms, like a
cuttlefish squirting out ink. In our age there is no such thing as "keeping
out of politics." All issues are political issues, and politics itself is a mass
of lies, evasions, folly, hatred and schizophrenia. When the general atmosphere is bad, language must suffer. I should expect to find—this is a
guess which I have not sufficient knowledge to verify—that the German,
Russian and Italian languages have all deteriorated in the last ten or fifteen years, as a result of dictatorship.

16 But if thought corrupts language, language can also corrupt thought.
A bad usage can spread by tradition and imitation, even among people
who should and do know better. The debased language that I have been
discussing is in some ways very convenient. Phrases like *a not unjustifiable assumption, leaves much to be desired, would serve no good purpose, a
consideration which we should do well to bear in mind,* are a continuous
temptation, a packet of aspirins always at one's elbow. Look back through
this essay, and for certain you will find that I have again and again committed the very faults I am protesting against. By this morning's post I
have received a pamphlet dealing with conditions in Germany. The author
tells me that he "felt impelled" to write it. I open it at random, and here is
almost the first sentence that I see. "(The Allies) have an opportunity not
only of achieving a radical transformation of Germany's social and political structure in such a way as to avoid a nationalistic reaction in Germany
itself, but at the same time of laying the foundations of a co-operative and
unified Europe." You see, he "feels impelled" to write—feels, presumably,
that he has something new to say—and yet his words, like cavalry horses
answering the bugle, group themselves automatically into the familiar
dreary pattern. This invasion of one's mind by ready-made phrases *(lay
the foundations, achieve a radical transformation)* can only be prevented if
one is constantly on guard against them, and every such phrase anaes-
thetizes a portion of one's brain.

17 I said earlier that the decadence of our language is probably curable.
Those who deny this would argue, if they produced an argument at all,

that language merely reflects existing social conditions, and that we cannot influence its development by any direct tinkering with words and constructions. So far as the general tone or spirit of a language goes, this may be true, but it is not true in detail. Silly words and expressions have often disappeared, not through any evolutionary process but owing to the conscious action of a minority. Two recent examples were *explore every avenue* and *leave no stone unturned,* which were killed by the jeers of a few journalists. There is a long list of flyblown metaphors which could similarly be got rid of if enough people would interest themselves in the job; and it should also be possible to laugh the *not un-* formation out of existence,* to reduce the amount of Latin and Greek in the average sentence, to drive out foreign phrases and strayed scientific words, and, in general, to make pretentiousness unfashionable. But all these are minor points. The defense of the English language implies more than this, and perhaps it is best to start by saying what it does *not* imply.

18   To begin with it has nothing to do with archaism, with the salvaging of obsolete words and turns of speech, or with the setting up of a "standard English" which must never be departed from. On the contrary, it is especially concerned with the scrapping of every word or idiom which has outworn its usefulness. It has nothing to do with correct grammar and syntax, which are of no importance so long as one makes one's meaning clear, or with the avoidance of Americanisms, or with having what is called a "good prose style." On the other hand, it is not concerned with fake simplicity and the attempt to make written English colloquial. Nor does it even imply in every case preferring the Saxon word to the Latin one, though it does imply using the fewest and shortest words that will cover one's meaning. What is above all needed is to let the meaning choose the word, and not the other way about. In prose, the worst thing one can do with words is to surrender to them. When you think of a concrete object, you think wordlessly, and then, if you want to describe the thing you have been visualizing you probably hunt about till you find the exact words that seem to fit. When you think of something abstract, you are more inclined to use words from the start, and unless you make a conscious effort to prevent it, the existing dialect will come rushing in and do the job for you, at the expense of blurring or even changing your meaning. Probably it is better to put off using words as long as possible and get one's meaning as clear as one can through pictures or sensations. Afterwards one can choose—not simply *accept*—the phrases that will best cover the meaning, and then switch round and decide what impression one's words are likely to make on another person.

---

* One can cure oneself of the *not un-* formation by memorizing this sentence: *A not unblack dog was chasing a not unsmall rabbit across a not ungreen field.* [Orwell's note]

This last effort of the mind cuts out all stale or mixed images, all prefabricated phrases, needless repetitions, and humbug and vagueness generally. But one can often be in doubt about the effect of a word or a phrase, and one needs rules that one can rely on when instinct fails. I think the following rules will cover most cases:

(i) Never use a metaphor, simile or other figure of speech which you are used to seeing in print.

(ii) Never use a long word where a short one will do.

(iii) If it is possible to cut a word out, always cut it out.

(iv) Never use the passive where you can use the active.

(v) Never use a foreign phrase, a scientific word or jargon word if you can think of an everyday English equivalent.

(vi) Break any of these rules sooner than say anything outright barbarous.

These rules sound elementary, and so they are, but they demand a deep change in attitude in anyone who has grown used to writing in the style now fashionable. One could keep all of them and still write bad English, but one could not write the kind of stuff that I quoted in those five specimens at the beginning of this article.

19   I have not here been considering the literary use of language, but merely language as an instrument for expressing and not for concealing or preventing thought. Stuart Chase and others have come near to claiming that all abstract words are meaningless, and have used this as a pretext for advocating a kind of political quietism. Since you don't know what Fascism is, how can you struggle against Fascism? One need not swallow such absurdities as this, but one ought to recognize that the present political chaos is connected with the decay of language; and that one can probably bring about some improvement by starting at the verbal end. If you simplify your English, you are freed from the worst follies of orthodoxy. You cannot speak any of the necessary dialects, and when you make a stupid remark, its stupidity will be obvious, even to yourself. Political language—and with variations this is true of all political parties, from Conservatives to Anarchists—is designed to make lies sound truthful and murder respectable, and to give an appearance of solidity to pure wind. One cannot change this all in a moment, but one can at least change one's own habits, and from time to time one can even, if one jeers loudly enough, send some worn-out and useless phrase—some *jackboot, Achilles' heel, hotbed, melting pot, acid test, veritable inferno* or other lump of verbal refuse—into the dustbin where it belongs.

A Modest Proposal

Jonathan Swift

Jonathan Swift was born in 1667 and educated in Ireland. In 1713 he became Dean of St. Patrick's Cathedral in Dublin, but he was soon recognized for his satire and criticism of the British government. His best-known work is Gulliver's Travels *(1726). Deeply concerned over the poverty and misery of the Irish peasants suffering under British control, Swift wrote this famous "proposal" in 1729.*

> *For Preventing the Children of*
> *Poor People in Ireland from*
> *Being a Burden to Their*
> *Parents or Country, and for*
> *Making Them Beneficial to the Public*

1   It is a melancholy object to those who walk through this great town, or travel in the country, when they see the streets, the roads, and cabin-doors crowded with beggars of the female sex, followed by three, four, or six children, all in rags, and importuning every passenger for an alms. These mothers, instead of being able to work for their honest livelihood, are forced to employ all their time in strolling to beg sustenance for their helpless infants: who, as they grow up, either turn thieves for want of work, or leave their dear native country to fight for the Pretender in Spain, or sell themselves to the Barbadoes.

2   I think it is agreed by all parties, that this prodigious number of children in the arms, or on the backs, or at the heels of their mothers, and frequently of their fathers, is in the present deplorable state of the kingdom, a very great additional grievance; and, therefore, whoever could find out a fair, cheap, and easy method of making these children sound and useful members of the commonwealth, would deserve so well of the public, as to have his statue set up for a preserver of the nation.

3   But my intention is very far from being confined to provide only for the children of professed beggars; it is of a much greater extent, and shall take in the whole number of infants at a certain age, who are born of parents in effect as little able to support them as those who demand our charity in the streets.

4   As to my own part, having turned my thoughts for many years upon this important subject, and maturely weighed the several schemes of other projectors, I have always found them grossly mistaken in their computation. It is true, a child, just dropped from its dam, may be supported by her milk for a solar year with little other nourishment; at most, not above the value of two shillings, which the mother may certainly get,

or the value in scraps, by her lawful occupation of begging; and it is exactly at one year old that I propose to provide for them in such a manner, as, instead of being a charge upon their parents or the parish, or wanting food and raiment for the rest of their lives, they shall, on the contrary, contribute to the feeding, and partly to the clothing, of many thousands.

5   There is likewise another great advantage in my scheme, that it will prevent those voluntary abortions, and that horrid practice of women murdering their bastard children, alas, too frequent among us, sacrificing the poor innocent babes, I doubt more to avoid the expense than the shame, which would move tears and pity in the savage and inhuman breast.

6   The number of souls in this kingdom being usually reckoned one million and a half, of these I calculate there may be about two hundred thousand couples whose wives are breeders; from which number I subtract thirty thousand couples, who are able to maintain their own children (although I apprehend there cannot be so many, under the present distresses of the kingdom); but this being granted, there will remain an hundred and seventy thousand breeders. I again subtract fifty thousand for those women who miscarry, or whose children die by accident or disease within the year. There only remain a hundred and twenty thousand children of poor parents annually born. The question therefore is how this number shall be reared and provided for? which, as I have already said, under the present situation of affairs, is utterly impossible by all the methods hitherto proposed. For we can neither employ them in handicraft or agriculture; we neither build houses (I mean in the country) nor cultivate land: they can very seldom pick up a livelihood by stealing until they arrive at six years old, except where they are of towardly parts; although I confess they learn the rudiments much earlier; during which time they can, however, be properly looked upon only as probationers; as I have been informed by a principal gentleman in the county of Cavan, who protested to me, that he never knew above one or two instances under the age of six, even in a part of the kingdom so renowned for the quickest proficiency in that art.

7   I am assured by our merchants that a boy or a girl before twelve years old is no salable commodity; and even when they come to this age they will not yield above three pounds or three pounds and half-a-crown at most, on the exchange; which cannot turn to account either to the parents or kingdom, the charge of nutriment and rags having been at least four times that value.

8   I shall now, therefore, humbly propose my own thoughts, which I hope will not be liable to the least objection.

9   I have been assured by a very knowing American of my acquaintance in London, that a young healthy child, well nursed, is, at a year old, a most

delicious, nourishing, and wholesome food, whether stewed, roasted, baked, or boiled; and I make no doubt that it will equally serve in a fricassee or a ragout.

10   I do therefore humbly offer it to public consideration, that of the hundred and twenty thousand children already computed, twenty thousand may be reserved for breed, whereof only one-fourth part to be males; which is more than we allow to sheep, black cattle, or swine; and my reason is, that these children are seldom the fruits of marriage, a circumstance not much regarded by our savages, therefore one male will be sufficient to serve four females. That the remaining hundred thousand may, at a year old, be offered in sale to the persons of quality and fortune through the kingdom; always advising the mother to let them suck plentifully in the last month, so as to render them plump and fat for a good table. A child will make two dishes at an entertainment for friends; and when the family dines alone, the fore or hind quarter will make a reasonable dish, and, seasoned with a little pepper or salt, will be very good boiled on the fourth day, especially in winter.

11   I have reckoned, upon a medium, that a child just born will weigh twelve pounds, and in a solar year, if tolerably nursed, increaseth to twenty-eight pounds.

12   I grant this food will be somewhat dear, and therefore very proper for landlords, who, as they have already devoured most of the parents, seem to have the best title to the children.

13   Infants' flesh will be in season throughout the year, but more plentifully in March, and a little before and after: for we are told by a grave author, an eminent French physician, that fish being a prolific diet, there are more children born in Roman Catholic countries about nine months after Lent than at any other season; therefore, reckoning a year after Lent, the markets will be more glutted than usual, because the number of popish infants is at least three to one in this kingdom; and therefore, it will have one other collateral advantage, by lessening the number of papists among us.

14   I have already computed the charge of nursing a beggar's child (in which list I reckon all cottagers, labourers, and four-fifths of the farmers) to be about two shillings per annum, rags included; and I believe no gentleman would repine to give ten shillings for the carcass of a good fat child, which, as I have said, will make four dishes of excellent nutritive meat, when he has only some particular friend, or his own family, to dine with him. Thus, the squire will learn to be a good landlord, and grow popular among his tenants; the mother will have eight shillings net profit, and be fit for work till she produces another child.

15   Those who are more thrifty (as I must confess the times require) may flay the carcass; the skin of which artificially dressed, will make admirable gloves for ladies, and summerboots for fine gentlemen.

16   As to our city of Dublin, shambles* may be appointed for this purpose in the most convenient parts of it, and butchers we may be assured
will not be wanting; although I rather recommend buying the children
alive, and dressing them hot from the knife, as we do roasting pigs.

17   A very worthy person, a true lover of this country, and whose virtues
I highly esteem, was lately pleased, in discoursing on this matter, to offer
a refinement upon my scheme. He said, that many gentlemen of this kingdom, having of late destroyed their deer, he conceived that the want of
venison might be well supplied by the bodies of young lads and maidens,
not exceeding fourteen years of age, nor under twelve; so great a number
of both sexes in every country being now ready to starve for want of
work and service; and these to be disposed of by their parents, if alive, or
otherwise by their nearest relations. But, with due deference to so excellent a friend, and so deserving a patriot, I cannot be altogether in his sen-
timents; for as to the males, my American acquaintance assured me from
frequent experience, that their flesh was generally tough and lean, like
that of our schoolboys, by continual exercise, and their taste disagree-
able; and to fatten them would not answer the charge. Then as to the females, it would, I think, with humble submission, be a loss to the public,
because they soon would become breeders themselves: and besides, it is
not improbable that some scrupulous people might be apt to censure
such a practice (although indeed very unjustly) as a little bordering
upon cruelty; which, I confess hath always been with me the strongest
objection against any project, how well soever intended.

18   But in order to justify my friend, he confessed that this expedient
was put into his head by the famous Psalmanazar,† a native of the island
Formosa, who came from thence to London above twenty years ago; and
in conversation told my friend, that in his country, when any young person happened to be put to death, the executioner sold the carcass to
persons of quality as a prime dainty; and that in his time the body of a
plump girl of fifteen, who was crucified for an attempt to poison the emperor, was sold to his Imperial Majesty's prime minister of state, and
other great mandarins of the court, in joints from the gibbet, at four hundred crowns. Neither indeed can I deny, that if the same use were made
of several plump young girls in this town, who, without one single groat
to their fortunes, cannot stir abroad without a chair, and appear at play-
house and assemblies in foreign fineries which they never will pay for,
the kingdom would not be the worse.

19   Some persons of a desponding spirit are in great concern about that
vast number of poor people who are aged, diseased, and maimed; and I

---

* Butcher shops
† George Psalmanazar was a Frenchman who defrauded readers in 1704 by pretending to
be from Formosa.

have been desired to employ my thoughts what course may be taken to ease the nation of so grievous an encumbrance. But I am not in the least pain upon that matter, because it is very well known, that they are every day dying, and rotting, by cold and famine, and filth and vermin, as fast as can be reasonably expected. And so to the younger labourers, they are now in almost as hopeful a condition: they cannot get work, and consequently pine away for want of nourishment, to a degree, that if at any time they are accidentally hired to common labour, they have not strength to perform it; and thus the country and themselves are happily delivered from the evils to come.

20   I have too long digressed, and therefore shall return to my subject. I think the advantages by the proposal which I have made are obvious and many, as well as of the highest importance.

21   For first, as I have already observed, it would greatly lessen the number of papists, with whom we are yearly overrun, being the principal breeders of the nation as well as our most dangerous enemies; and who stay at home on purpose with a design to deliver the kingdom to the Pretender, hoping to take their advantage by the absence of so many good Protestants, who have chosen rather to leave their country than stay at home and pay tithes against their conscience to an idolatrous Episcopal curate.

22   Secondly, the poorer tenants will have something valuable of their own, which by law may be made liable to distress, and help to pay their landlord's rent; their corn and cattle being already seized, and money a thing unknown.

23   Thirdly, whereas the maintenance of an hundred thousand children, from two years old and upwards, cannot be computed at less than ten shillings a piece per annum, the nation's stock will be thereby increased fifty thousand pounds per annum; besides the profit of a new dish introduced to the tables of all gentlemen of fortune in the kingdom who have any refinement in taste. And the money will circulate among ourselves, the goods being entirely of our own growth and manufacture.

24   Fourthly, the constant breeders, besides the gain of eight shillings sterling per annum by the sale of their children, will be rid of the charge of maintaining them after the first year.

25   Fifthly, this food would otherwise bring great custom to taverns; where the vintners will certainly be so prudent as to procure the best receipts for dressing it to perfection, and, consequently, have their houses frequented by all the fine gentlemen, who justly value themselves upon their knowledge in good eating; and a skillful cook, who understands how to oblige his guests, will contrive to make it as expensive as they please.

26   Sixthly, this would be a great inducement to marriage, which all wise nations have either encouraged by rewards, or enforced by laws and penalties. It would increase the care and tenderness of mothers towards

their children, when they were sure of a settlement for life to the poor babes, provided in some sort by the public, to their annual profit instead of expense. We should soon see an honest emulation among the married women, which of them could bring the fattest child to the market. Men would become as fond of their wives during the time of their pregnancy, as they are now of their mares in foal, their cows in calf, or sows when they are ready to farrow; not offer to beat or kick them (as is too frequent a practice) for fear of a miscarriage.

27   Many other advantages might be enumerated. For instance, the addition of some thousand carcasses in our exportation of barrelled beef; the propagation of swine's flesh, and improvement in the art of making good bacon, so much wanted among us by the great destruction of pigs, too frequent at our tables, which are no way comparable in taste or magnificence to a well-grown, fat yearling child, which, roasted whole, will make a considerable figure at a Lord Mayor's feast, or any other public entertainment. But this, and many others, I omit, being studious of brevity.

28   Supposing that one thousand families in this city would be constant customers for infants' flesh, besides others who might have it at merry meetings, particularly weddings and christenings, I compute that Dublin would take off annually about twenty thousand carcasses; and the rest of the kingdom (where probably they will be sold somewhat cheaper) the remaining eighty thousand.

29   I can think of no one objection that will possibly be raised against this proposal, unless it should be urged, that the number of people will be thereby much lessened in the kingdom. This I freely own, and it was indeed one principal design in offering it to the world. I desire the reader will observe that I calculate my remedy for this one individual kingdom of Ireland, and for no other that ever was, is, or I think ever can be, upon earth. Therefore let no man talk to me of other expedients: of taxing our absentees at five shillings a pound: of using neither clothes nor household-furniture except what is of our own growth and manufacture: of utterly rejecting the materials and instruments that promote foreign luxury: of curing the expensiveness of pride, vanity, idleness, and gaming in our women; of introducing a vein of parsimony, prudence, and temperance: of learning to love our country, wherein we differ even from Laplanders, and the inhabitants of Topinamboo:* of quitting our animosities and factions, nor act any longer like the Jews, who were murdering one another at the very moment their city was taken:† of being a little cautious not to sell our country and consciences for nothing: of teaching landlords to have at least one degree of mercy towards their tenants: lastly, of putting a spirit of honesty, industry, and skill into our shopkeepers; who,

---

* A part of Brazil
† A reference to the defeat of Jerusalem by the Romans in 70 A.D.

if a resolution could now be taken to buy only our native goods, would immediately unite to cheat and exact upon us in the price, the measure, and the goodness, nor could ever yet be brought to make one fair proposal of just dealing, though often and earnestly invited to it.

30   Therefore I repeat, let no man talk to me of these and the like expedients, till he hath at least some glimpse of hope that there will ever be some hearty and sincere attempts to put them in practice.

31   But, as to myself, having been wearied out for many years with offering vain, visionary thoughts, and at length utterly despairing of success, I fortunately fell upon this proposal; which, as it is wholly new, so it hath something solid and real, of no expense and little trouble, full in our own power, and whereby we can incur no danger in disobliging England. For this kind of commodity will not bear exportation, the flesh being too tender a consistence to admit a long continuance in salt, although perhaps I could name a country which would be glad to eat up our whole nation without it.

32   After all, I am not so violently bent upon my own opinion as to reject any offer proposed by wise men which shall be found equally innocent, cheap, easy, and effectual. But before something of that kind shall be advanced in contradiction to my scheme, and offering a better, I desire the author, or authors, will be pleased maturely to consider two points. First, as things now stand, how they will be able to find food and raiment for a hundred thousand useless mouths and backs? And, secondly, there being a round million of creatures in human figure throughout this kingdom, whose whole subsistence put into a common stock would leave them in debt two millions of pounds sterling, adding those who are beggars by profession, to the bulk of farmers, cottagers, and labourers, with the wives and children who are beggars in effect; I desire those politicians who dislike my overture, and may perhaps be so bold as to attempt an answer, that they will first ask the parents of these mortals, whether they would not at this day think it a great happiness to have been sold for food at a year old, in the manner I prescribe, and thereby have avoided such a perpetual scene of misfortunes as they have since gone through, by the oppression of landlords, the impossibility of paying rent without money or trade, the want of common sustenance, with neither house nor clothes to cover them from the inclemencies of weather, and the most inevitable prospect of entailing the like, or greater miseries, upon their breed for ever.

33   I profess, in the sincerity of my heart, that I have not the least personal interest in endeavouring to promote this necessary work, having no other motive than the public good of my country, by advancing our trade, providing for infants, relieving the poor, and giving some pleasure to the rich. I have no children by which I can propose to get a single penny; the youngest being nine years old, and my wife past child-bearing.

The Great Person-Hole Cover Debate: A Modest Proposal

Lindsy Van Gelder

Lindsy Van Gelder has been a reporter for United Press International and The New York Post, *a writer for* MS. *magazine, and a contributor to a number of other publications, including* Redbook, Esquire, *and* Rolling Stone. *Her most recent book is* The Girls Next Door *(1996). This essay was published in 1980 in* MS. *magazine.*

1   I wasn't looking for trouble. What I was looking for, actually, was a little tourist information to help me plan a camping trip to New England.

2   But there it was, on the first page of the 1979 edition of the State of Vermont *Digest of Fish and Game Laws and Regulations:* a special message of welcome from one Edward F. Kehoe, commissioner of the Vermont Fish and Game Department, to the reader and would-be camper, *i.e.,* me.

3   This person (*i.e.,* me) is called "the sportsman."

4   "We have no 'sportswomen, sportspersons, sportsboys, or sportsgirls,'" Commissioner Kehoe hastened to explain, obviously anticipating that some of us sportsfeminists might feel a bit overlooked. "But," he added, "we are pleased to report that we do have many great sportsmen who are women, as well as young people of both sexes."

5   It's just that the Fish and Game Department is trying to keep things "simple and forthright" and to respect "longstanding tradition." And anyway, we really ought to be flattered, "sportsman" being "a meaningful title being earned by a special kind of dedicated man, woman, or young person, as opposed to just any hunter, fisherman, or trapper."

6   I have heard this particular line of reasoning before. In fact, I've heard it so often that I've come to think of it as The Great Person-Hole Cover Debate, since gender-neutral manholes are invariably brought into the argument as evidence of the lengths to which humorless, Newspeak-spouting feminists will go to destroy their mother tongue.

7   Consternation about woman-handling the language comes from all sides. Sexual conservatives who see the feminist movement as a unisex plot and who long for the good olde days of *vive la différence,* when men were men and women were women, nonetheless do not rally behind the notion that the term "mankind" excludes women.

8   But most of the people who choke on expressions like "spokesperson" aren't right-wing misogynists, and this is what troubles me. Like the undoubtedly well-meaning folks at the Vermont Fish and Game Department, they tend to reassure you right up front that they're only trying to keep things "simple" and to follow "tradition," and that some of their best men are women, anyway.

9   Usually they wind up warning you, with great sincerity, that you're jeopardizing the worthy cause of women's rights by focusing on "trivial" side issues. I would like to know how anything that gets people so defensive and resistant can possibly be called "trivial," whatever else it might be.

10   The English language is alive and constantly changing. Progress—both scientific and social—is reflected in our language, or should be.

11   Not too long ago, there was a product called "flesh-colored" Band-Aids. The flesh in question was colored Caucasian. Once the civil rights movement pointed out the racism inherent in the name, it was dropped. I cannot imagine reading a thoughtful, well-intentioned company policy statement explaining that while the Band-Aids would continue to be called "flesh-colored" for old time's sake, black and brown people would now be considered honorary whites and were perfectly welcome to use them.

12   Most sensitive people manage to describe our national religious traditions as "Judeo-Christian," even though it takes a few seconds longer to say than "Christian." So why is it such a hardship to say "he or she" instead of "he"?

13   I have a modest proposal for anyone who maintains that "he" is just plain easier: since "he" has been the style for several centuries now—and since it really includes everybody anyway, right?—it seems only fair to give "she" a turn. Instead of having to ponder over the intricacies of, say, "Congressman" versus "Congress person" "Representative," we can simplify things by calling them all "Congresswoman."

14   Other clarifications will follow: "a woman's home is her castle" . . . "a giant step for all womankind" . . . "all women are created equal" . . . "Fisherwoman's Wharf." . . .

15   And don't be upset by the business letter that begins "Dear Madam," fellas. It means you, too.

CHAPTER

30

Literature

We Real Cool

Gwendolyn Brooks

Gwendolyn Brooks is an American poet and teacher who won a Pulitzer Prize for Annie Allen *in 1949. She is the author of many books of poetry, including* A Street in Bronzeville *(1945),* The Bean Eaters *(1960),* Riot *(1969), and* Beckonings *(1975). She has also written two autobiographical collections, a novel, and several books for children. This poem is from* Selected Poems *(1959).*

> *The Pool Players.*
> *Seven at the Golden Shovel.**
>
> We real cool. We
> Left school. We
>
> Lurk late. We
> Strike straight. We
>
> Sing sin. We
> Thin gin. We
>
> Jazz June. We
> Die soon.

* A Chicago pool hall.

Those Winter Sundays

Robert Hayden

Robert Hayden was a poet and professor at Fisk University and at the University of Michigan, who also served as Poetry Consultant to the Library of Congress. A Ballad of Remembrance *(1962) first won him international honors at the World Festival of Negro Arts in Senegal; many other volumes of poetry followed, including* Words in Mourning Time *(1970),* American Journal *(1978), and* Complete Poems *(1985). This poem originally appeared in* Angle of Ascent, New and Selected Poems *(1975).*

Sundays too my father got up early
and put his clothes on in the blueblack cold,
then with cracked hands that ached
from labor in the weekday weather made
5 banked fires blaze. No one ever thanked him.

I'd wake and hear the cold splintering, breaking,
When the rooms were warm, he'd call,
and slowly I would rise and dress,
fearing the chronic angers of that house,

10 Speaking indifferently to him,
who had driven out the cold
and polished my good shoes as well.
What did I know, what did I know
of love's austere and lonely offices?

A Mystery of Heroism

Stephen Crane

Stephen Crane was a late nineteenth-century American short story writer, novelist, poet, and journalist. His best-known novels are Maggie, A Girl of the Streets *(1893), originally rejected by publishers because of Crane's sympathetic portrayal of the main character, and* The Red Badge of Courage *(1895), a Civil War story told so vividly that many veterans claimed participation in its fictional events. Some of Crane's stories include "The Open Boat," "The Blue Hotel," and "The Bride Comes to Yellow Sky." This story was first published in 1895.*

1   The dark uniforms of the men were so coated with dust from the incessant wrestling of the two armies that the regiment almost seemed a part of the clay bank which shielded them from the shells. On the top of the hill a battery was arguing in tremendous roars with some other guns,

and to the eye of the infantry the artillerymen, the guns, the caissons, the horses, were distinctly outlined upon the blue sky. When a piece was fired, a red streak as round as a log flashed low in the heavens, like a monstrous bolt of lightning. The men of the battery wore white duck trousers, which somehow emphasized their legs; and when they ran and crowded in little groups at the bidding of the shouting officers, it was more impressive than usual to the infantry.

2   Fred Collins, of A Company, was saying: "Thunder! I wisht I had a drink. Ain't there any water round here?" Then somebody yelled: "There goes th' bugler!"

3   As the eyes of half the regiment swept in one machinelike movement, there was an instant's picture of a horse in a great convulsive leap of a death wound and a rider leaning back with a crooked arm and spread fingers before his face. On the ground was the crimson terror of an exploding shell, with fibres of flame that seemed like lances. A glittering bugle swung clear of the rider's back as fell headlong the horse and the man. In the air was an odor as from a conflagration.

4   Sometimes they of the infantry looked down at a fair little meadow which spread at their feet. Its long green grass was rippling gently in a breeze. Beyond it was the grey form of a house half torn to pieces by shells and by the busy axes of soldiers who had pursued firewood. The line of an old fence was now dimly marked by long weeds and by an occasional post. A shell had blown the well-house to fragments. Little lines of grey smoke ribboning upward from some embers indicated the place where had stood the barn.

5   From beyond a curtain of green woods there came the sound of some stupendous scuffle, as if two animals of the size of islands were fighting. At a distance there were occasional appearances of swift-moving men, horses, batteries, flags, and with the crashing of infantry volleys were heard, often, wild and frenzied cheers. In the midst of it all Smith and Ferguson, two privates of A Company, were engaged in a heated discussion which involved the greatest questions of the national existence.

6   The battery on the hill presently engaged in a frightful duel. The white legs of the gunners scampered this way and that way, and the officers redoubled their shouts. The guns, with their demeanors of stolidity and courage, were typical of something infinitely self-possessed in this clamor of death that swirled around the hill.

7   One of a "swing" team was suddenly smitten quivering to the ground, and his maddened brethren dragged his torn body in their struggle to escape from this turmoil and danger. A young soldier astride one of the leaders swore and fumed in his saddle and furiously jerked at the bridle. An officer screamed out an order so violently that his voice broke and ended the sentence in a falsetto shriek.

8   The leading company of the infantry regiment was somewhat exposed, and the colonel ordered it moved more fully under the shelter of the hill. There was the clank of steel against steel.

9   A lieutenant of the battery rode down and passed them, holding his right arm carefully in his left hand. And it was as if this arm was not at all a part of him, but belonged to another man. His sober and reflective charger went slowly. The officer's face was grimy and perspiring, and his uniform was tousled as if he had been in direct grapple with an enemy. He smiled grimly when the men stared at him. He turned his horse toward the meadow.

10   Collins, of A Company, said: "I wisht I had a drink. I bet there's water in that there ol' well yonder!"

11   "Yes; but how you goin' to git it?"

12   For the little meadow which intervened was now suffering a terrible onslaught of shells. Its green and beautiful calm had vanished utterly. Brown earth was being flung in monstrous handfuls. And there was a massacre of the young blades of grass. They were being torn, burned, obliterated. Some curious fortune of the battle had made this gentle little meadow the object of the red hate of the shells, and each one as it exploded seemed like an imprecation in the face of a maiden.

13   The wounded officer who was riding across this expanse said to himself: "Why, they couldn't shoot any harder if the whole army was massed here!"

14   A shell struck the gray ruins of the house, and as, after the roar, the shattered wall fell in fragments, there was a noise which resembled the flapping of shutters during a wild gale of winter. Indeed, the infantry paused in the shelter of the bank appeared as men standing upon a shore contemplating a madness of the sea. The angel of calamity had under its glance the battery upon the hill. Fewer white-legged men labored about the guns. A shell had smitten one of the pieces, and after the flare, the smoke, the dust, the wrath of this blow were gone, it was possible to see white legs stretched horizontally upon the ground. And at that interval to the rear where it is the business of battery horses to stand with their noses to the fight, awaiting the command to drag their guns out of the destruction, or into it, or wheresoever these incomprehensible humans demanded with whip and spur—in this line of passive and dumb spectators, whose fluttering hearts yet would not let them forget the iron laws of man's control of them—in this rank of brute-soldiers there had been relentless and hideous carnage. From the ruck of bleeding and prostrate horses, the men of the infantry could see one animal raising its stricken body with its forelegs and turning its nose with mystic and profound eloquence toward the sky.

15   Some comrades joked Collins about his thirst. "Well, if yeh want a drink so bad, why don't yeh go git it?"

16   "Well, I will in a minnet, if yeh don't shut up!"

17   A lieutenant of artillery floundered his horse straight down the hill with as little concern as if it were level ground. As he galloped past the colonel of the infantry, he threw up his hand in swift salute. "We've got to get out of that," he roared angrily. He was a black-bearded officer, and his eyes, which resembled beads, sparkled like those of an insane man. His jumping horse sped along the column of infantry.

18   The fat major, standing carelessly with his sword held horizontally behind him and with his legs far apart, looked after the receding horseman and laughed. "He wants to get back with orders pretty quick, or there'll be no batt'ry left," he observed.

19   The wise young captain of the second company hazarded to the lieutenant-colonel that the enemy's infantry would probably soon attack the hill, and the lieutenant-colonel snubbed him.

20   A private in one of the rear companies looked out over the meadow, and then turned to a companion and said, "Look there, Jim!" It was the wounded officer from the battery, who some time before had started to ride across the meadow, supporting his right arm carefully with his left hand. This man had encountered a shell, apparently, at a time when no one perceived him, and he could now be seen lying face downward with a stirruped foot stretched across the body of his dead horse. A leg of the charger extended slantingly upward, precisely as stiff as a stake. Around this motionless pair the shells still howled.

21   There was a quarrel in A Company. Collins was shaking his fist in the faces of some laughing comrades. "Dern yeh! I ain't afraid t' go. If yeh, say much, I will go!"

22   "Of course, yeh will! You'll run through that there medder, won't yeh?"

23   Collins said, in a terrible voice: "You see now!" At this ominous threat his comrades broke into renewed jeers.

24   Collins gave them a dark scowl, and went to find his captain. The latter was conversing with the colonel of the regiment.

25   "Captain," said Collins, saluting and standing at attention—in those days all trousers bagged at the knees—"Captain, I want t' get permission to go git some water from that there well over yonder!"

26   The colonel and the captain swung about simultaneously and stared across the meadow. The captain laughed. "You must be pretty thirsty, Collins?"

27   "Yes, sir, I am."

28   "Well—ah," said the captain. After a moment, he asked, "Can't you wait?"

29   "No, sir."

30   The colonel was watching Collin's face. "Look here, my lad," he said, in a pious sort of voice —"Look here, my lad,"—Collins was not a lad— "don't you think that's taking pretty big risks for a little drink of water?"

31   "I dunno," said Collins uncomfortably. Some of the resentment toward his companions, which perhaps had forced him into this affair, was beginning to fade. "I dunno wether 'tis."

32   The colonel and the captain contemplated him for a time.

33   "Well," said the captain finally.

34   "Well," said the colonel, "if you want to go, why, go." Collins saluted. "Much obliged t' yeh."

35   As he moved away the colonel called after him. "Take some of the other boys' canteens with you, an' hurry back, now."

36   "Yes, sir, I will."

37   The colonel and the captain looked at each other then, for it had suddenly occurred that they could not for the life of them tell whether Collins wanted to go or whether he did not.

38   They turned to regard Collins, and as they perceived him surrounded by gesticulating comrades, the colonel said: "Well, by thunder! I guess he's going."

39   Collins appeared as a man dreaming. In the midst of the questions, the advice, the warnings, all the excited talk of his company mates, he maintained a curious silence.

40   They were very busy in preparing him for his ordeal. When they inspected him carefully, it was somewhat like the examination that grooms give a horse before a race; and they were amazed, staggered, by the whole affair. Their astonishment found vent in strange repetitions.

41   "Are yeh sure a-goin'?" they demanded again and again.

42   "Certainly I am," cried Collins at last, furiously.

43   He strode sullenly away from them. He was swinging five or six canteens by their cords. It seemed that his cap would not remain firmly on his head, and often he reached and pulled it down over his brow.

44   There was a general movement in the compact column. The long animal-like thing moved slightly. Its four hundred eyes were turned upon the figure of Collins.

45   "Well, sir, if that ain't th' derndest thing! I never thought Fred Collins had the blood in him for that kind of business."

46   "What's he goin' to do, anyhow?"

47   "He's goin' to that well there after water."

48   "We ain't dyin' of thirst, are we? That's foolishness."

49   "Well, somebody put him up to it, an' he's doin' it."

50   "Say, he must be a desperate cuss."

51   When Collins faced the meadow and walked away from the regiment, he was vaguely conscious that a chasm, the deep valley of all prides, was suddenly between him and his comrades. It was provisional, but the provision was that he return as a victor. He had blindly been led by quaint emotions, and laid himself under an obligation to walk squarely up to the face of death.

52   But he was not sure that he wished to make a retraction, even if he could do so without shame. As a matter of truth, he was sure of very little. He was mainly surprised.

53   It seemed to him supernaturally strange that he had allowed his mind to manoeuvre his body into such a situation. He understood that it might be called dramatically great.

54   However, he had no full appreciation of anything, excepting that he was actually conscious of being dazed. He could feel his dulled mind groping after the form and color of this incident. He wondered why he did not feel some keen agony of fear cutting his sense like a knife. He wondered at this, because human expression had said loudly for centuries that men should feel afraid of certain things, and that all men who did not feel this fear were phenomena—heroes.

55   He was, then, a hero. He suffered that disappointment which we would all have if we discovered that we were ourselves capable of those deeds which we most admire in history and legend. This, then, was a hero. After all, heroes were not much.

56   No, it could not be true. He was not a hero. Heroes had no shames in their lives, and, as for him, he remembered borrowing fifteen dollars from a friend and promising to pay it back the next day, and then avoiding that friend for ten months. When, at home, his mother had aroused him for the early labor of his life on the farm, it had often been his fashion to be irritable, childish, diabolical; and his mother had died since he had come to the war.

57   He saw that, in this matter of the well, the canteens, the shells, he was an intruder in the land of fine deeds.

58   He was now about thirty paces from his comrades. The regiment had just turned its many faces toward him.

59   From the forest of terrific noises there suddenly emerged a little uneven line of men. They fired fiercely and rapidly at distant foliage on which appeared little puffs of white smoke. The spatter of skirmish firing was added to the thunder of the guns on the hill. The little line of men ran forward. A color-sergeant fell flat with his flag as if he had slipped on ice. There was hoarse cheering from this distant field.

60   Collins suddenly felt that two demon fingers were pressed into his ears. He could see nothing but flying arrows, flaming red. He lurched from the shock of this explosion, but he made a mad rush for the house, which he viewed as a man submerged to the neck in a boiling surf might view the shore. In the air little pieces of shell howled, and the earthquake explosions drove him insane with the menace of their roar. As he ran the canteens knocked together with a rhythmical tinkling.

61   As he neared the house, each detail of the scene became vivid to him. He was aware of some bricks of the vanished chimney lying on the sod. There was a door which hung by one hinge.

62   Rifle bullets called forth by the insistent skirmishers came from the far-off bank of foliage. They mingled with the shells and the pieces of shells until the air was torn in all directions by hootings, yells, howls. The sky was full of fiends who directed all their wild rage at his head.

63   When he came to the well, he flung himself face downward and peered into its darkness. There were furtive silver glintings some feet from the surface. He grabbled one of the canteens and, unfastening its cap, swung it down by the cord. The water flowed slowly in with an indolent gurgle.

64   And now, as he lay with his face turned away, he was suddenly smitten with the terror. It came upon his heart like the grasp of claws. All the power faded from his muscles. For an instant he was no more than a dead man.

65   The canteen filled with a maddening slowness, in the manner of all bottles. Presently he recovered his strength and addressed a screaming oath to it. He leaned over until it seemed as if he intended to try to push water into it with his hands. His eyes as he gazed down into the well shone like two pieces of metal, and in their expression was a great appeal and a great curse. The stupid water derided him.

66   There was the blaring thunder of a shell. Crimson light shone through the swift-boiling smoke, and made a pink reflection on part of the wall of the well. Collins jerked out his arm and canteen with the same motion that a man would use in withdrawing his head from a furnace.

67   He scrambled erect and glared and hesitated. On the ground near him lay the old well bucket, with a length of rusty chain. He lowered it swiftly into the well. The bucket struck the water and then, turning lazily over, sank. When, with hand reaching tremblingly over hand, he hauled it out, it knocked often against the walls of the well and spilled some of its contents.

68   In running with a filled bucket, a man can adopt but one kind of gait. So, through this terrible field over which screamed practical angels of death, Collins ran in the manner of a farmer chased out of a dairy by a bull.

69   His face went staring white with anticipating—anticipation of a blow that would whirl him around and down. He would fall as he had seen other men fall, the life knocked out of them so suddenly that their knees were no more quick to touch the ground than their heads. He saw the long blue line of the regiment, but his comrades were standing looking at him from the edge of an impossible star. He was aware of some deep wheel-ruts and hoofprints in the sod beneath his feet.

70   The artillery officer who had fallen in this meadow had been making groans in the teeth of the tempest of sound. These futile cries, wrenched from him by his agony, were heard only by shells, bullets. When wild-eyed Collins came running, this officer raised himself. His face contorted

and blanched from pain, he was about to utter some great beseeching cry. But suddenly his face straightened, and he called: "Say, young man, give me a drink of water, will you?"

71   Collins had no room amid his emotions for surprise. He was mad from the threats of destruction.

72   "I can't!" he screamed, and in his reply was a full description of his quaking apprehension. His cap was gone and his hair was riotous. His clothes made it appear that he had been dragged over the ground by the heels. He ran on.

73   The officer's head sank down, and one elbow crooked. His foot in its brass-bound stirrup still stretched over the body of his horse, and the other leg was under the steed.

74   But Collins turned. He came dashing back. His face had now turned grey, and in his eyes was all terror. "Here it is! here it is!"

75   The officer was as a man gone in drink. His arm bent like a twig. His head drooped as if his neck were of willow. He was sinking to the ground, to lie face downward.

76   Collins grabbed him by the shoulder. "Here it is. Here's your drink. Turn over. Turn over, man, for God's sake!"

77   With Collins hauling at his shoulder, the officer twisted his body and fell with his face turned toward that region where lived the unspeakable noises of the swirling missiles. There was the faintest shadow of a smile on his lips as he looked at Collins. He gave a sigh, a little primitive breath like that from a child.

78   Collins tried to hold the bucket steadily, but his shaking hands caused the water to splash all over the face of the dying man. Then he jerked it away and ran on.

79   The regiment gave him a welcoming roar. The grimed faces were wrinkled in laughter.

80   His captain waved the bucket away. "Give it to the men!"

81   The two genial, skylarking young lieutenants were the first to gain possession of it. They played over it in their fashion.

82   When one tried to drink, the other teasingly knocked his elbow. "Don't Billie! You'll make me spill it," said the one. The other laughed.

83   Suddenly there was an oath, the thud of wood on the ground, and a swift murmur of astonishment among the ranks. The two lieutenants glared at each other. The bucket lay on the ground empty.

Copyright Acknowledgments

Index